Contemporary Choreography

This innovative text provides a range of articles covering choreographic enquiry, traditional understandings of dance making and investigation, and research into the creative process.

Featuring contributions by practitioners and researchers from Europe, America, Africa, Australasia and the Asia-Pacific region, this reader investigates choreography in six broad domains:

- Conceptual and philosophic concerns
- Educational settings
- Communities
- Changing aesthetics
- Intercultural choreography
- Choreography's relationships with other disciplines

By providing a reference work that captures the essence and progress of choreography in the twenty-first century, *Contemporary Choreography: A Critical Reader* supports and encourages rigorous thinking and research for future generations of dance artist-practitioners and scholars.

Jo Butterworth directs a part-time postgraduate degree in Choreography at Fontys Dansacademie, Fontys Professional University, Tilburg, the Netherlands. She is a Board member of Random Dance, and Northern Ballet Theatre and has chaired SCODHE (Standing Conference of Dance in Higher Education) and the Dance Section of ELIA (European League of Institutes of the Arts).

Liesbeth Wildschut lectures in dance history and dance theory in the Department of Theatre, Film and Television Studies at Utrecht University. She is chair of the Dutch Society for Dance Research.

Contemporary Choreography

A critical reader

Edited by
Jo Butterworth and
Liesbeth Wildschut

LONDON AND NEW YORK

First published 2009
by Routledge
2 Park Square, Milton Park, Abingdon, Oxon OX14 4RN

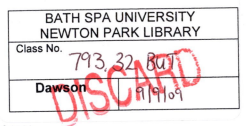

Simultaneously published in the USA and Canada
by Routledge
270 Madison Avenue, New York, NY 10016

Routledge is an imprint of the Taylor & Francis Group, an informa business

Typeset in Baskerville by
Bookcraft Ltd, Stroud, Gloucestershire
Printed and bound in Great Britain by
CPI Antony Rowe, Chippenham, Wiltshire

British Library Cataloguing in Publication Data
A catalogue record for this book is available from the British Library

Library of Congress Cataloguing in Publication Data
Contemporary choreography : a critical reader / edited by
Jo Butterworth and Liesbeth Wildschut.
p. cm.
Includes bibliographical references and index.
1. Choreography. I. Butterworth, Jo. II. Wildschut, Liesbeth, 1952-
GV1782.5.C66 2009
792.8'2--dc22 2008051953

ISBN10: 0-415-49086-3 (hbk)
ISBN10: 0-415-49087-1 (pbk)

ISBN13: 978-0-415-49086-3 (hbk)
ISBN13: 978-0-415-49087-0 (pbk)

Contents

Tables and illustrations

Front cover: *AtaXia* (2006) Wayne McGregor | Random Dance
Dancers: Antoine Vereecken and Lailla Diallo. Photo: © Ravi Deepres

Contributors

Philip Barnard is on the research staff of the MRC Cognition and Brain Sciences Unit in Cambridge, UK. Having spent much of his career researching human interaction with information technology, his primary research interests now lie in the area of human cognition and emotion. His experimental research focuses on how the mind processes meaning and on how that changes in disorders of cognition and affect like those that occur in states of depression, mania, anxiety and psychosis. He has participated in a number of interdisciplinary projects including arts–sciences collaborations involving both dance and cinematography.

Jo Butterworth directs a part-time postgraduate degree in Choreography in the Netherlands, and teaches at Liverpool Institute of Performing Arts (LIPA). Formerly Senior Lecturer in Dance at the University of Leeds, where she initiated the BA Hons Dance and MA in Performance Studies programmes. She received her MA from NYU and her doctorate from the LCDS, University of Kent. Research interests focus on dance making and its applications which led to the Arts Council-funded project *The Greenhouse Effect: the art and science of nurturing dancemakers* (1997–9); she has published articles on choreographic processes and teaching models. Jo is a Board member of Random Dance and Northern Ballet Theatre. She chaired SCODHE (Standing Conference of Dance in Higher Education) and the Dance Section of ELIA (European League of Institutes of the Arts).

Ya-Ping Chen is a dance critic and Assistant Professor at the Graduate Institute of Dance Theory, Taipei National University of the Arts, Taiwan. She holds a PhD in Performance Studies from the New York University. She served as the editor of *Taiwan Dance Research Journal* from 2003 to 2005. Her research interest includes history of Taiwanese contemporary dance, cultural and intercultural studies of dance, as well as dance criticism. She is a contributor to *Asian Dance: Voice of the Millennium* (2000, Malaysia), *Dance Research and Taiwan: the Prospect of a New Generation* (2001, Taiwan), *Thirty Years of Cloud Gate* (2003, Taiwan),

Legend of Cloud Gate: Lin Hwai-min's Masterpieces (2004, Taiwan), *Shifting Sands: Dance in Asia and the Pacific* (2006, Australia), *Pina Bausch: Dancing for the World* (2007, Taiwan) and *Dance, Human Rights and Social Justice: Dignity in Motion* (2008, USA).

Scott deLahunta works from his base in Amsterdam as a researcher, writer, consultant and organiser on a wide range of international projects bringing performing arts into conjunction with other disciplines and practices. He currently has the following long-term relationships: Associate Research Fellow at Dartington College of Arts (since 2000); Affiliated Researcher with Crucible, University of Cambridge (since 2001); Research Fellow, Amsterdam School of the Arts (since 2006) and he has been research coordinator with Wayne McGregor | Random Dance since 2001. He serves on the editorial boards of *Performance Research*, *Dance Theatre Journal* and the *International Journal of Performance and Digital Media*.

Ilythyia de Lignière studied at Higher Institute for Dance Lier (Belgium) and graduated with a BA in Dance. Since then she has explored her interest in the relationship between dance and music. In 2004 she received her MA in Choreography from the University of Leeds. She is currently active in Europe as a freelance dancer, choreographer and teacher. She teaches at Fontys Dance Academy Tilburg (the Netherlands) in the BA Choreography department and is part of the coordinating team for the non-Western Performing Arts minor modules in the Faculty.

Dirk Dumon studied at the Fontys Dance Academy Tilburg (Netherlands) and graduated with a BA degree in dance. After working several years with different groups in the amateur dance field in Belgium and the Netherlands, he became a teacher and choreographer at the Fontys Dance Academy. There he teaches in the theatre dance department, is the artistic leader of the BA choreography department and a member of the PG/MA Choreography teaching staff. In 2004, he received his MA in Choreography from the University of Leeds. He also works as a choreography coach for the CVA (Centrum voor amateurkunst Noord-Brabant) and for Station Zuid. He has an MA in Neurolinguistic Programming and works as a trainer/coach at a mind–body training centre for self-development.

Jeroen Fabius is coordinator of the MA in Choreography at the Theaterschool, the Amsterdam School for the Arts. He studied anthropology and communication science at the University of Amsterdam and choreography at the School for New Dance Development. He worked for ten years as choreographer, dancer and actor, and now regularly works as a dramaturge. Since 1991, he has been teaching dance history and anthropology at the School for New Dance Development. In 2007, he started doctoral research on the topic 'material political bodies in dance' at the University of Utrecht, supported by the Amsterdam School for the Arts.

Susan Leigh Foster, choreographer and scholar, is Professor in the Department of World Arts and Cultures at UCLA. She is the author of *Reading Dancing: Bodies and Subjects in Contemporary American Dance* (University of California Press, 1986), *Choreography and Narrative: Ballet's Staging of Story and Desire* (Indiana University Press, 1996) and *Dances that Describe Themselves: The Improvised Choreography of Richard Bull* (Wesleyan University Press, 2002). She is also the editor of two anthologies: *Choreographing History* (University of Indiana Press, 1995) and *Corporealities* (Routledge, 1996) and co-editor of the journal *Discourses in Dance*.

Soili Hämäläinen was appointed the first head of the Dance Department at the Theatre Academy of Finland in 1983. She was also among the founding faculty of the Department of Dance and Theatre Pedagogy of the Theatre Academy in 1996. Her teaching interests include improvisation, dance pedagogy and dance research. Dr Hämäläinen has studied the teaching and learning processes involved in choreography and explored ethical questions concerning dance teaching and evaluation in a dance class. She has focused on the meaning of bodily knowledge, sensations and feelings as a source in a creative process. She is currently interested in collaboration in artistic work and has published several articles on these topics.

Ninke van Herpt studied at the Rotterdam Dance Academy (the Netherlands) and graduated with a BA in dance education. She has followed additional courses in coaching, choreography and dance therapy. From 1998 she has worked almost exclusively in the amateur dance field in the Netherlands as a teacher, coordinator, coach and dance maker. In 2008 she completed her MA in Choreography at Fontys University Tilburg. Her interests lie in research and analysis of choreographic processes and reception theories and she is currently doing preparatory research for a PhD.

Sara Houston lectures in Dance Studies at the University of Surrey. She lectures and writes on social policy, community dance, professional development and aesthetics. Sara holds a doctorate from Roehampton University and she trained at the Laban Centre for Movement and Dance. She has choreographed for a variety of professional and community groups, working mainly with actors and singers. Sara is currently vice-chair of the Board of Directors and Trustees of the Foundation for Community Dance and serves on the Executive Committee of the Society of Dance Research.

Victoria Hunter is a practitioner-researcher and Lecturer in Dance at the University of Leeds. Her doctoral research is in site-specific dance performance exploring the relationship between the site and the creative process. Her research is practice-based; recent productions include *Beneath* (2004) situated in the basement of the Bretton Hall mansion building and *The Library Dances* (2006) situated in the Leeds Central Library building.

Larry Lavender is Professor of Dance at the University of North Carolina at Greensboro and a member of the Summer Dance faculty at Western Washington University. His areas of teaching and research are choreography, dance criticism, and creativity theories and practices. Larry holds an MFA in Dance from the University of California at Irvine and a PhD in Dance Education from New York University. His book *Dancers Talking Dance: Critical Evaluation in the Choreography Class* is widely used in dance departments and programmes worldwide.

Äli Leijen is a researcher at Viljandi Culture Academy of Tartu University in Estonia. Her academic background is in educational sciences (BA from the University of Tartu, Estonia, in 2001, and MSc from the University of Twente, the Netherlands, in 2004). Her PhD thesis, The Reflective Dancer: ICT Support for Practical Training (University of Utrecht, the Netherlands, 2008), was carried out in dance academies in the Netherlands. In several ways this project dealt with crossing borders between performing arts and educational science and dissolving different traditions. Äli's scholarly interests reflect her interest in combining different practices of knowing. Her research themes are: pedagogical practices of Performing Arts studies; supporting students' reflection and development of professional identity in educational settings; ICT as means for supporting pedagogy and implementing innovations.

Christine Lomas taught Dance in higher education from 1971 until her retirement in 2004 from the University of Leeds. From 1997 to 2003 she led the BA (Hons) Dance at Bretton Hall. Particular concerns were the development of the Community Dance module and through action research the application of 'Dance and the making of Choreography in Community contexts'. Following a presentation at the daCi Conference in Sydney in 1994, she published a chapter in *Dance, Power and Difference: Critical and Feminist Perspectives on Dance Education* (Shapiro ed. 1998). She presented papers at the Global Arts Beyond 2000 ICFAD Conference held in Auckland in 1999 and Pulses and Impulses for Dance in the Community Conference in Lisbon in 2003. She was a Director of Jabadao, a Community Dance resource company based in West Yorkshire, England, from its conception up to her retirement.

Sophia Lycouris is an academic researcher interested in interdisciplinary research methodologies and an artist with a background in dance and choreography. She was recently appointed Director of the Graduate Research School at the Edinburgh College of Art (Scotland, UK). She was Arts and Humanities Research Board Post-Doctoral Fellow in Creative and Performing Arts (2000–3), and a Reader in Interdisciplinary Choreography (2003–7) at the Nottingham Trent University (UK). Her research on interdisciplinary choreography interrogates the application of choreographic techniques on materials other than the dancing body and this informs her artistic work in the UK and abroad. Her current research activities include explorations in two parallel areas: the use of new technologies in interdisciplinary choreographic projects and the role of choreographic approaches in interdisciplinary projects, which address movement in the social and public space in relation to issues of architecture, urban planning and social exclusion.

Wayne McGregor studied dance at University College, Bretton Hall, and at the José Limon School in New York. In 1992 he founded his own company Random Dance, now resident company at Sadler's Wells. Recent works for Random include *Aeon* (2000), *Nemesis* (2002), *Presentient* (2003) and *Amu* (2005). His stimulus for *AtaXia* (2004) was a study of body–brain interaction during his appointment as Research Fellow at the Experimental Psychology department at Cambridge. His latest work for Random is *Entity* (2008). He has also created work for theatre, film and television including the choreography for the Warner Bros. movie *Harry Potter – The Goblet of Fire*. In 2006 McGregor made his opera directorial debut at La Scala, with *Dido and Aeneas*. He also created new works for NDT1, *Skindex* (2006) and *Renature* (2008), and for the Royal Ballet, *Chroma* (2006) and *Infra* (2008). He became Resident Choreographer of the Royal Ballet in 2007.

Shirley McKechnie is a pioneer of contemporary dance and dance education in Australia. She founded the Australian Contemporary Dance Theatre in 1963 and was Artistic Director until 1973. She subsequently founded the first dance studies degree course at Rusden College (now Deakin University) and was Head of the Dance Program between 1975 and 1984. She was Founding Chair of the Tertiary Dance Council of Australia (TDCA) in 1986 and served on national and international panels for the advancement of arts education and on research in dance. Shirley received the Medal of the Order of Australia in 1987, the Kenneth Myer Award in 1993, a Lifetime Achievement Award at the Australian Dance Awards in 2001, and an Honorary Doctorate from the University of Melbourne in 2007. She is Honorary Professor at the Victorian College of the Arts and a Fellow of the Australian Academy of the Humanities.

Susan Melrose is Professor of Perfoming Arts and Research Convenor, in the School of Arts, Middlesex University. Her research is focused on expert practices in the performing arts, and the specificity of a professional expertise in the performing arts that is widely ignored in Performance Studies writing in the university. She has worked closely, in recent years, with choreographers Kim Brandstrup and Rosemary Butcher, and her recent publications and conference presentations are either included or referenced on her website, at www.sfmelrose.u-net.com.

Francis Nii-Yartey has been in the forefront of dance theatre and contemporary African dance development in Ghana for many years. He was educated at the Universities of Ghana and Illinois, USA. He is the founder and director of the Noyam African Dance Institute in Accra. He was, until recently, the Artistic Director of the Ghana Dance Ensemble and the National Dance Company of Ghana. He is the author of a number of publications on contemporary African dance in Ghana. Nii-Yartey has over thirty choreographic works to his credit. Among his numerous awards is the Grand Medal (Civil Division) from the Republic of Ghana for his contribution to choreography and dance development. He was a visiting Cornell Professor at Swarthmore College, Pennsylvania, USA. He is currently a Professor at the University of Ghana and Ashesi University College, Ghana.

Mohd Anis Md Nor is Professor of Ethnochoreology and Ethnomusicology at the Cultural Centre (School of Performing Arts), University of Malaya in Kuala Lumpur. He has pioneered the study of Zapin dance and music in Southeast Asia and has published widely on the topic. Although his foremost research area is Malay dance and music in Southeast Asia, his current studies are on the interface of dance traditions among the Malayo-Polynesian societies in Southeast Asia and Polynesia and the making of new traditions through contemporary performances. Professor Anis is the curator for the Zapin International Dance Festival and the International Malay Performing Arts for the State Government of Johor in Malaysia. He was the 2007 recipient of the William Allan Neilson Distinguished Professor of Music, Dance and Theatre at Smith College, Northampton, Massachusetts, USA.

Anna Pakes is Senior Lecturer in Dance Studies at Roehampton University. She was educated at Balliol College, Oxford, trained in contemporary dance at the Centre National de Danse Contemporaine in Angers, and completed her PhD (about the impact of public funding on contemporary dance) at Laban Centre where she also taught for a number of years and led the MA Dance Studies programme from 1997 to 2000. Her major teaching and research interests are philosophy and aesthetics in relation to dance and she has recently published on the philosophical implications of practice-as-research as well as the mind–body problem in dance.

Scott Palmer is a lecturer in Scenography at the University of Leeds. His research interests focus on lighting design and the interaction between technology and performance. Current projects include *Projecting Performance* in collaboration with Sita Popat and KMA Creative Technologies, investigating the relationship between performer, operator and digital 'sprite'. Scott is the author of the Hodder and Stoughton *Essential Guide to Stage Management, Lighting and Sound* and has published numerous articles on technical training and lighting design practice in the British theatre. He is joint Editor of the Association of Lighting Designers' *Focus* journal.

Sita Popat is Senior Lecturer in Dance in the School of Performance and Cultural Industries, University of Leeds. Her research interests centre on dance choreography and new technologies. She is currently working on the *eDance* project, exploring Access Grid and e-Science technologies as platforms for performance and documentation (2007–9). She recently completed *Projecting Performance* (2006–8) in collaboration with Scott Palmer and KMA Creative Technology Ltd. This project investigated relationships between performer, operator and digital 'sprite'. Spin-off activities included research and development workshops with Lloyd Newson for DV8 Physical Theatre's *To Be Straight With You*. Her research on the Emergent Objects project applied dance knowledge to the design of robotic limb movement (2007–8). Her book on online choreography is published by Routledge, titled *Invisible Connections: Dance, Choreography and Internet Communities* (2006). She is Associate Editor of the *International Journal of Performance Arts and Digital Media* (Intellect Books).

Caroline Ribbers studied at Fontys Dance Academy (Netherlands) and graduated with a BA in Dance. As a professional dancer she has worked with Cirque du Soleil, Danstheater Aya and Olislaegers & Co. After completing a postgraduate programme in dance teaching, she became a teacher at Fontys Dance Academy. In 2004 Caroline gained distinction in her MA degree in Choreography from the University of Leeds. Since 2005 she has focused on Project Sally, an atelier which she founded with dance-artists Stefan Ernst and Ronald Wintjens. Together they create dance performances, dance-education projects and dance movies.

Bonnie Rowell is head of subject for music and dance in the School of Arts and principal lecturer in Dance Studies at Roehampton University. She researches and teaches on the dance analysis strand of courses. Research interests include dance and postmodern theory and the philosophy of dance. Publications include *Dance Umbrella. The First Twenty-One Years* (2000), a celebration and overview of the Dance Umbrella Festival's continuing support for postmodern dance in the UK; and contributions to *Dancing Off the Page: Integrating Performance, Choreography, Analysis and Notation/Documentation* (Duerden and Fisher, ed. 2007), *Europe Dancing* (Grau and Jordan, eds 2000) and *Dance, Education and Philosophy*, (McFee, ed. 1999).

Sarah Rubidge is a practitioner-scholar whose artistic activities as both creator and facilitator have been undertaken nationally and internationally. The focus of her artistic work lies in the dialogue between the body, movement and new technologies, in particular in interactive installations. Sarah is especially interested in developing installation spaces which are read through the haptic/kinaesthetic senses and performative installation spaces in which participants' movements become an integral element of the installation event. She has had her writings on dance and related fields published extensively in books and journals. Sarah is currently Professor in Choreography and New Media at the University of Chichester.

Jacqueline Smith-Autard lectured in Dance Education at Dartford College of Education (now Greenwich University), London College of Dance and Drama, Derby Lonsdale College (now University of Derby), Bedford College of Higher Education (De Montfort University) and Bretton Hall (University of Leeds). She is a dance educator of world renown, currently pioneering the use of multi-media resources in dance teaching through her work with Jim Schofield and the Bedford Interactive company. Her research through practice has provided a methodology for dance education across all sectors, primary, secondary and tertiary. She is the author of *Dance Composition* (1976), now in its 5th edition (2004), which has been translated into Japanese and Italian, and *The Art of Dance in Education* (1994, 2002) also recently translated into Korean, both published by A & C Black.

Catherine (Kate) Stevens is a cognitive psychologist who applies experimental methods to study cognition of complex auditory and temporal phenomena. Her doctoral research investigated musical training and pattern recognition in human listeners and artificial neural network models. In experimental research, Stevens and student collaborators investigate general mechanisms operating in the recognition of music and auditory signals. Collaborative research with Shirley McKechnie into 'choreographic cognition' has led to theorising and experimentation on creativity, memory for movement, and audience response to dance. Kate is an Associate Professor in Psychology, Associate Director of the Music, Sound and Action group in MARCS Auditory Laboratories at the University of Western Sydney (http://marcs.uws.

edu.au), and co-convenes the Australian Research Council Network in Human Communication Science (HCSNet).

Cheryl Stock works as Associate Professor at Queensland University of Technology across research, postgraduate supervision and teaching in the areas of dance, interdisciplinary, new media and site-specific practice, Asian performing arts and intercultural perspectives. She was Head of Dance from 2000 to 2006 and received the Lifetime Achievement Award at the Australian Dance Awards in 2004 for her outstanding contribution to contemporary dance as a performer, choreographer, artistic director, advocate, writer and leader in tertiary dance education. She created over 45 dance and theatre works, was the founding Artistic Director of Dance North (1984–95) and directed twenty cultural exchange programmes in Asia, with twelve in Vietnam. In 2006 she directed an interdisciplinary, interactive performance installation *Accented Body*, in collaboration with artists and technology experts from Australia, UK, Korea, Japan and Taiwan. Cheryl curated the 2008 World Dance Alliance Global Summit as Chair of the Program Committee and Conference Convener.

Liesbeth Wildschut graduated at the Fontys Dance Academy in 1973. As a dancer and choreographer she was involved in performances for young children. In 1995 she received her MA in Theatre Studies at Utrecht University (cum laude). Since then she has been lecturer and researcher at Utrecht University, Department of Theatre, Film and Television Studies. The subject of her 2003 doctoral dissertation was children's experience of theatrical dance performances. Her main research interests include emotional and physical involvement strategies of people watching a dance performance and the development of dance dramaturgy. She is chair of the Dutch Society for Dance Research and co-editor of the volumes *Danswetenschap in Nederland*. She was a member of the Boards of Springdance and daCi-the Netherlands, chaired the paper selection of the 2006 daCi Conference and edited the Proceedings.

Acknowledgements

The editors would like to thank a number of people who have offered support, inspiration and constructive criticism, or been influential in shaping this book through its years of development. In particular, Jo Butterworth's dance colleagues at the University of Leeds Bretton Hall campus where the original idea for a book about choreography in contexts emerged on the top floor of the mansion, and Sita Popat who was co-editor in the early stages; Jacques van Meel of Fontys Dance Academy who advised on the current situation in the Netherlands and made the introduction to Liesbeth Wildschut, who took over as co-editor; Paul Cowen, for his incisive editing of six chapters, and help with proof-reading; Conny van Bezu for her translations of two of the texts. For their advice, critique and suggestions we are very grateful to Ralph Buck, Christy Adair, Donna Davenport, Erik Kaiel, Sarah Gamlin, and Erica Stanton.

We would very much like to thank Minh Ha Duong for the initial support given to this project and to Catherine Foley for her enthusiasm, consistent professional support and friendship from the moment she became involved.

To all at Wayne McGregor|Random Dance, particularly Lailla Diallo and Antoine Vereecken, for providing a thrilling cover photograph taken by Ravi Deepres.

We are extremely grateful to all the contributors to this volume: their good will, hard work, patience and encouragement have been much appreciated. The journey has been very eventful and not always direct, but the original group have remained faithful and with those who joined us through recommendation more recently have given of their time and expertise very generously.

On a personal note, we feel it is extraordinary how well the 'job-share' has progressed: from our meetings, visits to Yorkshire, Oxford, Tilburg and Utrecht, emails and phone calls by the thousands; and through being strategic about our various roles, and taking morning walks, a true friendship has emerged.

The publishers, editors and contributors would like to thank those individuals and organisations who have been kind enough to allow their material to be reproduced herein. Particular thanks are due to *The Journal of Dance Education*, Cultural Centre University of Malaya, World Dance Alliance, *Research in Dance Education*, David Collins at the *International Journal of Performance Arts and Digital Media*, IFDR Seoul '08 and the 6th International Conference on Music Perception and Cognition, Keele 2006.

1 General introduction

Studying contemporary choreography

Jo Butterworth and Liesbeth Wildschut

Choreography is the making of dance. Dance, however, is not confined to theatrical contexts only. Contemporary choreography is concerned with dance making in an ever-expanding field of applications: from both viewers' and performers' perspectives, in live and broadcast media, in site-specific, applied, community and shared environments. Does the nature of choreography change with each new context, or is there a constant set of principles that define what choreography is, whatever the circumstance? This innovative text raises the question and, from a range of differing perspectives, challenges traditional understandings of dance making whilst promoting enquiry into the creative process as a whole.

The chapters in this book provide insights from individual dance practitioners who are also researchers. They are knowledgeable of their respective fields, and most are involved in choreographic processes from an internal, experiential or critical perspective. Thus they articulate practitioner concerns in intellectual form but are guided by empirical understanding. Readers will note the differences of style in these chapters, which are often connected to each contributing author's personal perspective or professional context.

This edition aims to interrogate the nature of contemporary choreography in selected contexts from a synthesis of practical and critical perspectives. The contributors are respected practitioner/researchers from Europe, Africa, America, Australia and Asia-Pacific; all are concerned to analyse personal practice within the wider contexts in which they find themselves. As such, these chapters build on and complement existing texts in the performance genre. They retain a strong practical inflection using a critical vocabulary suitable for both students and practitioners of dance and the performing arts. Unlike many existing texts that variously (and individually) discuss the philosophy of dance, or describe the practice of individual choreographers, or address the physical act of dancing, these scrutinise and contextualise choreographic practice within conceptual and critical frameworks appropriate for higher education consumption.

No attempt is made to provide an overview of choreographic practice, nor to explore norms of dance making by identifying common factors of intention, concept, generation of dance content, micro- and macro-structure, or rehearsal process. There is no reference to specific film, television or Internet approaches to choreography, except where such is an integral element in a live event or research imperative. Acknowledgement is given to a wide range of available texts that provide historical perspective, analytical framing and compositional know-how. But emphasis is on the here and now, on foregrounding practices that perhaps have been marginalised by lack of documentation or publication, and on identifying interrelationships with other disciplines that have developed that of choreography. The rationale is to disseminate forms of choreographic practice that are not widely accessible and to promote factors, issues and insights that are inherently interesting and worthy of documentation and publication. Focus, therefore, is on certain modes of performative practice, particularly those that challenge the conventional or orthodox, or that step beyond previous choreographic boundaries.

In the light of this, it is unsurprising that six of the chapters in this book engage with discussions about the use of technology, either in support of teaching choreography, or in the processes of making or performing, or indeed in terms of considering the potential of dance making. Five chapters converge around issues broadly dealing with questions of interculturalism and globalisation across international boundaries; two others articulate investigations into choreographic cognition from opposite hemispheres. Of common concern to the writers is the increased need for reflexivity and analysis, and the desire to investigate choreographic processes more thoroughly. This may have come about because of the growth of dance as a discipline in the university sector, but equally, because of the demands placed on dance artists to communicate their practice in languages other than dance. Funding bodies require articulated information about artistic vision in relation to new works; festivals, choreographic forums and post-performance discussions place exacting demands on dance makers to explain intention and process, and co-commissioning of collaborative projects by arts, science and other research funding put the onus on the artist to be a thinking, reflective and careful communicator. As choreographic boundaries expand rapidly and in unforeseen directions (as evidenced by the wide range of applications presented here), the need to develop and interrogate new theories grows.

The contributions of the authors are divided into six sections, namely:

- Conceptual and philosophical concerns
- Higher educational settings
- Communities
- Intercultural contexts
- Changing aesthetics
- Relationships with other disciplines

The main questions and themes of each chapter are introduced at the beginning of each section. Suggestions for further reading are provided beyond the texts listed in specific bibliographies.

There is no doubt that what is reflected here are some of the significant choreographic concerns of the first decade of the twenty-first century. Many of these themes will evolve and expand while others may become less important over time. As Randy Martin (1998: 1) believes: 'Dance lies at the point at which reflection and embodiment meet, at which doing and anticipation are intertwined'. Because of the range of topics, there is opportunity for everyone involved in this discipline – choreographers, students, teachers, and researchers – to find clusters of writing that have particular relevance to their own background and personal interests. No one is being asked to read the book from cover to cover, although should they do so, perhaps they will perceive a form of logic in its structure as chosen by its co-editors. We acknowledge that there are many other choices possible. Exciting cross-references are to be discovered as selected chapters are explored, allowing dance students, practitioners and researchers to find their personal focal areas within the choreographic landscape. But perhaps of greater importance is the congruence of these critical perspectives on contemporary dance-making practices from multiple points of view.

It is sincerely hoped that the book provides stimulus, and that new papers and articles will subsequently emerge to continue the dialogue and contribute to the literature. We are most grateful to all our contributors for sharing their experience and passion with us in the realisation of this book.

References

Martin, R. (1998) *Critical Moves: Dance Studies in Theory and Politics*, Durham and London: Duke University Press.

Section 1

Conceptual and philosophical concerns

Section introduction

Jo Butterworth and Liesbeth Wildschut

This section introduces the reader to chapters that reveal some of the philosophical arguments for and against the acceptance of choreography as a form of knowledge. In what ways is it possible to perceive choreographic processes and products as 'knowing', 'thinking', 'being' and 'interpreting'? How can a philosophic field of enquiry help us to understand, contextualise, interpret and unfold the significance of the dance? What are the seminal texts in this territory, and what are the 'well-rehearsed' and not-so-well-rehearsed arguments?

Historically, the dance discipline has been considered to have been neglected or undermined by a number of elements: its ephemerality and transience; little documentation and low social status; religion, especially Puritanism; the perception of dance as a female art; the lack of a canon of literature (Levin 1977, Sparshott 1988); and, as many have identified, its very nature seen as an activity of the body rather than mind where Western dualism since Descartes has privileged the cognitive over the corporeal, revealing the West's religious and ethical biases. One of the basic difficulties continues to be that bodily knowledge and artistry are not easily expressed in language, even where there is a will to do so.

Attempts to locate influential philosophical dance theories of the twentieth century inevitably reveal personal preference, but in the context of this edition, no doubt some of the consensual, if not seminal works include selected writings of Langer, Sheets-Johnstone, Best and Fraleigh. Between the 1960s and 1980s in particular, questions were raised about the origins and development of the aesthetic ideas that shape the nature of dance as an art form and as a cultural phenomenon. Philosophy as a mode of enquiry helps us to examine the authentic experiences of dance and dancing, how to understand concepts and to construct meaning (Hanstein 1999: 42). In the USA, Susanne Langer's oeuvre on the philosophy of art includes *Feeling and Form* (1953) and 'The Dynamic Image:

Some philosophical reflections on dance', published in the *Dance Observer* in 1956 (cited in Langer 1957). Acknowledging the work of Langer and Merleau-Ponty, the views put forward by Sheets-Johnstone (1966, 1979) draw on the phenomenological ideas of Husserl which encourage the dance writer to view the performer as a unified 'consciousness-body' (1979: 11–12), and foreground the lived experience, the consciousness of man and his fundamental interaction with his environment. Sondra Horton Fraleigh's *Dance and the Lived Body* (1987) examined and described dance through her consciousness of dance as an art, through the experience of dancing, and through the existential and phenomenological literature on the *lived body*.

Other texts from the UK included Betty Redfern's *Dance, Art and Aesthetics* (1983), written at a time when aesthetic enquiry in the realm of dance was notoriously sparse and few people involved in lecturing and learning about dance had even a limited understanding of formal philosophy. Graham McFee's (1992) textbook, *Understanding Dance*, explored the nature of understanding dance, and the arts more generally, particularly in the context of society and education, while David Best's *Philosophy and Human Movement* (1978), and *Feeling and Reason in the Arts* (1985) re-worked as *The Rationality of Feeling* (1992) gave 'cogent, powerful reasons for seeing the arts as agents of learning, of understanding, of development' (Abbs in Best 1992: viii).

These texts, supported by selected writings from Abbs (1987, 1989), Beardsley (1958, 1970), Dickie (1971, 1974), Margolis (1978), Reid (1961, 1969), Stolnitz (1960) and Wollheim (1973, 1980, 1987) among others, have provided generations of dance students with some fundamental questions about the nature of art in Contextual Studies modules and the like. Today, the use of the World Wide Web is an essential resource to aid further research, to locate and browse new texts and journal articles and enable the student and scholar to map the territory.

The chapters in this section provide juxtaposition of four contemporaneous yet distinct stances on choreography as a form of knowledge and as research methodology. The first two chapters in this section provide interesting dialectic on how we might define 'knowledge of choreography' in the current decade, contextualised specifically by the problematic of practice-as-research and artistry, scholarship and expert intuition. Readers will note that the two chapters that follow use theoretical and methodological frameworks beyond the disciplinary legacy of philosophy, drawing on psychology and gender studies to provide inter-textual methodologies. This demonstrates the considerable cross-fertilisation between disciplines that has aided the development of the study of dance in the last two decades.

Anna Pakes' discussion seeks to show how philosophical ideas about practical knowledge, reasoning and wisdom might be relevant to choreography and dance practice as research, helping us identify (at least part of) their epistemological value. Whilst acknowledging that this is not the only way in which the knowledge developed in and through dance making can be described, the discussion demonstrates the fruitfulness of the philosophical literature for attempts to think through the epistemology of choreography. She maintains that to think of choreography and choreographic research as dealing in practical knowledge helps to move us beyond dominant paradigms of knowledge, which deny that the practice of dance making has epistemological value.

Susan Melrose's chapter foregrounds artistry as she argues that the expert choreographer's expertise lies in her capacity to transfer an already modulated expert-intuitive product from the 'living body' of the immediate moment of discovery in the workshop or rehearsal room, to a further, production-specific apparatus. Second, it lies in the choreographer's capacity to make judgements about 'what works', at each stage of this transfer. Hereafter, she maintains, the expert-intuitive discovery can be 'artificially performed' outside the organic mind and body that lent themselves to its discovery. It is the choreographer who, by 'entrusting this process to a machine (both technological and methodological)', draws it into engagement with the performance-productive processes specific to the logics of production. The expert-intuitive outcome belongs to the choreographer, whose signature takes responsibility for the collaborative production. Melrose weaves into her discourse a critique of arts practices and conservative value systems in the present university 'economy' and in particular their failure to give a proper place to dance disciplinary specificity and mastery.

Chapter four, by Shirley McKechnie and Kate Stevens, probes for a microcosm of cognition in the creation, performance and appreciation of contemporary dance. This chapter applies contemporary psychological theory to the complex processes that mediate creation, performance and observation of contemporary dance. The term *choreographic cognition* is used to define collectively these perceptual, cognitive and emotional processes. Psychological investigations have tended to deal with dance as discrete movements or steps, and questions of memory and imagery have been unnecessarily confined to codes that are verbal or visual. McKechnie and Stevens propose that there is more: movement through space is continuous, it flows; transitions are the conveyors of information and form. In an effort to capture these temporal and spatial characteristics, the authors outline a theoretical approach that conceptualises choreographic cognition as an evolving dynamical system, suggesting how these might be addressed.

Finally, in chapter five, Susan Leigh Foster demonstrates an intertextual methodology that expands knowledge. She contributes to our understanding of how dance can propose a theory concerning gendered identity – how it offers to participants and viewers a conception of what gender might be and how it works. Moving alongside the many dance scholars, including Foster herself, who have argued for consideration of the gendered significance of dancing, this chapter evaluates gender's workings and effects in globalised culture, in a moment where popular images of femininity from Hollywood to Bollywood circulate rapidly through diverse mediatised formats. The focus of her inquiry, two recent works, one by British choreographer Lea Anderson and the other by the Japanese performance collective KATHY, draws upon images from Hollywood films to mount powerful critiques of contemporary femininity. In order to situate their arguments concerning gender, she examines two canonical works by US choreographers Martha Graham and Trisha Brown. Emblematic of key moments in the history of dance modernism, their theorisations of gender provide historical perspective on the contemporary choreographic practices of Anderson and KATHY.

References

Abbs, P. (ed.) (1987) *Living Powers: The Arts in Education*, London: The Falmer Press.

—— (1989a) *A is for Aesthetic: Essays on creative and aesthetic education*, London: The Falmer Press.

—— (ed.) (1989b) *The Symbolic Order: A contemporary reader on the arts debate*, London: The Falmer Press.

Beardsley, M. C. (1958) *Aesthetics: Problems in the philosophy of criticism*, New York: Harcourt, Brace and World.

—— (1970) *The Possibility of Criticism*, Detroit: Wayne University Press.

Best, D. (1978) *Philosophy and Human Movement*, London: Allen and Unwin.

—— (1985) *Feeling and Reason in the Arts*, London: Allen and Unwin.

—— (1992) *The Rationality of Feeling: Understanding the arts in education*, London: The Falmer Press.

Dickie, G. (1971) *Aesthetics: An Introduction*, New York: Pegasus Press.

—— (1974) *Art and the Aesthetic: An institutional analysis*, New York: Cornell University Press.

Fraleigh, S. (1987) *Dance and the Lived Body: A Descriptive Aesthetics*, Pittsburgh, PA: University of Pittsburgh Press.

Hanstein, P. (1999) ‘Evolving Modes of Inquiry’ in S. H. Fraleigh and P. Hanstein (eds) *Researching Dance: Evolving modes of inquiry*, London: Dance Books.

Langer, S. K. (1953) *Feeling and Form*, New York: Charles Scribner’s Sons.

—— (1957) ‘The Dynamic Image: Some philosophical reflections on dance’ in *Problems of Art*, New York: Charles Scribner’s Sons.

Levin, D. M. (1977) ‘Philosophers and the Dance’ in R. Copeland and M. Cohen (1983) *What is Dance?*, Oxford: Oxford University Press.

Margolis, J. (ed.) (1978) *Philosophy Looks at the Arts: Contemporary readings in aesthetics*, Philadelphia: Temple University Press.

McFee, G. (1992) *Understanding Dance*, London: Routledge.

Redfern, B. (1983) *Dance, Art and Aesthetics*, London: Dance Books.

Reid, L. A. (1961) *Ways of Knowledge and Experience*, London: Allen and Unwin.

—— (1969) *Meaning in the Arts*, London: Allen and Unwin.

Sheets, M. (1966) *The Phenomenology of Dance*, Madison: University of Wisconsin Press.

Sheets-Johnstone, M. (1979) *The Phenomenology of Dance*, London: Dance Books.

Sparshott, F. (1988) *Off the Ground: First steps to a philosophical consideration of the dance*, Princeton, NJ: Princeton University Press.

Stolnitz, J. (1960) *Aesthetics and the Philosophy of Art Criticism*, Boston: Houghton Mifflin.

Wollheim, R. (1970) *Art and its Objects: An introduction to aesthetics*, New York: Harper and Row.

—— (1973) *On Art and the Mind*, London: Allen Lane.

—— (1980) *Art and its Objects*, 2nd edn., Cambridge: Cambridge University Press.

—— (1987) *Painting as an Art*, London: Thames and Hudson.

Further reading

Adshead-Lansdale, J. (ed.) (1999) *Dancing Texts: Intertextuality in Interpretation*, London: Dance Books.

Franco, S. and Nordera, M. (2007) *Dance Discourses: Keywords in Dance Research*, London and New York: Routledge.

Hewitt, A. (2005) *Social Choreography: Ideology as Performance in Dance and Everyday Movement*, Oxford: Meyer and Meyer Verlag.

Lansdale, J. (2008) *Decentring Dance Texts: The Challenge of Interpreting Dances*, Basingstoke and New York: Palgrave Macmillan.

McFee, G. (ed.) (1999) *Dance, Education and Philosophy*, Oxford: Meyer and Meyer Sport.

Merleau-Ponty, M. (1972) 'Eye and Mind' in H. Osborne (ed.) *Aesthetics*, Oxford: Oxford University Press (first published in 1964 in J. Edie (ed.) *The Primacy of Perception*).

Weiss, G. (1999) *Body Images: Embodiment as intercorporality*, London and New York: Routledge.

2 Knowing through dance-making

Choreography, practical knowledge and practice-as-research

Anna Pakes

What does choreography have to do with knowledge? Clearly, choreographic works and the processes historically or typically involved in making them are the sorts of things we can know something *about*. But does the practice of choreography itself exploit, develop or demonstrate particular kinds of knowledge? Is it a way – or series of ways – of knowing in its own right?

The relationship between knowledge and dance practice has been explored by philosophers interested in dance and its role in primary, secondary and tertiary education. Writers such as Best (1985, 1987a, 1987b), McFee (1992, 1994), Carr (1984, 1987a, 1999) and Redfern (1982, 1983) are keen to assert the legitimacy and value of dance within educational curricula, and therefore emphasise how the practice of performance and choreography contribute to the pupil's understanding of the art form in general. They also (particularly Best and McFee) make a case for dance playing a role in emotional education – in developing students' understanding of life issues through the refined insight which engagement with dance works promotes. Much of this writing highlights the cognitive processes involved in making, performing and watching dance – clarifying the contribution dance can make to cognitive development. A clear connection between choreography and particular kinds or domains of knowledge is thus revealed.

More recently, debates about practice as research have again rendered urgent questions about choreography's epistemology.[1] If research (at least at higher degree level and beyond) is the generation of new knowledge, then treating dance practice as a form of research raises important epistemological issues. What kind of knowledge do choreography and performance generate? Is this knowledge specifically about the practice of dance, or also other domains? How does dance practice develop original insight, and how is this disseminated and shared? Unless we can identify the choreographer-researcher's claim to knowledge, it remains difficult to maintain that choreographic research has equivalent status with other, more traditional forms of scholarly enquiry. Within the broader university environment, the value of choreographic research also seems (at least partly) to hinge on whether it generates a distinctive form of knowledge, one that is not available by other means.

Western philosophy has traditionally conceived of knowledge as essentially 'justified true belief'. This conception can be traced back at least as far as Plato's *Theaetetus* and emphasises the importance of factual and theoretical knowledge over and above other forms. It is a conception of what it is to know which has intensified its hold with the ascendancy of positivist and scientistic forms of understanding in the modern world. One result is a contemporary situation in which ways of knowing that refuse or transcend the scientistic paradigm must often nonetheless be justified with reference to it, if they are to be recognised as valid. And against an epistemological framework in which factual and theoretical knowledge are accorded pride of place, practice as research is likely to be considered at best marginal, at worst illegitimate, as a form of scholarly endeavour (hence the scepticism with which dance practice as research is sometimes greeted by academics from other disciplines). Choreography is not (generally) a fact-seeking exercise, not (necessarily) a theory-building enterprise and rarely (if ever) a means to measure or quantify the objects of a supposedly mind-independent reality. So, what do and can we know through making dance?

One potentially useful route to an answer is mapped by philosophical discussions of practical knowledge. David Carr (1978, 1999) has explored these discussions' pertinence to the dance domain, examining generally how dance practice involves practical reasoning and wisdom. The discussion below is indebted to Carr's work and develops in more detail how the practical knowledge literature might be relevant to choreography and choreographic practice-as-research.

Knowing how

A well-known challenge to the factual and theoretical bias of Western epistemology is articulated in Gilbert Ryle's (1963) discussion of knowing *how* as distinct from knowing *that*. Against the background of a tradition preoccupied with 'investigating the nature, source, and the credentials of the theories we adopt' (1963: 28), Ryle's concern is to explore what it is to know how to perform tasks and what it means to act intelligently. His ideas are pertinent to choreography insofar as they outline a kind of knowledge embodied in dance, alongside other forms of practice.

The distinction between 'knowing how' and 'knowing that' can be illustrated using a simple example. Knowing how to ride a bicycle is clearly different from a theoretical knowledge of how the bicycle works, or of how the expenditure of human energy while pedalling results in forward motion. Factual and theoretical knowledge of the latter kind are not going to help the aspiring cyclist learn to ride – that can only be achieved through practice. Similarly, knowledge of how to make a dance work is distinct from being able to analyse existing choreography or explain how and why it is effective. By extension of Ryle's argument, the experienced artist's knowledge how would be embodied in her conduct of the creative process: it informs the way the choreographer relates to her dancers, generates movement material, manipulates and edits that material and orchestrates the variety of choreographic elements within the emerging work. It is not a case of having a prior theoretical knowledge of what should be done in a choreographic situation and then putting these ideas into practice; nor is it a question of envisaging the work in theory and then finding a physical form to illustrate that idea. Rather, the intelligence of the choreographer's action is embedded *in the doing*, of which she may or may not be reflectively aware. And this knowledge how is something that – like riding a bike – can only be developed through practice. It cannot be learned by rote or in the abstract.

For Ryle, then, knowing how is a legitimate form of knowledge in its own right, not a derivative operation premised on prior theoretical understanding. Thought and knowledge are embodied in the activity of those who know how. That intelligent action is not – as is often assumed – a two-stage process of thinking, then acting in accordance with the thoughts. With the skilful clown, the chess master, the experienced player of darts (and, by extension, the experienced dance artist), we admire what they do, not 'some extra hidden performance executed "in their head[s]"' (1963: 33). Ryle's claims about 'knowing how' form part of his broader challenge to dualist assumptions and to the paradigm of the 'ghost in the machine'. His ultimate purpose is to show the absurdity of positing mind and body, thought processes and physical action as separate, logically parallel entities. Dualism, for Ryle, rests on this fundamental category mistake. The 'intellectualist legend', which imagines intelligent practice as 'a step-child of theory' (1963: 27), previously formulated in the abstract and private space of the agent's mind, succumbs to the same fallacy.

Ryle's argument seems highly suggestive for the dance artist because it accords weight and value to the doing itself, instead of requiring a theorisation of practice to render it epistemologically respectable. Understanding is already embodied in actions the artist performs during the making process: there is no need to alter the nature of that process in order to give it credence as thoughtful activity. Ryle's view also chimes in tune with the claims of those choreographer-researchers who object to the idea that their practice must be informed, even directed, by a theoretical perspective or agenda in order to qualify as research. To assume that theory must be the driving force behind thoughtful choreography would be to succumb to what Ryle calls the 'intellectualist fallacy' and to ignore the intelligence intrinsic to practice itself.

Practical reasoning

Ryle's discussion thus resonates in the sphere of dance practice, but remains too schematic to probe the nature and parameters of knowing how. David Carr (1978) recognises and proposes to redress this by drawing on the writings of post-war analytic philosophers about practical inference (Anscombe 1963, Kenny 1966 and Von Wright 1963, 1971). These writings in turn refer back to Aristotle's exploration of forms of practical knowledge (2000), and to his 'invention' of the practical syllogism, which attempts to formalise the kind of reasoning typical of the sphere of practical action. Because this literature further elucidates the logic of knowing how, it arguably identifies principles of rationality embedded in dance practice, and may help clarify what constitutes choreographic knowing.

The mainstay of logical enquiry before Gottlob Frege, the syllogism, depends for its validity on certain rules that govern inference from premises to conclusion, a classic example being the following:

All men are mortal	Premise 1
Socrates is a man	Premise 2
Therefore, Socrates is mortal	Conclusion

In this example, the first premise states a universal law, the second an empirical fact, which falls under the province of that universal law, allowing the valid inference to another fact which is articulated in the conclusion. This pattern of passing from general premise to singular premise to singular conclusion is the 'canonical syllogistic form' (Carr 1978: 7). The syllogism presents a proof of the conclusion which follows necessarily from the premises, if the rules of logic are obeyed. This is a kind of reasoning about matters of fact and general principles, governed by a logic of truth and falsity: if the premises are true, then the conclusion will also be true. This kind of deductive inference plays a key role in scientific reasoning or explanation, though it is not the only form of reasoning present in that domain.[2]

The practical syllogism, meanwhile, articulates a different kind of logic, whereby one moves from intentions or purposes and consideration of the particular circumstances in play (the premises) to action (the conclusion), as in the following example from Carr:

> I intend to change the oil in my car;
> If I remove the drain plug, I'll be able to change the oil;
> There is no way to change the oil without removing the drain plug;
> I will/must remove the drain plug.
>
> (Carr 1978: 6)

In contrast to theoretical reasoning, this kind of logic is concerned with how we can fulfil our intentions rather than with moving from observations to statements about the world. Practical inference concerns 'the practical logic of our efforts to cope with and be effective in the world, not the theoretical logic of our thoughts about the world' (Carr 1978: 8). It takes into account the particularity of the situations in which action occurs. Where the first premise of a theoretical syllogism is invariably general (e.g. 'All men are mortal'), 'there is no general positive rule of the form "Always do X" or "Doing X is always good" (where X describes some specific action) which a sane person will accept as a starting point for reasoning out what to do in a particular case' (Anscombe 1963: 62). Aristotle and his modern followers stress that the conclusion to a practical syllogism is not a statement (though it appears as such in attempts to articulate the logical principles at stake) but an action. Thus, in the example above, the conclusion would be the actual removal of the drain plug not the thought that this would be a good idea, nor simply an intention to remove the drain plug (Carr 1978: 8–9). The conclusion 'is an action whose point is shewn by the premises' (Anscombe 1963: 60). The logical rules of theoretical inference ensure that one does not pass from true assertions to false conclusions; the rules of practical inference determine 'that in reasoning about what to do we never pass from a plan which will satisfy our desires to a plan which will not satisfy them' (Kenny 1966: 73). In this 'logic of satisfactoriness', the motivating desire is crucial as the touchstone against which action is measured.

Clearly choreographic making is a more complex, less predictable activity than changing the oil in one's car. But the choreographer's process entails a similar sort of practical engagement over and above any effort to theorise about dance works. It remains a question of acting in accordance with an intention, in a way that takes into account the prevailing circumstances, be they the precedents set by dance history, contemporary aesthetic conventions, or pragmatic considerations (like the available funds, dancers and rehearsal space). So the reasoning embedded in choreographic practice seems articulable in practical rather than theoretical syllogistic form. There are no general artistic rules to dictate what should always be done in particular choreographic situations; rather, the artistic intention is the starting point of the chain of reasoning. Relating that intention to the surrounding circumstances provides a justification or rationale for what choreographers do or the work they make (the syllogism's conclusion).

It is perhaps instructive to think of choreographers' verbal (spoken or written) accounts of their processes as articulating their rationality in this way. What such accounts often do is to show the sense of the artist's action, that is, they expose the logic embedded in what was done, which the choreographer may or may not have been reflectively aware of during the process itself.[3] Indeed, that logic arguably only becomes evident afterwards, when the work is complete and its connections with the original intention can be made. From this perspective, accounts of process are not so much causal explanations which trace chronologically what went on in the choreographer's head and the actions it provoked. Rather, they are teleological explanations which justify the activity in relation to its end. They lay bare the practical reasoning embedded in the choreographic process.

There is an issue here of how we can be sure that practical reasoning informs what the artist does unless that logic is somehow made explicit.

After all, as Ryle points out, 'there need be no visible or audible differences between an action done with skill and one done from sheer habit, blind impulse, or in a fit of absence of mind' (1963: 40). It is possible, if unlikely, that a successful choreographic work could be created by someone wholly inexperienced in the practice, because he just happens to hit on an idea, set of images or movement material that 'works'; he does not know how in the manner of the choreographer with thirty years' practice behind her, yet by happy accident produces a dance that gives the illusion that he does. But then being able to do is neither a necessary nor a sufficient condition of knowing how, since our inexperienced artist can choreograph without knowing how. Does this suggest that the artist's practical reasoning process *must* be formalised or symbolically articulated in a language other than that of the artwork in order to prove that it informed the action?

Requiring verbal articulation of the reasoning process seems to undercut the advances made by the notion of practical inference in the first place. It is one thing to say that such reasoning *can* be abstracted and formalised, another to argue that it *must*: the sense in which reasoning is embodied in the doing gets lost as soon as there is an expectation that it be reframed or articulated some other way. In their account of the practical syllogism, summarised above, both Anscombe and Carr emphasise how its conclusion is an action, not a statement of intention or a direction to act, both of which would suggest that a different, more theoretical kind of rationality is at stake. Equally, the choreographer might claim that – while she may choose to discuss her process and thus lay bare how it was informed by patterns of practical reason – such discussion does not alter the fact that her actions were reasonable and intelligent, embodying her knowledge how, regardless of whether or how what she did is subsequently described or paraphrased. Similarly, the practitioner-researcher might be uneasy that the requirement for a verbal account of his process, which exposes its reasoned character, shifts the focus of any assessment of his work from the practice itself to how well he writes about it even though it is the choreography he has made which really embodied his (practical) thinking and knowledge.[4]

One way around this problem might be to suggest that it is not so much the agent who should identify her reasoning process but rather those observing and evaluating what she does. Carr (1978) makes the point that we reason practically in the third person and past tense as well as in the first person and present tense. Practical reasoning is the means by which others' intentional actions are understood, 'a matter of perceiving the logical ties between their beliefs and intentions and the things that they do' (1978: 11). If we are to claim that a person has knowledge how, we need to be able to explain these logical connections implicit in their activity: 'the correct ascription of "knowing how" presupposes understanding of an agent's behaviour through practical reasoning' (1978: 14). An example of Ryle's (1963) may help to illustrate this point. Ryle imagines a chess game in which a drunkard novice makes a devastating move that flummoxes and, ultimately, defeats his more experienced opponent. However, the fact that the drunkard has proved able to do this, indeed has performed the move, does not mean that the spectators ascribe to him the quality of knowing how to play, or assume that his action was a planned move that had been carefully thought through. In fact:

> the spectators are satisfied that this was due not to cleverness but to luck, if they are satisfied that most of his moves made in this state break the rules of chess, or have no tactical connexion with the position of the game, that he would not be likely to repeat this move if the tactical situation were to recur, that he would not applaud such a move made by another player in a similar situation, that he could not explain why he had done it or even describe the threat under which his King had been.
>
> (Ryle 1963: 45)

This description highlights the many and various criteria against which spectators assess whether or not the move was intelligent.

A similarly complex, multifaceted set of considerations comes into play when judging a dance work as the outcome of a reasoned process. The audience or assessors will be interested in how different facets of the work relate to one another, to other instances of the choreographer's practice and, indeed, to works and strategies employed by others in the field. They will be concerned with whether the line a choreographer pursues at a particular moment (in the dance work, or more generally in her career) makes sense in relation to the surrounding circumstances – aesthetic, semantic, pragmatic – and in how the choreographer explains (or might explain) that action and/or the problematic it resolved (without requiring that the whole logic of her process be laid bare).[5] Evaluating practice in this way does not make the success of the action's outcome a condition of its intelligence. The experienced chess player may lose the game as a result of the drunkard's devastating move, but the spectators still recognise that he is the one who really knows how to play. Equally, the dance work performed as the culmination of the choreographer's process might be judged an artistic or aesthetic failure, but this would not necessarily disqualify the choreography – or the practice-as-research – as intelligent action.

Choreography as creative action

There is still, however, a major difficulty in adapting these ideas about practical knowledge to choreography and choreography presented as research. Carr, Anscombe and Kenny all treat practical reasoning as underwriting intentional action as such. Choreographic practice is clearly a form of intentional action – that is, it is not something we engage in by accident, or unwittingly (which is not to say that accidents and unexpected turns do not occur in the course of making); but it is also a highly specialised and distinctive activity which seems, intuitively, to be fundamentally unlike changing the oil in one's car or playing chess. These are much more clearly routinised actions, governed by norms or rules that make the reasoning about the means to achieve one's purposes relatively straightforward.

In one sense, of course, choreography is also a rule-governed activity: conventions do exist to render it both possible and identifiable, and even when breaking with these conventions one still operates with reference to them.[6] And yet, choreography's creative dimension transcends the norm-based character of the 'ordinary' activities with which the literature on practical inference is largely preoccupied. Ends and means are not as clearly defined in a creative situation. For one thing, the purpose or intention governing a choreographic process (and thus governing the logic of practical reasoning embedded in that process) may itself shift according to the circumstances that present themselves; it may also be *discovered* during that process rather than being identifiable in advance.[7] What is more, the requirement that practice at least aims at an *original* approach remains entrenched in the aesthetic-artistic environment in which most choreographers work. As soon as we begin to consider choreography as research there is an additional expectation that it generates *new* knowledge and makes an innovative contribution to the field, not necessarily only with respect to its *artistic* originality.[8] Can the practical reasoning model accommodate this creative dimension of choreographic (research) practice?

Carr, although concerned with dance education rather than dance research, recognises this problem within his early work on dance practice knowledge. He notes that ideas about practical inference seem able to account only for 'the acquisition of fairly routine or habitual techniques – staying well clear of the less predictable creative and imaginative aspects of dance practice' (1999: 126). His most recent solution to the dilemma is to further interrogate the range of Aristotle's distinctions between kinds of knowledge, focusing in particular on the notion of *phronesis* (practical wisdom). This notion is also interesting as a way of articulating the knowledge a choreographer or choreographer-researcher develops through her practice.

For Aristotle, practical knowledge is distinct from theoretical understanding (*episteme*), which is a demonstrable and teachable form of knowledge concerned with the first principles or causes of its objects. Thus *episteme* is objective knowledge in the traditional sense, linked to and demonstrated by the ability to 'give an account of the thing which traced it back, or tied it down, to certain principles (*archai*) or causes (*aitai*)' (Dunne 1997: 237–8) – the general laws of scientific understanding. The domain of *episteme* is thus the domain of things that cannot be otherwise – of natural laws that transcend human intervention in the world. In contemporary terms, a neuroscientific account of a choreographer's brain processes might provide this kind of theoretical explanation of practice. The domain of practical knowledge itself, meanwhile, 'lies forever outside the scope of theory'; it is a realm of 'contingent or variable being … and more specifically, those things which, subject to certain limitations, are within the rational power of human beings to change' (Dunne 1997: 243).

Aristotle also draws a distinction between two modes of practical knowledge, each associated with a different form of activity. *Techne*, or the skill of craftsmanship, is associated with making products (*poiesis*) through the interaction of the craftsman's skill with his materials, the product's evolving form and its ultimate outcome. This is a reasoned capacity to make, linked to theoretical understanding: the craftsman's *techne* is evident not just in the successful outcome of the making process, but in his capacity 'to give a rational account (*logos*) of his procedures – an account which is rational insofar as it can trace the product back to the causes to which it owes its being (Dunne 1997: 250). It implies a detachment of the maker from his product, in Dunne's words, he can 'stand outside of his materials and allow the productive process to be shaped by the impersonal form which he has objectively conceived' (1997: 263).

In Aristotle's world, art-making was (or was considered to be) essentially this kind of technical procedure, a species of craftsmanship in which skill was used instrumentally to achieve pre-conceived ends. In the context of contemporary choreography, *techne* is still involved in making processes where the end is clearly specified in advance – perhaps where a dance is created according to an exact specification, or within a well-defined style which already sets out the criteria for artistic or aesthetic success. Indeed, an element of *techne* may be present in all choreographic making, insofar as there are parts of the process where the aim is clear and a largely procedural approach is appropriate to fulfilling it. For example, a transition may need to be found between two distinct, already choreographed sections of a work, which gets the dancers from A to B in a manner which blends the movement motifs of the two parts. Or lighting may need to be designed which emphasises those elements of the movement that the choreographer has already highlighted as important (which is not to say that, in other cases, lighting design is not a less routine, more creative process). In these cases, the choreographer-craftsman works self-consciously within preconceived parameters to achieve an identified aim.

But Aristotle contrasts *techne* with a different mode of practical knowledge – *phronesis* or practical wisdom – which neither masters nor instrumentalises in this way. This is the knowledge associated with the domain of *praxis*, the variable and mutable world of human beings, intersubjective action and encounters; for Aristotle, the moral domain in which, as human beings, we try to live and act in ways beneficial to ourselves and the social group (*polis*). The kind of knowledge needed in this domain is not a technical understanding of how to manipulate processes, so much as a creative sensitivity to circumstances as they present themselves. *Phronesis* is not concerned so much with general principles, universal laws or causal understanding, but rather with what cannot be generalized. It is a kind of attunement to the *particularities* of situations and experiences, requiring subjective involvement rather than objective detachment; and it has an irreducibly personal dimension in its dependence upon, and the fact that it folds back into, subjective and intersubjective experience.

Although Aristotle's own analysis of *phronesis* applies to the task of cultivating moral virtue, Carr (1999) argues its relevance for contemporary artistic practice. In art-making, as in ethics, there is a focus on practice rather than theory and on the experientially particular rather than universal precepts or generalisations. It is what is done in particular situations that matters, and that is shaped by the nature of the particular situation, not by abstract reasoning about how things ought to happen. It seems rare that a dance be made in accordance with a theory defined in advance, according to generalised rules, or at least, choreography of this kind often lacks the interest of work made through a more aleatory, creative approach. Carr also points out that both moral and creative artistic action are intertwined with the expression and articulation of feeling, requiring sensitivity to the emotional character of situations, not detachment or neutrality. And it seems true that, even the choreographer who does not set out to make a dance which expresses a particular feeling or range of emotions still works with the emotional nuances of movement, light and sound, insofar as she is interested in the impact her work may have on a potential audience. Carr suggests that for the agent cultivating moral virtue or making dance, there is a comparable concern with personal development: in each case, the self is implicated, unfolded and cultivated, not something to be set aside in cool objectivism. There are, of course, exceptions to this in the world of choreography,[9] but in general it seems clear that making dance involves the artist as a person much more than, say, theoretical or scientific enquiry involves the researcher, or than a technical making process completed according to a predefined specification involves the craftsman. All of which suggests, in line with Carr's (1999) argument, that *phronesis* is a useful way of characterising choreographic as well as moral knowledge.

The concept of *phronesis* seems relevant to choreography not only because we can draw an analogy between dance-making and moral action. Choreography is itself arguably a form of praxis because it involves collective production. Choreographers work with others – performers, designers, audiences – to produce performance events. It is crucial, in this intersubjective context, to have a creative sensitivity to the others involved, the evolving situation and the experiences it generates. This creative sensitivity – and the ability to act in accordance with what it suggests to be the 'right' course – is arguably a fundamental part of any performing artist's practice. Decisions are not generally made according to a technically rational view of how to manipulate the relationships central to dance-making, but rather arise out of the circumstances of the moment and are governed by a different kind of rationality sensitive to contingencies and to the evolving nature of those relationships. Perhaps this is particularly true of choreography-as-research which tends to involve an increased self-consciousness about how the artist conducts herself within the making process. Research provides a space for reflection, often not afforded in the sphere of professional performance, geared as it is towards the production of works that can be exchanged as commodities within the dance market. With such reflection may come a heightened awareness of oneself and one's encounters as an artist as the basis of any performance event. And this awareness is arguably a form of phronetic insight developed through the practice itself.

Conclusion

This discussion has sought to show how philosophical ideas about practical knowledge, reasoning and wisdom might be relevant to choreography and dance practice as research, helping us identify (at least part of) their epistemological value. This is not the only way in which the knowledge developed in and through dance-making can be described, and it is not unproblematic.[10] For example, one might question whether theoretical and practical knowledge can be so sharply differentiated, whether *techne* and *phronesis* are distinct and mutually exclusive forms of practical knowledge and also whether the particularism of phronetic insight compromises its shareability and hence its very status as knowledge. All of these issues and more warrant more detailed investigation. But, hopefully, the discussion does demonstrate the fruitfulness of the literature for attempts to think through the epistemology of choreography. To think of choreography and choreographic research as dealing in practical knowledge does help move us beyond dominant paradigms, which deny that dance-making has epistemological value.[11]

Notes

1 Piccini (2003) gives a historical account and Thomson (2002) examples of the issues explored in these debates. Pakes (2003) explores some of these issues in the context of dance practice. The PARIP (Practice as Research in Performance) website includes links to a range of papers presented at its conferences, from a variety of disciplines in which practice is presented as research, including dance (http://www.bristol.ac.uk/parip/index.htm).

2 Inductive reasoning and inference to best explanation are also widely used patterns of inference, based on a logic of probability rather than truth and falsity. Popper (1968) proposes to refocus scientific reasoning around the principle of falsifiability rather than verification, recasting all inference in its deductive – and hence more reliable – form. According to Hempel's 'covering law model', meanwhile, the logic of scientific explanation is *essentially* deductive, since, when trying to explain the occurrence of a particular phenomenon, scientists tend to cite a general law from which the empirical facts follow (Hempel 1965).

3 A good example is Rosemary Butcher's reflections on her making processes, 2001–02, in conversation with Nikki Pollard: see Butcher and Melrose (2005: 66–85). Butterworth and Clarke (1998) furnish several other examples.
4 The necessity or otherwise of written documents accompanying practice-as-research is a contentious issue within the performing arts research community. For example, UKCGE (1997) claims that such documents play a 'pivotal role' in assessing doctoral submissions, where Rye (2003) argues that they may distort or alter the knowledge generated by practical projects.
5 These are the kinds of issues an examiner might consider when assessing a choreographic research project, but also typical questions posed in critical analyses of choreographers' work. See, for example, the essays in Bremser (1999) and Ploebst (2001).
6 On dance as a rule-governed activity, see McFee (1992: 52–5) and Carr (1987b).
7 For example, in Jonathan Burrows' conversations with six contemporary choreographers, both Michael Clark and Amanda Miller indicate that past choreographic projects have involved discovering a direction through the process (Burrows 1998).
8 See, for example, UKCGE (1997). Pakes (2003) explores further the issue of originality in dance practice-as-research.
9 Merce Cunningham's use of chance methods, for example, aimed to distance choreographic decision-making from his own will and personal resources (Greskovic in Bremser 1999).
10 Pakes (2004) develops a critique of the practical knowledge model and presents an alternative view of how knowledge is embodied in practice-as-research.
11 Early drafts of this material were presented to the PARIP 2003 conference, at PARIP and Roehampton University Dance Research Seminars, and to postgraduate students at London Contemporary Dance School and Laban between 2004 and 2006. Thanks to the audience on each occasion for its help in exploring and critiquing the ideas.

References

Anscombe, G.E.M. (1963) *Intention*, 2nd edn, Oxford: Basil Blackwell.

Aristotle, (2000) *Nicomachean Ethics*, translated and edited by R. Crisp, Cambridge: Cambridge University Press.

Best, D. (1985) *Feeling and Reason in the Arts*, London: Allen & Unwin.

—— (1987a) 'Creativity', in J. Adshead (ed.) *Choreography: Principles and Practice*, Guildford: NRCD.

—— (1987b) 'Feeling and reason in choreography and criticism', in J. Adshead (ed.) *Choreography: Principles and Practice*, Guildford: NRCD.

Bremser, M. (ed.) (1999) *Fifty Contemporary Choreographers*, London: Routledge.

Burrows, J. (1998) Conversations with Choreographers, London: South Bank Centre.

Butcher, R. and Melrose S. (eds) (2005) *Choreography, Collisions and Collaborations*, Enfield: Middlesex University Press.

Butterworth, J. and Clarke G. (eds) (1998) *Dance Makers Portfolio: Conversations with Choreographers*, Bretton Hall: Centre for Dance and Theatre Studies.

Carr, D. (1978) 'Practical reasoning and knowing how', *Journal of Human Movement Studies*, 4: 3–20.

—— (1984) 'Dance education, skill and behavioural objectives', *Journal of Aesthetic Education*, 18: 67–76.

—— (1987a) 'Reason and inspiration in dance and choreography', in J. Adshead (ed.) *Choreography: Principles and Practice*, Guildford: NRCD.

—— (1987b) 'Thought and action in the art of dance', *British Journal of Aesthetics*, 27, 345–57.

Carr, D. (1999) 'Further reflections on practical knowledge and dance a decade on', in G. McFee (ed.) *Dance, Education and Philosophy*, Oxford: Meyer & Meyer Sport.

Dunne, J. (1997) *Back to the Rough Ground: Practical Judgement and the Lure of Technique*, Notre Dame: University of Notre Dame Press.

Hempel, C.G. (1965) *Aspects of Scientific Explanation, and Other Essays in the Philosophy of Science*, London: Collier-Macmillan.

Kenny, A. (1966) 'Practical inference', *Analysis*, 26: 65–75.

McFee, G. (1992) *Understanding Dance*, London: Routledge.

—— (1994) *The Concept of Dance Education*, London: Routledge.

Pakes, A. (2003) 'Original embodied knowledge: the epistemology of the new in dance practice as research', *Research in Dance Education*, 4 (2): 127–49.

—— (2004) 'Art as action or art as object? The embodiment of knowledge in practice as research', Working Papers in Art and Design, 3. Available online at <http://sitem.herts.ac.uk/artdes_research/papers/wpades/vol3/apabs.html> (accessed 30 August 2008).

Piccini, A. (2003) 'An historiographic perspective on practice as research', *Studies in Theatre and Performance,* 23 (3): 191–207.

Ploebst, H. (2001) *No Wind, No Word: New Choreography in the Society of the Spectacle*, Munich: K. Kieser.

Popper, K. (1968) *The Logic of Scientific Discovery*, 2nd edn, London: Hutchinson.

Redfern, B. (1982) *Concepts in Modern Educational Dance*, London: Dance Books.

—— (1983) *Dance, Art and Aesthetics*, London: Dance Books.

Rye, C. (2003) 'Incorporating practice: a multi-viewpoint approach to performance documentation', *Journal of Media Practice* 3 (2): 115–23.

Ryle, G. (1963) *The Concept of Mind*, 2nd edn, Harmondsworth: Penguin.

Thomson, P. (2002) 'Notes and queries: practice as research', *Studies in Theatre and Performance*, 22 (3): 159–80.

UK Council for Graduate Education (1997) Practice-based doctorates in the creative and performing arts, Coventry: UKCGE.

Von Wright, G.H. (1963) 'Practical inference', *Philosophical Review*, 72 (2): 159–79.

—— (1971) *Explanation and Understanding*, London: Routledge and Kegan Paul.

3 Expert-intuitive processing and the logics of production

Struggles in (the wording of) creative decision-making in 'dance'

Susan Melrose

I want to start with a confession: I want to write '*about* dance' – almost as though, firstly, you and I were already in agreement as to what the latter means, or might mean; and secondly, as though I '*can write* about dance', even if it remains the case that my 'dance writing' can only be produced from my position as expert spectator, and on the basis of the relation to 'dance' that this spectating allows. *Spectating*, by the way, does tend to transform 'dance' into *spectacle*, by which I mean into an aspect of the wider, ubiquitous, pleasurable and very persuasive visual economy. Perhaps I should only write, on the basis of this limitation of mine, '*about* watching dance', where this shift in words would, at the very least, put me in my place: I am *not-a-performer*, at least as far as expertise in the performance disciplines is concerned, and I am *not-a-choreographer*. What am I doing here? (The first answer, of course, is *writing*.)

'Dance' as difference

Given my limitations as expert spectator and writer, even if I sit next to Rosemary Butcher, *watching dance*, at The Place, in London, as I have done a number of times over recent years,[1] it is absolutely clear to me that *how I watch*, *what I see*, and *what I make of it*, will be different from Butcher's own ways of watching, ways of seeing and experience of 'the work'. I have become aware, for example, while watching Rosemary Butcher watching 'dance', that whereas I can 'see dance' as though it were projected on a screen, Rosemary Butcher, sitting in The Place beside me, also 'sees dance' multidimensionally, and through the lens specific to expert-practitioner performance-making.

Butcher can see what is going on in those parts of 'dance' that my gaze fails to reach. She sees decisions made, opportunities lost; she sees what will come, in the moment before it arrives, and she tests what she sees and will see and doesn't see, in terms of an expert memory of 'dance' that stretches back at the very least to the 1970s and forward to the next pieces of work to be made – since Rosemary Butcher continues to make new work that others qualify as challenging. She sees *the other side of the dancer*, while I can only see the side I actually see. In the most banal and axiomatic of terms, then, 'dance', to the trained dancer and the experienced choreographer, is '*nothing like*' – or 'non-identical with' (Knorr Cetina 2001: 175–88) – the 'dance' that an expert spectator, reader and educator sees and appraises in terms of her or his own experience. And 'the dancer', of course, *can't see even what I see*, which means that '*the same dance*' is once again, in terms of the range of participants in it, *unlike*, or non-identical with itself.

Let's assume, for the moment, nonetheless, that we are, to some limited extent at least, sufficiently in agreement as to the meaning of 'dance', to enable us to use words to write and read about it here. Let's set aside, for the moment, the contentious issue of the authority upon which we might 'word', or name, or account for a complex system – or rather, systems – that operates, for the most part, *outside of language*. Operating in the main outside of language, it is neither 'structured like a language',[2] nor is it either 'textual' or 'non-textual' (the latter a negative definition); 'dance' is neither 'text-like', nor '*un*-like'. Its measure is taken from 'dance' and from other performance modes, not the linguistic/discursive. (It might be more appropriate, if we view language and text from the position of dance expertise, to argue that language-in-use by experts aspires to the choreographic;[3] aspires to the poetic – on which basis we might argue that certain poetic texts are '*dansant*', and their articulation 'choreographic', when they are delivered appropriately.)

'Dance', in fact, is always more than the word suggests, in the sense that real dancework, when it is expertly made, tends to bring together the input of a number of expert practitioners – such as, in the European tradition, 'dancer', 'choreographer', sound design/er, lighting design/er. Outside of language, 'dance' in that tradition tends, inasmuch as it operates effectively in the wider arts communities, to be signature-marked, by which I mean that the name of the choreographer, at least, tends to be a token of cultural exchange: that name figures, one might say, in the models of intelligibility specific to its practices. 'Rosemary Butcher' means, in the context of dance-making, much more than it says; it names a considerable body of work, in shorthand, and in this sense, the name is a professional dance signature.

'Dance' tends, on this sort of basis, and in the wider arts communities, to be *impressed with* the name/s of the expert practitioners involved, tends to be 'marked by' something (some 'things') associated with the name of an artist. I write these words with recent experience of Rosemary Butcher's 'dance' production processes in mind, and against the backdrop of my own long-established and *wordy* concern with the ways expert arts-making practices are approached in the university, and the former's uneasy relationships with text-production in the hands of the professional wordmakers and educators, that many academic researchers actually are. Is Rosemary Butcher's recent work on stage and film 'dance', 'dance on film', or 'dance on screen'? And if – in your view – it is 'not dance', how is it that so many of those who contemplate it do so through the lens and within the frameworks which apply to the dance and dance-related professions, in the wider arts communities?

On the precarious basis of an assumed degree of agreement about meaning-potential and the noun and verb 'dance', and my place (as word-maker) in or with regard to it, I argue that 'dance' – is whether or not one likes this notion – a discipline-specific complex practice or complex system of practices; relatively stabilised, as system, as well as repeatedly destabilised, from within. In short, 'dance' is a stabilised self-destabilising system, open to internal transformation, from which dance-makers select – explicitly or implicitly – a certain number of discipline-specific or related options with which they play; and to which spectators tend to bring modes of engagement that fall within a finite range of possibilities. In the case above, Rosemary Butcher's recent *work* (the dance event or the film), and her ways of working, are consistently calculated upon the input of a highly trained dancer. That work is, similarly, consistently informed by and attentive to dance production values that accrue to the dance professions as well as to 'new work', viewed from the perspectives of the wider arts communities, which are manifested in judgements of taste and value made by all involved. When Rosemary Butcher's *Hidden Voices*,[4] with dancer Elena Giannotti, reached the finals of The Place Prize in 2004, none who admitted that they found it challenging, or not to their taste, are likely to have claimed that it should not have been presented in the context of 'dance', at a major London dance institution. The Place, at least, recognised, and thereafter articulated, its place and function within the discipline.

What I want to entertain at this point is the possibility that, for some members of the audience at least,[5] Rosemary Butcher's *Hidden Voices* works in significant part because Butcher stages an expert dancer, in a pool or pools of light,[6] in order to constrain her, in order to require of her that she refrain from 'dancing' as such, while the work that emerges constantly bears the impress of Butcher's signature. On that basis the work is understood, irresistibly, in terms of its measure against a 'dance' that is itself understood in relatively conservative terms. I effortlessly view 'the dancer', in my mind's eye, when invited or required to, in terms that are actually banal. Let's acknowledge this: 'new dance', at its time, was measured, even by its most radical commentators, against a notion of 'dance' that remained relatively conservative. The discipline remained as such, especially when it was challenged. Hence 'dance' in the case of *Hidden Voices*, is irresistibly present, the more so at precisely those moments when a 'dance spectator' complains about its absence.

Dance is there *under deconstruction*, as some of us in the university might have written in the last decades of the twentieth century: 'dance', retained and relatively abstract as far as some of us are concerned, is brought by all of us who participate, even in the event that proclaims its own radicalism, and it hangs around that event in the ether. It is on this basis alone – that 'dance' is always present and in mind, as well as expected to reveal itself anew – that some of us can recognise that dance is *deferred* in Butcher's recent work with Giannotti.

What then, is 'dance'? It seems, to me at least, to be relatively abstract, yet formal, discipline-specific, stabilised, multidimensional, no doubt, and present to mind – yet it is differently present to Butcher's mind, and to my own. 'Dance' is similarly present and absent in the aura that accompanies Butcher's film *Vanishing Point*,[7] when it is viewed: it is retained, by spectators of dance, as a whole range of well-established, discipline-specific relationships and judgements of taste and value – all apparently insubstantial but determinant, which is why I represent them, metaphorically, in terms of *ether*. It's in the air, rather more than it is usefully qualified as virtual, yet variously so, dependent upon the degree of your own expertise and place in it. At the same time, some places breathe it in and out, and thereby cause us to re-articulate it as such.

'Dance', as discipline-specific, is also constitutively relational, which means that it is both here and there, and differently, as well as now and then and in the future. As both here and there, but differently, it necessarily entails an array of heterogeneous practices, some of which – significantly – I pay willingly to watch, and some of which – my own included – I would not. Based on this relationality, any attempt to account for 'dance', then, needs to be diagrammatic, multidimensional, rather than conventionally writerly. Butcher imagines the place of her spectator, in any performance-making decision she makes, even though she doesn't know the spectator and need not. Implicitly, she takes a spectator's ability to concentrate into account, as well as what she takes to be their wants – of 'dance', and of what for her is '*my new work*' – and interests. Her smallest decision tends to challenge an onlooker, but can only challenge inasmuch as they both have a notion of what 'dance' entails – something that might surprise her most challenged spectators. But in the making, her lucid concern is with the artistic and how she might make it emerge through her work with the expert dancer, and with one or two other performance professionals.

All the same, 'dance', in her new work, continues to occupy a relational framework, like a performance space at The Place, and it operates and intervenes relationally, between what the dancer brings, and how Butcher impresses into what emerges between them, her own highly particular signature. 'Impress', here, is active, high-energy, expert. The metaphor 'cartography', then, pleasing as it may seem to some writers, fails to allow us to work with a relationality which is not only multidimensional, but invested with energies that include those particular to the singular, disciplinary input of a number of expert practitioners. In place of the map, I prefer to use the term 'signature'. It is identified 'in the work' as singular, a mark of intellectual property ownership to which a name is given; but it is also a matter of heterogeneous particles, rallied by and impressed into, and partly transformed – thus constituting, in significant part – 'the work', or rather 'the dance work'.

In pragmatic terms, Butcher is a dance practitioner who impresses her mark, recognisably, into both the larger lines and the detail of the work, and in intellectual property terms, she legally owns that impress, despite the fact that it will almost certainly include within it those heterogeneous particles provided by other expert practitioners who have agreed to work with her, and whose input catalyses and is catalysed by her own. Now, different particles of what I call 'signature work' might well be copied by others, but not in such a way as to bear her (endlessly renewed) signature: one cannot 'copy' the input brought to Butcher by a chosen expert dancer, which, in that particular relationship, qualitatively transforms that dancer's own way of working. So while the attempt to copy Butcher's signature would have legal implications, that signature cannot, in fact, be extracted from the work; on the other hand, attempts to reproduce Butcher's stylistic choices have taken their place in Dance Studies programmes internationally, over a matter of decades.

The impress of a particulate signature is best identified in terms of a diagrammicity and rhythmicity (Deleuze 2003) that resonates with the name of the artist; it is likely to be multidimensional, hence it sits uncomfortably – as you can see here – in words, whether in writing, in expert-spectator interpretations or in journalists' renderings. Dance signature cannot be 'read' (all we really obtain thereby is the artist's name); nor indeed can it easily be accounted for, since any narrative constructed around it requires the writer's own inventive intervention, and tends, then, to be constructed in her/his own image. It can, however – and here lies the paradox – be recognised, even when the work is 'new'. I would argue that its paradoxical nature is such that 'we' might need to draw on a theoretics of choreographic composition, collaboration, and catalysis, if we are even to begin to grasp (at) it *in words*.

Discipline, discipline-specificity, and their troubled recent history

As intimated, the notion of 'discipline' itself has tended to receive a consistently bad press over the past few decades in published writing in Performance and Dance Studies – hence the crucial link with my concern with ways of *wording* 'things', *in* the university, when those things are specific to arts practices, as these are practised *outside* the university. It might be worth observing here that the ways arts practices are worded, in the university 'economy', are themselves contingent upon the 'ways of seeing' (Berger 1972) and models of intelligibility (e.g. 'new work'; 'liminal practices') that are dominant within that university economy. Repeatedly, in these sorts of terms, the inter-, post- and anti-disciplinary have been preferred to disciplinarity in performance-making throughout the university culture, over a number of decades, perhaps because practices in the realm of the 'inter-', the 'post-' and the 'anti-' are less difficult to resource in the university (as distinct from a specialist provider in the higher education sector) and tend to 'fit' with certain generations of academics' self-image.

Those who readily reject the term 'discipline', in Performance Studies writing at least, seem to associate it readily with what they take to be a conservative power structure imposed and 'measured' from above, entailing discipleship (hence obedience to a master), subscribing, necessarily, to conservative value systems, and associated with one or another elite. My own observation is that disciplinary mastery is indeed specific to an elite. You and I salute this, whenever we pay dearly to see the work of Pina Bausch or Robert Wilson: the mastery of the complex codes and the challenges specific to professional creativity are developed and engaged with by relatively few of us. To the university, sadly, the attempt to promote mastery is less sustainable than programmes with universal access (or – as the government discourse has it – 'widened participation').

The reasons for this tendency are complex, and they do also bear some relation to the coincidence, in post-WWII Europe and the USA, between the 'critical'-theoretical in writing in the university, and the avant-garde in arts production.[8] The 'anti-disciplinary', subscribing readily to a widely prevailing Hegelian logic[9] in post-WWII Europe and USA, implies radicalism and revolt, yet this so-called radicalism and revolt achieves nothing so much as to carry 'dance' with it, as implicit or explicit to it. 'Radical dance' still marks itself, explicitly, with the discipline. DV8, as they have found over more than a decade, cannot escape from this. Meanwhile, the 'inter-' of university programmes seems to place its emphasis, instead, on the multiple, on negotiation, on blurred boundaries, on liminality, on merging and hybridity – hence on difference and inclusivity, rather than the exclusivity that is proper both to radical refusals and to disciplinary mastery. Inter-disciplinarity still tends to be perceived, in the university in particular, as a positivity, although that is less the case in the wider arts communities. Inter-disciplinarity *theorises*, inasmuch as it tends to be dialogical, bringing together and attempting to resolve difference, and in historical terms it collocates with or is positioned alongside the feminine, the feminist and the 'queer', in contrast with the supposed masculinity of mastery – at least in the set-ups specific to the university and its dominant discourses.

I wonder whether those of us who operate in the university might 'de-gender' mastery and discipline, for a moment, for the purposes of the present enquiry into expertise and the expert, and ask how it is acquired, and how it might be understood? Unless we do so, we will continue to misrecognise an expertise (and associated 'production values') that always inheres in 'good work', whether that work is submitted for evaluation in the higher degree context or enjoyed in and by the wider arts communities. Until we begin to identify disciplinary mastery as such, in Dance Studies writing, we will remain unable to understand decision-making in the work of any of the notorious expert practitioners whose dance pieces tend to be cited in dance programmes across higher education institutions.

In order to demonstrate what I mean here, I focus in the next section of this chapter on what I have called the *expert-intuitive operations central to discipline-specific expertise in general, and to decision-making in dance and other performance modes in particular*.[10] The operation of the expert-intuitive in dance-making is central to the making processes (as it is, differently, to other disciplines), yet it is unavailable *as such* to the expert spectator whose own engagement with 'dance' tends to take product or outcome – 'the performance event', within which she can plainly take her place – as her primary focus. That is understandable. Besides, what is vitally important about expert-intuitive processes, central to creative invention, is that they are unavailable *as such* (because of expert collaborations and because of the catalytic effect attendant upon these[11]) to spectating, and to writing that is, implicitly at least, written from the position – and the times – of expert spectating.

Expert spectating (and what is lost to it)

Curiously, then, if in fact 'dance', as discipline, necessarily involves spectating (it is put in place, and aligned, with a spectator or spectators in mind, whether those spectators are viewed positively or negatively by the practitioners concerned), that dance's constitutive *expert-intuitive* processing occurs in a place and a time from which real spectators are absent. Spectating, always present in some part of the dance-maker's mind (even when she denies it), is retained, at these places and times, as virtual. Spectating's own times are both energetically charged and heightened, and they are extremely limited and limiting, as far as the performance knowledge economy is concerned. Dance-making processes and their knowledge status differ internally *in time*, as well as in type, from those available under the same disciplinary heading ('dance'; the show), to spectators.

In terms of access to knowledge, I have often, wearily remarked[12] that expert spectators *can only see what they can see*, but are trained to fill in the rest, often discursively, through a combination of *sensing* and of inferential processes that are normalised in many a university department. What by definition *can't be seen*, or *sensed* by a non-practitioner-spectator is that time when a discipline-specific inventiveness was summoned forth, juggled with, tossed about and tested, and in those processes catalysed and/or transformed, on the way to a production. A spectator can see the outcome of some of these operations (if indeed they are retained in the show itself), but not how the expert-intuitive emerged, nor in whose hands. Expert collaborations, common to much making in the performing arts, are largely mysterious to outsiders, not least because the discourse between expert collaborators is largely in a closed register, often cryptic and sometimes apparently imprecise (but actually entirely precise). What need hardly be spoken of, after all, between them, is that earlier signature work, through which these artists know or know of each other. As far as the expert practitioners involved are concerned, the exact source of a particular happy invention, catalysed by the collaboration itself, is rarely quarrelled over at the time, and they may not recall, when interviewed, who did or said what.

Now, the means to work in that manner can only be learned through active engagement in certain sorts of meaningful activities, in certain productive set-ups, with certain sorts of future activities – like 'making something new', or 'qualitatively transformed' – in view, under the constraints that those are specific to the discipline. These are largely closed to spectators, but more important here is the fact that the means to work in that manner cannot be acquired in most postgraduate settings, outside of the few specialist colleges in the higher education sector. Learning in the context of expert making operates best through something like an informal apprenticeship, rather than a postgraduate seminar, in that the former tends to expose the apprentice-practitioner to the ways of expert-intuitive and 'felt' knowledges that bring together the inventive and a keen grasp of production logics and production values, which are exercised in expert invention within a particular disciplinary field.

In the event, the dance event – where 'dance' goes public – differs markedly from that series of internal events that are vital to its constitution, even if it is also the case that the outcomes of this series of 'events', performed/produced by a range of expert practitioners, seem to meet, albeit momentarily, in that public event. The series of apparently internal, practitioner-specific events is itself internally differentiated in time and in type; they are marked internally by their different production stages and the processes that are associated with them; and it is worth noting of them that their outcome tends to be non-identical with the quest that drives the making.

When Lyotard (1991) asked something about time, then, in the mid-1980s, along these sorts of lines: 'what is the work that finishes the work?', his repitition of the noun 'work' seems to invite us to recognise that easy reference to 'the work' is problematic. The public event, despite the insistence of some performance theorists/expert spectators that it is 'never the same' from one night to the next, is, to the practitioners involved, almost always a compromise with time, made *just in time*; always a compromise with what's available; never quite as ready as spectators tend to imagine; and not quite loved – enough – by the practitioners who put their name to it, until it is ratified by positive feedback, which, besides, never really lasts. Therefore 'the event' is, for its makers, a pause in an ongoing making process whose duration is institutionally imposed on the discipline. It *always* (in *all ways*) informs the work in constitutive terms, and the work that finishes the work produces 'the work' – *just in time*. I would argue that it is in the work that finishes the work that the expert practitioner's signature emerges. The important point, with regard to time and expert practices, is that making takes place in discipline-specific stages. It is internally complex, in terms of those making processes. This makes 'the work', as it is experienced in the making, different from, or non-identical with, 'the work' that audiences experience in the event itself.

It takes a highly particular energy and forceful persuasion, a keen and practical grasp of production logics and production values, a contract or series of contracts, and professional respect between the artists concerned for expertise to reveal itself. It needs the artist's ability, at a certain point in time, to step out of the growing work, so that a third-person objectification and thematisation becomes possible, at the stage just *before* the work's public exposure, articulation, showing, in one or another of those highly particular set-ups whose 'apparatuses' serve to make dancework *dance*.

In relational terms, and in terms of the set-ups that articulate 'dance' on dance's own behalf, expertise recognises expertise, expert recognises expert, across the history of the discipline, in spite of historically specific stylistic differences within 'dance'. Dance experts tend, quite reasonably, to ignore academics, since they have no real need of them, but the opposite clearly is untrue. Most expert spectators as well as dance professionals know perfectly well, and *feel*, when work is expert and when it is not, even if many of those of us who are spectators are unable to identify precisely what it is, in the work, upon which that judgement is built, and what, precisely, might be done to retrieve it, when, as frequently happens, the work or aspects of the work falter.

The expert-intuitive, and logics of performance production

What is at stake in the ideologically based (but 'normalised' in the university) failure to give performance mastery, performance-making expertise, disciplinary specificity and professional production values their proper place in 'academic' registers of writing 'about' performance made by expert practitioners? I propose at this stage to take the expert-intuitive practices central to performance-making as exemplary of this failure or refusal. Perhaps I should clarify what I mean by the expert-intuitive before proceeding to demonstrate that what comes out of expert-intuitive processes is necessarily transformed, if it is retained, when it comes into inevitable contact with the logics of production. Gregory Ulmer is one of the few writers published on intuitive process as a vital aspect of invention (Ulmer 1994). I return to his approach below, but before I do so, I need to stress that the *expert*-intuitive is qualitatively different from the 'everyday-intuitive', in the sense that its intervention occurs within and in terms of the set-ups that apply to expert performance-making, with the development of creative performance-making in mind. By 'in mind', a potentially worrying term, I simply mean something acquired, retained, evaluated, trusted (to *work*), as part of expertise, that is brought by the practitioner.

We might account for the expert-intuitive as emerging from something like expert memory; it is part of a particular sensibility, which makes available a number of different apparatuses to the expert practitioner, who uses these very rapidly in everyday professional tasks as well as in invention in choreographic practice. As such, the expert-intuitive tends to intervene at particular points of time in producing quite specific and often arts-funded creative outcomes. That intervention, which recognises that the space for invention is time-limited, activates an array of mechanisms, professionally naturalised in the expert practitioner, which inform all of the everyday activities of making, as well as those that more explicitly target performance production. My *sense* is that these mechanisms are internalised in the expert practitioner, constituting a major aspect of that expertise; as such they can operate at lightning speed, so that the practitioner concerned will often describe them – wrongly – as 'just intuitive'.

The choreographer Kim Brandstrup, at work on a new project and with the date of the opening night in mind, seems to me to be juggling, at any moment in workshop or rehearsal, a number of time-sensitive set-ups, outlines and parameters, each of which – if you try to imagine them – is likely to be unfolded, apparently invisibly, at particular moments. Juggling these, he is likely to depend upon an intuitive sense of 'rightness', which enables him to identify new points of possible intersection, and to pursue them in practice. At such moments their use is likely (but it is not guaranteed) to reveal greater complexities and interesting possibilities; points and sites of meaningful intersection seem to reveal themselves, in the work of making, between options in a wide range of systems which tend to include the as-yet untested (the new dancer in the group, the new piece of music composed for the work). Process threads and thematic threads are partly revealed in this ongoing enquiry and based on a *sense of rightness*, these are likely to be taken up, tested, retained or cast aside.

Such 'set-ups and outlines and parameters' provide some of the conditions within which invention might occur – because such invention (and professional artists know this) *has occurred in the past*, and has been effectively exploited. In order to formalise these 'set-ups' and 'outlines' and 'parameters', I use the French term '*dispositifs*' (in the plural) to represent them. But I want to use the term, *dispositif* (meaning disposition, or grid), to signal something other than a map. Instead, it signals a productive apparatus that is made up of a whole range of smaller productive apparatuses that the choreographer, whose name we will at some stage remember, masters (even where, in her or his characteristic modesty, that choreographer denies this mastery).

The numerous *dispositifs* are something like multidimensional frameworks and mechanisms, juggled and brought into timely intersection by the artist; through these a heightened but generally quiet energy is channelled, not consistently, but in ebbs and flows that in professional inventive practice tend to accumulate (although rarely without interruption or blockage). They permit an inventive imagining, precisely because they are, themselves, specific to the discipline, rather more than they are specific to any individual imagination. In Brandstrup's work, for example, they bring the range of possibilities, for his imagining, that is specific to dancers from the Royal Ballet or the Rambert Dance Company: on this basis, his imagination can leap. In Butcher's work, her imagining is similarly facilitated by dancer expertise, although her signature-specific uses of it are different. Whereas the discipline itself means that these two choreographers have recourse to similar apparatuses, and can recognise this in each other's work, their imaginations have invested what is brought in radically different manner. This inventiveness tests the discipline, which in terms of its generative *dispositifs* can perfectly contain it.

Now, the collaborative framework of dance-making is such that we can multiply aspects (but not the whole) of this scenario, and the juggling central to it, across a range of inventive expert practitioners – named dancers, sound designer, lighting designer, and so on – whose contribution to the project has been sought by the dance-maker whose signature the outcome will bear. Ideally, what is produced at different stages of the process will come to achieve 'empirical fit' (Ulmer 1989) through transposition or transference, for the choreographer concerned, with what the others offer – and indeed, that choreographer is likely to have chosen collaborators on the basis of that expectation. Each collaborator is likely, as well, to bring to the project an aspiration to qualitative transformation (Massumi 2002) – the hope and expectation (as well as the anxiety) that the project will bring 'out of' her or his contribution something that he or she judges to be different from, and tentatively better than, her earlier experiences as a dancer or designer or composer.

Within this framework, where choreographer and collaborators juggle multiple *dispositifs*, specific to the discipline concerned, and are likely to generate 'new work', the quest to obtain 'empirical fit' with the choreographer's signature is both banal, affectively invested, existentially challenging (Osborne 2000), and likely to be fraught. It might well appear that production processes are blocked, despite an imminent deadline, when the creative input of one or another expert collaborator fails to achieve empirical fit with what the choreographer wants, which at the same time, she or he cannot yet identify. She wants – but cannot identify yet precisely what it is that she wants, because she wants it to surprise and excite her. She genuinely has not seen it before but waits for it to emerge, at which time she will be transported. When at length it finally occurs, the artist's recognition that empirical fit is momentarily achieved will almost certainly be *felt* by her or him, first, rather than experienced rationally – although after that feeling, *provided it holds*, practitioner expertise is such that s/he will be able to summon it forth again, albeit slightly transformed, in terms of the logics of production that apply and the *dispositifs* that are specific to directorial expertise.

What suddenly 'fits' seems to have been conjured up out of a nowhere of knowledge and a nowhere of individual intent: she cannot make it appear, but can bring to bear, with a semblance of patience, the various schemata that apply to the professional creative task, and wait. It – the intuitive 'product' (Ulmer 1994) – is likely to be felt by her, in its full impact, as something fragile, new, but 'right'. Ulmer, writing about what he called 'hyperbolic intuition', drew on the work of the educational theorist Tony Bastick to observe that what emerges, at such a moment of creative discovery and recognition, seems to be 'in the style of an "accident" that does not have a logical relevance to the problem that an invention addresses' – even though environment or place, he adds, is likely to play 'an instrumental role in insight' (1994: 141). In place of 'environment or place', I would prefer to identify the instrumental role of the set-ups, including production deadlines that are specific to a choreographer's invention. It emerges, instead, Ulmer writes, when something effectively invisible to the outside eye occurs, when 'emotionally-invested "sets"' are re-centred into a pattern (for example, a potentially choreographic pattern). Such emotionally invested sets are specific to the choreographer's endeavour, and they are specific, differently, to the other collaborators' roles, aspirations, and anxieties.

When the different productive mechanisms or disciplinary and other *dispositifs*, brought differently by each of these collaborators to the task, are suddenly aligned (and they are likely to be aligned, if the choreographer's ability to trigger them is effectively mastered, and where shared expertise and aspirations and disciplinary mastery, and a shared capacity for invention are in place), then something like repetition or reinforcement of the dominant set will suddenly 'produce ... a strong feeling of certainty', in many if not all of those involved. What seems to be at work at these moments, according to Ulmer, is a 'cross-modal transfer and transposition across emotional sets' (1994: 143) that are juggled, albeit differently, by all those involved.

The strong feeling of certainty tends to be short-lived, for some involved, but significant. It frees up partly blocked energies. It resonates throughout the relational set, even if its implications are not immediately apparent to all concerned. (Brandstrup's expert dancer is likely, then, in my experience, to murmur 'That feels great', or 'Yes, that works [for me]', at such a moment, even he or she is reluctant or unable, in the thick of it, to analyse its working. Brandstrup, meanwhile, will have nodded almost invisibly in recognition when what he wants to see, but has not yet seen, and cannot yet describe, among these particular dancers at work, suddenly emerges.)

The moment of strong certainty, 'of being "right"', of 'a feeling of "knowing"' with relatively little need to know how that knowledge occurred, involves, Bastick observes (in Ulmer 1994: 143), that precious and highly delicate aspect of expertise that is 'judgement'. He continues:

> The correctness of an intuitive product is judged by the intuiter according to the release in tension, anxiety, and frustration afforded by the product.
>
> (Ulmer, 1994: 143)

In the relational framework I have outlined, specific to collaborative input into choreographic signature in the expert or professional spheres, that 'release in tension' is likely to be shared, unevenly, amongst expert practitioners, for the moment, and its outcome to register as a moment of creative decision-making. Ulmer writes,

> Intuition in contrast to analysis, operates in a global or Gestalt mode, crossing all the sensory modalities in a way that may not be abstracted from the body and emotions.
>
> (Ulmer 1994: 140)

In dancework that intuitive material tends to be returned, by the choreographer, to expertly trained dancers' bodies and expert-emotional capacities, after s/he has processed it choreographically, not least in terms of those logics of professional production and the production values that accrue to expertise in that role. (It is illuminating to watch choreographers in training with Kim Brandstrup, first with his company, Arc Dance, and later at the Royal Ballet: highly trained dancers, Cathy Marston among them, learn, in whatever training or informal apprenticeships are available to them, to hold in store, and to reckon material in terms of an array of productive *dispositifs* that are specific to the knowledge-in-action of the expert choreographer, with which an expert professional dancer, like Darcey Bussell, might well choose not to engage *choreographically*. Yet these two, the professional choreographer and the expert dancer, might well be working with what seems to be 'the same' material. The same material, in other words, offers up a range of discipline-specific *dispositifs*, some choreographic and some dancer-specific, some specifically spectatorial.)

The (expert) choreographer's expertise lies first in her capacity to transfer this already modulated '[expert-]intuitive product' *from* the 'living body' of the immediate moment of discovery in the workshop or rehearsal room *to* a further, production-specific apparatus; second, in her capacity to make judgements about 'what works' at each stage of this transfer. Hereafter, the expert-intuitive discovery can be 'artificially perform[ed]' (Ulmer 1994: 143) 'outside the organic mind and body' that lent them to its discovery. It is the choreographer who, by 'entrusting this process to a machine (both technological and methodological'), draws it into engagement with the performance-productive processes specific to the logics of production. The expert-intuitive outcome effectively belongs to the choreographer, whose signature takes responsibility for the collaborative production. Her or his imprint, now, is on/in it, even though he/she knows that to conjure it required that the accidental destabilise what, in the discipline, may have been taken for granted by practitioners, spectators, and academic writers alike.

Notes

1 Choreographer Rosemary Butcher has held a Senior Research Fellowship at Middlesex University, London, since 2004. She transferred her postdoctoral AHRC Fellowship from the University of Surrey to Middlesex in 2005.

2 This notion is widely borrowed from the Lacanian psychoanalytic tradition – see for example J. Lacan (1977) – and has proved useful to the textual economy and its products, and rather less so to those who operate outside of it.

3 A wide range of writers in the final decades of the twentieth century have borrowed terms from linguistics and discourse analysis, applying them to fields as diverse as film studies, visual arts studies and even anthropology. A difficulty emerges for the arts discipline concerned as soon as one asks what the implications are, for the arts, of taking language and linguistics as the external measure of practices that are actually *un*like language.

4 *Hidden Voices*, The Place, London, 2004, was commissioned for entry into The Place Prize, 2004. It began as a five-minute piece, then extended to fifteen minutes, and performed over ten nights by Elena Giannotti. Butcher described it to Elena as an inner journey. It has been performed internationally since 2004. See R. Butcher and S. Melrose 2005.

5 The term 'the audience' is abusive because it bundles individual difference into a monolith. Words in use can 'ontologize': that is, their use can seem to bring something into being, as though it pre-existed that use of language.

6 Lighting design is by Charlie Balfour.

7 Butcher's film, with film-maker Martin Otter and dancer, Elena Giannotti, was first shown in 2004.

8 Many writers published at the end of the twentieth century and in the early years of the twenty-first, have identified this coincidence, and have pondered the implications for the theoretical itself. See, for example, C. Spinosa (2001). If theoretical writing is itself historically and ideologically contingent, rather than transhistorically valid, then we might want to consider whether or not that theoretical writing can be usefully applied in the context of an art-making that has consistent recourse to the discipline in question.

9 Suzanne Guerlac (2006) argues that Hegel's ('oppositional') philosophy displaced that of Bergson in Europe in the 1930s, via lectures presented by Kojève.

10 See, for example, '...just intuitive...' at www.sfmelrose.u-net.com

11 Catalysis or catalytic processes suppose mutual transformation of two or more elements, such that the outcome is greater than the simple sum of the two parts. My argument is that this applies widely in effective collaborations by expert practitioners working in different disciplines. Catalysis makes it singularly difficult to 'unpick' the choreographic material that emerges. Butcher's relationship, within the work, with dancer Elena Giannotti, is catalytic.

12 Cf. www.sfmelrose.u-net.com. I have described Performance Studies, over recent years, as a closet Spectator Studies that misrecognises itself as such. That is, its writers genuinely believe that they are writing 'about performance', whereas in fact they tend in the main to write about their own spectating, in the performance event.

References

Berger, J. (1972) *Ways of Seeing*, London: Penguin.

Butcher, R. and Melrose, S. (eds) (2005) *Rosemary Butcher: Choreography, Collisions and Collaborations*, London: Middlesex University Press.

Deleuze, G. (2003) *Francis Bacon: The Logic of Sensation*, trans. D. W. Smith, Minneapolis: University of Minnesota Press.

Guerlac, S. (2006) *Thinking in Time: An Introduction to Henri Bergson*, Ithaca and London: Cornell University Press.

Knorr Cetina, K. (2001) 'Objectual practice', in T. Schatzki, K. Knorr Cetina and E. von Savigny (eds) *The Practice Turn in Contemporary Theory*, London: Routledge.

Lacan, J. (1977) *Ecrits: A Selection*, trans. A. Sheridan, London: Tavistock Publications.

Lyotard, J.-F. (1991) *The Inhuman*, trans. G. Bennington and R. Bowlby, Stanford: Stanford University Press.

Massumi, B. (2002) *Parables for the Virtual: Movement, Affect, Sensation*, Durham and London: Duke University Press.

Osborne, P. (2000) *Philosophy in Cultural Theory*, London and New York: Routledge.

Spinosa, C. (2001) 'Derridean dispersion and Heideggerian articulation', in T. Schatzki, K. Knorr Cetina and E. von Savigny (eds) *The Practice Turn in Contemporary Theory*, London: Routledge.

Ulmer, G. (1989) *Teletheory: Grammatology in the Age of Video*, New York and London: Routledge.

—— (1994) *Heuretics: The Logic of Invention*, Baltimore and London: The Johns Hopkins University Press.

4 Visible thought

Choreographic cognition in creating, performing, and watching contemporary dance

Shirley McKechnie and Catherine J. Stevens

In the creation, performance and appreciation of contemporary dance we find a microcosm of cognition. Contemporary dance is at once non-verbal, communicative, and expressive; it is visual, spatial, temporal, kinaesthetic, affective, and dynamic. This chapter applies contemporary psychological theory to the complex processes that mediate creation, performance, and observation of contemporary dance. These perceptual, cognitive and emotional processes are termed collectively *choreographic cognition*. Psychological investigations have dealt with dance as discrete movements or steps, and questions of memory and imagery have been unnecessarily confined to codes that are verbal or visual. We propose there is much more. Movement through space is continuous, it flows; transitions are the conveyors of information and form. In an effort to capture the temporal and spatial characteristics, we outline a theoretical approach that conceptualizes choreographic cognition as an evolving dynamical system. We also pose research questions and suggest ways that these are beginning to be addressed.

Contemporary dance is defined here as a work in which the major medium is movement, deliberately and systematically cultivated for its own sake, with the aim of achieving a work of art. It shares with other art forms the possibility of being viewed either as non-representational/non-symbolic (typically termed 'formalist' in aesthetic theory), or of being representational or symbolic in some sense. Regardless of the approach that is adopted, time, space and motion are the media for choreographic cognition.

Correlative to the three aspects of the dance event (creation, performance and appreciation) are the three key actors: the choreographer, the performer, and the observer (Hanna 1979). For purposes of clarity and systematization, we consider each in turn (though it is important to bear in mind that, for many processes, the three are intimately connected). We begin with discussion of the choreographer and the psychological processes involved in the creation and composition of contemporary dance. In the next section, we focus on the performer, and then turn to the third key actor, the observer. Of necessity, we address a number of different 'levels' ranging from the basic neurophysiological and behavioural stage, through that described by dynamical systems theory, to the intentional or symbolic. These different levels of analysis correspond with different disciplinary approaches. For example, neuroscientists are interested in locations and networks of neural activity that underpin perception, memory, and motor acts and responses. Cognitive psychologists, by contrast, theorize about mechanisms involved in cognition such as attention, memory, and decision-making. Rather than analysing neurons, cognitive psychologists infer mechanism from behavioural responses such as the accuracy and speed of recall of material performed under different experimental conditions. Dynamical Systems Theory (DST) is a set of mathematical principles and tools used to explain complex natural systems such as the flocking of birds. In DST, complex wholes and forms emerge from chaos; each component acts and interacts with others in the system. Each state of the system determines the next state so that a structure or form evolves. Change occurs at many timescales, and change at one timescale shapes and is shaped by change at others. We apply ideas from DST to the creative process and actions and interactions between choreographers and dancers. Although not discussed here, DST may also be applied to the neural and motor aspects of human behaviour (Stevens *et al.* 2002, Thelen 1995). Finally, by intentional and symbolic forms of analysis, we mean language-based description of the drive or idea behind movement and ways of responding based on shared knowledge of signs, gestures, metaphors, and meanings.

Creating contemporary dance – the choreographer

One branch of cognitive psychology that may provide some insight into choreographic cognition involves theories of creativity and attempts to explain processes and circumstances that give rise to innovative thought. Creativity is almost universally defined in terms of novelty: a creative act, idea, solution, artistic form, or product, is novel and original, and incorporates substantial new ideas not easily derived from earlier work (Johnson-Laird 1988, Wales and Thornton 1994). For Simonton (1994), creativity is marked by an unending search for the new.

Boden (1996) alludes to the apparent difficulties inherent in studying the creative process, and refers to the perceived mystery that surrounds it: 'how could science possibly explain fundamental novelties?' (1996: 75). This almost mystical aura that surrounds the concept of creativity can be said to exist in the absence of a complete theoretical explanation of the phenomenon (Finke, Ward and Smith 1996). However, Boden suggests that creativity may be no more mysterious than other unconscious processes and systems such as vision, language, and common-sense reasoning (1996: 75). The essence of the novelty in artistic creativity may be metaphorical thinking. All humans are likely to use such thinking, and perhaps people who are creative, such as artists and scientists, simply use it more often or to more focused purposes (McKechnie 1996).

Alongside novelty, unconscious processes and metaphor, another element common to a number of accounts of creative thinking is the juxtaposition of two seemingly contradictory ideas. Rothenberg (1994) refers to this as a Janusian process: the ability to hold two competing, contradictory ideas, images or concepts in mind simultaneously. He proposes that creativity is the synthesis or coalescence of these. Koestler (1964) pointed to useful distinctions between creativity as it appears in humour (the collision of matrices or planes of thought), in science (integration), and in art (analogy). More recent accounts of creativity emphasize processes of problem solving and problem finding (Kay 1994, Wakefield 1994). Putting these notions together, Boden argues that a theory that considers unexpected combinations, together with a psychological explanation of analogy, may suffice as a theory of creativity.

By nature, contemporary dance is difficult to study as it is ephemeral and, unlike a musical score, painting or sculpture, there are few notes of the development of the work or even good records of all aspects of the performance. Fortunately, beginning in 1999 a collaborative research team involving the Victorian College of the Arts, dance industry partners, and researchers in Australia captured on digital video the inception and development of new dance works by two elite choreographers. We draw on this video and journal documentation seeking examples of problem finding and problem solving, metaphorical thinking, and evidence of the synthesis of competing ideas.

An important characteristic of creativity in contemporary choreographic cognition is that dancers and choreographers increasingly work together exploring, selecting, and developing dance material. Australian choreographer Anna Smith developed new dance material working closely with seven experienced and professional dancers over a period of six months, culminating in the work *Red Rain*. The dance materials were generated from improvisations of the whole group. At one stage, spoken cues were given to the dancers such as 'Right elbow behind back, shoulders tilting, left hand reaching' and each dancer interpreted the cue. Individual solutions were found and the group gradually selected and developed the interpretations made by one or more of the dancers. Importantly, the choreographer was not in control of the material thus generated but the choreographic exploration took place through interactive dance-making to which everyone contributed (McKechnie and Grove, 2000). An explanation of creativity in choreography must therefore address the complex of dynamics and interactions among dancers and choreographer in this community of creative minds. In addition to motivation, memory, and personality factors that underpin the individuals' thoughts and behaviour, there are dyads and triads within the group and concomitant ideas, tensions, conflicts, attractions and defences. The social and cognitive psychologist searching for a fresh domain to test current theoretical assumptions will be pleased with the uncharted territory offered by choreographer and dancer interactions.

Instances of problem finding and problem solving in choreographic cognition are easily found. The development of movement as art brings with it challenges of the limits of the human body and best use and negotiation of the dimensions of space and time. Although difficult to capture in writing, video footage of Smith and her team demonstrates the cognitive complexity of a segment that involved rapid and continuous whole body movement from all dancers with each performing a different series of complex transitions. As well as the motor and spatial complexity of each transition, the dancers were to carry out their individual movements while the group traced a DNA-like double helix. Before the sequence could be performed a logistical analysis to determine a way in which it could work spatially was carried out. Finally, movement of the complex spatial configuration of parts (dancers) and whole (group forming the helix) was realized using colour-coded paper trails of the path of each dancer. Thus, the spatial and temporal configuration was modelled with concrete materials and after much analysis and trial and error, it was achieved in real time and space.

In another example, the first author describes creation of a work commissioned for a very small dance space. The space elicited ideas and images related to the use of simple forms in small spaces. Pondering this problem led to images of ikebana, to the similar asymmetry of human lives lived in close contact in small rooms, to the alienation of separate lives closely entwined spatially but separated by emotional chasms. The source of the solution to the problem lay in synthesis between the imagery of confined spaces and the experience of contained tensions. A final example involves synthesis of real and imagined time in the perceptions of observers. *Amplification*, choreographed in 1999 by Phillip Adams, reflects an interest in the contemporary cult of the pornography of car crashes. The choreographer faced a problem of how to represent a distorted experience of time in dance terms. The seemingly endless expansion of time experienced by car crash victims during the few seconds of a violent accident became the source of a central image. The problem of conveying the nature of the experience in real time was solved by breaking up movement material into brief distorted and fractured components and performing a long and complex sequence of them at a tempo verging on the perilous: a feat accessible only to highly trained contemporary dancers. The presence of imagery is evident in these two examples and in most accounts of creativity. The examples also demonstrate that imagery can occur in all sensory modalities, but in contemporary dance, unlike other art forms, the creative search is embodied in the human form.

A theory of the dance ensemble as an evolving dynamical system

Drawing on contemporary writings (for example Clark 1997, Heylighen 2001, Kauffman 1995, Thelen 1995) and extensive studio investigations, we contend that collaboration in creative activities is something to be pondered to advantage, and theorize that a collaborative ensemble is a dynamical system. The work of physicists and biologists has revealed a universe that endlessly generates novelty where complex systems evolve by accumulation of successive useful (and at the time unuseful) variations (Kauffman 1995). We have observed this kind of complex system in the dance ensemble, revealed as vital and energizing for the artists involved (McKechnie 2005, 2007; Stevens *et al.* 2001, 2003). The studio process can be characterized as a 'community of creative minds' where cooperation and teamwork are essential elements of discovery and innovation.

Processes involving thought and action unfold in time. Substantial achievement is the result of the blossoming of ideas, the selective success and further evolution of some of these and the dying away or editing out of others. Charles Darwin's 'dangerous idea' (Dennett 1995) about the evolution of species can also illuminate the evolution of ideas in a creative process. Dawkins (1989) coined the word 'meme' as a cultural analogue of the gene. He proposed that our ideas, beliefs, values, actions and patterns of doing things are conceived and evolved in mind processes, just as genes are conceived and evolved in biological processes. But the meme, in this theory, is replicated, not in biologically defined cells, but in the minds of individuals and groups. Memes, he said, are also subject to variation (embellishment, modification) and to selection and replication, according to adaptive pressures. The nexus between memetic evolution and the concepts inherent in theories of self-organizing dynamical systems can provide new ways of thinking about how dances are made within a collaborative framework. In the creation of *Red Rain* we observed a movement subtlety seen in one dancer appearing in the body of another, changed, often extended or transformed by the individual length of an arm or leg, a subtle shift of focus, a sudden stillness, an inclination of the head, sometimes a radical recasting of the rhythmic tensions. Movement ideas, subtle rhythms and textures were progressively enhanced as dancers contributed some aspect of their own unique qualities of physicality and expression. This memetic process occurred throughout the development of the work.

These, then, are the two basic elements that form the basis of such a theory. First, the idea of a meme: a unit of culture, a pattern, a poem, a way of building a canoe, spinning a thread or a yarn, making a dance, or embellishing a particular style – the phenotype or distinctive expression of genotype in a given environment.[1] An idea is nurtured in minds and passed from one to another by a process of selection, elimination or adaptation. Second, the idea of the dance ensemble as a complex dynamical system adapting through time to the day-to-day changes inherent in any creative process. Such a system is sustained or not by its ability to adapt, to cooperate, to deal with ideas that are generated by group processes.

In the studio, many levels of thought, action, and interaction grow or evolve over time. These interactions sometimes resemble those of social exchanges, as dancers and choreographer discuss the associations and implications of a particular idea or image. One of the dancers working with choreographer Anna Smith on *Red Rain* commented on the amount of movement information the dancers had had to absorb. When the choreographer began to structure the material into complex layers and sections she felt it was an overload of information. She struggled to internalize both the semantics and the syntax or structures of the new 'language' to locate in her own body a new kinaesthetic sensibility in the movement-pathways and relationships. The choreographer, with a different perspective and a different responsibility, now conceived this material partly as extended sequences of movement, which needed to be brought into a coherent whole, and partly as material that found its own form. She wrote in her journal

> On Friday I had a great rehearsal; I think I passed through a difficult stage. I always feel as though I am over-anxious to know the work, what it is. But it is not alive yet so how can I possibly expect to know what it is? It has to breathe its own existence, and I have to be patient, to allow it to evolve itself. The work is an organism, which creates its own body, so to speak. Does this make sense? Perhaps I understand the dilemma much better now.
>
> (Smith 1999)

It seems that the choreographer is waiting for the dance ideas to appear and to find their own form – to 'self-organize'. It is a familiar phenomenon to artists and scientists, and in theories of creativity, where concepts of preparation, incubation and illumination characterize creative processes. In dance, the formal structuring of the overall design may also be 'discovered' in this way and shaped or enhanced by aesthetic considerations.

From the vantage point of a self-organizing dynamical system, the choreographer can be seen as a modern descendant of the shaman. In the examples we have studied the choreographer is many things – conceiver, creative thinker, teacher and learner; sometimes at the head of a centralized system in the role of initiator and arbiter of structures; sometimes as part of a more distributed system in which the thoughts and actions of individual artists contribute to a coherent and potent whole. Human cooperation harnessed in this way requires all parts of the system to contribute to the ongoing creation. The social and cultural forces that have shaped human evolution have been reliant on similar processes.

Memory and imagery in rehearsal and performance of contemporary dance – the performer

Although choreography and contemporary dance have only rarely captured the interest of experimental psychologists, classical ballet and contemporary dance have been used as tools to examine coding in human short- and long-term memory (Jean *et al.* 2001, Rossi-Arnaud *et al.* 2004).

Results include the observation that memory for complex movements is more kinaesthetic than verbal (Starkes *et al.* 1990). Anecdotal accounts suggest that recall is often multimodal such that activity in one mode triggers knowledge or recall in another. Smyth and Pendleton (1994) used an interference paradigm and measured effects of articulatory and movement suppression. Interference is used as a technique in studies of memory as a way to understand the form of the code in memory. If a particular task such as a verbal task is performed while new movement material is also being encoded, and the verbal task interferes with the encoding of the movement material (i.e., relatively poor recall of movement material), then we can infer that the underlying code for the movement has a verbal component. In Smyth and Pendleton's experiment, dancers' memory spans were longer than those of non-dancers for both classical ballet and modern movement and both articulatory and movement suppression decreased the dancers' spans. The latter result implies that material is coded at least in the short-term in both verbal and kinaesthetic form.

Solso and Dallob (1995) have examined long-term memory for dance material. They propose that a class of movements is represented abstractly in memory in the form of a prototype. Solso and Dallob conclude that there is an underlying scheme that governs the formation of body actions in general and dance routines in particular and that it may be possible to determine basic laws of motor performance and transformation as part of a comprehensive theory of dance 'grammar' and general kinaesthetic 'grammar'.

Of the experimental studies of memory for dance, most have used classical ballet in which a sequence of prescribed steps is drawn from an established repertoire of labelled formal movements. By contrast, contemporary dance frequently consists of idiosyncratic movement derived from the theme being explored and is less easily reduced to verbal description. At one point in developing *Red Rain*, for example, the dancers commented on the extraordinary amount of information they needed to retain while working with new and demanding movement material. On another occasion a dancer watched herself on video performing a slow and intricate move but had little recollection of performing the movement or how she made her body move in a particular way. Such observations have implications for memory in choreographic cognition. One testable hypothesis is that verbal labels or cues for single movements (such as 'Deirdre's wrist; Kathleen's sitting bones; Nicole's no. 3') are used initially. Over time, longer and more complex movements are sequenced, rehearsed, and chunked in long-term memory (for a review see Allard and Starkes 1991). A crucial question that arises is to ask, what is the nature of the representation in memory that stores and integrates visual, auditory, propositional, spatial, temporal, and kinaesthetic features?

Complex dance vocabularies challenge the view of human memory as a storehouse of linguistic propositions. Creating and performing dance involves knowledge that is procedural (implicit knowledge or knowing how to perform various tasks) and declarative (explicit knowledge or knowing about states of affairs such as dance and phrases of dance). The inspiration for the creation or the performance of phrases of dance material may be a concept, feeling(s), a space, texture, rhythm, lilt or sound. Contemporary dance declares thoughts and ideas not in words but expressed kinaesthetically and emotionally through movement. This may be achieved for example, through movement subtleties and qualities, contrasts between tension and relaxation, or contrasts between high degrees of physicality and absolute stillness.

Most often, communication in the studio is also through movement – 'Show me what you just did!' (Grove 2005). In the absence of skilled notation or multidimensional, multimodal recordings and archives of dance works, dancers' bodies are the repositories of dance works that they have composed and/or performed. The dancer's language (McKechnie and Grove 2000), is a kind of utterance of the body or the body being uttered by a language it doesn't entirely know. Verbal language, Grove says, is full of these unexpected 'knowledges', these potentialities and pressures, and it may be that dance-language is the same.

Communication through movement and dance – the observer

The power of movement and dance to evoke memories has been identified as an important factor in the communication achieved via contemporary dance. Hanna (1979) suggests that affect and cognition in response to dance are intertwined and she gives a broad account of the way in which emotion is communicated. For example, physical movements associated with affect may stimulate or sublimate a range of feelings and may be elicited for pleasure or coping with problematic aspects of social involvement. Adults may find succour and release cathexis in culturally permissible motor behaviour; this may be reminiscent of nurturance and protection of prenatal and infancy stages and imitates satisfaction of childhood behaviour. Dance may communicate a kind of excitement; may also provide a healthy fatigue or distraction that may abate temporary crises. Examples of the intoxication that occurs with rapid movement abound. Such therapeutic matters are unlikely to be of concern to the choreographer. However, such responses on the part of the observer constitute communication and reinforce the pursuit of dance as art or entertainment.

From the perspective of choreographic cognition as defined in this chapter, communication between dancers, between choreographer and dancers, and between dancers and audience occur in at least two ways: a) perception through neural mirroring and sympathetic kinaesthesia, particularly among experts; and b) extraction of and response to multimodal cues.

Mirror neurons, action observation and sympathetic kinaesthesia

Psychologists have long speculated that perception and action are intimately linked – that observing an action involves the same repertoire of motor representations that is used to produce the action (Castiello 2003). One implication of this view is that the capacity to understand another's behaviour and to attribute intention or beliefs to others is rooted in a neural execution/observation mechanism (Grèzes and Decety 2001). Using the brain-imaging technique, fMRI, Calvo-Merino *et al.* (2005) demonstrated neural mirroring and an effect of specialist expertise when dancers observed dance movement that they had learned to do (either classical ballet or capoeira) compared with movement that they had not learned to do (either classical ballet or capoeira). The results show an effect of acquired motor skills on brain activity during action observation – brain activity was affected by whether observers could do the action or not. Experts had greater activation when observing the specific movement style that they could perform whereas the same areas of neural activation in non-expert control subjects were insensitive to stimulus type. This neuroscientific research provides one explanation for why dancers observing dance report that they *feel* the movement or feel as if they are performing the movement.

Interpreting fMRI scans, Lee *et al.* (2001) suggest that novice observers perceive dance simply as movement whereas professional choreographers analyse movement with knowledge of choreography and the extraction of symbolic units that activate a semantic network associated with the meaning of particular gestures and actions. Calvo-Merino *et al.*, too, noted some (non-significant) activity in middle temporal areas suggesting semantic categorization of dance movement by experts. This is plausible given the labelled vocabularies of 'steps' that constitute classical ballet and capoeira repertoires and may again relate to the interplay or competition between procedural and declarative knowledge (Stevens and McKechnie 2005).

Extraction of multimodal cues

A large-scale experimental investigation of audience response (Glass 2006) involved the systematic manipulation of three variables or factors: choreographic intention (representational versus abstract), audience member expertise (experts (>10 years' training) versus novices), and pre-performance information (generic information session, specific information session, no information session – control group). The sample for the experiment was formed from 472 audience members with sessions conducted over a period of six months. Two new Australian works – *Red Rain* choreographed by Anna Smith and *Fine Line Terrain* choreographed by Sue Healey – were used as stimulus material with data collected from audiences attending one of seven live performances in city and regional centres in Australia. Approximately half of each audience arrived early

Table 4.1 Cues used to form an interpretation (Glass, 2006).

Cue	*Red Rain (%)*	*Fine Line Terrain (%)*
Visual elements	40.5	35.9
Aural elements	31.4	35.9
Movement	31.4	<10
Use of space	<10	63.1

to receive either a generic or specific information session concerning the work they were about to see. The remainder of each audience arrived just before the performance, thus forming a control group for the information variable (i.e. the control group received no information other than the title of the work and brief programme notes).

To evaluate information session effectiveness, we developed the Audience Response Tool (ART) – a new psychometric instrument for gathering psychological reactions to live or recorded performance (Glass 2005, 2006). The ART consists of three broad sections: a qualitative section that explores cognitive, emotional and affective reactions, a quantitative section that includes a series of rating scales that assess cognitive, emotional, visceral and affective responses, and a demographic and background information section (for example age, gender, dance experience, etc.).

Exhaustive qualitative and quantitative analyses of open-ended responses revealed that approximately 90 per cent of participants formed an interpretation of the dance work that they saw (Glass 2006). For the observer, contemporary dance can be viewed as non-representational or representational and various cognitive strategies may be called upon to extract representational content including (i) thematic analysis, (ii) metaphor, (iii) imagery, (iv) narrative-searching and (v) personal memory. Some of the cues used to form an interpretation included visual elements, aural elements, movement, and the use of space. Table 4.1 shows that the relative contribution of these elements in the two dance works differed. Information sessions did not impact on the tendency to engage with the piece but specific information sessions did affect the *content* of interpreted responses (Glass 2006).

More than 87 per cent of participants reported that they felt an emotional response. The results indicated that contemporary dance is a multi-layered event with numerous avenues for emotional and affective communication. Some of the reasons for the experience of emotion and enjoyment, as stated by participants, included visual and aural cues, dancer characteristics, movement, choreography, novelty, spatial/dynamic elements, emotional recognition, intellectual stimulation, the piece generally, and emotional stimulation (see Table 4.2). Audience members also noted higher-order relations between cues as being important for their enjoyment. For example, relations between dancer movement and music were mentioned; movement and music appeared to embody motion

Table 4.2 Reasons for enjoyment (Glass 2006).

Cue	*Red Rain (%)*	*Fine Line Terrain (%)*
Visual	32.4	51.3
Aural	28.4	28.3
Dancer characteristics	28.0	39.5
Movement	25.6	36.8
Choreography	10.0	18.4
Interpretation	7.6	25.0
Emotional recognition	3.6	6.6
Novelty	15.2	11.2
Spatial/dynamic	14.4	26.3
Intellectual stimulation	14.4	7.9
Piece generally	5.6	3.9
Emotional stimulation	7.6	9.2

expressed through structural variables such as dynamics and time (Glass 2006). Interestingly, some of the processes that we observed during practice-led research in creating a dance work (Stevens *et al.* 2003) were active as audience members watched contemporary dance – processes such as association, analogical transfer, synthesis and functional inference. Creative thinking was evident not only in the context of observers watching Smith's *Red Rain* (the dance work that we had studied from the perspective of creative choreographic cognition) but also in the context of a more abstract piece, Healey's *Fine Line Terrain*.

Conclusion

Creation, performance, and observation of contemporary dance provide a rich test-bed for theories and concepts of human perception, action, and cognition. We have considered the three actors – choreographer, performer, and observer – in turn, but recognize the complex, pan-directional connections between these three. For example, similar processes may be at work in creating and responding to dance, and processes of communication and knowledge transfer apply equally to choreographers interacting with dancers, and dancer–audience interactions. The present analysis has drawn on theories of creativity, memory, perception, and communication. In addition to outlining current theoretical views, we have sketched results of our studio investigations and experiments conducted in live performance contexts. Finally, dynamic systems theory has been considered as a high-level theoretical framework suited to the description of movement material evolving in the creation of new work.

A dynamical view of choreographic cognition has explanatory power with relevance to choreographer, performer, and observer. Our dynamical view proposes that the basis for an idea in movement can come from a pulse, concept, rhythm, or feeling. The task and artistry of the choreographer is to express the idea in visible, bodily form. The germ of an idea may multiply and develop so that from a single movement other variations, approximations, caricatures, and inversions emerge. At some later stage the movement may be described using verbal language or visual images – but this is not necessarily its original form. In dynamical terms, there may be structure and order, perhaps self-similarity, emerging from apparent chaos. Complexity increases when choreographer and dancers interact and dancers perform – transitions and explorations continue to be conceived as a state space of many dimensions. Finally, for the observer, there is an understanding from recognition, sometimes directly via neural mirroring and sometimes via analogy and metaphor, of conflicts, tensions, and resolutions in negotiating and navigating a world of time, space, objects, events, self, and others.

Acknowledgement

This research was supported by the Australian Research Council through its Strategic Partnerships with Industry Research & Training (SPIRT), Linkage Projects (C59930500, LP0211991, LP0562687) and Infrastructure (LE0347784, LE0668448) schemes, the School of Dance at the Victorian College of the Arts, and industry partners the Australia Council for the Arts Dance Board, Australian Dance Council – Ausdance, QL2 Centre for Youth Dance (formerly the Australian Choreographic Centre), and the ACT Cultural Facilities Corporation. Parts of this paper were presented at the 6th International Conference on Music Perception and Cognition, University of Keele, 2000. Further information may be obtained from Kate Stevens, email: kj.stevens@uws.edu.au, websites: http://www.ausdance.org.au/unspoken; http://www.ausdance.org.au/connections; http://marcs.uws.edu.au and search 'intention'.

Note

1 Phenotype refers to the observable physical or biochemical characteristics of an organism resulting from the combined action of genotype (i.e., genetic make-up or genome) and environmental influences.

References

Allard, F. and Starkes, J. L. (1991) 'Motor-skill experts in sports, dance, and other domains', in K. A. Ericsson and J. Smith (eds) *Toward a General Theory of Expertise: Prospects and Limits*, Cambridge: Cambridge University Press.

Boden, M. A. (1996) 'What is creativity?' in M. A. Boden (ed.) *Dimensions of Creativity*, Cambridge, MA: MIT Press.

Calvo-Merino, B., Glaser, D. E., Grèzes, J., Passingham, R. W. and Haggard, P. (2005) 'Action observation and acquired motor skills: an fMRI study with expert dancers', *Cerebral Cortex*, 15: 1243–9.

Castiello, U. (2003) 'Understanding other people's actions: intention and attention', *Journal of Experimental Psychology: Human Perception and Performance*, 29: 416–30.

Clark, A. (1997) *Being There: Putting Brain, Body, and World Together Again*, Cambridge, MA: MIT Press.

Dawkins, R. (1989) *The Selfish Gene*, London: Oxford Paperbacks.

Dennett, D. (1995) *Darwin's Dangerous Idea: Evolution and the Meanings of Life*, New York: Touchstone.

Finke, R. A., Ward, T. B. and Smith, S. M. (1996) *Creative Cognition: Theory, Research, and Applications*, Cambridge, MA: MIT Press.

Glass, R. (2005) 'Observer response to contemporary dance', in R. Grove, C. Stevens and S. McKechnie (eds) *Thinking in Four Dimensions: Creativity and Cognition in Contemporary Dance*, Carlton: Melbourne University Press.

—— (2006) 'The Audience Response Tool (ART): the impact of choreographic intention, information, and dance expertise on psychological reactions to contemporary dance', unpublished doctoral dissertation, MARCS Auditory Laboratories, University of Western Sydney.

Grèzes, J. and Decety, J. (2001) 'Functional anatomy of execution, mental simulation, observation, and verb generation of actions: a meta-analysis', *Human Brain Mapping*, 12: 1–19.

Grove, R. (2005) 'Show me what you just did', in R. Grove, C. Stevens and S. McKechnie (eds) *Thinking in Four Dimensions: Creativity and Cognition in Contemporary Dance*, Carlton: Melbourne University Press.

Hanna, J. L. (1979) *To Dance is Human: A Theory of Nonverbal Communication*, Chicago: The University of Chicago Press.

Heylighen, F. (2001) 'The science of self-organization and adaptivity', in *The Encyclopedia of Life Support Systems*, Oxford: EOLSS Publishers Co. Ltd.

Jean, J., Cadopi, M. and Ille, A. (2001) 'How are dance sequences encoded and recalled by expert dancers?', *Cahiers de Psychologie Cognitive*, 20: 325–37.

Johnson-Laird, P. N. (1988) 'Freedom and constraint in creativity', in R. Sternberg (ed.) *The Nature of Creativity*, Cambridge: Cambridge University Press.

Kauffman, S. (1995) 'Order for free', in J. Brockman (ed.) *The Third Culture*, New York: Simon & Schuster.

Kay, S. (1994) 'A method for investigating the creative thought process', in M. A. Runco (ed.) *Problem Finding, Problem Solving, and Creativity*, Norwood, NJ: Ablex Publishing Corporation.

Koestler, A. (1964) *The Act of Creation*, London: Hutchinson.

Lee, K-M., Kim, C-M. and Woo, S-H. (2001) 'fMRI comparison between expert and novice perception of dance', *NeuroImage*, 6: 907.

McKechnie, S. (1996) 'Choreography as research', in M. M. Stoljar (ed.) *Creative Investigations – Redefining Research in the Arts and Humanities*, Canberra: The Australian Academy of the Humanities.

—— (2005) 'Dancing memes, minds and designs', in R. Grove, C. Stevens and S. McKechnie (eds) *Thinking in Four Dimensions: Creativity and Cognition in Contemporary Dance*, Carlton: Melbourne University Press.

—— (2007) 'Thinking bodies, dancing minds', *Brolga: An Australian Journal About Dance* 27: 38–46.

McKechnie, S. and Grove, R. (2000) 'Thinking bodies', *Brolga: An Australian Journal about Dance*, 12: 7–14.

Rossi-Arnaud, C., Cortese, A. and Cestari, V. (2004) 'Memory span for movement configurations: the effects of concurrent verbal, motor and visual interference', *Cahiers de Psychologie Cognitive*, 22: 335–49.

Rothenberg, A. (1994) *Creativity and Madness: New Findings and Old Stereotypes*, Baltimore: The Johns Hopkins University Press.

Simonton, D. K. (1994) *Greatness: Who Makes History and Why*, New York: The Guilford Press.

Smith, A. (1999) 'Notes from daily journal', unpublished, School of Dance: Victorian College of the Arts, Melbourne Australia.

Smyth, M. M. and Pendleton, L. R. (1994) 'Memory for movement in professional ballet dancers', *International Journal of Sport Psychology*, 25: 282–94.

Solso, R. L. and Dallob, P. (1995) 'Prototype formation among professional dancers', *Empirical Studies of the Arts*, 13: 3–16.

Starkes, J. L., Caicco, M., Boutilier, C. and Sevsek, B. (1990) 'Motor recall of experts for structured and unstructured sequences in creative modern dance', *Journal of Sport & Exercise Psychology*, 12: 317–21.

Stevens, C. and McKechnie, S. (2005) 'Thinking in action: thought made visible in contemporary dance', *Cognitive Processing*, 6: 243–52.

Stevens, C., Malloch, S. and McKechnie, S. (2001) 'Moving mind: the cognitive psychology of contemporary dance', *Brolga: An Australian Journal About Dance*, 15: 55–67.

Stevens, C., Malloch, S., McKechnie, S. and Steven, N. (2003) 'Choreographic cognition: the time-course and phenomenology of creating a dance', *Pragmatics and Cognition*, 11: 299–329.

Stevens, C., Malloch, S., Morris, R. and McKechnie, S. (2002) 'Shaped time: a dynamical systems analysis of contemporary dance', in C. Stevens, D. Burnham, G. McPherson, E. Schubert and J. Renwick (eds) *Proceedings of the 7th International Conference on Music Perception and Cognition*, Adelaide: Causal Productions.

Thelen, E. (1995) 'Time-scale dynamics and the development of an embodied cognition', in R. F. Port and T. van Gelder (eds) *Mind as Motion: Explorations of the Dynamics of Cognition*, Cambridge, MA: MIT Press.

Wakefield, J. F. (1994) 'Problem finding and empathy in art', in M. A. Runco (ed.) *Problem Finding, Problem Solving, and Creativity*, Norwood, NJ: Ablex Publishing Corporation.

Wales, R. and Thornton, S. (1994) 'Psychological issues in modelling creativity', in T. Dartnall (ed.) *Artificial Intelligence and Creativity*, Dordrecht: Kluwer Academic Publishers.

5 'Throwing like a girl'?

Gender in a transnational world

Susan Leigh Foster

I hope to contribute with this chapter to our understanding of how dance can propose a theory concerning gendered identity – how it offers to participants and viewers a conception of what gender might be and how it works. Moving alongside the many dance scholars, including myself, who have argued for consideration of the gendered significance of dancing, this chapter functions, in particular, to evaluate gender's workings and effects in globalized culture, in a moment where popular images of femininity from Hollywood to Bollywood circulate rapidly through diverse mediatized formats.[1] The focus of my inquiry is two recent works, one by British choreographer Lea Anderson, and the other by the Japanese performance collective KATHY, that each draw upon images from Hollywood films to mount powerful critiques of contemporary femininity.[2] As a way to situate their arguments concerning gender, I detour through two canonical works by US choreographers Martha Graham and Trisha Brown. Emblematic of key moments in the history of dance modernism, their theorizations of gender provide historical perspective on the contemporary choreographic practices of Anderson and KATHY.

This chapter is also intended to promote debate on how to analyse a dance's movement. What rubrics of categorization can and do we implement? What criteria of observation and description can we utilize? And, perhaps, most important, how does the determination to use one system of analysis or another influence the findings? In an effort to foreground the possibility of implementing diverse frameworks for the analysis of dance movement, I have applied the criteria of spatial analysis proposed by philosopher Iris Marion Young in her pioneering study of gender and movement, *Throwing Like a Girl: A Phenomenology of Feminine Body Comportment, Motility, and Spatiality*, first published in 1980. Building on the work of Simone de Beauvoir, Young's unique system of analysis integrated patterns of movement with psychological orientations and social roles. She proposed to consider the feminine as a set of 'structures and conditions that delimit the typical situation of being a woman in a particular society' (Young 1990: 141). Most unusual for the field of philosophy, Young argued for consideration of movement patterns as part of those structures and conditions that define the feminine.

Analysing throwing

In *Throwing Like a Girl* Young argues that feminine experience, marked by a fundamental contradiction between subjectivity and being a mere object, can be observed in a woman's distinctive engagement with spatiality. Composed of both an apprehension of and response to space, this spatial awareness permeates female daily life, quotidian actions and cognitive calculations alike. Young identifies three principal features of this engagement with space: first, an ambiguous transcendence evidenced in the lack of forthrightness in women's gait and stride, and in a smallness in extending towards the limits of their reach; second, an inhibited intentionality, exemplified in a characteristic failure to commit the whole body to a particular task; and third, a discontinuous unity in which the feminine subject is unable to coordinate motions from different parts of the body towards a single intended action. In identifying these features of spatial engagement, Young implements criteria of size – the length of the stride – as well as of effort – the concentrated energy mobilized to execute a task. And she distinguishes between the whole body's interactivity with its surroundings and the organization within the body of its various parts.

Citing Merleau-Ponty (1962) that it is 'the body in its orientation toward and action upon and within its surroundings that constitutes the initial meaning-giving act' (1962: 147), Young asserts that women are not given access to an unambiguously purposeful sense of themselves in the world that Merleau-Ponty claims is a universal given. Instead, it is the masculine subject that actualizes as a fully confident and wilful being who experiences the body as a medium for the enactment or realization of aims, whereas the feminine subject experiences the body as a 'fragile encumbrance' (1962: 147). Women, she asserts, constantly vacillate between experiencing a primordial oneness with the body and a sense of distance from the body, prompted by the feeling that the body and its motions are 'not entirely under her control' (1962: 150). Furthermore, they experience themselves as embedded within a system of spatial coordinates that does not originate in their own intentionality.

According to Young, this 'inhibited, confined, positioned and objectified' sense of female identity is the direct outcome of sexist oppression in contemporary society. Such an identity is produced by girls' sedentary play, the assimilation of a feminine style of comportment in walking, standing, sitting, and gesturing, and in the generalized timidity inculcated by being told not to get dirty, not to get hurt, not to go too far from home, etc. It is equally the product of society's obsessive emphasis on female appearance, in which women learn to mould, groom, and decorate their bodies in conformance with a patriarchal standard of beauty.

In the same way that she de-centres Merleau-Ponty's claims for a singular relationship between body and consciousness, Young also insists on the historical specificity of the patriarchal authority that pressures women's physicality. She further grounds her observations in her own bodily experience, relating two anecdotes about her own tentativeness in crossing a stream and her juvenile efforts to learn a feminine walk. These reflexive comments on her own situatedness within the contemporary first-world patriarchy infuse her inquiry with modest particularity and also a lively sense of curiosity about one's own life in relation to the world.

Locating 'throwing'

Young's essay, from this early twenty-first century perspective, can now be located in relation to a twentieth century lineage of studies in corporeality prompted, in part, by sociological interrogations of the body in society, and in part, by phenomenological accounts of body. Where scholars such as Marcel Mauss (1973) in his famous essay *Techniques of the Body* or Michel Foucault's (1977) study of the penal system, *Discipline and Punish*, represent the former strand of inquiry, studies of perception, such as those of Merleau-Ponty represent the latter. Typically, these fields of inquiry are seen in opposition to one another, yet Young's approach provides an intriguing model for synthesizing these two distinctive forms of inquiry. In her analysis, she builds out from the individual's perceptual experience, while at the same time observing general trends in socialization. By focusing on the body's movement repertoires as a kind of interface between perception and action, she is able to integrate the external and internal structures through which identity is constructed.

Looking more specifically at the decades just prior to the essay's publication, the feminist movement of the late 1960s and 70s gave new momentum to studies of the body as did the emerging field of non-verbal communication. Feminist scholarship instigated a profound new interest in the body, yet the focus of most publications was to unearth repressed or neglected aspects of female anatomy and sexuality, to celebrate women's unique biological capacities, and to claim the rights to speak about the body publicly and without shame. Feminist inquiries focused on women's experience as a sexual and procreative being; with much research interrogating the body's status in intercourse, pregnancy, birth, motherhood, etc. The rest of woman's repertoire of physical behaviours and movements received very little attention. Young was among the first to investigate movement as one of the specific propensities of female physicality.

During these same years in the allied fields of psychology and sociology, non-verbal communication studies identified various repertoires of gesture and action as means for communicating. Typically, these repertoires of behaviour were construed as manifestations of subliminal or unconscious needs and desires. Researchers seldom conceptualized these repertoires as gender-specific or as manifesting a style of execution that was allied with a particular gender. Furthermore, the body's movement, always conceptualized as the effect or execution of the psyche's will, was never accorded agency. It remained a mute and dumb event, capable only of exhibiting the results of a person's thoughts or feelings.

In contrast to non-verbal communication studies, Young refrains from assigning movement a purely mechanical function. Nor does she invoke the binary that typically aligns speech with conscious, cognitive experience and movement with the unconscious, the libidinal, or the emotional. She does not enter into debates as to the conscious or unconscious valence of these movement vocabularies. Instead, she recognizes them as simply a part of the socialization process.

In this consideration of movement as part of acculturation, Young is aligned with the anthropological investigations of Alan Lomax, an anthropologist who studied the relationship between subsistence patterns and dance movement in a variety of cultures during the 1960s and 70s. Implementing categories of movement analysis corollary to Rudolph Laban's systems of movement analysis, Lomax and movement analysts Irmgard Bartinieff and Forrestine Paulay observed postural and movement flow patterns in films of dances from around the world. Envisioning dance as 'a representation and reinforcement of cultural pattern', they determined a strong correspondence between features of the movement repertoire utilized for purposes of subsistence and those invoked in dancing. These researchers found that the bodily stance and style of transition, whether 'cyclic, angular, rotated, or looped', among others, assumed while dancing correlated strongly with the 'rubbing, digging, or chopping', etc. entailed in food production (Lomax *et al.* 1968: 240–1).

Young's analysis, however, diverges from these findings in crucial ways. First, the categorization of movement implemented in Lomax's study presumes that features such as 'cyclic, angular, or rotated' are universals that are embedded and self-evident in all movement. Young, in contrast, proposed her categories as hypothetical tools whose application would yield specific kinds of insights. Second, Lomax's approach, in its efforts to compare all of the world's dances, establishes a hierarchy of cultures, moving from more 'primitive' to 'complex' social organizations. Young specifies that her study applies only to 'women situated in contemporary advanced industrial, urban, and commercial society' (Young 1990: 143), and she is not concerned with the potential application of her categories beyond that context. Whether or if they might illuminate the feminine in another locale would depend upon extensive and in-depth study of the distinctive epistemological assumptions about corporeality practised in that place.

Reading a feminist choreographer's dance as a feminist philosopher might

In her essay from 1998 reflecting back on 'Throwing', Young comments on the massive changes in social behaviours that distinguish her generation from that of her daughter. Able to wear jeans and take full advantage of athletic opportunities, Young's daughter and 'her friends move and carry themselves with more openness, more reach, more active confidence' than many of Young's cohort (1998: 286). Yet, Young finds that her essay remains pertinent to a significant number of undergraduate readers. How might the feminine have transformed so as to allow more 'openness' yet still exercise the oppressive influence that would make a new generation of feminists enthusiastic about Young's critique? For one answer to this question, I turn not to the everyday pedestrian events for signs of gender's construction that Young analysed, but to a highly staged event, Lea Anderson's *Yippee!!!* What follows is a detailed reading of Anderson's dance implementing the kinds of analytic perspectives that Young developed in her original essay.

The dancers traipse in, exuding a sultry glamour. Their arms poke at space with such ennui. They stare at the audience with a practised, bored blankness. Striking a statuesque pose, they slouch along in parade, their long mink stoles revealing a glimpse of a shoulder here, of a lower back there. Of course, any frisson that we receive from such a glimpse is dripping with irony, since all the bodies, male and female, are similarly naked – covered only with a translucent unitard that holds delicately in place massive quantities of fake pubic and underarm hair. They glide into ballroom couple poses and swirl gently around the stage. Other dancers pull on fur stockings and saunter in a circle. A livelier group wiggles their way onstage in grid formation, their complex rhythmic gyrations pulsing with fake euphoria.

At this point, the genre of this masquerade becomes identifiable: each scene is a take-off on filmed production numbers from Broadway-style entertainments. The dancers execute versions of the original choruses and follow their formations onstage, yet they break radically with the gender codes of those early twentieth century productions. Male and female bodies, sometimes indistinguishable with their slicked back hair and similarly muscled physiques, both inhabit the same roles. In scenes where male and female dancers would typically partner one another, men dance with men, women with women, and women with men. In scenes where the traditional chorus line consisted of all female dancers, both male and female dancers engage equally in the same feminine repertoires: broad smiles, mincing steps, gracious displays of the body, and daintily bound gestures.

The performance of such strongly gendered actions by both male and female bodies offers up a powerful representation of the feminine as a gendered construct. Anderson deepens this interrogation of the feminine through her choreographic strategy of faithfully copying sections from film or photographs. Even though the dancers precisely execute eighty-year-old choreography, they lack the accoutrements of the filmic scene that would ensure their reception as realistic actors. Either the movement sequences are not used in their entirety and thereby disrupt with their glaring beginnings and endings; or they lack the setting that would give them narrative coherence; or they are cobbled together in an absurd sequence; or they are repeated excessively such that their staging of exaggerated happiness becomes a most uncomfortable joke.

In all the obsessive repetition that overflows from the performance, what the dancers repeat most is the wiggle. They wiggle as their feet move from side to side in parallel. They wiggle as they skip. They wiggle as they shrug away any intimation of anxiety. Their wiggling is not quite naughty, not at all frenetic. Instead, the body pulls back from completely stretching one way and then the other. As a result, the figures look apathetic, even as they perform cheerfulness. Both the quality of the wiggle and the way it directs motion to one side and then the other signify a profound ambiguity. As in Young's initial observations about female comportment, these dancers can't decide which way to go, and even if they were to decide, so what?

From the beginning, the performance makes a convincing case for its artifice. The main action takes place within a set of lights on movable poles that the dancers re-arrange for different sections of the piece. Outside the lights dancers meander among racks of costumes, changing clothes, warming up, and watching the action. At one point, a seeming intermission, the dancers break to drink deeply from bottles of water stored in the open wings. At another, a dancer's fake dentures, enforcing his grotesque smile, pop out, and he fumbles frantically to reinsert them. Throughout, dancers stand in full view awaiting their entrances to the 'performance' inside the lights.

As they stand ready to make their entrances, each dancer's body musters all the concentration necessary to make the transition from 'off' stage to 'on', all the necessary energy that normally would explode with the vitality of 'dancing'. Yet instead, their onstage presence hails the viewer with an unbearable lack of zeal. So soft and subdued, so precisely directed yet fully lacklustre, each gesture underscores its own failure to show the audience vigour, excitement, the sheer joy and gusto of engaging with physicality. The driving rhythms of the live band upstage emphasize even further this restrictedness of motion.

How to describe this peculiar quality of restraint? In the history of modern dance, restrained movement has signified an internal struggle in which opposing motivations vie for control over bodily expression as vivified in the choreography of Martha Graham, Doris Humphrey, Anna Sokolow, and many others. Restrained motion is full of tension and drama, as the body seems to proclaim simultaneously, 'I will' and 'I won't'. The restraint evident in Anderson's piece, however, does not suggest a wilful subject. It is, to use Young's term, inhibited. These rubbery, resilient wigglers never extend themselves fully either towards effortful exertion or lackadaisical relaxation. In part, this inhibited exertion into space reproduces the qualities of effort evident in the production numbers that Anderson has copied. Without the full costumes or bubbly music of the original performances, however, and in contrast to the extreme exertion so prevalent on the concert stage today, these dancers purvey a remarkably fettered physicality.

Anderson's choreographic process of copying and then splicing together movement sequences from other sources also produces Young's third principle of feminine movement – discontinuous unity. Because of the process of copying the action, the dancers appear to wear the movement. Motions do not originate in the body's interiority, but instead get placed on the body's surface. The bodies execute the next action, as non sequitur as it might be, without any organic flow, any sense of movement's purposefulness.

The second half of the performance turns darker. The happy jumping becomes obsessive, meaningless – a kind of consumer frenzy on display. Now wearing black unitards with silver tap shoes, the dancers' formations become more austere. A 'Ballet Masteress' enters wearing a dark fur coat using a prosthetic foot as a cane. She rehearses the corps, adjusting posture, repositioning the dancers, counting and drilling them, then pronouncing their execution 'nice'. Anderson's critique of Tiller girls or Rockettes-type repetitive movement grinds forward, implementing the tyranny of the 8-count phrase. This nightmarish alternation between emphatic carefreeness and statuesque strutting summons up the underbelly of the beauty industry. Yes, women have more access to athletic pursuits in this culture of nip and tuck, where there is no gain without pain, and every repetition potentially enhances one's image.

Alternating between grid formations and the parade, the dancers seldom touch one another. Only one couple, adorned with red velvet vaginas over their noses and mouths, ever sustains physical contact. They perform failed versions of gags, and then re-appear dancing to the sounds of a tap dance, making reference to an African American duo such as the Nicholas Brothers on film. Cavorting, buffooning, they counterpoint the vacant monumentality of the larger production numbers.

For the finale, the dancers return to the ballroom, partnering up with partial tuxedos and strap-on feather boas in a last parade. Their fanciful strutting culminates in a single decorative tableau where all the dancers artfully drape their bodies across the front of the stage. Yet this final image produces no climax, no ta-da. As if to reassert, once again, the irony of the dance's title, the ending is as lame as the femininity, which it celebrates, is oppressive.

Gender's migration

In order to fathom the significance of Anderson's rendering of the feminine, I now look back at Martha Graham's solo from 1930 entitled *Lamentation*, made during the same time period as the material Anderson copied. This iconic work has served as a quintessential example of the modernist aesthetic, illustrating the tensile relationship between interiority and motion as well as the ability of the dancer to achieve a universality of subject position. If we look at the solo using Young's criteria, however, we also see how it mounts a critique of the feminine, one that comments on the same protocols of femininity that the Broadway musicals celebrate, but that completely contrasts with Anderson's argument. What Graham does is to dramatize the boundness and inhibitedness of the character's gestural possibilities, staging the limitations of the feminine, literally, as a tubular jersey that the self is struggling to transcend. Instead of the mincing, effervescent timidity of the Broadway productions that were taking place up the street from her studio, Graham creates a character that struggles valiantly against the confines of her situation. The body toils through oppositional torques, whose exertion on the body is manifest in the precarious positioning of the foot, straining to stay grounded as the arms heft the body skywards. The starkly-drawn diagonals, sweeping arcs, and monumental shapes, all testify to the labour of lamenting. The dancer persists in this exertion even as it threatens to wring her body of its life force.

Delving deep into the cloth's interior, the dancer shows woman as having superior access to deepest emotions. She, uniquely, is able to reach down to the bottom of the psyche. This interior, also womb-like, suggests the procreative power that is also uniquely feminine. Rather than succumb to the boundaries established for womanhood, the choreography constructs nobility and strength of character from limitations. Claiming women's unique work in mourning with such depth, the piece monumentalizes an intrinsic feminine. Where the Follies and musicals staged girls as delightful divertissements, Graham showed how they could accomplish much more. At a moment in US history when women had moved much more centrally into the public sphere, Graham's choreography thus presumes an essential femininity that it then works to ennoble.

Comparing Graham's vision of the feminine with that of Trisha Brown's in *Watermotor* from 1978, I find a marked shift in conceptions of gender. Whereas Graham's choreography stages a body that endeavours repeatedly and unsuccessfully to extend itself fully, Brown rarely extends to the full limits of her reach. At the same time, she shows many more possible articulations within a mid-range of motion than are normally conceivable. When she does, occasionally, extend a limb fully, it is followed almost immediately by its softening or by a collapse of the middle body, not, as in *Lamentation*, as a sign of defeat, but instead, as onward motion towards the next articulation. Thus Brown's body asserts a casual and relaxed familiarity that strives for nothing beyond the pleasure of enunciating its jointedness. And unlike Graham's piece which conveys the conflict between parts of the body that are differently directed, Brown revels in the potential of the body's parts to be disconnected. The choreography *never* coordinates the body towards a single action, and it frequently presents oxymoronic juxtapositions of incompatible movements. Where Graham works with Young's criteria to ennoble and glorify an essential femininity, Brown riotously multiplies the same directives into a myriad of possible articulations, laughingly dismissing their inhibitedness. In this way Brown doesn't deconstruct the feminine, so much as she explodes it.

Where Graham envisions gender as a natural and inevitable aspect of the human, one that entails a clear division of labour between the masculine and the feminine, Brown establishes a neutral body onto which gender can be placed. Her relaxed demeanour, pedestrian gaze, and refusal to offer up any spectacle all work to construct an androgynous physicality committed to a matter-of-fact exploration of its own possibilities. Admittedly, the palette of Brown's movement investigations tends towards softer and gentler motion, in strong contrast to Graham's effortful labour. Yet, her proclivities towards pliancy seem more geared to emphasize the relaxed and efficient quality of execution rather than any natural preference for a feminine grace. Where Graham dons a tubular jersey that references the Madonna, monastic life, and the depth of female subjectivity, Brown wears casual street clothes. Where Graham uses successive motion through functionally distinct parts of the body to represent the motionality of emotion, Brown inventories movement's possibilities, channelling motion one way and then another so that all pathways are equally plausible, all are equally capable of conveying the excitement of motionality itself.

The neutrality of the body cultivated by Brown and many of her contemporaries provided the baseline body onto which gender as a set of codes could be projected. Although she never inclined to explore gender as performance, some of her colleagues, notably Yvonne Rainer, and many artists in the next generation, Bill T. Jones, Anna Teresa de Keersmaeker, Meredith Monk, among many others, conducted extensive choreographic investigation of the citation as a means to put on and take off gendered identities. Alongside and enabling these performances of gender, however, was the non-gendered body that Brown had asserted.

Viewed from the perspective of these earlier works, Anderson's *Yippee!!!* maps the trajectory of the feminine from an essential identity through an androgynous neutrality with which the feminine can be performed and to a repository of codes that can be tapped to accessorize any body. Yippee! – we can be any gender we want. Yippee! – it's so much fun to play with the codes. Yippee! – now we know why Young's categories might still hold relevance for today's young women. The trope of the feminine, now uploaded into a sci-fi future where hybrid creatures with prosthetic smiles roam across the stage, continues to be celebrated. Perpetuating itself on and through billboards, television commercials, and each season's fashions, this rhetoric of femininity, Anderson seems to be claiming, is just as ambiguous, inhibited, and discontinuous as anything Young ever observed. Yippee! – one episode of glamour after another, each offering the consumer of gender construction a slightly different flavour of the feminine. Like the globally circulating flow of capital, feminine corporeality, equally pervasive through commodities and mediatized images, appears glamorous even as it pins the bodies that participate in it within the constrained, dislocated ambivalence of having to throw like a girl.

Gender's transnationality

Gender, now uploaded into a globally circulating set of codes, can be tapped for multiple purposes. As Shu Mei Shih (2007) has shown convincingly in her study of Sinophone cultures, constructions of the feminine can purvey distinctive sets of meanings within local, regional and national contexts. Shih untangles the many layers of significance embedded in visual images, paintings and films, as they travel across borders and are received by viewers who continue to affiliate with China while also identifying with their diverse local communities. She also demonstrates how multiple gazes – patriarchal, ethnic, post-Communist, and Orientalist – operate to influence a work's reception, but also how some of those gazes can be shown to be anticipated and rebuffed within a given artist's work.

Keeping Shih's insistence on the complexity of gender in the transnational sphere, I want to note the striking similarities between Anderson's *Yippee!!!* and work by the Japanese performance collective named KATHY. Where *Yippee!!!* presents a world of science fiction bodies draped with gender codes, KATHY members claim to be directed by an extra-terrestrial, or possibly an American, whose name is Kathy. In *Mission/K* (2002) three dancers cavort through a park-like landscape filmed by a camera whose fish-eye lens represents Kathy's omniscient presence. Sporting shirt-waist dresses and blonde page-boys, the dancers glide among vocabularies identifiable as derived from Broadway jazz, ballet, modern, can-can, tap, hula, children's games, and movie musicals – all performed to the effervescent sound-track of Debbie Reynolds singing 'Good morning' from *Singin' in the Rain*. Unlike Anderson's choreography, which cites a homogeneous group of production numbers, KATHY's sequencing selects from diverse genres, both popular and high art. Yet like Anderson's dancers, these women perform every move with a faint but discernible lack of gusto. They flop into arabesque, twirl with groggy abandon, and fall with a clunk; the ambivalence in their motion underscored by the black tights that cover their faces, legs dangling as two grotesquely deflated protuberances.

Where Anderson's dancers always perform just short of their full-out capability, KATHY's members occasionally demonstrate blatant failure at certain moves: the can-can makes them gasp for breath; the partner fails to catch the dancer as she lurches forward in arabesque. In these failures, the dancers underscore the pretence of their performance. They step into the camera's view, driven to execute a choreography that they show they have not fully mastered. Theatre scholar Nobuko Anan (forthcoming) argues that since the vocabularies they perform derive from Western and primarily US sources, their ineptness 'wittily de-naturalizes the "organic" beauty' of those forms.

Anan's analysis also points to several further layers of signification embedded within KATHY's choreography. Not only does the group's ineptness construct a send-up of Western dance, but their lack of virtuosity and gusto also signals the dancers' inability to 'live up to Americanization' in the post-war period, a mastery of American culture that Kathy is demanding. Anan argues that the performance shows their failure to assimilate American cultural values, while also revealing Japan's feminized status in relation to the US. Their little-girlness references Japanese citizens' identity as children in relation to US hegemony, stemming from the post-war occupation, but continuing into the present with the coercive demand that Japan assist US forces in Iraq. Analogous to the theory of super-flat launched by artist Murakami Takashi in which post-war Japan is seen as lacking the maturity, intellectually and ethically, to govern, KATHY displays the infantilization that has suffused US treatment of the Japanese. However, where Murakami focuses exclusively on boys, KATHY's performance introduces a feminist response. Their cut-and-paste sequencing of diverse movement traditions, as in Anderson's choreography, serves to deconstruct the femininity that was put on display in the original versions. As such, it destabilizes Japanese patriarchal assertions concerning an essential femininity, and refuses to return to the patriarchal hierarchies and values governing pre-war Japan.

Anderson's critique of the feminine in contemporary British society reacts against post-feminism and the residue of Prime Minister Margaret Thatcher's deregulated, free wheeling economy in which a libratory consumer culture poses as the equalizer of gender.[3] Her choreography also responds to the rise of commercialization within concert dance, evident in the large-scale and highly popular productions of choreographers such as Matthew Bourne, as well as the drop in state support for the arts resulting from globalization's financial crises. *Yippee!!!*'s finale is a painfully dreary and deflated celebration of just this glamorousness. Members of KATHY, in contrast, negotiate between different efforts to reassert Japanese identity, either through a return to traditional patriarchy or a super-flat aesthetics. They conclude their performance with a startling change in energy and direction, one that suggests an opening through which to imagine a future apart from the enduring colonial influence of the US: they abruptly abandon a swishy phrase of lyrical turns and gallops to march towards and then past the camera, their direct and confident stride certainly not that of a girl.

Throwing across cultures

Both Anderson and KATHY contest the traditional depictions of female dancers, deflating the shapely attractiveness, undermining the sexy presentation of an objectified body, and distorting the standard narratives upon which scopophilic and patriarchal pleasure depend. And both use startlingly similar choreographic tactics to stage their feminist antagonism. Young's categories of analysis provide an entry point for analysing these choreographed critiques. Her conceptions of space help us fathom how a 'girl' moves and how her movement is characterized by each artist. Still, the girl in Britain and the girl in Japan are also two different subjects. (And had there been space, it would be important to excavate the experiences of the girl from Graham's 1930s as well as Brown's 1970s.) Although both Britain and Japan are 'contemporary advanced industrial, urban, and commercial' societies for which Young's categories are applicable, Japan's history as an occupied country and the sustained hegemony of the US towards Japan create very different contexts for each feminist critique. Anderson's work rejects her own country's post-feminist consumer frenzy, whereas KATHY unsettles traditional Japanese patriarchal values as well as US dominance over its former occupied territory.

Young's categories, in and of themselves, could not have unpacked these differences. Even as Hollywood moves into the transnational as a salient repertoire of the feminine, the local histories of those who access it substantially influence its meaning. Nonetheless, Young's efforts to integrate psychological and social codings of the feminine, in their assertion that movement signifies in both realms, enable us to launch an inquiry into such differences and to track the experience of the feminine in diverse arenas. Perhaps they also suggest how a transnational feminism in dance scholarship could begin to choreograph itself.

Notes

1 See, for example, Cynthia Novack, *Sharing the Dance: Contact Improvisation and American Culture*, Madison: The University of Wisconsin Press, 1990; Christy Adair, *Women and Dance: Sylphs and Sirens*, New York: New York University Press, 1992; Susan Manning, *Ecstasy and the Demon: The Dances of Mary Wigman*, Minneapolis: University of Minnesota Press, 1993; Ann Daly, *Done Into Dance: Isadora Duncan In America*, Bloomington: Indiana University Press, 1994; Ramsay Burt, *The Male Dancer: Bodies, Spectacle and Sexualities*, New York: Routledge, 1995; Susan Leigh Foster, *Choreography and Narrative: Ballet's Staging of Story and Desire*, Bloomington: Indiana University Press, 1996; Ann Cooper Albright, *Choreographing Difference: Body and Identity in Contemporary Dance*, Middletown: Wesleyan University Press, 1997; Sally Banes, *Dancing Women: Female Bodies on Stage*, London: Routledge, 1998; Linda J. Tomko, *Dancing Class: Gender, Ethnicity, and Social Divides in American Dance, 1890–1920*, Bloomington: Indiana University Press, 1999; Thomas F. De Frantz, *Dancing Revelations: Alvin Ailey's Embodiment of African American Culture*, Oxford: Oxford University Press, 2006; Ananya Chatterjea, *Butting Out: Reading Resistive Choreographies Through Works by Jawola Willa Jo Zollar and Chandralekha*, Middletown: Wesleyan University Press, 2004; Janet O'Shea, *At Home in the World: The Bharatanatyam Dancer As Transnational Interpreter*, Middletown CT: Wesleyan University Press, 2007.

2 Anderson is an internationally recognized British choreographer who has achieved renown, in part, through her salient analyses of gender. Maintaining two companies, the all-female Cholmondeleys and the all-male Featherstonehaughs, Anderson has launched a number of humorous and insightful critiques on traditional gender roles in society and in dance. For a good overview of her earlier work, see Dodds (2001) and Briginshaw (1995/96); and for a lucid analysis of her choreographic strategies, see Hargreaves (2002).

KATHY is a collective of three classically trained dancers who perform primarily in visual arts venues. They never appear in public unmasked, and they circulate information about their projects and their history in the form of rumours via the internet. For an English-language analysis of KATHY, see Martin (2006).

3 For an expanded analysis of post-Thatcher theatre in Great Britain, see Kritzer (2008).

References

Anan, N. (forthcoming) 'KATHY's Parody of *Singin' in the Rain*: Reconsideration of Japanese Women's Bodies'.

Briginshaw, V. (1995/96) 'Getting the glamour on our own terms', *Dance Theatre Journal*, 12 (3): 36–9.

Dodds, S. (2001) 'Breaking the boundaries of high art', *Dancing Times*, 91: 433–9.

Foucault, M. (1977) *Discipline and Punish: The Birth of the Prison* (A. Sheridan, Trans.), New York: Pantheon.

Hargreaves, M. (2002) 'The cut-up pleasure and politics of Lea Anderson's choreography', *Dance Theatre Journal*, 18 (3): 16–19.

Kritzer, A. H. (2008) *Political Theatre in Post-Thatcher Britain*, London: Palgrave Macmillan.

Lomax, A., Barinieff, I. and Paulay, F. (1968) 'Dance style and culture', in A. Lomax (ed.) *Folk Song Style and Culture*, New Brunswick, NJ: Transaction Books.

Martin, C. (2006) 'Lingering heat and local global J stuff', *TDR*, 50 (1): 46–56.

Mauss, M. (1973) 'Techniques of the body', *Economy and Society*, 2 (1): 70–87.

Merleau-Ponty, M. (1962) *The Phenomenology of Perception* (Colin Smith, Trans.), New York: Humanities Press.

Shih, S. (2007) *Visuality and Identity: Sinophone Articulations across the Pacific*, Berkeley: University of California Press.

Young, I. M. (1990) 'Throwing like a girl: A phenomenology of feminine body comportment, motility, and spatiality', in *Throwing Like a Girl and Other Essays in Feminist Philosophy and Social Theory*, Bloomington: Indiana University Press.

—— (1998) 'Throwing like a girl: Twenty years later', in D. Welton (ed.) *Body and Flesh: A Philosophical Reader*, Malden, MA: Blackwell Publishers.

Section 2
Higher educational settings

Section introduction

Jo Butterworth and Liesbeth Wildschut

Research in dance education of the type included in this section was virtually non-existent in most European countries 40 years ago, although the USA could demonstrate pockets of dance research and publication, predominantly in the university sector, such as the writing of Margaret H'Doubler (1940, 1957). On the other hand, from the turn of the century until the Second World War, traditions of dance in British education could be categorised by emphases on social dance forms, folk forms, physical recreation and basic movement training. Subsequently, influences such as Emile Jacques-Dalcroze (eurhythmics), the revived Greek dance (Ruby Ginner) and Margaret Morris Movement could be seen to presage the work of Rudolf Laban (Bloomfield 1989). Though developed in Switzerland and Germany for application in the theatre and for amateurs and community groups, Laban's ideas had a profound influence on the physical education curricula in England from the 1940s through the introduction of Modern Educational Dance (Preston-Dunlop 1980; Foster 1976; Redfern 1973). In the next decades in the USA a number of dance compositional texts providing practical examples of the 'what' and 'how' of choreography were published (see for example Humphrey 1959; Turner 1971; Hawkins 1964; Louis 1980; Blom and Chaplin 1982, 1988). Additionally, the Nikolais/Louis methodology can be seen as the bedrock of choreographic pedagogy in some parts of the USA and still vitally informs practice at a large number of institutions internationally. The work of Sandra Cerny Minton (1985, 1997) and Daniel Nagrin (1994, 1997) is also influential; his *Choreography and the Specific Image: Nineteen Essays and a Workbook* (2001) completes a trio of complementary texts and Minton's *Choreography: a Basic Approach Using Improvisation* (2007) is now in its third edition.

More recently, the *Journal of Dance Education* in the USA and the journal *Research in Dance Education* in the UK have emerged as two specific publications where research into choreographic pedagogy has been disseminated. Publications such as Jacqueline Smith-Autard's *Dance Composition*

(2004), Alma Hawkins' *Moving from Within: A New Method for Dance Making* (1991), Larry Lavender's *Dancers Talking Dance: Critical Evaluation in the Choreography Class* (1996) and Valerie Preston-Dunlop's *Looking at Dances: a Choreological Perspective on Choreography* (1998) are examples of seminal texts which support teachers, students and artist-practitioners in developing awareness of approaches to the learning process in the dance discipline. In addition, conferences such as those organised by Dance and the Child International, the Congress on Research in Dance and the World Dance Alliance continue to offer teachers and lecturers the opportunity for the dissemination of ideas where others can be influenced by results of findings and may, perhaps, examine such ideas in practice. Consequently, publication and the empirical sharing of teaching methods have occurred, thus supporting teachers to reappraise their own methods in the classroom and studio both in theory and practice. However, the question of teaching choreography in higher educational contexts is often only tangential to some of these studies. This edition therefore provides a valuable contribution to the literature.

All the chapters in this section on choreography in higher education derive from the personal research imperatives of lecturers/professors who teach in the higher education context, predominantly in dance departments in the university sector.

The first chapter is by Larry Lavender, who extends his previous work on dance criticism and choreographic pedagogy. His interest lies in fostering aspiring choreographers to identify, manage, and ultimately to succeed in meeting the challenges of dance making. To assist teachers in working with students, he introduces three imaginative/critical facilitation practices – creative process mentoring, rehearsal criticism, and choreographic provocation – to supplement results-based dance criticism. Lavender's facilitation practices improve students' ability to gain deeper understanding and firmer control over all aspects of their work. Both experienced choreographers and those who are just starting out may benefit from the efforts of a teacher/facilitator with knowledge of these approaches.

Jacqueline Smith-Autard considers some conceptual opposites in the traditional professional training model and the Laban-based educational model: objectivity versus subjectivity, knowledge versus feeling/intuition, product versus process, learning of techniques versus personal explorations and didactic versus open-ended teaching methodologies. She introduces the use of a CD-ROM resource pack, created by the author herself in cooperation with Jim Schofield, to demonstrate how meaningful dance composition can result from a complex mix of objective learning and subjective, intuitive feeling entering into the process. The chapter concludes by reference to technologies such as the web, videoconferencing, video recording/playback, etc. and the employment of generalised software packages to advance and enhance teaching/learning in dance.

The following discussion interrogates the evaluation of student choreography. Soili Hämäläinen believes that evaluation has to do with questions concerning not only the teacher's authority, expertise and power, but also the student's ability, choices and independence as well as expertise regarding one's own body and the creative process. She focuses on three important questions in evaluation: what to evaluate, who are the evaluators and what is the meaning of evaluation? The chapter surveys a number of methods and concludes by identifying some directions that might illuminate and enhance the possibilities of evaluation.

Äli Leijen's chapter investigates how teachers can help dance students to reflect on their own practice. A short overview of three different theories of reflection in education is followed by analysis of common pedagogical practices in dance education, which led to the production of a model. She suggests that the focus of reflection in practical dance education concerns both the standards of the professional dance domain and the subjectivity of the dance students, describing how determinative and reflective judgements are encouraged during and after choreographic practice. Leijen provides a case study of a web-based learning environment to help support students' reflection.

Bonnie Rowell identifies some specific ways in which postmodern dances challenge the dance analyst. Rowell suggests ways in which these problems may be tackled through an integrative approach to teaching dance in higher education, specifically through a philosophical concept of embodiment that is useful in unravelling some of these dances' complexities. Problems to do with originality, creativity and value are addressed and these issues are teased out in relation to specific dance works. In particular, the model serves to explain our perception of dances as they are performed in relation to our experience of dancing.

The final chapter in this section focuses specifically on the postgraduate choreography student in academia. Jo Butterworth explores the dichotomy between professional apprenticeship and concepts of knowledge in academic practice, suggesting ways in which integration of theory and practice can be brought about in a taught master's programme. She proposes a range of investigative tools that can be introduced to artist-researchers in order to aid individual development, and identifies approaches that can guide them towards reflection, interrogation and articulation of their professional dance-making processes.

These six chapters represent a range of interests in choreographic pedagogy. The authors demonstrate the ability to develop their discipline and to gain credence for the subject domain. In so doing, the attempt has been made to engage with a variety of pedagogical issues from particular personal perspectives. The potential applications of this research could be used to benefit teaching–learning approaches, and possibly to influence curriculum design in higher education dance programmes.

Within the dance curriculum generally, the possibility for research to continue to develop through practice exists, either explicitly or implicitly.

In a number of these chapters the authors have chosen to engage/practice with students in order to explore new methods, to verify their research and to develop the knowledge itself. Here it is evident that the contribution of students in the outcomes of the research is both acknowledged and valued. Further, all these practitioners recognise the importance of dialogue between themselves and their students, as well as between academic and professional colleagues within and outside the university environment.

These chapters offer lecturers new mechanisms for the further development of students, linked to the aims of teaching. These methods can also inspire students with new ideas and concepts to initiate new avenues in their own learning – that is, to help identify their own interests and to pursue them. Of course, such inspiration may lead to artistic, conceptual or intellectual journeys, even where those interests go in their own direction, far away from the original research, by providing important new starting-points for the student. Equally, engagement with the personal research interests of staff can make students more involved, more critical and yet more knowledgeable.

In practice, professionally speaking, a choreographer's development most naturally or ideally takes place when working for a concentrated period of time towards a performance, engaged in the research and development of an initial stimulus or starting-point, through to the various stages of the rehearsal period and towards a full-length choreographic outcome. While similar processes can and do take place in the educational sphere, the norm for choreography teaching in the sector is in short, regular timetabled blocks. In the teaching situation, students tend to practise their skills through compositional tasks in 'bite-size' pieces – short sessions, a particular focus on elements, a brief culminating sequence or study. Teachers 'spotlight' one element of choreographic practice for further development, emphasising process rather than completed outcome, and then let it 'slot' back into the whole picture like pieces of a jigsaw puzzle. Gradually these exercises help the student to develop a toolbox of choreographic methods to apply in the creation of their own artistic work.

In the educational context, young choreographers crucially learn about reflection and evaluation of their own work; that is, applying the process of critical judgement. Increasingly this reflection is learned through the inter-relationship of practice to theory. In the dance studio, students generally gain experience through appreciation and analysis of their own work, and through observation and critical appraisal of the work of their peers. In the lecture or seminar, knowledge is gained through introduction to theoretical frameworks and analytical methods and their application to the choreographic work of professionals. This consideration of the inter-relationship with the professional dance world *and* with scholarship is crucial in terms of the artistic development of students.

Despite the pragmatic/empirical nature of these chapters, there are also important artistic imperatives in the work of these researchers. In fostering the development of aspiring choreographers – those who will become sympathetic to and knowledgeable about artistic professional processes – lecturers must be guided by their own depth of knowledge of the professional context, together with their own aesthetic sensibilities.

References

Blom, L. A. and Chaplin, L. T. (1982) *The Intimate Act of Choreography*, Pittsburgh: Pittsburgh Press.

—— (1988) *The Moment of Movement: Dance Improvisation*, London: Dance Books.

Bloomfield, A. (1989) 'The philosophical and artistic tradition of dance in British education', in *Young People Dancing: an International Perspective*, Conference proceedings Dance and the Child International, London: daCi.

D'Houbler, M. N. (1940, 1957) *Dance: a Creative Art Experience*, Madison: University of Wisconsin.

Foster, R. (1976) *Knowing in my Bones*, London: A & C Black.

Hawkins, A. M. (1964) *Creating through Movement*, Englewood Cliffs, NJ: Prentice-Hall.

—— (1991) *Moving from Within: A New Method for Dance Making*, Princeton, NJ: a cappella.

Humphrey, D. (1959) *The Art of Making Dances*, New York: Grove Press.

Lavender, L. (1996) *Dancers Talking Dance: Critical Evaluation in the Choreography Class*, Champaign, IL: Human Kinetics.

Louis, M. (1980) *Inside Dance: Essays*, New York: St Martin's Press.

Minton, S. C. (1985, 1997, 2007) *Choreography: A basic approach using improvisation*, Champaign, IL: Human Kinetics.

Nagrin, D. (1994) *Dance and the Specific Image*, Pittsburgh, PA: University of Pittsburgh.

—— (1997) *The Six Questions: Acting Technique for Dance Performance*, Pittsburgh, PA: University of Pittsburgh.

—— (2001) *Choreography and the Specific Image: Nineteen Essays and a Workbook*, Pittsburgh, PA: University of Pittsburgh.

Preston-Dunlop, V. (1980) *A Handbook for Dance in Education*, Harlow: Longmans.

—— (1998) *Looking at Dances: a Choreological Perspective on Choreography*, Ightham: Verve.

Redfern, H. B. (1973) *Concepts in Modern Educational Dance*, London: Henry Kimpton.

Smith-Autard, J. M. (2004) *Dance Composition*, 5th edn, London: A & C Black.

Turner, M. J. (1971) *New Dance: Approaches to Non-literal Choreography*, Pittsburgh: University of Pittsburgh Press.

Further reading

Alexander, E. (1998) *Footnotes: Six Choreographers Inscribe the Page*, G&B Arts International. (Essays by Douglas Dunn, Marjorie Gamso, Ishmail Houston-Jones, Kenneth King, Yvonne Meier, Sarah Saggs.)

Butcher, R. and Melrose, S. (2005) *Choreography, Collisions and Collaborations*, Enfield: Middlesex University Press.

Kreemer, C. (ed.) (2008) *Further Steps 2: Fourteen Choreographers in What's the RAGE in Dance?* Abingdon, Oxon, and NY: Routledge.

McCutchen, B. P. (2006) *Teaching Dance as Art in Education*, Champaign, IL: Human Kinetics.

Morgenroth, J. (2004) *Speaking of Dance: Twelve Contemporary Choreographers on their Craft*, New York and London: Routledge.

Theodores, D. (2000) *Writing Dancing, Righting Dance: Articulations on a Choreographic Process*, Cork: Firkin Crane, Dance Development Agency.

6 Facilitating the choreographic process[1]

Larry Lavender

Within the diverse field of contemporary concert dance, new works may be inspired by a vast array of ideas, and created through an equally vast array of rehearsal methods. However, unless a dance is to be improvised afresh each time it is performed, its specificities must in some way be 'set' through rehearsal. To create and set a dance a choreographer must continually make decisions to address both planned and unforeseen challenges.

Fostering in choreographers the capacity to meet artistic challenges is a complex undertaking. Certainly, choreographers need to learn and practise using diverse dance composition principles and approaches; college and university choreography curricula do a good job in providing such opportunities.[2] Yet there are vast differences among choreographers' ways of working, and in the help they may seek at any given moment. The only constant factor is that while potentially paralysing obstacles may arise during dance creation, artistic solutions from one dance rarely satisfy the needs of the next. Myriad features of a work – its rhythmic and other temporal qualities, presence in space, and other expressive subtleties – prohibit routine 'fixes' from resolving any but the most generic choreographic problems. For this reason all choreographers may benefit from the efforts of a skilled and nurturing facilitator.

Given the uniqueness of each dance-making context, it may seem as if facilitating choreographic process must remain an ad hoc activity, depending mostly on guesswork and luck. This view seems pervasive in academic settings where results-based criticism of complete or nearly-complete works has long been the primary, if not the sole, facilitating tool available to choreographers. Glossing over the intricacies of dance making, and giving little attention to the cognitive idiosyncrasies of creators' work styles, such criticism seeks to improve the stage-worthiness of the dance.[3]

Dances often do improve through sharp-eyed critical feedback. But as a tool for deepening choreographic know-how, results-based criticism falls short. In most cases, by the time a dance is 'set' sufficiently to receive critical attention the decisions through which the choreographer purposefully (or inadvertently) generated the work's structure and expressive qualities have been forgotten or remain only as hazy memories. Largely unaware of how and why they make their creative choices, many choreographers fall repeatedly into the same mental ruts no matter how often particular weaknesses (or strengths) in their works are identified by critics.

To do their best, choreographers need specific tools to address every aspect of dance making from idea construction to 'finishing touch' editing and revising, and they need help in gaining the meta-cognitive skills known to give problem solvers maximum autonomy over their work.[4] With the above aims in mind, I provide in this chapter descriptive models of the creative operations of dance making and of the kinds of intentions that choreographers commonly use to launch and sustain their work. Next, drawing upon research findings in creative cognition and many years of experience as a choreographer and choreography teacher/mentor, I introduce three facilitation practices that teachers and mentors may use to help choreographers to succeed: *creative process mentoring* clarifies otherwise blurry relationships among artistic intentions, in-studio practices, and emergent forms/meanings. *Rehearsal criticism* cultivates choreographers' invention and use of effective in-studio creation methods. *Choreographic provocation* devises and explores multiple pathways for choreographic intentions and dance structures.[5]

The creative operations of dance making: IDEA

There are four creative operations of dance making. Everything a choreographer does in making a dance is an instantiation of one (or more) of these operations. It is not that there are only four actions choreographers do; there are hundreds of things they do, myriad ways in which they do them, and a vast number of reasons why. Still, every action of dance making is an instantiation of one or another of the four operations.

The operations are identified through the acronym IDEA: *Improvisation*, *Development*, *Evaluation*, and *Assimilation*. (The names given to the techniques in this chapter are those that I have developed with students and colleagues; others may find that different names better suit their particular context.) The IDEA model is neither a method for making dances nor a progression of stages though which one passes in making a dance. Rather, it is a map of the intrinsic operations of dance making, each of whose challenges may arise at any time. Artists cannot predict which challenge will arise next, for that depends on their responses to realities before them and in their minds; they may suddenly need to improvise material, or to take apart and re-assimilate part of the dance. The IDEA model helps choreographers to discover their tendencies; what they do (or neglect to do, or avoid doing) as their dance making crawls or zooms along. With this insight, they can more readily regain direction when lost.

Improvisation

Within the IDEA model, *improvisation* refers to any means of generating or testing the potential artistic value of movement or dance-structure ideas. At any moment, choreographers may decide to invent or to reconfigure material mentally or directly on bodies. Experimental 'cutting and pasting', and trying out alternative versions of material are modes of improvisation.

Development

Choreographers regularly act upon material to change its expressive details and/or to shape its design. They *develop* movement and structural frames for movement through the application of choreographic principles and devices: they may lengthen, shorten, expand, or sharpen material, or change its speed or direction. They may infuse movement with a particular energy quality, or turn it upside down, and so forth.

Evaluation

Choreographers must *evaluate* (instantaneously or reflectively) their actions and outcomes.[6] When outcomes disappoint, one finds alternatives or gets stuck. In every case, to move forward (which may mean restoring earlier conditions) artists must evaluate the consequences of earlier choices and any new options they can envision.

Assimilation

Choreographers *assimilate* – provisionally or with feelings of certainty – bits of material into larger chunks that eventually coalesce into the entity called 'the dance'. With the final act of assimilation, a dance is 'set' for performance.

Dance-making intentions

Artistic challenges emerge (or are chosen by choreographers) in unique patterns and adopt different guises from one venture to the next. To assist choreographers in understanding and in responding imaginatively to challenges, facilitators must know how the artists mentally represent their intentions. A choreographer's intentions – motives and plans for creating – set the creative wheels in motion.

Intention framing

Intentions may remain steady or change during dance creation. To grasp a choreographer's current intentions, one may invite the choreographer to use one or more of the following sentence frames:

'I am making a dance by …' (a process for creating);

'I am making a dance in which …' (intended imagery);

'I am making a dance that …' (outcomes for the work to achieve);

'I am making a dance about …' (theme or subject-matter).

It is important to remember that choreographic intentions need not be eloquent, logical, comprehensive or firmly held. Indeed, even in stating what they are doing or intending to do choreographers may change their mind. This is not a problem; the purpose of intention framing is just to bring the relation between inspiration (even tentative inspiration) and creative action steps into focus, and thereby to gain a basis for understanding the choreographer's ways of engaging the IDEA operations.[7] There is no need to constrain the artist or to pin her down conceptually; intentions are only plans, not promises.

Process intentions

A choreographer says, 'I want to explore loneliness, so we'll improvise phrases based on that, and I will create the dance from there'. Emotion-based process intentions of this nature are common, as are design-based process intentions such as this example from Lucinda Childs: 'I was interested in exploring what would happen when two dancers paced an eighteen-count phrase on a semi-circular path while the other two dancers were executing a phrase of the same duration on a floor pattern that covered three quarters of a circle' (Morgenroth 2004: 75). Interestingly, while process intentions easily launch *improvisation*, they may do little else; one may sail easily with movement generation but struggle to perform the *evaluations* needed to *develop* and *assimilate* steadily accumulating material.

Image intentions

A choreographer says, 'I imagine a rough and tumble duet with neither dancer really taking the lead; I see a power struggle, with angular, distorted movement'. This idea names particular kinds of movement and specific qualities the movement (hopefully) will express, and it describes a social relationship. One might ask, 'Will you describe the relationship you envision, and have the dancers create movement, or will you create the movement first and set it on the dancers?' Such questions, even if not answered fully or clearly, nevertheless give the choreographer access to her operational thinking that she might not otherwise gain. It is helpful also to remind the choreographer that imagined movement might differ vastly from the same movement performed in real time and space. If the choreographer seeks to press predetermined images onto dancers – that is, to copy images from an imagined future and paste them into the present – she may become throttled by negative *evaluation* (insisting that reality conform to her vision) and neglect to discover through *improvisation* different, possibly richer, imagery.

Outcome intentions

A third choreographer says, 'I want my dance to make people do something about ...' (a pressing issue or cause). Many choreographers seek to achieve through dances laudable social/political outcomes.[8] But since laudable social aims for art do not necessarily produce laudable art, choreographers may need to be reminded that artistic challenges do not melt away merely because the intended outcome is not particularly artistic. If artistic thinking has little to do with specifically artistic matters – for example, the design and integration of movement, costumes, and sound – and does not contain or suggest criteria for assessing specifically artistic achievement, there may not be any.

'Aboutness' intentions

Many choreographers describe subject-matter for their dances to 'deal with' or 'be about'. For example, 'I am making a dance about jealousy' (or dolphins, or life on Mars). Such thinking is tricky: 'aboutness' is a slippery concept and there may be no reliable way to determine, as one creates, whether one moves closer to or further away from achieving 'aboutness'. An important question is, '*How* will your dance be about this idea? Merely thinking about jealousy, or being constantly jealous, will not make the dance about jealousy'. Choreographers with 'aboutness' intentions may need help in distinguishing between literal, denotative meaning and evocative, connotative meaning. Trapped by the ease of literalism, many choreographers rely on cliché imagery to illustrate subject matter.[9]

Each kind of intention engenders particular advantages and liabilities; whatever one approach contains in abundance, another may leave out. For example, even as two choreographers may be working with Schubert's *Impromptu in C Minor*, their plans and thus the challenges ahead may differ greatly. The music may give a strong 'aboutness' idea to one choreographer, but leave her empty of images. The other artist may possess strong images but struggle to combine them. The facilitator's job is different in each case.

Intention framing often elicits 'patchwork' ideas that combine the basic intention types. For example, 'I imagine smooth, gliding electronic music and randomly patterned group sections that we improvise each time. This dance is about layers of identity, and audience members will learn a lot about themselves.' Knowing that the components of patchwork ideas may mesh to fuel creative work, or clash in such a way as to undermine it, a facilitator may help the choreographer to understand how distinct aspects of an intention may coexist. Are all the parts of the idea really meant for one dance, or are several works trying to come out at once? Are some parts of the idea too open-ended, or restrictive? Considering such matters early avoids trouble later, and repeating the intention framing exercise as dance making proceeds helps choreographers to recognize changes to their ideas and adjust efforts accordingly.

Creative process mentoring

This practice involves pre- and post-rehearsal dialogue between a choreographer and a facilitator that takes place away from the rehearsal and focuses on the choreographer's dance-making intentions and perspectives on process. Using the IDEA model as a framework for pinpointing the challenges to which a choreographer may allude, the mentor poses clarifying questions and makes suggestions to prompt the choreographer to reflect on aspects of her activities that she might otherwise hold only vaguely in mind.[10]

For example, suppose a choreographer says, 'My dance is about the trials and tribulations of sisterhood': the mentor might help the choreographer to imagine images and/or to concoct improvisations to generate imagery. The mentor may also 'reflect ahead' with the artist about developing and employing images for maximum effect. Maybe the choreographer struggles in this area; an image sequence is clear but transitions are unsettled. The mentor may ask, 'Is there a particular effect you are seeking? Would a quick change or a slow fade work?' Such questions stimulate choreographers' deeper perception of their creative actions and promote further reflection on ways to create new options, or to revisit previously rejected ones.

A creative process mentor need not see the dance being made, for its appearance is of no direct concern to the mentor. Knowing that even mild commentary (or other reactions, including involuntary facial expressions) from an observer may over-influence a choreographer's conception of the dance, the mentor avoids exposing the choreographer to any signs of approval/disapproval of the work. By remaining unattached to outcomes the mentor protects the choreographer from any perceived need to justify or defend any aspect of the dance. Under these conditions choreographers tend to become more eager to describe deep details of their thinking and more able to think of new ideas to try in the studio.

Suspending dance-critical involvement positions the mentor to help the choreographer to understand why artistic clarity sometimes grows cloudy and confidence sometimes becomes shaken, and to learn to act effectively in such moments. It is not uncommon for a choreographer to become alienated from the dance; maybe it 'speaks back' and says something unexpected, or maybe it offers no useful clues about itself. Maybe a critic's remarks throw the choreographer into a crisis of faith in her ideas, or maybe she just runs out of ideas. At such moments choreographers working without support may default to quick fixes. Ever vigilant for signs of impasse, a critically neutral mentor may pull the choreographer out of panic, and help her to regain control of her process.

Rehearsal criticism

A rehearsal critic observes and analyses a choreographer's moment-to-moment in-studio engagement with the IDEA operations, and her interactions with dancers. Later, the rehearsal critic shares her observations and may provide suggestions to help the choreographer to modify her activities. *Rehearsal criticism* is an important facilitation practice because on the material plane rehearsal *causes* dances; it is in rehearsal, at each moment of creative action, when a dance, bit by bit, achieves its tangible identity.[11] Thus, as in *creative process mentoring*, in *rehearsal criticism* critical focus on the dance is suspended; the job is to ensure the choreographer's maximum understanding and ownership of her choreographic actions.

Prompts, manipulations, directives, and reactions

Of special interest to a rehearsal critic is the verbal communication between a choreographer and her dancers. Most rehearsal environments are rich with verbal activity. Indeed, as much talking as dancing may occur as a dance is created. The *evaluation* operation, in particular, generates a great deal of talk and stimulates transitions to and from the other operations, for to move forward a choreographer must signal her specific choices to keep, change, or erase and replace bits of material. To deliver evaluations and to explore their consequences choreographers perform such distinct 'speech acts' as *prompts*, *manipulations*, *directives*, and *reactions*.[12]

Prompts activate dancers' creativity to improvise and/or compose new material or develop existing material. For example, 'Try moving together, remaining close, but have a skirmish with your hands'. Prompts use dancers' imagination and their 'insider feel' for the dance to gain embodied propositions for the piece. The choreographer evaluates and makes decisions. I write more about the art of prompting later.

Manipulations generate movement possibilities without activating dancers' creativity. Here the choreographer draws upon her insights and her 'outside eye' to change one or more aspects of the choreography. For example, 'Turn that bit around backwards', and, 'Try that without the arms' are simple manipulations that may produce significant changes.

Directives change one or more aspects of dancers' performance of material without necessarily changing choreographic structure or generating new material. Such directives as, 'Make that turn sharp yet serene', bring both a technical and a qualitative adjustment to performance.

Reactions express immediate and uncensored feeling-based evaluations. Such reactions as, 'That pattern is lovely'; 'No, no, not like that', and 'I need to fix that transition' are common. 'Negative' reactions, such as the latter two examples, may fuel the next stage of work, or stall activity. To support creative flow a negative reaction must tacitly be understood by the dancers or reframed consciously for them as a *prompt*, a *manipulation*, or a *directive* so that specific action may be taken. Experienced dancers often respond to negative reactions either by seeking further description and directives: 'What is not working; what should we try?' or by proposing ideas: 'Maybe if we turn it around …' Less experienced dancers may stand mute and wait to be directed.

A rehearsal critic notices all in-studio talk/activity and senses its impact on the creation process. The operative questions are: How does the choreographer tend to the material? What is observed, what is overlooked? What is discussed, what passes unmentioned? Perhaps the process is deliberate and methodical, or maybe it is ad hoc and sporadic with the choreographer rarely pausing to decide anything, but staying open to opportunities for inventiveness, and veering off on tangents.[13]

Keyed to notice rapid progress and moments of fatigue and laboured effort, a rehearsal critic observes the management of dancers' time, energy, and tolerances for uncertainty, and gauges the choreographer's ability to inspire dancers to give their best, and to change course when needed to sustain rehearsal energy. Such factors exert immense shaping force over a dance. For example, choreographers uncomfortable directing dancers, or shy about manipulating 'set' material, may leave parts of their work unresolved to avoid confrontation. Others may neglect to prompt or direct dancers because they do not trust their own abilities to explain or demonstrate artistic aims.

The art of prompting

Because they embody choreographers' ideas in such a way as to engender dancers' creativity, prompts are the most potent of the speech acts used in rehearsal. Thus it is in the interest of choreographers to understand how they use prompts, and to grasp the connections between prompts and artistic consequences. For example, generic 'situation prompts' such as 'Imagine you are in a lonely mood …' barely constrain dancers' options; almost any movement will satisfy such prompts. Other prompts, particularly when aimed at revising material, tend to carry more specific restraints. For example, 'Try the lifts again but insert slow transitions', provides conditions to be met and thus reflects a specific (even if tentative) artistic choice. Below are typical kinds of prompts:

> *Amplification* prompts ask dancers to add emphasis to particular aspects of material. For example, 'Find more hostile tension even if the movement changes'.

> *What if* prompts, such as, 'What happens if you choose some shapes randomly, based on what you notice the other dancers doing?' and 'What if you transpose the standing phrase to the floor?' permit the choreographer to entertain possibilities without implying dissatisfaction with the dancers' choices or committing to using any particular outcome.
>
> *Insertion* prompts develop movement by placing bits of material inside already existing bits. 'Add a few steps and a turn every few seconds' and 'Try random pauses during this section' are simple insertion prompts.
>
> *Rapid response* prompts seize on surprises, even unhappy ones, to harvest their artistic potential. For example, 'Wow, that's weird, but I like it. Let's add it to the floor part' signals to the dancers that taking risks and even making 'mistakes' often go together, and are welcome in rehearsal.
>
> *Praise* prompts such as 'I like that choice; see where you can take it' generate cooperation from dancers by letting them know that their work is appreciated.

A rehearsal critic pays attention to when and how prompts and other speech acts are utilized in rehearsal, and how they influence the mood of the participants and impact the dance.

Pervasive evaluation

As mentioned earlier, the *evaluation* operation stimulates transitions to and from the other IDEA operations. This point warrants discussion, for many choreographers take pains to prevent 'the rational mind', especially 'evaluation', from 'controlling' the creative process. Clearly, hasty and/or too frequent evaluations (especially from third-party 'experts') may block the imagination, but evaluation in and of itself is not the problem, and is in fact central to creativity.[14] Evaluations must be made to move forward in creative work, and artistic challenges never melt away merely because one wishes to avoid evaluation.

Spontaneous and intuitive evaluations do differ from their analytical and reflective counterparts in terms of the speed and the emotional ease with which they are made, and because spontaneous/intuitive evaluations are usually not accompanied by verbal explanations – they just 'feel' right. This does not mean intuitive evaluations are arbitrary or irrational. It just means they are based on reasons that, while perfectly rational, are not processed consciously by the artist.[15]

Some artists appear quite willing and able as they work to access preconscious and/or unconscious levels of information, tapping easily into knowledge bases that are highly conducive to original thinking. These artists may find it natural to create, explore and evaluate material rapidly and intuitively. While there is no guarantee that intuitively made evaluations will differ from reflective evaluations with respect to the helpful and/or damaging artistic outcomes they produce, each creator should be encouraged to cultivate his or her own pace and style of evaluation.

For their part, facilitators need to be concerned only with how the process is actually going. If the choreographer 'over-thinks', fretfully undoing work and losing faith in the process, one might suggest that she work more spontaneously, perhaps prompt her dancers with improvisations, knowing that between sessions she can 'think' all she wants. Conversely, choreographers committed (or adhering blindly) to a strategy of 'under-thinking' their dances, or 'leaving it to the muses', may accumulate massive amounts of spontaneously fashioned material, all of which may seem worthy of inclusion because no particular artistic principle is in place on the basis of which *development* and *assimilation* evaluations might be made. Here one might suggest that the choreographer reflect on her goals to determine some basis for selection; not every bit of material necessarily belongs in the dance.[16] The point is that no matter how a choreographer works, the need for evaluation (spontaneous, reflective, intuitive or some other kind) is pervasive, for it is through evaluative choices that a work gets built up, shaped and completed.

Many experienced choreographers make deliberately quick, non-reflective evaluations when engaged in the *improvisation* operation. Later, in *developing* material, they reconsider earlier actions and decide more consciously what to keep, change, or erase and replace. As a general rule, *assimilative* evaluation is careful and reflective, for the explorations and choices that determine precisely where in a dance a particular image, pattern, transition or something else will be placed, repeated, embellished or echoed are the evaluations that mark the difference between run-of-the-mill dance craft and sophisticated choreographic art.

For all of these reasons rehearsal critics note carefully how choreographers' criticality manifests. Some choreographers pause frequently to evaluate and work on details. The risk is that obsession with detail can break flow and dampen dancers' enthusiasm. Other choreographers focus on the big picture for lengthy periods, fussing with details later. The risk here is that the longer a construct remains unchanged the more difficult it may be for some choreographers to make changes, and for some dancers to accept them, especially as fatigue sets in and deadlines approach. Each case is different, so a good rehearsal critic carries no preconceptions about how much and what kinds of critical activity are best. The important thing is to see how each choreographer's critical behaviour clarifies and nurtures rehearsal, or undermines it. In discussions with choreographers, the aim is not to instruct them as to what they *should* be doing but rather to help them to see what they *are* doing, so that they may determine the utility of their actions, and perhaps devise alternatives.

Red flag/green light

This is a reflective evaluation technique. A rehearsal critic may ask, 'Are there any red flags in your mind about upcoming plans, or about your work so far?' In responding, choreographers frequently discover small, disconnected, and/or previously unaddressed worries. One choreographer said to me, 'I realize I have too many competing elements; I need to pare down to what is essential, but how?' Noticing his problem could be divided, I suggested treating the first part – too many elements – as a gift, and treating the second part – deciding how to pare down – as the challenge. The problem became manageable for the choreographer as soon as the threat of 'losing' previously created material – a threat he had not previously recognized – became suddenly clear, and was removed. As concerns the establishment of priorities, he had intuitions in this direction but none that were decisive, so I suggested he do artificially, as a game, what seemed difficult to do naturally: 'Imagine each element individually as if it were the core of the piece, and then imagine how each remaining element might support/enhance the temporarily privileged one'. This mental excursion pushed him rapidly to select a main focus – a red flag became a green light.

Sometimes choreographers' red flags are 'cop-in-the-head' scripts; nagging inner voices that find fault incessantly, muttering such things as, 'That's not original', and 'Is that all you can think of?' Cop-in-the-head voices usually come more from repressed anxiety than from actual artistic problems and thus dissolve through discussion with a facilitator.[17]

A rehearsal critic may take the lead in raising red flags, and link them with green light alternatives. For example, 'I see you discarding options before they have a chance to work'. Here the green light suggestion to be more patient is implied by the description of the red flag. A second example, 'You issue so many directives in such quick succession that the dancers can hardly remember them, much less apply them … why not slow down a bit?' Here the suggestion is tagged on as a question. In each case further discussion might focus on spontaneous versus reflective decisions, ways to explore movement to reveal hidden aspects, and respect for the effort dancers put into rehearsal. Importantly, even as green light ideas may lean toward the prescriptive, the point is to suggest, not impose, new ways of working. Moreover, observations of perceived weaknesses in the dance should not be raised as red flags; rehearsal criticism is not dance criticism.[18]

Choreographic provocation

In all fields of creative work, it is easy to get used to doing things in the same way each time. Whatever has worked before (even if it did not work very well) seems to be the first option that comes to mind, and the mind often stops looking for options as soon as it has one;

the comfort of the familiar can numb curiosity and stifle the search for possibly better alternatives.

Creativity theorist Edward de Bono's 'provocation' technique (developed by de Bono without artistic creation particularly in mind) is a powerful way to challenge habits and generate new options. *Choreographic provocation* applies de Bono's ideas in the setting of dance rehearsal.

In contrast to *creative process mentoring* and *rehearsal criticism*, neither of which includes direct engagement with the dance under construction, *choreographic provocation* does address the dance, temporarily altering its character through playful 'what if' and 'let's try' suggestions. Released from creative management duties, and momentarily distanced from their dances, choreographers often gain startling new insights from provocation sessions.[19]

Choreographic provocation is based on the idea that there are always alternative versions of choreographic material as yet unimagined, any one of which versions may be as true to the choreographer's ideas as anything so far constructed. The technique works best for choreographers who are unalarmed by this fact and open to surprises. Ideally, a choreographer will invite provocation to take herself outside of habitual artistic grooves, knowing that from unlikely or strange ideas something useful may emerge.[20]

Genuine readiness for the new is difficult for some choreographers to achieve because they identify so closely with their dances as an aspect of 'self' that to see their works change unexpectedly is disturbing. Thus provocation is best undertaken once a work is set and has been practised sufficiently for the dancers to perform without gaps or hesitation, and for the choreographer to grasp the material as distinct from herself. If provocation is foisted on a reticent choreographer, or undertaken too early, the process will likely be uncomfortable and ineffective. In giving provocations, one may adopt a wide lens and provoke the work as a whole. For example, 'Pretend the floor is wobbly, and tilts in unpredictable directions; you constantly lose and regain balance'. At another moment the facilitator may focus on specific places within or aspects of the work. For example, 'Turn this way and whisper a secret each time you begin the circling phrase' elicits a particular artistic effect at one place within the dance. Performed outcomes may invite further provocation of the material at hand or suggest something to try elsewhere in the work.

A facilitator should adopt an attentive, curious, and critically neutral attitude in issuing provocations. The idea is to observe material without concern about whether or not it is 'good' or what it may need to 'get better'. Provocations are not 'feedback' and are not responsible for 'improving' material. Rather, provocations re-configure material in myriad ways to see what happens. Some outcomes are useful right away, some are bridges to new ideas, and some are rapidly discarded. All of that is up to the choreographer, later, when she next engages with the dance in rehearsal.

In producing outcomes whose value may be ascertained only through hindsight logic, *choreographic provocation* gives choreographers a powerful hands-on rehearsal tool for invention within the parameters of their existing material. It is often tempting for choreographers to lean heavily on foresight logic – that is, the logic of looking ahead, planning and preparing. Important as these capacities of mind are, they are not always the best for searching out or developing novel ideas. By offering fresh, and even deliberately outlandish, options for the choreographer to consider, provocations invigorate the creative process.

There are different types of provocations, some of which may suit the temperament of a choreographer and/or the work better than others. *Intention* provocations push in directions consistent with the choreographer's intentions. For example, 'You've really got the feeling of aimlessness in the meandering paths, so add body-part aimlessness'. In response, the dancers infuse into their bodies an already valued spatial quality of the choreography.

Image provocations push in directions suggested by the material regardless of the choreographer's intentions: 'The unison sections could be extended; add the arm circle in a couple more places and repeat the turns', and 'Take the movement to the floor, then improvise with the shapes from the other solo'. The results of such trials often lead choreographers clearly to grasp differences between where they may want to take material and where it may be trying to go. Choreographers often modify their ideas in accordance with newly configured material, or modify material to fit their ideas, or a little of each.

Adventure provocations focus on choreographers' intentions or images in the work, or both, to take the dance in unanticipated directions. One might expand, shrink, or reshape the performance space by making certain regions off limits. Or one may invent 'rules' for dancers to follow temporarily in different areas of the space and/or during different moments. Other adventures may address movement structure. For example, 'Move the arm-circle unison to the beginning, but make it jerky, then do the old beginning faster, then put the arm-circle in'.[21]

The different provocation types may be combined, but there is no need to use all types in every session. As a rule, initial provocations should be mild, aimed at producing slight adjustments. For example, a dance that is anchored in one area may be provoked to spread into the space. Mild provocations accustom the choreographer slowly to change and prepare the ground for more adventurous provocations should they be desired.

Provoking forward

While most provocations play with already-created material, choreographers often feel anxious about ideas that have yet to emerge into form. Whatever is not yet done is worrisome because it stands in a highly uncertain relationship both with that which is already done (even if only tentatively) and with the ideas that ostensibly motivate the creative process. Indeed, it is common to find a struggle between the ideas in the choreographer's mind and the material so far created; each seeks in its own way to control the character of the remainder of the piece. This struggle may be experienced as a small psychic itch or as real panic in the artist who at one moment may find her choreography perfectly expresses her ideas and at the next moment finds the ideas undermined by choreography with ideas of its own. In such cases, a choreographer working without support may default to easy fixes, or give up altogether.

Provoking forward neutralizes anxiety by generating 'possibility options' for not-yet-created parts of a work. For example, 'Let's use this material to make a duet to plug in before the exit'.

Obviously, *provoking forward* is not intended as a back door entry for criticism of a work: new possibility options are not critical imperatives. Provocations are put forth not because they are already believed to possess artistic value but only to find out if they do. As mentioned earlier, even when provocations deliver nothing particularly useful choreographically (which often happens), they may be stepping stones to new gains, sparking the choreographer to say, 'This does not work but it gives me a new idea'.

What about dance criticism?

In light of the benefits that choreographers may derive from *creative process mentoring*, *rehearsal criticism* and *choreographic provocation*, how might results-based dance criticism fit into the picture? Certainly straightforward criticism may provide to a choreographer a sense of how the work may be understood and valued by an audience. However, external criticism easily shifts artistic control from the artist to the critic, whose remarks (no matter how 'softly' delivered) may plague the choreographer as 'cop-in-the-head' warnings, curbing her appetite for experimentation. Especially at risk are choreographers struggling to gain clarity of their ideas and ownership of their rehearsal processes, for these artists are often not able to make any but slavish use of criticism.

Too often, results-based criticism is the first or only facilitation method used, and it silences other richer lines of investigation before they have even begun. This occurs commonly in academic settings, and for several reasons. First, choreography classes may be too large for teachers to give individual attention to students. Second, facing pressure to ensure that students' works are recognized by parents, colleagues, administrators, and the public as 'good dances', teachers may adopt a hurried approach to instruction that leans heavily on prescriptive criticism. Finally, since most teachers received no training in creative cognition and problem-solving skills per se, they lack the knowledge (and perhaps the confidence) to do much else with a choreographer and her dance besides to deliver an opinion of the latter, regardless of its relevance to the questions on the choreographer's mind.[22]

Ideally, teachers and other choreographic facilitators will understand the distinctions among the methods discussed in this chapter, and use each method alone or in tandem with others to discover and address each choreographer's particular needs.

Notes

1 Portions of this chapter have appeared in Lavender and Sullivan (2008), Lavender (2006) and Lavender (2005).

2 Choreographers routinely borrow and synthesize ideas and compositional principles/devices from Western and non-Western music, film, art, sports, and literature, and from myriad other cultural practices, rituals and ceremonies. Dance educators' efforts to teach domain-specific skills for choreography are supported by an extensive body of literature. Widely used sources include Blom and Chaplin (1982), Hawkins (1988), Hayes (1955), Hodes (1998), Humphrey (1959), Minton (1991), Morgenroth (1987), Nagrin (1993), Smith-Autard (1992), Tharp (2003), and Van Dyke (2005).

3 Interesting texts are available in which choreographers' artistic process thinking is detailed. See Alexander (1998), Butterworth (2004), Butterworth and Clarke (1998), Hanstein (1986), Kreemer (1987), Lavender (1997), Morgenroth (2004), Van Dyke (1996).

4 Smith (1995) provides findings on how and why creative problem solvers in all domains fall into mental ruts. See Jaušovec (1994) for detailed discussion of the role of meta-cognition in problem solving.

5 Lavender and Sullivan (2008) describe a fourth facilitation practice, *task activation*, designed especially for dance-pedagogical settings. Smith, Ward, and Finke (1995) present an excellent anthology of creative cognition research; the approach is grounded in the idea that creativity depends on how people think – that is, mental processes are the engine of all creative endeavours, including artistic ones. Runco (2006) provides numerous insights of relevance to choreography pedagogy.

6 Runco and Chand (1994) discuss evaluative processes associated with creativity. Hogarth (1980) analyses the predictive judgements people make in the decision-making process. Lavender (1997) describes two choreographers' accounts of self-criticality. See Hämäläinen (2002, and chapter 8 in this volume) for a survey of approaches to evaluation within choreography pedagogy.

7 See Weisberg (1995) for a good introduction to the concepts of mental representations of ideas and problem states, ways of restructuring mental representations at moments of impasse, and brief case studies of these phenomena drawn from diverse domains.

8 Spiralling social, economic, and environmental crises have pushed artists in all genres into having to justify their work (to art-world insiders, funding agencies and to the art-consuming public) in terms of its social utility. It is not clear how art can solve any but artistic problems, but many people insist that it at least try. See Gablik's *The Reenchantment of Art* (1991) for a powerful argument in this direction.

9 Subject-matter, or 'aboutness' ideas, particularly those related to issues of race, class, gender and identity are prevalent among choreographers as late-twentieth century theoretical rejections of 'art for art's sake' values have hardened into dogma. My concerns with 'aboutness' ideas are pragmatic, not political: such ideas tend to include little or no process/method or image-specific components and thus do little to fuel dancemaking. To know what one's dance is intended to mean or convey is one thing, but knowing how to use an intended meaning or message as the basis for design of a work is quite another. The distinction is important, for even dances packed with social, political or personal meaning must capture, sustain and reward spectators' perception. See Barrett (2003: 192–3) for a clear description of artistic denotation and connotation of meaning.

10 Choreographers must be encouraged to state ideas in their own terms. The idea is not for choreographers to produce theoretical treatises or easily

understandable explanations of their work, but simply to say aloud what they are already saying to themselves silently. If a choreographer sees creative process mentoring as involving the requirement to speak about her work in a forced or unnatural way she will likely tire rapidly of the process and discontinue it. Lavender and Predock-Linnell (2005) discuss a range of choreographic mentoring practices.

11 Obviously, dances are 'caused' by an array of social/cultural factors, not the least of which is the choreographer's ongoing exposure both to other dances and other kinds of art, and the creative insights she gains over successive dance-making ventures. My point is not that the activity of dance making is or can be one that exists in a cultural vacuum, but simply that rehearsal is the place where whatever influences that there may be on the shape and character of a dance actually exert their influence and gain 'embodiment' (quite literally) 'in' the dance.

12 The following discussion is informed by 'speech act' theory as articulated by Austin (1962) and Searle (1969).

13 Finke and Bettle (1996) provide intriguing techniques for the development of 'chaotic thinking' capacities that choreographers might well use to their advantage.

14 Thomas McEvilley (2005: 77–104) explicates the lineage of anti-cognitivist positions within arts discourses from Plato to the present. See Runco's (2003) *Critical Creative Processes* for an excellent collection of research findings on the criticality intrinsic to creative work. Amabile (1979, 1996) provides detailed findings and rich discussion on the nature and role of evaluation in creative work. In Chapter 4 of *The Mind's Best Work* (1981), Perkins provides valuable insights into the ways in which analysis and judgement exert shaping power over creative making activities.

15 Here I follow Baron (1988: 28–9), who characterizes 'rational thinking' as 'whatever helps us to achieve our personal goals. If it should turn out that following the rules of logic leads to eternal happiness, then it is "rational thinking" to follow the rules of logic. If it should turn out, on the other hand, that carefully violating the laws of logic at every turn leads to eternal happiness, then it is these violations that we shall call "rational."'

16 McLaughlin (1993) provides a thorough discussion of the *selection of emergent value* as a key to understanding creative processes.

17 See Boal (1985: 191–200) and Lavender (1997).

18 Segal (2004) describes research showing that incubation – that is, time spent away from direct work on a problem – may assist problem solvers in finding solutions by diverting their attention from the problem at hand, thus permitting unwarranted assumptions and other constraints to be released, and mental restructuring of the problem to occur. I believe that the red flag/green light technique, and other discussion between a choreographer and a creative process mentor and/or a rehearsal critic, functions as a kind of *conversational incubation*.

19 Perkins (2000: 46–66) provides cogent explanations of, and clear remedies for, four common thinking traps that stall creative work. See de Bono (1992: 104–28) for clearly articulated creative techniques. See also de Bono (1970: 265–74) for discussion of various 'blocks' to creativity. Provocation sessions may activate and/or refresh choreographers' use of schematic, associational and case-based knowledge useful to their work. See Hunter *et al.* (2008).

20 See Gordon (1961: 27–56) for useful descriptions of techniques for 'making the familiar strange', a key component of his *Synectics* process for enhancing creativity. *Choreographic provocation* works in a manner consistent with Gordon's research findings.

21 See Wakefield (1994); choreographers' empathy with, and critical under-

standing of, their material increases noticeably as a consequence of *choreographic provocation*. The use of *image* and *adventure* provocations makes *choreographic provocation* a 'deviation amplifying' practice in Maruyama's (1963) sense of the term even as the artistic permanence of each amplified deviation is a matter for the choreographer to decide.

22 To develop rehearsal skills choreographers need training in dance-critical operations, for learning to describe, analyse, interpret and evaluate dance works (and other works of art) trains the eye and hones artistic taste. See Lavender (1996).

References:

Alexander, E. (1998) *Footnotes: Six Choreographers Inscribe the Page*, Amsterdam: Gordon and Breach.

Amabile, T. (1979) 'Effects of external evaluation on artistic creativity', *Journal of Personality and Social Psychology*, 37: 221–33.

—— (1996) *Creativity in Context*. Boulder, CO: Westview Press.

Austin, J. (1962) *How to Do Things With Words*, Cambridge, MA: Harvard University Press.

Baron, J. (1988) *Thinking and Deciding*, New York: Cambridge University Press.

Barrett, T. (2003) *Interpreting Art*, New York: McGraw-Hill.

Blom, L. and Chaplin, L. T. (1982) *The Intimate Act of Choreography*, Pittsburgh: University of Pittsburgh Press.

Boal, A. (1985) *Theatre of the Oppressed*, New York: Theatre Communications Group.

Butterworth, J. (2004) 'Teaching choreography in higher education: a process continuum model', *Research in Dance Education*, 5 (1): 45–67.

Butterworth, J. and Clarke, G. (eds) (1998) *Dance Makers Portfolio*, Bretton Hall, Wakefield: Centre for Dance and Theatre Studies.

De Bono, E. (1970) *Lateral Thinking: Creativity Step by Step*, New York: HarperCollins.

—— (1992) *Serious Creativity*, New York: HarperCollins.

Finke, R. and Bettle, J. (1996) *Chaotic Cognition Principles and Applications*, Mahwah, NJ: Lawrence Erlbaum Associates.

Gablik, S. (1991) *The Reenchantment of Art*, New York: Thames and Hudson.

Gordon, W. (1961) *Synectics: The Development of Creative Capacity*, New York: Harper and Row.

Hämäläinen, S. (2002) 'Evaluation in choreographic pedagogy', *Research in Dance Education*, 3 (1): 35–45.

Hanstein, P. (1986) On the Nature of Art Making in Dance: An Artistic Process Skills Model. Unpublished Dissertation, Ohio State University, Columbus.

Hawkins, A. (1988) *Creating through Movement*, revised edition, Princeton, NJ: Princeton Book Company.

Hayes, E. (1955; 1993) *Dance Composition and Production*, Princeton: Princeton Book Company.

Hodes, S. (1998) *A Map of Making Dances*, New York: Ardsley House.

Hogarth, R. (1980) *Judgment and Choice: The Psychology of Decision*, New York: John C. Wiley & Sons.

Humphrey, D. (1959) *The Art of Making Dances*, New York: Grove Press.

Hunter, S., Bedell-Avers, K., Hunsicker, C., Mumford, M. and Ligon, G. (2008) 'Applying multiple knowledge structures in creative thought: effects on idea generation and problem-solving', *Creativity Research Journal*, 20 (2): 137–54.

Jaušovec, N. (1994) 'Metacognition in creative problem solving', in M. Runco (ed.) *Problem Finding, Problem Solving, and Creativity*, Norwood NJ: Ablex Publishing Corporation.

Kreemer, C. (1987) *Further Steps: Fifteen Choreographers on Modern Dance*, New York: HarperCollins College Division.

Lavender, L. (1996) *Dancers Talking Dance: Critical Evaluation in the Choreography Class*, Champaign, IL: Human Kinetics.

—— (1997) 'Making and un-making: intentions, criticism, and the choreographic process', in *Proceedings of the 30th Annual Conference of the Congress on Research in Dance*, University of Arizona, Tucson.

—— (2005) 'Rehearsal criticism', in *Proceedings of the 7th Annual Conference of the National Dance Education Organization*, Buffalo, NY.

—— (2006) 'Creative process mentoring: teaching the "making" in dance making', *Journal of Dance Education*, 6 (1): 6–13.

Lavender, L. and Predock-Linnell, J. (2005) 'Standing aside and making space: mentoring student choreographers', in J. Bennahum (ed.) *Teaching Dance Studies*, Florence, KY: Routledge.

Lavender, L. and Sullivan, B. J. (2008) 'Transformative systems for teaching and learning choreography', in T. Hagood (ed.) *Legacy in Dance Education: Essays and Interviews on Values, Practices, and People*, Amherst, NY: Cambria, pp. 176–217.

Maruyama, M. (1963) 'Deviation amplifying mutual causal processes', *American Scientist*, 51: 164–79.

McEvilley, T. (2005) *The Triumph of Anti-Art: Conceptual and Performance Art in the Formation of Post-Modernism*, New York: McPherson & Company.

McLaughlin, S. (1993) 'Emergent value in creative products: some implications for creative processes', in J. Gero and M. Maher (eds) *Modeling Creativity and Knowledge-Based Creative Design*, Hillsdale, NJ: Lawrence Erlbaum Associates.

Minton, S. (1991) *Choreography: A Basic Approach Using Improvisation*, 2nd edn, Champaign, IL: Human Kinetics.

Morgenroth, J. (1987) *Dance Improvisation*, Pittsburgh, University of Pittsburgh Press.

—— (2004) *Speaking of Dance*, Florence, KY: Routledge.

Nagrin, D. (1993) *Dance and the Specific Image: Improvisation*, Pittsburgh: University of Pittsburgh Press.

Perkins, D. (1981) *The Mind's Best Work*, Cambridge, MA: Harvard University Press.

—— (2000) *The Eureka Effect: The Art and Logic of Breakthrough Thinking*, New York: W. W. Norton.

Runco, M. (2003) *Critical Creative Processes*, Cresskill, NJ: Hampton Press Inc.

—— (2006) 'Reasoning and personal creativity', in J. C. Kaufman and J. Baer (eds) *Creativity and Reason in Cognitive Development*, New York: Cambridge University Press.

Runco, M. and Chand, I. (1994) 'Problem finding, evaluative thinking, and creativity', in M. Runco (ed.) *Problem Finding, Problem Solving, and Creativity*, Norwood, NJ: Ablex Publishing Corporation.

Searle, J. (1969) *Speech Acts: An Essay in the Philosophy of Language*, London: Cambridge University Press.

Segal, E. (2004) 'Incubation in insight problem solving', *Creativity Research Journal*, 16 (1): 141–8.

Smith, S. (1995) 'Getting into and out of mental ruts: a theory of fixation, incubation, and insight', in R. Sternberg and J. Davidson (eds) *The Nature of Insight*, Cambridge, MA: The MIT Press.

Smith, S., Ward, T. and Finke, R. (eds) (1995) *The Creative Cognition Approach*, Cambridge, MA: MIT Press.

Smith-Autard, J. (1992) *Dance Composition*, London: A & C Black.

Tharp, T. (2003) *The Creative Habit*, New York: Simon and Schuster.

Van Dyke, J. (1996) 'Choreography as mode of inquiry: a case study', *Impulse: the International Journal of Dance Science, Medicine, and Education*, 4 (4): 318–25.

—— (2005) 'Teaching choreography: beginning with craft', *Journal of Dance Education*, 5 (4): 116–24.

Wakefield, J. (1994) 'Problem finding and empathy in art', in M. Runco (ed.) *Problem Finding, Problem Solving, and Creativity*, Norwood NJ: Ablex Publishing Corporation.

Weisberg, R. (1995) 'Case studies of creative thinking: reproduction versus restructuring in the real world', in S. Smith, T. Ward, and R. Finke (eds) *The Creative Cognition Approach*, Cambridge, MA: MIT Press.

7 Creativity in dance education through use of interactive technology resources

Jacqueline Smith-Autard

This chapter introduces a specific resource-based teaching methodology in the context of teaching dance composition based on the conceptual 'midway' model for the art of dance in education defined by the author in her books *Dance Composition* (1976)[1] and *The Art of Dance in Education* (1994).[2] Consideration of the creative process as inclusive of both objectivity and subjectivity precedes detailed discussion of ways in which innovative digital technology alongside especially designed worksheets can promote creativity. A CD-ROM resource pack – *Choreographic Outcomes: Improving Dance Composition* (Smith-Autard *et al.* 2005) – is used to demonstrate how meaningful and competent dance composition can result from a complex mix of objective learning and subjective (intuitive) feeling entering into the process. The CD-ROM resource pack focuses on the former in providing students with the means of coming to understand and employ elements of form in their own creative work. With reference to philosophers' writings on the creative process, it is contended that absorption of the knowledge gained through in-depth analysis of composition as promoted in resources such as this one will lead to a richer reservoir of creative, intuitive and feeling responses that will emerge in students' future composition and appreciation undertakings.

Dance Composition (1976) began to delineate proposals for change in content and delivery of dance particularly for secondary and tertiary sectors with the proposal that dance should be taught as an art form through the processes of composing, performing and appreciating dances. These new ideas emerged from cognisance of what was then current 'good and valued practice' and from experimenting with and reflecting on studio practice.

Gradually, a model evolved that embraced elements of both the consensus Laban-based educational dance model practised in the 1960s and 1970s and that which emanates from theatre dance and can be described as a professional model. The former with its emphasis on process and personal development outcomes was under scrutiny in a climate of objective assessment of skills, knowledge and understanding. The latter, favoured for its reference to the public dance art world by some secondary and tertiary educators was criticised for its attempt to emulate the technical training model of conservatoires. Through distillation of 'best practice' in these extremes and taking account of the aims for the art of dance in education, a 'midway' model was fully conceptualised in *The Art of Dance in Education* (1994). This book provides a theoretical underpinning for the art of dance model[3] that is practised today in the UK and in a growing number of other countries.[4] It is the teaching and learning process itself that constitutes the 'midway' art of dance pedagogy in that it is proposed that there should be equal emphasis on conceptual opposites – product *and* process, subjectivity *and* objectivity, knowledge *and* feeling/intuition, learning of techniques *and* personal explorations plus didactic *and* open-ended teaching methodologies.

In the art of dance model, the third strand – appreciation – fully utilises public dance art works to inform tertiary students of traditions, developments and artistic practices that constitute the discipline. Yet, it often appears that such study is divorced from practical choreography and performance engagement. Focus on dance works of professionals provides an ideal opportunity for use of a resource-based teaching/learning methodology – an important feature of the 'midway' art of dance model. It is mooted here that the use of dance works as resources should be as apparent in practical performance and composition study as it is in theoretical lectures and seminars. Experience surmises that few institutions embed such study into students' practical dance activities. It is acknowledged, however, that to integrate all three strands, tutors and students need resource packs with full ranges of learning possibilities at different levels with potential to meet differing objectives. To date, there are few available but technology is now able to deliver the visual resources that offer an interactive environment for learners, for example, in setting problems and offering new and interesting ways of using the dance content to inform the student about choreography, performance or other related aspects such as its music and design elements. Alongside the visual interactive resource such as a CD-ROM or DVD-ROM there is need for pedagogy materials possibly in the form of worksheets that present questions and tasks under the headings of appreciation, composition and performance. Hence, a resource pack is created on the premise that in order to learn from complex and highly developed examples of dance works, students need to be guided through tasks which are sufficiently open for them to make their own responses to the art work, yet structured enough to aid progression and constructive learning.

In an article in the *Journal of Dance Education*'s special edition, 'Effective Pedagogy for Dance Composition', Morgenroth (2006: 20) acknowledges that such a practice is not yet common in the USA:

> Traditional composition classes teach the tools of choreographic craft, yet leave students in an odd limbo in which they create a special breed of 'college dance' that has little to do with the current dance world.
>
> (Morgenroth 2006: 19)

Her article then goes on to suggest that 'by trying out methods used by contemporary choreographers, students will discover and develop their own creative processes'. This approach of using professional choreographers' methodologies could be supported by a resource-based approach, which demands that there is constant interactive attention given to the live or recorded work/s of a choreographer through analysis and appreciation of the details in order to absorb and ultimately transform them into the students' own making processes. In support of this idea, articles included in the *Research in Dance Education*'s special issue in Technology and Dance (2008) suggest that:

> Today, the marriage of dance, education and technology is widely accepted – even expected – as our field maps new landscapes of meaning, builds new connections between ... communities, and embraces the promise of twenty-first century 'digital literacy'.
>
> (Warburton 2008: 111)

Until recently, tutors and students have had to use conventional linear video and, like Morgenroth, create their own structured tasks to make cross-references between the professional exemplars and the students' composing and performing activities. Such a laborious medium is somewhat outdated in our advancing technological environment.

DVDs of dance works are being produced, but there is still the limitation of linearity and nothing more on screen but the video itself. Computer-aided interactive technology can offer much more. Resource-based teaching/learning is best delivered through structured and guided tasks requiring students to analyse and appreciate details in a choreographed work and then to apply their learning in solving their own composition problems.

Creativity in dance education – objectivity and subjectivity

A brief exposé of theories that identify the interplay between objectivity and subjectivity in the creative process demonstrates one of the conceptual opposites in the 'midway' model. Here, rather than supporting the Laban-based educational model which aimed to develop creativity through encouraging students to make personal and individual responses to tasks, reference is made to philosophers such as Best (1985, 1992) who dispute that such development could occur through exploring movement for oneself and that creativity is an inborn facility which need not be educated.

> To be creative requires a grasp of the criteria of validity and value in the activity in question. Originality is given its sense only against a background of the traditional ... imagination is imagination only in so far as it operates within limits.
>
> (Best 1985: 78–9)

The Art of Dance in Education (1994, 2002) asked the questions: what are these criteria of validity, what is the background of the traditional and what are the limits placed upon imagination? The following answers are summarised (Smith-Autard 2002: 9):

- The art of dance, like other arts, is a public phenomenon which is removed from the everyday into the 'art world'.
- [Dance] is subject to the influence of public conventions, styles and meanings; pupils learning to 'create' in dance need to learn how to portray or discern meaning in dance movement and at the same time become aware of and use the shared public references.
- Creating dance is not going to advance beyond the cathartic release of personal feelings through unstructured and self-expressive movement responses unless teachers understand how creativity and imagination can be educated.
- This recognition does not prevent the individual's feelings and ideas from entering the expressive form.
- Creating and imagining in the dance context *depend* upon extending from the givens towards something new.

The above bullet points took cognisance of statements such as the following from Best, Redfern and Langer:

> A necessary condition for being creative is to have mastered at least to some extent the discipline, techniques and criteria of a subject or activity.
>
> (Best 1985: 89)

> What can be expressed is partly, and perhaps largely determined not only by what others have 'said' but also on how they have 'said it'.
>
> (Redfern 1973: 82)

These ideas are not new of course since Langer argued that:

> Art is a public possession because the formulation of felt-life is the heart of any culture and moulds the objective world for the people. It is their school of feeling and their defence against outer and inner chaos.
>
> (Langer 1953: 409)

Here, in the art-making process, we discern the inextricable link between knowledge and skills and feelings or intuitions. In terms of the latter, we acknowledge that:

> Intuition … is not without conceptualisation. Whatever we apprehend directly is inescapably apprehended in terms of concepts, is infused

> with, has assimilated an indefinitely large body of knowledge about things, knowledge-that.
>
> (Reid 1981: 80)

But at the same time, feelings should always play a role in the composing of dances. The interplay between objective knowledge and subjective feeling is difficult to describe; and it is not always possible to determine which comes first. Ultimately, as Reid says:

> What is needed is absorption of discursively reflective thinking and study, an assimilation of it, a conscious forgetting of it, and a return to illuminated intuition.
>
> (Reid 1983)

Taking account of the tensions between objectivity of knowledge/skills and subjectivity of feelings/intuitions, the table in Figure 7.1 may help to represent the composer's means towards undertaking a creative process in dance.

It is proposed here that meaningful and creative dance composition results from a complex mix of objective learning and subjective (intuitive) feeling entering into the process. This chapter goes on to show how a technology-based resource pack, focused on the former in providing students with the means of coming to understand and employ elements of *form* in their own creative work, can also lead to a rich reservoir of intuitive/feeling responses that will emerge in future composition and appreciation undertakings.

Choreographic Outcomes: Improving Dance Composition[5] – a CD-ROM resource pack

Briefly, the resource pack includes an interactive CD-ROM featuring video examples and a *Creative Practice Guidebook*. It also contains the 5th edition of *Dance Composition* (2004). The exclusive aim of this pack is to teach students how to create *form* in their dance compositions. This most difficult aspect is demonstrated on the disc through reference to and analysis of compositions created by professionals. The compositions, performed by professional dancers and young students, comprise a source solo and short composition outcomes in the form of another solo, four duos, a trio and a quintet. These outcomes are thus titled because each of the three choreographers was asked to use the source solo as a basis for development and variation. The aim is that both within each short composition – source or outcomes – and in comparisons between them, each aspect of form – motifs, developments, variations, contrasts, floor and air patterns, orchestration of dancers in time and space – can be studied and explored by the students in appreciation followed by or interspersed with practical composition tasks derived from worksheets in the accompanying *Creative Practice Guidebook*.

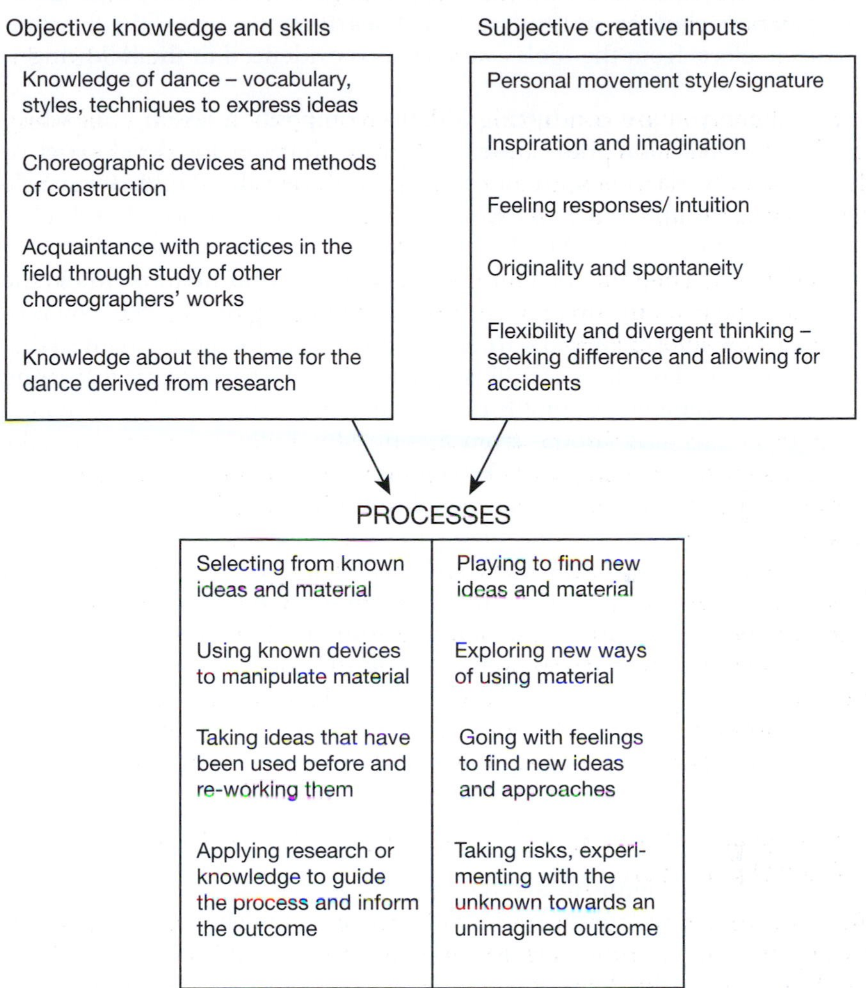

Objective knowledge and skills
Knowledge of dance – vocabulary, styles, techniques to express ideas
Choreographic devices and methods of construction
Acquaintance with practices in the field through study of other choreographers' works
Knowledge about the theme for the dance derived from research
Subjective creative inputs
Personal movement style/signature
Inspiration and imagination
Feeling responses/ intuition
Originality and spontaneity
Flexibility and divergent thinking – seeking difference and allowing for accidents
PROCESSES
Selecting from known ideas and material
Using known devices to manipulate material
Taking ideas that have been used before and re-working them
Applying research or knowledge to guide the process and inform the outcome
Playing to find new ideas and material
Exploring new ways of using material
Going with feelings to find new ideas and approaches
Taking risks, experi- menting with the unknown towards an unimagined outcome

Figure 7.1 The creative process in dance composition (Smith-Autard 2004: 138).

In commenting on the disc itself Warburton states that:

> *Choreographic Outcomes* takes full advantage of what computers do best. The multiple representations – from diagrams to videos – make it highly accessible, deepening the learning experience without sacrificing breadth of information. The ubiquitous views, perspectives, and thumbnail pictures make it easy to follow and fun to use. The logical structure, clearly marked buttons, and text directions support navigation through the sophisticated analyses.
>
> (Warburton 2005: 92)

There is no prescribed route through the resource, rather, in a dance composition class or in student-based learning contexts, the teacher/lecturer selects from the tools available as is evidenced in the following:

> Imagine you are conducting a dance composition lesson ... in which you are teaching your students various processes for developing, or creating variations of, dance motifs. You open the 'Motifs for a Solo Dancer' component of the *Choreographic Outcomes* CD-ROM and select the 'Library of Key Motifs.' You choose a motif and are taken to a menu depicting the total number of times that this motif occurs in the solo dance. By moving the cursor over each thumbnail video, you activate the video exemplars, whereupon you click for a full screen so that the entire class can view the sequences. After viewing and discussing several exemplars of motifs that occur in the solo, you click 'Potential Derivations' and choose from among four options for viewing solo, duo, and trio derivations of key motifs. So that your students can easily analyze the relationships between the original motifs and the variations, you select a function that places the source material and derivations side by side and 'volley' back and forth between the exemplars. After some discussion about the processes employed by the choreographers of the video examples, you have the students work in small groups to develop their own derivations of motifs they developed [themselves].
>
> (Cook 2005: 138)

Of course, along with other multimedia resources 'there is no simple answer to how one makes effective educational use of technologies ... how to integrate it in practice' (Warburton 2005: 93). He goes on to say that:

> Fortunately, Smith-Autard has brought her 'A' game to this issue. She understands learning, how diversified it is, and how important it is to develop methods and materials that are as articulated and flexible as the individuals utilizing them. For this reason the accompanying support materials are key to the effective use of this program ... Through a series of carefully constructed activities and worksheets, the Creative Practice Handbook demonstrates how to use the technology selectively to present dynamic models of key concepts or to enable students to participate together in disciplined inquiry.
>
> (Warburton 2005: 93)

Clearly then, *Choreographic Outcomes*, like any other resource, requires that teachers thoroughly explore the full range of materials and define ways in which reference to the interactive visual displays can augment and enhance their teaching and the students' learning. Importantly, students themselves should be able to access the resource through the intranet or networked computers so that they pursue further study of the concepts of form and apply their understanding in choreographic tasks

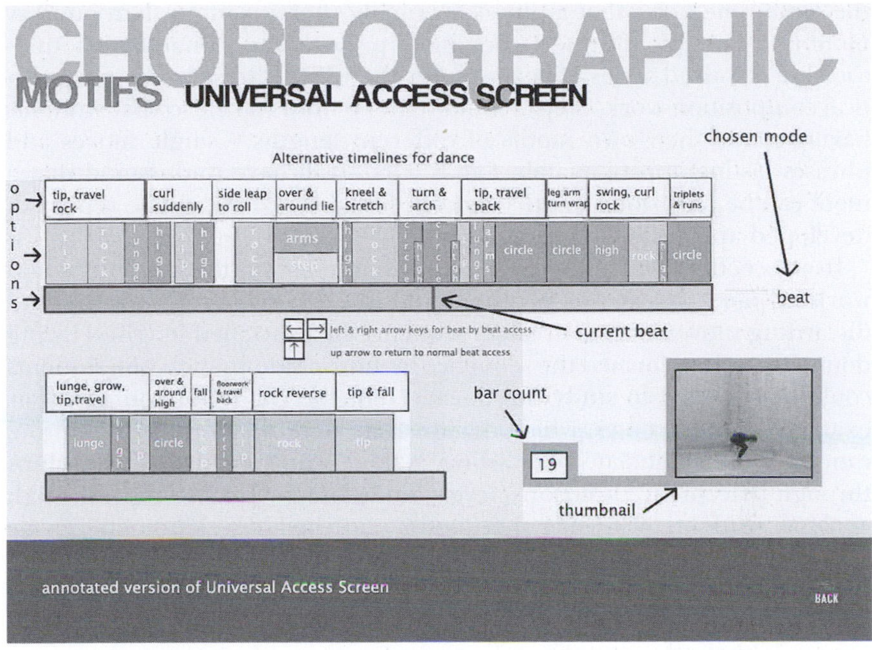

Figure 7.2 Universal access screen. Schofield (2005).

which can then be evaluated in class – or perhaps through download of their videoed responses via the web in a distance learning context for peer and teacher review.

It is difficult to describe and analyse an interactive resource that contains over 100 video clips and many layers of computerised tools such as immediate access to motifs, developments and orchestration of them in duos and groups, animated text, drawings, spatial patterning on the floor and in the air, form charts, phrase and rhythmic dynamics. It is evident that the resource needs to be seen and judged by users themselves. However, for the purposes of this chapter, an example as to how it can help students develop their own creativity whilst simultaneously gaining objective knowledge about form per se is provided below.

Innovations in teaching dance composition via CD-ROM technology

The scenario described by Cook (2005) above constitutes Step 1 in a lesson which could go on to explore longer phrase motifs having viewed what constitutes a phrase in the source solo dance on the CD-ROM. Access to the phrases and all other parts of the dance is made simple through a 'Universal Access Screen' (see Figure 7.2).

The user merely clicks on any of the 15 top white phrase boxes and at the same time notes that a phrase normally contains more than one key motif (for example, Phrase 1 contains Tip, Rock and Lunge key motifs – the blue coloured series of boxes under the white phrase boxes). In practical composition work, Step 2 could then be undertaken so that students having made their own motifs of different lengths – single moves and phrases lasting approximately 4 to 6 bars – will have understood that a motif can be of various lengths and once established should be repeated, developed and varied to create form.

In proceeding with the dance composition lesson, the students could work in pairs to learn each other's phrases – combining, refining and discarding movements to create a sequence of a specified length. Having done this and performed the sequence in unison side-by-side, the students could then be led to study duo form. Here the CD-ROM contains four example duo outcomes, which demonstrate time relationships – unison, canon, complementary, contrasting action – and spatial relationships through placement, directions, levels, floor and air patterning. Through analysis, students will learn that motifs and their developments can be presented simultaneously and that this results in complementary action. They will also learn that contrast can be produced through the two dancers performing different motifs simultaneously. Tasks such as that in Figure 7.3 help the students to first appreciate and learn from the examples on the disc and then apply such concepts and principles in their own compositions.

To summarise: through this resource-based teaching/learning methodology, by the end of this class, beginner students will have learned and applied some basic composition skills that help in achieving form. Starting from visual dance examples, answering tasks to describe, analyse and ultimately show understanding of the concepts and principles embedded in them through utilising these concepts and principles in their own ways requires that, rather than being taught, students learn for themselves. The value of reference to the CD-ROM resource in this learning cannot be overstated. The teacher's role here is one of guide and facilitator so that students' responses to the appreciation and composition tasks are appropriate, comprehensive, individually creative, and show depth of understanding. There are no answers given in the pack. Although most of the appreciation answers in Figure 7.3 can be judged right or wrong by the teacher, when it comes to the students' own creative composition responses, the teacher and the students themselves should formulate criteria to evaluate them. Clearly, the criteria in terms of understanding concepts of form will be derived from the content of the composition examples on the CD-ROM, but what constitutes a creative use of this understanding emerges through the teacher's and students' own views and values.

Appreciation

View the whole outcome as many times as needed and undertake the following preliminary tasks:

- Describe two moments of unison.
- Note two incidences of canon describing the action and the gap in time between the two dancers.
- Identify one moment of complementary action.
- Is there a moment when the dancers move in contrast?
- How many changes of level occur in this short excerpt and which dancer does each change involve?
- Note three changes of directional facings and say whether both or one dancer makes the change.
- Give a running commentary on the positioning orientation of the two dancers in relation to each other.
- What is the dominant spatial relationship?

Composition

Now use all the duo orchestration devices in Phrase 1 of Duo 1 on the CD ROM to orchestrate your duo. You can use the list in any order.

- Canon doing the same movement in opposition
- Canon into follow my leader
- Unison moving in the same direction
- Unison in opposition

Also use the same number of changes in relationship (three) and directional facings (three) as in Phrase 1 of Duo 1.

Figure 7.3 Creative Practice Guidebook (Smith-Autard 2005: 72).

Analysis of the example dance composition class (Figure 7.3) in terms of objectivity and subjectivity in the creative process

Guided through use of the CD-ROM and the accompanying books in the resource pack, students should develop objective knowledge and skills that include understanding that motifs can be as short as a single movement or can be much longer such as a phrase. They will learn how to link and dynamically phrase their movements, develop motifs and also how to orchestrate their motifs for two dancers in time and in space. They may also learn that complementary action is achieved through simultaneous presentation of the original motif and its development.

Interspersed with the above objective learning and acquisition of skills is a good deal of opportunity for subjective creative input. Given a theme, students explore their chosen single actions and ways in which they can be linked with dynamic and spatial variation. They can then explore different ways in which these moves can be developed, perhaps taking and adapting some ideas from the CD-ROM but also finding their own

Appreciation

- What movements from previous phrases are developed and how are they developed?
- Use slow-motion to identify where and how the following take place:
  - o Change from unison in opposition to unison
  - o Into canon
  - o Back into unison in opposition
- Describe the relationships and comment on the differences in this Phrase compared with previous Phrases.
- Compare Phrase 3 with Phrase 5 to observe and note the similarities and differences.
- What do you notice about the use of space that is different in this Phrase?

Figure 7.4 Creative Practice Guidebook (Smith-Autard 2005: 93).

ways. In orchestrating their motifs in pairs, they can creatively use the given list of devices in time and space in an organic way so that all duos in one class demonstrate different solutions to the same creative problem.

Since these hypothetical students are beginners in dance composition, there is likely to be more emphasis on the objective learning. Nonetheless, the opportunities for subjective inputs are inbuilt in the open appreciation and composition tasks that are characteristic of a resource-based teaching methodology.

In using the CD-ROM with a group of more advanced students, analysis and appreciation of the content is taken to a much deeper level to inform their own more intricately structured dance compositions. In guiding students to perceive detail in a composition each phrase viewed requires response to a set of questions. This is undertaken first by students viewing the whole duo, perhaps twice through. Ultimately, in viewing Phrase 5 in another duo, for example, the following questions and tasks from the *Creative Practice Guidebook* (Smith-Autard 2005: 93) require reference to previous phrases to discern ways in which previous motifs have been developed, varied, reversed, fragmented or re-echoed in part *and* the ability to identify the variety of temporal, spatial and relationship orchestrations that occur in the 8-bar phrase (see Figure 7.4).

Further such work on the other phrases leads towards the following practical composition work that would take at least two hours to complete (see Figure 7.5)

Analysis of the example dance composition class (Figure 7.5) in terms of objectivity and subjectivity in the creative process

Here, there is constant interaction with the example duo composition on the CD-ROM – to copy some of the movements thereby learning techniques

Composition

TASK: Select a piece of music or a sound track and create a Duo using some of the movement ideas and devices in Lisa's Duo 1. The duo could be based on a theme such as 'Play', 'An Argument' or 'A Windy Day'. Obviously, the dynamic and relationship content will vary according to the idea but motifs should emerge from the following explorations.

a) Work in twos to explore the following contact relationships taken from Lisa's Duo 1:
   - The lifting starting position – if this is difficult find an alternative position in which one partner takes the weight of the other off the floor.
   - Throw off from this hold – into different directions.
   - Pushing movements – shifting your partner – sideways, forwards or backwards. (See examples in Phrase 1 and 4 where there are two).
   - Lift and turn. There are all sorts of movements that can be done here. Try the lift and turn in Phrase 2 and Phrase 4 of Lisa's Duo 1 but others too.
   - The roll into the arms in Phrase 4.
   - The turning jump in contact in Phrase 6 and others that you can invent.

b) Next from the above exploration select and compose the following contact motifs:
   LIFT THROW PUSH LIFT & TURN ROLL INTO TURNING-JUMP

c) Now create some turning movements together. Take some ideas from Lisa's Duo 1 as follows:
   - Turn inwards initiated by a leg circling in action (Dancer B Phrase 2).
   - Turn inwards (pirouette) keeping the other leg held in position (Phrase 3 end).
   - Turn by rolling on the floor sideways (Dancer A Phrase 3).
   - Turning outwards on one foot the other leg behind (Dancer B × 2 Phrase 3).
   - Watch Phrase 4 and extract turns resulting from contact movements. Try adding turns resulting from your PUSH, THROW and ROLL INTO. Make the movement flow and appear logical.

d) Select 4 turning actions then develop or change them by adding hops, legs and arm positions or directions. This will result in you having the 4 initial turning movements and their respective developments to add to the vocabulary of your duo.

e) To explore travelling curving pathways access Phrase 5 and using running only, copy the travel forwards on opposite sides of a circular pathway in unison in opposition to meet then turn into unison leading and following but going backwards to end away from each other on a diagonal. Carry on into Phrase 6 and copy the pathways travelling forwards into a movement turning close then travel out to the diagonal again and then backwards into the spiral to end side by side facing the RDC. You should learn these pathways and changes of directions in order to utilise them in your duo.

f) Now use the above explorations in any order to compose your duo. It would probably be wise to decide on a starting motif – perhaps one of the contact moves – and then to feel what should come next – perhaps one of the turns into a curving pathway. This organic approach will work best if you consider the music and idea (if there is one). You should incorporate as many of the relationships that were listed in Lisa's Duo 1 as possible and use the devices of unison (both the same side and in opposition) and canon. Also, repetition, development and variation should be evident throughout.

g) Once the duo has been created and practised, write some questions on a feedback sheet to give to another pair. The questions should require the respondents to evaluate the duo as a formed whole making reference to all the devices in f) above. Use the evaluation to inform self-assessment of your duo.

Figure 7.5 Creative Practice Guidebook (Smith-Autard 2005: 94–5).

and to note complex use of development and variation through extraction of parts, addition, inversion, and so on. There is also analysis of the variety of ways a single move – the *turn* – is performed in the video duo followed by practical exploration of each of the different turns and adaptation of these with the students' own *lifts, throws* and *rolls into* movements. This demonstrates a depth in exploration which should inform students of the potential for exploration in other movement contexts. Composition task (e) requires students to extract and learn a phrase of movement from the CD-ROM duo. This inclusion of part of the repertoire, in this instance, creates a contrast of material to be incorporated in the students' own duo. It is anticipated that they would ultimately appreciate this subtle input and learn from it the need for contrast in a duo which consists mostly of very close relationship movements. All of this constitutes the objective learning and development of skills that is designed to take place through use of this resource pack.

Subjectivity also enters into much of the learning outlined above but it obviously takes a central role in the students' choice of idea, music and selection from the range of movement ideas explored with reference to the disc. Although imagination has been given several starting points in this instance, there are no limits on originality of the student outcomes. If, for example, lifts and/or throws were to be explored in a depth similar to exploration of turns in (c), students would be likely to experiment far beyond what they have seen in the CD-ROM duo and would certainly need to apply very different dynamic content if the idea selected were to be an argument, for example. The discipline required to include the devices in (f) and the given travelling pathway in (e) and the freedom to be able to utilise these features using their original movement responses to the other tasks implies that there is an interplay between knowledge and intuition/feeling. Moreover, under guidance of the teacher in use of the resource pack, it is anticipated that, to quote Reid (1983) again, 'absorption of discursively reflective thinking and study' through the appreciation tasks leads to 'an assimilation of it, a conscious forgetting of it, and a return to illuminated intuition' in the composing process.

Reflection on this example dance composition experience, with reference to the quotations that focus on what it is to be creative (Best, Redfern and Reid in particular), confirms that there is potential for developing creative responses within the context of structured tasks which also teach the discipline. In addition, if we look again at the bottom box in Figure 7.1 these hypothetical students are engaged in all the processes described as both objective and subjective.

How does use of the CD-ROM resource pack, **Choreographic Outcomes,** *develop creativity?*

Keeping a balance between the objective and subjective in teaching/learning dance composition is difficult and challenging but is also exciting and rewarding. The aim of the pack is to contribute technology tools to develop students' knowledge about and skills in creating form in their dances. It is also anticipated, however, that use of the pack will feed the intuitive/feeling side of the process through the viewing and study of 'well-made' dance composition examples as presented on the CD-ROM. Provision of visual demonstration of principles and concepts pertaining to form in dance composition, previously presented via the teacher and in book form only, certainly promotes learning that can be applied into the students' own work.

It is important to point out that 'this and the other Bedford Interactive resource packs constitute invaluable toolboxes that underpin paradigms for dance education' (Cook 2005: 139) – in this case relating to traditional practices in achieving form in dance composition. To this end, students are covertly presented with tools for analysis of the visual content on the disc and are then set tasks so that they can apply the concepts and principles gained in such analysis work to their own dance making and performing. The resource pack, therefore, is not instructional and

> is no "plug in and play" program. It is a sophisticated, deeply intelligent, effortful endeavour. ... [I]t embeds many important educational insights and practices into the very fabric of the program.
>
> (Warburton 2005: 93)

This reviewer clearly appreciates the intention to provide a flexible, intuitive bank of material that feeds both knowledge and imagination. Teachers' use of such technology with classes in practical dance studios – through distance-based learning modules, through self-directed responses to the tasks set on accompanying worksheets or in text on screen – will determine its value in dance education in the twenty-first century. As Risner and Anderson (2008) affirm:

> In dance technology education, there is a unique set of opportunities to present innovation in the context of tradition that might increasingly reaffirm creativity, discipline, and the centrality of the body in motion ... Dance is particularly well suited, given its visual and kinaesthetic grounding, for leading these kinds of innovative technological approaches.
>
> (Risner and Anderson 2008: 119, 123)

Conclusion

It is reported that 'little research has been conducted in the area of dance technology pedagogy or the impact of technology on dance learning' (Risner and Anderson 2008: 126). However, the Special Issue of *Research in Dance Education* (Volume 9, Number 2, 2008) in which Risner and

Anderson's article appears, contains an encouraging range of research featuring new technologies applied to dance education. However, the emphasis here is on the *application* of technologies such as the web, video-conferencing, video recording/playback, etc. and the employment of generalised software packages to advance and enhance teaching/learning in dance.

Through outlining the intentions of the authors of a resource that is specifically written to aid teaching and learning in dance composition, this chapter provides another perspective in demonstrating how 'the integration of dance pedagogy and technology [in] content-rich teaching resources' (Cook 2005: 140) can enhance the students' learning. *Choreographic Outcomes: Improving Dance Composition* (2005) delineates and progresses the 'midway' art of dance model in that, implicit in the appreciation, composition and performance tasks presented in tandem on the disc and its accompanying *Creative Practice Guidebook*, there is equal emphasis on product *and* process, objectivity *and* subjectivity, knowledge *and* feeling/intuition, learning of techniques *and* personal explorations together with didactic *and* open-ended teaching methodologies.

Clearly, further such resources that illustrate many other ways of achieving form in dance composition in addition to resources that focus on other aspects such as development of content and style should be developed to support dance composition teaching and learning. Moreover, resources should expose the multifarious ways in which professional choreographers employ choreographic devices so that students have banks of exemplars to inspire and inform them of a range of practices – past and present – that exist in the art of making dances. In all cases, however, such resources cannot be merely instructive nor merely entertainment. Rather they should contain rich banks of educational material and tools to promote students' own learning and creativity.

Notes

1 *Dance Composition* is now in its 5th edition (2004).
2 The *Art of Dance in Education* is now in its 2nd edition (2002).
3 To gain detailed information on the structure and content of the 'midway' model read Chapter 1 in *The Art of Dance in Education* (2002).
4 See National Curriculum guidelines – www.standards.dfes.gov.uk – Search for Physical Education – Dance activities. Also, General Certificate in Secondary Education (GCSE), Advanced Supplementary (AS 1 year course) and Advanced Level (A level 2 year course) examinations. See www.aqa.org.uk/ for detailed content. In relation to other countries, see for example, www.boardofstudies.nsw.edu.au – Select 'All NSW Syllabuses' and scroll down to Dance. The Syllabus Rationale for Years 7–10 (PDF page 8) indicates the influence of the midway model.
5 Authored by Smith-Autard, Schofield and Schofield (2005) and produced by Bedford Interactive Productions.

References

Best, D. (1985) *Feeling and Reason in the Arts*, London: Allen & Unwin.

—— (1992) *The Rationality of Feeling*, London: The Falmer Press.

Cook, W. (2005) 'Choreographic outcomes: improving dance composition', review in *Journal of Dance Education*, 5 (4): 138–40.

Langer, S. (1953) *Feeling and Form*, New York: Routledge and Kegan Paul.

Morgenroth, J. (2006) 'Contemporary choreographers as models for teaching composition', *Journal of Dance Education*, 6 (1): 19–24.

Redfern, H. B. (1973) *Concepts in Modern Educational Dance*, London: Henry Kimpton Publishers.

Reid, L. A. (1981) 'Knowledge, knowing and becoming educated', *Journal of Curriculum Studies*, 13 (2): 79–91.

—— (1983) 'Aesthetic knowing' in M. Ross (ed.) *The Arts – a Way of Knowing*, Oxford: Pergamon Press.

Risner, D. and Anderson, J. (2008) 'Digital dance literacy: an integrated dance technology curriculum pilot project', *Research in Dance Education*, 9 (2): 113–28.

Schofield, J. (2005) CD-ROM resource disc in *Choreographic Outcomes: Improving Dance Composition*, Dewsbury: Bedford Interactive Productions.

Smith-Autard, J. M. (1976, 2004) *Dance Composition*, 5th edn, London: A & C Black.

—— (1994, 2002) *The Art of Dance in Education*, London: A & C Black.

—— (2005) 'Creative Practice Guidebook' in *Choreographic Outcomes: Improving Dance Composition*, Dewsbury: Bedford Interactive Productions.

Smith-Autard, J. M., Schofield, J. and Schofield, M. (2005) *Choreographic Outcomes: Improving Dance Composition*, Dewsbury: Bedford Interactive Productions.

Warburton, E. C. (2005) 'Choreographic outcomes: improving dance composition', review in *Dance Research Journal*, 37 (2): 91–3.

—— (2008) Editorial in *Research in Dance Education*, 9 (2): 111–12.

8 Evaluation – nurturing or stifling a choreographic learning process?

Soili Hämäläinen

The most familiar form of evaluation in Western theatrical dance is aesthetic judgement, which considers dance performances as objects of art. This is how dance critics usually approach dance. Unfortunately, this approach is not uncommon in choreographic pedagogy either. However, there is more to evaluation than this. It also plays an integral part in learning: it can help a student develop skills in choreography as well as develop an aesthetic understanding of dance as art. I consider evaluation to be something that can nurture or stifle a creative process. Evaluation involves many questions concerning the teacher's authority, expertise and power, but also the student's ability, choices and independence.

This chapter discusses the nature of the choreographic process and some forms of evaluation used in choreographic pedagogy. Recent research on evaluation as an integral part of learning leads to the focus: what to evaluate and who are the evaluators? Also considered are students' experiences of evaluation and some ethical issues related to evaluation. The empirical material that details students' experiences has greatly affected my views on the topic. In pointing to some areas that might be illuminating and enhance the possibilities of evaluation, I focus especially on those features that are related to such pedagogic processes in which students choreograph themselves. My main experience as a teacher of choreography is with first-year contemporary dance majors and MA dance pedagogy majors in a university. However, these ideas are likely to be applicable to other age groups and dance forms.

Some views on the choreographic process

The first section discusses some of the central features through which choreography and the choreographic process are realized, addressing questions about the body, the tasks of the choreographer and the dancer, and the intentional and communicative aspects of dance.

The body is the core of experiences; it senses, feels, remembers and expresses what it has experienced. Dance is vividly present as long as dancers dance with or in their bodies. This makes dance, like the other performing arts, ephemeral. When dance is examined as a performing art, in addition to creating dance, a dancer's body is also the object of the spectator's gaze. As I see it, spectators can participate in the reception of dance through their own physicality, through their sensing and observing bodies. However, spectators also approach dance from visual and aesthetic points of view.

A dancer lives in her body. The body is a subject, a source in a choreographic process. The lived body is significant to a choreographer and is revealed as body awareness. Rudolf Arnheim (1971) points out that a dancer is bound to the given form of the human body and has to derive composition through it. One curious consequence is that a dance is created in a different medium from the one in which it appears to the audience. The painter looks at the canvas and so does the spectator. A choreographer creates mainly in the medium of the kinaesthetic sensations in her or his muscles, tendons and joints, but the spectator receives a visual work of art, even if a spectator senses it also with the body (1971: 393). When a dancer moves and sets his body in motion the dancing is perceivable, visible and audible to the others. According to Jaana Parviainen the dual nature of the body, that it is both sensing and sensed, allows for a sharp difference in its continuity that she calls an abyss or *écart* in at least two different manners:

> (1) in the dancing body itself and (2) between the moving body and the one who perceives it. An abyss in a dancer's experience of movement means that the dancing as experiential is never the same as it is 'moved', as it is visual. There is always an *écart* between moving and moved (visual) to the dancer her/himself.
>
> (Parviainen 1998: 66)

Parviainen (1998: 66) suggests that dancers, in order to express meanings through movements experientially lived, have to study 'the abyss between the experiential movements and their visual appearance, the moving-moved'. Despite reversibility between a dancer's movement and the audience's perception of it, this moving-perceived carries an abyss that is located in the difference of the self and other. A viewer's experience is different from a performer's experience of movement, although the audience and the dancer may pursue a shared experience of dance. Parviainen (1998: 71) believes that there is always an abyss between the self and otherness.

The choreographic process involves both a conscious and an intuitive process in which the body is simultaneously both the subject of the dance, the source of the experiential dimension of dance, and the object of observation. Because of the fusion of subject and object, dancers do not experience their dancing in the same way as the audience receives the work.

Lived body as a source in a choreographic process

Discovering the meaning of the lived body as body awareness and a source of creativity is the basis for composition in contemporary dance. It emphasizes the significance of a dancer's bodily knowledge, experience and memory, as well as a dancer's responsibility for her or his own body and its messages. According to Rouhiainen (2003) the way that we experience our body is connected to the history of our body, the way it has been used and the experiences it has had. The body memory brings into one's mind images of what the body has felt during certain moments and in certain situations. The emphasis on the body as subject or object in the teaching of dance composition depends on the pedagogical view and artistic methods utilized in teaching. Particularly important influencing factors are the teacher's relation to the body and understanding of its role, as well as the student's relationship with her or his own body in a choreographic process.

The objective of teaching composition so that the lived body or body as a subject is emphasized resembles Socratic maieutics, midwifery, where the 'midwife' does not create or give birth to the child, but merely helps in delivering it. A prerequisite to Socratic midwifery is the idea that there is something in the learner that can be revived, such as dormant talents or subconscious knowledge. The question is thus about finding the skills that already exist in the self, becoming conscious of the knowledge and creative potential that we have. The objective of maieutics is to provide a dancer with tools that can be used to observe and develop the possibilities and talents that lie concealed in the self. In this way, a choreographer can find her or his own creative potential, and by grasping it, she or he can further develop it.

Sherry Shapiro (1998: 9) also writes about the possibility of understanding one's body as subject rather than object, a subject which holds the memory of one's life, and defines one's racial identity, gender existence, historical and cultural grounding, indeed the very materiality of one's existence. I consider an ethical relationship with one's body to involve understanding the body as subject, born when a dancer questions general practices and clarifies her goals, and, above all, listens to her own bodily feelings. As a 'moral actor' (Foucault 1998: 132–5),[1] a dancer chooses to come to composition classes and to be the object of the teacher's assessment; that is, she chooses submission, in order to develop her bodily existence, creativity and entire way of being towards enhanced self-directedness and artistic growth. The questions and relationships between all these aspects described above are complex. Thus, they do not serve as an easy base for creating criteria for evaluation of a piece of choreography or the choreographic process. I have greatly emphasized here the value of lived body as a subject, a source in a choreographic process, yet I am aware that there are other approaches in choreographic pedagogy.

Evaluation in the tradition of choreographic pedagogy

In previous research (Hämäläinen 1999, 2002) I studied the traditions of teaching choreography. I will now describe some of the evaluation methods used in choreography classes and introduce some more recently developed ideas, which show how different teachers of choreography – Horst, Humphrey, Dunn, Hawkins, Smith-Autard and Lavender – have used evaluation in their teaching.

Louis Horst was one of the first teachers in choreography when he started working in New York in 1928, using music and the dances of the pre-classic period as a point of departure (Lippincott 1969). Horst emphasized the rules of composition when he gave students specific problems to solve. His students were encouraged to try different kinds of solutions while exploring the task but when they showed their work in class they had to be able to repeat it. In his feedback, Horst had a clear opinion of what was right and wrong in dance, which brought admiration as well as opposition. Lippincott (1969: 4) writes: 'His memory for the slightest detail of movement was amazing. He could tell a student exactly where changes should be made, to the precise measure and beat. On occasion he would demonstrate what he wanted, moving carefully with rather small movements despite his bulk.'

Janet Soares' experience of Horst's way to evaluate students' choreographies was less positive:

> Louis usually rejected most of what he saw, asking the student to change, edit, or reorganize certain sections on the spot, the rest of the class nervously watching – an ordeal that could take a few minutes to a half hour per student. Only when the entire class had finished the assignment to his satisfaction was he ready to go on to the next.
>
> (Soares 1992: 69)

This outlook on evaluation, based on behaviourist conceptions of learning, was common in the mid-1950s and it is still familiar to some choreography students.

Doris Humphrey's book on choreographic pedagogy, *The Art of Making Dances* (1959) introduces the basic elements of composition: design, dynamics, rhythm and motivation. For her the aim of studying choreography was to learn to understand and use these elements, which then played an important role in the choreographic evaluation process. Though Humphrey describes what is right and wrong in choreography on the basis of these elements, she also emphasizes the choreographers' roles in the evaluation of their work. In her opinion, choreographers should be able to consider and assess their work objectively. As Humphrey describes:

> The choreographer stands away from his work spatially as well – first in a literal sense, of space between himself and the dance, but also

> psychologically, so that he is sitting in an imaginary tenth row, looking at his dance for the first time, listening to the music, and receiving these impressions as an audience would, all just once through.
>
> (Humphrey 1959: 149)

Robert Dunn started to teach choreography at Judson Dance Theatre in 1960 to develop a more open approach to teaching and learning choreography. The students were post-modern dancers who sought to develop new aesthetics in dance (Banes 1983). In Dunn's workshops there was more interest in choreographic processes than products. His teaching method was very free – everyone choreographed a dance, performed it, and then it was discussed. The works were not evaluated based on some previously set criteria; instead, the teacher and the students discussed what steps might be taken to find solutions. Dunn's aim was to train dancers to watch and talk about dance (Banes 1983: 5). His teaching emphasized both individualism and sharing experiences. In his opinion, there were at least as many viewpoints and interpretations of things as there were people. The fact that dancers showed their works in progress, and the manner in which they were evaluated, differed significantly from earlier forms of teaching. As Dunn notes:

> Discussion should not be the prerogative of the teacher (with luck, a class can come to the point of 'teaching itself'), and [discussion] should be used to train the eye and the mind as to what has been there to be seen, rather than separate the sheep from the goats, whether movements, methods or choreographers.
>
> (Dunn 1972: 16)

Alma Hawkins (1964) did substantive research in the areas of creativity, movement exploration and choreography in the United States. Her book on choreographic pedagogy and the process-oriented approach considers the various phases of the creative process: sensing, feeling, imaging, transforming and forming (1991). Hawkins felt that when a young choreographer has clear motivation and is deeply involved in the process, the dance would take shape and have its own form. The teacher's task is to provide an enriched environment that motivates individuals to be self-directed and to make their own discoveries. Hawkins' approach to teaching and learning choreography is very holistic. She points out that students should be encouraged to be the evaluators of their work and to trust their inner voice in evaluation (1964, 1991). Trusting the inner voice is also an essential part of the artistic growth process. She argues that it is important to increase students' responsibility for their work and not to encourage them to expect answers from outside sources.

> There is less and less listening to the inner voice and more and more attending the outer voices. The individual is increasingly pressed

> to conform to external expectations, and the fear of not being right becomes a powerful force in shaping behavior. As a result, self-directed and creative responses happen less and less.
>
> (Hawkins 1991: 10)

According to Jacqueline Smith-Autard (1985: 92), there is no objective formula for the evaluation of a dance. She writes, 'A dance can only be measured as successful in a relative sense. Relative to the onlooker's experience and background and the composer's stage of development in composing.' She states that it is also valuable for pupils to learn to evaluate their own dances. When viewing dance, the teacher should give students special features to observe and then they should describe what they have seen by using the appropriate terminology. Smith-Autard (1994) suggests that Laban's framework can provide a checklist to be used in the observation and evaluation of a dance. This serves the choreography student well because it classifies movement into broad concepts, and each concept suggests a range of movement that can be explored in the choreography class.

Larry Lavender (1996) introduced the *order* approach to critical evaluation in choreography, outlining five steps: observation, reflection, discussion, evaluation and recommendations for revisions. He emphasizes that critical evaluation is a pedagogical method not a goal. Through this approach, he states that students learn to become choreographers through the development of critical consciousness. Lavender suggests that the teacher should give up some authority and show respect for diverse points of view. Lavender and Predock-Linnell (2001: 197) critically argue that dance works tend to be evaluated primarily in terms of their form and structure rather than in terms of expressive power.

The examples given above illustrate the diversity of choreography teachers' views on evaluation. Horst helped students by telling them where changes should be made. Humphrey emphasized the choreographer's own role in evaluation. Dunn's aim was to train choreographers to watch and discuss dance. Hawkins pointed out the importance of inner feedback and self-evaluation, while Smith-Autard suggested that Laban's analysis of movement could provide a tool for the evaluation of dance. Lavender and Predock-Linnell emphasized the value of the critical consciousness, which could be developed in an evaluation process.

Evaluation as an integral part of learning

Evaluation is an integral part of the choreographic process and product and can play a significant role in the creative development of the individual. As demonstrated, there has been a wide range of approaches to evaluation. The development of the various conceptions of learning is evident in the changes of the *principles* of learning as well as in the manner in which it is evaluated. In the early 1900s the behaviourist view of learning, which was based on measuring, became dominant. Evaluation of learning mainly involved the measuring of students' differences in knowledge and skill, and a great deal of emphasis was put on quantitative evaluation at the end of the learning period.

According to newer concepts of learning, evaluation is seen as an integral part of the learning process, showing interest in the results of learning but also in how people learn. Evaluation is therefore also directed at the process of learning, not merely at the product (Jakku-Sihvonen and Heinonen 2001; Kukkonen 1996). In the constructivist view of learning, *learners* are active and ambitious people who *have the ability to evaluate their own experiences* and activities and their significance. Learning is also an activity based on communal and social interaction (Jakku-Sihvonen and Heinonen 2001; Rauste-von Wright and von Wright 1994). The starting point here is the learners' ability and possibility for reflective evaluation of their experiences and activities (Jakku-Sihvonen and Heinonen, 2001). Rauste-von Wright and von Wright (1994: 117) argue that the learner reconstructs her or his earlier views and information based on the reflection of her or his performance and its results. They consider this reconstruction process to be the core of learning.

Harri Kukkonen (1996) puts forward an interesting view that evaluation cannot be artificially separated from an individual and their learning process without restricting and even hindering growth. He writes that no specific starting or finishing point can be set for learning and evaluation, which should be seen as an ongoing process both temporally and functionally. For Kukkonen, evaluation must be directed at processes as well as products. Quantitative evaluation of bodily knowledge and skills in a finished choreography, the final product, can cover only a minor part of the target of evaluation. For evaluation to be an essential part of the learning process, it should be focused on *working processes*, *works in progress* and *finished choreographies*.

Evaluation of working processes and works in progress

Reflective discussions on *working processes* are an essential part of self-evaluation especially when a student is dancing in her or his own work. Reflective discussions are based on reflective thinking, which means evaluative thinking directed at one's own actions, thinking and learning. Here it is significant that students learn to verbalize and reflect upon their experiences, emotions, images, observations, information and interpretation with other members of the group. It is essential to learn to examine and assess one's own working processes, but it is just as important to learn to watch, discuss and give constructive evaluation on other people's working processes, developing the ability to observe and to analyse movement. The viewer learns to verbalize and conceptualize the experiences dance arouses, and these discussions deepen the understanding of the artistic process. This type of common sharing of experience helps learning and facilitates verbalization of the working processes of creating choreography.

In addition to reflective discussions, students can contemplate and assess their working processes by keeping a journal of learning. The purpose of it is to collect the student's experiences, problems, solutions and notions in order to support the learning and evaluation. It is important that students write a journal for themselves, not for the teacher. In this way, they can more honestly evaluate their own work.

Showing *works in progress* and talking about them are an important part of the group's learning process. In my experience, students want to share their works and discuss them in various phases. Some wish to work alone for a long time whereas others want to receive feedback from the start. It requires confidence to show a work in progress. The students' different qualities should be considered in this respect as excessive criticism and fears are the greatest obstacles for presenting works in progress. Therefore, it is of utmost importance to create a safe and respectful atmosphere. It is also important that the person giving feedback does not take over as choreographer, but works in this process as the one asking questions and as a mirror in order to help the students find their own solutions.

Evaluation of choreography

One of the most difficult tasks of an art educator is the *evaluation of an art product*, especially if the teacher has to grade it. Since the evaluation of art tends to be based on personal experience and conception of art, there are few common measurements that can be used in the evaluation process. The results of my previous study (Hämäläinen 1999) showed clearly that quantitative evaluation is unsuitable for evaluating art works. There is no absolute truth; each evaluator sees and grades the work individually, using their personal conception of art as the basis of evaluation. Ben Shahn sharply criticizes quantitative evaluation of an art product:

> Can we say then, that the work of Picasso has better content than that of Dali, or better forms, or that Picasso is a more competent painter, or that his own values are better ones than those of Dali? Again no. For none of these qualities is an absolute in the light of which we can say that one thing is better or another is worse.
>
> (Shahn 1957: 93)

Susan Foster (1986: 41) points out that each viewer's experience is unique, not simply because each person has a different heritage of associations to the dance but because each viewer has literally made a different dance. According to Eisner, however, the fact that educational criticism is complex, subtle, and context-specific does not mean that we can avoid making judgements about the educational value of what we have seen. He writes: 'If we do not know what we have, there is no way of knowing what direction we ought to take' (Eisner 1991: 100).

How should an art product be evaluated? Should it be based on predetermined criteria? As Lavender (1996: 37) indicates, there are no fixed standards for judging art. He continues that the use of predetermined criteria prevents students from developing their own artistic values. In order for the evaluation to be a learning situation, students should be allowed to talk about their aims in the creating process and discuss how well they have fulfilled those aims. I consider the evaluation of choreography to be qualitative in nature. The criteria of evaluation should be based on the aims of the choreographer as well as the aims of the choreographic tasks.

According to Smith-Autard, 'that which is aesthetically pleasing will seem right, significant, complete, balanced and unified, and we feel these qualities rather than know them' (1985: 92). However, in aesthetic evaluation she trusts not only feeling but also knowledge, which plays an important role in intellectual reflections. The criteria of evaluation can also be based on the student's past and present performance. Eisner (1991: 102) calls this personally referenced evaluation; 'to make such comparisons requires the ability to appraise the qualities of the student's work and to have some sense of the direction in which it is going'. Eisner's point is important because this allows everyone equal opportunity to have experiences in succeeding. However, it requires sensitivity and a deep knowledge of the subject from the teacher. My next question is: *who is an evaluator?*, first focusing on *student as an evaluator*.

Student as an evaluator

Inkeri Sava (1993: 20) points out that only when students can analyse their learning and working processes can they become the subjects of their learning. If the teacher alone is responsible for evaluating the students' artistic achievements, the learners cannot develop an inner motivation or responsibility for their own actions. Then, the students are constantly dependent on their teacher's feedback. However, the learners' role as subjects and their autonomy in the learning process has not been sufficiently emphasized in choreographic pedagogy. We often lean on behaviourist learning concepts in teaching, in which teachers work as models and transfer their knowledge and skills to students. In a choreography class, for example, the teacher might give students suggestions on what they should change in their dance. This approach does not allow room for the student's holistic development and creative growth, nor does it develop the learners' responsibility for their learning.

It is important at the beginning of the creative process that the students trust their own intuition. Composition based on lived body and body as a subject emphasizes the individual's responsibility over her or his body. The significance of an individual's experience is also stressed as it highlights the fact that a dancer must take his place as an expert of his own body and its creation. In other words, when composing, a dancer must be aware not only of his movements but also of his sensations, and respect them. This awareness is not only verbal or conceptual; it is also tacit – intuitive and bodily – and cannot always be put into words. With the help of tacit knowledge, a dancer can return to the original, direct experience and activate the non-conceptual knowledge that lies in the self (Koivunen 1998: 201). Juha Varto (1991: 122) reckons that you cannot find the process for somebody else; you can only find yourself, your own personal process, your own transformation.

Most of the newer approaches to teaching and learning value the *student's role as an evaluator*. However, young dance students often lack the skill and courage to use their bodies as sources of knowledge and make choices to suit them, or they may not even be aware of the possibilities inherent to dance, motion, bodily expression and creativity. Students' own internal evaluation means that they have to make aesthetic judgement on their own and develop critical awareness that allows artistic growth. Yet young students aiming to become professionals are often dependent on their instructor's evaluation and feedback, and are not encouraged to take responsibility and exercise freedom and power regarding their own creative process. This may stem from the fact that the significance of the student's own bodily reflecting and evaluation process has not been sufficiently emphasized in dance studies.

Teacher's involvement in the learning process

If evaluation based on the constructivist view of learning strongly emphasizes the learner's role in evaluation, does it pay enough attention to the teacher's role? What *is* the teacher's task in evaluation? Pävia Tynjälä (2000) states that the teacher should explicitly express the forms and criteria for evaluation at the very beginning of a course because they affect the learning processes. The students should know who the evaluators are, what is being evaluated and when the evaluation takes place. However, the criteria should not only be based on the aims of the choreographic tasks but also on the intentions of the choreographer, which can help students to develop their own artistic values.

Reflective discussions have a great value in evaluation. The teacher can support these discussions by asking questions and introducing knowledge and stimulus to the learning situation. This helps students to understand and discuss their creative processes, which is a base for evaluation. The teacher also has the responsibility to support students' self-reflection so that they can find their own way of working and understand other ways as well. Through this, students learn to understand their strengths and weaknesses.

Hawkins (1991: 131) points out that the teacher can assist choreographers in seeing their work more clearly and in finding their own solutions. By using questions and comments, the teacher 'assists the choreographer in discovering what is happening in the movement event, clarifying what is desired and gaining insight about how to achieve that goal'. The role of a teacher in the evaluation process should be that of a facilitator rather than a controller. Hawkins (1991: 12) states that a teacher can help students become confident and proficient in self-evaluation; a teacher's task is to create a safe learning environment in the group so that students also start to trust themselves. Consequently, they are prepared to be more open both as evaluators and as the objects of evaluation.

It is therefore important that teachers are highly experienced in the subject content, capable of understanding the context, and possessing highly refined perception skills. Even an experienced teacher cannot be the expert of a student's lived body, feelings, experiences and thinking except through his or her own observations and interpretations.

Evaluation is learning together and it is part of human activity (Kukkonen 1996: 69, 76). This is a more fundamental phenomenon than merely checking on a student's progress and giving feedback. Ethics are at stake when a teacher chooses her or his own way of encountering a student, or when a student expecting feedback puts her- or himself in a vulnerable position. There has been little discussion on the *ethics of evaluation* even though evaluation has lately been a topic of active debate.

Ethical issues of evaluation

In spring 2003, I collected empirical material on experiences of evaluation and feedback from dance classes in collaboration with MA dance pedagogy majors in a university. The findings of this study engaged me in ethical questions of evaluation. I asked the students to reminisce about evaluation they had received in dance classes over the course of their studies, and to write about them in a 'stream of consciousness' style. Nine graduate students, ages 24 to 42, described their experiences (Hämäläinen, 2004).[2] Even when the students wrote about their experiences of evaluation in dance technique classes, I considered these findings applicable to the choreography classes as well.

The narratives in my study revealed that, in feedback situations, teachers also used their expertise, control and power over[3] students in ways that might have hindered learning experiences. The findings show that students have many *memories of negative evaluation*. It was clear that negative feedback made a lasting impression. Their narratives suggested that offensive feedback did not help the learning process and could ruin one's self-esteem and make one feel humiliated and worthless. Julia Buckroyd points out that children's and adolescents' identity is deeply invested in the body and the developing sense of mastery of it. At that stage of life, the sense of self is almost identical to the sense of one's body and physical self. Therefore, evaluation has the potential to either enhance and develop confidence and self-esteem or undermine and damage it. The results in both cases are likely to be long lasting (Buckroyd 2000: 3).

It is obvious that evaluation is not only a question of a person's learning and performance, but also concerns the individual human being as a whole.

Teachers need knowledge and understanding of the student's personality and life situation. In Kukkonen's (1996: 75–6) view, a teacher evaluating a student should treat the student as a conscious, thinking individual who sets goals for himself, plans his future and makes ethical choices. Maija Lehtovaara points out that the teacher's knowledge of herself or himself and of her/his self-image determines how her/his conception of other people is formed. The most important continuous task of evaluation is to study the pre-emptive understanding of the evaluator. The evaluator must critically dissect and analyse how she understood the subject of her evaluation, the student. Is she the victim of her own prejudices? Can a teacher separate himself/herself from the types and classifications he/she uses to look at students (Lehtovaara 1994: 57; Hämäläinen and Lehtovaara 2003)?

Traditional dance pedagogy views the skilful functional performance of taught dance movements from a third-person perspective. This means that the teacher views the body and its creation from an outside perspective: the body is defined as an objective entity, studied like any material object from the outside (Green 2002: 5). When assessing oneself according to these externalized norms and values, a composition student is in danger of losing the ability to listen to her/his own inner messages to aid creative process. Evaluation involves communication between teacher and student. The communication may be verbal or the message may be communicated through the body. Since communication always involves influencing another person, it also includes exercising power (Hämäläinen and Lehtovaara 2003). The use of power cannot be removed from teaching and evaluation situations, but should be made visible. Teachers should be aware of how power relations work in a dance class.

A teacher's task is to create space and opportunity for a student to grow. This means listening to students, trusting that they can find their own answers, giving students a chance to get to know their bodies and thereby make their own decisions in the creative process. A teacher should allow the student the freedom and chance to mature and the opportunity to think independently and creatively, retrieve and evaluate knowledge, and act ethically. In my view, space given by a teacher helps the student create an ethical relationship with her or his own body, thus enabling her or him to listen to and respect its messages in the choreographic process.

According to my study (Hämäläinen 2004), however, it seems that students do not have the courage to ask questions or to question the teacher's views, and equally, they think that the teachers assume they know what is best for the student.[4] In addition, students' emotional experiences in evaluation situations are not dealt with in the classrooms. These criticisms can be interpreted as one-way communication, which indicates *a lack of open dialogue*. Jorma Lehtovaara (1996) divides dialogues into open and technical dialogues, finding that a technical approach turns the world and other people into objects. Technical dialogue does not require a respectful and humble approach, and does not really allow listening to the other person. It is not a two-way relationship but a monologue dictated by one person only. Open dialogue is an attitude that leaves space for otherness, whereas a technical attitude denies it. The core of open dialogue is 'respectful and interested listening. Listening to the other as the Other, as what he or she truly is.'[5] The focus is on taking turns to listen rather than taking turns to talk. In an open dialogue, neither the intellect nor the will directs the attitude to reality. One is fully present, listening to it, looking and wondering about it – alertly and broadly. Thus, a teacher's total presence in evaluation situations enables open dialogue. In Lehtovaara's view, a teacher can genuinely encounter the other as the *Other* when she has mastered dialogue, that is, when she can honestly relate to the world as her true self without pretence (Lehtovaara 1996: 38–44).

Conclusion

The body is simultaneously the subject of a dance and the object of observation. Therefore, there is always an abyss between the moving body and the body perceived by another person. Even with a shared experience of subjective dance, a viewer's experience is different from a performer's experience of a dance. In addition, the ephemeral character of dance also makes it difficult to evaluate compositions. In the tradition of choreographic pedagogy, there are several approaches to evaluation that differ greatly from one another. It seems that the content and character of evaluation may promote or, in some cases, prevent positive learning experiences.

The aim of evaluation is to guide and encourage the student. Supporting evaluation does not mean that only the student's best qualities and successes are discussed. Evaluation should reflect students' accomplished skills and knowledge as well as the areas they still need to improve. The aim of encouraging evaluation is to help students develop into learners who are aware of their knowledge, enjoy learning and trust their learning skills. This can best happen in an open and supportive environment. The teacher's role is to create that environment and facilitate the learner to find her or his own answers. Teachers should also have knowledge and understanding about the student's personality and life situation and be aware of their own subjectivity and possible prejudices. It is also essential that teachers understand the importance of conversation and open dialogue in teaching and evaluation situations. This kind of attitude in evaluation creates room for the student to find her or his own potential and creative growth in the choreographic process. It allows the evaluation to support and nurture the learning process.

Notes

1 Foucault divided the study of morality into three parts. The first dimension consists of discourses that determine what is forbidden and what is permitted

as well as what is right and wrong. The second dimension is moral behaviour, which describes to what extent people comply with and apply the moral law. Between these two is the third dimension, which consists of the discourses that aim at controlling, advising, shaping, assessing and questioning the moral actions and the actor. This dimension connected to the moral control of oneself incorporates practices and models that the subject uses to form a relation with the self and shapes him- or herself into being a moral actor. Foucault considered this dimension as the primary area of ethics, and called these ethical practices the technique of the self. Techniques of the self are cultural models, with which individuals can affect their body, soul, thoughts, behaviour and the entire way of being. They are about actions where an individual, for instance a dancer, adopts the ethical dimension of self-direction.

2 Each person is a 'knower', who authors stories of their own experiences. A subjective perspective and personal meaning-making are worthwhile and valuable in researching human experience (Risner 2000; Stinson *et al.* 1990). Through these approaches, we can gain insight into personally meaningful reaches of our human world. By utilizing a hermeneutic-phenomenological approach (Van Manen 1994) to describe and analyse the students' experiences, my aim is to understand the nature and meaning of feedback.

3 Although he does not see all uses of power as negative, Clyde Smith (1998: 131) uses the words 'power over' to apply to situations in which a person controls an individual or group with the negative implications of authoritarianism.

4 Sue Stinson (1998) also points out that in most dance classes the teacher has the authority and is the only source of knowledge. Dance training teaches students to be silent and do as they are told. Stinson's research found that traditional dance pedagogy, with its emphasis on silent conformity, does not facilitate 'finding one's voice'. Dancers typically learn to reproduce what they receive, not to criticize or create (Stinson 1998: 28).

5 The Other (*l'autrui*) is one of Emmanuel Levinas' key concepts, the other two being 'the Countenance' (*le face*) and 'asymmetry'. In Levinas' view Otherness does not mean difference, rather he sees Otherness as a primary category: above all else, we are others to one another. The Other represents strangeness which remains mysterious and cannot be thoroughly known. The Other cannot be defined transparently. The Other is always more than I can conceive. What is important for dialogue is what is not said in words: in Levinas' view the silent Countenance of the Other (the concept of the Countenance refers to the entire body) invites others to respond and be responsible. These two words, respond and responsibility, are interestingly very much alike (Hankamäki 2003: 77–157).

References

Arnheim, R. (1971) *Art and Visual Perception: A Psychology of the Creative Eye*, Berkeley: University of California Press.

Banes, S. (1983) *Democracy's Body: Judson Dance Theatre 1962–1964*, Michigan: Umi Research Press.

Buckroyd, J. (2000) *The Student Dancer*, London: Dance Books.

Dunn, R. (1972) 'Can choreography be taught?', *Ballet Review*, 2: 2–18.

Eisner, E. (1991) *The Enlightened Eye: Qualitative Inquiry and the Enhancement of Educational Practice*, New York: Macmillan.

Foster, S. L. (1986) *Reading Dance*, Berkeley: University of California Press.

Foucault, M. (1980) *The History of Sexuality*, New York: Vintage; trans. Kaisa Sivenius (1998) *Seksualisuuden historia*, Helsinki: Gaudeamus.

Green, J. (2002) 'Foucault and the training of docile bodies in dance education', in *AERA Conference*, New Orleans: AERA Conference.

Hämäläinen, S. (1999) *Koreografian opetus – ja oppimisprosesseista – kaksi opetusmallia oman liikkeen löytämiseksi ja muotoamiseksi (Teaching and Learning Processes in Choreography – two approaches to find and form movement)*, Helsinki: The Theatre Academy, Acta Scenica 4.

—— (2002) 'Evaluation in choreographic pedagogy', *Research in Dance Education*, 3 (1): 35–45.

—— (2004) 'Ethical issues of evaluation and feedback in a dance class', in L. Rouhiainen, E. Anttila, S. Hämäläinen and T. Löytönen (eds) *The Same Difference? Ethical and Political Perspectives on Dance*, Helsinki: Theatre Academy, Acta Scenica 17: 79–106.

Hämäläinen, S. and Lehtovaara, M. (2003) '"Mute feedback": supporting or hindering learning to dance?', *Pulses and Impulses for Dance in the Community Conference*, University Tecnica de Lisboa, Departamento de Danca.

Hankamäki, J. (2003) *Dialoginen filosofia, teoria, metodi ja politiikka*, Helsinki: Helsinki University Press.

Hawkins, A. (1964) *Creating through Dance*, New Jersey: Prentice Hall.

—— (1991) *Moving from Within: A New Method for Dance Making*, Chicago, IL: A Cappella Books.

Humphrey, D. (1959) *The Art of Making Dances*, New York: Grove Press.

Jakku-Sihvonen, R. and Heinonen, S. (2001). 'Johdatus koulutuksen arviointikulttuuriin', in *Arviointi 2/2001*, Opetushallitus, Helsinki: Yliopistopaino.

Koivunen, H. (1998) 'Hiljainen tieto luovuuden lähteenä', in M. Bardy (ed.) *Taide tiedon lähteenä*, Helsinki: Stakes.

Kukkonen, H. (1996) 'Arviointi – yhdessä oppimista?', in J. Lehtovaara and R. Jaatinen (eds) *Dialogissa osa 2 – Ihmisenä yhteisössä*, Tampere: Tampereen yliopiston, opettajankoulutuslaitoksen julkaisuja A 8: 69–78.

Lavender, L. (1996) *Dancers Talking Dance: Critical Evaluation in the Choreography Class*, Albuquerque: University of New Mexico Press.

Lavender, L. and Predock-Linnell, J. (2001) 'From improvisation to choreography: the critical bridge', *Research in Dance Education*, 2 (2): 195–209.

Lehtovaara, J. (1996) 'Dialogissa – kokonaisena ihmisenä avoimessa yhteydessä toiseen' in J. Lehtovaara and R. Jaatinen (eds) *Dialogissa osa 2. – ihmisenä ihmisyhteisössä*. Tampere: Tampereen yliopiston opettajankoulutuslaitoksen julkaisu A 8: 29–55.

Lehtovaara, M. (1994) 'Tieto itsestä yksilön merkitysten kokonaisuudessa', in J. Lehtovaara and R. Jaatinen (eds) *Dialogissa – matkalla mahdollisuuteen*, Tampere: Tampereen yliopiston opettajankoulutuslaitoksen julkaisuja A 21: 57–79.

Lippincott, G. (1969) 'A quiet genius himself – Louis Horst', in M. Gray (ed.) *Focus on Dance*, Dance Division of the American Association for Health, Physical Education and Recreation.

Parviainen, J. (1998) *Bodies Moving and Moved. A Phenomenological Analysis of the Dancing Subject and the Cognitive and Ethical Values of Dance Art*, Tampere: Tampere University Press.

Rauste-von Wright, M. and von Wright, J. (1994) *Oppiminen ja koulutus*, Juva: WSOY.

Risner, D. (2000) 'Making dance, making sense: epistemology and choreography', *Research in Dance Education*, 1 (2): 155–72.

Rouhiainen, L. (1997) 'Tanssijana olemisen taidosta', in A. Sarje, (ed.) *Näkökulmia tanssin opettamiseen: Suomalaisten tanssitaiteilijoiden kirjoituksia*, Helsinki: Yliopistopaino, pp. 52–62.

—— (2003) *Living Transformative Lives: Finnish Freelance Dance Artists Brought into Dialogue with Merleau-Ponty's Phenomenology*. Helsinki: The Theatre Academy, Acta Scenica 13.

Sava, I. (1993) 'Taiteellinen oppimisprosessi', in I. Porna and P. Väyrynen (eds) *Taiteen perusopetuksen käsikirja*, Helsinki: Suomen Kuntaliitto.

Shahn, B. (1957) *The Shape of Content*, Cambridge, MA: Harvard University Press.

Shapiro, S. (1998) 'Toward transformative teachers: critical and feminist perspectives in dance education' in S. Shapiro (ed.) *Dance, Power and Difference*, Champaign: Human Kinetics Publishers.

Smith, C. (1998) 'On authoritarianism in the dance classroom', in S. Shapiro (ed.) *Dance, Power and Difference*, Champaign: Human Kinetics Publishers.

Smith-Autard, J. (1985) *Dance Composition: A Practical Guide for Teachers*, London: A & C Black.

—— (1994) *The Art of Dance in Education*, London: A & C Black.

Soares, J. (1992) *Louis Horst: Musician in a Dancer's World*, Durham: Duke University Press.

Stinson, S. (1998) 'Seeking a feminist pedagogy for children's dance', in S. Shapiro (ed.) *Dance, Power and Difference*, Champaign: Human Kinetics Publishers.

Stinson, S. W., Blumenfield-Jones, D. and Van Dyke, J. (1990) 'Voices of young women dance students: an interpretive study of meaning in dance', *Dance Research Journal*, 22: 12–22.

Tynjälä, P. (2000) *Oppiminen tiedon rakentamisena. Konstruktivistisen oppimiskäsityksen perusteita*, Helsinki: Tammi.

Van Manen, M. (1994) *Researching Lived Experience: Human Science for an Action Sensitive Pedagogy*, London, Ontario, Canada: The Althouse Press.

Varto, J. (1991) 'Laulu Maasta', *Filosofisia tutkimuksia Tampereen yliopistosta*, XXIII.

9 Supporting students' reflection in choreography classes

Äli Leijen

This chapter describes the main findings from my PhD research about pedagogical practices of reflection in choreography classes. This research was carried out in the Netherlands and aimed to explore pedagogical practices in higher professional dance education. In general, it can be classified as practice-led research, in that the relevance and aims of reflection, the distinction between the actual and desired situation of students' reflection, and the possibilities for bridging the two were determined by and based on teachers' visions, reservations and explanations embedded in their daily teaching practice.

In general, reflection in choreography classes is concerned with the individual agency of the student and her exploration process on the one hand, and the knowledge and skills related to the professional practice on the other. This allows the teacher to present what the professional domain stands for but it also gives space for the students to consider professional standards, to relate these to themselves, and their own work, and to select from the possibilities available in the diversity of today's practice of choreography. In order to connect these professional standards with one's own individuality, students need to be encouraged to reflect on themselves, their practice, and the dance domain.

This chapter is organized into three main sections. The first part gives a short overview of different notions of reflection in education, explains how these differentiate in terms of the focus and purpose of reflection and elaborates on the aims of reflection in choreography classes based on empirical findings. In the second part, I introduce the processes of reflection and give details of the difficulties choreography students might encounter while carrying out these processes. In the last section, I share the findings of a case study where streaming video and peer-feedback activities were used to support students' reflection processes in a choreography course.

Aims of reflection

Reflection can generally be defined as a cognitive process carried out in order to learn from experiences (Moon 2004) through individual inquiry and collaboration with others (Dewey 1933). It has been pointed out that reflection leads to deeper learning (Moon 2004), achievement of more complex and integrated knowledge structures, and more accessible and usable knowledge (Billing 2007). Despite consensus on the importance of reflection for learning, there are different interpretations of reflection in education. The three different perspectives are embedded in the philosophical traditions of pragmatism, critical social theory, and Kant.

In the tradition of pragmatism, reflection is concerned with becoming conscious of and thoughtful about one's actions, as opposed to using trial and error to deal with confusing and problematic situations (see Dewey 1933; Benammar 2004). Rational reasoning is often used to define a problematic issue, to map out a plan for dealing with the issue, and to carry this plan out. Since reflection is often aimed at improvement, very often the issues brought up for reflection are associated with apparent unsatisfactory aspects of one's own practice. Due to this, reflection in this tradition might be seen to foster a negative stance towards current practice.

The critical social theory perspective on reflection emphasizes the critical position of individuals and groups in relation to the actual situation. Reflection involves questioning existing assumptions, values, and perspectives that underlie people's actions, decisions and judgements. The purpose of questioning is to liberate people from their habitual ways of thinking and acting (for example Mezirow 1991). Gur-Ze'ev *et al.* (2001) feel that this practice of reflection is more related to alternative education and suggest that it is not possible in formal education owing to 'the hegemonic realm of self-evidence and the productive violence of social and cultural order' (2001: 93).

In addition to these two well-known approaches to reflection in education, a third approach was developed by Procee (2006). His systematic approach to reflection is based on Kant's distinction between *understanding* and *judgement*. The latter is associated with reflection: 'Understanding is related to the ability to grasp logical, theoretical, and conceptual rules; judgment is related to ability to connect experiences with rules' (Procee 2006: 247). As Procee argues,

> both are important in the field of education – students have to learn existing concepts and theories in their specialty (understanding), but they also have to learn to make connections between their state-of-art knowledge and the domains of reality in which they are operating (judgment).
>
> (Procee 2006: 247–8)

These connections can occur in two ways: either driven by pre-given concepts – *determinative judgement* – or driven by experiences – *reflective judgement*. Determinative judgement implies that a person stipulates and applies a set of rules or concepts in a particular practice. Reflective judgement is carried out when existing concepts or principles are limited and

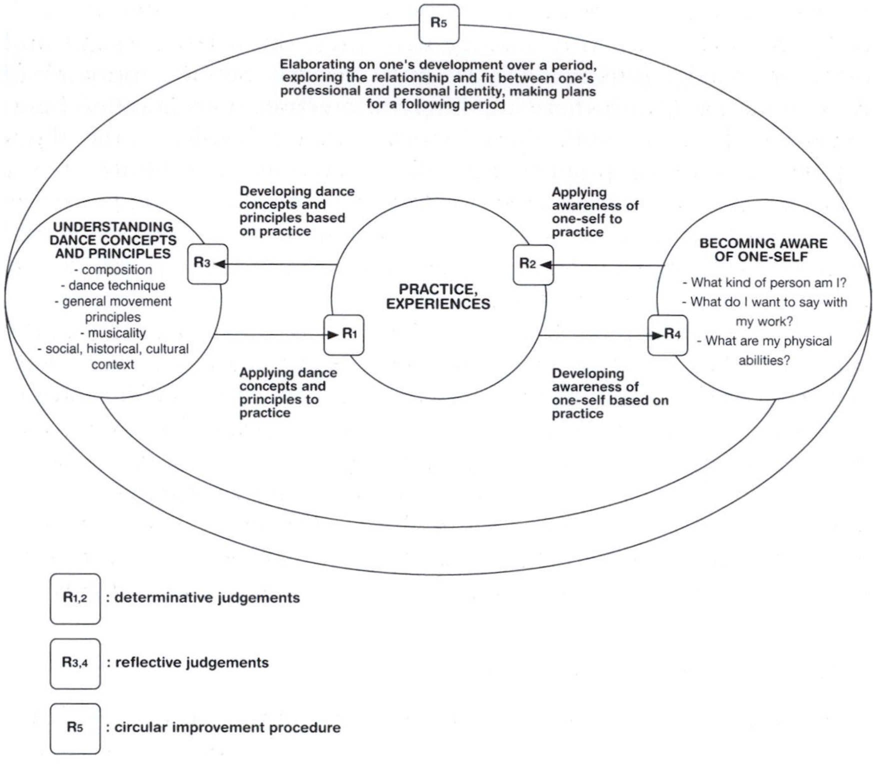

Figure 9.1 Leijen's model of pedagogical practices of reflection in tertiary dance education.

need to be developed based on a particular practice (Procee 2006). In accordance with the above, to reflect means both to compare and hold together one's conceptions and experiences in order to act with more self-confidence.

The research question of the study was the following: How can pedagogical practices of reflection in tertiary dance education be described in relation to the three different perspectives on reflection? The empirical study focused on the perceptions of choreography and dance technique teachers. Data were collected with semi-structured interviews. Researchers interpreted teachers' descriptions of supporting students' reflection using the three notions of reflection as sensitizing concepts (for a detailed overview of the methodology see Leijen *et al.* 2008).

Based on the series of data collection and analysis, a descriptive model (Figure 9.1) of common pedagogical practices of reflection was developed. The model incorporates five types of reflection. Four of the reflection types are related to the Kantian notion of reflection, where students are encouraged to reflect on: (1) how they apply concepts and principles related to dance disciplines in their dance practice, (2) how they apply concepts and principles derived from awareness of oneself and one's bodily possibilities in their dance practice, (3) which new concepts and principles related to dance discipline they have developed based on their dance practice, (4) which new concepts and principles related to themselves they have developed based on their dance practice. These types are mainly encouraged during the daily studio practice. The fifth type of reflection is related to the pragmatists' notion of reflection: (5) students are encouraged to elaborate on their development over a period of time, point out what needs further attention during a following period, and plan activities for enhancement.

The developed model of reflection does not include applications of the social critical notion of reflection. Although we found evidence of teachers encouraging their students to discuss issues related to the social, cultural, and historical contexts of the dance disciplines, arguably the main aim of such discussions is to develop understanding of the wider context of dance and appreciation of dance as an art form, and of other disciplines of art.

This model was developed based on choreography and dance technique teachers' descriptions of supporting students' reflection in their classes. Below I describe the reflection types regarding choreography classes.

Reflection in daily choreography classes

Regarding reflection on daily practice, we found from teachers that dance students are encouraged to reflect on the one hand on the core issues regarding the dance domain and profession and on the other hand on the self. This means that the focus of reflection in practical dance education concerns both the standards of the professional dance domain and subjectivity of the dance students. We explain below for what purposes choreography students are encouraged to carry out determinative and reflective judgements during daily practice.

Determinative judgements

Using the first type of reflection, students should analyse their kinaesthetic experiences in the light of predefined concepts and principles related to a dance discourse. These concepts and principles can be related to different dance styles, composition theories, or general notions, for example, postmodernism, related to a social, cultural, and historical context. Students are encouraged to elaborate on the extent to which they apply certain dance principles to their practice based on specific evaluation criteria that describe the accurate usage of these principles. For example, jazz dance choreography teacher A explained that she asks students to reflect on how they apply the form and structure of jazz dance in their own choreographic work. Prior to this, they have discussed in class the jazz dance forms and structures and the styles and dynamics related to specific forms.

Using the second type of reflection, students should analyse their kinaesthetic experiences in the light of the concepts and principles relating to themselves. These include personality, which includes the social and cultural background of the student; preferences, which point to interests a student wishes to share and express in dance art; and bodily possibilities. For example, modern dance choreography teacher B described how she often facilitates this type of reflection by asking students to prepare a text with their own story about something that is meaningful to them. Following this, students choose parts of the text and compose movements inspired by the selected ideas. The teacher emphasized that this assignment allows the students to bring in their own individuality and personal stories, and to reflect on how they apply those stories to their own artistic work.

Reflective judgements

Students are also expected to discover concepts and principles based on their own practice using reflective judgement; the third and fourth types of reflection are related to these judgements. The third type of reflection aims to create new dance concepts and principles. It can appear in two ways. First, learned concepts become more meaningful through practice when they are embedded in practical experiences or, based on their experiences, when students perceive a concept in a new way. Secondly, students develop new concepts or principles while practising. For example, modern dance choreography teacher C gave an example on how she encourages this type of reflection for learning about the use of different spatial levels in choreography. She sets a task based on rolling, kneeling and standing, and asks the students to create a compositional sequence exploring levels and differences between them.

Using the fourth type of reflection, students develop awareness of themselves, discovering personality traits or meaningful themes for choreographic work, or learning about their bodily possibilities and limits. Improvisation teacher D gave the following example of how she applies this type of reflection in her teaching:

> I do a lot of exercises where they have to work together in pairs, and that tells them a lot about how they communicate with other people in dance. For instance, you can be someone who likes an action–reaction form like in a conversation, but you can have also a conversation in dance. I do a movement and you react to that movement, and then I do another and you react again, so you get action–reaction. Or it is possible that you like to follow somebody, the other person; he or she takes the initiative and you follow. Or, you could be someone who copies, who does not have a lot of ideas of your own, but likes to copy the person you are working with. Those are things that you can reflect on: how does this work for me?
>
> (Interviewee D, November 2006)

Reflection over a longer period

Regarding reflection over a longer period, we find that students are encouraged to make explicit those aspects that can be improved in their practice. A linear procedure is applied for this type of reflection. Students write a reflective piece on a previous period, in which they give an overview of their development, pointing out areas of improvement and aspects that need to be further developed. They are asked to set goals for the following study period and realize these. During mentor meetings, students are expected to be able to motivate and further elaborate their viewpoints on their development. Mentors pose questions during the discussion, and give their views on matters under discussion. Semester reports and teachers' evaluations are also discussed at these meetings. In principle, this procedure of reflection is similar to the use of Personal Development Plans.

Besides encouraging the cyclical improvement procedures related to the pragmatists' notion of reflection, dance students are also encouraged to reflect on their professional identity. Students are supported to consider the relationship and fit between their personal and professional identity related to different agencies in the dance profession. Various questions are addressed here. For example, which area in the professional dance community might best suit me? What might be expected from me? What is missing in my 'toolbox'? At that point, the results from these distinct domains of reflection (the domain of dance and the domain of self) on daily practice become very informative. Besides the considerations and comparisons, it is here that the two areas become closely intertwined, so that students are able to make informed choices for specialization in studies and further career in the professional community.

Reflection on the developed model

The developed descriptive model of the practices of reflection incorporates the somewhat different views on reflection in dance education described in earlier studies. Anttila (2003) introduced the term *thoughtful motion*, where bodily sensitivity is coupled with thoughtfulness and fosters conscious reflection about dance experiences. Stinson (1995) also emphasizes sensory perception and reflection of the lived experience of the body. These ideas of reflection are mostly associated with reflective judgements, carried out to develop awareness about oneself based on practical experiences. Besides advocating the benefits of reaching reflection through internal inquiry of personal experience, other authors (Warburton 2004; Lavender 1996; Lavender and Predock-Linnell 2001) point out the need for developing dance students' critical thinking skills about their own and others' dance works. This perspective on reflection is associated with determinative and reflective judgements aimed to connect practical experiences with the concepts and principles generally related to the dance domain.

In brief, the descriptive model of these pedagogical practices of reflection can be of practical relevance for tertiary dance institutes since it presents five distinct types of reflection that dance educators can explicitly integrate in their teaching practices to support students' reflection activities. However, the model focuses specifically on the pedagogical aims of reflection. The next section describes which specific processes students are engaged in while carrying out the different types of reflection and touches upon some of the obstacles students can experience. These reported obstacles, like the pedagogical aims of reflection, are based on teachers' perceptions and experiences.

The processes of reflection

According to Procee (2006), the four general processes of reflection in an educational setting are: describing an experience, evaluating an experience, learning from multiple perspectives, and reflecting on the reflection process. The findings of a previous study (Leijen *et al.* 2007) suggest that the first three processes in dance education are often carried out to enhance students' professional competences during daily studio practice and the last is mostly associated with reflecting on how students see their learning process and their development over a longer period of time.

In the first reflection process, dance students need to look at their performance experience from a more objective perspective, as though they were the actions of another. Reaching this aim is challenging in performing arts (Leijen *et al.* 2007) owing to the fact that students' perception of their own experience is often influenced by implicit and explicit knowledge about the movement vocabulary and by feelings associated with concrete experience. What dance students think or feel about a movement often differs from the actual physical image of the movement.

Regarding the second reflection process – evaluating an experience – dance students should trust the validity of their experiences without spending a lot of time worrying about the judgements of others. The results of a previous study suggest that students tend to wait for the teacher to provide corrections instead of evaluating their experiences themselves (Leijen *et al.* 2007). In addition, it was found that dance students might lack the criteria for evaluation, or tend to focus on those aspects in which they made mistakes, and fail to notice positive aspects.

The third reflection process – learning from multiple perspectives – involves dance students considering their performance experiences from different viewpoints. These viewpoints can be embedded in different theoretical notions but can also represent the different perspectives of peers and the teacher. Leijen *et al.* (2007) point out that carrying out this process can be challenging, as it may be difficult for students to question teachers' comments, or indeed to share their own ideas with classmates. Students' responses might include feelings of vulnerability that follow from exposing their perceptions and beliefs to others. This occurs especially if the locus of control is not with the individual.

Finally, reflecting on the reflection process can also be challenging for students since it requires developing a meta-view over one's own learning process. Moreover, reflection on reflection also addresses the relationship and fit between the personal and professional identity of the students. Besides enabling awareness of the self, which can be challenging to recognize, reflection activities in an educational setting often imply that the private areas of learning become public. The latter can be a source of additional sensitivity.

In brief, reflection activities can be challenging for students. The next section describes how the processes of students' reflection can be supported more effectively.

Supporting the processes of reflection: a case study

In higher education, web-based learning environments are commonly used to support students' reflection on their competences. Video has become increasingly popular in professional learning because of its unique ability to capture the richness and complexity of practices for later analysis. This section describes a case study carried out in a composition class, where streaming video and peer-feedback activities were applied to support the processes of students' reflection and to facilitate ways of overcoming the difficulties of the reflection processes described in the previous section.

The case study relates to a short composition course where face-to-face classes took place four times per week over a period of two weeks. Students created short compositions during the course. Special attention was paid to exploring and applying personal intentions in these compositions, and to developing awareness about the use of space and how spatial decisions support students' choreographic intentions. To support the processes of students' reflection, assignments were designed in collaboration with the teacher.

Reflection assignments were carried out using a video-based learning environment DiViDU (see Figure 9.2). DiViDU is developed for supporting authentic learning tasks; it covers three learning processes: learning to analyse authentic situations, learning to reflect on these situations, and learning to demonstrate acquired competences. Based on these didactic models, the environment comprises three modules (analysis, reflection and assessment). The reflection module was used for this study. In this module, teachers can reuse and create learning tasks for students using templates. The learning tasks are carried out using a video recording of students' practices. Students make digital video recordings of their practice using a video camera, select video fragments during video editing and upload these on a streaming media server. All learning activities are integrated in one environment, this was also the main reason why

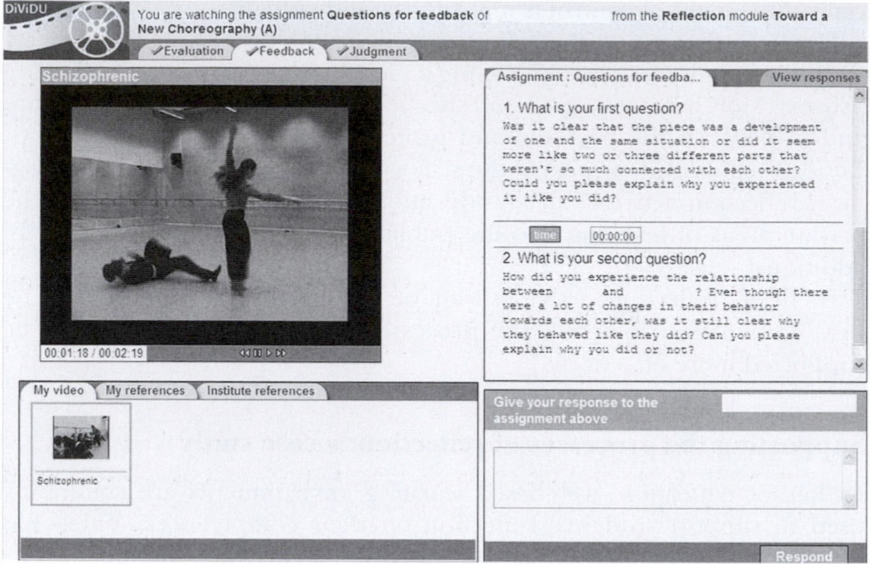

Figure 9.2 Screen capture of a reflection assignment in a choreography class in DiViDU environment.

DiViDU was chosen to facilitate the three processes of reflection in this case study.[1]

In our case study, students recorded their compositions on video, edited the videos (e.g., applied slow motion function on certain fragments) and uploaded them to the streaming video server. Viewing the composition on video aimed to facilitate students' description of their compositions. In order to evaluate the compositions recorded on video, students were asked to answer questions posed by the teacher. Students evaluated their experiences based on subjective criteria, for example,

> Please evaluate your own spatial decision making in relation to the outcome of your choreographic intentions. What worked, what did not work? Why? More importantly, as you look at the video, what new questions and impulses arise for you?

In order to learn from these multiple perspectives, students were asked to pose two questions for feedback. Each student received feedback from at least two peers. The use of streaming video influenced the three processes of students' reflections as perceived by the composition class students and the teacher in the following way.

Describing experiences

In order to support describing the experiences, students first edited their compositions (performed by peer students) and viewed them on video. Interestingly, video editing was often seen as a preliminary activity prior to reflection, though some students mentioned that editing helped them choose a starting point and was useful for describing and evaluating specific moments. Regarding video viewing, half of the students reported that the facilitation resulted in positive influences, and the other half indicated either a negative influence or no influence. Some students stated that since they had seen the combination already in class, viewing the recording of the composition was not useful. Others indicated that the video projected a more realistic view of the composition. Student A explained this as follows:

> In your mind, somehow, you can always make it richer than it actually was. So seeing it on video is more confronting, more real; you see it as it really was.
>
> (Interviewee A, March 2007)

Similarly, the teacher of the course indicated that viewing the composition on video helped students to describe it:

> They see a live performance, but seeing it on a real screen distances them from it; they see just what is happening. They don't, of course, see every element of the way they did it in real life, and the flatness has an effect, but I think it helps them to start to conceive a performance as an independent object outside the self.
>
> (Interviewee E, March 2007)

In addition, some students indicated that viewing the composition on video helped them to develop understanding of the composition as a whole or to consider the work from the audience's perspective.

Evaluating experiences

Students evaluated their compositions following the questions and criteria provided by the teacher. The majority of the students pointed out positive influences of the facilitation on their evaluation processes. The most prevalent positive influence was that answering the questions helped students to think and become more precise in reasoning. Student B explained this as follows:

> Becoming precise, because before it was more like a feeling and I didn't have clear arguments for why I did what I did. It helped me to write things down to get them clear in my mind, and to have not only

> a feeling but something concrete that I could start working on.
>
> (Interviewee B, March 2007)

Overall, the teacher was satisfied with the students' self-evaluations. He explained,

> DiViDU was a second forum where they could continue their thinking, and they were good. It was nice to see that the growth they made in class continued in the electronic medium ... everyone was quite clear, and I did not have a feeling that it was just writing for the sake of writing; they really thought about it, and this was the result of their thinking.
>
> (Interviewee E, March 2007)

The teacher also indicated, however, that self-evaluation did not include conceptualization of ideas and remained on the level of the concrete experience:

> I felt that most of the self-evaluation in DiViDU was at the level of functionality; like did it work, did it not work, and did it cohere with my intentions at the beginning?
>
> (Interviewee E, March 2007)

Learning from multiple perspectives

Peer-feedback activities were adopted to facilitate relating to multiple perspectives. Students posed two questions and received feedback on these from their peers.

In comparison to viewing oneself on video, and carrying out self-assessments, online feedback on compositions was considered the most influential facilitation for reflection by the composition class students. Feedback helped students to realize to what extent their choreographic intentions were manifested in the compositions, and provided alternative perspectives for their compositions. Student G indicated:

> It was really interesting to see the feedback, because sometimes your mind is really so closed: you have your idea and you go this way, and you can't see the other ways. The feedback was broadening, it helped me to see things differently.
>
> (Interviewee G, March 2007)

Both the teacher and students indicated that students felt safe sharing their ideas. The teacher explained this as follows:

> In this setting they do begin to articulate themselves, and because everyone articulated themselves, you know, regardless of language

> difficulties and whatever, I felt that it was a good egalitarian structure; it doesn't become some sort of social game, it is really just about the material.
>
> (Interviewee E, March 2007)

Finally, although the teacher agreed that alternatives were provided in the feedback, he also noted:

> It was focused on practicality, like what you need to do to fix things as opposed to what I imagine you are thinking about when I see this; it didn't get to the conceptual space behind the action, it dealt primarily with the physical world.
>
> (Interviewee E, March 2007)

Reflection on the case study findings and concluding remarks

The findings are encouraging since we demonstrated that video-based ICT facilitation can be valuable for supporting choreography students' reflection processes since it helps teachers guide their students and opens up new possibilities for students to take more responsibility and ownership in their learning.

Thinking 'outside the box' of one's experience and seeing it from a more objective perspective is a challenging task not only for choreography students but for people in general. It is easier to view others' experiences, and therefore it is easier for an experienced teacher to mirror the experiences to the students. However, the danger here is that students become passive and dependent on the teacher. This can increase the barrier for self-reflection since students may merely wait for the teacher to give corrections instead of evaluating their experiences by themselves. Moreover, since teachers are supposedly experts in a particular subject matter it can be difficult for the students to question the corrections and comments provided by the teacher. This is all despite the fact that the aim of the dance teachers is to encourage students to become active in learning and take more responsibility and ownership for it. The findings of the current study are therefore particularly important since we have shown that observing one's efforts on video can help students to observe their experience from a more objective perspective and notice new features about the experience.

Although seeing oneself on video is a powerful support for reflection, it can fall short on its own. While reflecting on experiences captured on video, students also need to choose a focus and evaluate a particular aspect. The challenge here is that students might not know which criteria are useful for evaluating a particular aspect of their experiences. What we have shown in the current study is that teachers can provide guidance for self-evaluation by posing questions and criteria. This, in turn, allows students to learn about the standards in professional practice and make use of them for considering themselves. As summarized by a student in the course, 'You can be your own teacher in a way'.

Besides describing and evaluating one's practice, reflection also entails considering an experience from multiple perspectives. For example, one can consider the experience in the light of different theoretical notions (e.g. specific composition theories in dance) or try to understand how the experience can be seen and interpreted by different bodies in a professional dance domain with audience members. The latter is especially important since dance is a performing art and besides becoming aware of how a student experiences dance by him- or herself it is important to learn how it can be interpreted by others. For that purpose, we decided to encourage students to give peer feedback. What we discovered is that viewing video of dance practice prior to giving feedback also supported peer students to become more specific in their feedback. Some students considered their feedback in the online environment to be more rational than in face-to-face situations. The assignment also fostered students to think how they can be constructive in their comments so that the feedback receiver can make the best use of it. These findings are interesting since we have found that students can also learn how to give feedback to their peers when facilitated by ICT.

Finally, some interesting findings regarding the reflection outcomes were reported by the teacher. These findings suggest that direct video observation guided by teachers' questions might not be sufficient for students' reflection on the conceptual questions and on a more general level of practical experience. Van den Berg (2001) noted similar results from research carried out in the teacher education context. She found that while reflecting on the exemplary teaching video footage, the student teachers presented well-defined images of the teaching shown in the video recording, but remained at low levels of abstraction in their ideas about teaching. Further research, therefore, should be focused on investigating more effective facilitation for supporting conceptualization of ideas used in practical experience and for helping students to develop a more general view of experiences as opposed to focusing merely on specific details.

Acknowledgement

I wish to thank dance teachers, who work in four different dance academies in the Netherlands, and students, who study in one Dutch dance academy, for sharing their ideas and experiences with me and for participating in this research.

Note

1 For further information about DiViDU, see http://info.dividu.nl/

References

Anttila, E. (2003) 'A dream journey into the unknown: Searching for dialogue in dance education', unpublished doctoral dissertation, Theatre Academy of Finland – Helsinki, Finland.

Benammar, K. (2004) 'Conscious action through conscious thinking – reflection tools in experiential learning', public seminar, Amsterdam: Amsterdam University Press.

Billing, D. (2007) 'Teaching for transfer of core/key skills in higher education: Cognitive skills', *Higher Education*, 53: 483–516.

Dewey, J. (1933) *How we Think*, Buffalo, NY: Prometheus Books.

Gur-Ze'ev, I., Masschelein, J. and Blake, N. (2001) 'Reflectivity, reflection, and counter-education', *Studies in Philosophy and Education*, 20 (2): 93–106.

Lavender, L. (1996) *Dancers Talking Dance: Critical Evaluation in the Choreography Class*, Champaign, IL: Human Kinetics.

Lavender, L. and Predock-Linnell, J. (2001) 'From improvisation to choreography: the critical bridge', *Research in Dance Education*, 2 (2): 195–209.

Leijen, Ä., Admiraal, W., Wildschut, L. and Simons, P. R. J. (2008) 'Pedagogy before technology: What should an ICT intervention facilitate in practical dance classes?', *Teaching in Higher Education*, 13 (2): 219–31.

Leijen, Ä., Lam, I., Wildschut, L. and Simons, P. R. J. (2007) 'Challenges to face: Difficulties dance students encounter with reflection and how to overcome these', presented at the conference Onderzoek in Cultuureducatie [Research in Culture Education], Utrecht, The Netherlands.

Mezirow, J. (1991) *Transformative Dimensions of Adult Learning*, San Francisco, CA: Jossey-Bass.

Moon, J.A. (2004) *Reflection in Learning and Professional Development*, New York: Routledge Falmer.

Procee, H. (2006) 'Reflection in education: A Kantian epistemology', *Educational Theory*, 56 (3): 237–362.

Stinson, S. W. (1995) 'Body of knowledge', *Educational Theory*, 45 (1): 43–54.

Van den Berg, E. (2001) 'An exploration of the use of multimedia cases as reflective tool in teacher education', *Research in Science Education*, 31 (2): 245–65.

Warburton, E. C. (2004) 'Knowing what it takes: The effect of perceived learner advantages on dance teachers' use of critical-thinking activities', *Research in Dance Education*, 5 (1): 69–82.

10 Dance analysis in a postmodern age

Integrating theory and practice

Bonnie Rowell

An important challenge facing teachers of dance analysis today is to achieve a balance between a systematic and thorough approach to dance study (including dance analysis and choreography – and I see these two as intimately linked) and one that is appropriately flexible, inclusive and open-ended. So one wants to draw upon sound theoretical foundations and encourage attention to detail, but at the same time avoid the prescriptive and formulaic. This, of course, is much easier said than done. Postmodern choreographies seem to pose problems for traditional models of dance analysis in terms of their choreographic construction, as well as the sorts of statements that they make. It follows that those concepts of dance analysis that base dance's perceptual features on temporal, spatial and dynamic qualities will be inadequate for the discussion of dances whose central concerns provide a challenge to these qualities, as postmodern choreographies arguably do. Yet such concepts are embedded in widely employed models for dance analysis.

These concerns may impinge on other areas of dance scholarship too, with students often seeing little connection between theory and practice: between problems with which they are asked to engage in 'academic' lectures that are to do with perception and understanding, and their focus in practice-based classes which they may perceive as calling only on their physical and creative capabilities. Some of the difficulties encountered in undergraduate teaching on university dance degree programmes arise because many of our students arrive with just this sort of dualistic attitude. The integration of theory and practice that tacitly underpins dance programmes cannot therefore be taken for granted and is by no means a given or even easily accepted principle, but is a process that needs to be taught. A dualistic attitude to dance as a medium is, in any case, everywhere embedded within the profession: for example, with the traditional notion that dancers are in some way the malleable material of choreographers and that their job is to do their bidding; with the notion that dancers somehow subjugate their bodies to the service of their art. This latter idea is especially prevalent at present with the cult of the 'sculpted' body: one that is honed and refined at the gymnasium in order to conform to a fashionable image. That these ideas still persist in an age where a holistic attitude to the self also prevails is perhaps surprising, but nevertheless the case. Sondra Fraleigh acknowledges the pervasiveness of this attitude – dualistic language permeates dance literature, she notes, with a tendency to objectify the dancer's body as instrument (Fraleigh 1987: 11). There is clearly a need to re-examine approaches and redefine the key areas for artistic attention, in the light of new ideas about dance making and critical practices.

There have been additional (but, I would argue, related) concerns in recent years with the whole vexed notion of artistic value and the status of meaning – how to foster the ability to make interpretative and qualitative judgements within a postmodern context which acknowledges the strengths of post-structural models for understanding (such as intertextual and deconstructive theoretical practices) without falling into some of their inherent pitfalls. The latter may include a tendency towards solipsism, an over-reliance on personal interpretation and an 'anything goes' ethos, a distrust of rigorous philosophical underpinning or worse, a distrust of philosophy. On this topic, I put trust in the slogan adopted by Graham McFee in acknowledging multi-layeredness and complexity in interpretation, that just because there is no *one* right answer, it does not mean that 'anything goes' (McFee 1992: 28–9),[1] the validity of which will become clear.

That intertextual and deconstructive strategies are valuable to dance studies is abundantly clear. The chief advantages of intertextual readings are that they recognise the complexity of artistic communication and acknowledge the active participation of the viewer. However, it is easy to mistake complexity for value under this model, and intertextuality appears to offer little by which an evaluative criticism may be made in terms of a moral position or worldview, over and above a *reflection* of the way in which we live.[2] It is questionable, too, whether an intertextual strategy is adequate to identify and then to convey the *artistic* and media specific significance of a dance, in particular, the affective quality of the movement, a component that it is possible to neglect under post-structuralist models. These issues – the importance of being able to judge artworks and the *artistic* significance of dance – are important issues for students to take on board, but are neglected in the current climate. It is also possible to underemphasise or even ignore the inherence of 'ideas' within the artwork, particularly in the case of dance, and consequently that these ideas originate from intentional human beings – choreographers and dancers. Recognition (and interrogation) of *their* roles would make it more likely that these ideas reveal more than just a reflection *of* the way in which we live, a reflection that predominates in models of meaning that are inspired by cultural studies, but a reflection *on* the way we live too.

The hallmarks of postmodern dance, then, are open-endedness of interpretative possibility together with the subversion of normative assumptions. These challenges, although they may not be quite as radical as they appear to be on the surface, do free up the role of the audience and place the emphasis on creativity and the imagination, in other words, on artistic qualities and this is all to the good. Another positive factor in deconstructive analysis is the rigour with which the text is interrogated. It is a shame then that the several advantages of post-structuralist models, frequently seem to coincide with a marginalisation of analytic philosophy, a marginalisation that is detrimental both to dance study and to philosophy of the arts.

In my own teaching, I attempt a pragmatic integration of the best that structuralist (Adshead *et al.* 1988), post-structuralist (Foster 1986; Adshead-Lansdale 1999) and analytic philosophical (McFee 1992) methodologies offer, by placing emphasis on attention to detail, but also by placing emphasis on how significance is determined in the first place – on what detail we are to attend to and how we recognise it. In this, I find myself drawing more and more upon students' embodied knowledge of technique systems and choreographic processes in order to tease out the nuances of meaning as well as the predilection towards certain kinds of meaning that appear to be embedded within movement vocabularies and choreographic relationships – in other words, the dancer–director/choreographer/creator–audience connection. Chris Challis argues that dance styles embody meaning in a fundamental way:

> Technique is not a system of training, but a system of education through which a dancer acquires not only bodily shape and facility but also learns the traditions, conventions and values which underpin the concept of dance being taught: the artistic body is thus skilful, intelligent and expressive of that form.
>
> (Challis 1999: 145)

If this is true, then this considerably strengthens the argument that a minimal physical accomplishment is necessary to understand a dance in that particular style. The least that can be suggested here is that investigation of models of embodiment in relation to dance understanding (and choreographic sensibility) would seem appropriate activities.

This chapter aims to address problems that are particular to postmodern dances; to suggest ways in which these problems may be tackled through an integrative approach in teaching, specifically through a philosophical concept of embodiment that is useful in unravelling some of their complexities; and to flag up ways in which this model of embodiment differs from how the term may be used elsewhere. In particular, it serves to explain and cohere with our perception of dances as they are performed in relation to our experience of dancing. I will first explain why I think that a philosophical model is so important in relation to teaching dance analysis and choreography; secondy, I will describe and explain in some detail a specific model of embodiment. I will then flag up ways in which this model may serve to underpin issues of originality, creativity and value in dance works – issues that have been particularly problematised under the conditions of postmodernity. Lastly, I will argue the implications for dance and explain how these ideas might work in practice.

Embodiment, dance and philosophy

Reasons for analytic philosophy's lack of toe-hold in university dance departments is partly due to contemporary philosophers' general lack of interest in dance,[3] in comparison to interest in the other arts, and this results in a lack of established philosophical aesthetics of dance (McFee 1999: 1). But analytic philosophy has had something of a bad press in recent years from dance theorists too,[4] so it has been a two-way distrust, with 'positivist', 'essentialist' or 'dualist' labels being ascribed to analytic philosophical positions. This distrust to some extent follows Derrida's project to undermine Western philosophical assumptions and values (Derrida 1978), but it is also due to a shift of focus away from a model of *dance as art*, towards a model of dance as cultural phenomenon. Challis discusses the loss of consideration of dance in its art object status in favour of an over-reliance on contexts in current dance theory:

> The fashionable idea in dance writing in the past decade has been to locate dance meaning within what Crowther (1997: 1) terms 'semiotic idealism', that is to say that the art object is not seen as an aesthetic object, but as a site for interpretation in terms of race, gender, sexuality and class.
>
> (Challis 1999: 143)

Interest in these areas of discussion was of course long overdue and the attention they attract now has immeasurable worth, but it has meant that interest in dance has in recent years favoured the social and political over the essentially artistic, to the detriment of both choreographic teaching and dance analysis. A balance needs to be struck.

In answer to the marginalisation of philosophy in relation to dance, I draw on McFee who argues that it is only the discipline of philosophy that can cohere other perspectives and who consequently outlines a commitment to three formative ideas:

> first … an honourable dance studies – one that [is] more than a collection of the history of dance, the sociology of dance, the anthropology of dance, etc. – would need a centre base in philosophy; second [is] the need for any philosophical investigations here to be consistent with, and to derive from, other philosophical commitment (since, as David Best put it, 'philosophy is one subject'); third [is] the need to preserve *roughly* the same account of dance as its practitioners give – that philosophy here should not be radically revisionary.
>
> (McFee 1999: 155)

So McFee, in urging consistency, is not just arguing for consistent treatment within the philosophy of the arts, though this would accord dance its long overdue recognition and status within them, but also consistency in relation to dance *as it is currently practised by its creators and performers*. A basic assumption that underpins this paper is that dance analysis has to be taught in tandem with aesthetic investigation into the medium and that what dance *is*, its nature, is of primary concern. A further implication is that it also has to be taught in tandem with practical investigation in order to preserve a holistic approach. Since the ontology of dance can only be discussed in terms of a philosophical framework, then that framework needs to be central to any account of understanding dance as art. But there is no overlooking the fact that the medium of dance involves the body,[5] and it is therefore crucial to clarify the nature of the medium, not just in terms of the body as site for political and social comment, but in relation to the body in its artistic transformation (see Challis 1999).

Theories of embodiment abound, but it is useful here to make a distinction between a philosophical concept of embodiment, one that interrogates the *nature* of the relationship between self and other, and notions of embodiment employed within other disciplines which primarily focus on the ways that different cultures conceptualise the body and draw upon cultural frameworks for that conceptualisation.[6] The areas overlap and get confused, but a philosophical concept of dance art foregrounds the body in an artistic dimension, with social aspects being dealt with contingently. Phenomenology has attracted many dance theorists for this reason. Francis Sparshott (1995: 5), for example, explains why dance is seen as a unique case amongst the arts, because the medium of dance involves the transformation of the dancer's self: it involves more than just the dancer's body. The consequences for Sparshott are that dancers are embodied minds, not minds attached to bodies. It follows that we simultaneously see persons dancing as well as persons transformed; that is, that we see embodied minds, but we see them in the context of artistic practice. Interestingly, the matter of how one is to 'read' the body in relation to person dancing or person transformed in an art context tends to be foregrounded in many current choreographers' work: for example, in works as diverse as those of Merce Cunningham, Mark Morris or Philippe Decouflé.[7]

Sparshott's analysis is specific to the case of dance, whereas art philosopher Paul Crowther's interest in embodiment theory pertains to a wider context of art. The latter incorporates a theory of perception and reception that concerns our interaction as human beings with the world, in which the interaction is reciprocal. In this, he draws upon the work of phenomenologist Maurice Merleau-Ponty (1972) who stresses the primacy of bodily experience in perception: in which consciousness is not a purely mental phenomenon, but a function of the integrated operation of all the senses. Perception is therefore acknowledged to be creative, as well as being pre-reflective and this idea has important consequences for our reception of postmodern artworks as well as for ways in which we value them, as we shall see.

A 'holistic' theory of embodiment

Thus Crowther (1993b) draws on ideas that derive from both the Western philosophical tradition and continental philosophy as well as post-structuralist readings, and draws what are often currently seen as irreconcilable positions together. In locating interpretation of artworks within this pluralist perspective, we have one of the main advantages of the model: that it presents a contemporary and non-positivist perspective that at the same time implicates notions of value. So while the importance and relevance of historical, social and cultural locations are appreciated, a more complex interaction with the artwork is explored, which at the same time denies any tendency towards absolutism or relativism.

Crowther suggests an account of art and embodiment that derives specifically from Merleau-Ponty's later theory of mind. Merleau-Ponty's account is attractive first and foremost because of its lack of distinction between subject and object, in favour of the notion that human beings 'inhere in the sensible' (Crowther 1993b: 1). In the relationship between the individual subject and the world, the special position of aesthetic perception within human perception is foregrounded and further, the special position of *artistic* perception within that field of value is privileged, and this is an important insight. This model reflects the fusion of the sensual and the conceptual that McFee (2003: 121–2) among others[8] also identifies as crucial to an understanding of the reception of artworks. Importantly, this fusion is also *reflected* in artworks.

So Crowther's 'ecological' theory of mind is predicated on reciprocity – it deals with the detail of our interaction with the world as well as with how we reflect upon the world and how we are reflected within it – a two way interaction. The artwork is accorded a special position in revealing the nature of our interaction with the world to us. The nature of our embodiment, the way in which human beings inhere in the world in this scheme, offers us an *explanation* of embodied knowledge that avoids dualism by addressing the notion of the embodiment of meaning as well as our physical embodiment as self-conscious beings. The interdependence of these two is consequently of particular interest to dance scholars.

This model of embodiment also serves to resolve some of the problems of indeterminacy that may pose a problem within some post-structuralist models of meaning (such as intertextual readings) and proposes an alternative view of postmodernity – one in which the notions of originality, value and decipherability may be included. To flesh out this account of embodiment, the nature of the relationship between ourselves and 'otherness' within this model is represented in my own diagram, Figure 10.1, which is freely adapted from the Crowther text.

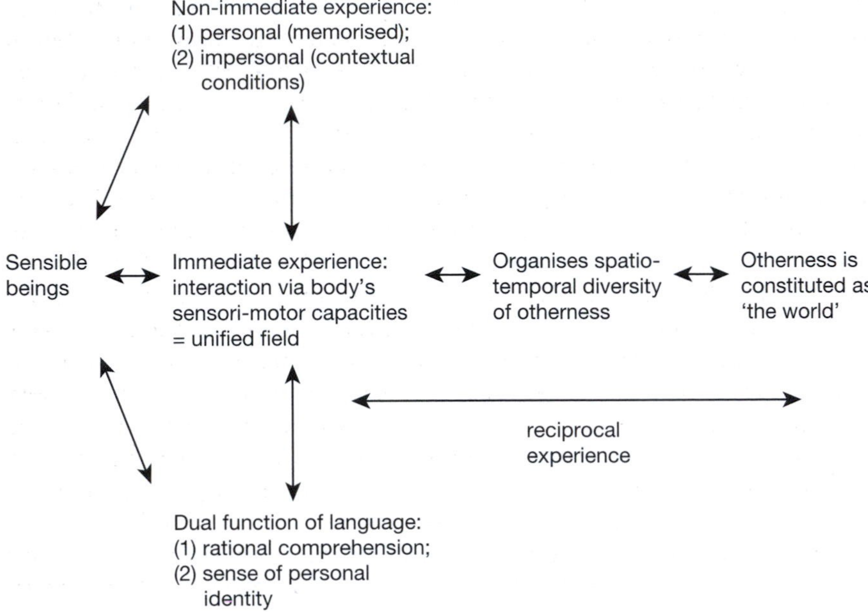

Figure 10.1 Rowell's diagram to illustrate Paul Crowther's (1993b) model for a reciprocal interaction with the world (adapted from the text).

These relations may be usefully summarised as follows: humans interact with each other and with the world in a sensual as well as psychological way, via the body's sensori-motor capacities, included in language on the one hand and memory on the other. Language has a dual function in that it gives us the ability for rationally comprehending the world as well as a sense of personal identity, and language thus plays a crucial and unifying role in our experience of self and other. Added to this, our interaction, as well as being informed by immediate physical and sensory conditions, is also informed by non-immediate experience. Thus the historical dimension, both personal in the sense of our memorised experience and impersonal in the sense of the contextual conditions surrounding our interaction (or, for example, the contextual conditions that surround the production of artworks), has another crucial role to play. In our interaction with the world and with others, we organise the spatio-temporal diversity of 'otherness', reconstituting it as 'the world'. But our current interpretation of events feeds back into the processes of our perception of future events, so that the process is reciprocal.

A dance example will help to clarify this rather complex description. In Mark Morris's 'Waltz of the Snow Flakes' from Act 1, *The Hard Nut* (1991), the viewer may take a sensual delight in the patterns that are created by the dancers, together with their manifest commitment; or, s/

he may be struck by the dangers inherent in fast spatial exchanges and nearly colliding bodies. S/he may also appreciate the humour of the situation – of large men in pointe shoes and tutus who are fully committed to balletic elevation, however improbable that appears. All of these impressions are immediate experiences in Crowther's model terms. The dance, though, also draws upon the viewer's memory (non-immediate experience) of previous *Nutcracker*s in a personal and in an impersonal way – we are reminded of previous productions that we have witnessed. We are, for example, aware of the contextual conditions of their production, the values inherent in classical ballet, of hierarchical order and of aspirations to a transcendent ideal of humanity. In other words, our knowledge of the contextual conditions surrounding the dance feed into and inform our direct experience of the current production. In this way, our experience of the artwork has brought us to re-evaluate our perceptions of a variety of things, with gender relations, dance values and conventions perhaps being foremost on the list. But experience of the dance will also affect our perception of those things in the future, such that our appreciation of, for example, future performances of *The Nutcracker* (including 'traditional' versions) will inevitably change.[9] The process has been reciprocal, in that our experience has shaped our perception of the artwork, but the artwork has also irrevocably changed our experience and perceptual processes.

The key point here is that, our experience of the world both physically and psychologically operates as a 'unified field'. It follows then that the relationship between the self and 'otherness' is one of reciprocity. For Crowther, this question takes on the emphasis of how to understand our interaction with the world without 'losing the sense of unity of the experience' (1993b: 2), hence he terms it an 'ecological' or holistic theory, in contrast to an analytic theory. In analysing, we fragment and lose the whole picture, and this, then, is where traditional philosophy fails, whereas an appreciation of the *unfragmented* experience can only be accomplished through an acknowledgement of our phenomenological inherence in the world. The way that we can grasp the totality of our interaction is via artworks – through their creation as well as through their appreciation. That is, in artistic creativity we fabricate complex entities that both reflect and give sense to our experience and in their capacity to function in multiple ways, artworks have the capability to reflect the complexity of our reciprocal interaction with the world, without fragmenting that experience. Art is appreciated in its objects; that is, it has a direct and physical or sensual dimension as well as a conceptual one. The artwork in its very nature thus reflects the complex inter-relatedness of our sensual and conceptual grasp of the world.

These insights have far-reaching consequences for our appreciation of artworks in general, but we can also see how important this account might be for dance, in which the materials of the art form are constituted in the intentional moving human body (intentional here on the part of the maker of dances as well as her material, the dancers). However, Crowther uses this model to propose a radical solution to problems involved in an account of artistic originality and creativity and as this too finds particular resonance with dance as an art form, a discussion of these ideas follows.

Originality, creativity and value

Under the conditions of modernism, the concept of value was intimately related to concepts of originality and authenticity and an artwork was only thought to be original if it broke entirely with traditional rules and radicalised the way in which artworks of its kind were both created and perceived. However, the capacities of originality and value have been problematised within the debate surrounding postmodernism, given two commonly held views of postmodern artworks: first, that innovation is an impossibility, given the condition of modernity,[10] and this produces a tension with the concept of creativity; and second, that evaluation is either irrelevant or in some way hierarchical and discriminatory (Banes 1987; Eco 1984; Jameson 1983).

For example, post-structuralist theory, such as that proposed by Roland Barthes, denies originality to artworks. Barthes holds that the work of art is a historically and culturally situated artefact that draws upon existing traditions and reconstitutes them. It cannot therefore be original (Barthes 1968). Arthur Danto (1981) similarly questions art's claim to originality but for different reasons: the project of modernity has gone as far as it can go along its stated path of self-definition and can go no further. Danto argues that the market still demands originality, but all it gets is pastiche – a re-arrangement of the superficial qualities of past style and past contents. Alternatively, there is the view that is held by 'social constructivists' who claim that human values are 'substantially defined by dominant power groups' (Crowther 1993b: 196). The result of all three positions, however, is to put in question or relativise issues of judgement and value.

Crowther answers all in the same way: creativity is not and never can be an 'at a stroke' absolute thing. Artistic originality 'is relative to, and embodies, specifiable traces of that form from which it develops, or against which it reacts' (Crowther 1993b: 197). In addition, an intertextual perspective may play a key role within artistic originality, in that subjectivity is one of creativity's pre-conditions: 'each of us qua embodied subject necessarily sees the world from a particular existential viewpoint which cannot be occupied by another person' (Crowther 1993b: 197). But the artwork's embodied status means that its materiality and meaning-bearing condition are one and the same, and this ties the concept of intertextuality to the artwork's autonomy, and hence to our freedom to respond, rather than to its social and historical context. So, while we perceive artworks from the standpoint of our own personal experience, this does not mean that the features are passively received, but rather that we are active in our assessment of them – they are 'queried, puzzled-over, taken apart, put back together again, qualified, compared, accepted, rejected, or thoroughly transformed' (Crowther 1993b: 197). In other words, we subject them to value judgements, and this is important. So contrary to some commonly held beliefs, the possibilities for creativity and originality are endless. Originality may be currently harder to achieve by the artist, and harder to perceive on the part of the audience, but that just means that artworks simply make greater demands. As Crowther puts it:

> From the audience this demands a sensibility orientated towards the disruption of the sublime rather than the felicities of the beautiful. From the critic it demands an expanded, specialist knowledge, and greater attentiveness to the nuances of the particular.
>
> (Crowther 1993b: 98)

So the current trend towards plurality of perspectives 'simply embodies an imperative to greater and more critical discussion' (Crowther 1993b: 199). Crowther is proposing that an alternative view of postmodernity is possible, one that can continue and build upon its original project, and moreover, one that includes notions of decipherability.

Crowther's holistic theory of art therefore has important consequences for a consideration of the concepts of originality, creativity and value. In this scheme, originality may be achieved, either by innovation or by the refinement of existing rules. If an artwork refines in some way 'existing rules or traditions of production' (Crowther 1993b: 182), it may be thought to be original, that is, its impact may not be radical, but it nevertheless extends the way other such artworks of its genre are perceived. By refining certain acknowledged modes, it is every bit as valuable as a complete rupture with past practice, which modernism tended to privilege but which resulted in artistic impasse.

Now in Crowther's (1993a) analysis of critical and non-critical postmodernisms, an appetite for innovation was encouraged to which the postmodern artistic response could be superficial. A superficial response is possible because of the conditions of postmodernity, which permit an easy assimilation of stylistic features that do not, however, fulfil the critical preconditions of modernity, but, in fact, merely serve to maintain the status quo, while in reality only affecting the superficialities of style of a radical position.[11]

> Neo-expressionism then, is to be seen as an exaggerated and empty response to the art market's demand for innovation. It provides, as it were, a show of newness, but in terms of strict artistic criteria, can only be an inflated repetition of what has gone before.
>
> (Crowther 1993a: 181)

Those forms of postmodernism that pose a valid critique of the status quo are thought to be truly innovative, while those that pretend to this status within their surface features alone are thought not to be.

A brief discussion of the choreographies of Merce Cunningham and William Forsythe may exemplify these important points in relation to dance. Here it is found that Cunningham raises profound questions about what art is, and in particular, about dance's ontological status – including, for example, the precise nature of the collaboration between dancer and choreographer. Moreover, the critical dimension is intrinsic to the dance's form and this is an all-important feature. When, in the first quartet of *Changing Steps* (1973), the male dancers change partners by ducking under the legs of the females who maintain balance, there is more than just a discussion of the duet form at issue. The testing of points of balance and dependency has been a feature of this section and has proceeded in (for Cunningham) a relatively lyrical way up to this point, with mutually dependent shapes melting into further explorations on the theme. The 'ducking' motif changes the mood abruptly to one of humour, even of absurdity, reminding us of the dancers' humanity, integrating their role and further challenging and redefining the nature of the medium in relation to dancers as people. This interpretation of Cunningham's work is supported in Roger Copeland's analysis of Cunningham's style. Copeland argues that:

> Cunningham's work may not *symbolize* anything; but it does serve an end beyond itself: that of *perceptual training*. The importance of Cunningham's work lies not only in what we're given to see and hear, but in *the way we see and hear what we're given*.
>
> (Copeland 1983: 322)

Thus Cunningham, for all his apparent radicalism, displays a very unified and consistent attitude to the world. Forsythe on the other hand tends to situate himself quite self-consciously within a deconstructionist ethos, one that prefers to remain open-ended rather than offer answers. Norbert Servos comments:

> The attitude [the choreography] displays towards the world is one of reason, hence philosophical. The fact that no precise conclusions are offered still remains one of Forsythe's best qualities.
>
> (Servos 1993: 24)

Forsythe's choreography displays a critical deconstructionism in that his work may be seen to question our assumptions about technique, structure and status. For example, in the duet of *Herman Schmerman* (1992), Sylvie Guillem's leg extension, quickly followed by misalignment of the hip, can be seen to undermine our preconceptions regarding classical ballet. In a similar way, the structure of a classical *pas de deux* is subverted, both in the ordering of its subsections and in its gender roles. The status of the *pas de deux* is also questioned, in relation to the classical concept of an 'ideal' partnership, and so on. The dancers (Guillem in particular) display their (human) relationship in a realistic way, for example, by shooting looks at each other or by tapping each other on the shoulder to gain each other's attention. Yet at no point is either dancer seen as less than 'ideal' in terms of their image or their accomplishment. A broadly similar critical dimension is evident as was seen in the Cunningham dance, but Forsythe overloads us with eclecticism and dramatic imagery and this has a tendency to connect with the viewer 'at the level of private and arbitrary association' (Crowther 1993a: 188) in which the lack of 'public or collective significance is taken as a signifier of the artist's profundity or depth of being' (Crowther 1993a: 188). I am not suggesting for one moment that this is Forsythe's problem, but rather that it is a problem inherent within our reception of postmodern dances, which takes eclecticism at face value. However, this example leads to a general consideration of the ideas of embodiment in relation to the special case of dance.

Implications for dance and conclusions

This discussion has argued for the centrality of the discipline of philosophy in dance teaching, especially teaching in relation to appreciation, understanding and creative work. It has also sought to approach the integration of theory and practice in relation to dance teaching by describing a theory of embodiment to support the argument; one that permits attention to the detail of an artwork, but that also places emphasis on how significance is determined in the first place, on what detail we are to attend to and how we know this. These are all questions of value. The theory of embodiment as outlined does not stress the conceptualisation of the body as in some other disciplines, but rather serves to emphasise the primacy of an artistic context, and to explain the special place of artworks in our understanding of how human beings operate in the world – how we integrate a perception of self and other. Lastly, I have argued that the very least that can be claimed for dance is that, contra to some philosophical writing, it is a very powerful example of art. An even stronger claim might be that it demonstrates and reflects upon our phenomenological existence in a more vivid and more integrative way than other art forms.

Crowther argues for the centrality of the artwork to our self-consciousness in that art is a means by which we both reflect and make sense of our experience of the world. But artworks are also embodied within physical particulars, thus reinforcing and strengthening our hold on the world. This then offers an adequate account of our position of relative stability within an unstable 'postmodern' world. Artworks embody ideas and as such, they resonate with us in a way that relocates us in relation to others and reaffirms our sense of self in relation to the 'self-ness' of others. We have a twofold embodiment in dance, in that the object that is the dancer embodies the choreographer's intentions, but the dancer is also an intentional subject. Susan Foster has drawn attention to this phenomenon, but only in so far as, what she calls, the 'dancer's subject' has a sense of self, dancing (Foster 1986). If, however, Crowther is right and art objects reaffirm our inherence in an unstable world, then dance may be seen to reflect upon our self-consciousness in a very special way.

In this model of embodiment, as we have seen, there are implications too for the perception and reception of postmodern dance works in terms of the possibilities for their originality over and above acts of imagination and/or the challenge to existing forms and conventions. Consequently, notions of value are inherent and trans-historical. Furthermore, if perception is creative (and the model endorses this position but within acceptable boundaries) there are further implications to do with ways in which understanding and critical judgement are intimately related. This is because understanding itself is embodied: perception of artworks implicates the senses and intellect, then it follows that understanding dance works involves the unified field of our sensori-motor capacities, drawing upon our physical experience of what it is to dance as well as on rational reflection.

If embodied knowledge of dance techniques aids or (put more strongly) is necessary to understanding dances, then there is a reciprocal argument that analytic understanding of how choreography works (by, for example, looking at a variety of dance forms and, dare I say, 'the choreographic canon'), far from impeding creativity, can foster critical practice and encourage experiment. There is a corollary to this position in relation to the interface between practice and research. To make art with any cultural relevance, one must have knowledge of and refer to that culture. Thus, the fact of the artwork and its context are intimately connected, but to assert that research can be completed by and within the artwork (as some have claimed) is to ignore that context and to ignore the artistic process. If the artistic process exists separately and historically from the fact of the artwork, then we can articulate, examine, and evaluate the processes of selection.

All of this is a very wordy explanation for something that in practice works in a fairly straightforward way. In dance analysis I stress the importance of choreographic intention, not in terms of what the choreographer has said about the work, but in terms of how the particular work relates to the choreographer's worldview, *as it is manifest in the choreography*. In other words, no dance can be analysed in isolation, but only in relation to knowledge about its wider context: the choreographer's other works; similar works by other choreographers of the time; other artists; other thinkers … and so on. Similarly, in choreography class, a heightened awareness of the processes of selection would seem appropriate and important in their articulation. 'Why this and not this?'[12] would seem a question that is valuable to ask at all stages of artistic creativity and appreciation, and at all levels of accomplishment.

Notes

1 For McFee, the issue hinges on misconceptions of the terms 'subjective' and 'objective' in relation to aesthetic judgement, specifically a misconception of objectivity that stems from scientific argument and that precludes disagreement. But, it is also useful to discuss the ethos of indeterminacy in relation to embodiment and critical deconstructionism, because the latter is a practice in which the notion of indeterminacy has found particular emphasis. As Crowther reminds us:

> The discourse of deconstruction hinges on such things as the problematics of determinacy of presence, the incongruence of signifier and signified, the false rigidity of oppositions such as inner and outer, etc.
>
> (Crowther 1993b: 143)

However, physical presence in art is undeniable by the very fact of its materiality, hence there is a contradiction at the heart of deconstructive practice. So, while meaning is dependent upon a seemingly infinite network of relational possibilities within a deconstructionist (or intertextual) model, in practice it is focused (and bounded) by our phenomenological existence in the world and this observation is relevant to all the arts, as well as being applicable to all of our social interaction (Crowther 1993b: 143–4). Crowther points up this contrast between theory and practice in a concise way:

> In theoretical terms the possibility of meaning and presence is determined by an item's location within an inexhaustible network of relations to other items. But in our direct experience this abstract structure is focused and fixed by our body's hold upon the world. Presence is paramount – despite its theoretical indeterminacy.
>
> (Crowther 1993b: 143–4)

2 An example of this practice is to be found in Susan Foster's seminal work *Reading Dancing: Bodies and Subjects in Contemporary American Dance* (1986) in which she argues the choreographic strengths of Meredith Monk and Grand Union in relation to their communal practices and social inclusivity, value judgements that are based upon social rather than artistic reasons.

3 There are many and varied reasons for this, but one reason that is often given by philosophers (see Carr 1999; McFee 1999) is the contentious status of notation in recording dance works, resulting in suspicion regarding dance artefacts which results in turn in an underdeveloped ontology of dance; a second reason, of course, relates to a traditional mistrust of the body within philosophical reflection and to dance's own critical history, with dance critics not always being the best advocates of dance art in this respect. See, for example, Theophile Gautier's accounts of Elssler and Taglioni reprinted in Roger Copeland's and Marshall Cohen's *What is Dance?* (1983: 431–7).

4 Briginshaw's assumption that 'the premises of Western philosophy [...] revolve around the concept of an ideal, rational, unified subject which, in turn, relies on dualist thinking that enforces seeing things in terms of binary oppositions' (Briginshaw 2001: 9), is a common view. These premises, we are told, result in subject/object distinctions in relation to dance: with audience as subject, dancer as object, a situation which some postmodern choreographers (like Bausch) challenge. Briginshaw's book *Dance, Space and Subjectivity* (2001) centres on dance analysis, but has sympathy with a focus beyond dance into contemporary critical theories 'beginning with feminist theory, and more recently with postmodern, postcolonial, queer and post-structuralist theories, which seek to deal with issues that have hitherto been ignored' (Briginshaw 2001: xiii), and these focuses are of course important. Fraleigh endorses this view, when

she posits an interest in feminism that has sought to redress the previously male dominated perspectives on art by looking to post-Freudian psychological insights, and writes on 'ways of seeing, such as voyeurism, fetishism and scopophilia' to shift aesthetics to a gendered perspective (Fraleigh in Fraleigh and Hanstein 1999: 206). The focus in both cases is amply justified, but the point I wish to emphasise here is that it can lead to the oversight of some, arguably equally important areas, to do with the identity of dance as an art.

5 The materials of dance, less still the medium, are not simply 'the body', as some schemes would have, but involve the body in a relationship that invokes Stanley Cavell's account of artistic medium, that it is 'materials-in-certain-characteristic-applications' (Cavell 1969: 221). In other words, the medium of dance is the body as intentional and intended.

6 I am indebted to my colleague Andrée Grau for the clear and concise account here.

7 I am flagging a contrasting range of choreographic interest here, with works that take an abstract/formalist approach, in the case of Cunningham; those that are interested in music/dance relations, in the case of Morris; those that are radically eclectic and boundary crossing, in the case of Decouflé.

8 Dance critic Deborah Jowitt (2001) argues a similar position.

9 For more detailed accounts of how meanings of dances can change through time, see Rowell (1999).

10 Umberto Eco makes the point: 'I think of the postmodern attitude as that of a man who loves a very cultivated woman and knows he cannot say to her, "I love you madly", because he knows that she knows (and that she knows that he knows) that these words have already been written by Barbara Cartland' (Eco 1984: 67).

11 Hal Foster (1983) makes a similar point in his analysis of a postmodernism of resistance and a postmodernism of reaction while Jameson's (1983) distinction between pastiche and parody relies upon a similar judgement.

12 I am prompted here by Stanley Cavell's question in relation to artistic intention (Cavell 1969: 227).

References

Adshead, J., Briginshaw, V., Hodgens, P. and Huxley, M. (1988) *Dance Analysis: Theory and Practice*, London: Dance Books.

Adshead-Lansdale, J. (ed.) (1999) *Dancing Texts, Intertextuality in Interpretation*, London: Dance Books.

Banes, S. (1987) 'Introduction to the Wesleyan Paperback Edition', *Terpsichore in Sneakers*, Connecticut: Wesleyan University Press.

Barthes, R. (1968) 'The Death of the Author', *Image Music Text*, London: Fontana, 142–8.

Briginshaw, V. (2001) *Dance, Space and Subjectivity*, Basingstoke: Palgrave.

Carr, D. (1999) 'Further Reflections on Practical Knowledge and Dance a Decade on', in G. McFee (ed.) *Dance, Education and Philosophy*, Oxford: Meyer & Meyer Sport.

Cavell, S. (1969) 'A Matter of Meaning It', in *Must We Mean What We Say?* Cambridge: Cambridge University Press.

Challis, C. (1999) 'Dancing Bodies: Can the Art of Dance be Restored to Dance Studies?', in G. McFee (ed.) *Dance, Education and Philosophy*, Oxford: Meyer & Meyer Sport.

Copeland, R. (1983) 'Merce Cunningham and the Politics of Perception', in R. Copeland and M. Cohen (eds.) *What is Dance?* Oxford: Oxford University Press.

Copeland, R. and Cohen, M. (eds) (1983) *What is Dance?* Oxford: Oxford University Press.

Crowther, P. (1993a) *Critical Aesthetics and Postmodernism*, Oxford: Clarendon Press.

—— (1993b) *Art and Embodiment: From Aesthetics to Self-Consciousness*, Oxford: Clarendon Press.

Danto, A. C. (1981) *The Transfiguration of the Commonplace*, Cambridge, MA: Harvard University Press.

Derrida, J. (1978) *Writing and Difference*, London: Routledge.

Eco, U. (1984) *Postscript to the Name of the Rose*, New York: Harcourt Brace Jovanovich.

Foster, H. (ed.) (1983) *Postmodern Culture*, London: Pluto.

Foster, S. L. (1986) *Reading Dancing: Bodies and Subjects in Contemporary American Dance*, Berkeley, Los Angeles and London: University of California Press.

Fraleigh, S. (1987) *Dance and the Lived Body: A Descriptive Aesthetics*, Pittsburgh, PA: University of Pittsburgh Press.

Fraleigh, S. and Hanstein, P. (eds) (1999) *Researching Dance: Evolving Modes of Inquiry*, London: Dance Books.

Jameson, F. (1983) 'Postmodernism and Consumer Society', in H. Foster (ed.) *Postmodern Culture*, London: Pluto, pp. 111–25.

Jowitt, D. (2001) 'Writing beneath the Surface', in A. Dils and A. Cooper Albright (eds) *Moving History: A Dance Reader*, Middletown, CT: Weslyan University Press.

McFee, G. (1992) *Understanding Dance*, London: Routledge.

McFee, G. (ed.) (1999) *Dance, Education and Philosophy*, Oxford: Meyer & Meyer Sport.

McFee, G. (2003) 'Cognitivism and the Experience of Dance', in A. Sukla (ed.) *Art and Experience*, Westport, CT: Praeger/Greenwood.

Merleau-Ponty, M. (1972) 'Eye and Mind', in H. Osborne (ed.) *Aesthetics*, Oxford: Oxford University Press; first published in 1964 in J. Edie (ed.) *The Primacy of Perception*.

Rowell, B. (1999) 'The Historical Character of Dances', in G. McFee (ed.) *Dance, Education and Philosophy*, Oxford: Meyer & Meyer Sport.

Servos, N. (1993) 'The World Topsy-turvy', *Ballett International*, 8 (8): 24

Sparshott, F. (1995) *A Measured Pace: Towards a Philosophical Understanding of the Arts of Dance*, Toronto: University of Toronto Press.

Videography

Caplan, Eliot and Cunningham, Merce (directors) (1989) *Changing Steps* [video], co-production of the Cunningham Dance Foundation and La Sept, reproduced for video, 1989, shown on *Dance International* series, directed by Bob Lockyer for BBC TV and Guillaume Gronier for La Sept [choreography, Merce Cunningham, 1973, first shown on BBC 2, 28 October 1989].

Diamond, Matthew (director) (1992) *Hard Nut*, [video] Robin Scott, prod. for NVC Arts, a production of Thirteen/WNET with NVC Arts in association with RTP, Portugal and VLE, Finland, National Video Corporation Ltd [choreography, Mark Morris, 1991, filmed live at the Théâtre Royal de la Monnaie, Brussels].

Large, Brian (director) (1993) *Covent Garden Winter Gala* [video], BBC2, Peter Maniura, prod. [duet from *Herman Schmerman*, choreography, William Forsythe, 1992, televised live from the Royal Opera House on 1 December 1993].

11 Choreographer as researcher

Issues and concepts in postgraduate study

Jo Butterworth

The central dichotomy facing the choreographer-researcher is usually created by the differences of skills, knowledge and processes of professional choreography on the one hand and of academic practices on the other. Traditionally, professional dance training has been dominated by methods of apprenticeship, whilst the choreographer, having served an apprenticeship as performer, has relied on artistic exploration driven forward by intuitive leaps. In the university sector, however, the processes of academic research are based on systematic methods of enquiry leading to an expansion of knowledge. Can this division of practice and theory be integrated? If so, how can choreographers be supported, inspired and challenged when they place themselves and their work in the academic arena as postgraduate students? What kinds of investigative tools can be introduced to artist-researchers to aid their development, and what approaches can be taken to guide them towards reflection, interrogation and articulation of their professional dance-making processes?

This chapter will first explore this dichotomy by mapping

- concepts of apprenticeship in professional dance training
- concepts of knowledge in the university sector
- ways in which a dynamic fusion of theory and practice can be brought about.

In seeking a synthesis of these two positions in order to develop appropriate theories of knowledge for the choreographer-researcher at the postgraduate level, three levels of enquiry are investigated:

- What do we mean by embodied knowledge?
- How can experiential learning be of benefit in developing skills of reflection?
- What disciplines and research methods provide appropriate tools for the artist-researcher?

Finally, in order to examine how these theories, methods and practices can be integrated and applied, two exemplars are discussed where theory underpins practice and practice illuminates theory.[1]

Apprenticeship in professional dance training

It is evident that vocational training practices first introduced from France, Italy, Denmark and Russia remained in the classical tradition, providing exemplars for Britain. Since the 1920s many of the major ballet companies have created a direct link with a school, and these have been concerned predominantly with training professional dancers for employment within these companies. These conventions have tended to exist also in the modern or contemporary dance domain. The main requirements of a performance graduate in the vocational sector in the UK, therefore, include a high level of executant skill, the ability to learn and remember repertoire, the ability to engage with the process of creating a complete new work in rehearsal, to interpret and perform choreography as set by a choreographer and to realise it and perform it as requested (Butterworth 2002: 121).

In professional dance contexts, including vocational dance training, dancers have evidently learned about choreography, even if they have not had the opportunity to do so formally. The 'osmosis' occurs through daily immersion in technique classes, in rehearsals with choreographers or *répétiteurs* where the concern is with the making of new works or with the re-construction of existing choreography and through the regular performance of completed works. With this work experience, dancers have tended to become choreographers through what might be termed the apprentice method, that is, by drawing upon their personal experiences as dancers in relation to the 'master' choreographers. Historically, this apprenticeship was often followed by the opportunity to make new works within a company framework, and to develop a personal signature as choreographer by evolving new languages and methods. There is little doubt that most dancers in training have been party to these practices at some time, in whichever country they are based.

Professional choreographers work in very specific contexts: they may enjoy the relative freedom of choice to make a new work in their own company, or are perhaps invited to make a new work for a specific ballet or contemporary, genre-specific company. Limitations of funding, rehearsal time, genre, style, length, dancers and collaborator choice may determine aspects of the outcome, yet these determinants are rarely made explicit. Artistic tradition has tended to privilege the 'secrets' and 'processes' of the artist. Historically the question of how an artist has achieved the making of a work has often been hidden, and is frequently considered irrelevant from the receiver/audience point of view. In validating the dance choreography product in the theatre, there is no requirement to explain, contextualise or reflect, though indeed all these activities may occur to some degree in applications for funding, marketing material and programme notes. Seminal texts such as Cohen's *The Modern Dance: Seven Statements of Belief* (1966) began to provide insights into artistic creation. More recently, publications investigating artistic process in more depth (for example, Jordan and Grau 1996, Butterworth and Clarke 1998, Burrows 1998 and Sanders 2004) indicate a growing interest in choreographic processes and procedures.

Educational dance

The history of educational dance in the UK until the mid-1970s demonstrates a radically different approach to learning. Indeed, the long separation of professional/vocational and educational contexts and the need for dialectic are themes that can be clearly traced throughout the *Dance Education and Training in Britain* (1980) report produced by Peter Brinson. In the educational sphere, social dance and physical recreation dominated until changes in the social and cultural context after World War II, when the 1944 Educational Act provided a new context of receptivity for the introduction of modern educational dance based on the principles of Rudolf Laban. Post-war education adopted teaching and learning strategies that were increasingly child-centred and process-oriented, influenced by Dewey (1934, 1958), leading to the acceptance of discovery methods and expressive creativity. By the 1970s, this form of expressive dance was being taught at many physical education colleges in the UK (Adshead 1981), and is well documented in terms of its philosophy, approach and application by practitioners such as Redfern (1973), Preston-Dunlop (1963, 1980), Foster (1977), Haynes (1987) and Russell (1969). It was not until the 1970s that dance was offered as a major study in a creative and performing arts programme, and the first bachelor's degree in dance in a British university was instigated in 1981.[2]

The situation in the USA, however, reveals a different history. Beckman (1981), writing about the relationship of American professional modern dance to educational dance, states:

> In tracing the relationship between professional modern dance and dance in education in the USA between 1930 and 1940 it soon becomes clear that it is impossible to separate the influence of one on the other because their development is so closely related and interdependent. Not only were they crucial to each other but they came out of what seems to be a strong historical trend in both education and the arts.
>
> (Beckman 1981: 26)

This strong interdependence of professional and educational domains at this period, and particularly through the university sector, meant that there was little conflict between the educational dance and the concert artist, and that aesthetic functions were viewed as compatible (1981: 31).

Beckman cites the involvement of professional dance pioneers such as Duncan, St Denis, Shawn, Graham, Humphrey and Weidman who taught and performed in the university sector with such innovative educators as Martha Hill, Bird Larson and Margaret H'Doubler. The summer school at Bennington College from 1934 to 1942 was a particular catalyst, becoming a perfect link between the two worlds, serving 'all types of dance students, teachers, professional dancers, those interested in the art as amateurs and as audience' (1981: 29).

Though dance development in many countries in Europe has been highly influenced by American modern dance styles, systems and teaching processes, and may indeed exhibit a similar interdependence, the British dance education system in higher education from 1980 still displays a vision of the continuing dichotomy between apprenticeship and knowledge. In the university, the subject discipline of dance is viewed as a vehicle for experiential learning and understanding. The acquisition of skills must be supported by the knowledge of principles and concepts and by the demonstration of understanding. That is, there must be justification for using skills, knowledge and experience. Thus, the development of technical and performance skill in the university dance department has rarely been adequately valued, while the ability to reflect, appraise and communicate analysis is overemphasised. Unfortunately, the lack of technical competency that is normally aided by learning repertoire or technical studies renders students incapable of reaching a level of performance proficiency that would allow them to join a professional company, or even to fully demonstrate the qualities of the choreographies that they, or others, have created.[3]

There is now general consensus that artists in training should develop the ability to be articulate about their practice. This position is evidenced by the many institutions, academies and university courses in Europe, where bachelor's degrees in dance include contextual studies, dance analysis and theoretical concepts which underpin and cross-reference practical learning in the dance studio, whether in technique, improvisation and/or composition. Ideally, the principles of technical mastery, critical faculty and creativity are pulled into correspondence. Once the dance-artist-in-training has completed an initial programme, choices are made as to future career as dancer, teacher, workshop leader, choreographer, collaborator, academic or other. Since many individuals combine two or more of these roles at different stages of their career, the skills of reflection, evaluation, documentation and discrimination are pertinent to both contemporary dance artists and dance practitioner-researchers, whatever their chosen sphere.

Student dancer/choreographers require a language with which to describe the fundamentals of dance making, first in the process of making dances, then in preparation for performance, and in analysis and reflection. The principles of Laban (1960, 1975) provide one useful method of identifying the components of dance into action/motion, dynamic, spatial

Table 11.1 Butterworth's four perspectives to choreography learning/teaching.

	Making	*Performing*	*Appreciating*	*Communication of Understandings*
Own	• Own works • Personal styles • Developing personal strategies	• Own works • Personal (inner) intention • Experiencing forms of communication	• Conceptual processes • Creative understandings • Self-reflection	• Log of dance-making process • Critical review of own work • Presentation of practical research
Peers	• Experiencing the work of peers • Technical and conceptual challenges • Shifts in group dynamic • Differences in leadership approach	• Performing the work of peers, leading to performance challenges which can be technical, conceptual or interpretative	• Understanding concepts • Cognitive understanding • Reflection of meaning, style, interpretation • Recognising appropriateness of form to content	• Writings on dance-making processes • Analysing those processes • Critical review of the work of others • Consideration of differences in concept, context and methods • Presentation of findings
Professionals	• Experiencing the work of professionals 1 Through learning repertoire 2 Through experiencing the choreographic process with professionals • Including differences in leadership approaches and in interrelationship within the group	• Performing the work of choreographers 1 Performing seminal, professional works through repertoire 2 Performing professional works through working with artists in residence	• Conceptual understanding • Cognitive understanding • Creative understanding of processes	• Writings on dance-making processes • Analysing those processes • Critical review of professional choreography • Consideration of differences in concept, context and methods • Presentation of findings
Applied	• Experiencing making of work for applied contexts • Intention • Awareness of group needs	• Experiencing a variety of performance intents, contexts and applications for dance making • Awareness of group needs	• Appreciating the differences of intent • Cognitive understandings of each process and context • Appreciation of group needs	• Writings on dance-making processes in applied contexts • Analysing those processes • Critical review of works made in applied contexts • Consideration of differences in concept, context and methods • Presentation of findings

and relationship concerns that can be used in an increasingly sophisticated way, offering a set of principles that can be used to conceptualise the non-verbal physical experience of dance without being style- or technique-specific. In an experiential approach to learning choreography, the interrelationship of theory and practice is both crucial and central. Theories and concepts from literature initiate practice in dance making, and practical studies and performances institute sharing, discussion and analysis of the particular underlying concept or theory to develop understanding. Arguably students benefit from being involved in making, performing, appreciating and communicating understandings of choreography from four perspectives: personal, peers, professional and applied. Table 11.1 explicates both what that entails, and how it can be seen to progress skills, experience, knowledge and understanding. At each stage, students should have opportunities for making choreography, performing it, developing concepts to appreciate it, and learning the mechanisms of documentation.

As the chart indicates, in the early stages of a choreography course students may be involved in making short choreographies, developing a personal style, experiencing the presentation of personal work in performance, understanding creative and conceptual processes, and researching and writing a log of the dance-making process to include a critical review of the outcome. They can also experience radically different methods and movement material by co-creating and performing the work of their peers, by learning and performing seminal professional works, and by involvement in devising processes with professional artists in residence. After experiencing the work of peers and professionals from equally broad perspectives, I suggest that students are encouraged to gain further experience working in applied contexts, perhaps working with the elderly, with special needs groups, in youth-group or wheelchair-user workshops, or other client-based situations. Here, they have opportunity to consider differences of concept, contexts and methods. Undergraduate and postgraduate might pursue similar interests, though essentially these are manifested at different levels of sophistication and probably with quite different outcomes. But by questioning the relationship of practice, theory and communication at every stage, and by maintaining a balance between making and doing, investigating and writing, these artists-in-training tend to develop the fundamentals of process, purpose and appraisal. These ideas can be seen as a blueprint for bringing about a fusion of practice and theory for the dance student in the university sector. Whether a career choice is in theatrical, educational or amateur-community contexts, dance artists-in-training need profound understanding of the methods of initiating, conceptualising and creating new work, the ability to trace its departure points and its lines of development, to place it in one or more contexts, to document it, to analyse and evaluate it.

The detached observer may attempt an analytical, critical and/or theoretical account of a choreographic work. This is the field of the scholar, the critic or the researcher, engaging in acknowledged research methods to question, identify objectives, plan and design, collect, analyse and present information systematically and objectively. However, these methods do not nullify the value of assessing a work from the inside, of investigating the *subjectivity* of the art practitioner-researcher. Here, reflexivity is essential. Several stages are involved: making conscious aesthetic judgements from the perspective of the artist; being what Shahn called the 'artist as critic' (1957: 34); reflecting on one's own practice and systematising its representation are all key elements. In investigating the nature of these skills of detached observation and reflexivity, an understanding of relevant theories of knowledge are crucial.

Theory of knowledge

Art, in all its various manifestations, is an 'appearance incapable of appearing', as Lefebre terms it (1991: 395). It appears to offer a doorway beyond mere perception. It certainly represents a plan of activity that cannot be strictly empirically understood, assessed or validated by traditional research methods. That is, its products, material and seemingly immaterial, cannot be reproduced or tested under controlled conditions (Dallow 2005: 133).

A consideration of how the revealing of art takes place, however, beyond randomness and serendipity, may be tackled through an investigation of 'the act of discovery' of creative practice. Research, or discovery, is about learning something we did not know. Art also is about learning something we do not know, or did not *know* we *knew* (Dallow 2005: 135). In order to investigate the creative act, to examine aesthetic knowledge and reveal something of the logic of arts practice, forms of systematised thinking need to be employed whereby artists continue to develop a sense of discrimination.

The artist-researcher in academia needs to present the research context and delineate the problems, methods and the relationship of his or her own approach to prevailing practices (Hannula, Suoranta and Vadén 2005: 160–2). The artwork or choreography might well feature as an outcome of the research practice, but the artist-researcher must also present theoretical viewpoints, from which to approach the object and data, and upon which he or she bases his/her interpretations. The artist-researcher must justify his/her decision-making and document it, and the reader must be able to follow the research process and scrutinise the results on page and stage. The epistemology must be sound.

Epistemology is used here to denote methods of justification, for helping to identify the grounds by which we can claim to know certain facts, and to help us answer the question, 'How do we know what we know?' Perhaps that is why one of the first tasks of the young artist in training is to be able to identify *what* they know, and then to question how they have assimilated certain forms of knowledge, both practical and theoretical.

Thereafter, they learn to codify, frame and categorise, identify and define. Hodder asserts that practical knowledge, like most cultural knowledge, 'is non-linear and purpose dedicated, formed through the practice of closely related activities' (Dallow 2005: 136). By reflecting on their own creative activity, artists in training gain further insight into their own aesthetic knowledge and taste, or perhaps question personal or national identity, cultural or semiotic systems in relation to their own work. Advanced competence in a range of methods, approaches and research techniques appropriate to the artistic and scholarly study of choreography can only support that quest. The growing disciplinary field of practice as research (PAR) or practice-led research thus offers valuable skills for the developing artist-researcher.

Some of the most significant published work in the philosophical field of *embodied knowledge* is by Anna Pakes. In the article 'Art as action or art as object? The embodiment of knowledge in practice as research' (2004) Pakes investigates the claim that practice as research (PAR) in the arts makes available a distinctive kind of knowledge not available to other domains, and inaccessible to other (more traditional) modes of enquiry. She specifically interrogates the nature of practical reasoning in terms of its epistemological validity, relating practical knowledge/artistic action as 'a form of insight embodied in what we do in the world ... underwritten by a logic that emerges in and through the activity itself' (2004: 2). The question is raised as to which element, the practice itself or the reflection upon it, embodies the knowledge that artistic action produces. Pakes introduces Aristotelean ideas, specifically the contrast between the terms *techne* (the skill of craftsmanship) and *phronesis* (the practical wisdom of acting well within the social and moral domains) (2004: 3). Whereas *techne* might involve instrumental skill, or understanding based on general laws and knowledge of causal connections, *phronesis* denotes a capacity to respond to the particularities of experience, and to evolving relationships with others. As far as performance practice is concerned, Pakes argues, characterising the epistemological modes as phronetic does help highlight important dimensions of art-making activity, particularly in terms of creative sensitivity:

> presenting practice as research – or, more particularly, as generative of phronetic insight – reasserts the nature of dance-making as intersubjective action and allows the artist a space to develop increased self-consciousness about her conduct in that making process. In her reflexive awareness of what she does, and of her relationships with dancers, other collaborators and audience members, the dance artist-researcher develops a kind of knowledge that is valuable in reflecting on both specifically artistic processes and, more generally, on the nature of social relationships.
>
> (Pakes 2004: 4)

However, since this kind of reflexive awareness comes about through a synthesis of craft and experiential knowledge, which heightens consciousness, we might claim its value for all kinds of artist, whether or not she is practising as artist or practitioner-researcher. Arguably, most established choreographers tend to engage in activities that juxtapose intuitive bursts with periods of reasoned decision-making. There may be key differences between practitioner-researchers and 'ordinary' artists in their practice with regard to how far they proceed with analysis or documentation, but for both, phronetic insight, or practical wisdom, must incorporate questions of intention, form, content, relationship and meaning in some form; the artistic activity of an experienced choreographer tends to follow an intentional model.

For those engaged in study for a postgraduate master's degree, the intentional action model is indeed one valuable approach to a heightened awareness of process: it raises questions about the intent and the context of a particular work, challenging the need for systematised and clearly articulated thinking about the various stages of the creative process. In the educational arena, these philosophical ideas can be read, discussed, sifted and juxtaposed with other theories, beliefs and opinions so that each artist/student benefits intellectually *and* artistically from the plethora of stimulating ideas. These can be explored through learning about a range of research tools, through studio exploration, through writing papers and giving presentations. Essentially each student aspires to developing the dual abilities of working as a professional choreographer in the chosen field of application, and of practising performance research, thus experiencing a little more deeply the dialectic of these two worlds.

An important objective is that these artist-students no longer make choreographic work exclusively from well-worn methods, personalised choreographic 'toolboxes' and personal intuitions, but that they begin to employ other approaches and tools of investigation. Which approaches can we introduce to guide artists towards articulation, interrogation and reflection of their dance-making processes, and how can an understanding of experiential learning methods benefit these developing skills?

Experiential learning

Brookfield (1983: 16) suggests that writers in the field of experiential learning tend to use the term in two contrasting senses. On the one hand, the term is used to describe the sort of learning undertaken by students who are given a chance to acquire and apply knowledge, skills and feelings in an immediate and relevant setting, or 'a direct encounter with the phenomena being studied' (Borzak in Brookfield 1983). This type of learning tends to be utilised in an institution and is often used in programmes of education and training, as will be demonstrated. The second type of experiential learning is defined as that which occurs through direct participation in events of life (Houle 1989: 221). Evidently, one of the most valuable and interesting elements to the teaching of a postgraduate choreography group is that each of them arrives with a phenomenal amount of prior learning, knowledge and skills derived from life and career experiences thus far, and this can and should be embraced within the study. Much experiential learning literature centres on the work of David A. Kolb with Roger Fry (1975), whose model of the experiential learning circle features four elements: concrete experience, observation and reflection, the formation of abstract concepts and testing in new situations. Essentially certain features characterise experiential learning: involving the student personally in active learning, delegating control, presenting students with management issues, etc. Key factors to success include relevant facilitation and guidance techniques, which empower individuals.

From the perspective of learning about choreography, one of the most relevant articles on experiential learning can be seen in the work of Jane Henry (1993), who suggests at least eight different approaches: personal development, action learning, prior learning, activity-based learning, placement, project work, problem-based learning and independent learning. The following discussion links some of these methods with practical application examples.

Henry suggests that the *personal development* approach

> usually focuses on affective development and uses a process of reflection as its route to empowerment. Practitioners typically employ a two stage model of experiential learning where an experience is followed by discussion and the learner is expected to articulate the nature of the experience and discuss the meaning of that experience for him, generally with or in the presence of others.
>
> (Henry 1993: 2)

In the Fontys PG/MA Choreography programme, this occurs almost daily, during or after practical choreographic problem-solving in the studio, and again during theoretical debates such as those on postmodernism, semiotics or cultural identity in dance. Students are encouraged to reflect on the nature of the particular experience in group conversation or in pairs, or by note-taking. Developing the ability to articulate these experiences is particularly important for those whose early dance or choreographic experience took place in a ballet or modern dance company where critical reflection may not have been encouraged. A key issue here lies in the development of appropriate language and terminology and the introduction of concepts and theories that can underpin and illuminate these experiences. Informal assessment may well be undertaken by peers, and the outcome over time generates student confidence in expressing who they are and what they want through taking part in reflexive conversations.

The programme focuses on *prior learning* as a way of accessing credibility of skills and knowledge, and in the process, identifies areas where further learning would be helpful. For example, over the course of a teaching block, each student in turn teaches 'class' to the group: that is, a warm-up and physical and mental preparation for the daily practical workshop, where skills and approaches to teaching in particular dance styles can be shared. Since all students take part in all classes, the sharing of prior learning crosses stylistic, cultural and personal boundaries, and at the same time establishes credibility and empowerment through the recognition of existing individual strengths. Equally, members of the cohort are encouraged to share their personal choreographic strengths and perceived weaknesses through working in small groups to problem-solve and challenge one another and by making performances designed to place peers in new performative positions either technically or stylistically. Other prior knowledge is initiated in group seminars through discussion of aesthetics or phenomenology, or of cultural or gender theories and the relationship to dance works known or viewed. As each cohort is culturally diverse, representing many countries in Europe, individual knowledge of companies, choreographers and genres is shared and discussed, and thus the prior learning of one student becomes new stimulus for fellow learners.

Project-based learning helps to develop autonomy. Students choose and take responsibility for devising a plan of action, researching relevant material and determining the organisation and presentation of the work; the outcomes may be choreographic assessments for performance, essays, or lecture-demonstrations. Like *independent study* or *problem-based learning*, tutorial guidance is offered to ensure that a project is feasible, focused and appropriate to context. Over time, these experiences make students capable of managing their own learning more effectively.

New knowledge

Choreographing in professional and applied contexts frequently introduces the need for knowledge of different kinds of research, often from different disciplines. Initially this might include theories from education (pedagogy, creativity), philosophy (aesthetics, perception, beauty, art), hermeneutics (meaning, interpretation), phenomenology (feeling, experiencing), criticism, community studies or human sciences – for example, from cultural studies, gender studies, anthropology or interculturalism. In the postgraduate Choreography degree students are introduced not only to concepts and frameworks from dance history and analysis but also from the broader field of performance studies – from the writings of Schechner (1988, 2002), Turner (1974), Carlson (1996), Campbell (1996), Pavis (1992, 1996, 2003), Counsell and Wolf (2001) and Shepherd and Wallis (2004). Performance theory will stimulate personal and specific interest in certain topics, leading to personal research for projects and essays, and new knowledge and understanding derived from these projects will often lead students to attempt new approaches in their personal choreographic work. New insights into or knowledge about performance – perhaps from the perspective of history, philosophy, semiotics, politics, gender, identity or ethnicity – can stimulate new artistic practices, thus offering a further way of bridging the gap between artistry and scholarship.

Research methods

The third area of development for the intending artist-researcher is in the field of quantitative and (more usually) qualitative research. Familiarisation with and application of various modes of enquiry and research methods gives a postgraduate student confidence and the ability to create new models for theory making and new knowledge creation:

> The researcher as scholar engages in careful study, examination and observation of facts, which often include what people say and do. Through a rigorous and systematic process using appropriate research methodologies and procedures, he or she gathers, scrutinizes and assesses the credibility of information. During this process of gathering and analysing data, themes emerge, ideas take shape, and meaningful interpretations are discovered. The researcher considers these interpretations within the context of the existing body of knowledge, advances new theories, and considers the significance of her or his discoveries.
>
> (Hanstein 1999: 23)

Though purposeful, scholarly research is often creative, interpretative and a process of discovery. It can be both constructive and 'in part constructively destructive' (Altick 1981: 22), meaning that in questioning the status quo, we might expose misinterpretations and spurious claims. The researcher must attempt to remain objective, sceptical and sharply focused whilst exhibiting the kinds of skills that choreographers often share: a problem-solving, discovery-oriented process. Both choreographer and researcher learn about the work as it unfolds, but the researcher normally adheres to a more rigorous and systematic process.

Other modes of research perhaps more pertinent to practice-led situations include ethnographic/participant observation, triangulation, action research, case study and grounded theory. The ethnographic/participant observation approach is heavily dependent on observation and on complete or partial integration with the society or group being studied (Bell 1993: 10). Anthropologists developed this style of fieldwork research, but it can also be applied to ensemble work in choreography, though it is time-consuming, and there may be problems of representativeness. Triangulation involves the comparison of approaches through documentation (through interview, diary or questionnaire) to assess the consensus view. Action research was essentially developed by teachers to review, evaluate and improve practice. It allows practitioners to analyse problems in a specific situation:

> the immediate aim then becomes that of understanding those problems. The researcher/actor, at an early stage, formulates speculative, tentative, general principles in relation to the problems that have been identified; from these principles, hypotheses may then be generated about what action is likely to lead to the desired improvements in practice.
>
> (Brown and McIntyre 1981: 245)

Essentially, action research is seen as cyclical, alternating action and reflection, a useful mechanism for students who need to design, manage and evaluate their own projects. Schön (1987) describes the reflection-in-action process as an intuitive process of trial and error. In working with student architects, he subscribes to the view that each stage in the process is followed by a period of reflection, and then the goals are set for the next stage. He notes that reflection might improve the planning of future events (1987: 28). Reflection then is related to self and improving future practice through a retrospective analysis of action. On the other hand, reflexivity as defined by Rothman (cited in Darling 1998) involves an interaction between the practitioner and their environment that influences the form of the reflexive process. It is a proactive process, as 'its focus is on providing practitioners with a tool that will simultaneously improve their communication and help make them aware of assumptions and priorities that shape their interaction with others' (Darling 1998). Rothman's concept was developed in the field of conflict resolution, which perhaps explains why it can be viewed as a useful tool in the performing arts where intervention takes place between dancers or actors and their collaborators. Paul Rae, in his paper 'Re:invention – on the limits of reflexive practice' (2003), writes:

> The inventive practitioner-researcher takes reflexivity as a given, to the extent that it is germane to the matter in hand, while sensing that such reflexivity will take different forms in different contexts. By understanding artistic and research practices as mutually implicated in a process of invention, one can be simultaneously invested in and led by the work as it unfolds, without ever fully relinquishing conceptual engagement (what the researcher fears), or artistically determined priorities (what the practitioner fears). This requires courage, for uncertainty is an integral part of the process. Operating across skewed temporalities, one is required to keep faith with certain features of a project even though they may pass temporarily from view, or even consciousness.
>
> (Rae 2003)

The notion of 'different forms in different contexts' and equally the question of the balance of consciousness are both important concepts for the choreographer-researcher, as will be demonstrated by the exemplars discussed in the last section of this chapter.

Two further methods of research are of particular use: case study and grounded theory. The case-study method gives opportunity for one aspect of a problem to be studied in some depth within a limited timescale. The researcher can concentrate on a specific instance or situation to identify, or attempt to identify, the various interactive processes at work (Bell 1993: 8). The relationship between variables can be studied through observation and interviews.

Grounded theory as defined by Strauss and Corbin (1990) is a form of qualitative research 'deductively derived from the study of the phenomenon it represents':

> That is, it is discovered, developed, and provisionally verified through systematic data pertaining to that phenomenon. Therefore, data collection, analysis and theory stand in reciprocal relationship with each other. One does not begin with a theory, then prove it. Rather, one begins with an area of study and what is relevant to that area is allowed to emerge.
>
> (Strauss and Corbin 1990: 23)

According to Borg and Gall (1989: 386), the qualitative researcher starts with a tentative design, gathers the data and then adapts the design to develop understanding. Bassey (1990: 36) speaks of 'the common-sense theory of hitherto unrecorded knowledge of practitioners ... [that] may be thought of as knowledge in action'. Creativity is considered to be a vital component of the grounded theory approach, necessary to develop an effective theory, concept or set of principles, though any categories or statement of relationship must be validated. It is evident that in the qualitative model, the researcher's biases interact with the data, and that the two influence one another and are inseparably interconnected. The research is value-bound because enquiry is inevitably influenced by the values of the researcher. The method is particularly useful to practitioners who have a great deal of prior experience in a particular field of performance, education or amateur dance.

In order to understand how this synthesis works and how we can bridge the gap, the final section of this chapter engages briefly with two examples of practice-led research drawn from professional choreographers who have interrogated their practice within a university setting while studying for a master's degree in choreography. How did such a focus affect their professional choreographic work?

Exemplars

Kevin Finnan engaged in practice-led research involving the exploration of traditional and innovative uses of space in dance theatre performance (underpinned by texts from Appia, Craig, Bachelard, Lefebre, De Certeau and McAuley). He choreographed a number of 'study' works to inform his research before going on to work with his professional company Motionhouse Dance Theatre on a full length work *Atomic* (1999),[4] and a performance event for the Tramway, Glasgow, in collaboration with the writer A. L. Kennedy and installation artist Rosa Sanchez. He wrote recently:

> I was initially concerned that the structures of academia would crush the creative spark of my work. Academic research has to conform to a particular structure of argument and justification. To engage with this it is necessary to learn a new way of thinking which appears trammelled and limited by comparison with artistic exploration. To my surprise, I found the clash between the two disciplines to be very creative.
>
> (Finnan 2006: 2)

Finnan went on to pursue a PhD at Warwick University. He had been making choreography with his own company for many years, often stimulated by the relationship between the physical spaces constructed through architecture, such as homes and work places, and the spaces that may be generated through social interaction as in personal relationships, and thus his academic enquiry followed similar lines. Later he wrote:

> The interesting thing was how the two ... enquiries led to a completely new direction for me. Academic research teaches many things ... how to open up a field of enquiry, not just to follow the leaps of your individual interest. In learning to broaden my research process and question basic assumptions my (theatre) work began to change.
>
> (Finnan 2006: 2)

Victor Choi Ma, a professional dancer/choreographer from Hong Kong, pursued an artistic collaboration with an actress, sculptor, musician and lighting/video artist for the Collaboration and Devising module of his MA degree. The performance was set up 'in promenade' inside a large space, with multi-layering of elements, absorbing inter-relationship of these elements, and the possibility of multiple perceptions in the 'reading' of the piece. The work was intriguing, rich and engaging, and the theme, *A Path to the Unknown Space, Tracking through the Body* ... was sufficiently flexible to be approached by all of the media, and in many different, inter-related ways. Ma was examined by contribution to performance, by workfile/process log, and by individual viva. The viva allowed him to explain clearly the intention of the project, his research into collaborative strategies and the nature of the dialogues between artists. In addition, he identified some of the perceived learning outcomes: self-sustainment, openness and ideas referencing working through sensation, visual imagery and motion. Ma noted ways in which collaboration can enrich one's own discipline, and also the part the common theme of 'tracking' played in stimulating each artist individually, in distinct narrative or non-literal ways, before these materials were amalgamated.

These examples help to qualify ways in which the choreographer and researcher strands can valuably feed each other, demonstrating plans of activity that aid empirical understanding, evaluation and validation. If art, and particularly the art of choreography, is fully to take its place in academia, then we must continue to find correspondence between arts practice and acts of research, between serendipity and a sense of discrimination, between objectivity and subjectivity, by understanding that artistic and research practices are mutually implicated in a process of invention, leading to a synthesis of performance, analysis and documentation.

Notes

1 All examples are drawn from the author's experience of teaching postgraduate degrees in Choreography, from University College Bretton Hall, the University of Leeds and LIPA in the UK, and the Dance Academy of Fontys Professional University in the Netherlands.
2 The first BA Hons Dance degree was approved by the Council for National Academic Accreditation for the Laban Centre in 1977. The University of Surrey BA Hons Dance in Society was validated in 1981.
3 There are of course a handful of exceptions to this general perception.
4 With the strap line 'once the equilibrium of a small space is disturbed, particles and people become unstable …'.

References

Adshead, J. (1981) *The Study of Dance*, London: Dance Books.

Altick, R. (1981) *The Art of Literary Research*, New York: W. W. Norton.

Bassey, M. (1990) 'On the nature of research in education (part 1)', *Research Intelligence*, British Education Research Association, Summer: 35–44.

Beckman, C. (1981) 'Performance and education: Survey of a decade', *Dance Scope*, 15 (1): 26–32.

Bell, J. (1993) *Doing Your Research Project* (2nd edn), Buckingham: Oxford University Press.

Borg W. R. and Gall, M. D. (1989) *Educational Research: an introduction*, London: Longman.

Brinson, P. (ed.) (1980) *Dance Education and Training in Britain*, London: Calouste Gulbenkian Foundation.

Brookfield, S. D. (1983) *Adult Learning, Adult Education and the Community*, Milton Keynes: Open University Press.

Brown, S. and McIntyre, D. (1981) 'An action-research approach to innovation in centralised educational systems', *European Journal of Science Education*, 3 (3): 243–58.

Burrows, J. (1998) *Conversations with Choreographers*, London: Royal Festival Hall.

Butterworth, J. (2002) Dance artist practitioners: an integrated model for the learning and teaching of choreography in the tertiary sector, unpublished PhD thesis, London Contemporary Dance School/University of Kent at Canterbury.

Butterworth, J. and Clarke, G. (eds) (1998) *Dance Makers Portfolio: Conversations with Choreographers*, Wakefield: Centre for Dance and Theatre Studies at Bretton Hall.

Campbell, P. (ed.) (1996) *Analysing Performance*, Manchester and New York: Manchester University Press.

Carlson, M. (1996) *Performance, a Critical Introduction*, London and New York: Routledge.

Cohen, S. J. (ed.) (1966) *The Modern Dance: Seven Statements of Belief*, Hanover, NH: Wesleyan University Press.

Counsell, C. and Wolf, L. (2001) *Performance Analysis: an Introductory Coursebook*, London and New York: Routledge.

Dallow, P. (2005) 'Outside "The True?": research and complexity in contemporary arts practice', in M. Miles (ed.) *New Practices – New Pedagogies: a reader*, London and New York: Routledge.

Darling, I. (1998) *Action Evaluation and Action Theory: An assessment of the process and its connection to conflict resolution*. Available online at http://www.lupinworks.com/ar/Schon/Paper6.htlm (accessed 2 August 2006).

Dewey, J. (1934) *Art as Experience*, New York: Mitton, Balch.

—— (1958) *Experience and Nature*, New York: Dover.

Finnan, K. (2006) *Making Perfect and Becoming a Doctor*. Available online at http://www.motionhouse.co.uk/documents/makingperfectandbecomingadoctor.pdf (accessed 14 August 2006).

Foster, J. (1977) *The Influences of Rudolf Laban*, London: Lepus.

Hannula, M., Suoranta, J. and Vadén, T. (2005) *Artistic Research: Theories, Methods And Practices*, Helsinki and Gothenburg: Academy of Fine Arts, Helsinki and University of Gothenburg/Artmonitor.

Hanstein, P. (1999) 'From idea to research proposal: balancing the systematic and the serendipitous', in S. H. Fraleigh and P. Hanstein (eds) *Researching Dance: Evolving Modes of Inquiry*, London: Dance Books.

Haynes, A. (1987) 'The dynamic image: changing perspectives in dance education', in P. Abbs (ed.) *Living Powers: the Arts in Education*, London: Falmer Press.

Henry J. (1993) 'Managing experiential learning: the learner's perspective', in N. Graves (ed.) *Learner Managed Learning*, World Education Fellowship and Higher Education for Capability.

Houle, C. (1989) *Continuing Learning in the Professions*, San Francisco: Jossey-Bass.

Jordan, S. and Grau, A. (eds) (1996) *Following Sir Fred's Steps: Ashton's Legacy*, London: Dance Books.

Kolb, D. A. and Fry, R. (1975) 'Towards an applied theory of experiential learning', in C. Cooper (ed.) *Theories of Group Process*, London: John Wiley.

Laban, R. (1960) *The Mastery of Movement*, 2nd edn, revised by Lisa Ullmann, London: McDonald & Evans.

—— (1975) *Modern Educational Dance*, 3rd edn, Plymouth, UK: MacDonald and Evans.

Lefebre, H. (1991) *The Production of Space*, Trans: Donald Nicholson-Smith, Oxford: Blackwell.

Pakes, A. (2004) 'Art as action or art as object? The embodiment of knowledge in practice as research', *Working Papers in Art and Design*, 3. Available online at http://www.herts.ac.uk/artdes1/research/papers/wpades/vol3/apfull.html (accessed 7 June 2006).

Pavis, P. (1992) *Theatre at the Crossroads of Culture*, London and New York: Routledge.

—— (1996) *The Intercultural Performance Reader*, London and New York: Routledge.

—— (2003) *Analyzing Performance: Theater, Dance and Film*, Ann Arbor: University of Michigan.

Preston, V. (1963) *A Handbook for Modern Educational Dance*, London: Macdonald and Evans.

Preston-Dunlop, V. (1980) *A Handbook for Dance in Education*, Harlow: Longmans.

Rae, P. (2003) Re:invention – on the limits of reflexive practice. Available online at www.bris.ac.uk/parip/webpaper_rae.doc (accessed 2 August 2006).

Redfern, H. B. (1973) *Concepts in Modern Educational Dance*, London: Henry Kimpton.

Russell, J. (1969) *Creative Dance in the Secondary School*, London: Macdonald & Evans.

Sanders, L. (2004) *Akram Khan's Rush: Creative Insights*, Alton: Dance Books.

Schechner, R. (1988, 1994) *Performance Theory*, London and New York: Routledge.

—— (2002) *Performance Studies: an Introduction*, London and New York: Routledge.

Schön, D. (1987) *Educating the Reflective Practitioner*, San Fransisco: Jossey-Bass.

Shahn, B. (1957) *The Shape of Content*, Cambridge, MA: Harvard University Press.

Shepherd, S. and Wallis, M. (2004) *Drama/Theatre/Performance*, London and New York: Routledge.

Strauss, A. and Corbin, J. (1990) *Basics of Qualitative Research: Grounded Theory Procedures and Techniques*, London: Sage.

Turner, V. (1974) *Dramas, Fields and Metaphors*, Ithaca, NY: Cornell University Press.

Section 3
Communities

Section introduction

Jo Butterworth and Liesbeth Wildschut

> Everyone has the right freely to participate in the cultural life of the community, to enjoy the arts and to share in scientific advancement and its benefits.
>
> (Article 27, The Universal Declaration of Human Rights)

The cultural needs of a post-modern society may in part be met by opportunities that stimulate and release the creativity of ordinary people, through emphasising accessibility and participation. Matarasso (1994) seeks to outline a coherent and workable theoretical underpinning for community-based arts work, defining art as a means through which:

> ...we can examine our experience of ourselves, the world around us and the relationship between the two, and share the results with other people in a form which gives free rein to our intellectual, physical, emotional and spiritual qualities. This definition characterises art by *purpose* rather than *type*, the distinguishing system favoured by the arts establishment. ... it places art's function of communication at the heart of its nature, so that any human activity which seeks to express individual or collective experience creatively may be termed art.
>
> (Matarasso 1994: 4)

This sense of purpose can be identified in each of the five chapters in this section which draws together contributions from the UK and from the Netherlands, two countries where there have been important developments in 'community dance' and 'amateur dance' in the past thirty years. Though these two terms 'community' and 'amateur' are often seen as problematic, in general we are speaking here of non-professional dance activity outside formal educational spheres, where the focus is on the value of social interaction *and* the personal interests of individuals in relation to the creation of dance. Undoubtedly, some problems of definition still exist, together with a general lack of common understandings and evident cultural differences in the areas of amateur dance in the Netherlands and community dance in the UK and Australia. But as Thomson (1988: 89) describes, the community dance movement 'might be characterised as an amateur movement led by professionals (and aspiring, when appropriate, to professional standards)', having the potential to bring dance back into the mainstream of our respective cultures. Normally, this means publicly funded dance projects, led by individual dance workers or small dance companies, which aim to 'stimulate, develop and coordinate dance activities within their community' (Rubidge in Thomson 1988). And crucially, it broadens the definition of the term 'professional'; we are not only speaking here about professional dancers, but about artist-practitioners who demonstrate the ability to teach, choreograph, workshop, facilitate, devise, organise, manage and coach.

The first chapter in this section, 'Too many cooks?', presents a framework for engaging in dance making and devising through a continuum of five distinct approaches to the generic choreographic process. This model is conceived for use as a teaching/learning tool with students at all levels who will emerge as dancers, choreographers, dance tutors and contributors to dance in education and community from different countries and contexts, or to experienced choreographers, whatever their genre or style, with refreshing new ways of thinking about key social and creative aspects of dance making. Jo Butterworth provides a rationale for the Didactic–Democratic model with further explanation of its guiding principles. She describes the design and development of the framework model detailing the original sources of research and findings. The current model is then explicated as a continuum of choreographic processes in which the roles of choreographer and dancer participants may change. The last section characterises and exemplifies collaborative processes within dance devising.

Christine Lomas offers further definitions to the community debate in the following chapter, where the concepts of interventionist and celebratory approaches to dance making are investigated in the context of a series of choreographic workshops held in a women's prison. She argues that in this circumstance, celebration is concerned with the recognition and valuing of oneself and others in relation to dance activity in the processes of making and performing (or sharing). Through sensitive facilitation of dance making by undergraduates, who are learning these skills and concurrently taking part, *all* participants have the opportunity to engage in activities that lead to empowerment for both the individual and the group.

Sara Houston engages with a social inclusion agenda which has gained momentum within mainstream politics and, concurrently, within the community dance sector in the UK. Dance projects for disenfranchised communities have augmented the profile of community dance as a socially valuable activity. Thus, in the context of a long line of such community dance initiatives stretching over a period of approximately thirty years, the chapter first examines the concept of participation benefit as it has entered political thinking, particularly within the framework of policies concerning themselves with social inclusion and exclusion. Secondly, Houston discusses the implications for choreographers working with the socially excluded within the context of the ongoing discourses concerning both inclusion and exclusion.

Caroline Ribbers and Ninke van Herpt describe in the following chapter what can happen when professional and amateur dancers share the same stage. The production of *TIJ* (which translates as 'tide'), created by choreographers Stefan Ernst and Ronald Wintjens, was performed by professional as well as amateur dancers as part of the 2005 Dutch Dance Festival in Maastricht, the Netherlands. The rehearsals and performances (in which Ribbers took part as one of the professional dancers) led to a number of interesting questions. What are the differences (perceived and actual) between these groups of dancers? What is the nature of the interaction between the groups, the creative process, performance outcome and audience response? What skills do the choreographers require to work with both professional and amateur dancers?

Dirk Dumon's research into choreography coaching in the field of amateur dance in the Netherlands is concerned with the perceived need to develop amateur dance as a performing art and with policy decisions formulated with the National Centre for Amateur Dance (LCA), an organisation now amalgamated into Kunstfactor. This chapter asks questions about the skills required by a choreography coach in order to guide the learning process of an amateur dance maker, what roles a coach can play and how the coaching process develops. Dumon offers a model to aid the development of different approaches to coaching for both coach and choreographer.

There is no doubt that amateur dance and community dance have different histories and socio-political drives, yet one of the perceived shared functions is to promote access and participation to dance. Theories, beliefs and approaches derive from the term 'community arts', and as Poyner and Simmonds argue in *Dancers and Communities* (1994), published by the Australian Dance Council, the community dance experience 'must be a possibility for all interested people regardless of age, social background, cultural difference, disability or previous experience in the art form' (1994: 20). One of the main features of community and amateur work is that the dance is rarely imposed and purely artist-led: rather, this kind of choreography might be devised through tasks or problem-solving in the studio, perhaps facilitated by an individual or through decision-making shared by a group. The work is possibly smaller and seen as less prestigious than professional dance work, and often the dance process, the actual dance making, is valued more highly than the final product.

The diversity of community-related activity in the UK and Australia makes it difficult to generalise, but essentially the dance practitioner is dependent upon the context and the brief of the job, the needs of the community and the interests of the individual. The traditional concepts of form, content and technical skill normally adhered to in professional dance performance may need to be adapted, or re-evaluated. Performance outcomes may be considered secondary to the development of self-esteem and empowerment that dance can offer. The LCA formulated a new policy of choreography guidance at the end of the 1980s in the Netherlands in order to stimulate and improve the quality of amateur dance. According to Dumon, dance-coach training was set up to develop dance-coaching skills and insights. This training was intended for dance teachers and dance makers in order to support children, young people and adults in the creation and presentation of their own dance work.

Amateur dance can engender a sense of freedom for a choreographer, as creative outcomes are not judged in the same way as professional dance outcomes. There may be little external critical review except for regional interest, but equally the work may be judged with different criteria. Perhaps there may not be high production values or long rehearsal periods, but often there are many other benefits for the choreographer or workshop leader. For example, exploration of movement ideas with less pressure, shorter projects, a spread rehearsal period which can allow gestation time, knowledge, self-awareness, new and more appropriate methods of generating dance content and of forming work, the experience of working with groups with different capabilities, including young people, people with disabilities, the elderly, etc. Besides their social engagement, choreographers are often interested in doing these projects for their own professional development, as the experience of choreographing work in this arena may develop new understanding or offer a place for practising or challenging creative skills.

Benefits for the community dance group might include the development of skills, knowledge, self-awareness, self-esteem and social relationships. Being accepted by a group, belonging to a community of shared interests and experiencing real involvement and a sense of ownership in creative dance are seen as important advantages to the participant over and above the possibility of improved dance technique or greater knowledge of making dances. Amateur and community dance work often has more immediate value for specific audiences too; the themes and ideas of these dances can be more accessible, and closer to their own experience than some professional work, and this allows greater insights into other people's issues or problems. The principle of communication is seen as central to the experience of making choreography in amateur and community settings, where both social and artistic experience matters for all participants, and long-term, to the potential of dance as an art form.

Regional or national cultural development often includes strategic community partnerships, pooling resources and expertise, leading to artistic pleasure of local artists with the empowerment of community participants. Another development that borders this domain focuses on art and well-being. However, globalisation, together with the development of technology, has impinged on this territory and contemporary communities of interest may now be global, engaged with communicating and choreographing via the World Wide Web as can be seen in the chapters of the following section on intercultural choreography.

References

Matarasso, F. (1994) *Regular Marvels: A Handbook for Animateurs, Practitioners and Development Workers in Dance, Mime, Music and Literature*, Leicester: Community Dance and Mime Foundation.

Poyner and Simmonds (1994) *Dancers and Communities*, Australian Dance Council.

Thomson (1988) 'Community dance: what community ... what dance?' in Glaister, I. K. (ed.) *Dance and the Child International Conference: Young People Dancing*, 3: 88–98, London: Froebel.

Further reading

Anttila, E. (ed.) (1997) *The 7th International Dance and the Child Conference: The Call of Forests and Lakes*, Koupio, Finland.

Armans, D. (2008) *An Introduction to Community Dance Practice*, Basingstoke: Palgrave Macmillan.

Fisher, J. and Shelton, B. (2002) *Face to Face: Making Dance and Theatre in the Community*, Melbourne: Spinifex Press.

Hanna, J. L. (2006) *Dancing for Health: Conquering and Preventing Stress*, Lanham, MD: AltaMira Press.

Hogan, C. (2003) *Practical Facilitation: Theory and Principles*, London: Kogan Page.

Jennings, S. (ed.) (1997) *Dramatherapy: Theory and Practice*, London and New York: Routledge.

Kelly, O. (1989) *Community, Art and the State: Storming the Citadels*, London: Comedia.

Liebmann, M. (ed) (1996) *Arts Approaches to Conflict*, London: Jessica Kingsley.

Macara, A. and Batalha, A. P. (eds.) (2003) *Pulses and Impulses for Dance in the Community*, Conference Proceedings, Lisbon: Universidade Técnica.

Matarasso, F. (1997) *Use or Ornament? The Social Impact of Participation in the Arts*, London: Comedia.

Matos, L. (ed.) (2003) Breaking boundaries: dances, bodies and multiculturalism, *The 9th International Dance and the Child Conference*, Salvador: FSBA.

Novack, C. (1990) *Sharing the Dance: Contact Improvisation and American Culture*, University of Wisconsin Press.

Oddey, A. (1994), *Devising Theatre: a Practical and Theoretical Handbook*, London and New York: Routledge.

Payne, H. (ed.) (1992) *Dance Movement Therapy: Theory and Practice*, London and New York: Routledge.

Shapiro, S. (ed.) (1998) *Dance, Power and Difference*, Champaign, IL: Human Kinetics.

Thompson, J. (ed) (1998) *Prison Theatre: Perspectives and Practices*, London: Jessica Kingsley.

Tuffnell, M. and Crickmay, C. (1990) *Body Space Image: Notes towards Improvisation and Performance*, London: Virago.

Wildschut, L. (ed.) (2006) *The 10th International Dance and the Child Conference: Colouring Senses*, Proceedings, The Hague, the Netherlands.

—— (ed.) (2006) *The 10th International Dance and the Child Conference: Colouring Senses*, Proceedings: keynotes, The Hague, the Netherlands.

Williams, D. (ed) (1999) *Collaborative Theatre: The Théâtre du Soleil Sourcebook*, New York: Routledge.

12 Too many cooks?

A framework for dance making and devising[1]

Jo Butterworth

During my doctoral studies, I constructed the Didactic–Democratic framework model for the teaching of choreography in the higher education sector in the UK (2002). Initially the model emerged solely from my personal experience as dance lecturer in the British university system; it was trialled over many years of programme and module design with colleagues and with undergraduate dance students following choreography modules through three years of full-time study. Briefly, the model presents a framework for approaching dance making and devising through a continuum of five distinct approaches to the generic choreographic process. The design of the model assumes that the dance practitioner has some knowledge and understanding of choreographic craft, and related contextual theory. The model puts forward a series of roles for the choreographer in relation to the dancer participants, and identifies shifts in skills, methods and interaction. The elements are placed into a flexible, working framework, organised in such a way as to demonstrate the value of approaching some aspects of choreography from a directed, 'teaching by showing' approach, termed 'didactic'; and dialogically, the value of learning to work in a shared, cooperative, collaborative approach, termed 'democratic'. It is understood that in practice there is slippage between these stages of the framework: that is, dance making in the studio may utilise several of these processes in the course of making a single choreography.

Through peer review, further research and the opportunity to teach in other European institutes it has became evident to me that the model has broader application than that for which it was initially designed. It serves as a powerful teaching/learning tool for use with students at all levels who will emerge as dancers, choreographers, dance tutors and contributors to dance in education and community from different countries and contexts, and it provides experienced choreographers, whatever their genre or style, with refreshing new ways of thinking about key social and creative aspects of dance making.

The chapter is organised in four sections. First, I provide a rationale for the model together with further explanation of its guiding principles, including the central concept of the dance artist-practitioner

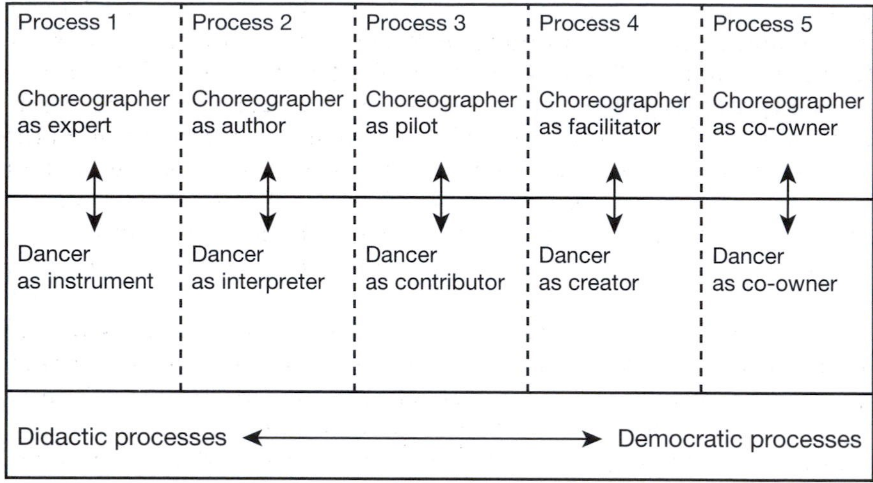

Process 1
Choreographer as expert
Dancer as instrument
Process 2
Choreographer as author
Dancer as interpreter
Process 3
Choreographer as pilot
Dancer as contributor
Process 4
Choreographer as facilitator
Dancer as creator
Process 5
Choreographer as co-owner
Dancer as co-owner
Didactic processes
Democratic processes

Figure 12.1 Butterworth's simple Didactic–Democratic framework model.

and his/her potential roles in a choreographic situation. Second, the design and development of the Didactic–Democratic framework model are described, detailing the original sources of research and findings. The current model is then explicated as a continuum of choreographic processes in which the roles of choreographer and dancer participants may change. Traditional approaches to choreography, in which the choreographer is considered expert and the dancer as instrument, are placed at one end of this continuum. At the other end lies the notion of co-ownership where, perhaps by collaborative methods, or by collective decision-making processes, the creation of dance as art is attempted by more than one artist working together. Finally, perceived strengths and weaknesses of these dance-devising processes are characterised, analysed and exemplified.

Within the Didactic–Democratic model, a dance artist-practitioner is defined as an experienced, multi-skilled individual: a dancer who may also choreograph and teach, a teacher who may also choreograph and dance, or a choreographer who may also dance and teach. The inference is that the dance artist-practitioner learns the basic principles and attributes of the model's differing roles in training, develops them in practice, and is able to apply them variously and relevantly through choice and opportunity. Choreographers may learn rather unconsciously to play these roles, but one specific value of the model is to make them more conscious about the choices they make. Figure 12.1 demonstrates the bare bones of the framework model.

The definition of the term 'didactic' here refers not only to the instructional element of 'teaching by showing', but also to the development of skill competency though repetitive practice. This dual sense of 'didactic' is grounded in educationalist Jerome Bruner's notion of 'apprenticeship' (Leach and Moon 1999: 10–12). I use the term 'democratic' as it was developed in post-modern dance in New York in the 1960s, particularly by members of the dance group Grand Union who rejected traditional hierarchies and demonstrated preference for equality, cooperation, and collective working situations (Banes 1987, 1994). My use of the term also conflates aspects of community arts theory and definitions put forward by such devising theatre groups as those documented by Alison Oddey in *Devising Theatre* (1994: 1–9). Thus there is no intention to suggest either negative connotation or purely political usage of either of the 'bookend' terms used within the framework, but rather to reconsider the origins of the Greek terms *didactikos* (to teach) and *demos* (the people), the latter denoting an egalitarian and tolerant form of society.

The model pulls together consensus practice identified in professional, vocational and educational domains in the twentieth century, drawing upon their evident differences of approach towards dance making. It serves as a tool for dance artist-practitioners working in a variety of dance contexts who seek greater understanding of the range of approaches available to them in the creation of choreography. It leads practitioners to appreciate more fully distinct dancer–choreographer relationships and their impact on dance creation. Specifically, the model helps dance workers to

- identify their personal preferences;
- recognise the specific needs of dancers or participants in the application of choreographic skills; and
- modify rehearsal processes in light of deeper understanding of the influence of contextual factors in the choreographic process.

Construction of the model

The research was initiated by a series of questions:

1. What range of choreographic processes and dancer–choreographer relationships currently exists in the UK?
2. What have been the dominant traits and significant shifts in the traditions of professional/vocational and educational dance-making procedures?
3. Why do methods of choreography need reconsideration for the twenty-first century?
4. What were the origins of my own ideas?

What follows is a brief documentation of the various aspects of the research that contributed to the organisation and structure of the model.

Influences from theatre dance

It became evident that any historical examination of choreography of the theatre domain had to be selective in terms of both genre and period. While acknowledging the richness and complexity of the choreographic field today, it can also be recognised that working practices in dance making are often in flux, merging the paradigms of orthodoxy with innovation, tradition with experimentation. Initial research investigated three distinct historical periods from Western theatre dance where clear, significant shifts could be recognised, giving temporal structure to the history of choreographic development. These related to developments in ballet, modern dance and New Dance in order to explore *genre-specific* choreographic methods and processes, and *particular* dancer–choreographer relationships. Decisions were also guided by the availability of data as the paucity of literature on choreographic processes per se reflects the ephemerality of the discipline and its comparative youth as an academic subject.

1 Identification of traditional styles of choreography from British classical ballet from 1930 to 1940, drawing on literature of Ninette de Valois and Frederick Ashton.
2 Exploration of the period 1967–77, when British choreography was heavily influenced by American modern dance through the practice of Glen Tetley at Ballet Rambert and Robert Cohan at London Contemporary Dance Theatre (LCDT).
3 Examination of British New Dance from 1977 to 1988, which revealed some choreographic characteristics taken from a range of sources, including Judson, and from contemporary practitioners.

The collated evidence provided some understanding of a wide range of choreographic processes that were then categorised by 'tendencies'. Whilst they indicate the norms of each period, these processes do not remain static: the range and complexity of choreographic approaches continue to be extended and enriched, and many of the working practices identified still have a place today.

British classical ballet 1930–40

The differences in approach between de Valois and Ashton became evident from texts such as Beaumont (1946), Haskell (1943), Vaughan (1977), Kavanagh (1996), Jordan (2000) and from de Valois's own writings (1942, 1957). For example, both de Valois and Ashton were influenced by the choreographic reforms of Michel Fokine, and both began developing their respective individual artistic skills in the 1930s. However, their social relationships with dancers could hardly be more distinct. While de Valois tended to be dictatorial and to impose her choreography, Ashton worked like an editor, using his dancers as inspiration and allowing them to contribute to the choreographic process. Annabel Farjeon, who was a member of Sadler's Wells Ballet Company throughout the 1930s, wrote:

> De Valois was cold and reserved, outwardly sure of herself, so that one was never exposed to her personal feelings or a sense of participation in the creation of a ballet. ... Although the prospect of a new ballet such as *Checkmate* ... was obviously of great importance to the company ... it always seemed to me odd that nobody ... in the corps de ballet knew what this creation was to be about ... We were never told. ...
>
> At the first rehearsal de Valois would remain cool, concentrated and often humorous. She was already primed with ideas and knew what she wanted: it had already been written down in a notebook. Save for a pianist or merely using the score, she had marked out the details of the whole ballet in private. She inclined to use dancers as puppets to be manipulated and there was little elasticity to the system. Now and then she would alter some step, rearrange a pattern, or bring a character more to the fore, but it was seldom necessary. Her private imaginings had been pretty accurate.
>
> (Farjeon in Carter 1998: 23–4)

Another dancer, Mona Inglesby (1995: 39), reinforces this opinion, recalling 'I was never happy in rehearsals, always feeling very apprehensive under de Valois' severe direction and forbidding personality'. This clear exposé of de Valois's authoritarian approach perhaps reveals the expected role of the dancer of that period.

Ashton too planned the overall structure of the work, familiarised himself with the music and/or text, and imagined tableaux and designs on stage. Yet, unlike de Valois, he only started to choreograph in any detail within the studio with dancers. He stated in an interview: 'I never choreograph until I'm with people ... I might have certain ideas but I don't do steps till then ... so I do make a certain structure' (Ashton 1984: 2–7). Farjeon describes the 'stillness and silence' in the studio on the days when Ashton had no ideas, or when he challenged the dancers to dance something which would then get him started. He would play and experiment with shapes, and manipulate his dancers to create images; 'on other occasions he knew just what he wanted, but movements were always open to improvements' (1998: 26).

> Often, after searching for clues among his dancers, Ashton would suddenly begin a flow of movement that seemed to take hold of choreographer and dancer alike, until both became instruments on which his imagination would improvise for hours with a facility and professionalism that entirely belied all that earlier agony and dither.
>
> (Farjeon 1998: 27)

For the dance artist-practitioner, knowledge of these contrasting approaches can help to define the ways in which we work as individuals in various dance contexts. Essentially, they raise questions about the social relationship norms that are created in the studio, and they may help the practitioner become more self-reflexive about personal interaction with dancers.

British contemporary dance 1967–77

The second historical period draws on choreographic tendencies identified from the decade 1967–77, collated from the investigation of Glen Tetley with Ballet Rambert and Robert Cohan with LCDT, including Pritchard (1988, 1996a, 1996b), Percival (1971, 1980) Mackrell (1992, 1997), Coton (1975), Clarke and Crisp (1974, 1989), Jordan (1992) and Adair (1992). The following characteristics were noted and illustrated.

Both companies introduced American dance techniques that allowed extension and modification of an existing dance language, particularly in the application of floor work. The standard of the technical ability of the dancers grew with the maturity of each of the companies. Tetley brought an exceptional understanding of how synthesis of technical languages, modern and classical, could be used to make a more expressive dance medium.

In terms of the creation of new work, fresh themes and ideas emerged, and contemporary social and personal issues utilised to stimulate and initiate choreography. Choreographers have always used the special capabilities and qualities of individual dancers, but the new techniques offered an even broader palette for the dance maker.

Methods of creation began to involve *improvisation* more frequently and the specific roles of choreographer and dancer became less discrete. The American modern dance tradition introduced to the UK the notion of the dancer/choreographer trained in improvisation and composition who could create and perform dance work. In turn, this allowed the choreographer a greater degree of internalisation of the characterisation or physicality and the dancer greater freedom to interpret and endow the dance. From interviews with Ann Whitley (dance choreologist, personal interview on 18 April 2000) and Yair Vardi (ex-Rambert dancer, personal interview on 15 April 2000) and from critical writings of Williams (1968) and Percival[2] it is evident that Tetley contributed important changes in the choreographic process in the UK. His intelligence, previous experience and broad knowledge of culture inspired and challenged the dancers cognitively, technically and phenomenally.

Robert Cohan's multifaceted role at LCDT included teaching, performing, choreographing and directing. He established a good technical foundation for the company based on his personal experience with Graham; indeed his choreography tended to reflect a reliance on the modernist aesthetic and symbolism of Graham (Williams 1969: 24).

Through the teaching of choreographic workshops, he passed on the principles he had learnt from Graham and Horst empowering dancers in his company by encouraging choreographic efforts from company members.

The significance of this factor cannot be underestimated in relation to the history of the dancer–choreographer relationship. For the dance artist-practitioner, we can identify from these findings the importance of employing task-based improvisations, developing compositional understandings and inspiring and challenging the skills, thoughts and experiences of their participant groups.

British New Dance 1977–88

Examples from New Dance, in the third phase, identified the dominant ideas stemming from the influence of the post-modern, alternative ideologies of independent dance making – that is, more democratic concepts of facilitation, dancer contribution, and dance devising, as documented by Adair (1992), Jordan (1992), Kaye (1994) and Mackrell (1992). There are some crossovers here with practices in dance education, concepts that are referred to later in this chapter.

Choreographic methods for generating dance content in New Dance tended towards experimentation and improvisation by dancers who were also aspiring dance makers, working alone, with partners or in small groups. The range of starting points relied on such elements as political stance, attitudes towards the body, the grouping and the environment. Setting movement tasks controlled by particular rules, or using chance scores or instructions, graphic notation or structures from other art forms such as music or painting, led to new movement invention. Chance work derived from the Cunningham tradition was favoured as a way of relinquishing any pre-planned meaning or movement material, and of getting away from the normal furrow of repeated improvisation (Charlip in Kostelanetz 1992). Contrasting approaches stripped dance down to the minimum, using formal structures, like accumulation or improvisation, as performance.

Collaborative pieces were common, often exploring political issues of sexism, elitism or feminism, or the ideological situation of arts practice. The growth of small groups and pick-up companies in the 1980s meant that a gradually increasing pool of experienced dancers was able to contribute to the creation and development of new pieces. New Dance works tended to be constructed through organic or collage structures, non-linear narratives or by deliberate juxtapositioning of discrete sections of separate material, and these structures could be negotiated.

New Dance practitioners tended to be questioning, consciousness-raising and unorthodox, critical of the mainstream and reflective of each other. Discussion and debate was an educative force, manifested in the development of more articulate dancers who also choreographed in new forms of critical writing in the journal *New Dance*, and in sharing and critiquing each other's choreographic work in progress. This challenged the perceived mindlessness of some forms of pragmatic, highly technical dance training and initiated the link between dance making and research. In the context of building this model, the philosophy of the thinking dancer and practitioner is possibly one of British New Dance's most important characteristics.

Influences from the domain of education

The research focused on dance in education and examined the learning and teaching of choreography in the maintained dance education sector during the twentieth century, where generic objectives related to the development of the child, pupil or student rather than to dance as an art form. From the social dance and recreational forms, existing pre-World War II exploration covered modern educational dance, expressive creativity and related issues of educational theory between 1945 and 1970; artistic discipline and formality as introduced into the British educational system between 1970 and 1988; and the influences of the National Curriculum from 1988 and beyond.

Findings demonstrated how the democratic and philanthropic impulse of the 1960s, where Rudolf Laban's principles were in ascendancy, shifted to critical scrutiny in the 1970s as arts practices in the education sector were required to develop theory to underpin practice (Laban 1960; Redfern 1973; Adshead 1981). Since the mid-1970s, when examinations in dance first became established in this sector, a balance of instructional and discovery methods, principles and techniques, theory and practice have dominated.

Laban (1975) believed in the dancer as creator as well as interpreter. He emphasised mastery of movement and personal expression, placed importance on dance play, improvisation and experimentation, and a desired synthesis between understanding dance and practising dance. These notions were adapted for use with young people in practical dance education sessions in school, but were also applied to the training of prospective teachers in colleges of education. It is also evident that modern educational dance outcomes – individually composed movement and small group interaction based on Laban's themes – required appropriate teaching methods to involve guidance, facilitation and encouragement.

Process-oriented approaches to the making of dance concentrate on open, even democratic methods using exploration, discovery and problem-solving to find movement content relating to body action, dynamic or spatial considerations. Using these methods, the teacher may act as initiator, guide, facilitator or collaborator, or indeed choose to utilise more didactic or instructive methods if and when necessary. A range of creative dance-composing situations can be chosen to engage students both practically and cognitively, demanding individuality, imagination and an element of ownership. Laban, Ullmann and other colleagues developed these approaches in schools and colleges, thereby offering non-specialist teachers a range of non-didactic dance-making methods and procedures.

Thus, this part of the investigation contributed to the framework the application of approaches *beyond* the instructional, including exploration/discovery, experiential, interactive and collaborative. These approaches are all part of the palette of the dance artist-practitioner.

The personal, experiential perspective

The third area of research to contribute to the model design was in-depth reflection on aspects of the author's personal career experiences. The frame of reference included five areas of enquiry: ideas originated from my student days at the Laban Art of Movement studio (1960s); those drawn from teaching dance in the state sector in London (1970s); experience of teaching educational drama methods at Bretton Hall (1979–88) and lecturing in dance (1984–2005); influences from post-modern dance and from performance studies during my MA study period in New York in the early 1980s; and research into community arts development in the UK in the mid-1980s. This experiential perspective contributed significantly to aspects of this model, and led in particular to the development of the term 'dance devising' to denote the creation of dance by more than one artist.

A review of current UK professional practice

The fourth and final area of research reviewed the developments and events related to professional dance practice in the UK from 1993 to 2001. Here I sought consensus views of the compatibility between choreographic practice and vocational training of the period; and identified perceptions of what was required in relation to future careers in dance. A brief evaluation of the dance culture in 2001 suggested a changing, evolving and eclectic context for the dance artist-practitioner. The review included material from several conferences, newspaper and journal articles, interviews, accreditation outcomes, *The Independent Dance Review* and other reports from UK dance organisations. From this extensive review, a wish list of qualities pertinent to the developing dance artist-practitioner model was selected (Butterworth 2002: 210–11):

Dancers/choreographers should be:

- widely educated, intelligent, curious and versatile;
- articulate, able to discuss and daring to question;
- adaptable in demonstrating technical facility and mastery and the ability to take direction, but equally able to experiment, improvise, devise and problem-solve;

- aware of the historical, social and cultural context of the art form;
- able to demonstrate, perform and interpret;
- cognisant of a number of approaches to the making of dances;
- an autonomous thinker, individual, able to demonstrate critical faculty;
- able to interact, collaborate, and negotiate.

Findings

The design and content of the framework model emerged from the development and synthesis of the salient ideas raised in these four areas of research. Summaries of the findings from theatre and education domains indicated that they had separate histories, little relationship, growing recognition of what is lacking but no consensus strategies for change. The education sector tended to exhibit little relationship with the legacies of dance as art form; the vocational sector demonstrated paternalistic and hierarchical attitudes within the academy, perpetuating a mid-body split in dance training (Butterworth 2002: 212). A common assumption suggested that choreography is a given talent, subliminal, intuitive, not learned, separated from conscious, articulated processes and not needing to be taught systematically.

As a result of the investigation and the concepts derived, some general principles emerged which were applied to the design of the model. Five distinct working processes were selected in order to construct a manageable framework, exemplar approaches as practised in the making of choreography in professional theatre, education and community contexts. These are presented as a viable palette of knowledge and skills in the twenty-first century.

The model

The Didactic–Democratic framework model proposes five distinct choreographic processes, detailing in each one some differences and distinctions between choreographers' and participants' roles. The model identifies the respective skills that are normally required, the type of social interaction, methods of leadership and possible approaches to participation by the client group. Each individual may be able to recognise his/her usual tendencies in terms of methods of working. No linear progression through dependence to independence (from Process 1 to Process 5) is advocated. Rather, the choreographer or workshop leader makes conscious decisions about the appropriateness of an approach at a particular point in time, depending on the context, the participant needs, and the intended outcome.[3] Table 12.2 clearly identifies differences of knowledge and skill for all participants in the creative situation.

The model has already provided a valuable resource to choreographers who have been introduced to it. Equally, there are benefits to dance participants, as follows:

Table 12.2 Butterworth's Didactic–Democratic spectrum model.

Process 1	*Process 2*	*Process 3*	*Process 4*	*Process 5*
Choreographer role:				
Choreographer as expert	Choreographer as author	Choreographer as pilot	Choreographer as facilitator	Choreographer as collaborator
Dancer role:				
Dancer as instrument	Dancer as interpreter	Dancer as contributor	Dancer as creator	Dancer as co-owner
Choreographer skills:				
Control of concept, style, content, structure and interpretation. Generation of all material.	Control of concept, style, content, structure and interpretation in relation to capabilities/qualities of dancers.	Initiate concept, able to direct, set and develop tasks through improvisation or imagery, shape the material that ensues.	Provide leadership, negotiate process, intention, concept. Contribute methods to provide stimulus, facilitate process from content generation to macro-structure.	Share with others research, negotiation and decision-making about concept, intention and style, develop/share/adapt dance content and structures of the work.
Dancer skills:				
Convergent: imitation, replication.	Convergent: imitation, replication, interpretation.	Divergent: replication, content development, content creation (improvisation and responding to tasks).	Divergent: content creation and development (improvisation and responding to tasks).	Divergent: content creation and development (improvisation, setting and responding to tasks), shared decision-making on aspects of intention and structure.

Continued overleaf

Process 1	*Process 2*	*Process 3*	*Process 4*	*Process 5*
Social interaction:				
Passive but receptive, can be impersonal.	Separate activities, but receptive, with personal performance qualities stressed.	Active participation from both parties, interpersonal relationship.	Generally interactive.	Interactive across group.
Teaching methods:				
Authoritarian.	Directorial.	Leading, guiding.	Nurturing, mentoring.	Shared authorship.
Learning approaches:				
Conform, receive and process instruction.	Receive and process instruction and utilise own experience as performer.	Respond to tasks, contribute to guided discovery, replicate material from others, etc.	Respond to tasks, problem-solve, contribute to guided discovery, actively participate.	Experiential. Contribute fully to concept, dance content, form, style, process, discovery.

Process 1: learning valuable skills about the making of dances, observing and learning from the choreographer's creative process, being inspired, learning about expected conventions, or engaging in new dance vocabulary.

Process 2: working with an expert, enjoying artistic and technical challenges, identifying one's own special qualities (including personal movement style), developing characterisation or individual interpretation.

Process 3: introduction to the process of devising, contributing to the choreography by responding to tasks through improvisation or problem-solving, identifying appropriate facilitation skills, comprehending and contributing to the choreographer's intentions.

Process 4: engaging in devising process, contributing to the whole creative process in negotiation, active participation in content creation and decisions about structure, applying analysis and evaluation to the dance work as it develops, interacting with group, personal involvement with the dance work.

Process 5: sharing ownership of the work from research, to negotiation and decision-making, sharing decision-making on content creation and development, intention and structure.

In the Didactic–Democratic framework, three distinct *dance-devising* processes are put forward where a clear shift in ownership is apparent from one process to another.

- Process 3: dancers contributing to the concept of a choreographer,
- Process 4: dancers collaborating with a choreographer, and
- Process 5: dancer-choreographers working together in ensemble.

What is dance devising?

Essentially 'dance devising' involves the dialectic between the acts of making and doing, of creating and performing, and of being an artist and/or interpreter. By implication, the roles and responsibilities are shared. Perhaps by collaborative methods, or through collective decision-making processes, the creation of dance as art is attempted by more than one artist. In 'Potholes in the Road to Devising' (2005), Joan Schirle provides ground rules for theatre devising, offering collaborative principles through which artists might develop trust and respect, come to common understandings and clarify intentions, roles and agendas:

> In the crucible of devising, each group must strike its own balance between the productive engagement of artistic egos and the generosity of the collaborative spirit.
>
> (Schirle 2005: 92)

Schirle points out the essential tension here. Since this means of working is often based on the intentional relation of artists who have chosen group creation (i.e., Process 5), there is some risk in the outcome, some compromise of personal artistic ideas and aesthetic. But there are also benefits. For a professional ensemble of dancer creators engaged in creating original work, the compounding ideas and energy provide personal knowledge of intent and context for all members. The developing work cannot be mindless; it demands critical thinking. Thomson affirms that:

> creativity not only demands critical thinking, but also is sometimes identical with it. Critical thinking similarly avoids judgement, preconceived and unexamined opinion, and champions risk, discovery and an appetite for the unknown.
>
> (Thomson 2003: 121)

In dance-devising situations it is recognised that there may be ambivalence or creative opposition between individual and ensemble needs and desires that requires more than an understanding of choreographic strategies, concepts and devices. In common with teachers and social workers, the skills of communication need to be refined: development of social interactive and facilitation skills and an understanding of the functions of leadership are required. Schirle argues that devising is a way for young artists to engage with each other 'in the stimulating territory where art and ideas commingle to generate excitement, provocation, even hope' (2003: 99). However, equality of responsibility or artistry within the group is not necessary: roles may be negotiated, as there exist as many models of devising as other processes of directing or composing.

In dance devising there may or may not be a choreographer present in the studio and indeed this role may be flexible and/or rotational. The central premise is that participants engage with, and contribute to, the various stages of the choreographic process, including the ability to function as a member of a team, and this may be in partnership with a choreographer. Devising methods tend to challenge each individual's knowledge and skills of dance making with an awareness of and sensitivity to the group as ensemble. Thus, awareness of artistic and social processes must coexist in parallel.

For the student, devising provides a laboratory for investigating the dynamics of choreography, for wrestling with social/artistic processes, learning to articulate opinions and recognising personal aesthetic decisions. As Thomson (2003: 120) describes, devising requires 'a high tolerance for open spaces, advanced skills in uncertainty, a hunger for the question, and a commitment to surpass what is routine'.

The notion of *shared endeavour* is a predominant mechanism for this work, and the use of facilitating skills that involve joint decision-making and open rather than closed strategies. Distinctions between performer and audience, creation and participation, and production and consumption tend to blur. In some contexts, such as dance with disabled groups or with mothers and toddlers, participants could value the creative processes more highly than the end product; any performance outcomes may be informal, or may not be appropriate at all.

Naturally, anxieties and critical prejudice about collaboration abound; that it eradicates individuality or artistic genius, or that it is the 'enemy of true artistic vision' (Frisch in Rudakoff and Thomson 2002: 283). Heaton[4] provides a critique on the nature of choreographer–composer collaboration thus:

> In reality the fruits of collaboration, with a meagre handful of notable exceptions, are like anything designed by committee: they creak with compromise. All the friction of two very different creative minds sparking together is dulled into bland, obscure banality by too much cooperation.
>
> (Heaton 1995: 12)

Pragmatically, however, group ensemble work is now a central feature of many areas of the performing arts, and allows a particular kind of process of engagement, a shared vision, the sharpening of problem-solving skills and accompanying discoveries that a single artist cannot achieve. In undergraduate dance and theatre programme workshops, as in amateur and community group activities, those who choose to work together invent methods for dealing with the reconciliation of difference. At the postgraduate and professional level, there may be radical differences in choreographic style, movement memory or technical performance ability that can be perceived as problematic, but the obstacles that are encountered lead to education and deeper understanding about how best to function in the task. Since I use these methods as aspects of my own teaching of choreography, quotations from MA students' process logs (from three different devising projects) provide some insight into personal experience:

> Student 1: Overall this workshop ... exceeded my expectations, as it became a happening on its own. After it turned into a group improvisation, it became so vibrant and alive; we were all in the moment, sharing an exciting experience.
>
> Student 2: My role in the group could best be described as 'undercover mediator'. ... We simply cannot have four captains on a ship. When there is already tension between two, others need to take another role. Adding to that the fact is that in different cultures we react differently to differences in opinion, we created an interesting cocktail of diplomacy skills.
>
> Student 3: Again, in my experience, the responsibility of each person is to be the best that they can be, to show kindness, compassion and interest in those around them, with no power play or domination. And most importantly, to be willing to trust the people around them,

and embark on a 'changing' transformation experience, without expectation or fear of what the outcome will be.

Student 4: It is only in hindsight that I realise what a great deal I have gained from being part of this dance-devising project. Never before, and possibly never again will I have the privilege of working alongside six highly experienced choreographers all with their own varied experience, knowledge and skill base.

Student 5: Compromises had to be made and individual tastes sacrificed, but overall the experience was a very positive and enriching one.

It is clear that 'dance devising' may not be an easy option, but it is perceived as a valuable learning experience. For the dance practitioner, these shared periods of involvement often provide a watershed of understanding, a relinquishing of self-consciousness, and recognition of the power of dance as a shared experience and an instrument of social change. It is in the *experiential* that the function of devising dance becomes validated. The value of didactic and instructional approaches should never be forgotten, however. Indeed, all five of the Didactic–Democratic model processes provide different nuances of role, relationship, skills and understanding, offering further choice to the choreography student, teacher, postgraduate or experienced practitioner, whatever their chosen style or genre.

A final question might be posed here in relation to the choreographer's acknowledgement of the achievement and input of dancers in performance programme notes. Since devising processes tend to heighten the visibility of the contribution of dancers to the work of a choreographer, and to clarify the intrinsic ownership of the final production product, might dance devising lead to further emancipation of dancers from the shackles of tradition?

Notes

1 Parts of this chapter were published as 'Teaching choreography in higher education: a process continuum model' in *Research in Dance Education*, 5 (1) 2004: 45–67.
2 Published in *Dance and Dancers* throughout the late 1960s.
3 It is well understood that choreographers tend to develop several operational choices, sometimes within the making of a single dance, but it is also important to consider a good match with participants' needs at salient times.
4 Roger Heaton, a clarinettist and composer who was Music Director for Rambert Dance from 1988 to 1993.

References

Adair, C. (1992) *Women and Dance: Sylphs and Sirens*, Basingstoke: Macmillan.
Adshead, J. (1981) *The Study of Dance*, London: Dance Books.

Ashton, F. (1984) 'Sir Frederick Ashton in Conversation with Alastair Macaulay', *Dance Theatre Journal*, 2 (3) Autumn: 2–7.

Banes, S. (1987) *Terpsichore in Sneakers: Post-Modern Dance*, 2nd edn, Middletown, CT: Wesleyan University Press.

—— (1994) *Writing Dancing in the Age of Postmodernism*, Hanover: Wesleyan University Press.

Beaumont, C. W. (1946) *The Sadler's Wells Ballet: a Detailed Account of Works in the Repertory with Critical Notes*, London: C. W. Beaumont.

Bruner, J. (1999) 'Folk Pedagogies', in J. Leach and B. Moon (eds) *Learners and Pedagogy*, London: Paul Chapman.

Butterworth, J. (2002) Dance Artist Practitioners: An integrated model for the learning and teaching of choreography in the tertiary sector, (unpublished doctoral thesis), LSCD, University of Kent at Canterbury.

Charlip, R. (1992) 'Composing by Chance' *Dance Magazine* (January, 1954) reprinted in R. Kostelanetz (ed.) *Merce Cunningham: Dancing in Space and Time*, London: Dance Books.

Clarke, M. and Crisp, C. (1974) *Making a Ballet*, London: Studio Vista.

—— (1989) *London Contemporary Dance Theatre: the First 21 Years*, London: Dance Books.

Coton, A. V. (1975) *Writings on Dance 1938–1968*, selected and ed. by Kathrine Sorley Walker and Lilian Haddakin. London: Dance Books.

Farjeon, A. (1998) 'Choreographers: Dancing for de Valois and Ashton', in A. Carter *The Routledge Dance Studies Reader*, London and New York: Routledge.

Haskell, A. L. (1943) *The National Ballet*, London: A & C Black.

Heaton, R. (1995) 'Music for Dance', *Dance Theatre Journal*, 11 (4) Spring: 12–15.

Inglesby, M. (1995) 'From the Cradle of British Ballet', *Dance Now*, 4 (1): 35–45.

Jordan, S. (1992) *Striding Out: Aspects of Contemporary and New Dance in Britain*, London: Dance Books.

—— (2000) *Moving Music: Dialogues with Music in Twentieth Century Ballet*, London: Dance Books.

Kavanagh, J. (1996) *Secret Muses: the Life of Frederick Ashton*, London: Faber.

Kaye, N. (1994) *Postmodernism and Performance*, Basingstoke: The Macmillan Press.

Laban, R. (1960) *The Mastery of Movement*, 2nd edn revised by L. Ullmann, London: MacDonald and Evans.

—— (1975) *Modern Educational Dance*, 3rd edn, Plymouth: MacDonald and Evans.

Mackrell, J. (1992) *Out of Line: The Story of British New Dance*, London: Dance Books.

—— (1997) *Reading Dance*, London: Michael Joseph.

Oddey, A. (1994) *Devising Theatre: a Practical and Theoretical Handbook*, London and New York: Routledge.

Percival, J. (1971) *Experimental Dance*, London: Studio Vista.

—— (1980) *Modern Ballet*, rev. edn, London: The Herbert Press.

Pritchard, J. (1988) 'Archives of the Dance: The Rambert Dance Company Archive', *Dance Research*, 6 (1): 59–69.

—— (1996a) (compiler) *Rambert: A Celebration*, London: Rambert Dance Company.

—— (1996b) 'Two Letters', in S. Jordan and A. Grau (eds) *Following Sir Fred's Steps: Ashton's Legacy*, London: Dance Books.

Redfern, H. B. (1973) *Concepts in Modern Educational Dance*, London: Henry Kimpton.

Rudakoff, J. and Thomson, L. M. (2002) *Between the Lines: The Process of Dramaturgy*, Toronto: Playwrights Canada Press.

Shirle, J. (2005) 'Potholes in the Road to Devising', *Theatre Topics*, 15 (1): 91–102.

Thomson, L. M. (2003) 'Teaching and rehearsing collaboration', *Theatre Topics*, 13 (1): 117–28.

Valois, N. de, (1937/1942) *Invitation to the Ballet*, London: John Lane, The Bodley Head.

—— (1957/1973) *Come Dance with Me*, London: Dance Books.

Vaughan, D. (1977) *Frederick Ashton and his Ballets*, London: A & C Black.

Williams, P. (1968) 'Tumbling and the Consenting Adult', *Dance and Dancers*, January: 12–14.

—— (1969) 'Sturdy Foreign Roots', *Dance and Dancers*, November: 23–6.

13 Doing time

A discussion of interventionist and celebratory approaches to dance making for undergraduates

Christine Lomas

A number of the concepts investigated in this chapter are informed by ongoing research with second year undergraduates in the context of dance-making workshops in a women's prison in West Yorkshire. In this project it was my intention to further the enquiry of dance art as a medium for intervention and celebration. Intervention in this context relates to the notions of empowerment and facilitation, where the focus is the relationship between the received experience and the response to it. The experiences afforded by this relationship are celebratory in nature. Celebration here is concerned with the recognition and valuing of oneself and others in relation to dance activity in the processes of making and performing; that is, the individual celebrates in and through the dance. Arguably, all performance should have elements of empowerment and celebration for both the dance maker and performer.

I wish to propose that art exists as an empowered interaction within our lives in our capacity to create metaphor, to be human. In my support for dance as interventionist and celebratory activity I am not conceding to populist persuasions; rather suggesting that elitist marginalization concedes to populist notions of quality and vice versa. The marginalization of dance in the 'high art' establishment negatively affects its accessibility to the wider population. In turn, other dance activity which is seen as neither part of the elitist model nor part of the populist model is doubly marginalized.

This chapter begins with a discussion of some issues related to differences between theatrical and applied dance making. More specifically it identifies the central curriculum concerns of a specific undergraduate degree in dance at Bretton Hall and the nature of undergraduate learning in the community dance context, where emphasis is placed on process and aspects of facilitation rather than choreographic outcome. The objectives and key concerns of the prison project are followed by analysis of the interventionist process, observation of selected aspects of the workshops and group evaluation of the participants' contribution.

The subjective body: a strategy for empowerment

Our engagement with the tradition of art forms is our heritage, but within a monetarist culture this heritage has been hijacked so that our lives in art have been marginalized. Involvement in dance making assists us in our reconciliation of irreconcilables, and seeks to mediate between sets of oppositions. In this sense it involves us in activities which acknowledge our capacity for hope, for belonging, for individual significance and group solidarity. In the era of postmodernity it can no longer be acceptable to see only the object on stage; the subject must be able to be referenced, the people and process as well as the dance product. Interaction with another person in dance brings more than awareness of 'other'; it also expands the image of self, whether as a member of an audience or as a participant in the dance-making process.

Higher education in the arts should not necessarily follow, if at all, a conservatoire model. If art is a mirror of our society, the art removed from our lives may afford us distorted images. There exists a long history of virtuosity in dance linked to virtuoso bodies; that is, emphasis on technique, on skill. However, it needs to be recognized that virtuosity does not necessarily lead to the essential transcendence of the whole being greater than the parts. As Shapiro observes,

> The body for the dancer was a tool, an instrument objectified for the benefit of the dance. ... The body that I had treated as an object to perfect both visually and technically can be a rich source of knowledge.
>
> (Shapiro 1998: 9)

Authenticity and feeling are no doubt aspects of that knowledge. It is with the subjective body, which is resonant with both natural and nurtured conditions that we might respond authentically within the dance, intuitively and with feeling. If we understand the vital relationship between the subject and the intention in dance making and performing, the conflict which describes certain people as achievers, or *able*, and which describes others as non-achievers or *unable*, may then be addressed. In her seminal publication, *Dance: A Creative Art Experience*, Margaret H'Doubler writes:

> In Dance, the dancer reflects through bodily tensions and disciplined movements the emotion and meaning he wishes to communicate ...
>
> (H'Doubler 1957: 25)

Initially I am particularly interested in what may be understood by 'disciplined movement'. Clearly, technical skills play a part in this notion of discipline, but what part? A technically good mover is not necessarily a good dancer; to dance well is to work beyond the constraints of technique.

Is it sufficient to have the right body, a dancer's body, or is there something else: the desire, response to a need to dance, as H'Doubler suggests, to explore, express through the dance activity something authentic of self, some sense of ownership. Shapiro (1998) argues that to engage in the art discipline, not merely the technical discipline, is a formative process with the body as a rich source of knowledge. This is the knowledge related to individual significance, that is, the conscious placing of oneself as subject in the dance activity where the notion of body as object is consciously engaged. Undergraduate education in dance should aim to facilitate the student's understanding of the power of dance, where dance technique is understood, not an end in itself, and where in some contexts it may have very limited currency, if any at all. I would argue that the power lies in the challenge to give form – art/aesthetic form – to significant experience, to value the ownership of the performer in the performed, and to recognize the individual.

The undergraduate legacy

For most undergraduate dance students, the legacy of the person-centric concerns of the modernists such as Graham and Cunningham are an important aspect of their studies. Often this dance theatre, or dance created for the theatre, is synonymous with technique which equals language and method. In effect it prioritizes content and form: in Graham's work the form often followed a narrative impetus, whereas for Cunningham the form was often created by the use of chance mechanisms, or indeterminacy. But still, these works were created for the theatre, though Cunningham delighted in placing the same material in other venues such as art galleries or outside spaces. What I continue to find quizzical is the fact that, in postmodern dance, 'new' dance and independent dance genres, having defined something to be *outside* the theatrical context, dance artists can be observed trying to do in the non-theatrical context what we find/observe *in* the theatrical context. In other words we do the same thing, but we are just in a different place. The notion of dance art as the institution of theatre, with technique as the major dynamic, still plays a huge role in our perception of dance activity.

Included in the curriculum for the dance undergraduate, alongside technique classes, improvisation, reconstruction, choreographic devising and direction, are the overarching concerns of the theatrical and the non-theatrical context. This chapter draws its examples largely from the community dance context. Our understanding of both theatrical and non-theatrical context is normally informed by a broad base of dance as art; yet, if we are able to think beyond the theatre as institution, the question which arises is whether dance activities need theatre or forums. Do we need a specific forum for artistic expression, for expression of the subject? If we consider dance more broadly, we no longer need to be concerned with spurious comparisons and definitions related to whether this or that performance is as good as another, but instead we are able to see, recognize and interact with the performative in relation to what it is. What it *is* can only be dependent upon our ability to experience it.

Process: the intrinsic experience

To experience the dance kinetically as performer or visually as viewer we have to be present to feel it, to see it. Preoccupations with the technical and with crafting concerns do not necessarily afford *dance experiencing* directly whether as performer or viewer. In addition, the dance undergraduate's developing understanding of the dance discipline is challenged, informed and progressed when he or she is exposed to contextual frameworks. All art is contextually ephemeral, and even though we have examples of long-lived artefacts, our response to them is dependent upon an interactive process which is in essence ephemeral. Investigating the historical perspective, that is, exploring where the dance has come from and where it may be placed now, is perhaps one of the most difficult areas of the curriculum. Beginning to understand a variety of genres and styles may well support the students' ability to embrace others' technical and choreographic styles, but essentially it also challenges them to reflect upon their present and inform their future, socially, culturally and choreographically. In students' work in the community context, as well as drawing from and continuing to develop upon adaptive, learned responses, they are challenged to recognize authenticity. And through working with improvisation, or on the facilitation of an event with the emphasis on process, the intent and context of the dance rather than its content and form is stressed.

The body in action, shaping energy and taking time are the three vital elements in facilitated dance activity which is celebratory, playful and empowering. Managed and organized expression can be experienced during facilitated workshops because participants are empowered by the process. Ann Holmes proposes that

> Empowerment is concerned with the processes whereby people are assisted to become powerful in this sense of being enabled to act.
>
> (Holmes 1992: 8)

The dance action (act) in the facilitated workshop is usually defined in relation to its purpose rather than its type. In this sense all facilitated dance activity could be described as interventionist, that is, aiming to actualize the potential of the individual in relation to themselves and their experience. An essential feature of facilitated activity is facilitators' ability to transfer their focus from the work plan to the participant so that self-directed and increasingly self-mastering experiences can occur. Dance offers the individual the opportunity to organize experience and to problem solve; and a process of reclamation can occur where the adaptive self, which has developed in order to achieve acceptability to the perceived world, is challenged and reshaped. Debatably, understandings occur which are more acceptable to the inner, deeply intuitive self. The revelation of our authentic selves to self and others employs the tools for dance expression – energy, time, space and flow – wherein the body does the knowing, creates, communicates and learns through dance (Lomas 1998). The facilitator is also a participant, prepared and able to risk and to move beyond tried and tested adaptive behaviours.

The project: actualizing potential

The project took place in the spring of 1999 in the second semester and second year of a three-year BA Dance degree at Bretton Hall College of Higher Education and formed an assessed part of the Choreography Applied module. Lectures, seminars and practical preparation preceded five workshop sessions with the client group, one day per week. Eleven students, who were both facilitators and participants, prepared and led workshop sessions in teams, supported by the author. The intention in the prison project was to encourage individual and group dance making via an interventionist approach, and the generation of movement content was through dance improvisation. The clients, nine women, were following a Business Studies course in the education unit of the prison and part of this course concentrated upon communication. Data from planning notes, written records of sessions with observations and reflections, student analysis and reflections between sessions and written submissions from both client group and students made it possible to chart key developments in the understandings of participants. From the project's outset, one day a week over five weeks, it was recognized that what we were aiming to do was afford a counter-culture contrary to the prison culture, which emphasized individual significance and group solidarity. In preplanning, the undergraduate students investigated further what facilitation in the community dance context and through intervention might be. Key concerns which emerged from these investigations were the potential dissonance for individual participants between the actualization of potential and hierarchy, as the need to value and evaluate caused a perceived re-imposition of hierarchy. The question posed, 'What if you actualize someone's potential and then don't like the results?' was responded to by a fellow undergraduate in the following way, 'By giving them freedom you have handed over responsibility, it is no longer yours to judge!'

Prior to the prison-based workshops, each undergraduate prepared a solo using self as stimulus; so that personal, implicit movement was stylized and emphasized to change the implicit to the explicit in the performative. Through this performance of self, the student chooses whichever 'self' to express and is therefore responding to the freedom and the responsibility which is offered in the interventionist process. In placing oneself as *subject* in the dance activity, the notion of body as object is consciously engaged. The reason for the creation of these solo dances was that they were later to be used as the vehicles for the animation of dance activity. The solo material was heightened choreographically by presenting it simultaneously, as duet form.

After the first workshop, discussion revealed that the dance undergraduates did not consider that they were achieving their aim of facilitating the dance making of the client group. They did not feel that they had observed any dance activity. However, more detailed reflections and reconstruction by the students of some of the dance activity which had taken place revealed that there *had* been, particularly in small-group interactions, some clear interventions and a conscious attempt made to recognize the ideas and contributions made by individual prisoners.

The prison group was asked to interpret the student duets; responses indicated that they were reading both movement content and relationships. Responses were quick and insightful, and included descriptions such as 'shyness', 'nervousness', 'low status', 'closed/open movements'. Their intuitive knowledge of movement was being tapped as a result of watching the students draw upon their own expertise in performance. The scene was set for all participants to seek vocabulary, and the undergraduates discovered that throughout their participation in the workshops quite an advanced movement vocabulary was appropriate. The first workshop led by the undergraduates opened with the duet watched by the group sitting in a circle. The sitting position of each individual was the starting point for the session. Postural shifts, body shape and spatial management were the key concerns from which trios were generated. Lisa and Diane from the prison and Karen from the college worked together. In the process Karen rolled over crossed legs to lie on her stomach: the verbal interaction between Karen and Diane was as follows:

Diane: We could do that, and then roll on our sides facing forward to that position.
Karen: OK, what next?
Diane: I don't know – you're the dancer! (Laughter)

Observations from individuals in the client group about the first session included reference to being taken away from being in prison and how hard it is to let your feelings out, 'but when you do it feels really good'. The education unit tutor assigned to the project was surprised at how quickly the two groups integrated. The undergraduate reflections supported this observation, noting that a feeling of equality was quickly achieved. Some possible reasons for this were identified: first, the prison group initiated the introductions; second, the learning frame was shared, as both groups were students, similar in age. Third, the leaders of the workshop were quiet and unthreatening in tone and voice levels in their presentation style.

The reservations held by the undergraduates in relation to the success of the first workshop were tested further in the second. The lively debate about facilitation and intervention which had occurred in the planning stages was now being put to the test. The second workshop was directed rather than facilitated. It consisted essentially of the presentation of a series of dance activities by the undergraduates. The model of the workshop emphasized dance knowledge, content and form, activity which could be termed 'the dance artist in the community approach'. An action of major intervention did occur, but not through the dance. A prison officer removed one of the participants for a 'room spin' (a cell search for drugs) and a strip search. Wendy returned to the session some time later, very distressed. The opportunity to welcome her back into the group via dance activity – perhaps through the use of the circle, the sculptural shape, or duet following and leading – was missed initially, but along with other similar experiencing of prison culture the undergraduates began to develop an understanding of the importance of the context and of their intention in relation to dance activity. The two student leaders of the second session considered themselves to have 'failed' in relation to the interventionist aim of the project; however post-workshop discussion identified key thoughts leading to planning for the following week.

The emphasis upon intent and context in itself challenges the further development of dance content and the necessary act of forming, in order to frame and articulate the moment and series of moments experienced as living in the prison context. David Best writes:

> if people succumb to popular pressures, and are thus limited to the circulating library of cliché forms of expression, then their capacity for *their own* individual thought and emotional experience is commensurately limited. ... They impede the possible development of genuinely individual feelings: they restrict personal possibilities.
>
> (Best 1992: 83)

This project, however, began to allow these individual feelings to develop. The content of the remaining three sessions was planned to reflect the growing sense of a collective resonance. The community which had begun to emerge was dependent upon recognition by others of the significance of the individual, which in turn afforded a sense of group solidarity (Lomas 1998). The introduction to contact improvisation work in the second session was built upon and further challenged; whole group sculpture building was developed to note and consider the dynamic, spatial and gestural concerns of individuals as they moved into the group and retuned to the outer circle again. Participants were encouraged to watch from the circle edge and to respond improvisationally to the activities of crossing the circle to replace someone on the other side, or bringing others into the circle before leaving, of passing touch around the circle, or of contact duets between couples across the circle. Sharing and an equality of leadership began to emerge. The tendency for the undergraduate students to panic in relation to 'what comes next' began to be replaced by seeing the *now*, by responding to the process in its immediacy. The duration of the project revealed significant development in all participants' abilities to improvise, to move spontaneously in increasingly mature, organized and reflective movement. Community dance does not empower communities; rather it nurtures individual empowerment, self-intimacy, interaction with one's authentic self, a sense of fulfilment and a feeling of achievement. All these qualities became apparent in the project's process, contributing to a larger 'whole' which we all experienced; the community of solidarity, the 'we' and the 'ours' which we sensed as individuals and as a community of individuals (Lomas 1998).

At the end of the project the undergraduates submitted final reflections. Julia wrote:

> One of the first major turning points in my conception of the project was the moment when we established, during discussion, some recognition of a level of personal intervention by some of the client group. Up until this point I had been unsure of the whole concept of an interventionist approach and how it worked practically, expecting some sort of climactic moment in which an individual achieved a sense of self worth and empowerment through the accomplishment of some aspect of the dance form. I did not expect that all the other packages that came with the experience – issues around prison life, my personal emotional state and interactions with individuals – would play such a major role. ... This I have attributed to the fact that I have been denied the privilege of being able to bring my own agendas, emotions and reactions into most previous dance experience. This project allowed me to really appreciate the role of the subjective body in dance.
>
> (Julia's process log: 11 June 1999)

Julia goes on to address and reflect upon her own intervention through the dance activity and to analyse how her own responses, using a dance-as-art framework, at times inhibited her involvement in the workshops and led to her own disempowerment. With the realization that the intended focus was not upon content and form, and without having to judge an end product critically, she was enabled to become involved in the experience, to focus on the felt, the moment of dancing. From observation there was little sense of two separate groups of people: she danced with individuals as the situation arose and felt the appreciation of and sensitivity towards each other's energy and agendas. With a clear emphasis upon intent and context all the participants became the group which danced, no longer concerned with their roles as defined by institutions. A sense of freedom and purpose was experienced in dance where issues and agendas could be addressed, not explicitly or superficially in the manner of 'let's do a dance about how we feel in respect of ...' but *implicitly* in the movement, the dynamics and the relationships.

In the fourth session, which drew upon the content and forming experience of previous sessions, a series of improvised duets emerged, framed within a whole-group shape. The motivation for this was Lisa's news at the beginning of the session that she was to be transferred to an open prison. Initially Lisa and Diane were talking verbally about the situation, but at the same time having a movement conversation which unequivocally spoke of support and friendship through sensitivity of touch and weight giving. Diane chose different music, *Teardrop*, and later *Safe from Harm* by Massive Attack, and the dancing continued with individuals from the prison group initiating throughout with a sense of ease and understanding.

A participant in dance improvisation usually draws upon a basic framework of experience in order to interact with self, others or both. This personal framework involves beliefs, experiences, emotions and knowledge which are drawn upon in a spontaneous process (Lomas 1998). From the initial naive, simple, responsive movements of Diane and Lisa, more mature, organized and reflective movements could be observed as the workshop progressed. Individuals drew upon the experience and/or knowledge gained from the previous three workshops in an intrinsic creative process and the formulation of the group's dance of celebration could be observed.

The requirement to take on simultaneous roles of facilitator and participant was a reoccurring concern for the dance undergraduates throughout the project. How can you lead a session, facilitate *and* be an interactive member of the group, all on an equal basis? At the outset the students had a propositional knowledge base (knowing that) but not an experiential one (knowing how) (Ryle 1949). Julia's reflections at the end of the project indicate significant development of understanding as a result of practical involvement and the intuitive knowledge to improvise within the facilitative situation. At the end of the fourth session students observed that an internal dynamic had been found which was sufficient to lead the improvisation, and that all were participants in an empowered event. At that point, the notion of leader/facilitator/participant as distinct roles is almost redundant. This state was achieved some way into the project when the students had begun to recognize their own energies, motivations, concerns, their own understanding of the reasons why they dance, their intention and their cultural context. Authentic movement, instinctive, felt behaviour and ownership, movement belonging in the moment to the creator was becoming increasingly paramount. The meanings were found in intent and context as well as in the content and form. The appreciation of the dance was occurring because of knowledge of intent and context, and confidence in self and the dance were gained simultaneously.

Inclusivity: the authentic self

The emphasis in the research-based community project is creative process through improvisation and a concern with the dance experience as intrinsic to the creation. Intuitive responses are used to create, and as we take part in or observe the process, we see the formulation of the creation. The participants are involved simultaneously in 'intended performance' managing and manipulating content and form, and in risk, uncertainty, trying and testing. Improvisation calls for honesty as its essence. Freed from the constraints of the dance-as-art aesthetic, the community dance artist nurtures and supports experiences and experiencing. In respect of experience, Turner's definition is particularly relevant:

> willing or wishing forward ... establishing goals and models for future experience in which, hopefully, the errors and perils of past experience will be avoided or eliminated.
>
> (Turner 1982: 18)

Accessing and revealing our authentic selves to ourselves and others through this form of dance making, where the body does the knowing – creates, communicates and learns – affords the possibility for understandings which challenge our adaptive selves. In our self-discovery we can reflect upon that which has shaped us and recapture our individual significance. As art, dance has an aesthetic significance in our lives. Aesthetic appreciation both of the process and the emerging dance product should not be exclusive. Not all performance is theatre. Much theatre is both objective and observable, with the emphasis being placed upon content and form. When a dance artist works in the community context a greater range of skills is required. The interventionist approach, person-centred work, with emphasis on the experiential, is concerned with the performative but also with challenging and developing skill. But its inclusivity acknowledges the potency of the individual in his/her capacity to create, to make sense of, to experience through art.

References

Best, D. (1992) *The Rationality of Feeling: Understanding the Arts in Education*, London: Falmer Press.

H'Doubler, M. N. (1957) *Dance: A Creative Art Experience*, Madison, WI: University of Wisconsin Press.

Holmes, A. (1992) *Limbering Up: Community Empowerment on Peripheral Estates*, Berkhamsted, UK: Delta Press.

Lomas, C. (1998) 'Art and the Community: Breaking the Aesthetic of Disempowerment', in S. Shapiro (ed.) *Dance, Power and Difference: Critical and Feminist Perspectives on Dance Education*, Champaign, IL: Human Kinetics.

Ryle, Gilbert, (1949) *The Concept of Mind*, London: Hutchinson.

Shapiro, S. (ed.) (1998) *Dance, Power and Difference: Critical and Feminist Perspectives on Dance Education*, Champaign, IL: Human Kinetics.

Turner, V. (1982) *From Ritual to Theatre*, New York: PAJ Publications.

14 Dancing around exclusion

An examination of the issues of social inclusion within choreographic practice in the community

Sara Houston

> Twelve men hang, heads down, from the balcony. Dropping to the ground they slowly press faces, hands and bodies against the unforgiving wall and anonymous cell doors. As the music builds in pace, so the performers increase speed, agility and risk with partner work, leaping into a physical maelstrom of high, twisting turns in the air to flatten on the ground, shoulder high, spinning lifts and *Matrix*-style fly jumps that launch bodies wheeling through the air, horizontal to the floor ...

Set within a wing of a prison in Staffordshire, England, the performance given by inmates in conjunction with Motionhouse Dance Theatre was the culmination of eighteen months of contact improvisation workshops.[1] The project, *Dancing Inside*, was characterised by its funder, the Arts Council England, as a social inclusion initiative giving those socially excluded from society – in this case, men serving long sentences in prison – a chance to experience art and potentially gain social and personal benefits from participation. In a long line of such community dance initiatives stretching over a period of approximately thirty years, it provides a focus for this chapter, the aims of which are to:

- examine the concept of participation benefit as it has entered political thinking, particularly within the framework of policies concerning themselves with social inclusion and exclusion;
- discuss the implications for choreographers working with the socially excluded within the context of the ongoing discourses concerning both inclusion and exclusion.

Social policy and the arts

The idea that people experiencing art might receive benefits other than merely knowledge of an art form is one underpinning most state-funded arts projects.[2] The nature of that benefit has been discussed since the time of Plato (Sorell 1992), but national and regional governments within Europe have continued to support the arts in varying degrees by buying into the notion that they augment the quality of lives of citizens and communities. The French Ministry of Culture and Communication states that, 'culture is not only a source of personal enrichment, but also a privileged means to strengthen social cohesion' (Le Ministère de la Culture et de la Communication 2003), whilst the British Department of Culture, Media and Sport proclaims that, 'the arts can offer innovative solutions, build bridges and express difference positively, not just for the individual but for whole communities. They can break boundaries' (DCMS 2006).

The notion that the arts bring benefits to individuals and communities, even contribute to social cohesion and social justice, is one aspect of a larger policy drive within the European Union, ever mindful of the taxpayer, under the heading 'social inclusion', a term appropriated in 1989 from France (Lister 2000). In the United Kingdom New Labour embraced 'social inclusion' as one of the cornerstones of its social policy after its rise to power in 1997, based on the Commission on Social Justice's 1994 report, in line with other European Union countries and Clinton's Democrats in the USA (Driver and Martell 1998).

New Labour's drive to combat social exclusion was embraced by the community dance sector in the UK, which had long sought recognition for its work in this area. Jill Green points out that because community dance emphasises the idea that anyone can dance, it 'has often been linked to disenfranchised populations such as the elderly, inner city, those with special needs and physical disabilities, those with health needs and "at risk" children' (Green 2000: 54). Possibly, because of its work with disenfranchised, 'hidden' groups who exude none of the glamour of the professional dancer, community dance has had to work hard to gain credibility and profile within the wider dance community (Devlin 1989, Clarke and Gibson 1998). Until New Labour introduced a policy of joined-up government where departments co-ordinated agenda and strategy, such as on social exclusion, community dance in Britain was considered by many, even in its own sector, as the ugly duckling of dance (Peppiatt and Venner 1993), despite having a reputation as a world leader in the field (Meyers, 2000).[3]

Prior to this, from the 1980s community dance had to contend with a New Right political agenda, ascendant in much of Europe and the USA, that was hostile to the concept of community, which, it argued, was detrimental to individual freedom. John Gray (2000) points out that global laissez-faire, the economic strategy of the New Right, 'is indifferent to social cohesion' and inhibited in its ability to 'repair the social injuries it has caused' (2000: 20).

The move in the mid-1990s to a more social democratic agenda brought the idea of community into focus. This was important for organisations like the Foundation for Community Dance, who believed that: '[dance] is largely a communal activity and creates a sense of belonging and significance, in other words, a sense of community' (Foundation for Community Dance in Meyers 2000: 39). Charles Landry, an expert in urban renewal and development, echoed these sentiments: 'planners should see the arts as one of their key tools in community and social development. Arts programmes can support public sector objectives from economic development to education'. Benefits include the arts' ability to 'support key areas of social policy, from education to social services', to 'foster community relationships, active citizenship and social cohesion' (Landry *et al.* 1996: 2).

According to Angus Stewart (2000), it is the realisation that unregulated market forces cannot create and nurture the structures necessary for social cohesion that drives governments to promote programmes of social inclusion. Whatever the reasons, arts professionals involved in creating work within the social inclusion bracket need to acquaint themselves with the vocabulary and intentions of such programmes, including issues of participation.

John Carey writes:

> Every child in every school should have a chance to paint and model and sculpt and sing and dance and act and play every instrument in the orchestra to see if that is where he or she will find joy and fulfilment and self-respect as many others have found it. Of course it will be expensive – very, very expensive. But then, so are prisons. ... It is time we gave active art a chance to make us better.
>
> (Carey 2005: 167)

Yet there is no simple correlation between government social policy and specific choreographic projects for socially excluded participants. Intentions and aims within dance projects can sit awkwardly within the expressions of the social inclusion agenda.

The discourses of social inclusion

Since its introduction the term 'social inclusion' has been appropriated by social, political, economic and artistic bodies to meet their own ends. Levitas (1998) and Stewart (2000) provide analyses of the various discourses. Dominant in the Western nation states is that of 'social amelioration' which Gray (2000: 22) describes as 'an ideal of common life'.[4] Gray argues that the central idea of inclusion is that 'every member of society should participate fully in it'. He goes on:

> The social ideal that inclusion expresses is an ideal of common membership: no one is denied access to activities and practices that are central in the life of society. An inclusionary society is a cohesive society.
>
> (Gray 2000: 22)

His thoughts are echoed in the slogan 'opportunity for all', found in the rhetoric of Scottish politician Gordon Brown, then New Labour's

Chancellor of the Exchequer in 1998. In a speech to the News International Conference, Brown stated that, 'a vital key to the dynamism and cohesion we need is opportunity for all in return for obligations shared by all' (Brown 1998). Brown sees the opening up of access to opportunities in life as the creation of a socially inclusive and cohesive society, and the end to social exclusion.

This has resonance for many dance organisations aiming to provide opportunity for inclusive participation, often for the very first time. For example, South East Dance, a UK National Dance Agency states that it aims to 'increase opportunity for people of all ages and ability to participate in dance' (South East Dance 2006); whilst Dance United, a British-based company set up specifically to work with young offenders, aims to 'inspire marginalised and socially excluded people to realise their full potential' (Dance United 2006). The opportunity to experience dance, to enrich lives, to learn new skills and realise latent potential, is central to a discourse of inclusion. In creating the opportunity of access to dance, organisations, companies and individual artists are reinforcing a value system that prioritises inclusion.

For some, like Dance United, this value system goes beyond the principle of access to one of social justice, not simply of including people in dance, but of surmounting exclusion and inequality. Owen Kelly (1984) champions a radical community arts perspective linked to the more radical notion of social inclusion, which is empowering. He writes:

> Implicit in the notion of 'working with' communities is very often the idea of the community as a blank canvas upon which 'experts' can paint ideologically correct pictures. Instead the question should be concerned with the nature of community that a group is working towards; that is, what community a group is *participating* in bringing into being.
>
> (Kelly 1984: 51)

Similarly, Sue Akroyd, community dance commentator and founder member of the community dance company Ludus, writes:

> The recognition that to offer and share something beyond the art form itself facilitates growth and change within the individual on a personal and social level (as opposed to merely physical) gives justification to a social imperative for dance that can claim to effect change in a wider social context.
>
> (Akroyd 1996: 17)

Angus Stewart (2000) argues that the extent of the prioritisation of 'agency' is a critical aspect of social inclusion. He explains that the argument is split between those who feel that integration of individuals into mainstream structures is sufficient, irrespective of any inequalities, and those who believe in the self-determination of life chances; meaning active involvement in opportunities and decisions. Kelly's thesis fits into the latter viewpoint, where people themselves build up structures.

The value of inclusion – whether for access or empowerment – is clear in the discourse of community arts commentators, who talk about the underlying principles inherent in their work. These principles such as social amelioration are also highlighted in dance organisation literature. In drawing attention to the social worth of the projects, the literature underlines that they are useful to society in a way that taxpayers, funders and politicians can understand. Yet although the choreographers involved in these projects may hold dear the value of inclusion, they also have other priorities and values that are integral to the creation of work in this setting.

The artistic impetus

For many choreographers, artistic impetus is more important than social imperative. Laura Woods is the co-ordinator of the Water Project, a joint initiative between The Place, the centre for contemporary dance in London, Cardboard Citizens, the UK's homeless people's professional theatre company, and Crisis, the national homeless charity. She argues that people are drawn to an artistic idea: 'often if you have a vision, people are more likely to buy into it' (Woods, interviewed 12 January 2006). If there is an artistic idea, not just a notion of social utopia, potential participants will see a way of working and be drawn into that vision. Prioritising the artistic impetus works for Woods in an immediate way, as participants have very diverse needs, problems and abilities, not necessarily addressed by a notional social imperative.

For choreographers, the importance of the artistic impetus is also inherent in the job of choreographing for community groups. Royston Maldoom, known for his work with young offenders and those at risk, as well as with disabled people and street children in Europe and Africa, states:

> I choreograph what I want to choreograph, I do not label or categorise the people I work with. If I am to work at my best, I must be doing what I want to do and what excites me as an artist.
>
> (Maldoom in email, 18 January 2000)

The artistic imperative lies at the heart of what he does. Speaking in a group discussion at a Dance UK's *Choreoforum* conference in 2000, he argued that as a choreographer his skills do not and should not lie in social work. Such skills should be provided by an organisation or individual who specialises in that area. The result, according to Maldoom, is often of a higher quality if there is an effective relationship between choreographer and social agency. The distinction for Maldoom is clear. As a choreographer, he must work as an artist; the social impetus has to be managed otherwise.

Kevin Finnan, Artistic Director of Motionhouse Dance Theatre, has worked in a variety of community contexts, including prisons. Like Maldoom, he is adamant that he must work as an artist coming with creative ideas rather than with notions of social imperative. Whilst working on *Dancing Inside*, Finnan states that what interested him about the project was the group of participants, not because they were socially excluded, but because they were boisterous (Finnan, interviewed 14 March 2003).

By approaching choreographic projects in social exclusion settings as vehicles for creativity rather than as instruments for social inclusion, choreographers, such as Maldoom and Finnan and project co-ordinators, such as Woods, are able to establish a different relationship with the participants than might otherwise have occurred. Maldoom refuses to categorise the dancers in his projects; Woods saw the labelling of participants of the Water Project as counterproductive. The Water Project was designed as an arts initiative that would allow participants to take a few hours out from the challenges of the streets and hostels by engaging in dance and drama activities. Just as the choreographers and workshop leaders came to the scheme in order to create work and teach dance, so the participants expected to join a dance class, but also expected to eat.[5] Woods felt that the treatment of the participants as dancers, rather than as homeless people was particularly important. By sending them on trips to the theatre and to dance classes, which were open to the public, the participants were treated as individuals who did not stand out as different but as 'normal'. One commented that 'it was nice to be treated like an average person … [rather than] as a number' (Alan, in Williams 2005). With spending money in their pockets for the theatre and new dance clothes for the classes, participants were able to experience and enjoy dance without feeling threatened by it.

This attitude was carried over into the three choreographic works the group produced, where they worked with professional artists and crew to perform to the public. Although each choreographer took a different approach to the process of creating material on or with the participants, none made an issue of homelessness. In the first choreographic project, Tara Herbert and Suz Broughton laid down their normal strict parameters for rehearsals: no cigarette breaks and full attention required in each rehearsal, something that was challenging for many participants whose lives were not structured in such a way. The subsequent dance film choreographed by Catherine Seymour was shown on its artistic merit without mention of homelessness.

By emphasising the artistic aims of the project, Woods argues, the creative vision was not restricted by generalisations of participants' backgrounds (Woods, interviewed 12 January 2006). Maldoom agrees: 'I try to provide a space where people can work without "labels" and where they can present themselves in the way they choose, not as others choose to see them' (Maldoom in email, 18 January 2000). Importantly, Woods argues that approaching the Water Project as an arts initiative, rather than a social inclusion project, meant that the volunteers could participate as interested individuals, often with something to share. This was not to shut out or deny the situations that the participants were in – indeed, participant Shauna argued that it was a help having other people there who had similar problems but who tried to surmount them (Shauna, in Williams 2005) – but to acknowledge that the project looked beyond a label-centric approach to engage with participants.

Nicholas Rowe delivers dance workshops to Palestinian communities, traumatised by the Arab–Israeli conflict. Rowe (2003) is very clear that his aim is not to heal the trauma, but to deliver dance:

> Whilst the work I am doing is within traumatised communities, it is not directly soothing the impact of the trauma. ... The dance education programs that I am involved with are, rather, attempting to maintain dance as a social medium, within a traumatised environment.
>
> (Rowe 2003: 126)

He argues that it would not be possible to attempt to address trauma directly through his work because the workshops take place within a chaotic environment where cultural and psychological stress is still on-going. Rowe addresses the issue of the artistic imperative from the point of view that, even if he had wanted to attempt a therapeutic approach, he would not have succeeded. The most his workshops can do is to create an environment where people are enabled to relate socially with one another and to use dance as a cultural pivot in their lives.

In the examples above, choreographers and project co-ordinators have attempted in their own ways to steer away from thinking of their work as combating social exclusion to concentrate on working creatively with a group. Although each choreographer takes a different view on how much to adapt to the specific group of participants, they are clear that their emphasis is to work in dance with their group. In focusing on art making, rather than addressing social exclusion issues, the dance artists and co-ordinators sidestep some of the accusations of paternalism levelled by social policy scholar Robert Furbey (1999). Reflecting the old Roman adage *mens sana in corpora sano*,[6] Furbey argues that regeneration strategies hint at the paternalistic social planning of the late nineteenth and early twentieth century when naturalist Charles Darwin's theory of the survival of the fittest was taken up as a theme for social planning. For the nation to achieve 'social fitness', its citizens had to be physically, mentally and morally fit. The poor, perceived as lacking all three 'qualities', had to be 'regenerated' (1999: 426) in order that the nation state could grow stronger. Furbey challenges this motivation:

> The association between 'regeneration' and prevalent 20th century concerns with individual transformation (particularly of poor people),

> and also with conservative, neo-liberal and 'top down' social democratic 'organisms' raises questions about its status as a genuinely capacious and radical idea.
>
> (Furbey 1999: 427)

Social objective initiatives imposed upon participants in order to achieve 'social fitness', through a 'top down' notion of what will be good for individuals and society, will create an excluded and reactionary moral underclass (Levitas 1998).

Concentrating on making art, rather than social cohesion, avoids such moral paternalism and choreographers who do so refrain from passing moral judgements. Suz Broughton, who works extensively within the criminal justice system, states that it is her belief that 'everyone can dance and it is simply our job as professionals in this field to be able to pitch the work at a level where this can be achieved' (Broughton 2004: 17). She frankly states that she never inquires into a participant's background because 'this information is not going to help me relate to that person in a professional and unbiased way. It will only serve to make me nervous at best and prejudiced at worst' (Broughton 2004: 17). Although some choreographers disagree that knowing nothing about the background of participants will aid the process of dance creation, Broughton's comments illustrate a firm attitude to an *artistic* process and outcome, rather than a process and outcome that focuses on regeneration.

Although choreographers like Broughton and Herbert plan sessions and compositions beforehand (Broughton 2004: 17), others see the process as a much more organic integration of ideas and work of participants and choreographer. Jasmine Pasch from Phew! Arts Company has choreographed for disabled groups in the UK and South Africa and has facilitated workshops for those with dementia. She sees herself as a 'maker' (Pasch, interviewed 6 April 2006). She works as a choreographer and movement facilitator who happens to have made a name for herself working with people on the margins of society. In this way, she is motivated by the artistic potential of a specific project.[7] Pasch characterises the choreographic contract as entering into a relationship with the commissioner and participants. She argues that the artistic process means 'taking on a bit of what you want and realising some of what they want: It's a dialogue and negotiation to arrive at solutions' (Pasch interview 2006). In her view, it is a dialogue with an open door. For Pasch, the choreographic process involves having a sense of what one wants to achieve, but keeping the door open for people to come with their ideas. It is a creative dialogue, where it is just as much, if not more, about the artistic visions of the participants rather than her own needs, and certainly not about prioritising a social inclusion agenda.

The prioritisation of agency

What Pasch advocates is listening to and acting upon the knowledge and experience that participants bring to a project, rather than assuming that the choreographer comes into the initiative as the carrier of all knowledge. Such a stance requires an acknowledgement that even participants who are deemed to be socially excluded have something to give creatively. Indeed, Pasch argues that the projects that she has been involved in have far exceeded everyone's expectations (Pasch interview 2006). This way of working has the potential to galvanise a sense of 'agency' amongst participants, although does not have a monopoly on so doing. After studying the different points of view on the make-up of an inclusion agenda, Stewart argues that 'inclusion is a matter … of participation in the determination of both individual and collective life chances' (Stewart 2000: 9). The prioritisation of agency, or taking a 'participatory' (Benhabib 1992: 78) perspective, allows a degree of self-determination of events by individuals that gives them the power to interact with and to act upon events positively. In giving participants a voice within the choreographic process and creating shared meaning, Pasch's work allows for a 'bottom up' inclusive process to happen.

In the view of sociologist and cellist Richard Sennett (2004), agency becomes important when people are faced with situations that deny them recognition and therefore respect. He describes his upbringing on a doomed housing project in Chicago, where scenes of race riots were common:

> The project denied people control over their own lives. They were rendered spectators to their own needs, mere consumers of care provided to them. It was here that they experienced that peculiar lack of respect which consists of not being seen, not being accounted as full human beings.
>
> (Sennett 2004: 13)

In becoming 'spectators', the residents of the housing estate remained passive and powerless. Sennett's way out of the cycle of deprivation, which afflicted so many of his neighbours, was through playing the cello. 'It was through learning an art', he states, 'that I began to leave the others behind' (Sennett 2004: 13). Sennett argues that it is the development of a craft – and so by implication, the *participation* in an art form – that gives the practitioner an 'inner sense of self-respect' (Sennett 2004: 13–14). Sennett found self-belief and respect, and therefore agency, within himself through his enjoyment and satisfaction from playing a musical instrument. He characterises respect as having two sides: the respect one receives from others for doing something valued and the self-respect that one generates from exploring how to do something. 'There's satisfaction in that', comments Sennett, 'by constructing an accurate, free sound I experienced a profound pleasure in and for itself, and a sense of self-worth which didn't depend on others' (Sennett 2004: 14).

Shauna, interviewed after participating in the Water Project, echoes Sennett's view. She describes how she and her fellow dancers were given the opportunity to create movement themselves, as well as being taught dance sequences. The creation of movement allowed her to 'explore parts of yourself' (Shauna, in Williams 2005). Shauna elaborated on this act of introspection:

> When I see an incredible dancer it is not when I see someone do loads of incredible moves, it's when I see someone who's free within themselves. Like you're seeing someone's spirit dance ... People were just wanting to explore that part of themselves ... So I'd come home buzzing on a high doing something creative with myself, not buzzing on a drug.
>
> (Shauna, in Williams 2005)

Shauna's poetic description of what she experienced reflects Sennett's idea of someone who by virtue of exploring how to do something, or creating something new, was enjoying an inner sense of self-respect and a renewed sense of action. In likening the experience to seeing 'someone's spirit dance', Shauna was describing a process of revival and active participation, in contrast to the dependency wrought by drug addiction.

So even if the artistic impetus is primary for many choreographers, their working process may open up the project to inclusory gains for participants, as seen in Pasch's work. Maldoom observes that although 'the artistic impetus must be what drives and motivates us in my projects the social imperative is addressed through the working process' (Maldoom in email, 18 January 2000). Broughton admits that by making the same demands on participants within the criminal justice system as on those outside it, behaviour patterns often change without much conscious effort on the part of the choreographer. Broughton believes this is because her aim is to get 'people to believe in themselves and [give] them an opportunity to express that with others through dance'. She goes on, 'my interest is in supporting people, by whatever method I have available in my experience, to make those human connections and take them to the level where they can become artists' (Broughton 2004: 18). As Sennett (2004) points out, for those who had no self-belief before, in becoming an artist, self-respect and a sense of agency can materialise.

Finnan develops this idea of agency within creative workshops. He argues that in giving participants the skills to interpret the movements given to them, and to create their own phrases of movement, the choreographer allows them the skill to make their own aesthetic choices. He believes that this can empower participants and brings value to what they achieve (Finnan, interviewed 14 March 2003). Participants' comments on Finnan's project were evidence to what worth they held their work.

Several commented that during the dance sessions, which were deliberately fast paced, they could be themselves, without needing to resort to aggressive attitudinal postures cultivated to fit into the prison environment. In having no time to think about how they looked, who they were dancing with and who was watching, participants had less time to feel self-conscious about themselves in their environment. Relinquishing these masks, some of the prisoners started to think about the value of relationships with others outside of the prison (Brown *et al.* 2004).

Rowe is another advocate of giving participants the metaphorical and literal space through dance to address concerns they might have. It is not himself, as the dance artist, who instigates this:

> I am not trying to inspire peace with Israel, challenge gender discrimination, convince kids not to fight their oppressors or present a variety of other social, political or religious agendas that I may or may not support. The goal of the work (that I am engaged in) is to provide a dynamic forum, a vibrant structure for dance activity in which these communities may then address various issues themselves. The goal is to keep dance alive as a medium, by ensuring it remains essential to the community's immediate needs and wants.
>
> (Rowe 2003: 128)

As a facilitator, the way in which he guides dance practice allows for a degree of agency to be taken up by participants should they wish to. Keeping dance as an important cultural and social activity within the community allows for a peaceful focal point for its members.

Building boundaries and structure

The idea of facilitation is echoed in South East Dance's Dansync project. Dansync was a dance initiative run by South East Dance with Pupil Referral Units in south-east England. As a three-year initiative, it was broken down into projects of approximately ten weeks in duration delivering dance to young people outside of mainstream education, who were at risk from offending, homelessness, or being sent into care. The projects often ended in a performance or informal sharing. Dansync was also a vehicle for training dance artists who wanted to specialise in working with vulnerable young people, one of whom, Maria Stylianou, took on the role as the workshop leader. Kyla Lucking, Programme Manager, was clear that Stylianou was regarded as a dance facilitator or practitioner (Lucking, interviewed 12 January 2006). She argued that there would have been problems if Stylianou had come in solely as an 'artist', with the young people as her tools of expression, as her predilections would have been addressed before the young people's needs. The participants of Dansync were the project's priority. This preference was seen in some of the very low-key performances in which the dancers took part. Instead of exhibiting what they had learned on mainstream choreographic or performance platforms with other youth dance groups, some participants preferred the anonymity of sharing work with only the eye of the video camera to witness their efforts. Some participants had a resistance to being watched by their peers, others had territorial issues that precluded them sharing a platform with other young people from nearby 'territories'. The artist in these cases was creating work on such an intimate scale that only the participants would appreciate it. Yet, paradoxically, Lucking commented that the more they 'let go' (Lucking, interviewed 12 January 2006) of seeing the project as an artistic initiative, the more the creativity and artistic qualities shone through. In concentrating on delivering dance for those specific groups of participants, the form as embodied by the young people was emphasised.

The form of dance Stylianou taught to participants required adherence to technical rules, although the technical style was varied on occasion to suit the tastes of each group of young people. For example, a more commercial style of street dance, or a fusion of forms could be used to interest a group if necessary. According to Lucking, the boundaries put in place by whichever technique was used were useful to participants (Lucking 2006). Unlike their often-chaotic personal lives, dance sessions were structured. The participants knew where they stood with the form and could therefore enjoy it without feeling undermined by it.

Likewise, in the Water Project, Herbert and Broughton, who took a similar approach to structuring sessions, facilitated one of the choreographed performances. In rehearsals, participants had to adhere to strict rules in order to be allowed to perform in the work: promptness, no fidgeting, no cigarette breaks and total focus during sessions were paramount. Shauna, who took part, surmised that those who dropped out of the performance did so not because of the rules, but because they had other problems with which they needed to deal.

> If you are doing a show it's got to be professional. ... By having that [strictness] it's like it doesn't matter what situation you're at, you've got to be there on time. I think that's good you don't need people making allowances for you because you live in a hostel. I think some people had problems to deal with within themselves that weren't part of the Water Project ... and that's why they missed out on doing things. I don't think it was anything to do with the strictness of the class. I think that's good because it's making you live to routine and that's what you're striving for.
>
> (Shauna, in Williams 2005)

According to Shauna, the need for routine was important in lives which had been led by the vagaries of the street and the need for a drug fix. So even though the rehearsals for this particular performance seemed to be too much for some of the potential participants, the structure given was an important life-skills lesson for those who stuck to the project.

Choreography and social exclusion

It is clear that individual choreographers working in social exclusion settings use different methods and processes based on personally formed values. Those studied here are primarily concerned with creating and facilitating dance with participating individuals and groups. Issues of social exclusion are secondary. However, by giving the participants a sense of their own abilities, by enabling them to create material by themselves, helped build in those individuals a sense of agency. Pasch (2006) emphasises that it is easy to get too serious about working with people on the margins and that play is an important part of relating successfully with the excluded, such as those with learning disabilities or dementia. Others identify the need for boundaries and structures within which individual expression can be found. Both approaches aim to promote a notion of 'common life' (Gray 2000: 22) and social cohesion. Few of these choreographers working in social exclusion settings would describe themselves as radical political activists, considering dance, the enjoyment of the act of dancing and the creating of movement with others of primary concern. For them dance acts as a subconscious guerrilla movement: on the surface doing one thing, but during that process, creating the momentum for something infinitely more radical; a redistribution of the power base for social inclusion.

There are major issues surrounding any project, such as the ability to sustain impetus, interest and to embed agency, for example. Short-term projects are likely to fall short of expectation and quantifiable results. However, Pasch's experience of working in special schools in South Africa demonstrates that participants can be galvanised to produce work beyond the expectation of all parties. Some choreographic projects do provide a map for participants to start a life-journey of their own making. Where exactly the journey leads or what path it takes will be the decision of the adventurer herself. Sociologist Pierre Bourdieu (1999) argues that suffering is 'positional' (1999: 4); that using one measure of exclusion as the only measure limits understanding of other forms and development of suffering. The measures taken by governments to alleviate social exclusion may only do so much because of the necessity to stipulate and ground agenda according to self-interest. It is therefore essential that there are other agents, such as choreographers, who are prepared to work with people who have been excluded to show that inclusion is a form of choice not necessarily formed by governments of their policies.

Notes

1 *Dancing Inside*, at HMP Dovegate, Staffordshire, England, project run by Motionhouse Dance Theatre, 2003–4.
2 See Tom Sorell (1992) for an overview.
3 Canadian Deborah Meyers writes: 'the dance infrastructure in Britain is so dazzling, relative to the Canadian experience' (Meyers 2000: 40).

4 Political analyst Jerry Cohen suggests that while ensuring 'an equal right to realise potential', inclusion means tacitly accepting 'the unfairness of natural disadvantage' (Cohen 1997: 16).

5 A free meal was offered to participants at the end of the session and many admitted that this initially drew them to the project (Williams 2005).

6 'A sound mind in a sound body'. In fact from medieval times onwards, the body politic has been symbolised by a healthy or a diseased body and mind, depending on the health of the kingdom. Jacques Le Goff (1989) relates that in the early fifteenth century, the head symbolised 'the unifying principle and assure[d] order within society and the state' (Le Goff 1989: 23). A chaotic kingdom, therefore, was symbolised by a diseased mind. Nearly two centuries later, Shakespeare makes this point in his plays *Hamlet* and *King Lear*. Similarly, Shakespeare created the deformed body of Richard III as the manifestation of his wicked mind.

7 Pasch also mentions the necessity of sustaining a livelihood as another basic motivation. Earning one's living as a choreographer does not get talked about much, possibly because it is seen as a vocation, particularly when associated with working with disadvantaged people, yet it is a fundamental part of any professional choreographer's needs.

References

Akroyd, S. (1996) 'Community Dance and Society', in C. Jones (ed.) *Thinking Aloud: In Search of a Framework for Community Dance*, Leicester: Foundation for Community Dance.

Benhabib, S. (1992) *Situating the Self*, Cambridge: Polity Press.

Bourdieu, P. (1999) *The Weight of the World: Social Suffering in Contemporary Society*, trans. by Priscilla Parkhurst Ferguson, *et al.*, Cambridge: Polity Press.

Broughton, S. (2004) 'Getting People to Believe in Themselves', *Animated*, Spring: 16–18.

Brown, G. (1998) 'Speech to the New International Conference' Idaho, 17 July.

Brown, J., Houston, S. and Speller, G. (2004) An Evaluation of Dancing Inside: A creative workshop project led by Motionhouse Dance Theatre in HMP Dovegate Therapeutic Community, Year Two Programme, Guildford: University of Surrey.

Carey, J. (2005) *What Good are the Arts?* London: Faber and Faber.

Clarke, G. and Gibson, R. (1998) *Independent Dance Review Report*, London: Arts Council of England.

Cohen, J. (1997) 'Mind the Gap', *Red Pepper*, 42: 14–16.

Dance United (2006) *Dance United*. Available online at <http://www.dance-united.com> (accessed 28 January 2006).

Department of Culture, Media and Sport, UK (2006) Available online at <http://www.culture.gov.uk/arts/arts_and_social_policy> (accessed 6 January 2006).

Devlin, G. (1989) *Stepping Forward: Some suggestions for the development of dance in England during the 1990s*, London: Arts Council of Great Britain Dance Department.

Driver, S. and Martell, L. (1998) *New Labour: Politics after Thatcherism*, Cambridge: Polity Press.

Furbey, R. (1999) 'Urban Regeneration: Reflections on a Metaphor', *Critical Social Policy*, 19 (4): 419–45.

Gray, J. (2000) 'Inclusion: A Radical Critique' in P. Askonas and A. Stewart (eds) *Social Inclusion: Possibilities and Tensions*, Basingstoke: Palgrave.

Green, J. (2000) 'Power, Service and Reflexivity in a Community Dance Project', *Research in Dance Education*, 1 (1): 53–67.

Kelly, O. (1984) *Community, Art and the State: Storming the Citadels*, London: Comedia.

Landry, C., Greene, L., Matarasso, F. and Bianchini, F. (1996) 'The Art of Regeneration: Urban Renewal through Cultural Activity', *Supplement to Social Policy Summary 8*, Joseph Rowntree Foundation.

Le Goff, J. (1989) 'Head or Heart? The Political Use of Body Metaphors in the Middle Ages', in M. Feher (ed.) *Fragments for a History of the Human Body, Part 3*. New York: Zone.

Levitas, R. (1998) *The Inclusive Society? Social Exclusion and New Labour*, London: Macmillan.

Lister, R. (2000) 'Strategies for Social Inclusion: Promoting Social Cohesion or Social Justice?', in P. Askonas and A. Stewart (eds) *Social Inclusion: Possibilities and Tensions*, Basingstoke: Palgrave.

Meyers, D. (2000) Animating Dance in Communities: A Discussion Paper, Canada: The Canada Council for the Arts.

Le Ministère de la Culture et de la Communication, France (2003) *Le Ministère de la Culture et de la Communication*. Available online at <http://www.culture.gouv.fr> (accessed 20 November 2003).

Peppiatt, A. and Venner, K. (1993) *Community Dance: A Progress Report*, London: Arts Council of Great Britain.

Rowe, N. (2003) 'Presenting Dance Workshops in Traumatised Communities', in *Pulses and Impulses for Dance in the Community: Proceedings of the International Conference*, Lisbon: Universidade Tecnica de Lisboa.

Sennett, R. (2004) *Respect: The Formation of Character in an Age of Inequality*, London: Penguin.

Sorell, T. (1992) 'Art, Society and Morality', in O. Hanfling (ed.) *Philosophical Aesthetics*, Oxford: Blackwell.

South East Dance (2006) *South East Dance*. Available online at <http://www.southeastdance.org.uk> (accessed 28 January 2006).

Stewart, A. (2000) 'Social Inclusion: an introduction', in P. Askonas and A. Stewart (eds) *Social Inclusion: Possibilities and Tensions*, Basingstoke: Palgrave.

Williams, C. (2005) *The Water Project*. Film, London: The Place & Crisis.

15 Sharing the stage

A case study of *TIJ*, a choreography for Dutch professional and amateur dancers

Caroline Ribbers and Ninke van Herpt

The main inspiration for this chapter is the production of *TIJ* (translated as 'Tide'), in which six professional and eleven amateur dancers collaborated. This work was created by choreographers Stefan Ernst and Ronald Wintjens and shown during the 2005 Dutch Dance Festival in Maastricht, the Netherlands. Caroline Ribbers took part as a professional dancer and helped create the related website (www.tijdewebsite.nl) with the intent to share experiences and insights gained during this project.

The intent of this chapter is to take a closer look at the Dutch setting in which collaboration projects with those other than professional dancers take place, the benefits for partaking dancers, choreographers and audience, and the questions raised. Furthermore, this chapter describes the aims of the Dutch Dance Festival in producing *TIJ*, the aims of the choreographers in creating it, the creation process of *TIJ* and the choreographic outcome from a case study perspective. Finally, some questions and answers related to the project are addressed.

Defining the Dutch focus – combined dancer projects in the Netherlands

Working with mixed casts is not new in the Dutch dance scene. In 2001 Ed Wubbe created one of the first professional dance performances for theatre setting with the *010 B-Boys* for Scapino Ballet, joining the forces of his contemporary dance performers with Rotterdam break-dance pioneers. Krisztina de Châtel has also initiated several collaborations with non-dancers, for example, *Onderstebavo* (2007) with her own dancers together with *Vanuit Marlies*, a group undergoing recovery from mental illness; and *Zooi* (2006) – translated 'mess' – danced with her own dancers and a real group of garbage collectors (dustbin men), which was performed in a former machine factory. De Châtel's latest combined dancer project *Cirklo* (premiered May 2008) includes professional dancers, dervishes and a twirling girl. Noticeably, most collaborative productions seem to work with either non-dancers or experts in certain dance styles that are not available for study in the Dutch organised professional dance education system. In a dance scene where the focus is shifting to 'generation mix' – that is, young makers who, according to Kocken and Tjon a Fong (2006: 9), aim for anthropological and interdisciplinary collaborations – it can become difficult to distinguish between the professional and the amateur. In this chapter, the definitions of professional and amateur dancers are based on the insights gained during the production of *TIJ*.

During participation in *TIJ*, some differences between amateur and professional dancers were discussed. The professional dancer was seen as a dancer who, before making a career out of dancing had followed a professional dance education. The amateur dances as a hobby, does not get paid for his dancing and has often followed a less intensive education. Based on these points of view, the following distinguishing features between the two groups can be identified: differences in the level of dance techniques, in body control, in spatial awareness and in the ability to learn dance movements. Professional dancers are capable of analysing and carrying out body actions more quickly and this makes them better able to 'translate' the dance material to their own bodies. Through years of training, professional dancers have taken these skills to a higher level compared to amateur dancers.

The amateur dancers involved in this project and those with the ambition to work on a professional level are not to be compared with any other amateur dancer: there must be a strong motivation, discipline and commitment to the production, in other words, a professional attitude. The definition of amateur dancers in this chapter excludes those dancers who have no ambition to be dance performers. The amateur dancer with the drive to be a performer has the tendency to look for opportunities to realise this ambition through working with professionals, the facilities offered in the professional circuit and the benefits of the existing knowledge.

In the Netherlands, a policy for culture is set every four years at governmental level. These culture policies set the political direction for art funding and the general direction for the arts. Different guidelines have recently been written, in preparation for the new national *Cultuurplan* 2009–12. The two main guides are *Innoveren, participeren!* (Innovate, participate), published by the *Raad voor Cultuur* (the Dutch advisory board on culture), discussing the general issues of all the arts in the Netherlands, and the dance specific *Dans zichtbaar beter* (Dance visibly improved) by the *DOD brancheorganisatie voor de dans* (organisation for dance), which based its advice on recent dance sector analyses. In the latter, one of the main issues, as expressed by Schots (2007: 31), is that 'the sector wants to discuss the different roles the dance artist should fulfil in society, and research how the connection between the professional dance arts and the amateur circuit can be improved'. This supports the conclusion that the professional field and the amateur dance circuit are two separate entities, with their own specific sector organisations. Although a strong focus is placed on talent development in *Innoveren, participeren!*, the collaborative projects focus mainly on receptive and cognitive exchange and art education instead of participation on an equal level in the performance circuit. There are hardly any productions by professional companies where amateur dancers are equally integrated with professional dancers that are considered to be professional productions. More often, with initiatives from the amateur scene and facilitated by institutes supporting the amateur arts, such as the national *Kunstfactor Dans* or the regional Centre for the Amateur Arts, production collaborations are set up between a group of amateur dancers and a professional dancer or choreographer. These productions are often considered amateur dance productions, regardless of the fact that there are one or more professional participants.

Working in the amateur circuit often involves taking a different choreographic approach. The choreographer needs to be able to find the strengths and capabilities of the performer. Many professional choreographers in the Netherlands such as Adriaan Luteijn, Helma Melis and Thom Stuart, have started working in both fields, specialising in choreography for both professional and amateur dancers. But, the joining of the two fields on stage is hardly ever seen within the context of a professional production.

In *Minister van Dans* Jos van der Lans (2007: 13) questions the assumption in *Innoveren, participeren!* that there 'is a world of difference between dance as social experience and dance as theatrical experience [...] and professional dance makers would like to bridge that difference'. Van der Lans wonders who these professional dance makers are that are willing to tear down the walls between high and low art, mass culture and elite entertainment, young and old, stage and street. We wonder if it is that drastic. When considering the amateur dancer as an artist with his specific contribution to dance other than the merit of the professional, will the combining of the two on the same stage not lead to a multifaceted choreography?

Dutch dance days – aims of producing *TIJ*

The city of Maastricht hosts the Dutch Dance Days Festival for one weekend every year. The most striking and important professional dance performances from the previous season are shown again in several theatres in the town. Each year, the festival initiates a choreography project in which a collaboration between professional and amateur dance circles takes a central part. The emphasis of these projects was, until the 2004 Festival, on the collaboration between choreographers from professional dance circles and amateur dancers. In the weeks prior to the festival, professionals created a performance with amateur dancers, which was then shown to the public. However, in the 2005 Festival a significant change in course took place. The focus of the choreography project shifted to the collaboration *between* amateur dancers and professional dancers where, under the direction of choreographers Stefan Ernst and Ronald Wintjens, amateur dancers performed with professional dancers in the production *TIJ*.

Leontien Wiering, director of the Dutch Dance Festival, writes in an article on the *TIJ* website that the rationale of the Festival to produce a project like *TIJ* is 'to bring amateur and professionals in contact with each other, in the dance studio and on stage, to share knowledge and passion with each other' (Wiering 2006). In the same article she also mentions that:

> Creative projects within the community embed the work of the dance artist in this surrounding. In this way the environment will be better informed about what the dance artist is occupied with and will therefore show a stronger commitment. By working in the field of amateur dance, the dance artist invests in the future and with that in potential talent and the relationship with the audience.
>
> (Wiering 2006)

Choreographers Ernst and Wintjens collaborated with seventeen dancers in the production of *TIJ*. *TIJ* strives to achieve an integrated completeness, where amateur and professional are involved and presented as equals. In doing so, the ambition to create a product that merges the expertise of performers gains shape and lifts the chemistry of interaction to higher level. The composition of the cast made the production different from other collaborating projects. The dancers in *TIJ* came from a wide variety of backgrounds: six of them were professional dancers with a modern dance company in the Netherlands. The other eleven dancers were amateur dancers. Their dance backgrounds varied from jazz, tango, break-dance and tap dance to flamenco. Ernst and Wintjens (2006) hoped to realise a number of aims:

1 In making *TIJ*, Ernst and Wintjens wanted to take the image of collaboration between professionals and amateurs to a different level. *TIJ* had to make both dancers and audience think again about the boundaries that exist between amateur and professional dance circles in the Netherlands. The experiences and results achieved in the performance of *TIJ* could support the debate about the importance and creation of similar collaborations. Van der Wiel (2007: 9) quotes Wiering when saying that one of the purposes of the Dutch Dance Days is 'to initiate reflection and discussion'. There has been a call for the development of a dance discourse and formulating vision on dance in the Netherlands. According to initiatives such as *Dansplan 20/20*, a discussion between Dutch dance makers is required on the future of dance in the country.
2 Ernst and Wintjens wanted *TIJ* to be an inspiring experience for the dancers. As choreographers who have gained experiences in both professional and amateur dance circles, they are convinced that establishing collaboration between dancers from these two worlds can be a source of inspiration for both parties and may broaden their outlook.

3 The final aim was concerned with their own artistic development. In their choreographies, the notion of *people* dancing plays a central part; that is, both makers think it is important in their work that the individuality of each dancer remains visible. The expression of the dancers is just as important as the technical performance and consequently Ernst and Wintjens prefer to work with dancers who have a certain charisma. It is therefore apt that their group of dancers consists of professional and amateur dancers with backgrounds in modern dance, street dance and tango. The choreographers acknowledged the importance of investigating which choreographic principles and methods were involved when dancers from various backgrounds danced together.

Setting *TIJ* in motion – preparation, work processes and the final product

The creation process of *TIJ* was divided into two stages: preparatory and rehearsal. The reason for this was to do with available funding and the availability of the dancers, which resulted in having only eight days to create *TIJ*.

In view of the very short rehearsal period, Ernst and Wintjens devoted a considerable amount of time to the preparation stage. The precious hours on the studio floor had to be used to accomplish an interaction between the professionals and the amateurs rather than on defining the concept or on organisational matters. Therefore, the rehearsal schedule was set up and choices made about the theme of the performance, the music, the stage settings and the costumes. Much thought had been given beforehand both to the working methods that Ernst and Wintjens wanted to use during rehearsals and to the macrostructure of the performance.

With the concept of *TIJ* in mind, Ernst and Wintjens went looking for dancers. The amateur dancers were found by holding auditions, which were very well attended. From all corners of amateur dance land, dancers applied, which resulted in the choice of a varied group of amateur dancers. The search for professional dancers was not that easy. Initially, the plan was to ask dancers from government-funded Dutch dance companies. However, the busy rehearsal and performance schedules of these companies did not allow the participation of their dancers. Thus, Ernst and Wintjens went in search of six freelance dancers to complement the cast of *TIJ*. All dancers – professionals as well as amateurs – had to possess a number of qualities defined by Ernst and Wintjens based on their predetermined concept. First, the dancers had to be open-minded about collaboration between amateurs and professionals. In addition, they had to be able to create their own dance material based on choreographic tasks and guidelines. Ernst and Wintjens do not support the opinion that dancers merely carry out the ideas of the makers. Instead, they wanted to challenge the dancers to contribute their own ideas and to let them take shape.

As far as dance technique was concerned, Ernst and Wintjens looked for dancers who had a feeling for their dance style. Finally, the choreographers were looking for individuality in their dancers. Ernst and Wintjens wanted to work with those who radiated individuality and self-assurance, which would in turn be reinforced by their personal dance style. Looking back, the choreographers were happy with the dancers they had chosen based on their selection criteria: 'The careful selection of the dancers provided the project with a firm basis to build on' (Wintjens 2006).

Significantly, the amateurs and the professionals each went through a different rehearsal stage. For the amateur dancers, the project began with three preparatory workshops during which the focus was on teaching the dance-style characteristics of the choreographers, and learning how to create and dance duets. The theme of the first workshop was based on the choreographers' viewpoint that the amateur dancers would need more time to familiarise themselves with the dance material supplied by the makers. The second workshop related to the role of the dance duets in the performance. In order to create interaction between the professional and amateur dancers a strong focus would be placed on dance duets, which require an optimal interaction between the dancers. More than in any other form of collaboration, dancers should be in tune with each other during the performance of these duets. Tuning in to each other is like making contact with the other person by using all your senses. The willingness to be 'intimate' with each other, touching the body of the other person and to feel body parts of the other on your own body may prove to be difficult if you are not used to it. The resulting discomfort may influence the creativity process. Because it was expected of the amateurs and professionals to create and dance duets together in this work, Ernst and Wintjens wanted the amateur dancers to be well prepared for this interaction.

After these workshops, the amateur dancers met the professional dancers for the first time. The choreographers gave a dance motif and showed a few steps of a dance duet. In order to learn the steps, a professional dancer was coupled with an amateur dancer and then the couples were asked to create their own dance duets based on the material given by the choreographers. The dancers were encouraged to contribute elements from their own backgrounds to the dance, so as not to let the individuality of each dancer disappear. During the following rehearsals, the choreographers went to work with the material created by the dancers. The shape of the movements, the placing of the dance material in space, and the quality of the performance were accentuated. In the last two rehearsals, they collected all the dance material created up until that point and arranged it into a composition. The structure of these compositions was established by Ernst and Wintjens beforehand, so their ideas now needed to be implemented on the studio floor. In the final stage of the project, the choreographers worked on the accuracy of the dance movements and on mixing the elements of dance, music, stage settings, lighting and costumes.

Ernst and Wintjens aimed to take the image of collaboration between professionals and amateurs to a new level. It was therefore of the utmost importance, from their point of view, to create an interaction between the dancers in the group as well as interaction between the dancers and the audience coming to watch *TIJ*. That is why interaction became the theme of the production.

A long line of hatstands with yellow raincoats hanging from them was placed in the foyer of the theatre. Members of the audience had to put on these coats and pull the hoods over their heads. While they were 'dressing up', they were joined by the dancers disguised in the same yellow raincoats. Together the dancers and the audience entered the dimly lit hall of the theatre. There were no seats. Soon it became clear that everybody had to stand behind the red line drawn on the floor. The audience had little space. They could feel the slightest movement from the person standing next to them through the raincoats, but everyone remained anonymous because the hoods were still pulled over their heads and the room was still in semi-darkness. Nobody had any idea who was standing next to him or her: it could have been a member of the audience or a dancer. In this situation, the boundaries between dancers and audience as well as the dividing line between professional and amateur dancers had disappeared. There must have been some dancers behind the red line – that much was clear – but nobody could distinguish between the professional dancer and the amateur. This question remained unanswered even after the first dancers stepped from behind the red line onto the dance floor. Only when the dancers took off their raincoats did they shed their anonymity. They went in search of one another and met in different formations. There were solos, duets, trios and group dances – but the duets formed the basis of the choreography. In most cases, the duets seemed to come about by coincidence, but this was not the case. Ernst and Wintjens had thought carefully about which dancers met where and when. As a result, the relation between the professionals and the amateurs on the dance floor was kept in balance, without seeming to be contrived. The interaction between the amateurs and professionals developed organically. It became irrelevant to know who was a professional dancer and who an amateur. What was more intriguing was the natural communication between the dancers, the way they looked at each other, touched each other. It was all about people dancing with each other, regardless of background, and this was reinforced by the context in which the dance was presented. The music, the lighting, the stage settings and the costumes were kept simple and this simplicity was well planned. As a result, the audience focused their attention on the events on stage. They could zoom in on the dancers and feel a connection with them, which resulted in establishing not only an interaction between the dancers but also between the dancers and the audience.

Part two of the performance felt like a visit to the museum, a promenade. In unexpected places in the theatre, such as the attic, the office and the foyer, the audience could stop to watch a dance duet. The dancers had created these duets during the rehearsals and these formed elements of the first part. The locations where these duets were presented could be visited in random order. It was up to the audience to decide where to go and when to move on. Part one and part two together gave the audience the chance to participate in, and to contemplate, the remarkably surprising results of collaboration between professional and amateur dancers.

Experiencing *TIJ* – raising questions, finding answers

The interaction between the two groups of dancers raised interesting questions, such as: what are the differences between the two groups of dancers and what specific skills should choreographers possess to work with both professional and amateur dancers? How might this collaboration influence the dancers and the audience?

Amateur dancer Selene Driessen states: 'Professionals have learned more, but sometimes their knowledge can be a burden' (www.tijdewebsite.nl). Professional dancer Liat Waysbort agrees with Driessen: 'I like the self-assurance of the amateur dancer. To them, making a mistake is not the end of the world. It took me some years to learn to think like that' (www.tijdewebsite.nl).

For Ernst and Wintjens, the most essential difference between professional and amateur dancers has to do with the individuality of the amateur dancers:

> The professional dancer has been taught to 'neglect' his individuality and to sound out first what the choreographer wants from him. It is easier for the choreographer to mould them. The trump card of the amateur dancer is his individuality, and it influences everything he does.
>
> (www.tijdewebsite.nl)

Amateur dancer Selene Driessen adds to this conclusion:

> To me, dance is not what I am capable of, but dance is what I am feeling. And I can express my feelings in this project. My dance technique is not my strongest point. I cannot but draw on inner resources.
>
> (www.tijdewebsite.nl)

Selene's description of the process fits in with what professional dancer Jesus de Vega Gomez notices of the way in which amateur dancers dance:

> I noticed how the amateur dancer experiences each new movement with great intensity. It reminds me of how it used to feel, when I started my dancing career.
>
> (www.tijdewebsite.nl)

But professional dancer Marc van Loon has different views on the subject. At first, he thought that the dancing of the amateur dancers lacked intention. He felt that the amateur dancers gave all their attention to the form of the dance and only at a later stage gave interpretation to the movements:

> From day one I know there will be an audience watching me. I immerse myself fully in the dance, with everything I have learned, everything I am. That is why I found it strange to see that people approached the dance in such a different way. At first, it was just the form. But now I can see that each movement gains meaning. It will come ... it just takes time ...
>
> (www.tijdewebsite.nl)

Amateur dancer Rodney Kasandrikomo agrees with Marc van Loon:

> The big difference between the professional dancer and the amateur dancer is that the professional knows how to give the dance a particular style, to improvise on the dance right away. He knows there is more than technique. He is jamming right away.
>
> (www.tijdewebsite.nl)

If we now shift perspective to choreographic skills, according to Ernst and Wintjens, a choreographer should understand that in a project like *TIJ*, choreographic process and outcome could not be viewed separately. In order to achieve the desired choreographic outcome, methods of guiding the creation process play an essential role. In their evaluation report on the *TIJ* website Ernst and Wintjens (2006) mention that they deliberately focused on creating mutual trust and establishing good communication between the dancers. Only when trust and clear communication have been established can the interaction between dancers and between dancers and choreographers come into being.

During the rehearsals with the professional dancers, it soon became evident that the preliminary workshops for the amateur dancers had turned out well. Wintjens said:

> The preliminary workshops proved their worth during the creation process. There was an enormous surge of mutual enthusiasm which made it possible to begin the interaction with a certain kind of 'greed'.
>
> (www.tijdewebsite.nl)

The successful outcome of these preparations is obvious in the reaction from professional dancer Liat Waysbort on her collaboration with amateur dancer Rodney Kasandrikomo:

> The experience that I could work together with Rodney on such an equal footing was a revelation to me. We really made the dance duet together, complementing each other all the way. That surprised me.
>
> (www.tijdewebsite.nl)

This aspect of the relationship between process and product also creates insight into the reasons why it was important to Ernst and Wintjens not to make a distinction between the professional and amateur dancers in the joint rehearsals. They approached both groups of dancers in an open and easy manner and showed the dancers that they were confident that an interaction between both groups could be established.

Because of the composition of this particular group, Ernst and Wintjens made slight adjustments to their manner of working. There were small differences in the way they addressed professionals and amateurs. This was noticeable, for instance, in how they chose their words. When talking to the amateur dancers, they limited their use of professional terms. At times when they had to use dance jargon, they used imagery to support their explanations. Another aspect they took into account was the work pace. The rehearsals were regularly interrupted by short breaks. Before providing the dancers with new information, they first checked if the information given earlier had been understood.

In making a production with professional and amateur dancers, it is also important that a choreographer is aware of and able to work with the boundaries of the performers. On the other hand, according to Wintjens

> We should learn to see the amateur dancer as a full performer. We should see the more limited possibilities of the amateur dancer as a base, not as a limitation. As a choreographer, it means you should learn to watch, listen and to be patient until you see the real person, the real power and specific colour of the dancer. Only then, one could unfold and really use these aspects in the process of creation and the final choreography.
>
> (www.tijdewebsite.nl)

This production of *TIJ* also made clear to Wintjens that

> because of the presence of the professionals, I physically demanded more of the amateur dancers and wanted them to reach higher levels. I noticed that they also wanted to find and push their own boundaries. The final results were surprising. This means that in the future I can put greater physical challenges to amateur dancers. Before, I did not think so much was possible.
>
> (www.tijdewebsite.nl)

Ernst and Wintjens were convinced that collaboration between professional and amateur dancers could be an inspiration to both groups and may broaden their outlook. Some of the professional dancers involved at first doubted this. What can the professional dancer gain from the experience? Is it not easier to suppose that, in the case of professional and amateur dancers working together, the amateur dancers are the ones who have more to gain from the collaboration? After all, professionals have trained for years, and know the ins and outs of their discipline. Does collaborating with amateur dancers add anything new for them? Ernst and Wintjens wrote on the *TIJ* website that 'in a collaboration between amateurs and professionals it is not only the amateurs who learn something new. The reverse is also true'. It seems that the dancers in *TIJ* are a good example of how this interaction influences both groups of dancers on different levels.

To the question of what professional dancer Jesus de Vega Gomez had learned from his meeting with amateur dancers, he answered:

> It is nice to follow your first impulse of movement, thinking: does it feel right or not? You have to start simply. I tend to forget that sometimes. To start simply is not such a bad idea.
>
> (www.tijdewebsite.nl)

Peter Berends, one of the amateur dancers, said about his participation in *TIJ*:

> The professional dancers move very expressively. Brilliant to watch. It made me aware of the importance of focus and intention.
>
> (www.tijdewebsite.nl)

In addition to the insights on the level of craftsmanship, two other reactions proved that collaboration between dancers from different backgrounds can lead to reflections on the dancers' different frames of reference. This may be the aesthetic frame of reference of a certain dance form or dance style, but also of the habits and traditions that go with this form, style or a specific area of dance. Juul Sadee, a passionate amateur tango dancer, said:

> More than a meeting between professionals and amateurs, to me this project is a meeting between several dance forms. The collaboration with professional dancers has brought me into contact with the essence of my dance language. Marc (professional dancer with a modern dance background) and I decided to take the tango as a starting point in our first improvisation together. We just stood there and nothing happened and then I said to Marc: 'Yes, the man leads! You have to start!'
>
> (www.tijdewebsite.nl)

Figure 15.1 TIJ rehearsal. Photo: © Willem Betlem.

Liat Waysbort, an experienced professional dancer, also changed her views on the dance profession as a result of *TIJ*:

> The amateur dancers totally dedicate themselves to dance. Their enthusiasm, although it may sound strange, has opened my eyes. For me, dance had become more of a job. This project brings back the spirit.
>
> (www.tijdewebsite.nl)

As turns out from Ernst and Wintjens' report of the production of *TIJ*, both makers share Liat's experience. In collaborating with amateur dancers, Ernst and Wintjens were constantly surprised by the dancers' dedication and their involvement with the project. During the creation phase of *TIJ*, Ernst received emails from the amateur dancers in which they expressed their enthusiasm about the project and offered suggestions for the next rehearsals.

The diversity of the audience that came to see *TIJ* was remarkable. Bringing together dancers with different backgrounds meant bringing together an audience with different backgrounds. Because of this, many audience members were brought in contact with dance styles they were not very familiar with such as tango, tap dance, flamenco, modern dance and body popping. But *TIJ* has also helped to open up the boundaries between the professional and amateur dance world in the Netherlands. Because, how regularly do professional dancers, choreographers and their audience visit an amateur dance performance? How often does the professional dance world carry out projects with amateur dancers? Moreover, how often do the field of amateur dance and its audience come to see a professional modern dance performance? It can be difficult for amateur dancers and their audience to understand the form and vocabulary of a modern dance performance. In our opinion, the professional dance world sometimes has the tendency to stay too much within its world. It seems that there is a gap between these two worlds of dance. By bringing professional modern dancers and amateur dancers together on stage, the relationship between these different worlds of dance can improve. This gap remains a peculiar issue; after all, did not every professional start out as an amateur? Additionally, we believe that the *form* of the performance used in *TIJ* has helped to build a bridge between the professional and amateur dance circle. Ernst and Wintjens subtly integrated the audience into the performance through which the relationship between dancers and audience was strengthened. This has helped to bring the world of professional dance closer to the field of amateur dance and vice versa.

Another way in which *TIJ* might have influenced the audience after the event is through the website, www.tijdewebsiten.nl. With reference to the production of *TIJ*, participants from the respective amateur and professional dance worlds thought about the way in which the insights and experiences gained in *TIJ* could be shared with the various target groups in the dance world. Ernst, Wintjens and the authors greatly value the exchange of acquired knowledge with dance colleagues, such as students of the fine and performing arts, dancers, choreographers, teachers from the amateur and professional dance circles and policy makers working in the dance world. In order to encourage this exchange of ideas, the created website is easily accessible and offers the option of online reactions to and discussions on the project.

Furthermore, this production might have influenced the audience by initiating a debate on the existing boundaries between the professional and amateur dance circles. During the Dutch Dance Festival and the *Danswerk4daagse* (a conference on the developments in amateur dance, organised by the Noord-Brabant Centre of Amateur Arts in April 2006), Ernst and Wintjens shared their experiences gained in producing *TIJ* with the audience in an open discussion. The project served as an example of how connections between amateur dance and professional dance could be established. Questions that should not be left out of such a discussion are the following: should we still talk about the differences between amateur and professional dancers when we are carrying out projects in which the two groups share the stage as equal partners? When we are referring to a collaboration form such as this, would it not be better to talk about dancers as each having their own qualities? Moreover, is it not strange that the amateur and professional dancers are not paid the same amount of money, even though they are treated as equal partners on the stage? We believe that if we really want to break the boundaries between the amateur and professional dance circles, we certainly have to take into account the questions raised above.

Note

This chapter was partially translated from Dutch by Conny van Bezu.

References

DOD, brancheorganisatie voor de dans & Stuurgroep Dansplan 20/20 (2007) *Dans zichtbaar beter, sectoronderzoek van de Nederlandse theaterdans*. Available online at <http://www.theaterinstituut.nl/nl/content/download/340/3105/file/Danszichtbaarbeter_zonderfotos.pdf> (accessed 6 November 2008).

Kocken, O. and Tjon A Fong, J. (2006) 'Voor mix gaat de zon op', *TM*, 10 (6): 8–10.

Lans, J. van der (2007) 'Minister van Dans', *Dans*, 08 (3): 13.

Raad voor Cultuur (2007) *Innoveren, participeren! Advies agenda cultuurbeleid & culturele basisinfrastructuur*. Available online at <http://www.cultuur.nl/files/pdf/vooradvies0912/innoveren_participeren/pdf> (accessed 6 November 2008).

Schots, M. (2007) 'Dans daagt zichzelf uit & Dans legt zichzelf over de knie', *TM*, 11 (4): 28–31.

TIJ, *De dansers vertellen*. Available online at <http://www.tijdewebsite.nl> (accessed 27 October 2006).

—— *Ronald and Stefan vertellen*. Available online at <http://www.tijdewebsite.nl> (accessed 27 October 2006).

Wiel, F. van der (2007) 'Leontien Wiering: Dansdagen moeten naar Amsterdam', *TM*, 11 (7): 8–10.

Wiering, L. (2006) *De Nederlandse Dansdagen produceerden TIJ*. Available online at <http://www.tijdewebsite.nl> (accessed 27 October 2006).

16 Choreography coaching in the field of amateur dance in the Netherlands

Dirk Dumon

Amateur dance in the Netherlands has gone through important developments over the past ten years. Increasingly more people want to create choreographies with and for the amateur dancer and there is a steady growth of amateur dance productions. This development is stimulated by national and regional art and dance institutions in the Netherlands and has contributed to the growth of the quality of the amateur dancer and the amateur dance productions. In addition, there has been expansive development of amateur dance circuits, choreography projects and festivals with a need for more stages/performance spaces to perform these productions. The increase of all these new dance productions and new stages has had a positive influence in the field of amateur dance, yet we are conscious that there are also some less positive aspects due to these developments. Many amateur dance choreographers do not practice the craft of choreography in a sufficiently competent and professional way and thus, many of the choreographies shown on these stages have been poorly crafted. Therefore, the same groups and choreographers win the prizes at festivals. The conclusion is that, though performance facilities have improved, the development of the craft of the choreographers has not developed accordingly. As a direct result, the National Centre for Amateur Dance (LCA) in the Netherlands developed a new project for choreography coaching in 1991.[1] This was the start of a structural approach to coach beginners and advanced choreographers to help them with the challenges, problems and questions they encounter in the studio.

The choreography coach (normally a choreographer with specially trained skills) actually coaches the choreographer during the working process. Yet the conception of the term choreography coach is still developing; there are different methods and approaches concerning the coaching of choreography. The 'dance coach' and 'choreography coach' are familiar terms in the Netherlands, yet, from a socio-cultural point of view, coaching has not yet found its niche. Both the term and practice cover a diversity of meanings. My point of departure in this chapter is from a personal perspective of a choreography coach in the field of amateur dance. I write with the aim of acquiring better insights into the development, possibilities and backgrounds of coaching in general, and in particular, choreography coaching in the amateur field. This chapter will therefore address four issues:

- the specific skills a choreography coach needs to acquire,
- how he/she can steer the learning process,
- what different roles he/she should be acquainted with, and
- how a positive choreography coaching process could evolve.

The answers to these questions will take into account the way choreography coaching could work in practice. It is important to indicate that it is not the intention here to describe a well-defined methodology. Indeed, I think it is not possible, given the fact that each coaching trajectory is different. Each situation is unique; there is no widely accepted format for coaching systems that can be adapted or offered as a model of best practice. 'One should also depart from the assumption that master key solutions exist because people can differ fundamentally from one another' (Van den Beuken 2001: 41). That is why it is necessary for every coach to have a wide range of personal skills and insights.

What skills should a coach possess?

The art of coaching consists of outward skills combined with inner skills. In my vision of coaching, I start with the inner skills a coach might possess. These ideas are concerned with the coach *himself*, not what he or she should *know* and be able to *do*, but rather what he or she should *be*. A coach is something you *are*. Robert Hargrove uses the following metaphor in this respect:

> The Japanese have the word *korkoro* which has to do with the perfection of one's own inner condition. In order to become a great swordsman, tea ceremony master or kojiki dancer, you do not only have to master the technique, but you also have to develop a way of being that corresponds with the discipline. Being able to teach people the road to the objective requires perfection of one's own inner nature.
>
> (Hargrove 1995: 35)

The first question to ask about being a good coach is not, therefore, what do I do, but how am I and who am I? Being a coach means having a commitment with respect to being a coach. The traditional way of teaching people how they should coach consists of indicating certain qualities of coaching, categorising them, gathering information about each of them and then offering them to people. This traditional approach works from the outside inwards, as opposed to Ofman's approach to being a coach:

> The more he discovers about himself, the better he will be able to understand others and the better he will play his role as a coach or a

> facilitator, because he has learned from his own development what is required for further development and growth.
>
> (Ofman 1992: 32)

Whitmore confirms this by stating that being a coach 'is a way of approaching people, a way of thinking, a way of being' (1995: 32). This suggests that the quality of the coach is first determined by his/her self-understanding and reflective ability and not so much through knowledge and skills. In other words, the choreography coach should have an insight into what Ofman calls his core qualities:

> Qualities which form a part of the essence (the core) of a person; which permeate the entire human being and put all of his more or less striking qualities in a certain light. A core quality colours a human being; it is a specific strength of which we think immediately whenever we think about him or her.
>
> (Ofman 1992: 32)

Ofman suggests that 'just like light and shadow, core qualities and pitfalls go together' (1992: 35). In other words, a coach should have an insight into both his qualities and his weaknesses and should learn how to deal with them. We are concerned with authenticity here. The coach should have a true and authentic interest in the coachee and the latter's questions, as Burger and de Haan state:

> We believe that spontaneous and true interests cannot be replaced by any training, study or supervision. In this respect, there is nothing better than a personal style of one's own of coaching.
>
> (Burger and de Haan 2004: 42)

Thus, a coach should have the following inner skills: the ability to show interest, be attentive, conscious, self-conscious, observant, patient, honest and, in conclusion, should have a passion to help others how to learn, grow and perform. In addition to the inner skills, a coach should have learned perceivable 'outward skills'. A thorough command of outward skills will lead to the art of coaching, and by 'outward skills' I mean the tools a coach should have at his disposal. McDermott and Jago state the following in this respect:

> Whether we are coaching ourselves or others, having the right tool for the job makes all the difference. As with any practical toolkit, coaching works best if the coach can draw upon different tools for different needs, and for each and every stage of the task in hand.
>
> (McDermott and Jago 2001: 22)

Eric Parsloe takes a step further by stating that:

> The competent coach will need the relevant knowledge and a set of skills. These can be classed as core skills, technique skills which relate to each learner being coached; and personal skills which relate to the style and tone of the coach behaviour.
>
> (Parsloe 1992: 63)

The coach should have extensive communication skills but this core skill in itself is not enough, as in my vision, the coach should have *other* basic skills. Schreyogg adds an element here which is sometimes overlooked but which occupies an important place in practice; that is, 'naming standpoints of one's own'. By this she means that the coach sometimes sees things that the client is unaware of (and therefore does not perceive as a problem) but the coach has the responsibility to make it clear (Schreyogg 1997: 25). It is important in coaching situations for a coach to voice a personal opinion when it has an added value within the coaching process. Peter Dalmeijer describes this as 'fair witness':

> Fair witness is a position we can take with respect to others and ourselves or, in other words, taking the position of an impartial.
>
> (Dalmeijer 2003: 29)

These basic skills have to be nurtured continuously, as Starr (2003: 106) suggests 'once skills are acquired, it's not like riding a bike – coaches do forget. These skills are more like muscles; they must be used regularly to keep them strong', which comes down to the fact that this repetition and usage becomes a fixed component of one's daily actions.

How can a coach guide the learning process?

In order to connect with a coachee, the coach needs an instrument that allows him to have insights into his own thinking process. This is to overcome the fact that otherwise a coach will soon be seduced into believing that *his* way of thinking applies to everyone, a pitfall that may lead to misunderstandings. In order to prevent this, the logical levels, which Robert Dilts developed, based on the theory of the anthropologist Gregory Bateson, could be of use:

> Logical levels are a way of identifying underlying structures and patterns in thinking about ideas, events, relationships or organisations. They help us understand what's involved, or what's going on. The logical levels form a hierarchy.
>
> (Dilts in McDermott and Jago 2001: 48)

Logical levels are a series of 'coaching tools' that a coach can use to initiate processes of change and learning. Bateson and Dilts developed six fundamental logical levels (Figure 16.1).

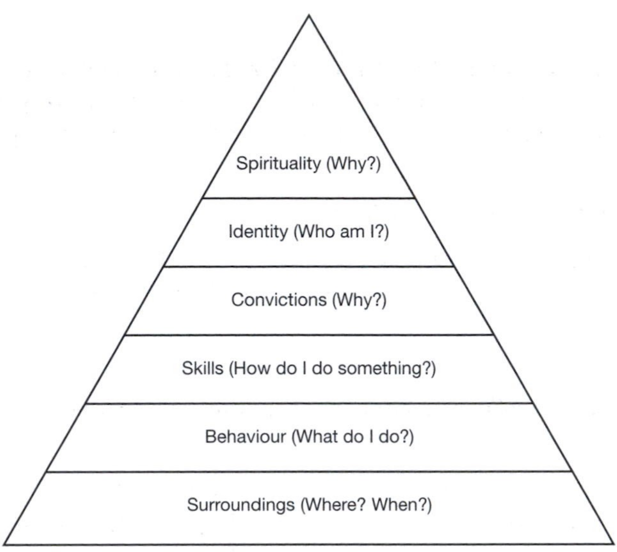

Figure 16.1 Six fundamental logical levels (Dilts in McDermott and Jago 2001: 48).

The levels are rendered as a triangle: 'the more you go down from the top of the triangle, the more concrete the thinking becomes' (Hoffman 1998: 24). The higher you go, the closer you get to your *being*. This triangle is a phase model.

> Each level results in a totally new way of looking at the world, a new standpoint, a new learning assignment, new challenges. Change is possible at each level.
>
> (Hoffman 1998: 25)

By establishing the level, the coach can focus his interventions on the area where development stands still or where the stagnating question is situated. The logical levels also clearly indicate 'where a problem originates, what the real issue at stake is and what the appropriate level for interaction or intervention is' (McDermott and Jago 2001: 49).

When and how can a coach use these levels?

Environment: Concerning where and when the question/problem is happening?

This level involves issues or details of context. It may mean a physical context, space or a particular room. It may also refer to a social context, for instance with a certain group of people or with an individual.

Behaviour: Concerning what do I do when a certain problem is involved?

This level involves mental and physical behaviour, that is, our activities or our actions, what you actually do or do not do. What are your actions, your thoughts? What are you doing well, and what can be improved?

Capability: How do I do something?

This level is about knowledge, skills, processes and capabilities. It attempts to answer the question: which capabilities do you have? What are you able to do?

Beliefs and values: Why do I address situations/problems in a certain way?

At this level there is a consciousness concerning our beliefs and values, our model of the world and our understanding of why things are possible or impossible for us. Beliefs and values provide us with a rationale for, and drive, our actions. Important questions are: What do you believe in? What do you feel is good? What do you like? What is important to you?

Identity: Who am I?

Identity is to do with one's sense of self. At this level, we discover who we are as a choreographer.

Beyond identity: For whom/what/why?

This level relates to a bigger picture or a larger system, where questions of a larger purpose come into play. What is your mission as a choreographer? What do you add to the world of choreography?

Essentially, Dilt's notion of logical levels (in McDermott and Jago 2001) provides ways of understanding to the coach and coachee of:

- what kind of information you are dealing with,
- where the problem or question originates,
- what the 'real' issue at stake is.

Logical levels can be used to monitor situations and to identify what the real issues are, or they can help to find the simplest or most effective point of leverage. They can also be used for rapport building.

What roles can a coach play?

The coach has to adopt appropriate coaching roles in addition to recognising and adapting to the level for interaction or intervention. What then are the coaching roles a coach can utilise? The answer is that coaches have certain preferences based on their own personalities, which means that a coach is more attracted to certain approaches and less to others. The central questions that actually preoccupy each coach most are: what works for this coachee? Which approach and method can I use to give the best support to this coachee with this presentation of the question in this coaching session? In my opinion, various coaching styles can be effective, depending on the situation, though a coach should understand his own preferred approaches and should know when to deviate from them if another approach proves to be more efficient. This flexibility in choosing his own approach may be the most important quality of the coach. Burger and de Haan (2004), Parsloe (1992) and Rubin (2000) all formulate good points of departure for a frame of reference for the coaching approach. Each approach offers other accents that can be useful at different moments and with different coaches.

The most basic and obvious coaching approach is *the directive approach* whereby the 'coach keeps a grip on the conversations and keeps the coachee on a leash as it were, encourages the coachee and helps him to solve his questions' (Burger and de Haan 2004: 50). This is a method frequently used by choreography coaches because many coachees still have little experience in making dances. Parsloe (1992: 54) calls working with inexperienced learners 'hands-on coaching'. In this case, the coach clearly takes control by structuring the conversations, suggesting solutions and/or giving assignments. It is an approach that works swiftly and effectively due to its steering character, and it fits in perfectly within the context of choreography coaching. Rivca Rubin calls this 'the skills coach' and describes it as follows:

> The skills coach can help you develop your particular craft, skill or technique, through focusing on your external technique and actions. This coach is most likely to be an expert in the same field and will create environments (physical spaces) and conditions that enable you to enhance through practice.
>
> (Rubin 2000: 15)

Interesting in this respect is what Rubin adds, that the coach has to be knowledgeable in the same working area. Within the context of choreography coaching, this means that the coach himself also has to be a practising choreographer or a choreography teacher. In a situation in which the coachee is a beginner choreographer or a choreographer with limited experience, I think this is very wise and necessary. This style relates to the logical levels of Dilts at the level of behaviour and skills, something Renske van Berkel (2002: 27) calls 'single-loop coaching' whereby the coach intervenes at the level of behaviour and skills.

Example 1

Linda was a young dancer of 18 who was making a solo on her own to perform during a national festival. She was working without any feedback from other people, and had a particular question about how she could use the music. At the stage that we met for a coaching session, she was using the music literally (this is often called 'Mickey Mousing'). She seemed unaware that there were other possibilities for using music in choreography, so I proposed to work with her on different ways of using her music and to concentrate on musicality. In fact, I used my skills and knowledge as a choreographer to let her experience different possibilities whereby she, by the end of the session, could make her own informed choice as to how she would like to use the music. In this situation, my hands-on approach was needed. I demonstrated my craft to give her the insight she needed to go on with her work.

The second coaching approach is *counselling coaching*.

> It is a form of coaching whereby the coachee is received entirely in his own terms and is given maximum space to work on his own questions in his own way.
>
> (Burger and de Haan 2004: 62)

Here, the coach refrains from any steering whatsoever as far as possible, only suggesting the minimum of new knowledge and advice and acting

Example 2

Marsha was already an experienced amateur dance choreographer. During her latest project, she became aware of the fact that she has occasional problems communicating her ideas to the dancers. I invited her to reflect on this issue and to talk freely about it. She was in control of the subject and the pace of our conversation. As the conversation continued I asked some deeper questions and she gave, through her reasoning, the answers she needed to gain more insight into her problem. My role was to listen, to give her the space she needed, not to impose a suggestion or feedback but just to support her own reasoning. At the end, without prompting, she identified a clear solution, that she wished to attend a workshop in communication techniques.

Example 3

John is a skilled and already established choreographer in the amateur field who knows clearly what his choreographies should look like. He was always well prepared; in fact, the choreography was already made in his head before he started to work with his dancers. But he still liked challenges, so he signed in for a coaching session. Instead of working in the studio, he and I had a long talk about his work and his convictions as to how a work should be processed. During the discussion, he became aware that because of the way he works, he hardly ever engaged his dancers in the working process. He realised that he had a directive (directorial) way of working in that he did not give space to the dancers to be involved. By mentioning the logical levels, questioning him on the level of his convictions and talking with him about his identity as a choreographer, he became aware that he wanted to start working in a different way, by involving the dancers more in the creative process of his next choreography, because he felt at that moment that this was the key to challenge him and to address new learning experiences.

The model diagram in Figure 16.2 offers an inventory of these coaching styles. One can observe that there is some commonality between the upper and the bottom row, as the arrows indicate that both use the counselling properties of coaching. One can look at this model as analgous to an iceberg. Behaviour and skills can be seen as the top of an iceberg but the part that we see is not an indication of what lies beneath the surface of the water. What people observe from each other are the behaviours, verbal and non-verbal, and the capability someone demonstrates. Sometimes a coach needs to work on the top of the iceberg because it is there that the answer can be found, but needs to be constantly aware that beneath the behaviour and the capability there is an underlying intention that in some cases needs to be addressed. That means that the choreography coach must address this intention at the level of 'convictions' and 'identity'.

instead as 'a kind of partner and fellow traveller in the development of the coachee' (2004: 62). One can argue in fact that the counselling approach is a fundamental skill for each form of coaching.

The third approach is *analytical coaching*, that is, looking for insight. Understanding from the inside takes centre stage in this approach, in the guise of a shared search between coach and the coachee. It is about enhancing the coachee's insight into his own questions and problems:

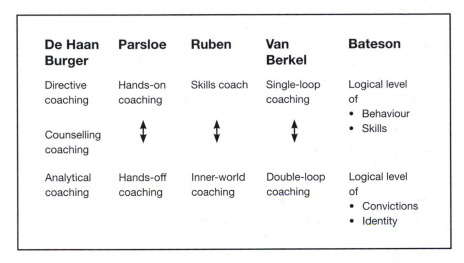

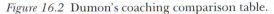

De Haan Burger	Parsloe	Ruben	Van Berkel	Bateson
Directive coaching	Hands-on coaching	Skills coach	Single-loop coaching	Logical level of • Behaviour • Skills
Counselling coaching	↕	↕	↕	
Analytical coaching	Hands-off coaching	Inner-world coaching	Double-loop coaching	Logical level of • Convictions • Identity

Figure 16.2 Dumon's coaching comparison table.

> The coach does not take the attitude of an expert or of someone who has gathered quite a lot of self-knowledge or insight into human character. His attitude is more one of an empirical expert – someone who has already been down this path of illumination and understanding before.
>
> (Burger and de Haan 2004: 69)

As in counselling coaching, a key factor in analytical coaching is listening carefully to the presentation of the question. This skill is specifically important during discussions of concepts to find the choreographer's intention. This approach links with what Parsloe calls 'hands-off coaching', used

> when developing higher performance with experienced learners. This coach is relying almost entirely on questioning to enable learners to develop their own improvement plan and to own the responsibility for achieving it, and at the same time developing the mental attitude necessary for success.
>
> (Parsloe 1992: 54–5)

Rubin states: 'The other type of coaching approach ("inner-world" coaching) is to work with the way you represent the world to yourself – your maps, models, beliefs and values' (Rubin 2000: 15). This form relates to the level of 'convictions' of the logical levels of Dilts, such as double-loop coaching 'which is about learning at the level of insight, what are the underlying motives' (Van Berkel 2002: 26).

How does the coaching process develop?

I conclude that it is on the one hand necessary for a coach to have his coaching style link up with his own personality and, on the other hand, important that he expands his coaching style by also trying out other methods. Each coaching trajectory runs differently, each situation is unique and most of the time coaching will turn out to be an adventure. Nevertheless, there is more to say about the travel plan of the adventure, an overview stating what the start of coaching is, how to go about it and how the process runs. This raises the issue that a proper support structure is essential to the overall success of a coaching assignment. I emphasise once again here that it is not my intention to introduce a fixed methodology. I simply wish to outline possible routes which originate from my own practical experience, supported by literature from Parsloe (1992), Scheweer (2000) and Starr (2003) together with the manual 'Danscoach Training' (Dance Coach Training) of the Centrum voor Amateurkunst Noord-Brabant (Centre for Amateur Art Noord-Brabant).

Scheweer departs from three phases in each coaching trajectory: first,

> The harmonisation phase in which coach and collaborator get on the same wave length, they gear the learning goal, the learning style and the approach during coaching towards one another.
>
> (Scheweer 2000: 153)

Parsloe calls this the 'analysis and assess the situation' period (1992: 62). However, Scheweer's additions to Parsloe's ideas are important because a choreography-coaching trajectory may sometimes be preceded by a concept discussion. Here the coach and the choreographer discuss the choreographer's intention and what he or she wants to elaborate. Some subdivisions can be added to this harmonisation phase. Initially this phase is where coach and coachee get acquainted with each other and rapport is established. The coach clearly indicates to the coachee what he/she can do and cannot do. The coachee indicates what the content of the question or problem is. The working frame is set, in which, as Starr (2003: 41) indicates, 'the context for the coaching is established' by the participants. The concept discussion is a part of the harmonisation phase. Once the frame is set, coach and coachee can initiate a concept discussion. Through questioning and discussion, the coachee is helped to formulate his concepts/goals/learning strategies and his choreographic outcomes. Scheweer mentions that a so-called contract is concluded in this phase or 'a more or less explicit agreement on the goal of and the working method during coaching' (2000: 156). This is necessary, especially when working with youths and young makers. This framework makes it clear to both parties how they will work and what they can expect.

The second step is the key phase. 'Coach and coachee analyse the current approach to the problems by the coach, and they look for a more adequate approach' (Scheweer 2000: 153). This does not always have to

Phase	Steps	Content
Harmonisation phase	Preparation Concept discussion Harmonising	Initial ideas, as yet undeveloped Analysis and assessment of situation Goals orientation Rapport Setting the frame
Key phase	Analysis Intervention	Looking for starting points Coach works actively
Completion	Process evaluation Product evaluation	How did coach and coachee experience the whole process? Coachee learns about himself as a choreographer Coachee learns about his choreography Next steps Future pace

Figure 16.3 Dumon's choreography coaching graph.

be a problem per se; it can also be a presentation of the problems that the coachee experiences. It may be possible in this phase that a choreography coach starts working actively with the coachee himself or with the product made. Sometimes it is more convenient to work with the product because it allows the coach to see what can be done differently. The question as to whether a choreography coach has to be a professional expert also presents itself here. If he wants to intervene at the product level, it is imperative he has expertise, but this is not relevant to all situations. Starr (2003: 77) refers to this phase in the following words: 'to create insight and direction' in which answers and solutions are sought in a dedicated manner in association with the coachee.

The last step consists of the completion:

> In this phase, the coach and coachee look back on the coaching trajectory and they wonder how the coachee wants to continue his development in the future.
>
> (Scheweer 2000: 153)

Two things have to be achieved in this phase, first evaluation and then completion. The evaluation has two aspects: The first relates to the process: did the coach and the coachee experience the entire process as being good, interesting, efficient and useful? The second aspect deals with the product evaluation, which also consists of two parts: what did the coachee learn about himself as a choreographer and what has he learned about the product he created? The latter is described by Scheweer as 'what does he learn about the world, meaning that someone acquires knowledge about the way something works' (2000: 161). Within the context of coaching choreographers, functional knowledge is involved. Starr calls this 'Confirm learning' (2003: 77), by which she means that what has been learned has to be repeated for the person we are coaching so that the latter can make a link between what he learns and the benefit he experiences from it. During the completion of the coaching trajectory, the coach and the coachee once again list all the agreements and look at the continuation. Possibly, a future coaching discussion may be arranged. Even if the trajectory is nothing more than one meeting, the phases of harmonisation, change and completion have to be dealt with. The graph in Figure 16.3 gives an overview of the entire process. It is subdivided into the *phases* one goes through, and the *steps* one takes that relate to them, and the potential *content* one deals with.

Conclusion

Robert Hargrove states that 'coaching is a voyage, not a destination' (1995: 14). This chapter has attempted to show a number of routes which may lead to a destination, but the terrain has to be explored further. I want to demonstrate that coaching choreographers is infinitely more than offering a tool. Coaching is an art and a skill. In my opinion, there are no rules of best coaching practice, yet different coaching styles are effective in different situations. The talents and the personality of the choreography coach, the questions and the personality of the coachee, the objectives of the coaching and the context within which all this takes place, all determine the effectiveness of each approach. Choreography coaching is also about learning by doing; it helps the coachee to be clear about what he is going into, what he wants to focus upon and to be open for opportunities to experiment with the creative process. A coaching project should be formed around the specific requirements of the individuals involved and should empower the choreographer to help him gain support and development.

Choreography coaching is a new form of conversation, but it needs to be given shape and still has to acquire its own socio-cultural place within the world of dance. We are still only at the beginning. This phenomenon still has to be embedded in our culture so that it becomes a self-evident value. This provokes the question, how can we develop and stimulate a coaching climate internationally in the world of dance?

I offer some informed suggestions: we need to

- identify cultural and systems barriers to developmental behaviours. Executives as lecturers in dance education all too often hide behind tested formulas; they need to be convinced that coaching requires other approaches, creating new opportunities.

- establish a coaching climate, with much more concentrated, integrated and coherent approaches. This means that dance academies as well as regional and nationally supported organisations should develop clear guidelines and enter into cooperative structures from which the work can be done.
- initiate research into the effectiveness of choreography coaching and publish articles to clarify this method of guidance.
- provide clear definitions for choreography coaching.

I therefore offer my own formulated definition of choreography coaching:

> Choreography coaching is a present-day guidance tool which can free up the potential qualities of each choreographer and the self-development qualities in the profession via an individual goal-orientated learning process so that the coachee is empowered to perform to the best of his abilities.
>
> (Dumon 2004: 50)

Note

1 This organisation was amalgamated in Kunstfactor in 2007.

References

Berkel, R. van (2002) *Coachen met het eneagram*, Deventer: Kluwer.

Beuken, J. van den (2001) *Acties die coachen tot een succes maken*, Soest: Uitgeverij H. Nelissen.

Burger, Y. en Haan, E. de (2004) *Coachen met collega's*, Assen: Koninklijke van Gorcum B.V.

Dalmeijer, P. (2003) 'Zelfcoaching', *Mind & Body Coaching*, 2: 29–58.

Dumon, D. (2004) 'A research into the art of choreography coaching in the field of Amateur dance in the Netherlands', unpublished MA Dissertation, University of Leeds.

Hargrove, R. (1995) *Masterful Coaching, extraordinary results by impacting people and the way they think and work together*, San Francisco: Jossey-Bass/Pfeifer.

Hoffman, K. (1998) *Werken met NLP*, Amsterdam: Uitgeverij Schors.

McDermott, I. and Jago, W. (2001) *The NLP Coach*, London: Paitkuss.

Ofman, D. D. (1992) *Bezieling en kwaliteit in organisaties*, Utrecht: Servire uitgevers B.V.

Parsloe, E. (1992) *Coaching, Mentoring and Assessing, a Practical Guide to Developing Competence*, London: Kogan Page.

Rubin, R. (2000) 'Coaching: developing the person', *Animated* (summer): 15–17.

Scheweer, E. (2000) *Veelzijdig coachen*, Schiedam: Uitgeverij Scriptum.

Schreyogg, A. (1997) *Coaching*, Amsterdam: Prentice Hall.

Starr, J. (2003) *The Coaching Manual*, Harlow, Essex: Pearson Education Limited.

Whitmore, J. (1995) *Succesvol Coachen*, Soest: Uitgeverij H. Nelissen.

Section 4

Intercultural contexts

Section introduction

Jo Butterworth

This section presents selected current writings about choreographic issues arising from using or blending or evolving traditional or indigenous dance making within contemporary arts and contexts. The current buzz words are 'hybridity' and 'fusion', used to denote work which moves away from singular meanings, homogeneous movement styles or disciplinary norms towards multiplicity and complexity.

In the twentieth century, mainstream dance has often looked to 'other' cultures to enrich its language, whether in terms of European–American modern dance from non-Western dance cultures, or simply from one style of dance to another. In some circumstances these influences evolve when choreographers or dancers move from one context to another: see for example, the recognisable shifts in the content and form of such choreographers as Richard Alston in the journey from Strider to Rambert Dance Company; Itzak Galili's relocation from Israel to the Netherlands; or Lin Hwai-min who studied Chinese opera movement in his native Taiwan, modern dance in New York and classical court dance in Japan and Korea before founding Cloud Gate Dance Theatre in 1973.

In other cases, these interdisciplinary tendencies demonstrate deliberate attempts by groups or individuals across international divides to explore personal or cultural identity, or to look for ways in which cultural borrowing can enrich the dance of the home state. Schechner (2002: 226) suggests that many artists intentionally create post-colonial, post-modern work, respectful, ironic or parodic, to overturn or subvert the colonial horror of 'mixing' or 'impurity'. More recently, both performers and scholars have gone beyond the deconstruction of dance traditions or the tendency to focus on cultural difference, in favour of encompassing commonality (Shapiro 2008: viii). Significant artist collaborations have been set up by choice to provide cross-cultural dialogue and allow choreographers to 'embrace positively the problems and advantages inherent in the unpredictable interplay between different sets of experiences' (Sanders 2005:1). Arguably, scholarship focusing on representation of culture, identity, gender and race in choreography, and on ways in which dance has been analysed and interpreted, elicits new understanding and provides impetus to the creation of new choreography.

The first chapter in this section by Francis Nii-Yartey discusses dance in many traditional African communities, where creation and practice are viewed as collective responsibilities and integral components of the life of the community. Even though this creative responsibility usually falls on a few active individuals and small groups, the ownership of traditional dance forms is usually not attributed to an individual choreographer. It is, therefore, the community that usually sets the norms guiding dance creation and practice. However, the introduction of formal dance education and the advent of communication technology, as well as artistic and other social affiliation through participation in international, national and regional arts festivals, workshops, seminars and other cultural and artistic programmes has created unprecedented opportunities and advantages as well as challenges for the African choreographer today. Nii-Yartey discusses some of the norms guiding contemporary choreography in Africa, specifically Ghana; he explores how the African choreographer reconciles tradition with modernity, as he constructs the new from the old within the framework of the principles and philosophy of African dance creation and practice.

Ilythyia de Lignière is a Belgian dance maker who collaborated on a project with Victor Phullu, a Nigerian choreographer. The chapter documents some aspects of the process of the *Dance Fusion Project*, investigating how a 'style loan' from one culture to the other can work, and discussing in some detail the content, form and performance realisation. She applies practice-as-research methods to evaluate the creative process, documenting the actual making of the art work and using triangulation to form an integral part of the research process. This personal evaluation relies on a supporting framework of established theories from Preston Dunlop & Sanchez-Colberg (2002), Pavis (1992) and Jeyifo (1996). De Lignière attempts to illustrate a pattern of intercultural collaboration with Victor Phullu by giving insights into their personal cultural parameters and the reference points they most rely on in choreography.

An Australian perspective of contemporary intercultural practices is offered by Cheryl Stock, who argues that whilst the sharing of culturally specific, body-centred practices still has a strong place, many intercultural dance artists now work in the globalized context of interdisciplinary mixed-media practices. This shift has augmented and refined modes of intercultural exchange, which she identifies as belonging to four categories: in-country cultural immersion, collaborative international exchange/sharing of culturally diverse practices, hybrid practices of diasporic artists, and implicit intercultural connections. Two interconnected aspects are at the heart of all four proposed models: identity and transformation. Whilst contemporary interculturalism may or may not derive from long-standing traditions, questions of continuity and identity remain inherent in the practice. Stock provides an example of the 'implicit intercultural connections' model: *Accented Body* was an interactive, international, multi-site performance installation which took place across six live sites in Brisbane, Australia, with distributed presences in Seoul and London. The two-year process began in 2005 when she invited 30 key artists from five countries in the areas of dance, performance, visual and sonic media, to respond to the 'accented body' brief, which was deliberately open-ended – the body as site and in site, and the notion of connectivities. The site teams coalesced around this brief, which additionally was about architectural, personal and cultural transformation.

Mohd Anis Md Nor examines how multiculturalism and intercultural discourses in contemporary Malaysian dance are observed as a confluence of relationships reflecting all aspects of life where personal world view and national gestalt are intertwined in all forms of contemporary artistic expressions. He describes how contemporary dance in Malaysia not only deals with issues of performing and choreographing dance for intercultural dialogues but it also acknowledges diversities as substantial constructs in dance discourses. After a brief history of the colonisation of the geographical area, Nor shows how, through political will (in particular a socio-economic affirmative action plan introduced in the 1970s), cultural diversities are deliberately engaged in order to emphasise uniqueness in form and styles of contemporary Malaysian dance. Thus, intercultural elements are visibly noticed as choreographers of different ethnicities vie to construct new works through contemporaneous movements amidst familiar but culturally engaging dialogues.

These chapters reveal the fluidity and diversity of dance practice, developed within particular historical or socio-cultural contexts. Certainly, the underlying causes of these developments may lie with such societal factors as globalisation, political shifts or technological improvement, or with new trajectories within aesthetic or artistic domains. It is evident that, like many other human experiences today, dance and choreography are affected by globalisation, and that migration, technology and growing connections transform our sensibilities and our understanding:

> These transformations are not always easy, since they disrupt our [existing] assumptions … Traditional forms of belief and expression are undermined by the influx of alternative visions and values. Yet … these changes are generative; they produce new and sometimes startling forms of art, they help to create new identities formed from disparate histories and experiences, and they help us rethink how we value one dance form over another.
>
> (Shapiro 2008: vii)

Theoretical underpinning of these global and intercultural positions can be found in the performance theories of Pavis (1996, 2006), Schechner (2002: 226–72), Bhabha (1990, 1994) Bharucha (1993) and

Fischer-Lichte (1996) and are applied, often in intertextual ways, in the dance writings of Franko (1995, 2007), Manning (2006) and Martin (1998) among many others.

What we might call an intercultural trend has progressed, thankfully, beyond the adoption of foreign or 'other' dance and theatre traditions or mindless eclecticism. We present here examples of intentional networking; attempts to create work that is culturally grounded for political purpose in post-colonial times; overt and deep recognition of artistic possibilities within a multicultural dance society; or deliberate global collaboration for artistic and research purposes. These processes of cultural transformation in choreography often result in new integrated forms, ones that can be understood universally, but perhaps an examination of the intercultural aspects can only be fully understood or explained in the context of the particular culture concerned.

References

Bhabha, H. K. (1990) *Nation and Narration*, London and New York: Routledge.

—— (1994) *The Location of Culture*, London and New York: Routledge.

Bharucha, R. (1993) *Theatre and the World: Performance and the Politics of Culture*, 2nd edn, London and New York: Routledge.

Fischer-Lichte, E. (1996) 'Interculturalism in contemporary theatre' in P. Pavis (ed.) *The Intercultural Performance Reader*, London and New York: Routledge.

Franko, M. (1995) *Dancing Modernism/Performing Politics*, Bloomington and Indianapolis: Indiana University Press.

—— (2007) *Ritual and Event: Interdisciplinary Perspectives*, London: Routledge.

Jeyifo, B. (1996) 'The reinvention of theatrical tradition: critical discourses on interculturalism in the African theatre', in Pavis (ed.) *The Intercultural Performance Reader*, London and New York: Routledge.

Manning, S. (2006) *Modern Dance, Negro Dance: Race in Motion*, Minneapolis and London: University of Minnesota Press.

Martin, R. (1998) *Critical Moves: Dance Studies in Theory and Politics*, Durham and London: Duke University Press.

Pavis, P. (1992) *Theatre at the Crossroads of Culture*, London and New York: Routledge.

—— (ed.) (1996) *The Intercultural Performance Reader*, London and New York: Routledge.

—— (2006) *Analyzing Performance: Theatre, Dance, and Film*, translated by David Williams, Ann Arbor: The University of Michigan Press.

Preston-Dunlop, V. and Sanchez-Colberg, A. (2002) 'Current modes of enquiry in choreological practice', *Dance and the Performative*, London: Verve Publishing.

Sanders, L. (2005) 'I just can't wait to get to the hotel': *zero degrees*. Available online at <www.akramkhancompany.net/html/text_akct_essays.asp> (accessed 20 October 2008).

Schechner, R. (2002) *Performance Studies: An Introduction*, London and New York: Routledge.

Shapiro S. B. (ed.) (2008) *Dance in a World of Change: Reflections on Globalisation and Cultural Difference*, Champaign, IL: Human Kinetics.

Further reading

Birringer, J. (2000) *Performance on the Edge: Transformations of Culture*, London and New Brunswick, NJ: The Athlone Press.

Castaldi, F. (2006) *Choreographies of African Identities: Negritude, Dance and the National Ballet of Senegal*, Urbana, Chicago: University of Illinois Press.

Franko, M. (2002) *The Work of Dance: Labour, Movement and identity in the 1930s*, Middlestown, CT: Wesleyan University Press.

Lepecki, A. (2006) *Exhausting Dance: Performance and the Politics of Movement*, New York and London: Routledge.

Nor, M. A. (ed.) (2007) *Dialogues in Dance Discourse: Creating Dance in Asia Pacific*, Kuala Lumpur: Cultural Centre University of Malaya and Ministry of Culture, Arts and Heritage Malaysia, and World Dance Alliance – Asia Pacific.

Nor, M. A. and Murugappin, R. (eds) (2005) *Global and Local in Dance Performance*, Kuala Lumpur: Cultural Centre University of Malaya and Ministry of Culture, Arts and Heritage Malaysia.

Van Erven, E. (2001) *Community Theatre: Global Perspectives*, London and NY: Routledge.

17 Principles of African choreography

Some perspectives from Ghana

Francis Nii-Yartey

My objective is to explore, from a Ghanaian perspective, how the African choreographer can reconcile tradition with modernity through constructing the *new* from established principles and philosophy of African dance. Few articles on African dance have been written by practitioners and even fewer on choreography itself. The substance of this chapter relies on those few listed in the reference section and my own thirty years' practice as choreographer and dance researcher.

The chapter is in two parts: part one is an overview of the role of dance in traditional African communities, detailing its basic choreographic characteristics and how knowledge of its practice is acquired. Part two discusses the impact of the new paradigm in choreographic practice in Africa – and specifically, Ghana.

African dance context

In Africa, dance serves as an index to the value systems that enable the community to interpret and express the various events of life. Participation in dance and other forms of artistic expression is a community experience. Dance provides the necessary linkages based on kinship, religion and common language that ensure meaningful social relationships, mutual respect and a sense of belonging among members of the various communities. Its creation and practice are viewed as a collective responsibility and integral to the life of the community. It is, therefore, the community that sets the norms guiding dance creation and practice. Knowledge and appreciation are acquired through legends, folk tales, songs, riddles, and dance itself; essentially through participation.

Opoku (1966) defines choreography from an African perspective as

> the putting together of carefully selected movements which express clear ideas, a style or character combined with form ... drum rhythms, voices, costumes, and mimed gestures, etc.
>
> (Opoku 1966: 53)

According to Nketia (1970: 71), traditional African dances are created by homogeneous communities with the responsibility falling on a few creative individuals, active social groups and households who may have been assigned this responsibility. However, the outcome and ownership of such creative pursuit is not usually attributed to the individual creator, but invariably considered community property; the creation and sustenance of dance depends on the ability of such creators to arouse and inspire emotional involvement, and to translate the symbolic and aesthetic qualities of the dance.

A whole range of social, religious, ecological, environmental, climatic and historical factors affect the characteristics of a dance. Royal dances, for example, can be exclusive. The *Kete* royal dance of the Ashanti of Ghana was originally the preserve of the king and his wives only, while only specific sections of the *Obonu* royal dance of the Ga may be enjoyed by a dancer on the lower scale of the royal ladder.

In religious dances one has to be 'chosen' by a particular deity to qualify to dance – the dance, in this case, is a gift from the gods to the community through the priest or priestess. So usually, it is the priest or the priestess who serves as medium, and occasionally, their assistants and advisers who may perform. However, everybody has a role in the performance, so the rest of the community may help with the provision of music or aspects of rituals associated with the performance.

In occupational dances for men, such as the *Abofoo* of the Ivory Coast and Ghana, or the *Inakpale* of Togo, one may have to belong to a guild of hunters, either as a professional hunter or in a position one has inherited from family tradition, to participate in these dances.

In dances associated with war, the dancers are usually male war veterans due to the violence associated with the performance, but in some cases individual women of outstanding physical and/or mental attributes may perform such dances. Yaa Asantewa of Ghana and Queen Amina of Nigeria are historical examples of such women associated with wars. Women usually perform special ritual dances at home when the men have gone to war to ensure victory for the latter. Kwakwa (1994) observes that:

> In Asante there is a most interesting female dance ritual which, in the past, took place during periods of crisis such as outbreak of war and epidemics. … mothers, sisters, wives and daughters of the fighting men … took charge of affairs at home ... to fight a spiritual warfare on behalf of the men. This … took the form of a processional dance ritual, *mmobome. Mmobome* combines song, hand clapping, dance, and ritual performances …
>
> (Kwakwa 1994: 12)

In Zimbabwe, both men and women perform the *Muchongoyo* dance in preparation for war and celebration of victory. The men perform the main and more energetic movements, while the women do improvised shuffling movements and help with the playing of musical instruments and singing (Asante 1998); while participation in some traditional warrior dances like the *Asafo* of the Fante of Ghana is based on automatic patrilineal inheritance for both men and women.

African cosmology reflects a continuity of experience and a re-occurring relationship between the past and the present; the ancestors and the living; the unexpected and the familiar. Repetition and improvisation are products of this concept. Tierou observes that:

> Africans tend to be uninterested in any art that lacks improvisation. … Every innovation and creation involves a thorough knowledge of technique which can then be 'forgotten' in order to allow spontaneous personal interpretations … In every traditional African dance the dancer is free to improvise because traditional African dances depend both on the repetition of the basic movements and improvisation around those movements ... Improvisation in Africa is not a result, as in the West, of spontaneity, but much more of the creative imagination of the improviser who applies himself to a given subject known to everybody …
>
> (Tierou 1989: 18–19)

Through the performer's 'innovation' the communal experience is heightened, common values refreshed, and aesthetic values enhanced. 'Beauty' is perceived in terms of curves and circular movements. The body is almost always slightly rounded, the knees relaxed, while the weight of the movement is earth bound. The belief is that circular images give a sense of perpetual motion and completeness of being. Many African dance movements follow the natural functions and form of the body. Any unexplained departure from this by overstretching, extension or any form of rigidity is viewed as exaggeration and therefore, considered aesthetically inappropriate, though local variations abound.

> the Akan people of Ghana emphasize the use of the arms, hands and feet in their dances … the Anglo Ewe of Ghana and those of neighbouring countries, the Republics of Togo and Benin, concentrate on movements of the upper torso in their dances.
>
> (Kwakwa 1994: 11)

Similarly, in the dances of the Lobi of Northern Ghana, the upper torso is brought into prominence in the *Sebre* dance, while the Frafra, also from the same region, prefer a combination of arms, shoulder movements and feet stamping in the *Bima* dance.

In the Ghanaian dance tradition, even though weight and centre are established through the pelvis and manifested in the hips, usually the various parts of the body come together to perform simultaneous movements at different times, speeds and qualities in multiple directions to create a harmonious and organic whole. This combination fosters power and economy of movement to help evoke the necessary aesthetic qualities and meaning of the dance. The knees are flexed; the feet well grounded and the arms rounded. From these basic positions, they extend, contract and contrast to define the core and subtle movements emanating from the torso and the pelvic regions – the centre.

This dynamic interplay of energy, time, gravity and rhythm in relation to the appropriate body stance is usually exemplified in the movement qualities assigned by society to men and women, the old and the young, the king and the ordinary citizen – dictating how the dancer in each dance genre and context should employ these movement qualities. Thus, in the *Adowa* dance of the Ashanti a female solo dancer uses the various parts of the body, including the head, to correspond to specific rhythmic patterns of specific musical instruments at different times, while the feet and hands may be moving independently in different directions. In this case, the movement of the torso articulates the subtle movements of the pelvic region while it performs its own independent movements. When the *Adowa* dance is performed in pairs, the dancers may relate their movements to each other in a reciprocal manner. They may also decide to interact with the spectators instead.

Even though most traditional African dances are abstract in form there is always some kind of story – either personal or around the community experience. Nketia (1988) has observed three forms of dramatic forms in traditional African society,

> 'ceremonial' drama – dramatic expression associated with social, ritual or ceremonial occasions. … 'Narrative' drama, a composite of speech (narrative and dialogue), music and mime … It finds its most elaborate expression in … story-telling … 'dance-drama' … expressed through music, poetry, mime and movements of dance.
>
> (Nketia 1988: 29)

Dance in its various forms is an inextricable part of these three categories. In the *Adevu* hunters' dance of the Ewe of Ghana for example, a sudden and abrupt stop or an intuitive emotional outburst in the course of the performance may underline the motivation, mood and characterization behind a personal experience on hunting expedition. *Adevu*, which may be considered a traditional dance-drama, is full of unexpected dramatic moments and tension accompanied by appropriate facial expressions and movement actions, drumming and songs to narrate the hunting experiences of the hunter. The dancer's actions are characterized by slow, fast and sudden stops as he stalks his prey. He takes short, rhythmic but careful steps in a crouching position, his face focused towards the direction of the elusive animal. Suddenly, his movement pattern changes, when the difficulty in locating the animal is resolved. Through his performance, the dancer is able to invite the spectators into his world of anxiety in locating his prey – his disappointment when he fails to kill the animal in his first attempt. When finally he succeeds in killing the imaginary animal, his movements become bigger and more outward and expressive.

Each dance, therefore, is specific; function, aesthetic and symbol being a consciously manipulated formalization of cultural and social patterns expressed through movement and story typical of customary behaviour. Appreciation by the community is only earned if the dance conforms to the canons of the community's dance traditions. To understand and appreciate the dance therefore, one must also understand the context of the occasion and its inherent symbolic purpose. The royal *Obonu* dance of the Ga people of Ghana, for example, may be performed during the funeral of a royal or a prominent member of the community using movements denoting the sad nature of the occasion, as well as the good or bad deeds and other attributes of the deceased. On another occasion, such as the celebration of war victory, the same dance might be performed with more aggressive movements and gestures, using battle motifs and scenes depicting battle. These changes can also bring alterations in rhythmic patterns, costumes, props and make-up and contribute to the final choreography.

Music

In Africa, it is often said that, 'When the beats of the drums die down, usually the dancing also ceases …' (Nketia 1963: 163) The key factor that an African dancer will always look for in both music and dance is the rhythm. Rhythm remains the central core to any expression of African culture and consequently the centre of any analysis that is conducted (Asante 1998: 207). It is usually rhythm that determines the structure and sequence of the dance. Depending on the requirements of the dance and the complexity of the music that accompanies its performance, the rhythmic patterns may be melodic or percussive, either linear or multi-linear. Nketia explains this phenomenon in the following:

> The music for a specific dance may consist of a number of individual items of songs, instrumental pieces or both. … linear rhythms are organized in sections within a time span delineated by handclapping, the beats of a bell or some such idiophone or a drum … In multi-linear rhythmic organization, the durational rations observed horizontally may also be organized vertically. While one instrument is playing two or four equal notes to the measure, a second instrument may be playing three or six against the same measure …
>
> (Nketia 1965: 92–6)

The dancer, therefore, looks for the primary regulative beats of the music for his or her performance. He or she then builds on these and other musical elements such as speed, time and alternative rhythmic patterns being provided by supporting instruments to phrase and elaborate his or her movements to help advance the performance generally.

Costumes

The part played by costume in traditional communities is indicative of social, political and financial status and also of appropriateness. The wearing of adornments in a manner other than accepted by society is seen to be rebellious and disrespectful (see Gyeke 1996). Both regional variation (for example, the smock and pantaloons worn by the men of north Ghana, compared with the eight to nine yards of wrapped-around linen used by the men in the south) and dress for occasion are important. Serious or sombre occasions require the wearing of blacks, reds or russets, with brighter, lighter or even white for joyous ones. In dance forms the costumes become animated and adapted (see Nketia 1988: 23–31 for further accounts).

In some dances, the performers may be elaborately or scantily dressed depending on the requirements of the particular dance. Some dances are designed to reveal certain parts of the body to draw attention to details of particular movements, as in the *Sebre* dance of the Lobi of Ghana where the main feature of the dance is in the vibratory movements of the upper torso. In other dances elaborate costumes are used to disguise the dancer's identity as he takes on the role of a spiritual entity, found in the *Bolohi* panthers' dance performed at the enthronement and funeral ceremonies of the Senufo of Côte d'Ivoire.

Props

Implements such as bows and arrows, horse or cow tails, and wooden staffs are used for historical and aesthetic reasons, as well as for identification purposes. In the *Lilek* the performers use bows and arrows to re-enact how the Builsa people in northern Ghana defended themselves against slave raiders during the period of slavery in Africa.

In some communities it is believed that the horse-tail or cow's tail contains spiritual powers and helps to protect the user against possible spiritual reprisals by enemies. In others their use is important in the identification of social positions of community members and their ancestral connections. The horse's tail in the *Nakwaawa* butchers' dance of the Dagomba of northern Ghana plays a significant part. The Dagomba are patrilineal; therefore, only if one's father, or mother's father, is a butcher, is one qualified to perform the *Nakwaawa*. If the dancer holds the horsetail with the left hand and raises it above the head while performing, it is an indication that he or she inherited the position through the mother's family. If the inheritance is directly through the father's lineage, the dancer performs holding the horsetail with the right hand raised above the head. The use of such special items in the dance and other social situations are limitless in African communities.

Make-up

The use of make-up in Ghanaian dances by choice is not as elaborate as one finds in other parts of Africa, except in the religious and initiation dances. The *Akom* and *Kple* religious dances, and the *Dipo* and *Otufo* puberty dances of the Ga-Dangbe people are typical examples where sometimes the whole face, torso, arms and legs of the dancers are smeared with *ayelo* (white clay). Markings of *ntsuma* (red clay) on specific parts of the body are associated with funerals and war situations while *ayelo* and *kloboo* smearing is identified with festive and ceremonial occasions. Among the Dagomba and other ethnic groups of northern Ghana, *Kooli*, a shiny grey powdery substance, believed to contain medicinal properties that help maintain healthy eyelashes, is usually used to decorate the eyelids while *lenle* (substance made from the henna leaf) is used to dye the feet in the case of married women.

Choreography

Choreographic knowledge and craft are acquired through kinetic experience gained from customary activities and behavioural patterns in the community. Complex rhythmic combinations in African recreational activities such as the Ghanaian *Nteewa* hand clapping and *Ampe* multi-rhythmic games for women, and *Djama*, a rhythmic game-of-strength for men, help to instil rhythmic sense, movement awareness, discipline and trust in the dancer from an early age. Later in life, re-enactments of past events such as hunting expeditions, wars, ceremonial rituals and festivals and story-telling sessions, provide movement resources for creative and technical foundation for choreographic exploitation. Of great importance in African dance creation and performance is that the choreographer must also be a good dancer, because:

> the ability to express one-self competently and to communicate ideas, emotions, and knowledge through the language of dance is recognized as an important attribute of a cultured, educated citizen … training lasts throughout the dancer's life time. A sense of rhythm and timing are taught through voice simulations of drumming with hand clapping, miming to work chants, and the recitation of dramatic incidents in folk tales at storytelling sessions. This sustained training programme makes it possible for a dancer to meet several dance situations, even the most technically demanding.
>
> (Opoku 1987: 194)

The new choreographic context

Today, the old African cultural values have significantly changed and the socio-economic and cultural conditions that nourished them are rapidly diminishing. This is due largely to the introduction of formal education, the advent of communication technology, creation of social affiliations and participation in international, national and regional arts festivals, as well as social programming. While there is no doubt that African traditional cultures have consistently influenced artistic development in Western and other cultures for centuries, African cultural traditions have also been impacted and enriched by other cultures. Fodeba (1957: 205–6) recognises the need to acknowledge the hybridity of African folklore (culture). The phenomenon of duality of old and new norms guides the texture of life generally in almost all communities on the continent and continues to stimulate the creation of new traditional cultures in Africa.

New discoveries and different approaches to dance practice are evident in many African countries today. Through the establishment of national dance companies, teaching and research institutions for dance and other formal educational facilities in some African countries in the wake of their independence from colonialism, respect for dance has grown beyond its traditional context. The African choreographer has been accepted as a legitimate product of the new socio-cultural, artistic and economic dispensation of the African continent. A major contributing factor to this recognition is due to the policies of African political leaders who, in the late 1950s and early 1960s, on attaining independence,

> implicated dance in the making of a national culture, reconfiguring local dance traditions as vehicle of historical memory and continuity. African Ballets (African Dance Companies) linked to the newly independent state to the cultural patrimony of a pre-colonial past, uncontaminated and cleansed of the influences brought about by colonization. At the same time, they established a dialogue between western modernity and indigenous forms of art, like the new nation itself established continuity between the inherited colonial structure of state and the Africanization of its personnel and goals.
>
> (Castaldi 2006: 9)

President Sekou Toure of Guinea established the Les Ballets Africaines, Kwame Nkrumah inaugurated the National Dance Company of Ghana, and Leopold Sedar Senghor founded the National Ballet of Senegal. Those of the Gambia, the Ivory Coast and Uganda were established as a viable vehicle for their Pan-Africanist and nationalistic ideology and their determination to reverse the negative legacy of Africa's colonial past. The responsibility for giving direction to these companies fell on the shoulders of creative individuals who were formally educated outside the continent and at the same time intimately rooted in the artistic traditions of

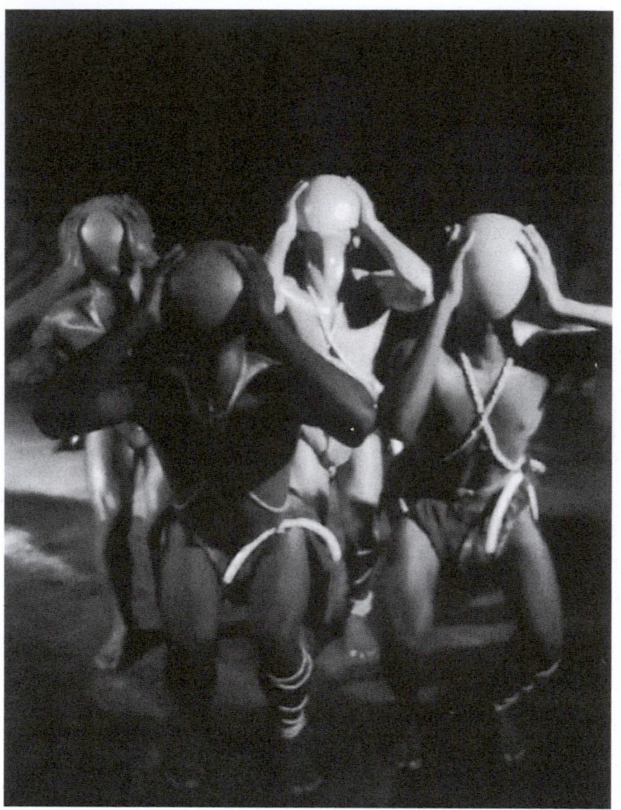

Figure 17.1 Koom (1998) a contemporary African dance choreographed by F. Nii-Yartey and performed by the Noyam African Dance Institute. Photo: © F. Nii-Yartey.

their people. To these creative artists, the challenges and responsibilities associated with the patterns of change in the African artistic milieu were as profound as they were exciting and fulfilling. They saw each creative process as stimulating the kind of consciousness that transcended the existing artistic and cultural heritage of Africa.

This commitment enabled these artists to follow a path of development and processes that allowed the vitality and unique impulses of African dance as well as 'making allowances for new constructions, meanings and a richer and more extended vocabulary' (Opoku 1969: 1). This is evident in the compositions of pioneers like Mawere Opoku of Ghana and Keita Fodeba of Guinea who present the two main approaches to neo-traditional dance on the continent.

Fodeba developed a style of narrative in dance-theatre format, combining traditional instrumental music, dance, gesture, songs, legends and elaborate costumes, including the offerings of the modern conventional theatre, to create some of the most formidable choreographic works produced in Africa. Opoku on the other hand, focused on the representation of the traditional dances as individual forms on the conventional stage with no definite narrative intent, even though his only major work in the narrative, *The African Liberation Dance Suite* (1965), was equally highly successful.

During the period of political agitation for independence, a concept known as the 'African Personality' was conceived by the architects of the independence struggle in Ghana. Led by President Kwame Nkrumah of Ghana, the concept helped to shape government policies on arts and culture in the country. A National Theatre Movement emerged to help bridge the existing gap between the acquisition of theoretical knowledge and performance ability in the arts (and between African and Western artistic values) and to create viable artistic products of music, dance and drama (Sutherland 2000: 45). In furtherance of this, specific cultural, artistic and academic institutions based largely on Western educational structures were established, such as the Institute of African Studies based at the University of Ghana. The Institute was charged with the responsibility of studying the arts of Africa: a School of Music, Dance and Drama and a National Dance Company operated for the purposes of teaching, research and performance. Students from other African countries came to study and to share their knowledge of African music, dance and drama and related subjects. Traditional dancers and musicians from all over the country were recruited and integrated to form the nucleus of the Dance Company.

As a result of this cultural and artistic re-awakening, three phases of dance development – *neo-traditional*, *dance-theatre*, and *contemporary dance* have emerged in Ghana alongside the traditional forms. The process of traditional dance development and training is relatively slower and less formal in approach than the neo-traditional and contemporary forms. Unlike these last two forms, collective inputs are paramount in traditional dance creation and very rarely are creations of particular dance forms attributed to individual choreographers.

Opoku, who pioneered the neo-traditional phase in Ghana, explains,

> the neo-traditional … seeks to extend and enhance the content of the traditional forms with an eye towards clarity in the creation of the salient qualities of the repertory of dances from many regions and stages. This presupposes that the audience will be largely non-participating. … It does not in any way distort the structure of the dance nor does it in any way debase the traditional execution of the dances.
>
> (Opoku 1999: 85–9)

Neo-traditional dance

In this phase, Opoku brought together existing traditional dances from around the country – outside their usual rural community context – and

Figure 17.2 *Sochenda* (2000) a contemporary African dance choreographed by Nii-Yartey, performed by dancers of the Noyam African Dance Institute. Picture: © Karla Hoffmann.

carefully re-arranged their movements to suit the conventional stage. He explored and exploited the related art forms, such as music, costume, and props of traditional dance forms. The rearrangement was meant to suit the taste of the usually mixed audiences who patronize the theatre by shortening their original forms to save time and to enhance their appreciation.

Dancers who usually danced towards the musicians or were encircled by them in the course of the performance, were redirected to allow greater visibility of the movements of the bodies from different angles. Important movements, which otherwise might not have attracted the attention of the audience due to the distance created by the conventional stage setting were also 'amplified' for clarity. Modification of costumes was done in a way as to maintain their specific cultural nuances and authenticity.

Even though the traditional ways of dressing are still fashionable, our modern life-style has brought about new tastes in fashion that are allowing contemporary African choreographers, unlike those in the neo-traditional dance forms, to significantly modify traditional costumes and create new and refreshing ones to suit new choreographic taste even within the traditional idiom.

Dance theatre

In phase two, the development of a distinct Ghanaian dance theatre emerged. The use of modern production methods did much to bring the many elements represented in this form of dance presentation into a coherent unity of expression of various themes. The first serious dance-theatre production in Ghana was Opoku's *African Liberation Dance Suite* (1965). Set in four movements, the first movement dealt with the exploitation and enslavement of the sleeping giant Africa; movement two dealt with the awakening, restlessness, agitation and call to arms; movement three with lamentation for the dead and dying freedom fighters and movement four dealt with the struggle for freedom which will continue till victory is won.

The treatment of this choreographic work advanced flexibility, variety, and fluidity in the visual flow of thematic content of dance composition in Ghana. The overwhelming success of the *African Liberation Dance Suite* opened the floodgates for the creation of dance-theatre productions like Nii-Yartey's *The Lost Warrior* (1978), *The King's Dilemma* (1979), *Atopre* (1983), *Bukom* (1986), *Atamga* (1989), and *The Legend of Okoryoo* (1991); *The Maidens* by Patience Kwakwa; *The Orphan* (1996) and *The Palm Wine Drinkard* (2002) by Ofotsu Adinku; and *Odwira* by Asare Newman. Since African dance is integrative – that is, it combines dance with music, drama, poetry, costumes for its expression – these choreographers used adventurous and provocative movements with music, dramatic and the other artistic elements to help maintain the traditional marriage between dance and these art forms.

Contemporary African dance

The third phase emerges from these experiences – contemporary African dance. What the word 'contemporary' represents here is, in many ways, different in the African context from what pertains in the West as it deliberately creates from, and at the same time advances, the traditional classical forms. Its language, inspiration, content and symbols are drawn from the African experience. However, to advance African dance *beyond* the old form, and for its appeal to transcend its original community context, universally proven and acceptable methods and techniques of dance composition developed from within and outside Africa. They are based on informed and compatible creative impulses and experiences and are required to achieve a viable and credible contemporary choreographic creation in Africa.

Contemporary African dance must negotiate between the old dance traditions of Africa and the impulses and issues of our new generation. It must redefine and distil the intrinsic values, vitality and contradictions of the African dance tradition to sketch out something unique, but still 'African', that opens up the art of dance and reasserts it in the contemporary idiom and to a higher and universal level of artistic consciousness. Essentially, contemporary African dance must transverse both time and space. Its aesthetic standard and means of expression must help to articulate the lives, views and innovations of African people in the context of today. Contemporary African dance must also thrive on innovation, technical skill and originality in evolving its own choreographic language.

Contemporary African dance is being developed by choreographers and other creative people with formidable artistic insights and technical skills. These are creative people who, through exposure to local and international artistic forms and products, have acquired a holistic outlook that informs their teaching, choreographic and technical methods. Pioneers who are helping to change the face of African dance through their writings, teaching, choreographic works and performances in their respective countries and beyond include Germaine Acogny of Senegal, Alphose Tierou and Adiatu Massidi of Côte d'Ivoire, Kofi Koko of Benin, Elsa Wolliaton of Kenya, Achille N'Goye of the Congo, Sylvia Glasser of South Africa, Salia Sanon, Seidu Boro and Irene Tassembedo of Burkina Faso, Nii-Yartey of Ghana, Peter Badejo of Nigeria and Kariamu Welsh of the USA.

At the forefront of the development of contemporary African dance in Ghana is the Noyam African Dance Institute. *Noyam*, which translates as 'development' or 'moving on', was set up in 1998 with the endorsement of the Ghana Education Service (GES), Ministry of Education and with initial funding by the Danish Development Agency (DANIDA) to operate as a private dance institution in the country. The Institute provides opportunity for diverse groups of young people with differing educational backgrounds to access knowledge of dance and to help advance the development of contemporary African dance in Ghana. This includes the development of a 'Noyam' technique derived from the movement characteristics, aesthetic qualities and philosophy of the African dance traditions and from the enormous movement and rhythmic resources in traditional games, such as the *Nteewa*, *Ampe* and *Ntoosa* rhythmic games for girls and boys. In developing this technique, my colleagues and I looked at compatible elements from international artistic forms and products, and drew from the dynamic experiences of dance practitioners involved in the development of dance in Ghana. The style and vocabulary of Noyam is based on the philosophy that the human body as a tool for the creation and dissemination of dance should not be limited in its ability to absorb movement, from wherever it comes.

Today's student must therefore, acquire the movement skills needed for the effective execution and definition of this form of dance. To achieve this, students are taken through a selection of traditional dance movements, ensuring that they learn the proper execution and details of each dance as done elsewhere. The Institute pays particular attention to shape, dynamics, contextual and emotional qualities of the movements. Kinetic energy derived from such everyday human activities as falling, lifting, jumping, walking, clapping, rolling, pushing and pulling, running, and the natural undulation of the spine, as well as facial expressions of all sorts are employed in the process of building the vocabulary.

Movement phrases for a particular dance composition, for example, are guided and defined by the evolving choreographic language of contemporary African dance based on the creative principles and processes of the African dance tradition yet determined by the dynamics and compatible elements of modern techniques and processes of dance creation. From these, some elements are applied in their original form or abstracted, extended, stylized and filtered into the choreographic works of the Institute.

Conclusion

Dance addresses fundamental issues of human existence. In Africa, dance and the related arts of music, drama and the visual arts permeate all activities of the life cycle – birth, work and death. Over the years however, through contact with the outside world and within the continent itself, Africans have acquired new ways of addressing the many issues confronting them today. There has been a tremendous impact of foreign values as well as dynamic internal changes on the arts, including dance.

The challenge for African choreographers is, therefore, to find efficient ways of pushing spatial, stylistic, creative and technical boundaries beyond their present limitations, and to formalize and codify the results of their creative energies, inspired by criteria and processes accepted by most in the artistic world. Since there are diverse approaches to dealing with creativity and technique, it is necessary for the African creative artist to look at the wide-ranging and integrated training programmes available within the continent and elsewhere in order to develop a viable, three-dimensional and distinct African dance vocabulary, style and technique.

The new African choreographer is able to draw on a wide range of creative impulses, based on his or her experiences and perceptions of the world around him *and* from his perspective as a choreographer living in Africa. The acquisition of this artistic ability is what evokes the required emotional, spiritual and social meaning of the dance in the community and beyond. Arguably, the new African dance expert should examine the inadequacies of the African traditional systems of documentation of the body of knowledge on dance and make the effort to help expand the existing structures, as well as aiding the development of a new vocabulary and codification system. For, as Acogny observed,

> Instead of letting the development [of African dance] take its own way, we Africans should take it in our hands and make it become indigenous modern dance … because traditional dance is meaningful only within a given socio-cultural context.
>
> (Acogny 1988: 24)

Work achieved by established dance practitioners and researchers like Kariamu Welsh Asante, Germaine Acogny, Alphose Tierou and others in the area of contemporary African dance need to be encouraged by African governments and other stakeholders interested in a holistic development of the continent. Their financial and institutional support will greatly facilitate the future merging of these seemingly scattered but similar developments into one coherent African dance technique and vocabulary comparable to any system elsewhere in the world.

References

Acogny, G. (1988) *African Dance*, Frankfurt: Verlag Dieter Fricke.

Asante, K. W. (1998) 'Zimbabwean Dance Aesthetic: Senses, Canons, and Characteristics', in K. W. Asante (ed.) *African Dance: An Artistic, Historical and Philosophical Inquiry*, Trenton, NJ: African World Press.

Castaldi, F. (2006) *Choreographies of African Identities: Negritude, Dance, and the National Ballet of Senegal*, Urbana and Chicago: University of Illinois Press.

Fodeba, K. (1957) 'La Danse Africaine et la Scène', *Presence Africane*, 14–15 (June–September): 202–9.

Gyeke, K. (1996) *African Cultural Values: an Introduction*, Philadelphia, PA, and Accra, Ghana: Sankofa Publishing Company.

Kwakwa, P. A. (1994) 'Dance and African Woman', *SAGE*, 8 (2) Fall: 10–15.

Nketia, J. H. K. (1963) *Drumming in Akan Communities of Ghana*, London: Thomas Nelson and Sons.

—— (1965) 'The Interrelations of African Music and Dance', *Separatum, Studia Musicologica Tomus*, 11(fasc.): 91–101.

—— (1970) 'The Creative Arts and the Community', *Proceedings of the Academy of Arts and Sciences*, VIII, Accra, Ghana: 71–6.

—— (1988) *Ghana: Music, Dance and Drama*, Accra, Ghana: Information Services Department Press.

Opoku, A. M. (1966) 'Choreography and the African Dance', *Research Review University of Ghana Institute of African Studies*, 3 (1): 53–9.

—— (1969) 'The African Choreographer's Problems', *Research Review University of Ghana Institute of African Studies*, 5 (2): 1–8.

—— (1987) 'Ashanti Dance Art and the Court', in E. Schildkrout (ed.) *The Golden Stool: Studies of the Ashanti Center and Periphery*, Anthropological Papers, New York American Museum of Natural History, 65: 192–9.

—— (1999) 'African Dance Perspectives: Review of Basic Concepts', unpublished manuscript, Institute of African Studies, University of Ghana: Legon.

Sutherland, E. T. (2000) 'The Second Phase of the National Theatre Movement in Ghana', in K. Anyidoho and J. Gibbs (eds) *FonTonFrom: Contemporary Ghanaian Literature, Theatre and Film*, special edition of the journal *Matatu* 21–2: 45–57.

Tierou, A. (1989; 1992) *Dooplé: The Eternal Law of African Dance*, Paris: Harwood Academic Publishers.

18 An intercultural encounter

The *Dance Fusion Project*

Ilythyia de Lignière

To me as a Belgian artist, an evolution in one's personal choreographic style is accelerated when one is involved in different projects, working with other people and interacting with unfamiliar cultures. I was therefore delighted to have the opportunity to set up the *Dance Fusion Project*, an intercultural choreographic collaboration with an African choreographer.

The project was realized in Lagos, Nigeria, by Victor Phullu, a well-respected contemporary choreographer and author, supported by the Dance Guild of Nigeria and by the Alliance Française as one of its cultural activities. The intention was to present a performance where the synergy of our personal choreographic skills created a new language. A secondary aim, to document and analyse the event as a research project was set up after these plans had been finalized but before rehearsals began.

Before and during this process, it was apparent that Victor and I perceived things differently: our interpretation of themes or ideas, uses of techniques and compositional forms varied substantially. It is exactly these differences, and the constant moving between the two cultures, that triggered the dialogue between the participants and made the project a unique experience.

This chapter documents the process of the *Dance Fusion Project*, investigating how a 'style loan' from one culture to the other can work, and discussing in some detail the content, form and performance realization. The methodology used to describe and evaluate the creative process is that of practice as research, where the actual making of art forms an integral part of the research process. Its success relies on a strong supporting framework of established theories.

Thus, the ideas and theories that I have applied to guide my work as researcher are:

- Preston-Dunlop and Sanchez-Colberg (2002) – the perspectives of *experience, experimentation, documentation and analysis*.
- McNiff's (1988) *action research* principles for the evaluation and development of rehearsals in the session sheets.
- Pavis' (1992) *hourglass* model to inform how effectively cultural information is transferred.

- Jeyifo's (1996) guiding *questions* on measuring intercultural transfers.
- Butterworth's (2004) *Didactic–Democratic Continuum* model to assess the roles and decisions in the process of choreographers.

To structure this chapter, I reflect upon the design of the hourglass used by the Pavis model (1992: 4). By using this model in the context of the *Dance Fusion Project* I illustrate a pattern of intercultural collaboration between Victor Phullu and myself, by giving an insight into our personal cultural parameters and the reference points we most rely on in choreography.

The design of the hourglass is crucial to the meaning of the Pavis model. When turned, the informative sediment of the source culture will trickle down towards the target culture. The hourglass neck acts as a filter and the speed and ease with which information will be received at the bottom will depend on the receptive ability of the target culture. The model also represents the numerous possibilities by which the sediments of both cultures will mix and flow. The superior bowl of the hourglass represents the source culture as it is conceived and formalized before the actual work of adaptation begins. The inferior bowl represents the performance itself and deals with the receptive ability of the target culture.

In order to trace the progress of how a 'style loan' from one culture to the other works, I take a closer look at the inferior bowl of the hourglass. I refer to what Pavis calls 'the theatrical production' (1992: 185) as the process and performance realization of the *Dance Fusion Project*, and to 'the reception by the audience and target culture' (1992: 185) as the evaluation of the project, though limited in this chapter to my own perception.

The process of the *Dance Fusion Project*

Rehearsals for the project were conducted at the National Theatre in Nigeria, Lagos. Victor Phullu and the author were the joint choreographers for this project, and together with dancers Maxwell Smith and Justin Ezirim we formed a group of four dancers to perform the piece on 13 August 2004 at the French House in Lagos. In the time between the very first meeting and the final performance, the group interacted during twenty-one rehearsals, out of which a total of nine studies were retained.

Before we started rehearsals, Victor and I discussed our intentions for the *Dance Fusion Project*. We decided that the research process would be an outcome of several dance studies concentrating on the fusion of the two different styles of *Bata* and Western contemporary dance. It was agreed that 'kinaesthetic stimuli' would govern most of the movement creation (Smith-Autard 1976: 28) and that there would be no other communicative goal.

I designed and kept a process log that included the rehearsal session sheets, written in note form, and video data. The session sheets are a compilation of the factual details from the rehearsal process. They also contain notes on group discussions and feedback, and my personal responses; excerpts from this log are quoted in this chapter. For each rehearsal we had an action plan that defined the aims of the session and guided our creation process. The names and order of the separate studies were given by the choreographers to aid their discussions. Six examples are given below.

In preparation for our first rehearsals I looked for information about the *Bata* tradition but because of the limited published or visual information on the history of Nigerian dances, I depended on Victor's knowledge. Therefore, we decided that it would be useful to spend the first session working with the *Bata* style as we got to know each other. It would give me time to gain some insight into this kind of tradition so that we could start from a shared base. Victor created an original movement sequence, which was an interpretation based on the abstract movements of the *Bata* tradition and I gave my response to this.

Study 1 – **Bata** *1*

Before going to war, men and women from the south of Nigeria performed certain movements from the *Bata* dance tradition. The structure of this dance can be divided into two parts. One part consists of movements with proverbial significance. The other part consists of movements that are not significant in meaning, but rather 'abstract' – they are included for their beauty only. In the movement phrases that Victor created he had only used the 'abstract' movements. In addition, this phrase was an individual interpretation of the authentic actions. This is apparent in the qualities of the movement, and more specifically in the applied dynamic and efforts.

I felt that it was difficult to utilize the typical body techniques of the African dance, because my body is trained differently. I noticed this especially in the isolation of the shoulder movement, and the continuous performance of the bouncing in the legs when they are already bent. The *Bata* never uses stretched legs, or straight body, rather a sitting position, but different parts of the feet (heel, ball, toes, sides).

Victor's phrase had an even amount of standing and repeated movement and was static in space. As I wanted to break with the overall rhythm of this phrase I began to explore more time- and space-related features. For example, I introduced ideas like uneven amount of repetitions, coincidence, floor patterns and reversal of movements. In addition, I added two improvised tasks: first, I asked Victor to pause at a point in time and to interact freely with the duration of this stillness before shouting 'GO' and continuing with the next movement; second, the context of the space was manipulated when the dancers started to dance as they would in the disco.

As a continuation of the idea of 'meeting each other's cultures' we switched the choreographers' roles. For this study I created the original movement sequence and Victor gave his response to it. My intention was to create a sequence in my personal style which contrasted with the movement material of *Bata 1*.

Study 2 – Firewood

This sequence focuses on the body and its design in space and on the movements of isolated parts of the body as well as the whole. It is performed in variation and with a diverse phrasing of the qualities. For example, these include: the emphasis on the pelvic region to initiate and cause momentum, tension between high and low levels, floor work, the use of the torso, turned-out feet and stretched legs. In contrast with *Bata 1* this phrase is less energetic and gentler. It no longer has a driven and rhythmical character and because of its new continuous flow it creates a timeless feeling.

Victor made some alterations mainly concerning time and spatial features, for example, when Maxwell and I started at a different time and place. In addition he edited some movements at the beginning of the sequence, adding mimed and new movements.

> Victor found it very hard to manipulate movements that were unfamiliar to him. To him, the movements were too abstract and it had no context, therefore, he needed to add a context.
>
> (De Lignière 2004: 4)

Throughout the whole creation process we were continually looking for a balance where each one could work on his/her personal needs. Since I was interested to learn more about the authentic *Bata* vocabulary and Victor's personal need was to work with the idea of creating characters through movement, we created new dance material through characterization of movements derived from *Bata* tradition.

Study 3 – Footwork

To elaborate on the *Bata* vocabulary we focused on the virtuosity of the footwork. After Victor had demonstrated more of the authentic *Bata* steps, we all worked individually on our interpretation of the examples that we had seen. Towards the end of the creation session we taught each other's phrases and made one composite phrase. In the outcome of the new sequence the predominance of the authentic *Bata* movement was replaced by a focus on fast footwork, which took on an amusing feel and created funny characters.

With the following study I realized that for Victor it was important that the choreography had a narrative and that each group of abstract movements could be related to reality.

Study 4 – Streets

At the start of the rehearsal Victor asked me: how different is Antwerp from Lagos? Next, Victor set a task for the dancers to mime the actions of the street scenes in Antwerp and Lagos. This resulted in two contrasting mimed scenes. Antwerp was represented by actions that reflected its quiet order whilst the actions representing Lagos were loud and chaotic.

> I explained to the group that I had no personal interest in purely creating mime scenes, because to me this does not serve the project. However, I am interested in working with this idea as a starting point, and in particular to research how we can develop the mimed actions in a more abstract way.
>
> (De Lignière 2004: 8)

In order to accentuate the contrast between the scenes I decided to make the mimed actions in the Antwerp streets more abstract. Originally, I intended to use improvisation to involve the African qualities that the dancers might express to explore movement. The *Streets* section was originally a study based on improvisation but what emerged was not really an exploration of movement vocabulary but rather an exploration of cultural scenes and lifestyle differences. Improvisation became the tool responsible for translating mimed actions in the project to abstract movements.

As the dancers were not familiar with the freedom involved in improvisation, Victor and I were forced to guide them strongly through the assignments. In the end, as both parties had such different levels of experience with improvisation, the abstraction of the project became purely intuitive – movements were not necessarily studied, they were chosen as an extract of the mimed actions that fitted the choreographic idea. Thus, intuition was an important factor for decisions taken about the degree of abstraction.

The outcome was an abstract scene alluding to its intercultural nature as to the reserved atmosphere in Antwerp, followed by a scene of dance drama expressing the exuberant character of Lagos.

Another good example of our particular method of improvisation is demonstrated in the opening movement of *Positions*. In search of understanding the other choreographer's view about the host culture, each choreographer created movement material in the foreign style.

Study 5 – Positions

Victor created a phrase by giving an interpretation of my personal style. His opening movement was a mimed action of him approaching me, me looking at him and then moving away. I suggested changing the intention of the action and reaction because to me this had the meaning of rejection or ignorance, and this was the opposite of the *Dance Fusion Project*'s intention.

Therefore, the motivation of the movement was turned into a game of 'cat and mouse', and the movements became an abstraction of that idea.

The continuation of Victor's idea was to perform the first part in canon and the second part in unison. In order to make it more 'cat-and-mouse-like', I suggested developing this phrase by focusing on the structure of a unison canon. The result was that the original sequence developed through use of canon in a playful way that focused on time elements.

Victor tended to use unison movement quite often as a choreographic pattern, and therefore the orchestration of the group became an important feature in our creative process. The main movement material was originally created for a duet, but we decided to translate it into a group piece so that we could explore the group relationship. Victor felt that a group sense was created by all four dancers dancing in unison all the time.

It was clear to me that Victor was familiar with working with aspects of space and time with the same movement, but that he was less familiar with applying these ideas using complementary movements, contrasting movements, or background and foreground movements (Smith-Autard 1976: 59). I challenged him with different ideas of spatial and time design. Consequently, most of the space and time elements that emerge throughout the project are a result of my personal interest in expanding Victor's choreography beyond his cultural norms.

In my opinion it is very important that the group development is shaped to enhance the dance idea. In *Looking at Dances*, Preston-Dunlop (1998: 183–8) articulates how different group formations serve to strengthen the nuances intended by the choreography. Instead of performing the group pieces all in unison towards the public as is traditional in African dance, I felt that we needed more variation in group formation to add interest to the study. We achieved this and investigated group development by varying the number of dancers performing, the divisions within the group of dancers performing, and where they are in relation to each other's kinaesphere and the total space. We also reduced performing the same movements in unison by using time elements. For example: in *Positions*, Victor and I initially danced a duet in unison but we developed this by using an overlapping canon. In addition we developed a duet for Maxwell and Justin that is synchronously performed on the background. As a result, the phrase was instantly more interesting visually.

The starting idea of the next study was the same as the study above, but now I was to create a phrase that was an interpretation of 'African' movement. I focused on repetition in unison and at the same time I also used variation and contrast.

Study 6 – African

Repetition in its truest sense means that a movement is replicated a specific number of times. It is a powerful element in traditional African dances. It is in this way that Victor understands repetition. In my opinion, repetition is one of the most valuable ways of creating and highlighting content. Also, without it the spectator would forget movements and therefore never grasp the ideas communicated through the choreography. However, unlike traditional African dance, in Western dance repetition is usually achieved through performing several variations of the movements which are crucial to the choreographic idea. It is this idea that I attempted to communicate to Victor.

The fact that I had chosen to work with repetitive symmetrical movement made me choose easy and short movements. I also decided to dance it in typical African unison. To break the perfect repetition and unison, I chose to make small and detailed variations. Variation was the principal way in which we developed the movement. For example the main content of the opening movement is repeated approximately thirty times but the emphasis of the focus regularly changes. Other examples of where variations are utilized as a compositional tool can be seen in changes of direction or time. For example, movements are performed in canon. It was interesting that, although I thought I had created an interpretation of African movement, the dancers had difficulty learning it! But they found a way to understand and perform these 'unfamiliar' movements.

By using variation, we were able to develop movements that were appropriate to a study, but by changing the way in which that movement was performed we encouraged the dancers, the audience and ourselves to understand the relevance and importance of that movement.

The performance realization

Our aim was to achieve equilibrium when we knitted the studies together so that a unity in the performance would become apparent. In order to achieve this, we constantly reviewed the structure of the nine studies during the last six rehearsals.

Firstly, both choreographers needed to determine what range of material was suitable for the total dance. Once this was achieved, the effect on the final performance by each study was evaluated together. It was from here that we could decide what proportion of the performance to dedicate to each study.

The performance begins with a movement interpretation of the motivation behind the *Dance Fusion Project*. It conveys a message of collaboration between two choreographers from very different backgrounds. *Bata 2* opens with four dancers performing traditional *Bata* movements in canon. It is an expression of the ritualistic and the artistic. And it is an expression of how these two different philosophies can be used together to generate a dance performance. When looking at the nature of each section, we observed that in each study there existed some highlights. These appeared like little sparks of interest and had been created throughout the exposition of the collaborators' ideas on the merging of the different styles. They built up slowly and the ultimate development at the end of the piece is the climax.

The overall performance results in a binary structure: the first half of the dance performance sharply contrasts with the second half. The movement in section A is slow and gentle and that in section B fast and strong. The main reasons for this are the cultural and stylistic differences that existed between the choreographers. Despite this, the exploratory nature of the *Dance Fusion Project* unified all these contrasts by expressing them as cultural awareness.

The music functions as an aural frame and alludes to a mood; the movement is more important than the sound. The chosen music includes: a bird soundtrack, traditional 'a cappella' song and pure instrumental parts with a jazzy atmosphere. The beginning and the end were performed without music. The music fades in and out at each new dance section. As the movement material is not fixed on the music, there is always some element of coincidence involved. For the second half of the dance, the music functions in coexistence with the dance. This coexistence method (Preston-Dunlop 1998: 214) combines the visual and aural elements in the choreography, not giving more importance to one or the other. At this stage the music and the dance share the same space and time and give freedom to each spectator to interpret this coexistence.

Evaluation of the *Dance Fusion Project*

What are the stylistic Western and African elements in the Dance Fusion Project?

From the dance studies, it is clear that several methods of construction continually appear to affect our creative process. These are unison, repetition, abstractions of mimed actions, contrast and variation. Throughout the studies we dealt with the elements of repetition, unison and use of mimed actions as being important in African dance. It also highlights that I, as a Western choreographer, use a lot of abstraction, variation and contrast in the creative process.

Towards the performance realization it became very clear that the stylistic element most apparent in Victor's work was its percussive quality whereas that in my work was the sustained quality. The different dynamics in action in the *Dance Fusion Project* occur in the layering of contrasting sustained and percussive qualities. My Western style has a sustained quality and possible variations of performing these are with a slow or fast speed, and with high or low energy. Victor's African style has a percussive quality and is mainly performed with fast speed and high energy. A hybrid form is created by synthesizing both styles and their qualities.

What motivates the interaction and combination of our cultures in the Dance Fusion Project?

In answering this, I refer to the first part of the inferior bowl of Pavis' hourglass. When creating an intercultural performance the interaction and combination is strongly motivated by the reception of the creator(s) and more particularly influenced by:

- the perspective of the adaptors and their work of adaptation;
- the preparatory work of the choreographers and their choice of theatrical form;
- their theatrical representation of the culture;
- their reception adaptors (adapted from Pavis 1992: 15–17).

Throughout the performance creation of the *Dance Fusion Project* the focus was on the teamwork between two choreographers from different cultures. Thus it is pertinent to look at the different relationships between two choreographers in a devising process.

To discuss the different choreographic roles that Victor or I practised in a process of collaboration, I refer to Butterworth's Didactic–Democratic Continuum model (2004: 55). In order to utilize this model more effectively, I have adapted it to the context of the *Dance Fusion Project*. I no longer refer to a choreographer and a student, but to choreographer 1 (myself) and to choreographer 2 (Victor). Although it is clear from the session sheets that both choreographers' roles often overlap during one session or at different stages, a clear pattern is recognized in three phases.

As is clear from the earlier description, the first phase of the collaboration was intended to be a time of experimentation in which choreographers and dancers could get to know each other's style and processes. Throughout this period three roles are identified. In the first process both choreographers engaged in a method of dance devising, that is, Victor was the *pilot* and I the *contributor*, or vice versa. This is followed by a second process where the role of choreographer 1 is to be the *facilitator* and choreographer 2 to be the *creator*. When both choreographers fully contribute to the concept, content, style and form as a team, a third kind of relationship is recognized: both choreographers are *collaborators* and *co-owners*.

In phase two of the collaboration we focused on the refinement of the content towards the final result of the project. As we progressed in the refinement, the choreographic process became more didactic as I took on the role similar to the *author* and Victor the role similar to the *interpreter*. In phase 3, towards the performance realization we selected the definitive material that would be performed on stage as the *Dance Fusion Project*. The choreographers' relationships changed again as I took the role of *expert* and Victor the role of *instrument*. These, in brief, are the five choreographic roles which motivated the interaction and combination of our cultures in the project.

How do social and ideological elements facilitate or impede the intercultural fusion of both cultures?

When Pavis discusses the second part of the hourglass' inferior bowl, he argues that the reception of a performance by the audience or the target culture is an important part of the cultural transfer in his model. He explains that *readability* or level of reading varies from one culture to the other. The *given and anticipated consequences* in a performance are more or less freely decided by the memory of the audience. Thus, the audience's reading of the performance is influenced by their own memory of that performance (Pavis 1992: 17–19).

During my observations of the Lagos dance scene, it quickly became apparent that I did not have an objective viewpoint. I found that my initial analysis of contemporary African dance was based on Western dance. As a result I was experiencing a feeling of 'déjà-vu' originating in the past aesthetic values of European dance. The aesthetic procedures, production methods, representation and structure of performance appeared outdated and old-fashioned. As Pavis implies, reaching a pure state of objectivity was an unlikely goal but it soon became clear that my critical viewpoints should not be restricted to form and aesthetic style.

In comparing these areas of difference:

> the radical potential of dance as a producer of the grounds for cross-cultural transgression begins to come in view. ... they are also the grounds that can enable new forms of tolerance, understanding, and cross-cultural respect at profoundly personal levels of awareness.
>
> (Ness in Morris 1996: 246)

Ness writes with great accuracy about one of the most striking features of interpretation of dance within a foreign culture. In the beginning I had so many conflicting questions and ideas, wanting explanations for everything.

In spite of all these queries it was clear to me that there was no point in trying to understand the Lagos dance scene from my solely Western knowledge – that would take a lifetime. I realized that an interaction between both worlds, a dialogue between my dance world and theirs, between Belgian and Nigerian, would be the key. A pathway of personal interventions could make both cultures communicate. Both sides can identify themselves and realize that their explorations can only be put into practice by means of some basic compromises in order to relate to each other.

African dance uses completely different dynamics, rhythm, time and space and the nature of the bodily actions contrasts sharply with Western dance. Once I became conversant with these elements I was able to examine them more closely by developing and manipulating these elements using Western choreographic techniques. Through attempting this I learned other ways of fusing two different styles by taking a traditional/original movement and then making it behave in a way unconventional to its mother culture.

In addition, Victor's presence was indispensable in translating my ideas to the dancers from English into Pidgin English and the other way around. English is the national language of Nigeria but most people speak Pidgin English, a curious dialect that is a hybrid form of the Nigerian and English languages. It contains many colloquial words and is extremely difficult to understand even if your mother tongue is English. I had not anticipated this language barrier. There were also cultural nuances in body language and social behaviour that led to discrepancies in intended and received information. The participants in the *Dance Fusion Project* communicated in 'real time' and 'real space', and all had the opportunity to ask for clarification and to give direct feedback. However, it usually took me some time to realize that my messages had not been understood or had been misinterpreted, as no one would come forward to ask for clarification.

In my view, our individual depth of knowledge about choreography both facilitated and impeded in our project. Fortunately both of us accepted this situation and our tolerant attitude towards it allowed the smooth interaction between us as individuals and as representatives of our cultures.

I organized the *Dance Fusion Project* in a way that would give me the best opportunity to apply practice-as-research methods to gain an insight into my own choreographic process. This methodology helped me to be aware of the conscious steps I have taken right from the beginning of the creation. As so little research has been published on Nigerian traditional dance, and African contemporary dance, I could not rely only on the use of this established material. The practice-as-research approach helped me in setting out realistic, measurable and comparable results about the Nigerian dance field in Lagos.

Because Victor followed a very different choreographic pattern, I was challenged with my own observations of how to explore movement and evaluate it in terms of dance fusion. I observed how Victor repeatedly used the same method of creation and this allowed me to review, revise and practise a variety of fundamental choreographic skills.

Practice as research also made me look into my intuitive patterns in the context of an intercultural collaboration. It revealed that although I am very intuitive during the creative process, I tend to follow a basic formula. I gather material, mostly using improvised tasks that I set for myself and then choosing from these movements the ones that feel right. The movement is then translated for the dancers depending on their capabilities. I then zoom out on this bank of phrases and work on the structure of the whole dance by continually matching the choreography with the intended theme. This is followed by a period of refinement.

Living and working in Nigeria, with such different dynamics in both life and dance, has certainly enriched my choreographic style. As the *Dance*

Fusion Project was a practical activity in choreography, personal experiences have been investigated. This type of practical research has highlighted issues that purely theoretical methods could not have done, allowing me through reflection an in-depth understanding of my own choreographic patterns and consideration of further personal development.

References

Butterworth, J. (2004) 'Teaching Choreography in Higher Education: A Process Continuum Model', *Research in Dance Education*, 5 (1): 45–67.

De Lignière, I. (2004) 'Practice as Research in Dance Fusion: an Intercultural Choreographic Collaboration', unpublished MA thesis, University of Leeds.

Jeyifo, B. (1996) 'The Reinvention of Theatrical Tradition: Critical Discourses on Interculturalism in the African Theatre', in Pavis, P. (ed.) *The Intercultural Performance Reader*, London and New York: Routledge.

McNiff, J. (1988) *Action Research: Principles and Practice*, London: Routledge.

Ness, S. A. (1996) 'Observing the Evidence Fail: Difference Arising from Objectification in Cross-cultural Studies of Dance' in Morris, G. (ed.) *Moving Words Re-writing Dance*, London: Routledge.

Pavis, P. (1992) *Theatre at the Crossroads of Culture*, London and New York: Routledge.

Preston-Dunlop, V. (1998) *Looking at Dances: a Choreological Perspective on Choreography*, Ightham: Verve Publishing.

Preston-Dunlop, V. and Sanchez-Colberg, A. (2002) 'Current modes of enquiry in choreological practice', *Dance and the Performative*, London: Verve Publishing.

Smith-Autard, J. M. (1976) *Dance Composition: a Practical Guide for Teachers*, London: A. & C. Black.

19 Beyond the intercultural to the Accented Body

An Australian perspective

Cheryl Stock

> dance occupies a fabled continent, to enter which you need no visas or passports. This is its true subversive potential in an era of flattening sameness. Dance still possesses the power to make new forms and new audiences.
>
> (Menon 2005: 40)

Contemporary choreography – a personal history

Once, the concept of choreography seemed quite straightforward. As a young dancer I thought it was simply 'dance-making' in which I was privileged to be the interpreter of the dance made for me or even with me. Later, as a young choreographer, a useful working definition was the creation and manipulation of movement in time and space. This was not to discard the integral contribution of sound, visuals and lighting as fundamental to the staging of most works, but it did not seem fundamental to the concept of choreography itself.

In the early 1980s I had the privilege to work as a dancer and then rehearsal director with a Chinese Malaysian artist Kai Tai Chan who came to Australia to study architecture and remained to become one of Australia's most innovative and probably first 'intercultural' choreographers with his One Extra Company.[1] At that time in Sydney, dance theatre was a popular contemporary genre and the works in which I was involved with One Extra Company, such as *One Man's Rice*, did not seem so unusual with its cast of Chinese, Anglo-Australian and Aboriginal dancers. Perhaps this was partly because of the demographic in which I lived and worked – inner city Glebe and Newtown.

Kai Tai Chan's hybrid choreographic style drew on image- and situation-based improvisations together with phrases and sensibilities derived from his Chinese heritage and movement approach; it occasionally incorporated the fusion style coming from the early experiments of AIDT (Aboriginal and Islander Dance Theatre), as well as drawing on contemporary dance and theatre. Given our cultural environment, such hybridity was an accepted part of the creative process, such as learning a Chinese ribbon dance and Torres Strait Islander dances and songs. The works created at that time were strong social and political commentaries about the world in which we lived, in multicultural Australia, with its inherent tensions and contradictions, challenges and opportunities, joys and tragedies. But, I was unaware at that stage of the term 'intercultural' in reference to the company's work.

It was several years later as a director, when I became intensely involved for over a decade in collaborative work with dancers in Vietnam, that I confronted philosophically and conceptually intercultural contestations of 'self and other'; ideas about 'the dominant' in intercultural exchange; guilt about the dangers of appropriation; and 'orientalism', most famously investigated by Edward Said (1995). I encountered the writings of nomadic theatre director Eugenio Barba (1982, 1986, 1988) about the nature of cultural exchange as 'barter'; the elegant definitions of theatre scholar Patrice Pavis (1992, 1996) re inter/cross/trans/intraculturalism; and the differing approaches of, and strident debates between the American Richard Schechner (1982, 1990, 1991, 1993) and Indian author and cultural activist Rustom Bharucha (1984a, 1984b, 1993, 1994, 1997). It is with Bharucha that I connected most deeply and who assisted me to understand and interrogate my own intercultural practice of the 1990s, predominantly in Vietnam. It was a painful, exhilarating, humbling and ultimately rewarding decade of intercultural engagement.

Contemporary choreography – a multimodal practice

It is not necessarily that the above issues are no longer relevant, but that the ground has shifted and our choreographic landscape has become more layered and nuanced, complicated by increasingly digitised and online communication and expressive encounters in virtual as well as 'real' space. At the end of the first decade of the twenty-first century, how can we frame choreographic concepts and practices – intercultural or otherwise – in a globalised environment of blurred boundaries, interdisciplinary processes and the slipperiness of provisional knowledge? Contemporary choreography grapples with a multiplicity of patternings within and across bodies and 'messy' practices; a polyphonic overlay of rich and bewildering possibilities, conceptually, technologically, culturally and socially. Choreography's reach and scope has expanded, perhaps in some cases beyond recognition.

Indisputably, choreography now commonly embraces elements beyond those that are dance specific. Taiwanese dancer Ko-Pei Lin who undertook further training in Australia as a dancer and choreographer, traces the evolution of her growing understandings:

> As I gradually gained more experience, I started to appreciate that the concept of 'choreography' was not just about combinations of different movements. ... [it] oftentimes involves the process of

> digesting all your memories, tracing your own thoughts and reflecting on the idea of your creations. In my view, choreography extracts all the possibilities and ideas and manages these arrangements and connections so that they may be communicated. In other words, in my current understanding, choreography is about connecting ideas and/or concepts with the audience.
>
> (Lin, K.-P. in personal correspondence in e-mail (22 August 2008))

Connections and connectivity currently often appear as key descriptors in choreography. Perhaps nothing has changed our choreographic landscape more than the networked and interactive rich media environment of the last decade. Rubidge and Sky (2006a, 2006b), referring to an interactive dance-based project *Accented Body*, speak of:

> expanded notions of choreographic form through an integrated interconnectivity with digital interfaces and computational programs, such that the movement of the performers equally [address] the real time orchestration of image and sound generation, and simultaneously ... their distribution to both actual (built environment) and virtual projection screens and spatialised sound systems.
>
> (Rubidge and Sky 2006b: no pagination)

As an interdisciplinary artist with a background in Butoh, Akido and performance studies, Maria Adriana (Mariana) Verdaasdonk (personal correspondence, e-mail (7 September 2008)) also views choreography as a process which 'involves coordinating the composite elements of bodies, visual imagery and sonic media by devising a compositional framework, often metaphorical, that works as a fluid and improvisational structure that is activated through the live performance'. For Mariana, choreography becomes 'a kind of pathway or journey: whilst some aspects may be predetermined, the overall sequencing is seen as an unfolding of temporary forms, with the potential for evolving "in-between" spaces'.

Whilst the body and movement are still central to the above understandings of choreography, notions of coordination, connectivity and the management of complex interdisciplinary systems are equally significant in the creative process and the emergent definitions of what choreography is today.

Contemporary intercultural practices – an overview

These expanded notions of choreography have similarly affected intercultural performance. Although the sharing of culturally specific, body-centred practices still has a strong place, many intercultural dance artists now work in the globalised context of interdisciplinary mixed-media practices. This shift has augmented and refined modes of intercultural exchange, of which there are at least four, which I have grouped as:

1 in-country cultural immersion;
2 collaborative international exchange/sharing of culturally diverse practices;
3 hybrid practices of diasporic artists;
4 implicit intercultural connections.

Issues of identity and transformation

Two interconnected aspects are at the heart of all four proposed models: identity and transformation. Whilst contemporary interculturalism may or may not derive from long-standing traditions, questions of continuity and identity remain inherent in the practice. Menon (2005: 34) refers to this as dealing with 'our individual and collective pasts with empathy, intensity, involvement and insight'. In a similar vein, Indonesian choreographer Bambang Besu Suryono refers to 'the biography of the body' and to 'honouring this awareness of our life stories in our bodies' (in Murgiyanto 2005: 283). These bodily stories are of course rooted in our culture(s) and form a large part of who we are and what we present to others, thus contributing to our various evolving identities. Australian dance artist Vivienne Rogis refers to the body as a 'geographical place of identity ... in the cultural scape of interconnection between the individual and the wider social collective' (2005: 339).

Whether viewed as biography or geography, identity in intercultural dance is a site of ongoing transformation through construction, deconstruction and reconstruction, both conscious and unconscious. Maggi Phillips, grappling with 'that elusive phenomenon, the one or multiple Australian identity' describes the current dance scene as 'additionally shaped by Indigenous Australian and immigrant Asian artists' (2005: 86). In Australia as elsewhere, the varying cultural influences that contribute to forming an identity are not always overt. Since contemporary choreography is in many ways a search for self through movement practices adapted to and for our individual body, cultural influences on our practice may well be 'indirect, attitudinal rather than visible in vocabulary or approach', as Phillips suggests (2005: 86).

Where recognisable regional and cultural similarities exist, an intercultural rapprochement appears more achievable. Within Asian dance practices, Menon (2005: 33) speaks of 'a common conceptual sky' emerging from the work of Lin Hwai-min in Taiwan, Ea Sola in Vietnam and Sardono Kusomo in Indonesia, which stems from 'a deep-seated desire of the community of artists and thinkers in this part of the globe to re-negotiate their artistic identities from within their own rich resource of a plural form-language' (2005: 33). Although these artists draw on their respective cultural traditions through form or content, or both, their work is conceived very much in the present. Birringer refers to 'historical trajectories and multiple identities realiz[ing] themselves in culture as overlapping circles of consciousness' (2000: 172). Such overlaps create an interstitial place and time where a process of evolving identities, transformation and aesthetic transfer create intercultural possibilities, through the four modes of practice discussed below.

In-country cultural immersion

In the first mode of interchange, intercultural possibilities are realised as individual artists immerse themselves in another culture drawing on its influences either as a solo practitioner or in collaboration with artists from that country. In relation to her own experience of working in Japan, Australian choreographer Sue Healey refers to this process as 'positive dislocation'; a way of unsettling familiar artistic processes through encountering unfamiliar cultural and geographical environments.

In a collaborative setting, this model can also be seen from the in-country artists' perspectives, where the 'positive dislocation' can sometimes be experienced within one's own surroundings through the 'intervention' of a visiting artist. An example of this stems from my long-standing collaboration with the dancers of the Vietnam Opera Ballet Theatre in Hanoi. We were experimenting with movement and voice in three languages and gestural styles in a work called *Through the Eyes of the Phoenix* (*Qua Mat Phuong Hoang*). I had worked with most of the dancers over many years, and knew that they all had a good working knowledge of music and trusted Pho Duc Phuong, the Vietnamese composer with whom we were collaborating. Although rehearsals seemed to be fun, there was a certain discomfort and resistance. Dancer Bich Huong reported that the dancers felt it was confusing and difficult to sing and move. Other sources of discomfort for them were the minimalist staging and costumes, the use of pedestrian movement and the distillation of everyday gestures, so different from their own rich aesthetic and stylised formal movement. However, in the liminality of performance this sense of 'dislocation' disappeared. A senior dancer, Thuc Anh, struggled to express the transformation that occurred:

> it is difficult for me to explain it, but I can feel it – very touching ... the dancers think it is strange, but when we are on the stage, it is very quiet and everyone in the audience was very quiet too so maybe they feel the same thing.
>
> (Bui Thuc Anh in Stock 2000: 258)

Australian designer Michael Pearce also felt this ineffable sensation and spoke of a 'real hush in the audience, a magical thing' (in Stock 2000: 259).

Collaborative international exchanges/sharing of culturally diverse practices

Closely linked to these two examples of the cultural immersion style of intercultural performance is the second model in which a group of artists from several cultures gather together to make a collaborative work through sharing creative cultural processes. In discussing the complex interactions of his international performance group, which works from an improvisational basis with artists from a range of cultural backgrounds, Birringer (2000: 6–8) refers to a continual shifting of identity that occurs during the creative and performative process. He reflects on:

> possible forms of belonging or not belonging that are not subject to constricted or generalisable notions of an intrinsic identity, national, cultural, or other. The issues of 'alien nation' … surfaces in the work of collaboration, of course, since we spend a good deal of time translating, learning each other's languages of practice and imagination, making contact with each other's bodily vocabularies, movements, and boundaries.
>
> (Birringer 2000: 7)

Whilst improvisatory methods can open up spaces for the transformative in intercultural work, Birringer reminds us that transformation occurs through 'the necessarily constant struggle to welcome the widening range of the unexpected, the unpredictable' (2000: 7). Misunderstanding is ever present. One of his collaborators Sarries-Zgonc, a Catalan choreographer, remarks:

> Working with the diversity of cultures in the ensemble was eye-opening. I learnt how difficult dialogue can be, how we misunderstand. Avanthi [an Indian dancer in our ensemble] used to say: 'We don't speak the same language.' Nevertheless we practiced tolerance, dancing as a kind of listening to the various points of view we exchanged.
>
> (in Birringer 2000: 97)

Perhaps the most fundamental challenge of intercultural dance experiments is in listening to the way the body moves and accepts/incorporates/rejects alternative ways of moving.

In an Australian context, this model of collaborative international exchanges (predominantly with Asia) has become more prevalent over the last 15 years. Given the complexities of attempting to consciously embody another aesthetic, musculature and technical particularities of unfamiliar dance styles, especially when very different cultural sensibilities come into play, Hilary Crampton questions the value of short-term cross-cultural exchange projects, although she concedes that 'risk and the opportunity to break personal boundaries are some of the factors driving artists to step outside their cultural comfort zone' (2007: 6). Sue Healey concurs, writing about her time on an Asialink grant in Japan:

> Quite simply I could not have created this work in Australia. The Japanese environment facilitated risk-taking and 'seeing' in a new

> light. ... [and] not only affected the movement aesthetics captured in the film but gave it thematic depth.
>
> (Healey 2007: 21)

Hybrid practices of diasporic artists

Whilst the cultural immersion and collaborative exchange models continue to permeate the contemporary dance field and are popular festival fare in small experimental and large-scale mainstream formats, the third model, that of the 'hybrid', diasporic artist, is an increasingly strong contributor to intercultural choreography.

What differentiates this third mode of intercultural exchange is that that interculturality already resides within the artists' own body and practice, played out in a multiplicity of ways through their choreography and performance.[2] What is of interest here is how diasporic dance artists view their situatedness in relation to their work.

Diaspora in dance

The meaning of 'diaspora' – originally coined to describe the dispersal of the Jews to various parts of the world between the sixth and eighth centuries – has been expanded to refer to multiple émigré communities 'of dispersed peoples maintaining common identity across borders', with a growing focus 'on the particular consciousness that diasporic groups have developed' (Burt 2004). The term 'diaspora' often contains a sense of the loss of homeland, whether in one's own lifetime or that of previous generations, linked to notions of displaced identity. However, many intercultural artists draw on their diasporic experience of living in two or more cultures simultaneously, or living between cultures, to create new performance vocabularies that reflect their particular aesthetic and creative landscape. The term 'positive dislocation' mentioned earlier takes on a different meaning for a diasporic artist.

Briginshaw (2001: 98), discussing the work of UK-based choreographer Shobana Jeyasingh, refers to Rosi Braidotti's concept of 'nomadic subjectivity' (1996), which encompasses the optimistic notion of having the capacity to (re)create a home anywhere; it suggests the possibility of new horizons rather than the need to re-create from the past to compensate for loss. Interrogating diasporic experience through this perceptual lens, Jeyasingh refers to 'imaginary homemaking' and discusses how she and similar artists 'illustrate a pattern of belonging that is multi-dimensional' in which their 'unhoming has been a source of immense creativity' (1995: 192). Born in India and migrating to the United Kingdom, Jeyasingh has a highly developed practice in the classical Indian form Bharata Natyam, which she has contemporised by drawing on other dance processes and cultural influences. Such mixes of cultural and stylistic influences are not uncommon in a globalised environment but are arguably reshaped differently by the diasporic artist who inhabits multiple worlds to varying degrees on a daily basis.

Concepts of hybridity

Notions of hybridity in which cultural traditions are reworked and synthesised are therefore inextricably, but not exclusively, linked to concepts of diaspora. Certainly artists such as Jeyasingh and Akram Khan in the UK, and Tony Yap and Yumi Umiumare in Australia have contributed to a shift from the binaries of East/West, high art/low art and self/other to more complex, hybrid practices as the result of their diasporic experiences. In relation to the space/place where the creation of a new dance language through hybridity can occur, Jeyasingh (1995) refers to 'that imaginary homeland of the Diaspora' (1995: 192), which Menon (2005) similarly calls 'invented homelands'.

If diasporic artists reject as simplistic and reductive the notion of a fusion or joining together which hybridity may imply, what forms and processes do hybrid practices embrace? For some, it may be a complex layering through the body of diverse stylistic and cultural practices, resulting in the 'overlapping circles of consciousness' to which Birringer refers (2000: 172). Or it may be in the gaps between these forms and processes, which Bhabha's theory of hybridity (1994) calls the 'in-between spaces'. This in-between place of space-time resonates in many cultures. According to Trinh T. Minh-Ha (1991: 7), it is the third element between the *yin* and the *yang*, a place 'of stillness and action', which brings about an 'in-between state of mind'. This concept has parallels with the 'in-betweenness' of the Japanese *ma*, and both comprise an interstitial place where new things emerge, evolve and are created.

With regard to formal properties in intercultural performance, Joanna Bosse (2008: 49) points out that dance genres are 'filtered through a variety of movement dialects to create something stylistically different and new'; and that the resultant 'stylistic transformation is driven by a number of factors that are themselves rooted in notions of transformation at a personal and cultural level' (Bosse 2008: 61). This is not an easy process. Akram Khan, who began training in Kathak Indian dance at the early age of seven, and later trained in classical ballet, Graham, Cunningham, Alexander, release-based techniques, contact improvisation and physical theatre, reports that 'as a result of going to university and studying contemporary dance, my body got confused so my body started making decisions for itself' (in Burt 2004). The way through this confusion according to Burt, was to

> focus deeply on the internal, somatic sources of dance movement within his neuro-skeleto-muscular continuum. To try to identify these sources as clearly as possible became a way of letting himself gradually discover how he could move.
>
> (Burt 2004)

In terms of Khan's intercultural practice, experiments between contemporary Western forms and traditional South Asian Kathak, form and structure are paramount, especially 'mathematical elements that comprise each dance style'. These have created what he calls 'Contemporary Kathak' (Khan 2002).

One of Khan's most famous collaborations is *Sacred Monsters* (2006), a duet with ballerina Sylvie Guillem, which subliminally explores affinities between two classical dance forms, Kathak and ballet. Gallasch (2008: 32) describes *Sacred Monsters* as 'a work of reflection and cross-cultural kinship'. The word kinship is interesting in this context, referring perhaps to the 'family' of dance where the homeland is familiar whilst the genres differ. Some assume that the refined virtuosity of these two extraordinary performers, encoded with different aesthetics and styles, comes together through the medium of contemporary dance, seen as a broad-based genre that allows hybridity to enter its processes and vocabulary. I believe, however, that it is the consummate and deep kinaesthetic knowledge of each artist's own bodily practices that has made this collaboration of seamless difference possible.

Beyond the theoretical constructs of diaspora and identity, and shared experiential artistic understandings, the artist has an individual voice, rooted in the sum of his/her experiences. As Khan said of his creative process in 2006:

> There are no formulas. It never feels the same twice and never approaches you in the same way twice. I believe the mind and body are like a library that holds not only your own experiences but also those of your ancestors, and so when external forces (like watching a film, or studying a picture, or experiencing a theatre piece) are presented to you, it triggers something within the library of your memory bank and suddenly the file that is triggered opens, and the language of inspiration begins.
>
> (Khan 2006)

Spirituality

Whilst space prevents an in-depth discussion of the place of spirituality in intercultural practice, it would be remiss not to mention its significance for many artists for whom it is integral to their practice. These artists link with traditions rooted in religious or philosophical beliefs from cultures where dance is 'acknowledged as the very force of creation and destruction and is duly assigned a divine intent' (Menon, 2005: 28). For example, in discussing understandings and practices that inform hula dance, Sharon Mahealani Rowe (2008: 38) points out that knowledge itself emerges from the spiritual context of the culture and its dance. The link of spirituality to knowledge and meaning in dance is often made though sometimes described in more secular terminology. Indeed Rowe believes that 'any culture recognizes artists ... [who] tap into something that transports themselves and the audience to an ineffable place of meaning' (2008: 38).

On the other hand, this 'ineffable meaning' may not be so easy to access. Crampton (2007: 4) points to the 'difficulties of shared understanding when artists seek to cross the cultural divide' and, one might posit, also the spiritual divide. In reviewing *How Could You Ever Begin to Understand* by Australian Asian performer/choreographers Tony Yap (Malaysia) and Yumi Umiumare (Japan) she makes the following observation:

> Drawing on Shamanism and Japanese Butoh, exploring mysticism and the spiritual dimension that seems so appealing and so unattainable to Western eyes, their performances leave one with the sense they have journeyed to a place we can never find.
>
> (Crampton (2007: 4)

Even in a work as accessible as Guillem/Khan's *Sacred Monsters*, the spiritual is subtly present. Reviewer Keith Gallasch notes that the work's 'roots in Hindu culture ... suspends our sense of time, if speed is more often its means than stillness' (2008: 32). The assumption that suspending time occurs through a sense of stillness is here turned on its head. In this instance suspending time through speed may also be a result in part of the meeting of two genres from two cultures – for example, the fast footwork and rhythms contained in both Indian Kathak and European ballet.

Whilst some contemporary diasporic artists, such as Khan, draw on formal aspects of spiritual traditions, other artists infuse contemporary practices with the essence and meanings behind spiritual traditions; for example, Korean choreographers who re-interpret shamanistic dances such as Salpuri, or Tony Yap who works through a Malaysian shamanist dance tradition. In these instances, it is a particular transmission of energy and timing in combination with a charismatic presence that often makes the work appear distinctive.

Implicit intercultural connections: a case study

The three intercultural performance models outlined so far assume that deep structure embodied experiences inform the practice of the performer/choreographer. In the fourth model (implicit intercultural connections) international collaboration is based on a premise other than conscious exchange or assimilation of different cultural practices – what Flynn and Humphrey (2006) refer to as 'culture-residue'; where intercultural processes are implicitly embedded in the project, resulting in more ambiguous and less recognisable intercultural aesthetics, form or content.

The first two models of intercultural choreography differ from the 'accented' body, which does not consciously share vocabulary, narratives or genre-/culture-specific practices, but rather reveals nuances and traces of differing cultural aesthetics that subliminally transform time and space as well as movement interpretation and invention. In the implicit intercultural model, motivations to come together in a collaborative space are less about cultural traditions and processes than other artistic concerns and subject matter which become 'inflected' by the cultural backgrounds of the collaborators.

An example of this model is *Accented Body*, an interactive, international, multi-site performance installation that took place across six live sites in Brisbane, Australia, with distributed presences in Seoul and London. This two-year process began in 2005 when I invited 30 key artists from five countries in the areas of dance, performance, visual and sonic media, to respond to the 'accented body' brief, which was deliberately open-ended – the body as site and in site, and the notion of connectivities. The site teams coalesced around this brief, which additionally was about architectural, personal and cultural transformation. It was an opportunity for independent artists and small project groups to work together on something of scale, to consolidate existing artistic relationships and to form new collaborative partnerships. Beyond that, the intention was to open up our practices and find new ways of communicating and being together, through the body '[bringing] to the site its full history – social, cultural, personal' (May 2006).

Underneath the meta-narrative was an exploration of how cultural notions of space, time and site are encoded on the body, and how they encode the body in a mutually transformative process. All the performers, to varying degrees, brought with them the influences of their dance practices, which included Butoh, ballet, contemporary dance, Malaysian trance dance, Chinese classical and folk dance, various forms of Asian martial arts and Bharata Natyam. With the exception of Tony Yap's contribution, these genres were not specifically explored in the project as a prime motivation. However, intercultural processes were embedded implicitly across site teams.

One of the key investigations of the project, which was spread over predominantly outdoor sites, was the integration of interactive technology and rich media. Rubidge and Sky described this as employing 'contemporary channels of communication between cultures and countries' as well as exploring the accented body at a 'micro level ... emphasising the flow of movement within the body ... at cellular, muscular and motional levels, and relating this to the flow of data between cultures' (2006a: no pagination).

The shift between macro and micro approaches conceptually and geographically could be seen in the differences between the two site teams who used interactivity to connect sound, visuals and the body; *Global Drifts* directed by Sarah Rubidge and Hellen Sky, and *Living Lens* directed by Maria Adriana Verdaasdonk. Whilst the former utilised almost all the outdoor sites connecting them via the two 'global drifters' (dancers Liz Lea and Bridget Fiske) in real and virtual manifestations by way of seven outdoor screens across several sites, the latter worked in an intimate 'black box' immersive indoor environment.

Conscious cultural inflections in Living Lens

The *Living Lens* team comprised four dancers, two of whom were from Taiwan and trained in ballet, contemporary and Chinese dance styles, whilst the two Australian dancers were predominantly contemporary trained. The key artists for visuals and sound were from Japan and not only brought a high level of technological skill to the project, but also a highly refined contemporary artistic sensibility and aesthetic that bore traces of their culture. Mariana, too, bridges the worlds of Australia and Japan, having lived and worked in Japan for over ten years. In many ways, she is the inverse of the diasporic artist:

> My creative practice initially blossomed in Japan, through the dual influences of Butoh and Aikido, practices I studied for several years concurrently. The seeds of this practice, however, germinated in Australia, where initial exposure to performance via undergraduate theatre studies, whetted a curiosity for ways to locate the human body within imaginary landscapes. Here, in this vast shared continent, experiences in the horticultural and adventure industries fostered a deep interest in the organic world. In Japan, I became aware of a cultivated sensibility to nature, for example, in the metaphors of the cosmos found in Zen gardens and the association of seasonal life cycles with death and rebirth.
>
> (Verdaasdonk, personal correspondence 2008)

An ongoing interest in cycles and the natural world became the subject of an extended work originally called *Patchwork in Motion*, which was the creative development stage of *Living Lens* in *Accented Body*. In the 'patchwork' iteration, Mariana experimented with a system she named the 'body texturiser', in which the 'performing body can interactively shape the visual and sonic textural layers through motion sensors and camera tracking' (Verdaasdonk 2006a: no pagination). In order to do this successfully she reported that 'for the contemporary dancers, this has meant breaking through encoded movement patterns and techniques to explore a more organic movement inherent in the body itself' (Verdaasdonk 2006a: no pagination). The patchwork metaphor also referred to the 'assemblage' of artists from diverse backgrounds and practices who collaborated 'to create an emergent hybrid life form' (Verdaasdonk 2006a: no pagination).

The concepts from this version were further refined into *Living Lens*, which Mariana described in the program notes of *Accented Body* (2006) as a 'three-dimensional living painting'. The notion of cycles and the natural, organic world was still paramount in the immersive performative installation. This included a large floor to ceiling serpentine screen crossing the

Figure 19.1 Ko-Pei Lin in *Living Lens* from *Accented Body*. Photo: Ian Hutson.

space, which performers and audience moved around and between. In order for the performers to realise the conceptual complexities and also handle effectively the technological complexities within the site, Mariana worked 'through an image-based approach derived from the Japanese dance-theatre known as Butoh' (2006).

Over almost 18 months, it was interesting to witness the performers' struggles to incorporate new approaches into their highly trained and technically refined bodies. This required letting go of familiar movement patterns without obliterating them altogether. The most fascinating example of the transformation of integrating new patterning into the body was Ko-Pei Lin whose highly articulate fingers and hands from her Chinese training took on a new dimension when combined with the extreme facial gestures and grounded organic movement of Butoh. This was further enhanced by the altered retention of the precision and high extensions of her ballet training and the fluid torso of her contemporary practice into what appeared a natural bodily 'habitus', despite these supposed conflicting aesthetics and kinaesthetic patternings. Ko-Pei herself reports (2008) that she '[does] not usually have any problems with dealing with different cultures in daily life. However, certain … types of dance that require exaggerated emotions or facial expressions can be challenging to me'. She is aware of her layered Chinese and Western dance identity stating that '[my] training in different oriental dances influences my understanding and appreciation of Western dances … [and] definitely influences the way I dance' (2008).

From Mariana's point of view as director, her own choreographic approach was both expanded and challenged in 'applying Butoh to contemporary dance practices' and she was 'opened up by the compositional approaches of the dancers where they developed short phrases of movement and then shared them with each other by arranging them in a variation of numbered orderings' (Verdaasdonk 2006b). A specific intercultural task that Mariana investigated in *Living Lens* was to use 'Japanese concepts and Chinese characters as a way to explore movement and artistic ideas' (2006b: no pagination). Rather than a deliberate intercultural approach, Mariana describes a 'kind of biotope; an assemblage of diverse "life-forms" coming together through a unifying concept' (2006b).

Unconscious cultural inflections in Global Drifts

Whilst intercultural inflections were evident though not foregrounded in *Living Lens*, they were quite subliminal in the performances of the *Global Drifts* dancers. This is particularly fascinating since in *Living Lens* all the performers identified as contemporary dancers, whereas in *Global Drifts* Liz Lea is well known for her intercultural practice, which combines Bharata Natyam and the martial arts Kalariapayattu and Chauu with various Western contemporary forms. Lea saw her role in *Global Drifts* as that of a contemporary dancer with the added challenge of working with interactive technology. In an interview with ethnographer Jean Bowra (Liz Lea interviewed on *Accented Body* (2006)) she says:

> I've never actually been in a pure contemporary dance work before because I normally work in classical Indian dance and martial arts – so that's been a challenge for me … to try and fall into a totally different choreographic path, someone else's choreographic path and one that doesn't necessarily draw specifically on the training and the techniques that I've been employing within my own career for the last fifteen years or so.
>
> (Lea 2006, in interview)

There was a noticeable difference in comparing her dancing to that of her contemporary dance-trained partner Bridget, despite their stylistic compatibility. Liz used a more directed and intense eye focus as well as a more detailed, nuanced and precise use of footwork and hand gestures, which echoed these qualities from her intensive Indian dance training over many years. When I pointed this out to Liz two years after the *Accented Body* project, she was very surprised. In a personal communication (personal correspondence: e-mail, 16 August 2008) she wrote:

> I was just very aware that you had really gone out on a limb to bring me all the way over from the UK, partially because of what I specialise

Figure 19.2 Liz Lea in *Global Drifts* from *Accented Body*. Photo: Ian Hutson.

> in and that those skills were not directly referenced. I see now the indirect reference was what worked. These are good things to know.
> (Lea 2008, personal correspondence)

Although the project is over, its intercultural inflections continue as Liz reports on her new collaborations with artists from *Accented Body*; with Korean media artist Hyojung Seo in Seoul and Japanese Australian sculptor Naomi Ota. She acknowledges that 'the *Accented Body* legacy lives on – for me in a whole new field' (2008).

As seen above, collaborative projects spawned by diverse intercultural practices contribute to survival and renewal for professional artists in a global and networked environment – whether collaboration occurs in real time and space, or virtually. In terms of intercultural choreography and performance, it is clear that the landscape has changed since its rise to prominence in the 1980s. Notions of exchange, hybridity and transformation remain as new forms evolve and coexist with older models of practice. Whilst the cultural immersion, international collaborative change and hybrid diasporic practices are still strongly present, we are moving beyond the concept of the intercultural to the 'accented' body of nuanced traces and inflections, which infuse rather than foreground our practice, and which reflect the interdisciplinary and interactive thrust of twenty-first century arts practice.

Notes

1 For more information on Kai Tai Chan see: *Australia Dancing*. Available online at <http://www.australiadancing.org/subjects/19.html> (accessed 24 September 2008). See also Lester (1998).

2 It is beyond the scope of this overview to delve into the already much theorised areas of notions of diaspora and hybridity, as seen through the writings of authors such as Homi Bhabha (1994), Benedict Anderson (1991), James Clifford (1988, 2005) and Stuart Hall (1993).

References

Anderson, B. (1991) *Imagined Communities: Reflections on the Origin and Spread of Nationalism*, London and New York: Verso.

Barba, E. (1982) 'Theatre Anthropology', *The Drama Review*, 26 (2): 5–32.

—— (1986) *Beyond the Floating Islands*, New York: PAJ Publications.

—— (1988) 'Eurasian Theatre', *The Drama Review*, 32 (3): 126–30.

Bhabha, H. K. (1994) *The Location of Culture*, London: Routledge.

Bharucha, R. (1984a) 'A Collision of Cultures: Some Western Interpretations of the Indian Theatre', *Asian Theatre Journal*, 1 (2): 1–20.

—— (1984b) 'A Reply to Richard Schechner', *Asian Theatre Journal*, 1 (2): 254–9.

—— (1993) *Theatre and the World: Performance and the Politics of Culture*, 2nd edn, London and New York: Routledge.

—— (1994) 'Somebody's Other: Disorientation in the Cultural Politics of our Times', *Third Text*, 2: 3–10.

—— (1997) 'Negotiating the "River": Intercultural Interactions and Interventions', *The Drama Review*, 41 (3): 31–7.

Birringer, J. (2000) *Performance on the Edge: Transformations of Culture*, London and New Brunswick, NJ: The Athlone Press.

Bosse, J. (2008) 'Salsa Dance and the Transformation of Style: An Ethnographic Study of Movement and Meaning in a Cross-Cultural Context', *Dance Research Journal*, 40 (1): 45–64.

Braidotti, R. (1996) *Nomadic Subjects*, New York: Columbia University Press.

Briginshaw, V. (2001) *Dance, Space and Subjectivity*, Basingstoke: Palgrave Macmillan.

Burt, R. (2004) 'Contemporary Dance and the Performance of Multicultural Identities'. Available online at <http://www.akramkhancompany.net/html/text_articles.asp?id=7> (accessed 6 September 2008).

Clifford, J. (1988) *The Predicament of Culture: Twentieth-century Ethnography, Literature, and Art*, Cambridge, MA, and London: Harvard University Press.

—— (2005) 'Diasporas', in A. Abbas and J. Nguyet Erni (eds) *Internationalizing Cultural Studies: an Anthology*, Malden, MA: Blackwell Publishers.

Crampton, H. (2007) 'Dancing Across the Cultural Divide', *Neon Rising: Asialink Japan Dance Exchange*, Melbourne: Asialink.

Flynn, M. and Humphrey, T. (2006) 'Accented Body', unpublished Artistic Acquittal Music Report.

Gallasch, K. (2008) 'Dynamic Duets', *RealTime* 84 (April–May): 32.

Hall, S. (1993) 'Culture, Community, Nation', *Cultural Studies*, 7 (3): 349–63.

Healey, S. (2007) 'Will Time Tell?', *Neon Rising: Asialink Japan Dance Exchange*, Melbourne: Asialink.

Jeyasingh, S. (1995) 'Imaginary Homelands: Creating a New Dance Language', in

C. Jones and J. Lansdale (eds) *Border Tensions: Dance and Discourse*, Guildford, Surrey: University of Surrey.

Khan, A. (2002) Interview. Available online at <www.londondance.com> (accessed 6 September 2008).

—— (2006) 'Divine Inspiration', *The Observer*, 12 March. Available online at <http://www.akramkhancompany.net/html/text_articles.asp?id=6> (accessed 6 September 2008).

Lester, G. (1998) 'Kai Tai Chan: part one, fingers dancing in the dark', *Brolga*, 8 (June): 7–17.

May, Elise (2006) 'Accented Body', unpublished Artistic Acquittal Report.

Menon, S. (2005) '"Passports, Please!" Border-crossings in the Invented Homelands of Dance', in M. A. Nor and R. Murugappin (eds) *Global and Local in Dance Performance*, Kuala Lumpur: Cultural Centre University of Malaya and Ministry of Culture, Arts and Heritage Malaysia.

Murgiyanto, S. (2005) 'In Search of New Paths', in M. A. Nor and R. Murugappin (eds) *Global and Local in Dance Performance*, Kuala Lumpur: Cultural Centre University of Malaya and Ministry of Culture, Arts and Heritage Malaysia.

Pavis, P. (1992) *Theatre at the Crossroads of Culture*, London and New York: Routledge.

—— (ed.) (1996) *The Intercultural Performance Reader*, London and New York: Routledge.

Phillips, M. (2005) 'A Narrative of Structure: Sue Peacock's Metaphorical Moves', in M. A. Nor and R. Murugappin (eds) *Global and Local in Dance Performance*, Kuala Lumpur: Cultural Centre University of Malaya and Ministry of Culture, Arts and Heritage Malaysia.

Rogis, V. (2005) 'Same but Different: Globalisation and Identity Negotiated through Inter-cultural Dialogue in Dance', in M. A. Nor and R. Murugappin (eds) *Global and Local in Dance Performance*, Kuala Lumpur: Cultural Centre University of Malaya and Ministry of Culture, Arts and Heritage Malaysia.

Rowe, S. M. (2008) 'We Dance for Knowledge', *Dance Research Journal* 40 (1): 31–44.

Rubidge, S. and Sky, H. (2006a) 'Accented Body', unpublished Creative Development Report.

—— (2006b) 'Accented Body', unpublished Artistic Acquittal Report.

Said, E. (1995) *Orientalism: Western Concepts of the Orient*, 2nd edn, London: Penguin Books.

Schechner, R. (1982) 'Intercultural Performance', *The Drama Review*, 26 (2): 3–4.

—— (1990) 'Magnitudes of Performance', in R. Schechner and W. Appel (eds) *By Means of Performance: Intercultural Studies of Theatre and Ritual*, Cambridge and New York: Cambridge University Press.

—— (1991) 'Intercultural Themes', in B. Marranca and G. Dasgupta (eds) *Interculturalism and Performance: Writings from PAJ*, New York: PAJ Publications.

—— (1993) *The Future of Ritual – Writings on Culture and Performance*, London and New York: Routledge.

Stock, C. F. (2000) 'Making Intercultural Dance in Vietnam', unpublished Ph.D. thesis, Queensland University of Technology.

Trinh, T. M.-H. (1991) *When the Moon Waxes Red: Representation, Gender and Cultural Politics*, New York: Routledge.

Verdaasdonk, M. A. (2006a) 'Accented Body', unpublished Creative Development Report.

—— (2006b) 'Accented Body', unpublished Artistic Acquittal Report.

20 The confluence of multicultural and intercultural discourses in Malaysian contemporary dance[1]

Mohd Anis Md Nor

Multiculturalism and *interculturalism* are buzzwords for many affirmative action plans in countries that have large numbers of migrant population. Yet these words share many ambiguities, meanings and intentions. *Multiculturalism* has many definitions: Pavis terms it the 'dominant cultural model in Europe … within which all differences are invited to converge, while preserving a certain autonomy…' (Pavis 2006: 283). In some countries like Malaysia it may emerge as a public policy approach for managing cultural diversity in a multi-ethnic and multilingual society, a state apparatus to develop mutual respect and tolerance for the multiplicities of cultural differences within the borders of nation states. When a policy on multiculturalism is instituted by the state, it officially places importance on the unique characteristics of different cultures that are represented within the communities of a nationality or nation. It idealises the preservation of cultural mosaic where separate cultural identities and ethnic groups are placed together harmoniously in a tolerant society, unlike a *melting pot*, where all the immigrant cultures are mixed and amalgamated without state intervention. This notion of multiculturalism can lead to anxiety about the stability of national identity, in spite of its ability to induce cultural exchanges in performance, literature, art, dress and nouvelle-cuisine that benefit cultural groups. However, it remains debatable as to whether multiculturalism is about culture or the practice of cultures.

Interculturalism, on the other hand philosophises the exchanges between cultural groups within a society. It may be seen as a method of approach with an inherent openness in order to expose the cultures of the 'other' for an ensuing dialogue, which becomes a very powerful tool in enhancing fusion of commonalities of cultures in constructing a new world culture, particularly in terms of performance (see for example Schechner 2002; Pavis 1996, 2006; Bhabha 1990, 1994). States may institute interculturalism as a policy that seeks to encourage the socialisation of citizens of different ethnic origins as an instrument to fight racism and overcome prejudice against others. *Interculturalism* refers to the creation of new cultures along with existing ones, focusing on possible trajectories for the near future while *multiculturalism* endeavours to cherish and celebrate existing cultures, looking at history as bench markers. However, the perception of *multiculturalism* being 'a theory (albeit vague) about the foundations of a culture rather than a practice which subsumes cultural ideas' (Harrison in Gunew 1990: 99) could perhaps be further understood as an equally important component of intercultural performances. Pavis' anthropological approach to intercultural analysis assumes:

> *Multiculturalism* is an *interculturalism* in which each culture reflects the complexity and variety of an overall society, absorbing all influences without being overpowered by any one in particular: a meeting and absorption no longer conceived as a melting pot or crossroads, but rather as a confluence.
>
> (Pavis 2006: 280)

It is within this context that multiculturalism and intercultural discourses in contemporary Malaysian dance are observed as a confluence of relationships reflecting all aspects of life where a personal worldview and national gestalt are intertwined in all forms of contemporary artistic expressions. Contemporary dance in Malaysia not only deals with issues of performing and choreographing dance for intercultural dialogues but it also acknowledges diversities as substantial constructs in dance discourses. Cultural diversities are engaged to emphasise uniqueness in form and styles of contemporary Malaysian dance. In this sense, the term 'contemporary' specifically refers to 'contemporaneous or current' dances that are non-traditional and are non-generic to the genres already known in the country.

However, narratives or traditions sourced from existing literature from many communities in Malaysia together with dance techniques from the various dance forms are extensively utilised in choreographic forays by Malaysian artists. Intercultural elements are visibly noticed as choreographers of different ethnicities vie to construct new works through contemporaneous movements amidst familiar but culturally engaging dialogues.

Multiculturalism and interculturalism: the Malaysian formula

As in many post-colonial nations, Malaysia seeks to find ways to navigate theories of multiculturalism and interculturalism in the social and cultural reconstructions of its citizenry in spite of their seemingly contrasting dichotomies, in order to find middle ground and breed social-cultural-religious tolerance through dialogues and discourses in the arts and culture.

The pre-independent colonial constructs of British colonies in Malaya, Singapore and Borneo[2] were divided and ruled by the British in the late eighteenth and nineteenth centuries as Federated States, Straits Settlements, Crown Colonies and British Protectorates through the constructs of multicultural colonial states with different cultures, histories and origins.[3]

Indigenous populations were kept separated from immigrant workers who came as bonded or indentured labourers. Each community lived within the myriad societies as individual and separate groups with little or almost no dialogues or interactions. The separate communities reported all of their affairs to their chieftains, clan heads, or sultans under the watchful eyes of the British colonial government. Hence, multicultural Malaya continued in the new nation state of Malaysia. Malaysia had inherited colonial-era multiculturalism where diversity and multiplicity of cultural representations between indigenous and immigrant population posed strategic problems for political stability and national identity. Wide chasms of economic divide between indigenous and immigrant population continued to be awkwardly problematic during the post-colonial period. Independence, which was peacefully gained in 1957 for Malaya and in 1962 for Malaysia was severely tested by the economic and political divides that were kept in place for more than 130 years under British rule. The precarious but assumed perception of national unity was ultimately tested in the 1969 race riots.[4]

Not wanting to disband multicultural identities or to coerce monoculture identity, a socio-economic affirmative action plan was introduced in the form of the New Economic Policy (NEP) in 1970. This five-year economic development programme was devised to engage and privilege indigenous and non-indigenous population to share the economic pie and to propagate cross- and intercultural awareness for dialogues and exchanges amongst the diverse cultural groups. Without negating the importance of multiculturalism, interactive blending and fusions of cultural experiences through intercultural experiences have provided an influential 'formula' for Malaysia to develop and construct a possible Malaysian race or *Bangsa Malaysia*.

Malaysian contemporary dance: from multiculturalism to interculturalism

Ramli Ibrahim, dancer-choreographer-curator of the Sutra Dance Company, succinctly places the 1970s as the nascent period of contemporary dance in Malaysia:

> the emergence of the first conscious seed of modern ideas in dance probably appeared in the early seventies. However, an exciting and identifiable Malaysian 'modern' dance movement with a distinctive indigenous Malaysian identity only began to appear in the late seventies and early eighties with the advent of pioneer choreographers who returned from abroad (USA, United Kingdom and even Australia) with fresh new 'modern' ideas.
>
> (Ibrahim 2003: 29)

Being a dancer of ballet, *Bharatanatyam*, *Odissi*, and contemporary dance, Ramli Ibrahim is a multicultural performer-artist whose observations on the making of contemporary dance in Malaysia mirrors his own initiatives in learning *Bharatanatyam* from master-teacher Adyar K. Lakshman and *Odissi* from Guru Deba Prasad Dasi in India while he performed ballet and modern dance with the Sydney Dance Company in Australia, New York, London and Europe in the 1970s. Born in a Malay-Muslim family he rigorously maintains his birthright and identity while he practises multicultural dance forms as a professional. He sees how the efficacious use of artistic ideas and creative innovations, stemming from multicultural experiences and intercultural awareness, has given birth to distinctive indigenous Malaysian identities in modern dance in Malaysia.

However, the notion of contemporary dance in Malaysia needs clarification. Contemporary dance here does not mean Western modern dance or post-modern dance but denotes contemporaneous dance with an effective post-colonial re-invention of dance traditions through the processes of intercultural dialogues by its culturally diverse dancers and choreographers such as Lee Lee Lan, Mohd Ghouse Nasharuddin, Marion D'Cruz and Lari Leong. These intercultural dialogues tend to form the 'creative backbone' for many contemporary dances in multicultural Malaysia.

Malaysia's contemporary dance today is a far cry from the days of isolated community-based dance events observed during the days of British rule and during the early years of Malaysia's independence from Britain. The emergence of a new Malaysian society in the 1990s has not only transformed Malaysia's economic and political standing in the new world order but also values the ethos of artistic works by Malaysian artists (Nor 1997: 51). Contemporary dance in Malaysia is about inventing new movements and improvising new ideas as extensions of multicultural experiences.

> The course of the decades of the 1970s to the twenty-first century as the time frame is deliberate and intentional. This is the period where a new generation of Malaysian dancers and choreographers emerged, whose environments oscillate between the local and the global. Most of them find the narrowness of the canon of western theatre art dance challenging in the context of the Malaysian soul. Rather than overturning the status quo, Malaysian choreographers embarked on the search to gain a more balanced perspective on the practice of dance by confronting under-investigated genres and cultural practices in tandem with mainstream paradigms in Asian contemporary dance.
>
> (Nor 2003a: 2)

The greatest impetus to the awareness of dance as a manifestation of multicultural identities vis-à-vis the cosmogony of multi-ethnicity came in the 1990s. The need for state-assisted coercive persuasion to develop a national dance culture, an obsession that had haunted state bureaucrats and dance artists alike from the 1970s to the 1990s, was based on the 1971 National Culture Policy's three main guiding principles: the affirmation of indigenous Malay culture, acceptability of other cultures suitable to be part of the national culture, and Islam as an important component to the moulding of the national culture. However, these became superfluous when dance artists began to develop local and indigenous dance styles without sacrificing the quintessential elements of identity, sense of belonging and heritage that speak of them as Malaysians of multi-ethnic descent groups. Cross- ethnic borrowings or in other words, multicultural experiences, were appraised and reconstructed to build new dances that were contemporaneous and innovative (Antares 2003, Daneels 2003, Chan 2003, Mukriz 2003, Weldon 2003, Murugappan 2005, Siew 2007, Shunmugam 2008).

By the late 1990s, a new generation of dance artists had emerged. They were either recent Malaysian returnees from America, Europe and the Asia-Pacific region or local artists who had undergone thorough metamorphosis for new ideas while retrospectively looking into their past and their present. Aida Redza, Michael Xavier Voon, Joseph Gonzales, Lena Ang Swee Lin who were trained in America or Europe; and Vincent Tan Lian Ho, Choo Tee Kuang, Loke Soh Kim, Anthony Meh, Lee Swee Keong, Suhaimi Magi, Aman Yap, Umesh Shetty, Mohd Arifwaran, amongst others who had their training locally or in the Asia-Pacific region, create collages of multicultural expression in their dances that are grounded in techniques gathered from multitudes of dancing experiences, from the West, the East and indigenous traditions. The creative endeavours of Mew Chang Tsing, Loke Soh Kim, Anthony Meh and Umesh Shetty, for example, are based on issues drawn to reflect the awareness of their well-being as Malaysians. Mohd Arifwaran, Aida Redza, Marion D'Cruz, Leng Poh Gee, Michael Voon, and Lee Swee Keong on the other hand create works that are abstractive, narrative or even realistic in form and structure. Their styles are peculiar, entertaining, at times confusing but overwhelmingly individualistic and modern. Some of the issues raised in their choreography deal with matters of cultural, individual and national interest, which reflects both multicultural and intercultural expressions. These thematic issues may be juxtaposed with other significant elements of performance such as stagecraft, lighting, multimedia presentation and installation work. The extent of their usage and level of implementation by the dancers and choreographers depend largely on their backgrounds (training and experiences) and on the nature of the dance spaces made available for their work. Thus, dance pieces are often adjusted to the locality of their performance spaces (Nor 2003b: 18–19).

Multicultural and intercultural discourses are intertwined in Malaysian contemporary dance. Arguably, this sense of personal worldview by multicultural artists and national gestalt as aspired through intercultural dialogues and exchanges form substantial constructs for contemporary Malaysian dance. Cultural diversities are engaged to emphasise uniqueness in form and style of contemporary dance in Malaysia. To highlight the points discussed above, works of three Malaysian choreographers of different ethnic-descent groups are illustrated: Suhaimi Magi, a Malay man of Javanese descent; Umesh Shetty, a man of Indian descent; and Mew Chang Tsing, a woman of Chinese descent are chosen as exemplar case studies of multicultural artists in an intercultural world of contemporary dance in Malaysia. They have one desire in common, aspiring to be some of the best Malaysian contemporary dance artists without sacrificing their identity, ethnicity and their perceived notions of membership of a larger multicultural community of artists, performers and equally as citizens of a nation that does not shy away from intercultural experiments.

Suhaimi Magi

Born in a central Javanese migrant family in the village of Tenom in the East Malaysian state of Sabah (formerly British Borneo), Suhaimi began dancing from the age of 10. He performed professionally for the Ministry of Culture, Youth and Sports in Sabah for four years before embarking on eight years of study at the Jakarta Arts Institute (Institut Kesenian Jakarta) supported by a Sabah Foundation scholarship (1980–8). Upon completion of his studies, Suhaimi worked for five years with the Sabah Cultural Board before migrating to Kuala Lumpur where he was with the National Arts Academy (Akademi Seni Kebangsaan) until 2002. He is now the Dance Executive at the PETRONAS Department of Performing Arts. Suhaimi specialises in the regional art forms of Sabah, Sarawak, Peninsular Malaysia, Indonesia and the Philippines. Spirituality and traditional elements are the hallmarks of his powerful, contemporary works. Suhaimi's initial choreographic endeavour in contemporary dance was with the ASK Dance Company of the National Arts Academy in 1994.[5] His first works with ASK Dance Company were *Berasik*, premiered at the 3rd Indonesia Arts Festival in 1994; *Serkam*, choreographed for the KIDE 95 Festival in Seoul, South Korea; and *Akar*, which was co-choreographed with Aida Redza and Joseph Gonzales and premiered at the Dance On 97 Festival in Hong Kong in 1997. All of these choreographies showcase Suhaimi's curiosity and awareness about the spiritual realms of many indigenous cultures in Borneo couched within the familiar semiotics of traditional dance forms from Sabah and Sarawak. Suhaimi's choreographies were organic, earthy and almost constantly weighted downwards, as though pulled by the unseen forces of gravity and of Mother Nature.

His most recent works, premiered at the National Arts Academy *Jamu* (2006), demonstrated that Suhaimi is further experimenting with mixing and interweaving. Two new dance pieces, *Liuk* and *Paut* were presented. While the former retained many of Suhaimi's familiar movements and their derivatives, the latter was completely revolutionary. *Paut*'s synopsis was described in one single but broken sentence, 'Paut berpaut ... tetap berpaut ... saling berpaut', which literally means 'Cling or hold on tightly ... always clinging ... clinging and holding on to one another'. While its literal meaning denotes an overemphasis on clinging to someone or something tightly, which was visually represented through a *pas de deux* by

Shafirul Azmi Suhaimi and Ismadian Ismail,[6] its abstract form represents a mixture of specific indigenous dance idiom and intercultural experiments with movement symbols, icons and semiotics.

Paut is a simple but organic choreography. Symbols of cultural identities of separate ethnicities are clearly represented by the Malay music and dance *ambiance*, curvilinear arm movements, flexing hands and implied 'Malayness' of dance properties such as sarongs and umbrella. However, it also explicitly reveals the 'other' within the 'familiar Malayness'. Wide and expansive body movements, low but pliant pliés and dominant use of lifts and carriage, which are characterised within and beyond the threshold of 'traditional or conventional' dance movements signify affinities to dances of the immigrant cultures that have become part of the multicultural identities of Malaysia. Hence, *Paut* has enabled Suhaimi Magi to dwell on intercultural dialogues utilising multiple signs in constructing his movement vocabulary. *Paut* has not only allowed Suhaimi to step beyond his 'familiar threshold' but has also given intercultural *gaze* to the multicultural specificities of the *Malay gaze*. In this context, the concept of the gaze is drawn from Lacan's (1978) theory of the dialectic gaze between the ideal-ego and the ego-ideal. Suhaimi Magi is the ideal-ego who finds himself as the Malay intercultural artist while the spectators' view of Suhaimi's work is an imaginary gaze of Suhaimi's ego-ideal, a contemporary Malay choreographer pursuing Malay and intercultural identities.

Umesh Shetty

Umesh Shetty is known throughout Malaysia as the Indian danseur extraordinaire from the illustrious family of Gopal Shetty,[7] who fathered, mentored and taught Umesh formal Indian classical dance training from the age of six. His father played an important role in introducing and the teaching of *Bharata Natyam* classical Indian dance in Malaysia. He was instrumental in setting up the renowned Temple of Fine Arts in Kuala Lumpur in 1981 with the equally illustrious Indian dance master, V. K. Sivadas. This pioneering endeavour in setting up the Temple of Fine Arts (TFA) in Malaysia with the assistance of their respective wives, Radha Shetty and Vitsala Sivadas under the spiritual guidance of an Indian Swamiji, Swami Shantanand Saraswathi, has led to the prominence of many classical Indian dances in TFA's repertoire. Umesh Shetty acquired the skills of dancing the *Bharata Natyam*, *Odissi*, *Kathak* and various folk styles of India from his parents, from Pandita Rohini Bhatte of Pune, India (*Kathak*) and other teachers brought in by TFA. Equipped with the knowledge and grand narratives of classical Indian dance, Shetty read for his dance degree at the Edith Cowan University in Western Australia. His return home was a watershed for contemporary dance in Malaysia when he introduced an eclectic fusion of Indian classical dance and modern dance movements in his new choreographies. His strong knowledge and skills in Indian classical dance befits his goal to extend the dreams of his

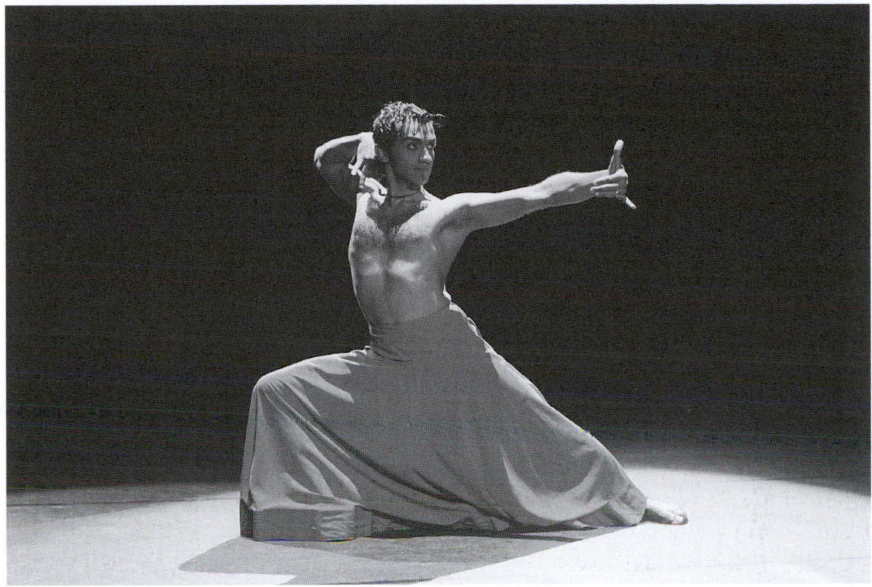

Figure 20.1 Umesh Shetty.

late father in preserving the dance traditions of greater India, essentially yearning to identify his ethnicity as a stakeholder of yet another multicultural identity of Malaysia. On the other hand, he is also keen to forge deliberately intercultural experiments to redefine the shape and styles of Malaysian contemporary dance.

One of his most recent nationally acclaimed contemporary dance pieces that showcases this eclecticism of multicultural/intercultural interfacing of Indian dance and contemporaneous arrangement is *Alarippu* (2005). The term *Alarippu* normally comes from the repertoire of the *Bharata Natyam* dance, which essentially means 'blossoming'. As the first dance in the repertoire of *Bharata Natyam*, *Alarippu* greets the audience and pays obeisance to the gods of Hindu mythology. In its traditional context, *Alarippu* is a pure dance piece that is accompanied by rhythmic syllables or *sollukattus*; outstretching of arms, moving the neck, eyes, major and minor limbs from slow to medium and ending in fast tempo signifies the accentuated gestures and rhythms, which ushers the dance into a sequential string of repertoire: *Jathiswaram*, *Sabdham*, *Varnam*, *Patham*, and *Tillana*. However, as a contemporary dance piece, *Alarippu* frames the dance with gestures from the traditional version but stretches the imagination of symmetrical dance phrases to a sequence of movements fused from asymmetrical and non-linear conjecture of modern and non-Indian dance motifs. The narrow and earthy conventional dance space of the classical Indian dance, synonymous with the space of obeisance for *Alarippu*, was reconstructed to embrace new vertical heights, wider stage depths and horizontal spaces. The juxtaposed dance space was consumed with dancing bodies from different ethnic groups as they conditioned their movements both to the required Indian dance idioms and to non-Indian contemporary dance expressions, contesting traditional Indian classical dance movements *and* modern dance within an assortment of specific Indic dance styles and intercultural extractions. Shetty attempted to indulge in new trajectories of expression and stylistics in choreographing *Alarippu*. While retaining the signs of *Bharata Natyam* through the integration of *mudra* (symbolic hand gestures) and *hastas* (defined form of hand gestures), and of *Nritta* (pure dance) signifying symbols of Indian ascendancy and hegemony, new symbols from intercultural dance gestures alien to classical Indian dance motifs were introduced to pierce through the barriers of multiculturalism signifying this new *Alarippu* as both Indic and Malaysian in origin.

Mew Chang Tsing

Mew Chang Tsing graduated from the Hong Kong Academy of Performing Arts and the University of Surrey (MA Dance). She formed her own dance company, the Rivergrass Dance Theatre and Rivergrass Dance Academy, in 1996 to promote her belief in redefining Malaysian culture by venturing into the roots of cultures to seek their respective contributions to contemporary Asian arts: 'tomorrow's dance is created by returning to the basic elements of culture, be it Malay, Chinese, Indian, Aboriginal, or Western … it can only discover its future cultural identity by first returning to and examining its multi-cultural roots' (Rivergrass 2003). This motivation has become an important factor in creating, inventing and producing her dances. Her interest in the search for her roots and the position of heritage in the multicultural facets of Malaysian life are both passionate and influential. Yet she is equally zealous in intercultural dialogues to advocate the idea of intercultural Malaysia rather than a singular mission of preserving her Chinese identity vis-à-vis multiculturalism. She reflects these in almost all of her choreographies except those that are specific to South-east Asia or to the Chinese Diaspora. She is an accomplished Chinese dancer and an extraordinary performer of Malaysian and Indonesian traditional dances.

Mew Chang Tsing's *A Journey with Li Yu*, premiered in July 1995 and, for example, tries to find a balance between non-Western conceptions of dance and the Western perception of how dance is constructed. Her attempt to abstract the emotions of the tragic life history of the Chinese Emperor Li Yu as analogous to her struggle to search for her own identity conjured subtle images of Malaysians confronting cross-cultural issues within a multicultural society that are poignant and real (Nor 1996: 55). Another particular example, which conjures similar emotive issues, is in *Re: Lady White Snake*, a piece of work that has been restaged more than seven times. The piece was choreographed with Lee Swee Keong (choreographer and a member of Nyoba & Dancers Dance Company) and over the years from 1996 to the

Figure 20.2 Mew Chang Tsing (L) with Lee Swee Keong (R) in *Re: Lady White Snake*.

present, they have both felt that they grew as people and artists through the ever-evolving work of *Re: Lady White Snake*. Through it Tsing was able to realise some of her aims; developing a new dance vocabulary with strong South-east Asian flavour, developing a new form of theatre that is rooted in Asia, and conveying her view (and that of Keong) of the duality of human personalities and complexities of relationship that sees no boundaries in time, space and gender. By using several dancers over the period of restaging this work (1996 to 2003), Tsing was able to use different dancers to display innately the traditional forms in the bodies, which need not necessarily be restricted to the races living in contemporary Malaysia.[8] She sees Malaysia as a land where traits of numerous cultures from different parts of the world and of different times can be found, observed and be used to express the multicultural dimensions of dance as an artistic journey. Although this dance has evolved over the years and has its own life and energy, her initial intention of creating something original, unique and representing the region's intercultural quality has not changed (Nor 2003b: 20–1).

Championing diversity

Suhaimi Magi, Umesh Shetty and Mew Chang Tsing represent a new breed of Malaysian contemporary dancers and choreographers who not only create contemporary dances as an extension of their ethnicity but also deal with issues of intercultural dialogues to champion the diversities of culture and traditions in multicultural Malaysia. Awareness of diversity as discourse for new choreographies in contemporary dance, in Kuala Lumpur in particular, has continued to provide the avenue for many young artists such as A. Aris A. Kadir, Jack Kek Siou Kee, Kiea Kuan Nam, Amy Len, Ravi Shankar and Elaine Pedley to showcase their newest works, which are often inspired by the works of others from diverse cultural backgrounds.

Historically, the processes of interfacing and acknowledging the confluence of diversities in creating, reconstructing and inventing intercultural contemporary dances in Malaysia began with the appropriation of multiculturalism as a state apparatus to develop mutual tolerance to cultural diversities as an aftermath of the turbulent years of the 1960s. Not wanting to be subjected to narrow definitions of cultural practices, dance artists began to investigate intercultural dialogues by learning diverse dance forms, either as participants or observers, to overcome their own prejudices. By sensitising their understanding towards the diverse 'others', dance artists accumulate their awareness and understanding of being polyglots, multi-ethnic, and multi-believers in a multicultural nation in order to cope with cultural diversities while harnessing their own unique traditions and heritage. Not wanting to carry post-colonial cultural baggage, Malaysian contemporary dancers and choreographers are more interested in the present state of intercultural experiences rather than indulging in re-creating the past to idealise separate cultural identities, which is often confronted with chasms of socio-religious divide. Suhaimi Magi, Umesh Shetty, and Mew Chang Tsing are amongst the many contemporary Malaysian choreographers who exemplify the myriad energies that abound in the spirit of interculturalism within multicultural societies of Malaysia:

> All of these have greatly influenced the temperament, composition and multicultural make-up of the contemporary dancer, choreographer, inventor, and creator of kinaesthetic nuances that is embodied in a culturally structured contemporary movement system, which in essence is the Malaysian contemporary dance.
>
> (Nor 2003b: 25)

Notes

1 This chapter is adapted from the article 'Convergence of diverse cultural backgrounds as discourse of contemporary dance in Malaysia' published in Mohd Anis Md Nor (ed.) (2007) *Dialogues in Dance Discourse: Creating Dance in Asia Pacific*, Kuala Lumpur: World Dance Alliance – Asia Pacific, Ministry of Culture, Arts and Heritage Malaysia, and Cultural Centre University of Malaya.

2 Comprising the ancient Malay peninsula, the old Sriwijayan colony of Temasik, Kingdom of the White Rajah in the former territorial domain of the Brunei Sultanate and British North Borneo in the hegemonic periphery of old Brunei and Sulu territories.

3 During the late eighteenth and nineteenth centuries, Great Britain established colonies and protectorates in the area of current Malaysia; these were

occupied by Japan from 1942 to 1945. In 1948, the British-ruled territories on the Malay Peninsula formed the Federation of Malaya, which became independent in 1957. Malaysia was formed in 1963 when the former British colonies of Singapore and the East Malaysian states of Sabah and Sarawak on the northern coast of Borneo joined the Federation. The first several years of the country's history were marred by Indonesian efforts to control Malaysia, Philippine claims to Sabah, and Singapore's secession from the Federation in 1965. Available online at <http://www.cia.gov/cia/publications/factbook/geos/my.html>, accessed June 2006.

4 As an aftermath of the 1969 racial riots, which brought heavy loss of life, property, foreign investments and political uncertainty, a national cultural policy was formulated by the governors of the National Culture Congress in 1971 to steer the country and its people towards a socially and culturally engineered programme of national unity. The policy was drawn to determine the direction of the nation in achieving a national identity, a sense of belonging and self-esteem as a sovereign nation that was almost torn apart by highly polarised societies that had taken roots in extremist political movements.

5 In 1994, the ASK Dance Company was established by the Dance Program of the National Arts Academy, Ministry of Culture, Arts and Tourism. The company was created with the intention to further promote local performances and to encourage the creative development of its lecturers and students. It was in this fertile soil of cross-cultural exchange that the founding members Suhaimi Magi, Aida Redza, Lena Ang and Joseph Gonzales worked, striving to break contemporary boundaries, redefine forms and norms to build the base of a unified dance culture in Malaysia. The company has built its reputation on the strong use of traditional elements, spirit and vocabulary as the starting point of its creative discovery.

6 Shafirul Azmi Suhaimi, born in Sabah is the son of Suhaimi Magi. A graduate of the National Arts Academy, Shafirul has shown extremely promising talents in many dance works choreographed by Malaysian choreographers. He was the principal dancer in the 2003 production of *AWAS!* by Joseph Gonzales for ASK Dance Company and Cross Roads Dance Ensemble. Shafirul is following his father's footsteps by conducting research on indigenous dances of Borneo such as the Cocos Malays in Tawau, Sabah. He is currently a dance tutor at the Academy, works with several colleges and institutions in Kuala Lumpur and is a freelance performer. His female dance partner, Ismadian Ismail is an accomplished dancer whose grasp of traditional and modern dance is equally strong.

7 Born in 1930 in India, Gopal Shetty began dance training under the tutelage of Mr. K. K. Shetty from the renowned Bharathya Kala Mandal at the age of thirteen. His earlier dance compositions in Bombay were aligned to the styles of Uday Shankar before he joined a world tour in 1954, which brought him to Malaya. His choreographies became staple entries in the early years of television in Malaysia in the late 1960s but it was his meeting and collaboration with V. K. Sivadas that made both men the pioneering icons of Indian dance in Malaysia. Gopal Shetty married one of his early students, Radha Saravanamuthu, who was instrumental in assisting his career in dance training and choreographies in Malaysia.

8 As this is a contemporary dance drama, the dancer has to be expressive and since *Re: Lady White Snake* deals with the complexity of human nature, the dancers must be able to convey such maturity. White Snake is elegant and beautiful, fierce and seductive but firm in her pursuit of true love. Green Snake is detached from the happenings around him, is playful and follows his own instinct without much thought. The Scholar is good-looking yet has no mind of his own in spite of being able to give his true love to White Snake. The Monk on the other hand, is powerful, righteous but merciless with a crooked

mindset. All these qualities are carried by the dance vocabulary, created out of the movement improvisations that are emotive and soul-searching.

References

Antares (2003) *Temu: Trance as Performance*. Available online at <http:www.kakiseni.com> (accessed 1 July 2003).

Bhabha, H. K. (1990) *Nation and Narration*, London and New York: Routledge.

—— (1994) *The Location of Culture*, London and New York: Routledge.

Chan, S.-P. (2003) *Get Ready for Sutra*. Available online at <http:www.kakiseni.com> (accessed 13 May 2003).

Daneels, J. (2003) *Making a Better World through Dance and Theatre*. Available online at <http:www.kakiseni.com> (accessed 24 September 2003).

Gunew, S. (1990) 'Denaturalizing cultural nationalisms: multicultural readings of Australia', in H. K. Bhabha, (ed.) *Nation and Narration*, New York: Routledge, Chapman and Hall Inc.

Ibrahim, R. (2003) 'Indigenous ideas and contemporary fusions: The making of Malaysian contemporary modern dance', in M. A. M. Nor (ed.) *Diversity in Motion*, Kuala Lumpur: MyDance Alliance and Cultural Centre University of Malaya.

Lacan, J. (1978) *Seminar Eleven: The Four Fundamental Concepts of Psychoanalysis*, New York and London: W. W. Norton and Co.

Mukriz, A. T. (2003) An email interview with Dr. Mohd. Anis Md. Nor. Available online at <http:www.kakiseni.com> (accessed 24 September 2003).

Murugappan, R. (2005) 'We still haven't found what we're looking for'. Available online at <http:www.kakiseni.com> (accessed 13 January 2005).

Nor, M. A. M. (1996), 'Dance in a multicultural society: The Malaysian dance scene today', *Ballet International-Tanz Aktuell* 11, 54–5.

—— (1997), 'Abstract: Celebration of diversity in dance', in *ASEAN Dance Symposium* at the 4th ASEAN Dance Festival Singapore, Singapore.

—— (2003a) 'Dance research: transference and reconstruction in contemporary Malaysian dance', in M. A. M. Nor (ed.) *Diversity in Motion*, Kuala Lumpur: MyDance Alliance and Cultural Centre University of Malaya, 1–22.

—— (2003b) 'Confluence of diversity: inventing contemporary dances in Malaysia', in *Dancing New Asia: Southeast Asian Dance Showcase and Forum*, Hong Kong Arts Festival 2003, Fringe Club.

Pavis, P. (ed.) (1996) *The Intercultural Performance Reader*, London and New York: Routledge.

—— (2006) *Analyzing Performance: Theatre, Dance, and Film*, translated by D. Williams, Ann Arbor: The University of Michigan Press.

Rivergrass Dance Theatre (2003) Homepage. Available online at <http://www.rivergrass.com.my/about/> (accessed 13 January 2005).

Schechner, R. (2002) *Performance Studies: An Introduction*, London and New York: Routledge.

Shunmugam, V. (2008) 'A Year the Arts Showed the Way'. Available online at <http:www.kakiseni.com> (accessed 13 January 2008).

Siew, Z. (2007) 'Bumps in the Landscape'. Available online at <http:www.kakiseni.com> (accessed 19 January 2007).

Weldon, L. (2003) 'Mew Chang Tsing and her vision of a new Malaysian dance'. Available online at <http:www.kakiseni.com> (accessed 25 August 2003).

Section 5
Changing aesthetics

Section introduction

Jo Butterworth and Liesbeth Wildschut

The chapters of this section on the changing aesthetics in choreography focus on specific challenges to traditional or conventional choreography, albeit that they concentrate on choreography in very different contexts. In our editorial conception of this section of the book, we determined to go beyond orthodox understandings of choreography, rather choosing to promote enquiry of the creative processes of dance making on a wider scale, foregrounding practices that extend or transgress boundaries or which result in new modes of performative events.

As contemporary choreographers investigate and re-chart their own 'artistic topographies' (Birringer 1993: xi) in terms of communication, attitude, structure and roles in their approaches to human movement, there is a need for greater investigation of issues such as how movement is perceived and executed, how choreographers wish to see bodies move, and how choreographers want the audience to experience bodies moving. Across the performing arts, traditional lines of demarcation shift, strain and shatter; but whereas historical moments of revolution, challenge and shock leave their own recognisable legacies and have been reasonably well documented, the chapters in this section indicate individual quests, unfinished, inquisitive, postmodern, resonant. Without literal narratives, stylistic movement or symbolising functions, contemporary choreography proves challenging, almost defiant in its complexity and multiplicity.

The first chapter in this section by Ya-Ping Chen bridges the issues of both the last section on the intercultural and on changing aesthetics. She introduces the concept of 'Asian modernity' as intrinsically defined by a dynamics of dialectic dualism: national/individual identity quest, colonial/post-colonial power structure, modern/traditional polemics and globalisation/indigenisation impetus. She argues that it is exactly this constant need to be in active interaction with its Western counter-part on the one hand and the incessant internal adjustments in response to historical conditions on the other that make Asian modernity a unique and vibrant phenomenon rather than a branch development of a Western original. The Cloud Gate Dance Theatre of Taiwan stands as an illustrative example in the histories of Asian cultures' pursuit for modernisation and contemporary expression, and in the second part of the essay Chen analyses in some depth how Lin Hwai-min, the company's founder and artistic director since 1973, negotiated between the strategies and/or necessities of emulating Western models, self-discovery of cultural roots and identity construction through artistic creation, to create a new body aesthetic.

Jeroen Fabius explores the interest in kinaesthetics held by three late twentieth-century choreographers, distinguishing three different approaches: first, a conceptual approach by Boris Charmatz, who uses the obstruction of sight to present perception as the central idea of the performance, and allows the spectator room to reflect on the role of kinaesthetics and other senses in choreography. In the work of Meg Stuart, a reductive, 'microscopic' approach permeates the visual with the sensual, creating what Deleuze calls haptic vision, where sight takes over the role of touch. Finally, in William Forsythe's work the dancers' application of their kinaesthetic sense organises the dance movement, resulting in choreography that is a product of collaborative production during the performance.

All three choreographers combat notions of conventional choreography: Charmatz strives for illegibility; Stuart wants to reduce 'danciness'; Forsythe explodes ballet vocabulary into an effect of disappearance. This focus on kinaesthetics creates different approaches to space and relations for the spectator: new perspectives on embodiment of subjectivity, less on body images, body language, representation and distance, more on process and the dynamic connections between action and reflection, material and virtual.

Sophia Lycouris explores recent shifts in traditional choreographic practice that have occurred as a result of the use of new technologies in contemporary dance work. She focuses on the dialogue between choreography and new technologies, examining interactivity and other varieties of material as choreographic components. Through reference to her own artistic journey, she addresses the impact of interdisciplinary practice and technology on aspects of contemporary choreography, citing three specific works which each challenge the perception and role of the viewer in their different ways.

In the final chapter of this section, we continue to identify works that might fulfil some of the criteria of stepping beyond previous choreographic boundaries. Sarah Rubidge examines choreography and performativity in interactive installations in relation to her 2003 collaboration *Sensuous Geographies* with the composer Alistair McDonald. She identifies and interrogates three specific types of performative and/or choreographic installations: first, choreographed performances that take place in an installation rather than a stage environment; second, choreographed or improvised performances in an installation environment which incorporate a measure of interactivity between responsive technological systems and performers; and thirdly, interactive engagements in an installation environment between 'audience' members and responsive technological systems that give rise to informal performance events.

In each case, readers will no doubt query these explorations, which might be considered boundary breaking but might also be perceived as simply building on artistic ideas appropriated from visual and performance arts, or from other cultures. An important question might be posed, do such explorations result in interesting pieces? Certainly, we are faced with different perspectives from inside and without traditional choreographic norms. For example, Rubidge interrogates the performative through description and appraisal of her choreographic installation: first sharing the intention, the objectives of the piece, the collaborative decision making and the elements involved, but also critiquing the work in performance, identifying changes which occur because of differences in environment, audience interaction and composer choice at each performance. This demonstrates the ability of the artist to objectify, to be critically reflective of creative process *and* final product.

Works such as those described in this section inevitably provide challenges to audience and critic perception. As at other non-evolutionary moments of dance history, we are provoked by choreographic works that make audiences set aside their usual ways of looking/perceiving. Audience expectations and their ways of looking, listening and sensing continue to be challenged for many diverse reasons. They may view work perceived as illogical or alogical, performed in a dance vocabulary that seems strange, physically dangerous or merely undance-like. Imagine initial responses to works that ask audiences to view an inordinate amount of dance material at the same time, or choreographies where spectators have been asked to participate in the performance.

Ramsey Burt's recent essay on 'Resistant Identities' (in Franco and Nordera 2007: 208–20) provides an exemplar. Burt examines the Berlin-based choreographer Felix Ruckert's deconstruction of the performer–audience relationship in *Hautnah*. He describes negotiating a fee, going upstairs with a dancer to a small cubicle, watching her dance, alone with her, responding woodenly to her obvious invitation to dance a 'duet' and finally being dismissed with an 'adieu'. His interpretation is an assumed rationale; the piece was used strategically to unsettle the spectator-participant, to stop him viewing the work in the habitual manner normally adopted, and thus created a heightened physical sensitivity. *Hautnah* disrupts the feeling of being distant in a performance; Burt smelled garlic and nicotine on the dancer's breath, his arms and legs were touched and moved, he was alone, he felt unsure, as Ruckert intended.

The chapters in this section raise such questions about passive, active or interactive audience engagement and/or involvement, about various forms of consciousness, and about kinaesthetic, intellectual, sensorial or emotional responses to dance work. They also question other notions of interactivity – that is, between dancers, or dancers bridging cultural norms; between performers and technology; or between audience–performers–technology. Technology in performance can bring a number of different approaches (Dinkla and Leeker 2002) – from the use of intelligent lighting and projections to musical technology, live and mediated dancers, real time, liveness, interactivity, embodiment and transformation, as discussed in the work of Auslander (1999), Birringer (1998, 2000), Chapple and Kattenbelt (2006) or Broadhurst and Machon (2007). Technology can evidently create different awareness of self in relation to others in the performative situation, or become another heterogeneous element of a performance, but it can also take the place of the live performer altogether in favour of the mediated or virtual body. Digital practices provide choreography with potential for numerous creative and aesthetic possibilities.

Further ways of choreography 'expanding' itself can be seen in terms of interactivity between the work itself and the environment: questions of location (where it is performed), in terms of place as inspiration (site-specific work) and in terms of created environments which may or may not be referred to as installations. Indeed, much contemporary choreography plays with fusion or hybridity between genres and styles, between culturally determined conventions, and between artistic movements, in the attempt to go beyond what already exists. Choreographers can no longer be reliant on intuitive, 'embedded' responses – they recognise the need for conceptualising, for being aware of the particular imperative in each artistic process, and of their specific intentions. If, as the second section of this book demonstrates, dance students are now engaged in the kinds of learning methodologies that may develop intelligent, dexterous and versatile dance practitioners as well as autonomous thinkers who are able to demonstrate critical faculty, then there can be no doubt that growth and expansion of the dance discipline will continue unabated.

References

Auslander, P. (1999) *Liveness: Performance in a Mediatized Culture*, London: Routledge.

Birringer, J. (1993) *Theatre, Theory, Postmodernism*, Bloomington: University of Indiana.

—— (1998) *Media and Performance: along the border*, Baltimore and London: Johns Hopkins University Press.

—— (2000) *Performance on the Edge: Transformations of Culture*, London: Continuum.

Broadhurst, S. and Machon, J. (2007) *Performance and Technology: Practices of Virtual Embodiment and Interactivity*, New York: Palgrave Macmillan.

Chapple, F. and Kattenbelt, C. (eds) (2006) *Intermediality in Theatre and Performance*, Amsterdam, New York: IFTH.

Dinkla, S. and Leeker, M. (eds) (2002) *Dance and Technology: Moving Towards Media Productions*, Berlin: Alexander Verlag.

Franco, S. and Nordera, M. (eds) (2007) *Dance Discourses: Keywords in dance research*, London and New York: Routledge.

Further reading

Fischer-Lichte, E. (2008) *The Transformative Power of Performance: A New Aesthetics* trans. Saskya Jain, London and New York: Routledge.

Gitelman, C. and Martin, R. (2007) *The Returns of Alwin Nikolais: Bodies, Boundaries and the Dance Canon*, Middletown, CT: Wesleyan University Press.

Lansdale, J. (ed.) (2008) *Decentring Dancing Texts: The Challenge of Interpreting Dances*, Basingstoke: Palgrave Macmillan.

Midgelow, V. (2007) *Reworking the Ballet: Counter Narratives and Alternative Bodies*, London and New York: Routledge.

Mitoma, J. (ed.) (2002) *Envisioning Dance on Film and Video*, London and New York: Routledge.

Preston-Dunlop, V. and Sanchez-Colberg, A. (eds) (2002) *Dance and the Performative: A Choreological Perspective – Laban and Beyond*, London: Verve.

21 In search of Asian modernity

Cloud Gate Dance Theatre's body aesthetics in the era of globalisation

Ya-Ping Chen

Modernity, as a West-originated idea, carries far more complex meanings for Asia than for Euro-American culture. Its evolvement in this part of the world has been closely intertwined with its history of colonisation, both by external and internal colonialists and in modes of political, cultural and economic colonialisms. As a result, the concept of 'Asian modernity' is intrinsically defined by a dynamics of dialectic dualism – national/individual identity quest, colonial/post-colonial power structure, modern/traditional polemics, globalisation/indigenisation impetus, among others. It is in fact the tension and negotiation within and between these dual structures that distinguish Asian modernity. I would argue that it is exactly this constant need to be in active interaction with its Western counterpart on the one hand and the incessant internal adjustments in response to historical conditions on the other that make Asian modernity a unique and vibrant phenomenon rather than a branch development of a Western original.

The Cloud Gate Dance Theatre of Taiwan stands as an illustrative example in the histories of Asian cultures' pursuit for modernisation and contemporary expression. Since its founding in 1973, the company's trajectory of development in terms of the style and content of its dances testifies to Asian contemporary art's endless struggle and continual negotiation between the strategies and/or necessities of emulating Western models, self-discovery of cultural roots and identity construction through artistic creation in this era of (post-)colonial globalisation.

Asian modernity – a process of continuous negotiation

In *Five Faces of Modernity*, literary historian Matei Calinescu identifies certain essential features of European modernity: (1) a *strong sense of time* as an irreversible linear development characterised by *dramatic ruptures in history* as well as a sharp distinction between the past (the ancient) and the present (the modern); (2) an urgent sense of *existential crisis* resulting from the demise of Christianity and the drastic social changes brought about by the Industrial Revolution; (3) an emphasis on *change* in response to the ever-changing environments of industrialised urban centres, which led to the emphasis on newness and innovation in the arts as opposed to repetition and continuity (Calinescu 2003: 13–92, emphasis added).

Inaugurated in the intensive interaction with Western colonial powers in the nineteenth and early twentieth centuries, Asian modernity bears the imprint of the characteristics above; yet due to the colonial situations many Asian countries were subjected to at the time, these features have been complicated by the colonial power relationship as well as the internal struggles of the Asian countries' attempt at self-rejuvenation and modernisation. First of all, the opposition between the present and the past was often cast as the conflict between the modern, which equalled the West or the coloniser, and the ancient, which meant the Mother culture. Consequently, this temporal/historical rupture was much more painful than in Western modernity, entangled with complex feelings in Asia since the embrace of the present/modern implicated a rejection of the self and its memory. Concomitant with this anxiety was an urgent sense of national crisis both politically and culturally. Rather than the existential crisis of the individual in Western modernity, Asian modernity in many cases was actually born of a national existential crisis under the threat of colonialism. In order to survive nationally, the pursuit of change, especially material and institutional changes, was desired; yet, the need to preserve self-identity also meant that 'tradition', or memory of the past, would continually be revisited and would re-emerge in different forms, especially in times of crisis, to reaffirm the integrity of the self-image.

To complicate the matter further, modernity as represented by colonial power and culture, though a potential threat to national existence and identity, has sometimes been a liberating experience for certain Asian individuals, especially through the practice of modernist arts. Modernism's emphasis on innovation and individual expression has lent Asian artists an effective means to counter the conservative forces in their own culture; for instance, women created and performed in modern dance in defiance of patriarchal repression of the female body. At the same time, under the mandate of national cultural rejuvenation as a resistance to colonial oppression, modernist language has often been integrated with so-called 'essential' elements of national culture to create contemporary art forms with distinct national identity.

Hence, when the Cloud Gate Dance Theatre was founded in the early 1970s with the slogan of 'Composed by Chinese, choreographed by Chinese and danced by Chinese for the Chinese audience', the blending of Peking Opera movement vocabulary and Martha Graham technique, as best exemplified by *Tale of the White Serpent* (1975), was considered a progressive move.[1] On the one hand, the aesthetics of modern dance allowed Lin Hwai-min, the company's founder and artistic director, to instill his personal interpretation of the conflict between law and desire into the centuries-old Chinese folk tale; on the other hand, the hallmark acrobatic movements drawn from Peking Opera endowed the dance with an 'authentic' Chinese identity. The increasing emphasis on Taiwanese cultural elements in the company's repertoire in the late 1970s and 1980s reflected the vicissitude of cultural and national identity within the island at the time.[2] Yet when viewed within the framework of Asian modernity illustrated above, the evocation of Taiwan's history in dances like *Legacy* (1978) and *Liao Tien-tin* (1979) could be regarded as a reaffirmation of collective identity at the time of statehood crisis faced by the Republic of China on Taiwan in the international political arena during the turbulent 1970s.[3]

Lin Hwai-min – an Asian subject in the era of (dance) globalisation

In retrospect, the second half of the 1980s marked a turning point in Lin's artistic vision and paved the way for the pan-Asian cultural identity characterising some of his most important works in the 1990s, most notably *Nine Songs* (1993) and *Songs of the Wanderers* (1994). Lin once recounted:

> *Nine Songs* can be seen as the confession of my middle-age years. … There were two major themes in my life: one was the drastic changes [in the world] and the other was the strong sense of yearning and attachment symbolized by the lotus flower.
>
> (Lin Hwai-min *et al.* 1993: 18–19)

The drastic changes included, in addition to the temporary folding of Cloud Gate from 1988 to 1991, the lifting of martial law in Taiwan and the resumption of cross-straits exchanges between Taiwan and mainland China in 1987 after forty years of separation; and the dissolution of major Communist states around the world, as well as the Tiananmen Square incident in 1989. Bringing about hope or destruction, these changes complicated Lin's world view and prompted him to reconfigure his relationship to his immediate surroundings and to the world. This readjustment of his perception not only of the world but also of himself was further enriched by his many journeys to Indonesia, Nepal and India since 1986. 'After being immersed in Western culture for too long a time, I finally began to know my neighbouring countries and through them to know myself', said Lin in an interview (Lin Hwai-min interview, 7 January 2003). The statement suggests a shift of Lin's identification from a 'Westernised' Chinese/Taiwanese subjectivity to a Taiwanese/Chinese/Asian identity.

Lin's transformation as a choreographer and as an Asian subject has to be read against the development of globalisation sweeping across the world since the late 1980s. Taiwanese scholar Chen Kuan-hsing, in his groundbreaking study *Towards De-Imperialization: Asia as Method*, argues that the implementation of the Cold War in the 1950s, with its engulfing ideology of anti-communism, deferred the process of de-colonisation and de-imperialisation after the end of the Second World War, even though many colonised nations won independence in the post-war years. China's opening-up toward the world in the late 1970s softened the rigid Cold

War structure, which was further encroached in the late 1980s due to the crumbling of Communism in many areas of the world. The end of the Cold War in the early 1990s boosted the development of globalisation thanks to the lifting of political barriers and the free flow of capital to almost every corner on earth. Yet Chen warns about the reincarnation of imperialism under the guise of neo-liberalist globalisation and insists on the dual task of de-colonisation within the former colonised nations and de-imperialisation among the former colonisers in this so-called 'post-colonial era' (Chen Kuan-hsing 2006: 3–21).

The dissemination of American modern dance to many parts of the world, including Taiwan, in the 1950s and 1960s, was part of the Cold War strategy of cultural exportation exercised by the US State Department to enhance American image and influence in the Third World (Prevots 1998). Taiwan's deep reliance on American military and financial aid at the time entailed its susceptibility as well as subjection to American culture, from Hollywood films to Jackson Pollock and Martha Graham. The modernist aesthetics of modern dance helped Lin Hwai-min's generation to create alternative dance languages to rebel against *minzu wudao*, the official Chinese national dance implemented by the Chinese Nationalist government (the KMT) in the 1950s as part of its anti-communist ideological warfare.[4] The strong presence of American modern and later post-modern dance has persisted not only in the training systems of major dance companies but also in the curricula of dance academia. The influence was so permeating and prevalent that there emerged in the late 1980s a phenomenon called 'Eastern body aesthetic dance' to counter the hegemony of Western dance techniques.[5]

If the task of Taiwanese modern dance in the 1960s and 1970s was to go beyond the stagnant *minzu wudao* and solve the problem of Chinese culture's modernisation, and if its mission in the 1980s was to confront and cope with the drastic socio-political changes within Taiwan society, then the principal concerns of Taiwanese choreographers in the 1990s were how to define their cultural identity in the sweeping flow of (dance) globalisation, best exemplified by the growing scale and number of international festivals, and the ensuing challenge of how to compete on these global dance stages. In other words, the emphasis changed from re-affirming 'authenticity', a modern version of Chinese/Taiwanese culture with tradition or history as the primary reference, to establishing 'difference', with the Western 'other' as the referential counterpart. In fact, the Eastern body aesthetic dance phenomenon, besides being a counter-movement against Western dance aesthetics, was itself an artistic strategy aimed at earning recognition in the flourishing market of international arts festivals by the aesthetics of 'difference'.

The creation of *Nine Songs* and *Songs of the Wanderers* by Lin in the early 1990s can be regarded as part of this self-reflective and simultaneously globalising trend. It reflected the shift in Lin's world view, a growing identification with Asia on the one hand and the international strategy adopted by Cloud Gate after its hiatus on the other, as an active response to the scenario of intensifying dance globalisation. Economically, Cloud Gate needs the international tours to sustain the company's high-standard production costs and professional administrative operations given the extremely small internal market of Taiwan. Furthermore, international exposure also meant more sponsorship from both governmental institutions and private sectors. If *Nine Songs*' 1995 tour to BAM's Next Wave Festival in New York opened the door for Cloud Gate to major theatres and festivals worldwide, the cultivation of a new body aesthetics and correlatively new dance theatre aesthetics since the late 1990s has established an *Asian modernism*, which I would define as extolling 'authorship' more than 'authenticity' and pursuing 'innovation' in addition to 'difference'.[6]

Cloud Gate's new body aesthetics

In 1996, Cloud Gate dancers began training in *Tai-chi Tao-yin*, a form of *chi-kong* developed by master Hsiung Wei in Taiwan, which draws upon the Taoist philosophy and the primary principles of three different schools of *Tai-chi Ch'uan* (shadow boxing) originating in mainland China. Three major features characterise this unique system of body–mind training: (1) circular or spiral courses of movement; (2) uninterrupted and continuous flow of energy; (3) intense attention to the reciprocal relationship between tension and release, motion and stillness, interior and exterior of the body. Engaged in a mode of long, deep, unhurried breathing centred at the abdomen (*tan-tian*), *Tai-chi Tao-yin* trains the nine major joints of the body by twisting and spiralling movements that wring muscles and bones inch by inch to achieve thorough flexibility (*sung*), a state of suppleness not only physically but also mentally and spiritually.[7]

According to master Hsiung, the human body is structured like an exquisite network defined by two crossing axes, each starting from the fingertips of one hand and ending at the tiptoe of the opposite leg. In *Tai-chi Tao-yin*, movement travels along the axes in spiralling fashion; as a result, all actions are three-dimensional rather than flattened as in straightforward motions (Hsiung interview, 29 January 2005). Like the curved line between *yin* and *yang* in the *tai-chi* icon, which symbolises the endlessly recycling and mutually reinforcing mechanism between the two states, the spiralling passage of movement in *Tai-chi Tao-yin* explores the infinite space within the human body – the 'micro-cosmos' which resonates with the 'macro-cosmos' of the outside universe according to the Taoist philosophy. Moreover, the cultivation of *chi* (breath or vital energy) enables the spiralling motions to reach and affect the innermost depth of the body. In this ideal state of 'thorough flexibility', the *chi* travels inside the body without any hindrance, and one could summon and direct it freely in the performance of any movement. '[When the *chi*] fills and resonates inside the body, one could be as soft as spring breeze and sprinkles or as strong as lightning and thunder', as stated by master Hsiung (Hsiung interview, 29 January 2005).

As a result of the systemic and regular training in *Tai-chi Tao-yin*, Cloud Gate dancers internalise its principles and philosophy into their bodies, undergoing fundamental changes not only in exterior appearance but also in the texture and inner logic of their movement. Unlike Eastern body aesthetic dance, which deliberately rejected Western dance techniques, Cloud Gate dancers integrate teachings in modern dance and ballet with *Tai-chi Tao-yin* and later Chinese martial arts and the practice of calligraphy. The result is more than 'hybridity', one of the favourite post-colonial keywords for describing the mixing of and negotiation between different cultures or cultural forms (Bhabha 1994, Lin Yatin 2001). The strength and resilience, the intense reciprocity between mind and body, and the highly controlled circular flow of *chi* – qualities gained from the Chinese body–mind training systems – transform the kinetic texture and expressive tone of the Western dance techniques used in the Cloud Gate repertoire. In other words, what has been achieved is nothing less than an alteration of the genes of modern dance and, in rarer cases, ballet.

Moon Water

The dance that inaugurated Cloud Gate's new body aesthetics and correlatively its new dance theatre aesthetics, drawing upon *Tai-chi Tao-yin*, is *Moon Water* (1998) choreographed to the music of J. S. Bach's *Suites for Solo Cello*. The choreography explores the principles of *yin* and *yang*, whereby the essence of nature is encapsulated in a highly calculated artistic creation, which aspires to delivering an intense experience of aesthetic beauty. In the video version of *Moon Water* published in 2002, the dancers calmly hold the energy or *chi* at the centre of their bodies while keeping their limbs in a supple state. Their spiralling gestures and movements, initiated in the lower abdomen (*tan-tien*), are never fully outstretched and always return to the centre with retrieving energy. The water-like fluid quality of the movement creates a breathing kinesphere around the dancers' bodies and sends the energy through their extremities into the surrounding space, a simple black stage with a few cursive white strokes brushed on the floor echoing the circular path of the dancers' movement and flow of *chi*.

An abstract dance without characters and story lines, *Moon Water* is a study about the passage of time, or the course of nature, demonstrated through the ways dancers enter and exit as well as in the inter-relationship between them in space. In the second act of the dance, a woman (Chen Ch'iu-yin) slowly walks in to join a man (Wang Wei-ming) onstage to begin a duet. At the first note of 'Sarabande' from *Suite No. 2*, the dancers, facing each other and standing far apart, sink their knees gently at the same moment before rising up to draw their arms apart with a slightly raised leg as counterpoint. As if mirroring each other, they repeat the movements again in the opposite direction before diverging into different motions. There are only rare moments like these in the duet when the dancers perform the same gestures. Yet the man and woman, who are never in direct physical or eye contact with each other, perform a partnership of deep resonance. Riding on the flow of the cello music, they are perfectly in tune with each other in their prolonged unhurried rhythm of breathing and in the push and pull of their gestures that form delicate counterpoints in time and space. Performing strings of different movements, they coincide sporadically in a sinking posture, in a spiralling turn that ends a movement phrase, or in an emphatic stroke of their lyrical arms, all of which are merged seamlessly with the unusually long breathing flow of Mischa Maisky's interpretation of Bach's score. As the duet proceeds, a story of encountering seems to be unfolded – an encountering between a man and a woman, between two forces in nature, or perhaps between two planets in the lonely universe.

While the couple is still onstage, a group of dancers enter with flowing *Tai-chi* gestures like a cloud drifting into the stage landscape. After the man has departed, the woman lingers for a short while to interact with the group, a transitional passage bridging the two episodes. After the group moves slowly to centre stage, another woman and man (Wen Ching-ching and Bulareyaung) break away by emerging with higher bodily posture from the ensemble, who pose in a prolonged deep squat following a slow swaying of the bodies in unison. In contrast to the meditative mood of the music so far, the new duet is danced to the lively tune of 'Prelude' from *Suite No. 5*. Full of spiralling turns, brisk falls and rises, and sweeping gestures of arms and legs, the duet offers an interesting comparison to that in the second act. While it retains the principle of having both forceful and retrieving energy in both the female and male dancers, this pair of equal partners seems to present an unusual performance of femininity and masculinity. The movement quality of the female dancer is more grounded and solid while the man is aerial and lyrical. Drawing upon the nature of the two dancers' bodily texture, the duet resists the conventional gender dichotomy seen in modern dance and ballet.

After a powerful leap and a few rapid twirls by the woman, the couple merges back into the group. As they become one again with the ensemble, they are subsumed not just into the unison gestures but more importantly into the breathing rhythm of the larger body, a choreographed 'natural' transit which reminds one of meeting clouds or merging streams. Throughout the energetic duet, the group maintains a steady flow of *Tai-chi* movements and energy in the background, as if embodying the unmoved and ever-ongoing passage of time. The breaking away and re-merging of the dancers can be read as a study of the course of nature, the conglomeration and dispersion of elements such as air or water, which form the transformative nature of the universe.

In *Moon Water*, a profound intercultural exchange took place in the Cloud Gate dancers' bodies, and as a result modern dance, the West-originated dance genre, underwent a unique and highly original evolution, a journey that continues in *The Cursive Trilogy* and Cloud Gate's later works. Being extensively trained in modern dance, especially the Graham technique, the Cloud Gate dancers are familiar with expressing emotions and symbolic meanings with their torsos. This expressive capability adds the desired performative effect to the originally neutral expression of the *Tai-chi Tao-yin*-derived vocabulary in *Moon Water*. Conversely, the intricate circular course of movement, permeated with the flow of *chi*, opens up an enormous space within the dancers' bodies – the somatic space for more refined and more protean bodily expression as well as the mental space for performing the interior landscape of spirituality on stage.

Through the emphasis on the rhythm of breathing, the intricate cursive pattern of all movements, as well as the often-meditative pace of the episodes, *Moon Water* highlights the process and transformative nature of things, an effect reinforced by the unusually slow and highly personal interpretation of Bach's score by Maisky. The last act of the dance begins with a line of female dancers entering one after another from stage left and exiting at the other end, as if a long scroll of painting slowly unfolded to the audience. At this moment, water seeps imperceptibly onto the stage, gradually transforming the floor into a mirror reflecting the image of the dancing figures. The multiple reflections created by the water and several mirror panels hung at different angles on the backdrop result in many layers of space, both real and illusionary, echoing the Buddhist verse of 'a thousand moons reflected in the water of a thousand streams', a phrase about the relationship between one and many, between essence and appearance.[8]

The Cursive Trilogy

While *Moon Water* is a philosophical meditation on *time* through space, *The Cursive Trilogy* (2001, 2003, 2005), a series of three evening-length dances inspired by Chinese calligraphy, is an aesthetic and spiritual exploration of *space* through the dancers' bodies and other theatrical means, including sound, lighting and stage design. 'I have harboured the thought of dancing calligraphy since the 1970s. Now we found *chi*, so we do it', said Lin (Lin Hwai-min 2003). After *Moon Water*, Lin knew that the Cloud Gate dancers were ready to take the challenge, not to imitate the exterior shapes of the strokes and lines of calligraphy but to capture the aesthetic essence and life energy of this ancient art form.

In order to prepare his dancers for this challenge, Lin invited martial arts master Hsu Chi to train them in various Chinese martial arts forms. While *Tai-chi Tao-yin* emphasises 'thorough flexibility' in the body through deep spiralling movement and the cultivation of *chi*, martial arts aim at the perfect control of energy as well as the efficient coordination of different body parts through enhancing the power and stability of *hsia-pan*,[9] thus bringing about rich variations and precise execution of all movements in speed and strength. The stronger dynamics of martial arts complements perfectly the softer tone of *Tai-chi Tao-yin*, endowing the dancers' bodies with an exceptionally protean ability capable of strong dramatic attacks on the one hand and fluid lyrical expression on the other. In addition, Lin also invited scholars in Taoist philosophy and Chinese aesthetics to nourish the dancers' understanding of the artistic value, history and spirituality of calligraphy. Then beginning in 2001, the dancers started regular calligraphy classes with Huang Wei-chung, a Chinese arts scholar and calligrapher, to experience physically the intricate control of *chi* and the rhythm of breathing in the process of manipulating the writing brush.

After these bodily, intellectual and philosophical preparations, Lin asked the dancers to improvise in front of the enlarged projection of characters written by calligraphy masters from various Chinese dynasties, a method not unlike the first step taken by neophytes in calligraphy training called *ling-muo*. The process was composed of carefully designed progressive stages prescribed by Lin. At first, the dancers could only use their torsos to imitate the brush strokes. This was to train the core of the body in the coordination between neck, spine and *tan-tien* as well as in the deftness of controlling *chi* and weight shifting. In the second stage, they were allowed to use the limbs but with a high awareness that all movements need to come from the core of the body. Only in the third stage were they given the liberty to incorporate bigger locomotion to interpret strings of different characters. The strict prescription of these measures was to ensure the freedom that comes at the end when the dancers go beyond the exterior form of the written characters by embodying the rhythm of breathing, in other words the 'vibration of *chi*', embedded in the shades and lines of the brush strokes (Tsou Chi-mu 2004: 156). In Lin's words, it was 'to absorb the energy in the [calligraphy] masterpieces and to re-create [from] them' (Lin Hwai-min 2006).

This evolutionary training and choreographic process is captured in the second act of *Cursive I*. In front of a white screen, a woman (Chou Chang-ning), dressed in black sleeveless top and trousers, traces the strokes of the character '*yung*' (forever) with her limbs and torso, each gesture clearly synchronised with the ordered appearance of the strokes in the style of *kai-shu* (standard script) on the screen.[10] After repeating the same series of movements at a faster pace, she proceeds to interpret the same character in the cursive style (*hsing-ts'ao*), which replaces the previous projection on the screen, with freer flow of bodily motions. Forsaking the imitation of the lines, the dancer enacts the breathing flow, the transition of energy, and the punctuation of weight inscribed in the brush strokes. Finally, as if to outdo the explosion of energy in the twirling black ink written in the wild cursive style (*kuang-ts'ao*) fading in at the end, she wheels her arms rapidly and then waves them with absolute fluidity in all directions like a pair of serpentine whips full of undulating rhythm and energy. The powerful strength of her grounded *hsia-pan* endows her whole body with enormous freedom and fluidity.This is the only scene in the dance where the relation between dancer's movement and specific calligraphic characters is decipherable. Like the cursive style, which frees calligraphy from the linguistic meanings and prescribed strokes of the Chinese characters, the Cloud Gate dancers also seek the liberty of artistic creation by going beyond the lines and shapes of the written scripts while echoing the beauty and spirit of the masterpieces.

In *The Cursive Trilogy*, a peculiar concept of 'space' is evolving in the Cloud Gate choreography, which encompasses several layers and aspects of performance: the interior and exterior space of the dancer's body, the space created by sound as an environment for dance, the space of the stage as a field of *chi* or energy, and the spiritual space created by the dancer's intense body–mind concentration. The awareness of space is first brought to the attention of the audience in *Cursive I* by the visual design of rectangles of light projected on the floor. Giving form to the invisible and intangible space, their shape and colour remind one of scrolls of rice paper while the dancing figures are like calligraphy inscribed on them. The images of masterpieces appearing on the stage backdrop in various scenes, against which the dancers perform, further enhance this understanding. Often partially selected and being blown up to enormous size, these cursive writings, rather than conveying the meanings of words, are actually a display of the lively interplay between the black ink and white space in calligraphy.

The concept of space is further enriched in *Cursive II* choreographed to the music of John Cage. Instead of the motif of black and white in *Cursive I*, the follow-up choreography is dominated by the colour white, especially the enormous white floor on the stage and the flowing white trousers of the female dancers. Compared to the more forceful and solid movement quality in *Cursive I*, evidence of heavy influence from martial arts, the bodily texture in *Cursive II* is more airy, serene and meditative. One characterising feature is that, after each exertion of force, there is often a sudden softening in the movement flow with long slow drawing of bodily gestures full of retrieving energy. The emphasis is obviously on the quieter movements and lingering breath, which feed into the emergence of another exertion of force leading into a new cycle of movement.

For all the three dances in the trilogy, Lin chose music that is non-melodic, composed of sounds and silence. Commenting on the music of John Cage, Lin said, 'There's always a great sense of immense space and flowing breath that goes on and on, layers after layers' (Lin Hwai-min 2006). The extremely long breath of the wind instruments in the Cage scores opens up temporal as well as mental space for the dancers while the sporadic poundings of the percussion create emphatic force that resonates with the punctuating energy in the dancers' movement flow.

The last chapter of *The Cursive Trilogy*, *Wild Cursive* is a celebration of nature and spontaneity. The humming of summer cicadas, gusts of wind, waves breaking on a pebbled beach, the sound of dripping water and foghorns are interwoven into the choreographic soundscape against which the dancers' rhythmic breathing, forceful foot stamps and occasional vocal exertions are effectively accentuated.

Scrolls of metre-wide white paper banners are alternately lowered or raised during the performance. Streams of black ink that drip from invisible pipes above seep onto the paper and create calligraphic patterns at an imperceptible speed, resulting in 'installations in progress' that differ each night. With the illumination of the lighting design, the white paper scrolls conceal or reveal dancers, adding layers of spatial dimension to the stage environment.

Yet the true magic belongs to the dancers. After years of immersion in the Chinese body–mind disciplines, the Cloud Gate dancers have acquired incomparable flexibility and strength in their bodies, which gives tremendous freedom in the execution of all movements. With the weight of their bodies firmly grounded, their limbs and torsos dance at extremely fast speed – spiralling, twisting and turning as if flying off into all directions and yet with perfect control. The richness in energy variations and the ever-evolving shapes of the gestures constitute an amazing feast for the eye and the kinaesthetic sense. This untamed and vibrant energy, which breaks the rules of all dance vocabularies and yet adheres to the essentials of truly organic movement, captures brilliantly the spirit of *kuang-ts'ao*, the wild calligraphy, which inspires the choreography.

Formulating an Asian modernism

The exploration of the concept of space in *Moon Water* and *The Cursive Trilogy* brings into relief the more non-material and seemingly more passive elements of the dances, for instance the empty space between dancers, the silence or quiet moments in the music score, the meditative mode of dancing, the stillness of the body between bursts of action, among others. In other words, it connotes the force of *yin* in the Taoist philosophy – the more subdued yet more resilient energy in the universe – which acts as the counterpart of the more aggressive force of *yang*. Lin's recent choreographies have been interrogations of these two fundamental forces.

Chinese literary scholar Tseng Tsu-yin, in his book *The Fields of Ancient Chinese Aesthetics*, discusses the relation between *hsu* (immateriality) and *shi* (materiality), the aesthetic counterpart of the philosophical dyad of *yin* and *yang*, as one of the primary principles of Chinese aesthetics. Though emphasising the importance of basing artistic creation in reality – *shi* – Chinese arts valorises the ability to transform and transcend the reality to achieve more abstract and non-material expression – *hsu* – for instance, the emotions or intricate mental states evoked by descriptions of natural phenomena in poetry or the empty space (*liu-pai*) in Chinese landscape painting which stands for the sky, mist or stream in the scenery. It is *hsu* which inspires the spectator's imagination and shows off the artist's aesthetic sophistication and spiritual aspiration. A truly successful work of art, according to Tseng, relies on the 'breathing reciprocity' (*hu-hsi chao-ying*) between *hsu* and *shi*, and as a result a devotion to the 'aesthetics of space', physical, imaginary as well as spiritual space (Tseng 1987: 177–204).

Figure 21.1 Huang Pei-hua in *Wild Cursive* (2005), Cloud Gate Dance Theatre. Photograph by Lin Ching-yuan.

While echoing the essential aesthetics of traditional Chinese high arts, the concept of space explored in *Moon Water* and *The Cursive Trilogy* also enriches the modernist sensibility characterising Cloud Gate's recent work. The rectangles of light projected on the floor in *Cursive I*, besides alluding to scrolls of rice paper, correspond to the simplistic formalism of minimal art. The correspondence is further enhanced by the motif of black and white in the dance. The backdrop of blown-up images of ice-crackles on porcelain from the Sung Dynasty in *Cursive II*, while highlighting the aesthetics of *tan* (*forte* white) found in Chinese painting and calligraphy,[11] also suggests an abstract beauty similar to that in modernist art such as abstract expressionism.

The valorisation of the aesthetics of *hsu* as well as the interrogation of the abstract forces of *yin* and *yang* in Cloud Gate's recent work find a congruent partnership with modernism's anti-representational proclivity. Though sharing the same vigorousness in the modernist inquiry into the essential nature of the arts and the enthusiasm for innovating formal languages, Cloud Gate's dances go beyond the modernist tenet of 'form is content' by always referring to something beyond the materiality of the body and stage effects – that is the spiritual-mental space created by the dancers' bodies and all the theatrical means. Furthermore, unlike Western modernism's rejection of tradition, Cloud Gate's version of modernist creation attempts to come to terms with history, to 'systematically link present action with a meaningful past and endow [the] particular cultural form with value and authority', to borrow dance anthropologist Brenda Farnell's argument about the transformation of indigenous peoples' dance in various colonial/post-colonial contexts (Farnell 2008: 159).

On the one hand, the vibrant spirituality and the historical connection with ancient Chinese aesthetics endow the Cloud Gate repertoire with an unquestionable Asian identity; on the other, it also enjoys the benefit of 'universalism' associated with modernist art, especially with regards to abstract expression. This particular combination of uniqueness and universality situates Cloud Gate strategically in the global dance market, which incessantly seeks new experience within a certain limit of familiarity. Yet this high art aesthetics, derived from both Chinese and Western arts traditions, though perfectly suiting the taste of international critics, may present a new challenge for Cloud Gate domestically – an increased detachment from the issues of the Taiwan society, which were once crucial elements in the company's earlier work. This dynamic and uneasy tension between the company's globalised Asian modernism and the specific local communication desired by some of its audience at home deserves further interrogation in future studies on Cloud Gate.

Notes

1 Though this Chinese theatre has been known as *jingju* on mainland China after the Communist revolution, it was called Peking Opera (*ping-chu*) in Taiwan until the 1990s. The Peking Opera in Taiwan before the 1980s was considered more conservative in terms of performance style and stage setting when compared to its counterpart in China. This is because Peking Opera's status as *guo-chu* (*the* national theatre) in Taiwan, and its adherence to tradition was essential to the KMT's claim of cultural 'authenticity'. To maintain this distinction, I use the term 'Peking Opera' here.

2 Beginning in the 1970s, there emerged in Taiwan society a wave of nativist consciousness, which emphasised a strong connection with the land and culture of Taiwan, as a counter-force against the Sinocentric policy implemented by the KMT government on the island since the end of the Second World War.

3 In 1971, the Republic of China on Taiwan was forced to give up its China seat in the UN to the People's Republic of China on the mainland, which was followed by the severance of diplomatic ties with many countries around the world. The biggest blow came in 1978 when the US terminated formal diplomatic ties with the ROC and normalised its relations with the PRC.

4 For more discussion on the phenomenon of *minzu wudao*, see Chen Ya-ping's 'Dancing Chinese Nationalism and Anti-Communism: *Minzu Wudao* Movement in 1950s Taiwan' (2008).

5 The 'Eastern body aesthetic dance' deliberately rejected Western-originated modern dance techniques and resorted to Eastern body–mind teachings such as meditation, yoga and *tai-chi* for inspiration. It was also deeply inspired by the Japanese avant-garde dance *Butoh* spiritually if not aesthetically or technically. For more discussion on this phenomenon, see the chapter 'Claiming of Difference: the Aesthetics and Politics of Eastern Body Aesthetic Dances, 1987–1997' in Chen Ya-ping's 'Dance History and Cultural Politics' (2003).

6 The concept of 'authorship' and its relation to 'authenticity' as used here is inspired by Brenda Farnell's 'Indigenous Dances on Stage – Embodied Knowledge at Risk?' (2008).

7 The nine joints include three joints in the arm (shoulder, elbow and wrist), three joints in the torso (lower spine, upper spine and neck), and three joints in the leg (crotch, knee and ankle) (Hsiung 2002: 3).

8 The thousand moons in the thousand streams are in fact the reflections of one moon in the sky.

9 *Hsia-pan* includes the lower torso, hips and legs. The training in the strength and stability of *hsia-pan* is the foundation of all Chinese martial arts.

10 The Chinese character '*yung*' is the first word every calligraphy student begins his/her lesson with, since it contains the eight typical strokes of calligraphy writing. *Kai-shu* is the standard script of calligraphy, and is the style beginners often take on in learning the art.

11 There are five shades of ink in calligraphy and traditional Chinese painting, *hei*, *nong*, *shi*, *kan* and *tan*, which can be roughly translated as blackness, heaviness, wetness, dryness and *forte* white (Tseng 1987: 195).

References

Chinese

Chen, Kuan-hsing. (2006) *Towards De-Imperialization: Asia as Method*, Taipei: Hsing-ren Publishers.

Hsiung, Wei (2002) *Tai-chi Tao-yin*, Taipei: The United Daily Press.

Lin, Hwai-min, Hsu Kai-chen and Chi Hui-ling (1993) *On Nine Songs*, Taipei: Min-sheng News Press.

Tseng, Tsu-yin (1987) *The Fields of Ancient Chinese Aesthetics*, Taipei: Tan-ching Publishers.

Tsou, Chi-mu (2004) 'Aesthetics in the White Cosmos – *Cursive I*', in *Legend: Masterpieces of Lin Hwai-min*, Taipei: The Cloud Gate Foundation.

English

Bhabha, H. K. (1994) *The Location of Culture*, London and New York: Routledge.

Calinescu, M. (2003 [1987]) *Five Faces of Modernity*, Durham: Duke University Press.

Chen, Ya-ping (2003) Dance History and Cultural Politics: a Study of Contemporary Dance in Taiwan, 1930s–1997, unpublished dissertation. New York University.

—— (2008) 'Dancing Chinese Nationalism and Anti-Communism: *Minzu Wudao* Movement in 1950s Taiwan', in N. Jackson and T. S. Phim (eds) *Dance, Human Rights and Social Justice: Dignity in Motion*, Lanham, MD: Scarecrow Press.

Farnell, B. (2008) 'Indigenous Dances on Stage – Embodied Knowledge at Risk?', in *Taiwan Dance Research Journal*, 4: 151–80.

Lin, Hwai-min (2006) 'Dragon Flying and Phoenix Dancing' (television essay), *Cursive II DVD*, East Sussex, UK: Opus Arte.

Lin, Yatin (2001) 'Dancing in the Age of Globalization – Cloud Gate Dance Theatre and the Political Economy of Touring', in *Dance Studies and Taiwan: the Prospect of a New Generation*, Taipei: the CKS Cultural Centre.

Prevots, N. (1998) *Dance for Export: Cultural Diplomacy and the Cold War*, Hanover and London: Wesleyan University Press.

Videography

Moon Water (2002) Directed by Ross MacGibbon, Well Go USA, Inc.

Cursive I (2003) Directed by Chang Chao-tang, Taipei: Jingo Records.

Cursive II (2006) Directed by Ross MacGibbon, East Sussex, UK: Opus Arte.

Wild Cursive, unpublished video recording provided by the Cloud Gate Dance Theatre.

22 Seeing the body move

Choreographic investigations of kinaesthetics at the end of the twentieth century

Jeroen Fabius

> From the speakers explode, 'It's real. It's a game.' Everything is both too much and without any further use or application. Not body language, but body sensation is the focus, for the dancer as much as the spectator. ... Traditionally distanced spectators are converted into virtually-wired sensors, plug-ins to the mise en scene: the public experiences rather than watching *decreation*. ... Instead of begetting a performance, the public lives it, through 'skin, brain and hair'.[1]
>
> (Boenisch 2004: 59)

As staged within Western theatre dance, dance, the art of the moving body, is made to be seen. The contradiction here lies in the fact that dance is created through the experiences of moving bodies while primarily accessed visually by its spectators. In the above quotation from Peter Boenisch, writing about *decreation* (2003) by the William Forsythe company, a bodily experience is described that is not just for the dancers, but for the spectators; not just for the eyes, but for the entire body. How do spectators gain information about movements done by other people, and how does this information give rise to kinaesthetic experience? Kinaesthesia, introduced by Bastian in 1888 (from *kinesis*, Greek for motion and *aisthesis*, for sensation), is defined as the ability to feel movements of the limbs and body (Longstaff 1996: 34). Choreography has specialised both in training dancers to develop kinaesthetic expertise and in creating formats for spectators to access particular fields of movement experience. In this chapter, I analyse the work of three late twentieth-century choreographers, namely Boris Charmatz, Meg Stuart and William Forsythe, whose preoccupation with kinaesthetics has altered ways of seeing dance.

I propose that their preoccupation with the sense experience of the moving body has led to new strategies for choreography, challenging the dominance of visuality in the aesthetics of dance. Their work has been described as obstructionist, reductionist and concerned with an aesthetics of disappearance. Rather than engaging with the entire historical development of the role of kinaesthetics in the twentieth-century dance, I discuss a work from each choreographer in order to illuminate their respective approaches to kinaesthetically-based choreography. In these three cases, I focus on kinaesthetics as: (1) the subject matter of the performance; (2) a mode of presentation; (3) a principle of choreographic organisation. This allows me to delve into the overall trends and to think about kinaesthetics in relation to choreographic analysis.

Boris Charmatz: obstructing vision

Boris Charmatz is a prolific dance maker. The works he has made since the early 1990s with Association Edna (Paris) span a wide range of media and collaborations; he has made films, installations, lectures, and even, in *Bocal* (2003), a school as an art project, as well as many combinations of dance with film, video and sculpture. He actively explores the engagement of the sentient and sensual body with the world around it; all his pieces reveal an interest in exploring questions of modes of perception and questions of embodiment. In *Entretenir* written with Isabelle Launay in 2003, he reflects on a broad spectrum of issues in relation to a contemporary dance practice, including his own development as an artist. In his description of his own works it becomes clear how strong his focus is on the body as a central vehicle in the art of dance, and that he proposes an arts practice that stimulates criticism of its own means (Charmatz and Launay 2003: 54). This critical approach leads him to question the modes of perception found in the theatre, and to present the spectator with perception as the central concept of performance.

How is it possible to present perception as subject of the performance? In the two Boris Charmatz productions discussed below, questions of perception are the starting point of the choreography, presented so as to make the spectator aware of and to reflect on how perception occurs. *La Chaise* (2002) does this through obstructed vision. One person is seated in front of the audience, blindfolded, while another person dances for this person. Even though vision is denied, it is immediately clear that the blindfolded person nevertheless perceives the dance. The watching audience is challenged to consider what is possibly being imagined by the seated person, and to explore how the perception of dance cannot be reduced to its visual properties. Jeroen Peeters (2004) speaks of mental reconstruction: we have both direct and indirect access, first by seeing the dancer ourselves and second through the blindfolded person. The piece 'deconstructs the visual regime, also provides an alternative space in which the mental theatre is addressed through a physical theatre … the gaze is confronted with a complex internal sensoriness' (Peeters 2004: 5). We are thus made aware that the process of perception, in this case visual, functions within a web of interconnected systems. While watching this dance it becomes possible to infer the various ways that the blindfolded person perceives the dance: through sound, touch, by the air that is moving along the dancing body and perhaps lifting the hair of the sitting person. We can say that Charmatz makes the seeing spectator conceptually explore these aspects of perception.

Con forts fleuve (1999) is conceptually not as transparent as *La Chaise*, but its aims are similar. Both the stage and seating are kept half-empty so that the audience is sitting only in the right half of the theatre. A dancer comes in from the outside, from the back of the seating area, and descends through the unused seats to the stage. Carefully he climbs over each row of the empty chairs to join the other performers on the dimly lit stage. They wear clothes, jeans, on their heads, thus rendering the dancers anonymous, a crowd of bodies within which it is hard to identify personalities. The scene creates associations with violence (they could be terrorists), or fools (stumbling around, blundering about the stage). There is no moment of revelation during the piece, nothing to soothe the audience into feeling that normality will prevail. It is an ongoing game to speculate about the identities of the figures, there are no conventional codes provided. Performers seem lost in space and time, shaking and disorganised, crawling at one point over one another like worms in a tin can, at other moments roaming about the stage without any sense of direction. There are unpredictable dynamics, no transitions. The obscure, barely lit stage and the covered bodies all contribute to the creation of obstacles, to the identification of what is going on. A big blanket falls down from the ceiling, the dancers wear pants over their heads; there is a reversal of what is up and what is down. Lacking conventions with which to understand this performance, the basic sensory information has to be called upon in order to understand what is going on. Charmatz calls this a 'mistreatment' of the theatre (Charmatz and Launay 2003: 25). All the normal perspectives of seeing theatre are purposely abused, creating spatial disorientation and the consistently anonymous performers.

The obstacle of readability is explicitly formulated by Charmatz as 'I want to put into peril the readability of the writing, the clarity of the exchange' (2003: 42). The covered figures force the dancing body to be oriented toward listening, and re- or disorientate the gaze of the spectator. Charmatz goes even further by assigning one of the dancers to improvise in order to mess up the mechanism: two figurants, who do not know the piece, are there to hinder the whole event. All these elements complicate the audience's ability to interpret. The audience has to decide what to do with the inhibited perception of the bodies, how they are lost in space and time, shaking and disorganised. In this purposeful chaos, Charmatz defines presence as 'a heterogeneous collection of projections, internal fictions, decompositions, imaginary reconstructions, both on the side of the dancer as well as the spectator' (2003: 31). Through all these obstacles the spectator becomes aware of the flux of multiple perspectives in perception of the performance, an awareness that is intensified because any externally referenced orientation by the dancers is drastically hindered, first by the clothes and later by the blanket that covers their eyes. This orients the performers toward feeling, self-reference and body

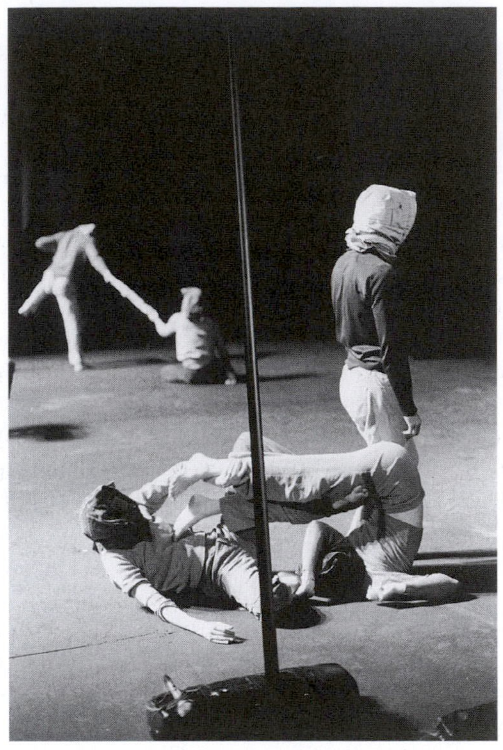

Figure 22.1 Con forts fleuve (1999) Boris Charmatz. Photo: Laurent Philippe.

part displacements, all of which affect the gaze of the spectator. Charmatz confirms that for him the piece presents questions about perception:

> This performance poses the central question of the body, precisely because one can hardly see it. The problem is not of the order of visibility but consists in knowing what the body is doing underneath these rags.
>
> (Steinmetz 2002, translation by the author)

What the body is doing under the rags the spectator can only speculate. But what is clear is that whatever movements the dancers are making, the movements are not made for visual perception by either the dancers or their public. Movement quality is determined by the physical conditions. What then is kinaesthesia? Earlier, kinaesthesia was defined simply as the experience of movement of the body. Kinaesthetic experience itself is not a singular event, but is composed of information derived from many bodily sources. Kinaesthesia is also called proprioception, the perception of one's body, in motion, according to Longstaff:

> Kinaesthesia is identified as arising from sensory stimulations via receptors in muscles, tendons, joints, skin, vestibular apparatus, eyes, ears, and also from an interior knowledge of motor commands (efferent data). This assortment of stimulation from throughout the body is derived into perceptions of balance and equilibrium, self-motion, limb-motion, limb position, and force or exertion.
>
> (Longstaff 1996: 42)

This extensive list makes clear that, as was proposed by *La Chaise*, perception is not a singular matter and kinaesthesia even less so.[2] This may account for why discussion of the term is a relatively recent matter, the term dates only from the 1880s. Longstaff suggests that that is why Aristotle, for example, only mentions five senses, omitting kinaesthesia (1996: 34).

As the darkness obscures detail, and makes it hard to distinguish the bodies in their mingling, we are invited to imagine what the body is doing under the clothes. Then the *imagined* sensation of movement, kinaesthesia, is stimulated. The re- and disorientating strategies of *Con forts fleuve* propose a non-visual sensation of space, one that privileges proprioception. The bodies do not travel to landmarks according to pre-established visually recognisable patterns, discernible by the spectator. All that is seen is the messy displacement of body parts, leading to no apparent conclusion. The scene demonstrates how proprioception contributes to human movement. Proprioception is a self-referential sense, egocentric, related to the body itself, whereas vision is an external referential sense that produces allocentric cognitive maps to support spatial orientation. Spatial orientation through proprioception works through a continual succession of information about displacement of body parts in relation to each other. Massumi proposes that proprioception presents an experience of space that is not in accordance with the Euclidean parameters of height, depth and width but instead through trajectories made up from individual displacements of the parts of the body (Massumi 2002: 179; see also Berthoz 2000: 110). Thus, it allows a process-based and dynamic sensation of space. Charmatz has strengthened this impression by reversing the spectator's associations of 'top' and 'bottom'.

These two works by Charmatz present perception as the subject matter of performance. The works engage the spectator in such speculation through a negative procedure of obstruction. In *La Chaise,* the obstruction of vision leads to consideration of the interconnectedness of the various senses. In *Con forts fleuve,* obstruction of the dancers' vision makes apparent to spectators how other senses are at work as the performers orientate themselves in space, and how proprioception, as part of kinaesthesia, creates a different sense of dynamic space rather than reliance on vision as the central organising sense.

Meg Stuart: reduction

The question that was raised with reference to Boenisch, of how the sensation of movement in others is perceived by a spectator, still remains to be answered. Meg Stuart uses reduction of choreographic information to create a microscopic effect: bodily movement is perceived through the reduction of movement to create a perspective on bodily movement that is *not* illusive, artificial, a product of choreographic design. This microscopy is achieved by using nearly still bodies, minimal movements, and exposing both personal and bodily experience, all characteristics of the work she has been making (mainly in Europe) since the early 1990s, after working with Randy Warshaw. 'The whole process was to do with elimination and [with] coming to terms with the fact that there really could not be this "*dancey*" part' (Stuart 1993: 10). What motivates her is the idea of exposure of the body in front of a live audience:

> Dance, by its very nature, is an exposure of the body, and this is why theatre, as one of the few places where people collectively experience a physical event, can only become more extreme.
>
> (Stuart in van Imschoot 1997: 24)

The body has become a central concern in her work, giving kinaesthetics, or the movement experiences of the body, a central place in her aesthetics. 'I always start from the body. But I put it into situations that imply a problem, that squeeze and constrict, that I investigate for their potential as physical narrative' (1996: 26). She calls this method 'asking questions in action'; by putting the body in impossible situations, the narrative possibility is induced by solutions that are not conceptually conceived but emerge from the physical action, 'There is always this task, this intention, this "*have to*" and then the body moves ... you just do' (Stuart 1993: 9 and further). That 'just doing' is an indicator for a kinaesthetic approach, and thus information will be derived from the doing, not an a priori conceptual or thematic decision. Rather than producing particular gestures or vocabularies, she is looking for uncontrolled, or involuntary, movement: 'I am fascinated by involuntary movements and what I call "*physical states*" or "*emotional states*" in the body'. By speaking of *states* it is clear that in Stuart's work the visual is informed by something physical rather than by a projection of gestures.

Indeed, Stuart infuses the visual with the kinaesthetic. In the last scene of *Splayed Mind Out* (1998), dancer Christine De Smedt repeats a short movement phrase over and over. In the phrase, she draws lines with her fingers on her body and from her body to the floor (on which she stands) and back onto her body again. The active finger is the sentient finger, perceiving the different textures and warmth of the surfaces it travels and also objectifying what is being touched, both body and floor. It thus unites the body with its surroundings; all are part of the perceived world.

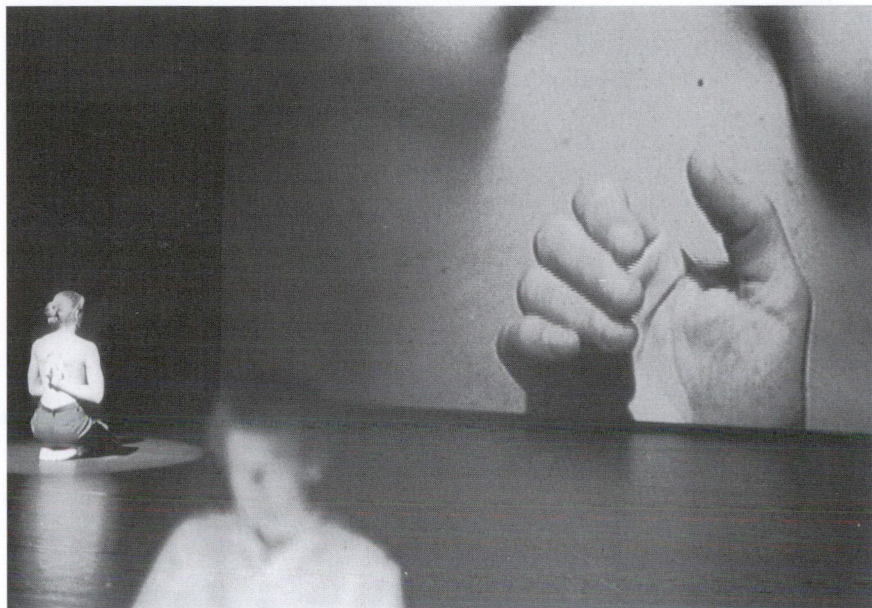

Figure 22.2 Splayed Mind Out (1998) Meg Stuart. Photo: Chris van der Burght.

Repetition of this movement strengthens this impression. In the observation of the choreography, a sense of synaesthesia is generated, and the audience is pulled into the tactile sensation of the hand touching, as if the eyes take over the function of the hand. The visual here aims to give us access to physical sensation, a kind of haptic aesthetics.

Haptic vision is a notion that Deleuze (2003) introduces in his book on Francis Bacon. Although Deleuze speaks of painting, his discussion is relevant here as he asks how to render the non-visible visible, that is, how to render sensate forces that are not themselves sensate. Deleuze speaks of haptic vision in relation to Bacon's use of colours, which creates an optical space that maintains virtual referents to tactility. It is a kind of seeing distinct from the optical, a close-up viewing in which 'the sense of sight behaves just like the sense of touch' (Smith, 2003: ix). The effect of close-up viewing is not very different from what André Lepecki (2000) calls the microscopic, that is, how Stuart makes the spectator look at minute movement in the body, vibrations rather than movement.

The microscopic effect has been achieved by Stuart through 'dance with unmoved bodies' (Husemann 2002: 33). This is a transgression of conventions of dance making and the idea of dance vocabulary. The bodies come to near stillness, which is, she says, 'not frozen, it's liminal. Liminal is when something is becoming but not quite becoming' (Husemann 2002:

34). The stillness is still charged with dynamic; there is virtual movement, which is not yet happening, but felt. Stuart speaks about a way of stretching time which results in the creation of 'over-time'. By slowing down the actions of the dancers, the spectator is given more time to see:

> You see beyond the first and then you are forced to see more in multiplicity, more than form, image, and more than one relationship. You start to have association beyond.
>
> (Husemann 2002: 61)

The stillness allows for associations beyond immediate perception, that is, how it mobilises virtual meanings of the event. Stillness also allows for the perception of physiological processes in the body, breath, heartbeat, or reflexes such as the blinking of the eye. But the concept of haptic vision does not entirely account for the perception of these events. Although touch is a component of the sense perception of kinaesthesia, it does not equate entirely to kinaesthesia.

So the question still stands, how are kinaesthetic experiences perceived by the observer? And can these observations give rise to kinaesthetic experiences in the spectator? Susan Leigh Foster (1998) has traced the genealogy of what she calls 'kinaesthetic empathy'. In early dance literature John Martin, advocate of the beginnings of Modern Dance in the 1930s, gave the most outspoken reference, speaking about 'inner mimicry', a capacity to mime muscular action, intrinsically intertwined with emotion:

> We shall cease to be mere spectators and become participants in the movement that is presented to us, and through all outward appearances we shall be sitting quietly in our chairs, we shall nevertheless be dancing synthetically with all our musculature.
>
> (Martin 1968: 53)

From recent fMRI research, it has been shown that 'spectators can internally simulate movement sensations of speed, effort, and changing body configuration' (Hagendoorn 2004: 3). So rather than think of the spectator as passive, 'spectating' on a cognitive level, perception in general is extremely active. Alain Berthoz is at pains to state that the sense of movement is constructed; before we become aware, the body is busy making movement *and* the perception of the movement. He calls perception 'simulated action' (2000: 9). If the perception of our own movement is constructed and it anticipates our conscious awareness, then perhaps that will be the case with perception of movement of others as well. Thus, Martin's text originally written in the 1930s has received strong resonance in recent neuroscientific literature.

Susan Leigh Foster and others argue however, that Martin's idea of the spontaneous and mechanical connection is problematic, and poses a rather simplistic universalism (1998: 248; Franko 2002: 116; Bleeker 2002: 156). Foster traces kinaesthetic empathy back to conceptualisations of sympathy in the writing of Adam Smith, which was connected to moral considerations in observing movement of other people. She proposes viewing kinaesthetic empathy from a political point of view: 'bodies must assess how they are connecting one with another as well as what they are feeling from that connection' (1998: 255).

Dee Reynolds (2007) attempts to sort out the connections between the physiological and neurological on the one hand, the unconscious anticipation of movement, and the social and political question of relation on the other hand. She relates thinking of the virtual to the concept of kinaesthetic imagination. Even though dancers probably develop greater sensitivity in observing movement in others, it is not necessary to have experienced the movement one perceives others doing. Reynolds states that 'acts of kinaesthetic imagination comprise both virtual, imagined movements and innovative effort actions that transform uses of energy' (2007: 188). In this way, she addresses both the active construction of perception and the problem of the mechanical connection objected to by Foster and others.

In the case of Meg Stuart's work, this debate comes to light in her approach to the mode of performing. The instruction to the dancer is to forget about projection and the distance between performer and spectator, and to concentrate on the dynamics of being seen. This increases the tension between the body's visual aspects, between posing and exposure and the intimacy of the live performance in front of the audience. The dancer is in command but at the same time allows us a more than normal view of his or her body in positions that are not everyday and often uncomfortable (Laermans 1995: 56; Lepecki 2000: 362). The spectator has no choice but to keep looking at the slowly evolving actions, and cannot avoid seeing different possible readings of the event. The work therefore does not propose linear narratives, but rather associative readings. This can lead to misunderstandings about how the work should be read, as with *Disfigure Study* (1991), which was interpreted to be about AIDS, although this was not Stuart's intention (Stuart 1993: 11). The dance crossed over into that area, she says, via a physical task or problem of isolating body parts. Perhaps her approach can best be described as combining Elisabeth Grosz's concepts of 'inside out', where Stuart is looking for intense physical states, and 'outside in', by allowing the spectator to read all kinds of ways in which the body is inscribed by social and cultural contexts (Grosz 1997). Grosz's image of the Möbius strip to describe how these two movements move in and out of each other, intertwined in a dynamic relationship that contains no definitive caesuras, perhaps comes close to reflecting Stuart's work. The 'states' she is looking for are exactly on the edge between the consciously executed task and the physical (physiological) processes going on in the body (Grosz 1997: 209).

Meg Stuart starts from the body, the kinaesthetic experience, as she is interested in 'physical states'. This has led her to a process of elimination of physical activity to heighten kinaesthetic experience of the performer as well as intensity of the attention of the spectator. She provides a microscopic approach to theatre, a visuality that is infused with bodily sensation.

William Forsythe: aesthetic of disappearance

Forsythe's use of kinaesthetics has influenced his dances through the processes of choreographic production. The dancers' experiences of their moving bodies contribute to making of the choreography in real time, that is, according to improvised decision-making. Here I explore how the choreography of Forsythe presents kinaesthetics as a generative force, focusing on A L I E/N A(C)TION (1994).

After the first moments, calm is established. We see a black floor with white straight lines arranged in all kinds of diagonals, creating a dynamic multi-directionality. Along one of these diagonals, a woman is seated on a chair, next to a cupboard, and next to the cupboard, a dancer is moving. He gradually moves towards the centre of the space, focusing attention on his figure. His movements are composed of all kinds of swaying limbs. It seems he is repeating movements, but on closer inspection, he is not. Every time the timing is just a bit different; he might just step away from the diagonal a little further, or another little movement is inserted between one of the swinging limbs we recognise from a moment before. It is hard to tell whether his phrasing is starting over again, or whether he is floating with a kind of ebbing tide between the diagonal he came from to the centre of the space. The dynamic of the phrasing is unpredictable and there is no way of getting a sense of his trajectory; as spectators, we can only go with where he is and where he was.

The range of movement is not totally arbitrary, but seems to hover around particular options, avoiding others. It has to do with the particular dancer's body, his long arms and legs, his strong erect body that keeps shifting these swaying limbs forward and backward from the diagonal. At the same time, the woman on the stool is talking as if she is holding a telephone conversation, leaving gaps for the answers. Shifting attention back and forth between them, one loses track of where they were in their respective processes. The simple opposition of these two activities, the dancing figure and the talking figure, makes one aware that the sound of breathing does not come from her. As it follows the rhythm of the dancing, it is probably the dancer's breath. Then other dancers join in, and another voice joins the conversation, a process of accumulation happens in which, as Boenisch said in the opening quotation of this chapter, it is all too much to take in. With every added dancer the unpredictability increases, and the information provided very quickly amounts to overload. The spectator is dealing with a continuous sense of loss, the incapacity to absorb the excess of

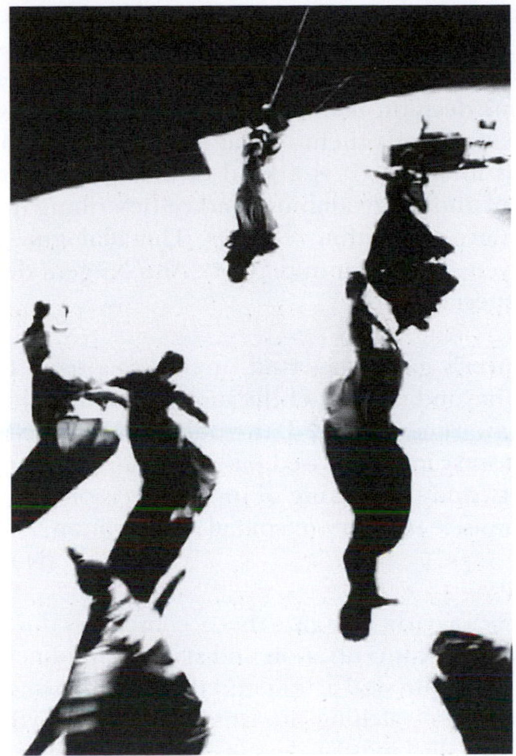

Figure 22.3 *Eidos Telos* (1994) William Forsythe, dancers of the Forsythe Company. Photo: © Dominik Mentzos.

impressions. From this follows the qualification of Forsythe's work as embodying the poetry or architecture of disappearance (Baudoin and Gilpin 1991; Sulcas 1991).

The sense of disappearance is achieved by the shared contributions of the dancers. Forsythe does not directly determine the event the audience sees; the choreography acquires a degree of complexity one person could never produce or conceive of. The dancers work with assignments or algorithms, which produce a choreography that is created in real time. In the case of A L I E/N A(C)TION the algorithm was called the iterative process, in the words of dancer Dana Caspersen:

> Iterative algorithm: examining where I was, what I did, re-describing it, and folding the results back into the original material, lengthening the phrases with these inserts and repeating the process several times.
>
> (Caspersen 2004: 29)

This is what we see in the solo dancer described above: Caspersen's description confirms it was not random freedom, nor choreographed dance, but decided upon on the spot. This approach has a component of kinaesthetics. In the execution of the assignments the dancers cannot rely on conscious decision making but have to rely on ways the movement of their bodies leads them to the next options, similar to Stuart's asking questions in action. It is a kind of dialogue between the execution of movement and the examining and re-describing the actions of the body, as the iterative algorithm requires. This dialogue has been called 'thinking in movement' (Siegmund 2004). Ann Nugent describes the way it looks for the spectator:

> Often a dancer's gaze is averted or the eyes seem to look inward, rather than beyond the line of the movement, as if thinking is honed to an inner awareness. Indeed, the muscular knowledge, or proprioception necessary in improvised passages, requires concentration and mental acuity, and the making of instant decisions that connect mind to body, or muscle memory to spatial organization.
>
> (Nugent 2007: 32)[3]

Nugent describes a particular gaze that accompanies this way of working, one that expresses the concentration and state of mind needed to execute the dialogue between physical action and the restructuring of the physical actions. In contrast to watching Stuart's work, in Forsythe's work there is no time to watch all kinds of details of the body. The inward gaze is connected to a stream of decision-making in action.[4] Boenisch describes this as a process of 'un-writing': 'the fractal texture of the dance undoes the body as projection screen, and destroys, disturbs, detracts, flees, escapes body images' (Boenisch 2004: 61, translation by the author). For Boenisch, this accomplishes a sense of bodily experience for the spectator as much as for the dancer. The central role of kinaesthetics in the production of the choreography has made it impossible for the spectator to cling to body images and has given an immediate sense of kinaesthetic experience.

In conclusion, kinaesthetics plays an important role in the performing of Forsythe's choreography, delegating as he does the final design of the dance to the engagement of his performers, organised through a range of algorithms. The experience of disappearance for the spectator is caused by the excess of activity and the complexity of the decentred conception of the choreography. And finally, the experience of disappearance can be perceived as a kinaesthetic experience.

Break from the dominance of the visual in choreography

This chapter has explored the interest in kinaesthetics held by three late twentieth-century choreographers, and investigated how they have changed ways of seeing dance for their audiences, and perhaps for their dancers. I have distinguished three different approaches: first, a conceptual approach by Boris Charmatz, who uses the obstruction of sight to present perception as the central idea of the performance, and allows the spectator room to reflect on the role of kinaesthetics and other senses in choreography. In the work of Meg Stuart a reductive, 'microscopic' approach permeates the visual with the sensual, creating what Deleuze calls haptic vision, where sight takes over the role of touch. Finally, in William Forsythe's work the dancers' application of their kinaesthetic sense organises the dance movement, resulting in choreography that is a product of collaborative production during the performance.

Some observations can be made. All three choreographers combat notions of conventional choreography. Charmatz strives for illegibility; Stuart wants to reduce 'danciness'; Forsythe explodes ballet vocabulary into an effect of disappearance. Historically one can place these tendencies within a larger historical development: from a more ocular-centric approach to choreography in the eighteenth and nineteenth centuries, to twentieth-century developments in which the material experience of the body proposes new notions of subjectivity (see Siegmund 2005, Jowitt 1988, Reynolds 2007 and Stüber 1984). This focus on kinaesthetics has created different approaches to space and relations with the spectator, creating new perspectives on embodiment of subjectivity, less focused on body images, body language, representation and distance but rather on process and the dynamic connections between action and reflection, material and virtual, in a movement such as the Möbius strip where inside and outside keep feeding back into each other.

Finally, the sensation of the moving body, kinaesthesia, is obviously crucial to the art of dancing. But its elusive complexity has contributed to it being neglected as the 'sixth sense'. However, as contemporary choreographers investigate its role in human movement, and as they share their findings with spectators, there is a need for greater understanding of the ways in which kinaesthetics contributes to issues such as how movement is perceived and executed, how choreographers see a body move, and how choreographers want the audience to experience bodies moving.

Notes

1 Translated by the author. In German 'mit Haut, Hirn und Haaren', playing on the expression with skin and hair, meaning the entire body, Boenisch has added the brain in the equation.

2 Arguably, one could also add visceral perception to Longstaff's list: a type of sensory system active within the internal organs. This system operates largely outside of consciousness, producing 'hidden' internal signals originating in the alimentary tract, the cardiovascular system, and the kidneys that may influence emotional states. Think of the sensation of rollercoaster rides in relation to movement experience.

3 In this citation, Nugent speaks of proprioception as muscular knowledge or muscle memory. Corinne Jola in her article 'Begriffskonfusion' (Jola 2006) considers the kind of language that has developed within dance practices as a

form of phenomenal language, that is, derived from the experience of movement. A cognitive psychologist, Jola explores some of these concepts (like 'muscle memory' and 'muscle knowledge') and argues for a broader understanding of the brain in these processes of movement coordination. This role is perhaps not experienced with the same immediacy by dancers and perhaps that is why more attention is given to muscles than to the brain.

4 Here the discussion about kinaesthetics leads to a discussion of epistemology. The term muscular knowledge can stand for what in other literature is called bodily knowledge or what Varela calls introspection (Varela in Obrist and Vanderlinden 2001). Varela speaks about introspective knowledge as a kind of knowledge that cannot be formulated discursively but is nevertheless displayed in bodily activity, as simple as the tying of shoelaces for example.

References

Baudoin, P. and Gilpin, H. (1991) 'Proliferation and perfect disorder: William Forsythe and the architecture of disappearance', Ballett Frankfurt website. Available online at <http://www.frankfurt-ballett.de> (accessed 1 July 2006).

Berthoz, A. (2000) *The Brain's Sense of Movement*, trans. [from French] by Giselle Weiss, Cambridge, MA: Harvard University Press.

Bleeker, M. (2002) 'The locus of looking: dissecting visuality in the theatre', PhD, Universiteit van Amsterdam.

Boenisch, P. (2004). 'Ent-körpern, ent-schreiben, ent-schöpfen. Wie sich die Tanztheorie von Forsythes "Decreation" zur Dekonstruktion der Diskurse über das Ballett verleiten liess', in A. Wesemann and H. Regitz (eds) *Ballettanz: das Jahrbuch 2004: Forsythe, Bill's Universe*, Berlin: Friedrich Berlin Verlag.

Caspersen, D. (2004). 'The company at work. how they train, rehearse, and invent. The methodologies of William Forsythe', in A. Wesemann and H. Regitz (eds) *Ballettanz: das Jahrbuch 2004: Forsythe, Bill's Universe*, Berlin: Friedrich Berlin Verlag.

Charmatz, B. and Launay, I. (2003) *Entretenir. À propos d'une danse contemporaine*, Paris: Centre National de la Danse and Les presses du réel.

Deleuze, G. (2003) *Francis Bacon: The Logic of Sensation*, trans. D. W. Smith, London: Continuum.

Foster, S. L. (1998) 'Kinesthetic empathies and the politics of compassion', in D. Tércio (ed.) *Continents in Movement: Proceedings of the International Conference, The Meeting of Cultures in Dance History*, Lisbon: FMH Editions.

Franko, M. (2002) *The Work of Dance: Labor, Movement, and Identity in the 1930s*, Middletown, CT: Wesleyan University Press.

Grosz, E. (1997) *Volatile Bodies. Toward a Corporeal Feminism*, Bloomington and Indianapolis: Indiana University Press.

Hagendoorn, I. (2004) 'Some speculative hypotheses about the nature and perception of dance and choreography', *Journal of Consciousness Studies*, 11: 3–4.

Husemann, P. (2002) *Ceci est de la danse. Choreographien von Meg Stuart, Xavier Le Roy und Jérôme Bel*, Norderstedt: Books on Demand.

Imschoot, M. van (1997) 'On the edges of deserts: an exploratory discussion with Meg Stuart', *Carnet*, 12: 24–31.

Jola, C. (2006) 'Begriffskonfusion. Körperkonzepte im Tanz und in der kognitiven Neurowissenschaft', *Tanzjournal* 5: 31–5.

Jowitt, D. (1988) *Time and the Dancing Image*, Berkeley and Los Angeles: University of California Press.

Laermans, R. (1995) 'Dramatic Images: Meg Stuart's dance theatre reflects on communication in an autistic society', *Ballett International Tanz Aktuell*, 8–9: 55–9.

Lepecki, A. (2000) 'Still: On the vibratile microscopy of dance', in G. Brandstetter and H. Völckers (eds) *ReMembering the Body, Körperbilder in Bewegung*, Ostfildern-Ruit.

Longstaff, J. S. (1996) 'Cognitive structures of kinesthetic space; Reevaluating Rudolf Laban's choreutics in the context of spatial cognition and motor control', unpublished PhD thesis, London: City University, Laban Centre.

Martin, J. (1939, 2nd edn 1968) *Introduction into the Dance*. New York: Dance Horizons.

Massumi, B. (2002) *Parables for the Virtual. Movement, Affect, Sensation*, Durham, NC: Duke University Press.

Nugent, A. (2007) 'William Forsythe, eidos: telos, and intertextual criticism', *Dance Research Journal*, 39/1 Summer: 25–48.

Obrist, H.U. and Vanderlinden, B. (2001) *Laboratorium*, Dumont Antwerpen Open, Roomade.

Peeters, J. (2004) *Lichamen als filters. Over Boris Charmatz, Benoît Lachambre en Meg Stuart*, CC Maasmechelen.

Reynolds, Dee (2007) *Rhythmic Subjects: Uses of Energy in the Dances of Mary Wigman, Martha Graham and Merce Cunningham*, Alton: Dance Books.

Siegmund, G. (ed.) (2004) *William Forsythe. Denken in Bewegung*, Berlin: Henschel Verlag.

—— (2005) 'Vers une histoire alternative de la danse: Le visuel dans le Ballet de cour, le Ballet d'action et le Ballet romantique', unpublished lecture from International Symposium *TransFormes*, Centre National de la Danse, Paris, 14 January 2005.

Smith, D. W. (2003) 'Deleuze on Bacon: Three Conceptual Trajectories in *The Logic of Sensation*. Translator's introduction', in *Francis Bacon: The Logic of Sensation. Gilles Deleuze*, trans. D. W. Smith, London: Continuum.

Steinmetz, M. (2002) 'Boris Charmatz présente au Théâtre de la Ville Con forts fleuve, oeuvre radicale créée en 1999', *Journal l'Humanité*, 10 June 2002.

Stuart, M. (1993) *Meg Stuart in Discussion with Staff and Students of CNDO*. The CNDO transcripts, Exeter: Arts Archives.

Stüber, W. J. (1984) *Geschichte des Modern Dance. Zur Selbsterfahrung und Körperaneignung im modernen Tanztheater*, Wilhelmshaven: Heinrichshofen.

Sulcas, R. (1991) 'William Forsythe: The poetry of disappearance and the great tradition', *Dance Theatre Journal*, 9 (1), Summer: 4–7, 32–3.

23 Choreographic environments

New technologies and movement-related artistic work

Sophia Lycouris

This chapter explores recent shifts in traditional choreographic practice that have occurred as a result of the use of new technologies in contemporary dance work. I am interested in whether, when and how the use of new technologies informs traditional techniques for the development of movement material and structures, and ultimately transforms traditional approaches to choreography. If an established notion of choreography changes, the accompanying definitions of dance as art form may adjust accordingly. This is a circular process: new techniques inform the development of new conceptual positions. Yet, once the conceptual boundaries about what can be accepted as 'dance' become looser, artists find it easier to see what their tools can do; and through developing increasingly appropriate novel techniques, they discover ways to push technical experimentations to extreme places they had not envisioned before. Furthermore, technical experimentation accompanied by appropriate conceptual freedom also stimulates questions about how artistic work is presented; fresh artistic and technological discoveries require fresh forms of presentation. This is a slow process and, in many ways, organic, although often extremely complex.

The discussion takes into account a variety of forms of presentation of contemporary choreographic work which uses new technologies, including live performances in proscenium (and other) theatre spaces, site-specific installations, performance/installations and interactive events. Examples in which performers are part of the work are discussed, as well as others in which there are no performers in the traditional sense. In some of these cases, audiences share the same physical space with the work and assume a performative function through becoming 'performers' as the work requires their physical involvement in order to manifest itself. Valerie Preston-Dunlop and Ana Sanchez-Colberg (2002: 1) suggest that 'performative events are ones in which "actors" and "spectators" engage in an exchange of some sort'. In considering choreology as the scholarly study of dance, they discuss the performative nature of human movement in relation to the concepts of *embodiment* and *corporeality* and the importance of the performer as primary communicator of the meaning of the choreographic work. Beyond acknowledging that audiences can operate as performers, this chapter will also discuss the performative potential of the movement of objects, artefacts, sounds and images, the function of which has become increasingly prominent in current choreographic work, often due to new possibilities made available to choreographers by new technologies.

These approaches are not necessarily incompatible with Preston-Dunlop's choreological perspective, which explains that choreology 'has to articulate a position and concurrently allow for expansion and contradictions of this sort' (Preston-Dunlop and Sanchez-Colberg 2002: 113). To reinforce this point, in *Dance and the Performative: a Choreological Perspective – Laban and Beyond* (2002), Sarah Rubidge was invited to discuss her choreographic work with digital installations as part of a series of case studies on the performative aspects of dance practice. However, in choreographic work that manifests itself in the form of digital installations, *embodiment* and *corporeality* function beyond the traditional audience–performer relationship, as there is no physical divide between audience and performance or involvement of performers in the traditional sense. This chapter explores the role of *embodiment* and *corporeality* in examples of choreographic work which propose new relationships between audience and performers; or fully subvert such relationships through inviting audiences to become physically involved with the work and, in this way, function as performers; or work which offers appropriate conditions for audiences to experience images and sounds as choreographic components through drawing attention to their dynamic qualities and the physicality of their presence.

Building on Preston-Dunlop's ideas on the performative in dance and focusing on the dialogue between choreography and new technologies, this chapter examines how interactivity and the use of a variety of materials (including the human body) as choreographic components can generate work which is communicated to the audience in a corporeal, highly experiential, almost visceral manner. However, this discussion cannot be undertaken effectively without addressing the impact of *interdisciplinary practice* in contemporary choreography, asking how this contributes to the emergence of an expanded definition of choreography and questioning the role of new technologies in these developments. Without bypassing Preston-Dunlop's emphasis on the performative nature of choreographed movement, this expanded definition brings a radical shift in both the making and understanding of dance as art form, through introducing the idea that, in certain types of choreographic work, it may not be possible to separate between 'actors' and 'spectators' and, as a result of this, *embodiment* and *corporeality* become located with the viewer. Of course, in the history of choreography there are few clear-cut moments of change. Transitions are always crucial aspects of this process and examples of work are later discussed which mark significant transitional moments in the fascinating journey towards this radical transformation.

The digital revolution and interdisciplinary choreography

My proposition of the term *interdisciplinary choreography* is the product of long negotiations between myself as a person with a natural tendency to ask questions about everything in life including dance, and a number of cultural, artistic, political, conceptual and philosophical contexts I confronted since the early days of my engagement with dance in my native country Greece. In the early 1980s, I was trained in ballet and Graham technique with a view to becoming a dance teacher and part-time dancer/choreographer. The journey took place in a highly animated cultural and political environment, as Greece was still in a post-dictatorship climate. As a dance student, I became involved with various politically orientated youth organisations, which put me in direct contact with students in music, theatre and film. As a young artist, I grew up in an environment where questions were asked on a daily basis, primarily in relation to the function of art as a tool for political transformation.

My early involvement with choreography happened in mixed environments and had a focus on 'making a difference', which would have political repercussions. My work was created for political youth festivals as part of collaborative events involving musicians, film-makers and actors. It was presented in temporary performance spaces, without dance floors, proper theatre lights, dressing rooms, sometimes in spaces designed for other purposes, where, in order to 'make a difference', I was trying to differentiate stylistically from traditional art practices by doing things such as 'dance' and 'speak' simultaneously, which was extremely radical at the time. By the end of the 1980s, there was not much spark left in Greek progressive artistic circles, so I moved to England to study for a Master's degree (MA) in dance. This relocation made available to me a wealth of theoretical tools which could be used to create new choreographic work that would 'make a difference', although no longer in relation to agendas other than my own.

Disillusioned with the pointlessness of overt political aims, I was particularly resistant to choreography with social meaning, which was fashionable in the UK during the early 1990s. I became highly interested in understanding how dance is physically 'experienced' by both performers and audience. As a dancer, my body always had to reach a particular physical state, otherwise I had a peculiar sensation that it 'was somehow ahead of itself and I was trying to catch it during the performance'. On the other hand, as a member of the audience, I was aware that my breathing was affected by the dynamic qualities of the dance I was watching and that, during these moments, I was experiencing a heightened awareness of my body as a physical entity. Some of this work had a meditative effect on me, through managing to draw my senses and thinking process into a highly absorbing experiential event.

I became interested in the experiential value of the 'moment' of dance and started exploring how I could create choreography that communicates states rather than stories, by totally focusing on the communication of the physicality of movement. In their initial introduction of the concept of *corporeality*, as the sum of all physical qualities of movement that reveal the multi-dimensional yet person-specific character of dance, the authors underline the importance of expressionism within the lineage of dance theatre and argue against narrative and the hierarchical relationship between body and language:

> where there is an emphasis on emotion and, with it, a focus on the performer's presence as a central factor of the event, a corporeal work emerges. Such a work embodies an anti-mimetic attitude towards the performance event where narrative is subsumed in corporeal form [...], corporeality [...] dealt directly with the polemic of the body on stage and the body's contentious relationship to a language structure.
>
> (Preston-Dunlop and Sanchez-Colberg 2002: 9–10)

Following the completion of my MA, I undertook doctoral research where I was soon attracted by the thrill of free improvisation as performance mode. In free improvisation there is no predetermined purpose or meaning; the performers have nothing to use as support, they are totally exposed in front of an audience and the only skill they can develop through training is their ability to read the character of the 'moment' and provide the most appropriate responses, both physically and intellectually. My thesis argued that, as in music, free improvisation in dance is a form of real-time composition, in which informed choices take place in the 'moment' of dance which are no less valuable than choices made by choreographers in their studios and then mediated to audiences by performers (Lycouris 1996). This kind of improvisation subverts the traditional power relationships between choreographers and performers and challenges the notion of authorship. This allowed me to suggest that improvisation is a form of choreography.

However, my doctoral research did not take place in a welcoming dance environment. In the early 1990s it seemed that improvisation in dance in the UK was still primarily understood as a form of movement therapy or technique for choreographers to stimulate their dancers to produce 'spontaneous' movement material that could be later shaped into repeatable movement phrases with choreographic value. This situation forced me to seek like-minded artists in other fields. At the time, the British improvised music scene was very active, drawing from a rich tradition of at least twenty-five years. Like dance artists Katie Duck and Julyen Hamilton, whose pioneering improvisational work I researched extensively, I worked with various musicians as well as visual artist Gina Southgate who, during our performances, was building and dismantling temporary structures through focusing on the sonic properties of the materials. To make sense of what we were doing in this context I had to think about movement and sound as part of a single compositional system. I saw my dancing body as an instrument contributing to hybrid musical compositions, in which movement in counterpoint with sound was part of a complex meta-system, somehow following rules of musical composition. At the same time, I experienced the presence of the musicians in the performance space, their movements and the movement of the sounds they were producing across this space, as aspects of its dynamic qualities. Their physical presence was contributing to a similar meta-system, in which the dynamic qualities of all elements, including sounds and movements, followed choreographic principles. A basic interdisciplinary approach allowed me to consider sonic elements from a choreographic perspective and vice versa.

In their discussion of *nexus* as a concept which describes complex interrelationships between the four strands of the dance medium (performer, movement, sound, space), Preston-Dunlop and Sanchez-Colberg (2002: 49) address in great detail possible types of connection (or non-connection) between sound and movement. During the late 1990s, my explorations engaged with similar questions, seeing that some examples of choreography can be understood as the product of complex negotiations between heterogeneous elements such as movement and sound. I argued that it is possible to develop tailored compositional meta-systems to support the creation of new choreographic work (and work incorporating new technologies in particular) in which the relationships between all heterogeneous components can be defined in a coherent manner (Lycouris and Kosmides 2000; Lycouris 2000b).

In order for this approach to work in the most efficient way, it is important to remain as open as possible to what can be understood as choreographic components. Language becomes instrumental in this instance because it offers the tool of metaphor, a linguistic device through which 'one field of reference is carried over or transferred to another' (Wales 1989: 295), allowing us in this way to move across the whole spectrum of both literal and metaphorical interpretations of the components of dance (Lycouris 2000a). As becomes evident later, this ability to move comfortably across the whole spectrum of such interpretations is sometimes the only way to make conceivable choreographic work that integrates new technologies. In such work, the four strands of the dance medium (performer, movement, sound, space) operate across various combinations of the 'physical' and the 'digital', which are materially different. Therefore, the development of compositional meta-systems, which can support the coherence of choreographic work created through the use of materially heterogeneous components, is an important aspect of choreographic practice that incorporates new technologies, since such practice is always constituted with reference to both the physical and digital. Even in examples of work that operate exclusively within the digital realm, in terms of both making and presentation, the terminology and concepts used to introduce and refer to this work come directly from the physical world of choreography. For example, the virtual installation *Hand Drawn Spaces*, created in 1998 by Merce Cunningham, Paul Kaiser and Shelley Eshkar has been described in the following way:

> The virtual dancers appear as life-size drawings emerging from the darkness and moving in an apparently limitless three-dimensional space. Though the dancers are visible on three screens, they move through a much larger virtual area, and so travel in and out of projected image, often traversing the spectators' space. The spatial sound-score by Ron Kuivila evokes their positions in space, making their presences felt even when not seen.
>
> (Kaiser 2008)

Through adopting the idea of choreography as a technique of movement composition which operates at a meta-systemic level in order to bring heterogeneous components to a coherent whole, it becomes possible to argue that the human body is not the only site in which the four strands of the dance medium can manifest themselves physically and provide conditions for the creation of what I call *movement-related* artistic work. The introduction of the term *movement-related* brings another shift into this discussion through liberating choreographers from the assumption that only movement which is 'dance' can be used choreographically; by no means a new idea. As Preston-Dunlop and Sanchez-Colberg remind us, the American choreographer Alwin Nikolais coined the term 'motion' to 'distinguish disembodied movement from movement mediated by an intended and committed dancer' (2002: 41) and they refer to work integrating intricate movement of dancers, objects, sculptural costumes and light, Nikolais's most significant contribution to the tradition of modern dance. Replacing the term 'dance' with the wider notion of 'movement' facilitates the task of exploring the performative aspects of choreographed movement produced through and manifested in elements other than the physical bodies of dancers. Thus, *interdisciplinary choreography* may include the application of choreographic techniques on materials other than the dancing body, for example, images and sounds that can assume performative presence. This does not exclude human bodies from being part of a wider, yet heterogeneous, pool of choreographic components; in fact human bodies become fully present in these meta-systems, particularly when the choreographic work is interactive and audiences become performers through triggering interactive mechanisms which activate these works.

Technology has always facilitated such expansions, and Nikolais's work is an obvious example in this area. His technical and conceptual breakthroughs were achieved through his critical engagement with a materially homogeneous world and the development of appropriate choreographic strategies, which were meant to challenge this world. The difference between old and new technologies[1] is that the 'digital revolution' brought into the physical world and people's everyday lives a number of elements inaccessible to our senses, which coexist with others fully accessible to our senses. The world became a complex combination of heterogeneous elements and we had to develop new strategies in order to be able to operate in this rapidly transforming reality.

When digital media interact with the traditional practice of choreography (or for that matter with traditional practices in other art forms) similar conditions emerge, and this affects how we create and experience contemporary choreographic work, which incorporates digital and interactive technologies. What the introduction of digital technology has mostly challenged in our relationship with the physical world is the perception of space, as we are surrounded by intricate combinations of physical and digital forms that are materially different. Through an extension of Preston-Dunlop's ideas about the importance of space in dance and choreography, perhaps an understanding of multiple conceptions of space across the full range of its literal and metaphorical interpretations is necessary in order to develop appropriate tools and approaches for both the creation and appreciation of contemporary choreographic work. I also propose that interdisciplinary methodologies can accommodate the problem of processing heterogeneous components and can therefore facilitate the use of materially different notions of space within the context of a single choreographic work, which can be communicated in highly experiential and visceral ways. Examples of such work will be explored in the next sections of this chapter to illustrate the ideas introduced so far.

New considerations of space

Contemporary choreographic work, which makes possible new articulations of the performative through use of new technologies in contemporary movement-related artistic work, often challenges the traditional physical boundary between performance and audience by allowing audiences to share a common physical space with the work. In addition, such work often becomes an instantiation of highly intricate combinations of physical and digital notions of space. This section explores how these characteristics are manifested in choreographic work that typifies crucial transitional moments in current movement-related artistic work.

BODYSIGHT (2001),[2] created by digital artist Konstantinos Papakostas and myself, is a choreographic audio-visual installation which explores views of selected London sites (London Eye, Hyde Park and Camden Market) from the perspective of a dancer's body as she performed choreographic material *within* these sites especially developed *for* the selected sites. The video images were created with a small digital camera, which was attached to five different points of the body of performer/dancer Debbie Ward using accessories created by costume designer Katia Fiorentino. The purpose of the cameras was to capture visual and sonic fragments of the three environments, which surrounded the body of the dancer when she danced in the three London sites. The video material with sound processing by composer Phil Durrant is presented as a five-monitor circular installation, in which each monitor presents a video loop created from images of all three sites which were recorded from a single perspective of the camera (for example when the camera was attached to the leg of the dancer). All monitors face inwards and the viewers are expected to be in the centre of the circle in order to experience the installation. The aim of this arrangement is to map within an exhibition space fragments of the original spaces in which the filming took place.

In this work, the use of new technologies (digital video[3] in this instance) changed my approach to composition and development of movement material and structures, as well as the mode of presentation. This shift was necessary in order for one of the main purposes of the piece – to address the traditional role of the dance performer – to be fulfilled. Rather than offering a dancing body as an object to be looked at by a passive audience, this piece offers the audience an opportunity to adopt a physically active role through placing themselves in the assumed position of the dancer in the centre of the circle; through experiencing the audio-visual material of the installation from this particular position, the viewers are offered a taste of what the dancer's body 'saw' and 'heard' when she was dancing in the three sites selected for this piece. In addition, this piece advocates the unique qualities of movement created through use of media other than the dancing body, which have, however, been processed from within a choreographic perspective. *BODYSIGHT* has been designed to show that, if the movement of a video camera is directly controlled by a dancer's body in action, the video images produced through this method have a unique quality. Furthermore, this work reveals that if the editing of the video material follows choreographic principles, the final result has unique aesthetic qualities which could possibly not be generated in any other way.

During the development of this piece, I was always driven by its material presence in the space, and found it helpful to think about it as a sculpture, video sculpture in particular, which also credits my continuing fascination with the work of American video artist Nam June Paik (Paik 2006). In terms of its relationship with the audience, *BODYSIGHT* also functions as a sculpture, with particular reference to the principles set by Minimal sculptors in the 1960s and 1970s. Although Michael Fried (1998) used this as a criticism, his idea that Minimal sculpture had an element of theatricality is useful here. Minimal sculptors created work of large scale, and, as a consequence, the viewers were placed in a physically active position: to experience these sculptures, the viewers had to walk around them (Colpitt 1990). This also meant that a temporal element was introduced in sculptural work. According to Fried (1998), this temporality was a characteristic exclusive to theatre. In *BODYSIGHT*, the audience is similarly expected to move around in the space of the installation in order to experience the work. Since the monitors are facing the centre of the

Figure 23.1 BODYSIGHT installation. Photo: Sophia Lycouris.

circle, the viewers need to (at least) change the direction of their bodies in order to watch the video sequences, which are different on each monitor. Photographic and cinematic methods were introduced into the choreographic method of this piece; through use of editing techniques, the space inside the frame of the monitors became a choreographed space. Editing shaped the internal dynamics of the resulting images, as well as their dynamic relationship with each other, through determining how and when video sequences appeared, disappeared and were repeated. In the absence of live dancing bodies, such choreographic elements questioned traditional assumptions about performance presence and explored the performative qualities of the monitors.

The uniqueness of this piece stems from the fact that there is a distinct emphasis on the dynamic character of the installation space. *BODYSIGHT* explores ways in which especially designed dynamic changes (through manipulations of sounds and images) can be introduced in the physical space of the viewer. In accordance with Preston-Dunlop's choreological perspective, this piece exemplifies a shift 'from dance perceived as an art object to dance seen as a participatory human' and rather emphasises 'the participatory aspect of corporeality ... and the richness of the experience of the participants' (Preston-Dunlop and Sanchez-Colberg 2002: 10) who are physically surrounded by the dance installation and therefore may experience physically the dynamic changes which take place in the installation space.

However, although *BODYSIGHT* placed the viewers in the centre of the work offering them in this way a primary role, it was not an interactive piece, as the unfolding of the audio-visual sequences in time was fixed and could not be triggered or activated by the viewers. In this piece, only the viewers were 'activated' by the work. The work of New York-based dance company Troika Ranch (Coniglio and Stoppiello 2008) is a good example of interactive dance performance, which is created for proscenium theatre stages, yet uses new technologies (interactive in this case) in order to challenge the role and use of space in the production of meaning through choreographic means. This piece exemplifies a complex fusion of physical and digital manifestations of space in dance that intensifies the materiality of emerging movement and foregrounds *embodiment* through offering highly tangible kinaesthetic manifestations of stories and states. The key to an understanding of Troika Ranch's work is that it uses interactive systems both to critique and expand ideas of narrative, plot and character; ideas which have been extensively used in traditional choreographic practice. The company uses Isadora, a specifically developed software which translates visual information detected through sensors (programmed to record predetermined aspects of the movement of the dancers) into instructions for triggering audio-visual effects (Coniglio and Stoppiello 2008). In this way, projected images and processed sound become functional choreographic components to join the rest of the 'live' action in order to inform the dynamic qualities of the live event in very particular ways.

In the performance piece *16 [R]evolutions* (2005–6),[4] composer/media artist Mark Coniglio and choreographer Dawn Stoppiello worked towards a specific message they wish to communicate to the audience, as evident in their online publicity:

> The work focuses on a single evolutionary path: how the animal drives of our pre-human ancestors have become sublimated to the point of abject confusion and disconnection. ... *16 [R]evolutions* asks the question, can we reconnect with our core needs to feed, fight and reproduce while continuing to evolve into beings of light and intellect?
>
> (Coniglio and Stoppiello 2008)

Audio-visual effects have been used in this work to insert fragments of imaginary space into a tangible, loosely narrative situation in which schematic human characters are in action to portray the development of various narrative threads. With a distinct expressionistic flavour, the audio-visual effects bring the non-material space of thoughts, desires and 'animal' drives straight into the physical space of the performance, yet in a completely physicalised, materially based and visceral mode, which is what constitutes the significance of this work.

Both the visuals and sound become an integral part of the 'live' action in the performance area and a new hybrid space is generated, emerging

Figure 23.2 16 [R]evolutions, Troika Ranch. Photo: © A.T.Schaeffer.

through a complex synthesis of physical and digital elements, no less alive, physical and materially present than the performance space of 'traditional' dance pieces which do not use interactive or other technologies. This integration is achieved because of the artists' particular approach to choreographic composition, according to which the necessity to work meticulously with dynamic qualities from within multiple perspectives and at multiple levels is fully acknowledged. Coniglio and Stoppiello are deeply concerned with highly precise choices in their decisions about the dynamic qualities of the audio-visual materials and how these materials coexist with the 'live' action of the dancers in the shared physical space of the performance event. It is because Troika Ranch is prepared to engage with narrative structures and devices that their compositional techniques work so well. Because they commit themselves so strongly to drawing the viewers into a certain kind of material world and its stories, their interactive devices work both against and in favour of the realism of the 'live' action, as they come at key points to give to this clearly defined world an unexpected surrealistic twist, which, however, remains clearly physical and materially defined. The crucial strength I perceive in this work is that the audio-visual effects have been fully integrated with the 'live' action, so that the viewers sense them kinaesthetically. There have been numerous explorations in the work of other choreographers with both linear and non-linear (interactive) audio-visual elements, in which such integration has not been successful.

Attempting to identify the source of the effectiveness of Troika Ranch's method, I suggest that this is because of the artists' highly developed compositional skills and their deep understanding that what matters in dance is ultimately the sophistication of the physicality of the work, and that all ingredients should serve this purpose as much as possible. Otherwise, the work cannot be experienced by the viewers in its full kinaesthetic potential and this could seriously compromise its immediacy and visceral impact.

Choreographic environments and the role of the viewer

Sensuous Geographies (2002)[5] created by British choreographer Sarah Rubidge in collaboration with British composer Alistair MacDonald goes one crucial step further and brings within the concrete time and space of a single interactive performative event the challenges introduced by both *BODYSIGHT* and *16 [R]evolutions*: the physical involvement of the audience with the work within the installation space and a fusion of physical and digital notions of space which intensifies the materiality of the emerging movement and the kinaesthetic experiences of the participants.

As described in the online publicity of the piece, this work 'is a responsive sound and video environment'. Like *16 [R]evolutions*, the interactive mechanism works with sensors that record the performers' movements, and this information is translated into instructions that trigger audio effects. More specifically, the interactive mechanism is based on colour recognition; colours determine sound textures and this is why the visitors of the installation are offered loose, large costumes in different bright colours, which they wear above their own clothes. However, in this work, there is no boundary between audience and performers, the visitors are also the performers of this piece, as their movement is the only trigger of the interactive mechanism. Like *BODYSIGHT*, this piece is time-based and has the spatial arrangement of an installation. The visitors are 'surrounded' by the work simply because they are an integral part of the work's 'operating system': its materialisation depends on their physical activity. This work does not exist without its viewers and their movement, which activates its interactive mechanism.

Sensuous Geographies also has an interesting element of theatricality, not only because it is experienced through the unfolding of the interactive process through time (and, as mentioned earlier, according to Fried, any artistic work with temporal elements is considered as 'theatrical'), but also due to the visual impression that it offers to any new visitor when he or she enters the installation space. Provided that there are already viewers in action within the installation space, each newcomer who enters the room faces an almost traditional theatrical setting; a number of human figures dressed in theatrical costumes move in different speeds and qualities within a black box lit in a theatrical way with theatrical lights; this visual impression is accompanied by a sonic element, as sounds reach the space from speakers pointing in various directions.[6]

Like *16 [R]evolutions*, *Sensuous Geographies* also engages with elements of narrative, although this occurs in a more abstract and improvisational manner. There is simplicity at the first level accompanied by a simultaneous complexity at a deeper level; the result depends on the degree of each visitor's engagement with the interactive mechanism. The installation is supported by the live presence of composer Alistair MacDonald who makes decisions in real time about the association of pre-programmed sounds with colours. Thus, the composer assigns a dedicated sound texture to each newcomer and this sound mimics the person's trajectory in the space across speakers. Depending on the quality, speed and intensity of the movement of the viewer, the sound texture assigned to each person inhabits the installation space in a unique way. The texture of each sound creates specific associations in the minds of both the persons who trigger the sounds and all the others who share the installation space or are observing from the outside. In this way, snapshots of stories and states are generated for the viewers. After a given period of time, the composer adds a new layer in the sound processing, so that the movement of the viewer/user becomes a trigger which affects the structure, timing and quality of the assigned sound texture, perhaps making reference to how people express themselves differently according to their personalities. Finally, there is a third layer of complexity in the interactive mechanism, which is determined by relationships of proximity between the active colours. In this phase, the sound textures associated with specific colours exist, develop and inhabit the space in ways that are defined by the spatial relationships between the different colours. Again, it could be argued that this final phase engages with how people use space differently due to differences in their personalities (Rubidge and MacDonald 2004).

It is important to clarify that the main reason why the artists designed this piece in the above way was to bypass problems of predictability with interactivity. The three layers of interactive response of the mechanism, in combination with the real-time involvement of the composer, create a large number of possible sonic outcomes and reduce predictability. These technical/structural devices both affect the meaning of the piece and determine its physical manifestation, and consequently, the way in which the work is perceived kinaesthetically by the visitors/performers. The degree of immediacy and viscerality of the experience in this work is higher than in traditional theatre spaces. This is because the movement that the visitors/performers perceive kinaesthetically is their own movement, which takes place within their own bodies and they experience it as such. In addition to this, they are in a position to also perceive, again kinaesthetically, the movement of other visitors, who use the installation space at the same time – often in close proximity. *Sensuous Geographies* is a typical example of an 'open work' in Umberto Eco's (1989) sense, in which the active receivers of the meaning also contribute to the creation of the work's meaning. Although Eco's approach has been developed for literary texts, it is even better suited to time-based media with interactive elements. The open character of such work, apart from determining its meaning, also affects its very existence in time and space; it establishes its physicality and materiality.

In considering the physically active role of the viewer in works such as *BODYSIGHT* and *Sensuous Geographies*, it is helpful to think of the installation space as an environment that contains the viewers. To emphasise that such environments have emerged through considerations of choreographic rules, methods and techniques, or perhaps a kind of choreographic thinking, I suggest that *choreographic environment* is an appropriate term for installative or performative work which requires physically active viewers, whether the work is interactive or not, and whether it is presented in art spaces such as theatres and galleries, or in non-art related sites. This terminology also covers my most recent work, which uses new technologies in combination with interdisciplinary choreographic techniques to explore the dynamics of urban space.

Contemporary architectural theorists and practitioners have explored dynamic definitions of architecture, through examining the experiential impact of architecture for human beings who move in and around these buildings, and, consequently, how this could affect principles about architectural design. The work of American architect Peter Eisenman (1999) has significantly contributed to a new understanding of non-linear conceptions of space by challenging the idea of static architecture, and exploring notions of fluid environments that exist in perpetual motion through constantly shifting the perspective from within which the viewer/user experiences the architectural space. From a choreographic point of view, the advantage of fluid environments is that they have greater potential to stimulate corporeal responses in the viewer.

The developing intricate relationships between the disciplines of architecture and choreography manifest the importance of interdisciplinary methodology in current choreographic practice. Eisenman's ideas are examples of how contemporary architectural discourse can support the expansion of traditional choreographic concepts. His work makes possible a dynamic understanding of the element of space. This allows for the development of new methods of production of organised movement (be it movement of human bodies, other elements such as images and sounds, or various combinations of them). His ideas provide an appropriate extra-disciplinary 'vocabulary' that can be used to expand and develop choreographic methodologies to highly challenging levels and facilitate the refinement of a process, which aims at the creation of works that remain open at the level of structure, meaning and materialisation. This is distinctly evident in current choreographic work, which invites the users to interact physically with the work and intensifies the users' experiences of the materiality of space using new technologies.

Notes

1 For the purposes of this discussion, this can be also understood as the difference between analogue and digital technology.
2 This work was created with a Capture Award offered by Arts Council England.
3 Some may argue that digital video is not new anymore, especially when recording, editing and presentation of the work function in exactly the same way as in analogue video, however with reference to the history of dance and choreography, digital video material created as a result of movement generated through a dancer's body was new at that time in both fields of dance and video art.
4 The piece was created with British performers and the support of *essexdance*, centre for dance and technology in Chelmsford, UK, along with the Arts Council England East and the International Workshop Festival.
5 This work was created with the support of a Creative Scotland Award from the Scottish Arts Council.
6 In *BODYSIGHT*, each newcomer is faced with a theatrical atmosphere, although less intense. What they see once they enter the installation space is one or more persons standing in the centre of a circle (in their own clothes), lit from five flickering 'footlights' as the only light source in this work, which is the light coming from the monitors of the installation that are placed at floor level and slightly tilted upwards through the use of special raising platforms built as 'wedges'.

References

Colpitt, F. (1990) *Minimal Art: The Critical Perspective*, Seattle: The University of Chicago Press.

Coniglio, M. and Stoppiello, D. (2008) *Troika Ranch Website*. Available online at <http://www.troikaranch.org> (Accessed 4 July 2008).

Eco, U. (1989) *The Open Work*, Cambridge, MA: Harvard University Press.

Eisenman, P. (1999) *Diagram Diaries*, London: Thames & Hudson.

Fried, M. (1998) *Art and Objecthood*, Chicago: University of Chicago Press.

Kaiser, P. (2008) 'Hand-Drawn Spaces', page in *The Open Ended Group Website*. Available online at <http://www.openendedgroup.com/index.php/artworks/hand-drawn-spaces-1998/> (Accessed 4 July 2008).

Lycouris, S. (1996) 'Destabilising dancing: tensions between the theory and practice of improvisational performance', unpublished PhD thesis, Guildford: University of Surrey.

—— (2000a) 'Reconsidering the medium, composition and the space: movement-based live performance work incorporating webcast elements', *TRANS electronic journal*, 9. Available online at <http://www.inst.at/trans/9Nr/inhalt9.htm> (Accessed 4 July 2008).

—— (2000b) 'Performance/Installation STRING: a case study towards a definition of Internet-based live performance work with dance elements', *1ères Rencontres Internationales, Arts, Sciences et Technologies*, La Rochelle, France, 22–24 November 2000, Maison des Sciences de l'Homme et de la Société de l'Université de La Rochelle in collaboration avec le Ballet Atlantique Regine Chopinot. Available online at <http://www.univ-lr.fr/recherche/mshs/axe2recherche/art_science/colloque/publications/LYCOURIS.pdf> (Accessed 4 July 2008).

Lycouris, S. and Kosmides, M. (2000) 'The theatre of mixed-means in the age of information technology', Proceedings of the 12th International Conference on Systems Research, Informatics and Cybernetics, Systems Research in the Arts, vol. II, Music, Environmental Design and the Choreography of Space, Ontario, Canada: The International Institute for Advanced Studies in Systems Research and Cybernetics.

Paik, N. J. (2006) *Nam June Paik's official website*. Available online at <http://www.paikstudios.com> (Accessed 4 July 2008).

Preston-Dunlop, V. and Sanchez-Colberg A. (2002) *Dance and the Performative: a Choreological Perspective: Laban and Beyond*. London: Verve Publishing.

Rubidge, S. and MacDonald, A. (2004) 'Sensuous geographies: a multi-user interactive/responsive installation', *Digital Creativity*, 15 (4): 245–52.

Wales, K. (1989) *A Dictionary of Stylistics*, London: Longman.

24 Performing installations

Towards an understanding of choreography and performativity in interactive installations

Sarah Rubidge

In 2003 in collaboration with composer Alistair MacDonald, I mounted a large-scale interactive installation entitled *Sensuous Geographies*. When the visitors stepped into *Sensuous Geographies*' central (interactive) space they found themselves generating and modulating a complex multi-layered sound environment in real time, which emerged as a response to the direction and speed of their movement.[1] After much deliberation we decided to call *Sensuous Geographies* a 'performative' installation, on the grounds that it simultaneously generated a new sonic environment in response to the behaviours of each grouping of visitors as they engaged with the installation *and* an emergent choreographic event as they moved through the space in response to the sounds they were generating. The use of this term concerned critics such as Ellie Carr (2003) who had not encountered the term 'performative' before, nor indeed the term 'immersive', which is also regularly used when referring to installations of this kind. That this is so is, perhaps, unsurprising, for installations such as *Sensuous Geographies* are developing a new mode of choreographic practice, one which might result in performative events but does not entail what is conventionally considered to be performance. This raises questions for artists and critics concerning, on the one hand, the nature of the works artists are developing in this field, and on the other, ways of describing them.

Although works such as *Sensuous Geographies* step beyond previous choreographic boundaries, as will be seen, these works are not without precedents, particularly with respect to the use of installation environments for performative events. As early as the 1960s in the USA, choreographers involved in the Judson Church Dance Theatre began to experiment with abandoning the conventional theatre space in favour of installation environments as the site for performance. In the UK in the 1970s and 1980s, experimental dance artists involved in the New Dance movement followed suit, as did Rosemary Butcher with *Spaces 4* (1981), *Shell: Force Fields and Spaces* (1982) and *Touch the Earth* (1987).[2] These artists were, however, ahead of their time, for it was not until relatively late in the 1990s that the use of built installation environments as sites for performance became more than an occasional feature of the choreographic terrain. At the cusp of the twentieth and twenty-first centuries more choreographers have become involved in extending the frame of the performance environment through an exploration of the potential of non-theatre spaces and installation environments as sites for choreography.[3] Performances now regularly take place in built environments or specially built installation environments, for example Carol Brown's *Shelf Life* (1998) and *Machine for Living* (1999), and La Ribot's *Still Distinguished* series (2000). Many of these choreographic installation works see the audience either standing or sitting around the designated performance space in close proximity to the performers. This changes the relationship between performer and audience and between audience and the work, aligning this form of choreographic work with installation art, which 'dissolve[s] the borders between the work and the field of observation surrounding it' (Nollert 2004: 11).

A more radical development of this expanding mode of choreographic practice has emerged in contemporary digitally enhanced performances. Here the performance environment itself, which is in part composed of virtual imagery and electronically generated sound, is modified by the choreographed behaviour of performers using interactive technologies. Although some of this work constitutes choreographed 'interactive' performances which take place on a conventional stage set-up, with performers on the stage and viewers seated in an auditorium,[4] choreographic artists working with installation environments are also experimenting with new technologies in their installation performances. Carol Brown, for example, has incorporated interactive digital technologies into *The Changing Room* (2004). The combination of built and virtual environments featured in these works provides a new frame for choreographic explorations. Choreographers such as Ruth Gibson of Igloo (*Winterspace* 2001–5), Susan Kozel and Gretchen Schiller (*trajets* 2001) and myself (*Sensuous Geographies* 2003) have embraced the challenge and begun to consider the choreography of the digital audio-visual environment as an integral, even central, part of our choreographic practice.

Performance events that take place in installation environments are sometimes described as 'performative' events. The notion of performativity is more complex than this usage implies however, for its roots lie in philosophical rather than performance discourses, and goes beyond the notion of artistic performance *per se*. In the context of the arts, performativity is a complex concept and two different types are often invoked. On the one hand, the term 'performative' can be loosely applied to performance practices *per se* (Nollert 2004). On the other, it can be applied to events in which the environment in which they take place is modified as the events progress, leading to the emergence of new imagery and/or new configurations of the elements present in the environment. It is this last example that exemplifies a philosophical use of the term 'performativity'[5] in the context of arts practice.

Linguistic philosopher John L. Austin coined the term 'performative' in relation to speech acts in 1962. Austin argues that a performative utterance actively produces the state of affairs to which it refers, contrasting it with a constative utterance, which describes or represents a state of affairs. Thus, in the right circumstances, saying 'I pronounce you man and wife' simultaneously brings into being the married state for the couple involved.[6] In this discussion the importance of the notion of the performative utterance, which here can be taken as the 'performative event', is that it brings a new state of affairs into being. Consequently, a performative utterance, which Semetsky (2003) notes can be couched equally in words, images, music or movement, is a creative utterance. It either generates a new state of affairs, or modulates an existing one to create new configurations in the existing set of artistic conditions. Performative language and/or events thus do not *re*-present what is already known, but create and present something new.

Judith Butler (1990) approaches the notion of the performative from the perspective of identity formation. She suggests that through the act of expressing, or performing, her gender (i.e. performing bodily actions which are understood in a given society as representative of 'woman') a female subject is actively constituting her gender identity, for 'there is no gender identity behind the expressions of gender; that identity is performatively constituted by the very "expressions" that are said to be its results' (Butler 1990: 25). Here two senses of the performative intersect, for the performance of (acting or staging) an identity brings that identity into being. Butler notes that this is a continuous process, suggesting that the simple reiterative enacting of an identity does not lead to a final identity, for it is necessary to allow for a re-inscription of any identity which is performatively generated, to 'learn a double movement; to invoke the category, and hence *provisionally* to institute an identity' (Butler 1993: 222, author's emphasis). This has implications in the context of the performative event in which any set of conditions that obtain is always provisional.

At one level, Butler's notion of performativity has a resonance with contemporary performance art practice, particularly that of the 1980s and 1990s, which addressed issues concerning sexual, ethnic, and other forms of identity. It could also have resonances with the very notion of stage performances in general. Just as one can form a socio-cultural identity by repeating certain active tropes, in a stage performance actions (and identities) are executed repeatedly, giving rise (in the moment) to fictional identities and/or states of affairs. They are thus, at one level, performative, but not in the strong sense. In conventional theatre performances, the identities and state of affairs generated by a performance are not open to re-inscription. Rather than the moment of performance being the source of a new event, or a radical modulation of the scripted events, the play or dance is intended to be repeated as a predetermined form. Thus, they are only performative in the sense that they involve performance.

In relation to stage performances, the term 'performative' is thus primarily a linguistic relation and constitutes performativity in the 'weak' sense.[7] The 'strong' sense of performativity needs to take into account the original Austinian sense, that is a performative event is an event (which may or may not entail a conventional performance) not concerned with representing the known, but rather with bringing new states of affairs into being. Although performance events of many kinds are often endowed with the descriptor 'performative' (Nollert 2004: 25), in a live performance context only a special kind of performance – improvisation – meets the philosophical conditions of performativity outlined by Austin. Only in improvisation can a new state of affairs be brought into being (one in which the precise form is not predictable when the improvisation begins). Improvisation in performance consequently is performative in the strong sense.

This chapter interrogates the notion of the performative within the framework of arts practices, which either involve installation environments or have a choreographic tenor. These can be referred to as 'performative' and/or 'choreographic' installations. Three types of work will be used as a frame for my musings. These are:

1 choreographed performances that take place in an installation rather than a stage environment;
2 choreographed or improvised performances in an installation environment which incorporate a measure of interactivity between responsive technological systems and performers;
3 interactive engagements in an installation environment between 'audience' members and responsive technological systems that give rise to informal performance events.

It is notable that 'performative' installations are becoming a feature not only of choreographic but also of fine arts practice.[8] In the fine arts, performative installations have been described as

> a synthesis of art event and art work, of presence and representation, of materiality and immateriality … [with] the fleeting moment as both a generative and constitutive element of the installation.
>
> (Nollert 2004:4)

This implies that the activity that takes place within them is as important as the built environment in determining their character as art 'works'. Nevertheless, claims to the performativity of a fine art installation are often generated by the fact that an installation entails a performance of some kind (Nollert 2004). This seems to align the notion of 'performativity' with performance, rather than with installation art.[9] It is worth noting that the use of the term 'performance' in performance art differs subtly from the notion of performance in conventional theatre contexts. Garoian (1999), for example, claims that performance art is performative

> in that the artist is concerned with doing not with meaning. [S/he]

> does not start with an attempt to represent or signify. [S/he] acts rather than acting.
>
> (in Linker 2003: 18)

That is, in contrast with conventional theatrical performance events, performance art is primarily presentational rather than representational. This is also a feature of installation art (Bishop 2005).

Many performance art events take place in installation environments, leading to the claim that these are 'performative' installations.[10] However, the installation space and the ensemble of objects and elements, which lie within it, are generally not the central feature of the work. Rather, it is the performance itself that occupies this position, for it is performance that primarily reveals the 'content' of the piece. In contrast, performative installations, which acknowledge the philosophical implications of the term performative frequently, reveal themselves and their content as much through the *visitor's* behaviour facilitated by the design of the installation space and the placement of elements within it as through any predetermined performance event. Indeed, the 'performance' element of the installation frequently lies in the *viewers* rather than the performers 'actively, flexibly and reflexively stag[ing] their actions within a space' (Jacucci 2004: 3).

A prime example of such an installation is Robert Wilson and Hans Peter Kuhn's *H.G.* (1995). Wilson set up a series of connected installation environments in various rooms and areas in the Clink Street Vaults in London.[11] Having entered alone and moved through a small dusty 'Victorian' parlour, viewers emerged into the vast space, and wandered at will from one installation environment to another. Each setting was composed of fragments of the built environment and carefully arranged artefacts. The materials in each area (beds, shoes, plants, papers) were associated directly with human activity and/or events. Placed with great attention to detail they implicitly and subtly encouraged particular forms of behaviour in the viewers, creating repetitions of pausing, looking up to the ceiling (to see where the sound was coming from), leaning forward (to peer through a small opening), and so on. As they viewed the individual installations, the visitors became an integral part of the larger installation environment. Here performativity is associated with a simultaneity of action and the production of the conditions that give rise to the experience, for as the installation is viewed, 'the event aspect of artistic production … continues to take effect within the installation' (Nollert 2004: 13). As they view the installation, the visitors' behaviour becomes a performance element in the installation environment.

In some installations, viewers' behaviour leads to a reconfiguration of the material environment, as in Yoko Ono's 1997 exhibition *Have you seen the horizon lately?*. Here viewers enter a gallery and are confronted by a 'ray' of ropes fanning downwards from a skylight and two piles of rocks, one on either side of the installation. They are invited to pick a rock from one pile and place it on the other pile, thus very gradually changing the material configuration of the installation. More frequently, as in Stefan Kern's *No Title: Sofa Sculpture* (1994), the material environment might remain constant, but require that viewers actively make a decision as to how to negotiate the installation environment.[12] In *Sofa Sculpture* four sofa-like seats are arranged in a square facing each other. Visitors can choose whether they will clamber over the backrests of the sofa in order to enter into, and thus engage with the installation, or stand outside the square of sofas and view the installation as an artefact from the 'outside'. If they choose the former they find themselves sitting on a sofa facing others who have also made this decision, and thus in a position whereby they must choose either to stay and communicate with their fellow viewers, or to clamber over the backrest again to attain a more distanced observational position. Here, even though the installation's material environment has not changed, a new set of conditions is created within the installation through the visitors' actions.

However, *Sofa Sculpture* extends beyond the experience of the participating viewers. Whilst the viewer activity is taking place *in* the installation those viewers who have remained behind the backrests of the sofas looking at the installation from the outside find themselves seeing the behaviour of the more active participants as part of the installation, even as part of an informal 'performance'. In these performative installations such as *Sofa Sculpture* and *H.G.*, the viewer oscillates back and forth between the positions of viewer and of being perceived as a 'performer'. Indeed, one could find a reverberation here with Merleau-Ponty's notion (1969) that human beings have the unique capacity to occupy simultaneously the position of both perceiver and the subject of a perception. He notes that 'between my body looked at and my body looking, my body touched and my body touching, there is overlapping or encroachment' (1969: 123). In many of the performative installations that are set up such that the visitor is simultaneously looked at by other visitors whilst engaged in the act of looking, there is an explicit intention that an overlapping of the roles of performer and viewer takes place.[13] However, in such installations, and this is what could be said to transform them into performative rather than *performance* installations, wittingly or unwittingly, the viewer is also engaged in the process of creating a new event and thus a new state of affairs.

Whilst *Sofa Sculpture* invites action on behalf of the viewer, that action becomes an integral part of the installation environment and is thus specifically *performative* (Saltz 1997). However, it is only incidentally 'choreographic'.[14] The notion of a *choreographic* installation would incorporate the conscious attempt by the artist to organise movement in space and time within the installation environment. It is clear that choreographic installations need not be constrained to installations generated by choreographers, as is evidenced by Wilson's *H.G.*[15] As an example, in one of *H.G.*'s multiple installation environments a body wrapped in bandages was laid out on the floor of a large crypt-like cellar in the windowless space. The 'entrance' to the cellar was as wide as the cellar itself. In the walls behind the body were two small arch-shaped niches, one to the right of centre and one to the left. Both were dimly lit. Faded flowers and handwritten letters had been placed in the niches. The placement of the bandage-wrapped body on the floor of the large empty space seemed to invite the viewer to come forward and view it at close range. Time after time different viewers stepped up the single step into this 'room', moved towards the body, stood and stared down at this curiosity, their backs customarily to the 'entrance' arch. Many viewers glanced up from the body and saw one or other of the niches on the back wall. The niches seemed implicitly to excite the curiosity of the viewers, tempting the viewer to move closer to them and lean forward to see what secrets they hold. Indeed with extraordinary regularity viewers moved diagonally towards one or other of the niches to peer down at its contents. They then turned and moved away, past the body, perhaps pausing briefly, perhaps with a glance down as they left, then moved out into the broad central 'passage' which led to other *H.G.* installations.

The repetitive, seemingly deliberately structured, movement events, which occurred in the cellar environment, became like a choreographic performance event when viewed from a distance. Indeed, movement behaviours amongst viewers that exhibited an apparently deliberate structure were observable throughout the multitude of discrete environments that constituted *H.G.* For example, in one space, sound emitted from an opening in the ceiling, causing viewers to pause and look up into the source of the sound. In another, viewers needed to climb a ladder to peer into a hole in the wall that contained artefacts placed there by Wilson. This implies that Wilson was aware of the performance-like behaviour that might be generated by the structures of the environments.

But, does this make *H.G.* a performative installation? In a choreographic context the first type of potentially 'performative' installation mentioned earlier, which sees performances taking place in an installation environment with audience standing, or sitting within or around it, includes works such as Siobhan Davies's *13 Different Keys* (1999), Charlotte Vincent's *On the House* (2000; reworked 2003), Carol Brown's *Machine for Living* (2000) and Charlie Morrissey's *The Palm House* (2005). These pieces take place in and around constructed or built installation environments. In most of these installations, as the performance event unfolds before them, the audience can determine their own viewing position in relation to the performance. When viewing the work-event, each mobile audience member individually foregrounds and backgrounds the visual details of movement images by moving from place to place within the performance environment. Viewers find themselves constantly reconfiguring the balance of the performers' respective relationship to each other, to the viewers and to the environment (of which the viewers have become a part), thus generating unique perceptions of the spatial relationships of the performers and the choreographed movement materials.

In works presented in this way, even if the presented choreographic form might be 'the same' each time it is performed,[16] each audience member is seeing perceptually 'different' works, and thus between them creating a multiplicity of what appear to be 'new' states of affairs at the same moment in time.[17] By virtue of this, in spite of the emphasis on a predetermined performance event, these works *could* be called 'performative' installations in that, perceptually, different 'states of affairs' are brought into being by each viewer. This, however, is using performative in its weak sense. These works are perhaps more accurately described as *performance* installations,[18] for neither performers nor audience members are expected to intervene in the predetermined structure of the event, and thus do not modify the event in any way other than in their perception of it. If the term performativity is invoked in relation to such installations, it has more to do with a linguistic relation to 'performance' than with the philosophical conditions of performativity discussed earlier.

In choreographic performative installations that are more closely tied to the Austinian notion of performativity, performers actively intervene in the development of a choreographed performance event as it unfolds (e.g. improvised events) and/or change the shape or texture of the environment in which they are performing, either through the structure of their movement, or the more subtle and variable dynamic qualities with which it is performed. Since the 1990s this type of performance event has tended to be characterised by the use of interactive technology.[19] Here performers actively modify the visual or sonic environment in which they are moving *as* they dance, thus generating a 'performative' event in the strong sense. The event might be pre-choreographed, involve an element of pre-choreographed performance, or be improvised.

In Carol Brown's *The Changing Room* (2002), the performers actively affect certain details of the installation environment. Here a predominantly pre-choreographed performance takes place in a digitally augmented installation environment, which has three distinct performance areas, each with its own spatial orientation. Viewers move from one to the other as they view the choreographic event. This links *The Changing Room* inextricably with performance installations. However, in this discussion, the performativity which is most significant lies less in the fact that a performance is taking place and more in the manner in which the performers actively modify the environment in which they perform through their engagement with an interactive computer program. During a performance of *The Changing Room*, the performers periodically generate and modulate computer-generated avatars through their actions. These avatars become virtual co-performers, 'dancing' alongside the live performers. Through their actions, the live performers are creating new 'states of affairs' (the presence of new entities) in the installation environment and simultaneously inhabiting, performing in and 'performing' the installation.[20]

In other performative installations of this kind, performers might have a more substantial effect. For example, they might create and modulate

Figure 24.1 The Light Room (2002).

a large-scale visual environment and/or sonic texture and thus generate a range of moods and atmospheres through their actions and the details of their performance. Company in Space's *The Light Room* (2002) is an example of the complex, multifaceted interactions between computer technologies and performers that can take place in installation environments. Set in a glass installation designed to create several distinctive performance areas (or 'rooms'), each constructed from glass upon which digital images are projected, *The Light Room* is a complex interactive performance event for five performers.

It integrates choreographed movement, sung and spoken voice and interactive sound and video imagery to create, through the performers' behaviour, an ever-shifting world of sound and image, which is simultaneously live and virtual. Like *The Changing Room*, *The Light Room* is performative both in the 'weak' sense (i.e. it entails a performance) and in the 'strong' sense (i.e. through that performance activity a change is brought about in the detail of the visual and sonic installation environment). Nevertheless, the types of performative installation event represented by *The Changing Room* and *The Light Room* are still primarily under the moment-by-moment control of the artist, and sit firmly within the conventional notion of choreographic performance.

A third type of performative installation with a choreographic tenor represents an even stronger sense of performativity. Installations in this category sit on the edge of the genre of choreography, aligning themselves with the performative installations developed by visual artists and with notions of performative architecture. These extend the frame of choreography to incorporate informal choreographic events and performances generated from the functional behaviours of viewers or visitors within the installation. Such installations adopt some of the principles that underpin performative architecture, for the artistic emphasis is not solely on the appearance of the installation, but on designing the environment on the basis of the dynamics of behaviour it initiates and the spatio-temporal poetics to which it gives rise. Additionally, the perception of the activities which take place in these installations as 'performances' exhibits an implicit association with the work of the 'postmodern' dance artists of the 1960s and 1970s. In their works, these artists celebrated the 'performative' qualities of everyday or functional movements, that is, their potential for becoming performance actions. A subtle, and significant, transformation of the notion of performance takes place when it is applied within such frameworks. In everyday life, functional actions are performed with scant attention to the act of performance itself; rather attention is on what the action can achieve. In an artistic performance, which uses everyday or functional movement as its material, the mode in which actions are performed is more attentive to the actions themselves than to their function. The action thus becomes concerned with the *performance* of that action, rather than the simple execution of that action for functional purposes.

In this context, although the functional actions might be performed for an audience, they are attended to by the 'performer' for their own sake, even though they are knowingly being 'performed' for others. This has implications for developing an understanding of the performative nature of audience-activated interactive installations,[21] in which the design of the interactive system subtly guides visitors' behaviours, through requiring 'functional behaviours' from visitors for the interactive system and the installation imagery to be activated. In a choreographic digital interactive installation designed for audience interaction, visitors tend to both 'perform' the installation and perform *in* the installation. The participants' behaviour in these instances lies somewhere in between; that is, the performance of an action for functional reasons (in this case action intended to trigger the interactive system, and thus 'perform' the installation), the performance of an action being attentive to the nuances of the action itself (and thus perform *in* the installation), and action as performance to be viewed.

Such installations exemplify David Saltz's notion of performative installations. Saltz (1997) suggests that for an interactive installation to be performative, the interactive behaviour of the visitors itself must become part of the aesthetic event, rather than merely the trigger for audio/visual digital activity. Additionally, he argues that a *performative* interactive installation is one which is 'clearly designed to give rise to performances and explicitly accounts for the audience's role within [its] performances' (Saltz

1997: 119).[22] In installations such as these the interactive interfaces must be designed to implicitly guide participants' behaviours in such a way as to generate an overt modification by audience members of the visual and/ or sonic detail, and thus the spatio-temporal appearance of the environment, *and* to make the audience's behaviour an integral part of the installation event. Indeed, in many audience-activated performative installations the interactive interface is intended to subtly guide visitors' propensities with respect to spatio-temporal behaviour in a manner similar to that of an architectural space designed with the dynamics of human behaviour in mind. This affords visitors some possibilities that extend further than the triggering of images and sound, moving them into the realms of reconfiguring the content and texture of the installation environment from moment to moment. In this sense, the installations can be called performative in the strong sense, as a new state of affairs is generated by visitors in each installation event.

Susan Kozel and Gretchen Schiller's *trajets* (2001) and *Sensuous Geographies* (2003) are both examples of this kind of installation. Although neither of them features professional performers or pre-choreographed events, 'performances' constituted by the visitors' actions do emerge. In these installations, audience behaviour does not only generate the modulations of the installation environment but also becomes an integral part of the performance event that is emerging from the installation. Their movement becomes another strand of the choreography of the installation, another layer in the choreography of sound and image. In performative installations such as *trajets* and *Sensuous Geographies*, visitors do not see themselves as primarily performing for others. Rather they are busy attending to their own actions, either as a means of generating the audiovisual detail of the installation environment, or for their own sake. They are thus *unwittingly* performing for the other participants who inhabit the installation space but temporarily take the role of viewer.

In *trajets* visitors are invited into a central space hung with closely spaced banners, upon which subtle video footage of close-ups of human movement is projected. The visitors are surrounded by subtly flowing light from the digital projections and gently rotating banners. As the participating viewers move through the space the banners turn on their axis in response to the viewers' motion and the proximity of the viewer to the banner.[23] The tempo (and thus dynamic quality), spatial orientations and direction of the rotation of the banners is directly affected by the behaviour of the viewer. Unwittingly, the viewers, in the act of simultaneously viewing the imagery and experiencing the installation, become at the same time the instigators of the 'choreography' of the banners and performers in the 'performative' event embodied in the installation environment. Schiller (2003) has noted that those standing outside the constructed environment of the installation waiting to enter, frequently find themselves viewing the event their fellow participants are generating as a kind of performance.

Sensuous Geographies (2003), which features a spatialised sound environment devised with choreographic principles in mind,[24] also sees visitors enter an electronically sensitised space. The event is akin to a theatre spectacle. Before they enter the active central space visitors don richly coloured silk robes of red, green, blue or yellow; this allows colour-sensitive tracking technology to individuate the trajectory of each visitor's motion as they move in the central area of the installation. The interactive system thus allocates a sound to each visitor as s/he enters the active space. Each sound tracks 'its' visitor, appearing to 'follow' him or her through and around the space. The interactive system responds directly to the velocity and direction of the movement of the visitors and their proximity to each other by applying electronic processes to the sounds (e.g. slowly increasing their tempo, raising or lowering their pitch, granulating the sound, and so on). The result of these processes is that each visitor is able to control the modulation of 'their' strand of sound by changing direction or moving faster or slower. They generate an ever-shifting spatial flow of sounds, each with a constantly changing texture. As the visitors move through the space, although attentive to the effects their individual actions have on the sound environment, as a collective they generate, modulate, and spatialise and thus could be said to be 'choreographing' a complex, textured multi-stranded sonic environment. At the same time they are generating emergent group choreography. As with *trajets*, the visitors in the central active space are engaged in their interaction with the installation, as visitors standing outside that space see an informal choreographic event emerge from the costumed visitors' actions.

Garth Paine's *MAP 2* (2000) is another example of a sound installation that generates an informal choreographic event. This interactive sound environment is sited on a constructed platform in a gallery space. The movement of visitors' bodies in the space initiates and modulates an immersive sound environment within the installation space. As they realise the effect their presence has within the installation, visitors begin to gesture, duck down, and move around the space as they attempt to generate sound strands in the environment. The visitors in this electronically sensitised space appear to be engaged in some strange dance within a choreographic event. Although primarily a sound installation, like *Sensuous Geographies*, *Map 2* generates an emergent choreographic event as visitors improvise within it.[25]

What is common to these installations is that, not only do they allow visitors to actively modify their audio/visual environments, but they are also designed such that people waiting to enter the 'active' (that is interactive) area of the installation spaces can stand on the periphery and perceive the performative event taking place before them. When viewed from the outside the 'active' visitors appear to be engaged in something more than simply viewing the imagery in the installation, or listening to a sonic environment. Their behaviour appears attentive, purposeful, and is performed with an overt and concentrated intention.

Figure 24.2 Sensuous Geographies (2003).

The visitors are, in Jacucci's words, 'reflexively stag[ing] their actions within a space' (2004). The installations are consequently performative in two senses. They are performative within the context of performance *per se*, in the weak sense. They are also performative in the Austinian sense, for the installations themselves guide the visitors' behaviour as they negotiate the installation environment and bring a variety of unique virtual 'worlds' (or new states of affairs) to presence. The elements from which the virtual worlds are generated are lodged in the unseen interactive structures and image banks that constitute the computer program, and emerge as unique forms as the interactive system responds to the motion of the visitors. In this way the installations present, rather than represent the ever-changing events that have been brought to presence. Finally, because the design of the interactive interface in all these installations requires full body movement for it to be activated, the combination of the viewer's behaviour and the movement of the imagery and/or sound appears to the casual viewer as a choreographic event.

The notion of the performative in choreographic installations thus ranges across a continuum that moves from formally choreographed works, performed within an installation environment, to audience-activated interactive installations in which the audience become the performers as they engage in a dialogue with the interactive system. To varying degrees, these require levels of performative behaviour from viewers and participants that bring about not merely a performance event, but also a change in a state of affairs, which is a central feature of Austin's notion of performativity. However, it is the third type of performative installation, in particular the digitally generated interactive installation, that embodies the paradigm of performative installations in the strongest sense, for in these the participants not only bring about unpremeditated changes in the material form of the installation environment through their actions, but they also unwittingly generate informal performances as they engage with the installation. This fulfils both Austin's and Saltz's requirements for performativity in an installation context.

When they are devised by, or in collaboration with, choreographers, these installations could be seen to constitute a new mode of choreographic activity. Not only are they designed such that emergent choreographic events are created unwittingly by the participants' actions as they engage with the installations, but also such that the visual and or sonic imagery is subjected to spatio-temporal, and thus choreographic manipulations as the interactive interface mediates sound and image in relation to the spatial and dynamic qualities of the visitors' behaviours. This gives the installations choreographic content at several levels and can lead to plausible claims regarding their choreographic nature, not only of the kind of installations discussed above, but also those that might present choreography without live performance. Indeed, it is not beyond the bounds of possibility that in the future, installations that comprise visual imagery and sound which are generated, spatialised and their qualities modulated by visitors' behaviour in the installation environment might eventually be understood as 'choreographic' installations, even though no live dance performance is involve.

Notes

1 Tracked using a video tracking system.
2 See Butcher and Melrose (2005) for further information.
3 See Dixon and Smith (2007) for an overview of contemporary digital performance and installation practices.
4 Companies such as Troika Ranch (Mark Coniglio and Dawn Stoppiello: e.g. *16 [R]evolutions*, 2006), Palindrome (Robert Weschler: e.g. *Jenseits der Schatte*, 2006) and Company in Space (Hellen Sky and John McCormick: e.g *The Light Room*, 2002) develop performances of this kind.
5 Although, as with all philosophical concepts, there is considerable debate between linguistic philosophers, such as Austin, who work within the English-speaking traditions and those from post-structuralist traditions, such as Foucault and Derrida, who extend the linguistic aspects of the performative to incorporate sociological and subject-critical applications.
6 Austin notes that the same utterance (e.g. 'I pronounce you man and wife') might not be performative on all occasions, for the performativity of the utterance depends on the intention of the speaker and the context in which the utterance is made. The same utterance can therefore be 'used on different

occasions of utterance in [two] ways … performative and constative' (Austin 1962: 121).

7 The terms reference a philosophical distinction which posits the weak sense as the use of a term in the 'ordinary' sense, and the strong sense as the use of a term in a 'philosophically stringent' sense.

8 Whilst fine art installations have their roots in the work of Marcel Duchamp, 1960s/1970s neo-dadaists, and artists such as Vito Acconi, choreographic performative installations have their precedents in experimental dance and performance practice that took place in the 1960s and 1970s in the UK (happenings, performance work developed and presented in lofts and other sites).

9 Performance art constitutes work presented in a visual arts context in which the actions of an individual or a group, rather than an object, constitute the work. Installation art constitutes spaces that viewers can physically enter, and which, although the installation space might contain collections of objects/elements, both space and elements are considered to be a singular entity (Bishop 2005).

10 A search of the Internet under the term 'performative events' reveals that many performance artists describe their work as 'performative'.

11 The site of a medieval prison and later the storage space for seizures of contraband by Customs officials. Built of old red brick the vaults comprised passages, open spaces and crypt-like rooms, all of which Wilson used in this vast installation.

12 Details of this installation can be found in Nollert 2004: 106.

13 Interestingly, in *H.G.* I found that once I had experienced the role of observing other viewers, from time to time when I myself was engaged in the act of viewing I was conscious that I was being viewed. This brought another dimension to the elided roles, that of conscious rather than non-conscious performance behaviour in the 'active' viewer.

14 Here I use 'choreographic' to mean the organisation of motion in space and time.

15 Perhaps unsurprisingly, Robert Wilson is a theatre director rather than a fine artist.

16 The notion of the 'same' is a contested notion in the context of performance (Rubidge 2000; Van Camp 1981). Here the 'same' does not mean identical in every way but substantially the same in terms of the choreographed form associated with the piece in question.

17 Danto (1981) argues that at each viewing of a work a new work of art is created, inasmuch as each viewer perceptually configures the features of the work of art differently according to their interests.

18 As indeed Carole Brown calls *Machine for Living* (2000) and *Never* (2000) performance installations (www.carolbrowndances.com).

19 Here 'interactive technology' refers to multi-stranded interactive systems which use performers'/participants' behaviour to activate them and the imagery to which they give rise. Dynamic tracking systems (e.g. video tracking, radio tags) or 'switch' sensors such as pressure pads send messages concerning the activity of performers/participants to a bespoke computer program to activate the interactive technology. Through the participant behaviour tracked by these sensors the volume and texture of sounds might be modified, video images or computer graphics blurred, distorted, multiplied, changed in size or colour, or overlaid with other images, or the rhythm or spatial positioning of virtual images or sounds altered. Parameters of participant behaviour used to alter the imagery include direction or velocity of travel in the space, the size or velocity of an action, the proximity of participants, either to each other or to designated features in or of the installation environment.

20 Interactive installations are designed to generate a delimited range of spatial and/or temporal behaviours of images and/or sounds when activated by visitors, much as a score for a structured improvisation is designed to generate delimited structures of sound or motion. Because the behaviour of the imagery is initiated and shaped by the behaviour of interactors it can be argued that the installation is being 'performed' by interactors.

21 'Interactive installation' here refers to digitally activated interactive installations.

22 In the first instance Saltz refers to the performance engaged in by the interactor, in the second to the 'performance' of the installation.

23 The banners are driven by motors linked to and activated by a computerised interactive system.

24 That is applying a choreographic understanding of space to the programming that generates the trajectories of the movement of sound strands through the installation's space, and an understanding of the compositional values of velocity in movement in a choreographic context.

25 The use of the term 'choreography' in relation to these installations is intended to acknowledge the fact that, as with Wilson's *H.G.*, the spontaneously generated forms and structures of the movement behaviours that emerge within the installations resemble those associated with choreographic works. It is perhaps significant that, as composers, both Paine and MacDonald have for several years been involved in collaborations with choreographers.

Bibliography

Austin, J. (1962) *How to Do Things with Words*, 2nd edn (1975) ed. J. O. Urmson and M. Sbisà, Oxford: Oxford University Press.

Bishop, C. (2005) *Installations: A Critical History*, London: Tate Publishing.

Butcher, R. and Melrose, S. (eds) (2005) *Rosemary Butcher: Choreography, Collisions and Collaborations*, London: Middlesex University Press.

Butler, J. (1990) *Gender Trouble: Feminism and the Subversion of Identity*, New York and London: Routledge.

—— (1993) *Bodies that Matter: On the Discursive Limits of 'Sex'*, New York and London: Routledge.

Carr, E. (2003) 'Sensual healing that's a real audience turn on' *Sunday Herald*, Glasgow, 9 February, p. 11.

Danto, A. (1981) *The Transfiguration of the Commonplace*, Cambridge, MA and London: Harvard University Press.

Deleuze, G. and Guattari, F. (1987) *A Thousand Plateaus: Capitalism and Schizophrenia*, Minneapolis and London: University of Minnesota Press.

Dixon, S. and Smith, B. (2007) *Digital Performance: New Technologies in Theatre, Dance, Performance Art and Installation*, Cambridge, MA: MIT Press.

Garoian, C. R. (1999) *Performing Pedagogy: Toward An Art of Politics*, Albany, NY: State University of New York Press.

Jacucci, G. (2004) 'Interaction As Performance: Cases of configuring physical interfaces in mixed media', unpublished PhD thesis, University of Oulu. Available online at <herkules.oulu.fi/isbn9514276051/isbn9514276051.pdf> (accessed January 2009).

Langenbach, W. R. (2003) 'Performing the Singapore State 1988–1995', unpublished PhD thesis, University of Western Sydney. Available online at <http://arrow.uws.edu.au:8080/vital/access/manager/Repository/uws:576> (accessed January 2009).

Linker, J. A. (2003) 'Aesthetics in an Expanded Field: Towards a performative model of art, experience and knowledge', unpublished PhD thesis, Pennsylvania State University. Available online at <http://www.sova.psu.edu/arted/grad/Phd/dis.htm> (accessed January 2009).

Merleau-Ponty, M. (1969) *The Visible and the Invisible*, trans. Alphonso Lingis, Evanston: Northwestern University Press.

Nollert, A. (ed.) (2004) *Performative Installation*, Cologne: Snoeck.

Rubidge, S. (2000) 'Identity in Flux: A Theoretical and Choreographic Enquiry into the Identity of the Open Dance Work', unpublished PhD thesis, Laban Centre/City University, London.

Saltz, D. (1997). 'The Art of Interaction: Interactivity, Performativity, and Computers', *Journal of Aesthetics and Art Criticism*, 55 (2): 117–27.

Schiller, G. (2003) 'The Kinesfield: a study of movement-based interactive and choreographic art', unpublished PhD Thesis, University of Plymouth.

—— (2008) 'From the Kinesphere to the Kinesfield: Three Choreographic Interactive Artworks', *Leonardo*, 41 (5): 431–7.

Semetsky, I. (2003) *An Unconscious Subject of Deleuze and Guattari*, Melbourne, Monash University, Centre for Comparative Literature and Cultural Studies. Available online at <www.arts.monash.edu.au/cclcs/research/papers/docs/Unconscious-Subject.pdf> (accessed March 2008).

van Camp, J. C. (1981). 'Philosophical Problems of Dance Criticism', unpublished PhD Thesis, Temple University. Available online at <http://www.csulb.edu/~jvancamp/diss.html> (accessed January 2009).

Choreographic references

Claid, Emilyn (1999), *Shiver Rococo*. Available online at <http://www.embamb.com/>.

Butcher, Rosemary (2001) *Scan*, Rosemary Butcher Dance Company. Available online at <www.rosemarybutcher.com>.

Flexer, Yael (2003–6) *Shrink'd*, Bedlam Dance Company. Available online at <http://bedlamdance.com>.

Vincent, Charlotte (2000; reworked 2003) *On the House*, Vincent Dance Theatre. Available online at <http://www.vincentdt.com>.

Davies, Siobhan (1999) *13 Different Keys* Siobhan Davies Dance Company, Available online at <http://www.sddc.org.uk>.

Brown, Carol (2000) *Machine for Living*, Carol Brown Dances. Available online at <http://www.carolbrowndances.com>.

Morrissey, Charlie (2005) *The Palm House*, Small Wonder. Available online at <http://www.small-wonder.i12.com>.

Sky, Hellen and McCormick, John (*2002*) *The Light Room*, Company in Space. Available online at <http://cis.com>.

Kozel, Susan, Schiller, Gretchen, *et al*. (2001) *trajets*. Available online at <www.trajets.net>.

MacDonald, Alistair and Rubidge, Sarah (2003) *Sensuous Geographies*. Available online at <www.sensuousgeographies.co.uk>.

Paine, Garth (2000) *MAP 2*. Available online at <www.activatedspace.com>.

Kuhn, Hans and Wilson, Robert (1995) *H.G.* London, Artangel. Available online at <http://www.artangel.org.uk/pages/publishing/v_wilson.htm> (accessed January 2009)

Section 6

Relationships with other disciplines

Section introduction

Jo Butterworth and Liesbeth Wildschut

All the chapters in this section discuss choreography in relation to one or more other disciplines, including dramaturgy, architecture, scenography, technology and cognitive science. The rationale for doing so differs in each case, either through a research imperative centred on discipline clusters, by concentration on artistic development, or through seeking connections between arts and sciences, an area of fruitful experimentation that has been widely funded in the recent past.

Liesbeth Wildschut examines the possibilities and challenges of the relationship between dance dramaturge and choreographer. She provides an historical overview of traditional concepts of theatre dramaturgy as connected to the development of theatre. Focusing on current theatre and dance practices in the Netherlands, she questions the diversity of roles for a dance dramaturge, from helping to establish the choreographic concept, to providing critical reflection during the choreographic process, and beyond. One of the important issues raised is the identification of initial resistance of some choreographers, who tend to feel that their intuitive decision-making in the studio might be hindered by dramaturgic scrutiny or the need for rational explanation too early in the creative process. This chapter goes on to give various examples of the possible contributions that a dance dramaturge has to offer a choreographer, not only aiding with text or narrative, but above all with the movement material of the dance. The dramaturge, she argues, can play a role in articulating theories about the choreographic process, which might otherwise remain hidden or unpublished.

Victoria Hunter questions the relationship between the site and the creative process in site-specific dance performance, interrogating the nature of the interaction between site, choreographer, performer, performance, and audience. The chapter begins by addressing initial questions of how we experience, perceive and interact with spaces. The discussion draws upon the work of architectural and philosophical theorists concerned with the experiencing of space including Lefebvre (1974, 1991), Lawson (2001), Tuan (1974, 1977) and Bachelard (1958). These theories are placed alongside those selected from choreographic and performance theory offered by Briginshaw (2001) and Preston-Dunlop (1998), drawing parallels between the philosophical and practical areas of dance and spatial theory. The paper explores concepts concerned with the physical design and construction of spaces, leading to social, phenomenological and personal interpretations that are integral to the experience of perceiving and 'reading' the site. In an attempt to unravel the relationship between site, choreographer and performance, the author utilises practical exemplars from her own site-specific choreographic work to discuss the phenomenological experiencing and embodying of site as experienced by the choreographer, performer and audience.

In 'Dancing with sprites and robots: New approaches to collaboration between dance and digital technologies', Sita Popat and Scott Palmer address the challenge of collaborative research between dancers, scenographers and digital technologists, seeking a model by which a common language can be developed between the collaborators. The chapter describes how the Performance Robotics project achieved cycles of iterative knowledge exchange between dancers and robotics engineers through embodiment exercises. Using similar open-ended creative processes, the Projecting Performance project resulted in computer operators 'dancing' via the control of animated sprites projected on stage alongside performers. The chapter proposes that dancers' knowledge of movement principles and qualities can inform and be informed by rich dialogues with digital technologists.

The last chapter in this section concentrates on issues to do with collaboration between the arts and the sciences, with reference to a joint research project Choreography and Cognition initiated by arts researcher Scott deLahunta with choreographer Wayne McGregor and neuroscientist Phil Barnard. The project engaged practitioners from the field of cognitive science in seeking connections between creativity, choreography and the scientific study of movement and the mind. Together with other selected scientists from neuroscience, cognition and brain science and experimental psychology, they began by exploring their own individual research interests brought about by the stimulus of observing creative processes in the dance studio between choreographer and dancers. At all times the collaborators maintained the integrity of the modes of looking and questioning pertaining to their own research areas, which were extremely open-ended, and thus allowed the chance for making unforeseen discoveries. Crucially, no concrete artistic product was demanded as a condition of outcome, although naturally, new works have been created and presented, and journal articles published.

Together these four chapters demonstrate the growing interest and importance in the discipline of choreography in relation to other disciplines. Sometimes the juxtaposition of dance with another discipline allows deeper understandings to develop, or extends our knowledge of its boundaries, as in Hunter's investigation of the nature of space emerging from architecture or phenomenology. Wildschut's chapter points out how the dance artist can use the knowledge of another discipline to gain deeper insights in his or her own working process. The essential difference here is that whilst Hunter is integrating both artistic and academic knowledge at a personal level as artist-as-researcher, for Wildschut the dance dramaturge acts as ally to the choreographer so that new knowledge may be integrated in and through the artwork itself. It seems that there is an element of chameleon in the dance dramaturge who may take a different role in each collaboration – that of friend, critic, mentor, spokesperson, negotiator or 'therapist'.

Where a number of disciplines choose to collaborate for the purpose of exploration, investigation, play or inspiration, as in these chapters, the nature and methods of the communication are always important factors. Since artists have personal ways of thinking and working, choreographers working with composers or with digital artists can find that they are actually pursuing different aims, or that their ideas are considered subordinate to those of their artistic partner. It is vital to set ground rules for collaboration, to identify the common aim, to maintain dialogue, to understand how to negotiate and to manage the obvious co-dependence. With open, rather than closed objectives, documentation of process becomes an increasingly important factor.

The reasons for interaction with other disciplines are numerous – personal inspiration, new ideas or approaches, the artist's desire for new knowledge or inspiration, or new contexts to work within – in order to extend their own experience as artists. For the choreographer, artistic interaction with another artist can provide a new framework, opportunity or limitation that can open up new challenges or interventions. Perhaps a funding initiative, invitation or commission can seem like an attractive opportunity, but without thinking through the particular compromises often inherent in such situations, artists may find these experiences very frustrating. This is not to say that these encounters might not be valuable to the development of the artists, especially after reflection and in hindsight. Such collaborations can provide new ways of thinking about one's own practice or might identify the need for re-assessment of a personal choreographic process to determine artistic direction. New expectations can be provided by these inter-disciplinary possibilities, and even if those expectations are not met, other valuable experiences may occur.

These notions of collaboration are not new. We can identify many examples of integrated performance work (as defined by Wagner's theory of *Gesamtkunstwerk*) or work which follows the principles of separation or peaceful coexistence. Diaghilev's Ballets Russes initiated the bringing together of a number of experienced artists in their individual fields, integrating as aspects of the production, whereas Cunningham and Cage's collaborations with visual artists initiated many opportunities for the interrelationship of artistic work, though repudiating any notion of integration which might signify specific meaning or symbolism. Cunningham's insistence on freeing choreography from any dependence on music or setting creates intentional disunity, separating all the elements, to preserve the spectator's perceptual freedom. This pendulum swing of integration–segregation continues to provide choreographers with a continuum of choices, without the need for assimilation or annihilation.

The study of choreography has developed in the academy through its engagement with music and scenography, and equally with ideas and theories from aesthetics, cultural studies, anthropology, gender studies, semiotics, performance theory and the like. Now, increasingly, choreography becomes the catalyst for activity/exploration and research in other disciplines – cognitive science, psychotherapy, robotics engineering or medicine. Perspectives on choreographic practice can only expand and deepen as rapprochement and exchange continue.

Further reading

DeLahunta, S. (ed.) (2007) *Capturing Intention: documentation, analysis and notation research based on the work of Emio Greco*, PC and Amsterdamse Hogeschool voor de Kunsten.

Hamera, J. (2006) *Dancing Communities: Performance, Difference and Connection in the Global City*, Basingstoke: Palgrave Macmillan.

LaMothe, K. L. (2006) *Nietzsche's Dancers: Isadora Duncan, Martha Graham and the revaluation of Christian values*, New York: Palgrave Macmillan.

McCarren, F. (1998) *Dance Pathologies: Performance, Poetics, Medicine*, Palo Alto, CA: Stanford University Press.

Oddey, A. and White, C. (2006) *The Potentials of Spaces: the theory and practice of scenography and performance*, Bristol: Intellect.

25 Reinforcement for the choreographer

The dance dramaturge as ally

Liesbeth Wildschut

From 28 October to 11 November 2006, the thirteenth occurrence of the CaDance Festival took place in The Hague, the Netherlands. According to the festival programme, CaDance is a modern dance festival where the audience can admire works by both young talented choreographers and experienced makers, which are performed by young dancers at the start of their career as well as by acclaimed and experienced dancers. Mirjam van der Linden, a Dutch reviewer, wrote in the daily newspaper *De Volkskrant* of 10 November:

> In dance, all attention is drawn to the body. As we could see again, it is the power of the flesh, the physical intuition that distinguishes dance from other art disciplines.[1]
>
> (Van der Linden 2006)

It was striking that several choreographers, presenting themselves during the festival, reported their co-operation with a dramaturge. Whereas theatre makers have a long tradition of working together with dramaturges, the dance dramaturge is quite a new phenomenon in the Netherlands. In the 1980s, a discussion was launched both in professional journals and in debates on whether or not it was a good idea to employ dramaturges in dance performances. Undoubtedly, a dance performance involves a certain dramaturgy, but whether a choreographer needs a dramaturge was (and remains) the question. Utrecht University, after having first gained experience in developing a curriculum in this subject, is the first Dutch university to offer MA students of Contemporary Theatre and Dance Studies a path in dance dramaturgy. This means a step forward in professionalizing dance dramaturgy.

The aim of this chapter is to shed some light upon the possibilities and challenges for dance dramaturges and choreographers when collaborating on the creation of a dance performance.

I will first give a historical overview: when did the profession of theatre dramaturge come into being? We will see that the development of dramaturgy is logically connected to developments within the theatre. I will discuss several views of dramaturges, both historical and current, on how they perceive their role, focusing on theatre and dance in the Netherlands and Flanders. There is currently a growing interest in the role a dramaturge may play in the choreographic process, but there is resistance as well. I will give a description of the dance dramaturge's tasks, which are different for each stage in the making process. Several levels may be focused on, leading us to wonder what knowledge dance dramaturges need to possess.

In this chapter, I elaborate on these developments and argue in favour of the dance dramaturge as the choreographer's ally in the quest for the ideal performance. I am convinced that dramaturges may contribute to a further development of theories about the creation process of a dance performance.

Historical development

The word dramaturge originates from the Greek *dramatourgos*. Although Aristotle's *Poetica* laid the foundations for Western theatre dramaturgy, the German Gotthold Lessing (1729–81) is considered to be the first dramaturge (Brockett 1987: 402). In his *Hamburgische Dramaturgie*, he gave a description of his work as literary adviser of the Hamburgische Nationaltheater where he greatly influenced the choice of repertoire and the text handling. He analysed and evaluated theatre texts for their quality and suitability as repertoire and looked for concrete staging options of theatre texts, whether or not adapted. Nowadays, such activities may still belong to the dramaturge's tasks.

A new kind of dramaturgy came into being under the influence of Bertolt Brecht (1898–1956), who sometimes spent more than five months on rehearsals with his Berliner Ensemble, using all available theatrical means to get the interpretations developed in advance across to the theatre text. The process was recorded in *Modellbücher* (model books) which inspired many theatre makers who themselves never saw the performances of Brecht's plays (Brockett 1987: 655; Styan 1981: 154).[2] The dramaturges who collaborated with Brecht in East Berlin during the 1950s arrived at the core of theatre making, that is, the creation process itself. From there on, guarding and developing the concept belonged to the dramaturge's tasks. His work became based on continuous reflection on the factual staging process. In the 1970s, Peter Stein collaborated with a whole team of dramaturges who acted as group ideologists. In those days, dramaturges contributed to defining the performance's ideological objective by means of background research and discussion, and together with the other makers evaluated the social relevance of the theatre production.

In the development described up to now, the starting point for the production is a text, which is analysed and adapted even before rehearsals begin, and worked out into a concept. The idea has taken root that dramaturges in contemporary theatre practice tend to guard the execution of this dramaturgical concept, developed beforehand, thereby limiting the director's artistic freedom (Bleeker 2003: 164). The unwillingness of some theatre and dance makers to collaborate with a dramaturge has its origins in this attitude. However, developments in the theatre have made room for working methods in which the concept can gradually change or develop. Marianne van Kerkhoven states in an interview:

> Most performances I have worked on are of the work-in-progress type: we start with all kinds of materials and during work we are searching for a place where we will end up.
>
> (in Groot Nibbelink 2005: 3)

The starting points have been created deliberately, but there is no binding concept. Moreover, the stories told are usually no longer linear stories. As in post-dramatic theatre, the theatrical signs are arranged in another way; the performance can be composed of a series of events which have no causal connection. It is rather about presenting a 'different' theatrical reality as such. The audience are often invited to experience the events with all their senses and are given the freedom to bring their own interpretations to what is shown.

As a result of the use of digital media in live performances, great changes that are important to dramaturgy have taken place. By using video, images recorded beforehand as well as live recorded images can be integrated into the performance, forming a relationship with the flesh-and-blood performer. This makes other perceptions and other experiences possible. Chiel Kattenbelt (2004) suggests that the audience was used to viewing spatial totality and an unchanged notion of distance and perspective in the theatre, but through the introduction of the video camera these principles are extended, with spatial fragments and a changeability of distance and perspective. The static character is neutralized; the spectator has to move because he has to reposition himself every time the camera angle changes. But the position of the actor or dancer changes as well. The camera shares the responsibility for their presentation and achievement. Digital media also play a part in the use of decision rules during the performance, which has consequences for the dramaturgy, a method of working which has often been applied by William Forsythe. In his performances, the movement finds justification in the dancer himself, who continually makes choices based on the formal rules and the stimulations offered (Siegmund 2004).

Over the past fifty years, influenced by changes that took place in the theatre landscape, the tasks of the dramaturge have become more varied and numerous. Robbert van Heuven states in *TM*, a Dutch journal for theatre and dance:

> The primacy of the text has disappeared. Other disciplines such as music and movement have become just as important and in some cases even more important. This means that theatre involves more multimedia. All those media generate theatrical signs which are either

> complementary or conflicting. The interpretation of a theatrical text in the broadest sense of the word has more layers and is therefore more complicated.
>
> (Van Heuven 2006: 41)

The dramaturge offers support and reflects on selecting and arranging theatrical signs, so that coherence is created within the scenes and in the sequence of scenes. The many tasks that once belonged to the dramaturge's responsibilities still exist, but in addition, we can see a number of shifts in accent and new tasks. This extension of approaches resulted in dramaturges specializing and developing in disciplines in which text does not play a (dominant) part, such as mime or dance. Choreographers like Pina Bausch and William Forsythe have employed dramaturges. In the Netherlands, some choreographers also began to collaborate with dramaturges, and in the 1980s, discussion was launched about employing dramaturges in the choreographic process.

From theatre to dance

In the 1980s in the Netherlands, the help of a dramaturge was solicited when a choreographer wanted to use text as a source of inspiration, or if he[3] wanted dancers to recite texts. In these cases, the dramaturge could point out several interpretations to the choreographer, as dramaturge Ivo Kuyl and choreographer Hans Tuerlings described in *Notes* (1989). In the journal's following issue Frits Humme disagreed with this sentiment, as he could not see why a dramaturge should only be involved the moment text starts to play a role:

> Dance practice, at home as well as abroad, shows that the dramaturge is not only used because of his knowledge of (drama) texts, but also with a view to structuring the 'performance text', the performance as meaning entity. Dramaturges can be used in mime performances, non-abstract dance performances and musical theatre performances.
>
> (Humme 1990: 30)

A year earlier, Gerdie Snellers had visited dramaturges who were involved in dance productions. It turned out that they indeed worked mainly on productions in which dance was combined with text, mime or film, because 'in such novel combinations the old "dance laws" no longer apply, calling for structure and interpretation' (Snellers 1989: 10). Other new developments in the theatre during the 1980s, such as the appearance of montage performances and post-dramatic theatre as defined by Hans-Thies Lehmann (1999) made it easier for dramaturges to begin collaborating with choreographers.

During the 1980s, the Amsterdam Summer University organized a series of workshops and discussions about what was then called 'new dramaturgy'. People were interested to know how bearers of meaning other than words could be coherently arranged now that the drama text no longer determined all aspects of design. Maart Veldman concluded from her report on this Summer School that, on the one hand, choreographers were attracted to the support dramaturges have to offer in evaluating (often improvised) dance material. On the other hand, they were afraid they would have to defend their intuitive decisions against rational arguments (Veldman 1991: 16–17).

These fears have not disappeared and often have to do with the unknown. Maaike Bleeker (2003: 170) is of the opinion that the practice of dramaturgy as it has developed during the last decades has undergone such profound changes that it seems highly unfair to keep on denouncing it on the basis of what it once may have been. Choreographers' views about the use of employing dramaturges are only slowly changing. Young choreographer Bruno Listopad, for example, was willing to be supported by the CaDance Festival programmer, but his ideal coach would never be a choreographer or a dramaturge: 'such a person is only using you to create his own performance' (Smeets 2002: 17).

Different methods of working also create confusion. Bart Dieho (2005) distinguishes two typical forms in theatre. On the one hand, the dramaturge and director can formulate their view on the working material beforehand, which they subsequently communicate to the audience by the staging of the performance. The dramaturge would then wish to guard this view during the creation process. At the other end of the scale, the staging of the performance does not come into being through deliberate intention, but by experiment with all kinds of materials carried out during the rehearsals. Instead of a concept worked out beforehand, there are only images and trends (Dieho 2005: 72).

The idea of the dramaturge as guardian of the concept is less appealing to many choreographers, as they work intuitively and do not want to be distracted by an inquisitive dramaturge. Before the rehearsals start, there is nothing tangible. There is an idea, surely, but everything revolves around the development of the dance material, which is only created on the dance floor. Intuition, defined as a hunch that is not based on logical reasoning, is a concept obtained by inner thoughts (Van Dale 1993: 1295). Intuition implies unconsciously using all the knowledge you have within. Choices which are made in this way can, however, be made consciously again afterwards through reflection, and as a result, the choreographer gains more insight into his own process, thereby expanding his knowledge. A dramaturge can play a supportive role here, by asking rational questions.

According to Janine Brogt, most people know very little about a dramaturge's activities because they are, by definition, invisible in the performance (in Van Heuven, 2005: 41). Differing from the contributions of designers or composers, their work dissolves into the production. There is also a confusion of terms. In the Netherlands, there is a discussion going on about the boundaries between coaching and dramaturgy.

Their tasks are often mingled because there is an overlap in the activities (Rinsma 2008).[4]

So the confusion originates partly from the overlap between different tasks, partly from a narrow or traditional view of the role of a dramaturge, but also from the diverse ways in which dramaturges see their tasks. However, the broad spectrum of possibilities offers choreographers the opportunity to collaborate with a dramaturge who can connect seamlessly to their needs, needs that might be different at each stage of the creation process and possibly at each performance. Some choreographers might benefit from collaboration with a theatre dramaturge, who is an expert in the field of attributing meaning where the relations between the different sign systems are concerned. Others might need a dance dramaturge who has a special knowledge of movement. Below I give a broad outline of possible tasks.

Dramaturgical tasks in a dance performance

Dramaturgy has a lot to do with making connections, with building bridges. Van Kerkhoven sees these connections as links between the performance and the outside world, between the performance and previous performances, between the fellow workers, between the other texts by the same author, between other texts from the repertoire, between cultural inheritance and current affairs, between theory and practice, between the inner world and the outside world (in Groot Nibbelink 2005). Profiting from his background in theatre studies, the dramaturge has the tools to analyse the performance and the creation process. In addition, reading a lot, seeing a lot, having conversations and travelling are indispensable activities. By being open-minded, by being interested and curious, the dramaturge builds up his knowledge of dance, theatre, expressive arts, philosophy, architecture, films, music, etc. At each developmental stage of the performance, the dramaturge has different tasks. It is of the utmost importance that each party knows what to expect.

The position of the dramaturge

Depending on the needs of the choreographer, the character of the dance piece, the expertise, temperament or preferences of the choreographer, and the available budget, the collaboration will vary in intensity during several stages. However intense the collaboration may be, dramaturges agree that the director or choreographer *must* have the final responsibility. Brogt says: 'It must always be clear: there is one person in the performance who decides and that is the director. Otherwise it will be chaos, unless you are working in a collective' (in Groot Nibbelink 2003: 6). As a rule, the dramaturge does not take decisions, but reflects, gives advice and makes suggestions.[5] In certain cases, particularly when the choreographer is also a dancer or participates in the dance piece as a dancer, the dramaturge may be given power of decision. Some choreographers look for someone to carry, support and advance their artistic ideas, in the concept stage as well as in the rehearsal stage. Choreographer Nanine Linning and Peggy Olislaegers worked that way in *Cry Love* (2006). Others have artistic ideas and want them to be transformed by the dramaturge's input, turning them into a common starting point, which is the way favoured by Gabriël Smeets (Groot Nibbelink 2004).

Choreographer and dramaturge participate in the same creative process, but each has a different perspective. The dramaturge reflects on the ideas of the choreographer, on the material being created during the rehearsals and on the audience's reactions to the performance, which may cause the performance to change again. He inspires and challenges the choreographer. A discussion on the way in which the role of the dramaturge is shaped during the various stages in the creation process follows.

The starting point of the performance

During the stage of concept development, the dramaturge will no doubt ask questions to get a clear definition of the choreographer's ideas, for example, ideas about motivations, themes and social involvement. Does the choreographer want to comment, expose something, or deliver experiences? By asking questions, the dramaturge can provide support in understanding fascinations and goals, in separating main issues from side issues, helping to deepen, broaden or nourish the theme to be pursued. He can carry out research with an eye to inspire the choreographer and to provide insights into the debates being held on this theme in society and dance. He can sort out how the theme is connected with what occurred before in terms of the history of dance or in current dance practice. By using images, research, poetry, biographies, music, films, people's experiences, desires, etc., he can supply information about the historical, current, social and political contexts of the subject. The task includes not only finding sources, but also analysing them and communicating the results in a clear and inspiring manner to the choreographer.

The dramaturge's questions can also relate to the staging: how does the choreographer want to translate the theme into dance, sound, design, projections, costumes, lighting, etc.? What style does the choreographer want to present? With which audience does he want to communicate? How large is that audience? Does the course of the story run smoothly or is it broken down in fragments? Is there one climax or a succession of smaller climaxes? Is there a musical structure? What skills do the dancers need? What kind of bodies should be on stage and to what extent might they be abstracted? How does the casting take place? Sometimes choices are made as a matter of course. The dramaturge will keep asking the whys and wherefores of the choreographer's choices and preferences or suggest alternatives. What are the possibilities and the consequences of the various options? What limitations need to be taken into account?

The concept may be regarded as a point of reference during the rehearsal stage. The choreographer may regard this concept as a goal that must be realized in the staging or as a basic idea that can be extended, adapted or changed during the creation process. The dramaturge's task is to observe what is happening during the staging process, and, by asking questions, identify what has changed in the original ideas, or to point out options that have not yet been researched. Sometimes there is little left of the original concept in the final performance.

The rehearsal stage

In the studio, ideas are translated into dance. The presence and the role of the dramaturge are determined by the needs of the choreographer. In the initial stage, the choreographer usually focuses intensely on developing dance material. The dramaturge reflects on what is being created, points out what associations and meanings are evoked by the material and underpins the reasons why. He keeps an overview of the performance and may offer suggestions for a possible structure. He reflects on the consequences of the choreographer's particular choices, which were made unconsciously or based on practical considerations. Providing material for inspiration may still play a part at this stage.

The dramaturge will often adopt a modest attitude in the initial stages. Some choreographers do not want a dramaturge present at an early stage because they are bothered by all his comments. Others do not object at all to his presence, because a dramaturge will view the process from a distance and is able to open things up when progress is 'bogged down' by too much detail. Peggy Olislaegers thinks that a dance dramaturge must adhere to 'behavioural codes':

> The choreographer is in the middle of the creative process, is deeply involved, and is surrounded by chaos which is essential to creation. The dramaturge is involved in another way and looks at the dance piece from a greater distance. The dramaturge must remain aware of the fact that his position makes reflection and analysis easier. That is why the dramaturge should respect the vulnerability of the profession. Adopting an arrogant attitude is simply not done.
>
> (Olislaegers in an interview, November 2006)

From time to time, the dramaturge will distance himself from the work process and play the role of the first, critical and curious spectator. He describes not what he would like to see or what is not there yet, but what he is seeing, what he is experiencing and what his associations are, linking them to his observations. In this way, he should be able to answer questions on why some things work and others do not. This does not mean that only one meaning can be attributed to the piece, as often a dance performance can be interpreted in many different ways, making it more interesting. The audience, unaware of the starting points for the performance and the developments which took place during the making process, should be able to follow a form of logic (of course, the logic could be that there is no logic). It often emerges that a choreographer is interested in a personal opinion from the dramaturge, but a dramaturge must remain constantly aware of the differences between an analysis, a grounded interpretation and personal taste.

At a later stage, he may look at the coherence within a scene and the relationships between scenes. Pina Bausch collaborated extensively with dramaturge Raimund Hoghe (e.g. *1980* and *Waltzer*) while ordering the material which resulted from asking her dancers personal questions. Here the dramaturge is occupied with questions like: What is the sequence? How do the transitions take place? How does the dance piece end? What are the possible consequences of leaving out, adding or repeating dance phrases or larger segments? How is the tension built up? What possibilities are there to guide the audience's observations? Are the several sign systems complementary or in contrast with one another? The dramaturge, in accordance with the choreographer, can maintain contact with the other participants in the project, such as composers and designers.

The performance stage

Even at the performance stage, the performance 'text' keeps developing. The dramaturge can moderate the changes in the performance and discuss these with the choreographer and/or the dancers. By mixing with audiences after the performance, the dramaturge may catch their reactions and as a result suggest changes, or adjustments might be required on tour because of new performance locations.

The outside world

Usually, the dramaturge is the link between the dance company and the outside world: for instance, by requesting subsidies, writing press releases or texts for the programme, although not all choreographers are interested in or familiar with writing texts. As a result of his involvement in the creative process, the dramaturge may introduce the performance to the audience (pre-performance talk) or lead the discussion afterwards (post-performance discussion).

The speciality of the dance dramaturge

Many of the dramaturge's tasks in a dance performance are carried out by dramaturges with a background in theatre studies, focusing on text theatre. They have become dance dramaturges because of their personal interest in or preference for dance, mime or post-dramatic forms of theatre. This implies that they have often developed their own methods of reflection on dance material in practice.

A dance dramaturge who knows how to analyse dance material and to define the various aspects, can underpin his interpretation with specific and perceptible observations, and, as a result, can act with more conviction. His arguments are based on his accurate observations, making his feedback more detailed and his remarks more profound. This enhances the communication between the dramaturge and the choreographer (and the dancers).

The dramaturge can analyse dance at several levels. He can focus his attention on the movements of the dancers, on the dance composition, on the relationships between dance and other sign systems, and, finally, on the structure of the dance piece.

The movements of the dancers

Dance is always about the body. There are numerous nuances and possibilities in bodily expression. To give shape to certain content, a choreographer develops dance material. Therefore, it is important that a dance dramaturge's understanding of the dancer is based on the dance material. In a dance performance, a character, in his various degrees of abstraction, is directly related to movement. Concerning the dancer's movements, a dance dramaturge can focus on the style in which the movements are performed; the quality of the movements related to the use of time, weight and space and the use of flow; the lines being created in the body and in space; the speed of the movements and the onset of the movement; the precision with which the movements are performed; the use of focus (of the body and eyes); the way in which awareness is projected into space; the use of facial expressions; the use of tonus and the use of the spinal column; the use of visible, invisible, fast or slow breathing; the switch between dance phrases; and the differences between moving dancers.

Dance may be experienced in many ways: as narrative, thematic or abstract. When a dance dramaturge not only defines the effect of a dance phrase but also points out the cause of this effect, a choreographer can change his dance material effectively. By changing certain aspects, a whole new interpretation can be created. Choreographer Hans van Manen convincingly showed this principle when, in his capacity as professor occupying an endowed chair at Nijmegen University, he made a short choreography in the lecture hall for dancer Rachel Beaujean (2 February 1988). After her performance, Van Manen asked her to dance the same choreography again, but this time she had to look at him as much as possible, and he had to look at her. 'And indeed, the second time the movements have a completely different connotation. One of seduction' (Lustig 1992: 18).

To provide understanding of the ways in which a dance dramaturge can use his skills to analyse movement, I discuss the example of tonus, based on a study by Vera de Vlieger (2006). Tonus indicates the muscle tension in the body. Each dance language has its own use of tonus. In Butoh a very high tonus is used. In modern dance, there are several techniques based on the contrast between tension and relaxation, like Graham, Horton and Limón techniques. A dancer who is broadly trained will be able to vary his tonus with more awareness.

During her collaboration with Olislaegers, De Vlieger discovered that the use of tonus deserves the dramaturge's special attention. Although it is often used unconsciously, it may be of significant consequence to the meaning of dance. She distinguishes three tonus variants: the functional muscle tension is the tension the body needs to carry out tasks. The personal tonus or representation tonus is different for each person and is, among other things, dependent on mood, emotions, temperament and the person's situation. As a third variant, she mentions the tonus that a person can add himself, consciously or unconsciously, but which is not necessary to carry out movements (De Vlieger 2006: 14). The muscles of dancers are usually clearly visible and one can observe whether the muscles are tensed (flexed) or not. Of course, tension in the muscles can increase or decrease during movement. If there is forcing, a certain woodenness or a certain resistance in the movement, then the tonus will be higher than what is needed to carry out the movement. The personal tonus of a dancer can be seen in dance, for instance, when his movements are similar to daily routines.

De Vlieger argues that tonus cannot be analysed as a separate aspect, because meaning is always dependent on context. Tonus is connected to all other aspects of movement; for example, in abstract dance, when the dancers are required to move in unison, the aim is uniformity and consequently, equivalence in tonus as well. Tonus that is unconsciously higher or lower than intended can cause noise or lack of clarity in dance. By pointing out this unintentional effect to the dancers and the choreographer, tonus can be managed at a conscious level and the dance will become more pure and, in a dramaturgical sense, sharper or more exciting.

According to De Vlieger, the dance dramaturge can note the use of tonus in dance in several ways. For instance, does the level of tonus give the correct or desired quality to the movements? Is the personal tonus of the dancer visible and does it fit in with the context? If uniformity is aimed at, is the tonus of the dancers equal? Is a specific use of tonus visible from other dance languages and is it a consequence of anything done previously? When a dancer just walks, is there a remainder of the tonus left from the section he just finished? Does the tonus shift in the course of the piece and does it happen consciously or unconsciously? If an adjustment to tonus might be a solution to a particular problem, the dance dramaturge may point this out and make suggestions for change.

De Vlieger concludes her research by providing an analysis of Dylan Newcomb's performance, *Burn* (2006). She looked at the use of functional, personal and added muscle tension and its interpretations. Based

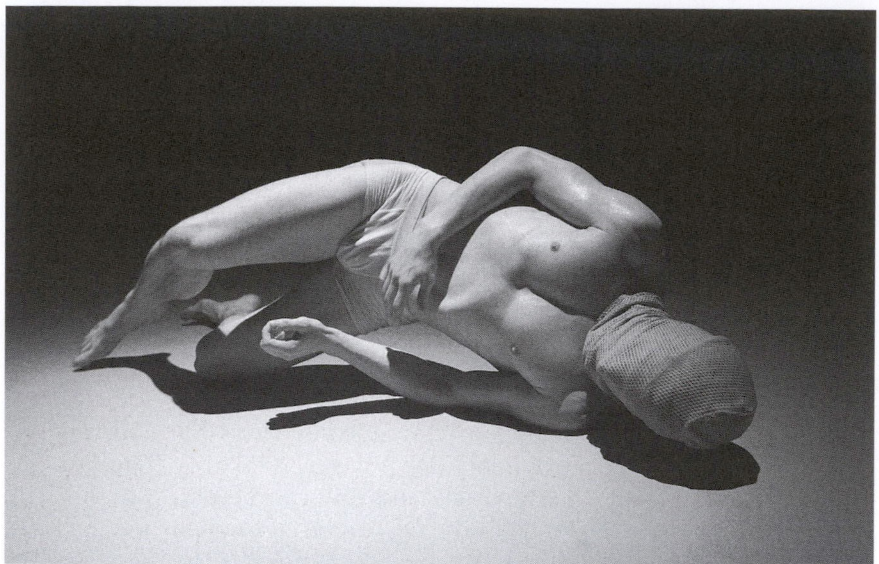

Figure 25.1 Burn (2006) Choreographer/dancer: Dylan Newcomb. Photo: © Robert Benschop.

on her observations she concludes that in this performance a high tonus is consistently used at moments when the character's inner self is expressed. The audience also has an important role. Newcomb tries to involve the spectators in several ways: at certain moments, he takes up the same tonus as his audience and he tries to increase the tension in the bodies of the spectators by addressing them at a physical as well as an affective level.

The composition of the dance

The second category that a dance dramaturge can focus on is related to the composition: the positioning of dancers in space and in relation to each other and to any objects in space; the movement in space and its relation to other dancers, audience and objects; the patterns in space, the repetition of the dance phrases, etc. Does the choreographer want his dancers to make their movements close to the audience, or far away, in the centre or in the periphery? Does he make use of effective ground patterns such as circles or diagonals or are the patterns not clearly discernible or chaotic? Where do the dancers enter and leave the stage? In which way does the choreographer mark out space or open it up?

Repetition is an important choreographic principle. Repetition makes the audience *see*. Does the choreographer have repetitions take place in time (consecutively), in space (in another spot or by using a different body part), in quality (such as intensity) or as multiplying at the same moment? A movement carried out by ten dancers becomes abstract, whereas the same movement carried out by one dancer is regarded as behaviour. How far can a movement phrase be developed still to be recognized as a repetition? Are there moments or aspects that may not be missed by the audience? If so, how is the eye or ear of the spectator guided? In what ways is the choreographer playing with expectations of the audience?

These are a few examples of choreographic principles through which the dance dramaturge can trace the effects of a scene to provide the choreographer with deeper understanding about when, why and in what way changes are desirable.

The relationships between dance and other sign systems

The third category on which the dance dramaturge focuses his analysis has to do with the relationships between the dance composition and other sign systems: sound, lighting, costumes, stage settings, props and video projections. Contemporary dance performances are often multidisciplinary, and an important task for the dance dramaturge is to investigate by means of synchronic or vertical analysis (Whitmore 1994) the effects of this multidisciplinarity. Interactions within and between the several sign systems create meaning, and whilst the dance material is being developed, the dance dramaturge will already make connections with existing ideas about music, costumes, lighting and stage settings. Which hierarchy is apparent and do we want it to be there? What you are hearing influences what you are seeing: how does music guide the interpretation of the movements? Are the movements strengthened or hindered by the costumes? How do the projected images relate to the performer?

The dance dramaturge makes the choreographer realize what effects the interaction of the several sign systems may have on the dance. Of course, the separate development and simultaneous presentation of, for instance, dance, sound, lighting, etc. is nothing new. However, with greater access to the use of digital techniques, the options of choreographers and designers have increased considerably. The dance dramaturge can play a part in keeping choices *and* consequences well organized. It is a major and necessary task, according to Heidi Gilpin, dramaturge for Forsythe, for the dramaturgy of contemporary movement performances to expose and explore how this multidisciplinary quality functions at the compositional level in the creation of these productions, as well as in the development of new discourses through which to interpret them (Gilpin 1997: 87).

The structure of the dance piece

The next category consists of aspects relating to the structure of the piece: the order of the scenes, the transitions between them, tension building and the temporal development of the dance piece. As the dance occurs in time, repetition is frequently applied to choreography to ensure coherence. Certain aspects of a scene may return a different level of movement content in the following scenes, causing longer lines in the composition. Smeets collaborated with choreographer Nora Heilmann on the structure and coherence of *Spunk* (2004) by plotting and schematically drawing several lines: the line of physical presence and absence, the energy line (increase, decrease and ebbing away of energy, recharging energy), and the line of the sounds the body produces in that particular space – when is something really visible and when is it not? Based on these lines, Heilmann and Smeets made their particular choices (Groot Nibbelink 2004).

By using diachronic or horizontal analysis (Whitmore 1994), the dance dramaturge makes the choreographer understand the effects of interaction. Scenes often have certain dynamics of their own, but the relationships between the scenes receive little attention. By reflecting on how one element reacts to another, scenes can be arranged more carefully and may be improved by slowing down or accelerating transitions between scenes. In determining the scene order, logic is an important factor, but practical considerations also play their part, such as the physical stamina of the dancers.

Finally

The dance dramaturge will consider the several categories discussed above separately and in terms of their coherence. They touch upon the essence of the performance: 'the power of the flesh ... that distinguishes dance from other art disciplines', as Mirjam van der Linden expressed it at the beginning of this chapter. Personally, I am convinced that dramaturges who understand how to apply their knowledge and skills to the effects of the bodies on stage can contribute positively to the further development of dance in their collaboration with the choreographer.

A look into the future

Many choreographers are willing to communicate their own experiences and understandings by interviews, for example see *Dance Makers Portfolio: Conversations with Choreographers* (Butterworth and Clarke 1998); *No Wind No Word* (Ploebst 2001) and *It's life Jim. But not as we know it* (Van den Braembussche 2001). There is literature in abundance discussing work of choreographers, but these verbal and written accounts of choreographers about their experiences are mostly reflections on their processes *afterwards*.

In my opinion, dance dramaturges can and must contribute to the further development of theories about choreographic creation processes. They should be able to describe, document, analyse and comment on the making processes while evolving. When choreographers and dance dramaturges act as allies, dramaturges have access to the creation process, gaining more understanding of the intuitive stages and the way in which choices are made. By keeping dramaturgic files and by not only describing but also analysing choreographic creation processes, the manner in which the choreographer's working methods evolve can be identified. By comparing creative processes, similarities and differences can be analysed and explained and more understanding can be acquired of the dynamics of creation. This can be helpful for the choreographer involved as well as for colleagues to reflect on their own making processes, decision making and intuitive knowledge. More documented knowledge would be useful as a bridge towards inviting spectators into the performance and giving them keys to develop other ways of looking. This need for additional knowledge (through pre-performance talks and post-performance discussions, for example) is related to the changing role of the spectator as an active interpreter and/or participant.

Notes

This chapter is translated from Dutch by Conny van Bezu, subsidized by the KNAW (Royal Netherlands Academy of Arts and Sciences).

1 Translated from Dutch.
2 Nowadays, we speak of dramaturgy files. Such a file was kept during the process of making *Bartók Aantekeningen* (Bartók Notes 1986), in which the Belgian choreographer Anne Teresa de Keersmaeker and the dramaturge Marianne van Kerkhoven collaborated. Afterwards, a book of the dramaturgical material was published, of which, in the end, a large part was not used in the performance (De Keersmaeker and Van Kerkhoven 1987). The work sketches and notes can be viewed online at <http://ltd.library.uu.nl/doc/601/bartok.pdf>.
3 In order to improve the readability of this chapter I have used the terms 'he' or 'his' where 'she' or 'her' would also have been appropriate.
4 See also the chapters by Larry Lavender and Dirk Dumon.
5 The collaboration between dancer and choreographer Emio Greco and dramaturge Pieter C. Scholten is an exception, which finds expression in the way their company is named: *EG|PC*.

References

Bleeker, M. (2003) 'Dramaturgy as a Mode of Looking', *Women & Performance: A Journal of Feminist Theory*, 26 (13/2): 163–72.

Braembussche, A. van den (2001) *It's life Jim. But not as we know it*, Amsterdam: Stichting Zwaanproducties.

Brockett, O. (1987) *History of the Theatre*, 5th edn, Boston: Allyn and Bacon.

Butterworth, J. and Clarke, G. (eds) (1998) *Dance Makers Portfolio: Conversations with Choreographers*, Wakefield: Centre for Dance and Theatre Studies at Bretton Hall.

Dieho, B. (2005) 'Syllabus Dossier Theaterdramaturgie', unpublished, Utrecht University.

Gilpin, H. (1997) 'Shaping Critical Spaces: Issues in the Dramaturgy of Movement Performance', in S. Jonas, G. Proehl and M. Lupu (eds) *Dramaturgy in American Theater: A Source Book*. Orlando: Harcourt Brace College Publishers.

Groot Nibbelink, L. (2003) *Over Dramaturgie – een gesprek met Janine Brogt*. Available online at <http://ltd.library.uu.nl/doc/307/interview.htm> (accessed 27 October 2006).

—— (2004) *Over Dramaturgie – een gesprek met Gabriel Smeets*. Available online at <http://ltd.library.uu.nl/doc/709/interview_smeets.htm> (accessed 27 October 2006).

—— (2005) *Over Dramaturgie – een gesprek met Marianne van Kerkhoven*. Available online at <http://ltd.library.uu.nl/doc/611/interview.htm> (accessed 27 October 2006).

Heuven, R. van (2005) 'De dramaturg #1. Janine Brogt', *TM*, 10: 40–2.

—— (2006) 'De dramaturg slot', *TM*, 10: 40–1.

Humme, F. (1990) 'Een dramaturg kan meer dan lezen', *Notes*, 1: 30–2.

Kattenbelt, C. (2004) 'Theater en Technologie in het Perspectief van Intermedialiteit en Mediavergelijking', in C. Kattenbelt, P. de Kort and D. Mesker (eds) *Zoekboek 1*, Toneelacademie Maastricht, Hogeschool Zuid.

Keersmaeker, A. T. de and Kerkhoven, M. van (eds) (1987) *Bartók/Aantekeningen*, Gent: Snoeck, Ducaju.

Kuyl, I. and Teurlings, H. (1989) 'Tussen hoofd en hart', *Notes*, 10: 12–15.

Lehmann, H.-T. (1999) *Postdramatisches Theater*, Frankfurt am Main: Verlag der Autoren.

Linden, M. van der (2006) 'Festival CaDance viert kracht van het vlees', *Volkskrant*, 10 November.

Lustig, D. (1992) *Tot U Speekt ... Hans van Manen, bijzonder hoogleraar*, Amsterdam: Nederlands Instituut voor de Dans.

Ploebst, H. (2001) *No Wind No Word*, München: K. Kieser Verlag.

Rinsma, I. (2008) 'Wie coacht de individueel choreograaf?', Utrecht: Theater-, Film- en Televisiewetenschap, Doctoral Thesis.

Siegmund, G. (2004) *William Forsythe: Denken in Bewegung*, Henschel Verlag.

Smeets, G. (2002) 'Een reddingsboei voor de choreograaf', *TM*, 11: 16–18.

Snellers, G. (1989) 'Eureka! Daar zijn de dramaturgen', *Notes*, 10: 8–10.

Styan, J. L. (1981) *Modern Drama in Theory and Practice. Expressionism and Epic Theatre*, Cambridge: Cambridge Univerity Press.

Van Dale Groot Woordenboek der Nederlandse Taal (1993) Utrecht, Antwerpen: Van Dale Lexicografie bv.

Veldman, M. (1991) 'Doe het onlogische: Dans als dramaturgisch proces', *Toneel Theatraal*, 11: 14–17.

Vlieger, V. de (2006) *Spanning! Tonus als dansdramaturgsch aspect*, Utrecht: Theater-, Film- en Televisiewetenschap, Doctoral Thesis.

Whitmore, J. (1994) *Directing Postmodern Theatre*, Ann Arbor: University of Michigan Press.

26 Experiencing space

The implications for site-specific dance performance

Victoria Hunter

Site-specific dance performance is a response by a choreographer to a particular location. That location, environmental or architectural, is the stimulus for performance. Though types of site (or location) and choreography will vary widely, two components remain common – the use of the site and its space. There is a specific interdependence between the site and the performance. Move the performance from the location and its significance will be either lost completely or weakened dramatically. The relationship between the spatial/experiential components and the choreographer and the consequent creative process leading to performance is the subject of this investigation.

Drawing upon the work of architectural and philosophical theorists concerned with the experiencing of space, including Henri Lefebvre (1974, 1991), Brian Lawson (2001), Yi Fu Tuan (1974, 1977) and Gaston Bachelard (1964), initial questions of how we experience, perceive, and interact with space are explored. These theories of space and spatial interaction are placed alongside those drawn from choreographic and performance theory offered by Valerie Briginshaw (2001) and Valerie Preston-Dunlop (1998) in an attempt to begin to draw parallels between the philosophical and practical areas of dance and space theory. Concepts of social and personal space, ways of constructing, experiencing, perceiving, and reading them and the implications for site-specific dance performances are all considered. This exploration will focus on architectural and constructed spaces and will not concern itself with landscape or geographical environments. Though the existence of dance-specific spatial components implicit in choreographic creation is acknowledged, they are not scrutinized here.

Finally, a 'model of influence' is presented as an illustration of how the various approaches to experiencing space can be of influence upon the creative and interpretive process.

Perceiving, constructing and experiencing space

For the purposes of this discussion, the process of perceiving space can be defined as a form of absorbing and ordering information gained whilst experiencing and interacting with space. Perception can be seen as a process of 'making sense' of this information, a process that is particular to each individual. Further definitions are provided by Brian Lawson (2001) and Christian Norberg-Schulz (1966):

> Perception is an active process through which we make sense of the world around us. To do this of course we rely upon sensation but we normally integrate the experience of all our senses without conscious analysis.
>
> (Lawson 2001: 85)

> Our immediate awareness of the phenomenal world is given through perception.
>
> (Norberg-Schulz 1966: 27)

These definitions imply that perception is distinct from analysis and is an active process, occurring subconsciously, almost instantaneously. The act of perception is a personal one, subject to many variables; space and spaces therefore can be experienced and perceived in many different ways by many individuals. Towns, cities, and buildings however are constructed spaces, 'concrete' in dimensions and form, so how can such 'closed' structures produce a variety of responses and interpretations?

Lefebvre (1991) and Lawson (2001) suggest that environments and spaces are 'constructed' in a variety of ways. Lefebvre considers concepts of 'socially' and 'personally' constructed space as 'mental' or 'real' space. Linked to this is the practice of architecture itself. Whilst many architects are assigned (or assign themselves) to a particular architectural 'school' and/or movement, few provide a concise, generic definition of the term 'architecture'. For the purposes of this discussion therefore, an appropriate definition of architecture is provided by the dance scholar and architectural user and 'consumer' Valerie Briginshaw:

> spaces that are structured actually or conceptually according to ideas associated with building design.
>
> (Briginshaw 2001: 183)

On first inspection, this definition appears straightforward enough. On closer inspection, however, it begins to raise questions regarding authorship and construction. Buildings do not simply appear; they are subject to complex processes of planning, designing, and re-designing, eventually culminating in construction and realization. Likewise, towns and cities evolve according to a number of factors including history, economic growth, social migration, and national and international policy. Buildings, towns and cities, largely speaking, are subject to rules and regulations regarding planning. They are constructed environments and, as such, dictate and influence how we experience and ultimately interpret them.

An examination of the use of scale in construction can serve to illustrate this point. Brian Lawson (2001: 29) observes: 'Scale is one of the most important elements in the social language of space.' He then cites the example of the city of Prague dominated by the grand Hradčany castle built at the top of a hill overlooking the city. He describes how housing built at the foot of the hill is small and increases in size and stature towards the top of the hill nearest the castle, reflecting the social hierarchy in existence at the time of construction (Lawson 2001: 50–1). This use of scale indicating wealth and status is still prevalent in Western society today. Large houses are deemed 'grand' and 'imposing' conferring social and economic status upon the occupants. Similarly, the size and scale of many civic buildings reflects the importance of the activities taking place within. Notions of power and control can also be associated with large civic and corporate buildings.

> As a social construct space is not transparent and innocent, it is imbued with power of different kinds.
>
> (Briginshaw 2001: 30)

Briginshaw's observation highlights how particular elements of location, scale, construction, and design can be interpreted and imbued with meaning according to the dominant ideology of a particular society. Historically, in the UK for example, we associated the term 'inner city' with notions of poverty and deprivation, whilst 'the countryside' carried with it images of peace and tranquillity.[1] Social construction of space can be seen therefore to develop through associations and connotations assigned to particular environments and spaces. Through common usage these associations become part of the common psyche. Thus, cities, spaces, and environments can be seen to be 'constructed' on a number of levels including physical and social as influenced by ideology.

Such social and ideological factors can influence the way in which we interact with and experience spaces. However, the physical construction and design of spaces and buildings directly dictate the manner in which we physically engage with space. Road systems and one-way traffic management schemes dictate how we enter cities and towns. Entrances and corridors determine how we navigate our journey through buildings. Lawson describes architectural and urban spaces as:

> Containers to accommodate, separate, structure and organize, facilitate, heighten, and even celebrate human spatial behaviour.
>
> (Lawson 2001: 4)

Here, Lawson is referring to a degree of architectural 'control' examined later.

Constructed environments inevitably provide us with a wealth of formal and informal spatial information. Whilst we may not consciously be aware of their impact upon our perception of space, Lawson explains how our brains prioritize these elements over others when later attempting to recreate a space in our 'mind's eye'. He (Lawson 2001: 62–8) identifies these elements as:

- Verticality
- Symmetry
- Colour
- Number (of windows, columns, doors, etc.)
- Meaning (i.e. 'labels' church, gallery, etc.)
- Context (our context when entering a space)

The first four elements listed here refer to an interaction with the more formal and structural elements with space, leading perhaps to an aesthetic response. The remaining two elements, meaning and context, both relate to the social and personal construction of space and require further examination.

The dominant ideology of any given society attaches labels of meaning to particular buildings and environments. These meanings are often constructed externally via architectural design and internally through conventions of use. This type of functional inside/outside interface is also facilitated via the internal design of the building serving to orchestrate and engineer the individual's interaction with the space and ultimately the institution it houses or represents. Lawson provides a pertinent illustration of this process when describing the conventions surrounding the construction of and interaction with church buildings:

> The Christian church not only organizes space for ritual, but also uniquely locates each of the roles in the special society of worship. The chair, the congregation, and the clergy each have their own place, and a Christian visiting a strange church will have little difficulty in knowing where to go and how to behave.
>
> (Lawson 2001: 26)

Lawson implies that the 'meaning' of the space refers not only to its external facade, but also indicates the building's function and the social norms employed when interacting with the space. These meanings and social norms attached to certain buildings can be culturally determined and are often identifiable only to those familiar with the conventions of usage. For example, an individual well versed in the conventions and social norms of a church building may be unfamiliar with the conventions employed within other places of worship. The individual's subjectivity and the context in which they experience a particular building or site may also impact upon their experience and perception of the space.

Personal, social, time-based, environmental, cultural, geographical, and political contexts can influence and impact upon our experience of place, to quote the Dutch architect Aldo Van Eyck:

> Whatever space and time mean, place and occasion mean more. For space in the image of man is place, and time in the image of man is occasion.
>
> (Van Eyck in Lawson 2001: 23)

Again, using the example of a church space, we can see how our experience and interaction with the space can be radically altered according to the context of the occasion occurring within the space. Weddings, funerals, and christenings all elicit differing responses to and prescribe differing interactions with the space, whilst the internal and external architectural make-up remains essentially the same. Choreographers engaging in the creation of site-specific work need therefore to research experientially the site on a number of occasions and from a range of social, cultural and contextual perspectives prior to embarking upon the creative process (see Hunter 2007).

Whilst 'external' factors focus the experience of space, therefore, 'internal' elements add contextual meaning. Erving Goffman (1969) highlights how the 'performance of self' affects the way in which we interact with any given space and Gaston Bachelard (1964) emphasizes the psychological associations we make with spaces, suggesting that attics, for example, relate to the 'super ego' (1964: 19) whilst basements connect to 'the dark id' (1964: 19); the home remains a haven, an 'ideal' space. Lefebvre, however, urges that both external and internal spatial factors operate upon our experience and perception of space.

> In actuality each of these two kinds of space involves, underpins and presupposes the other.
>
> (Lefebvre 1991: 14)

Thus both external and internal 'contexts' influence and inform our experiencing of space implying a two-way interaction between individual/space and space/individual.

Notions of a passive, arbitrary interaction with spaces are further challenged when exploring Lawson's earlier reference to architectural 'control'. He argues that our experience of space is managed by architects, designers, and town planners in particular ways. In this sense, space is both 'product and producer' (Lefebvre 1991: 142). It is produced by the architect and planner and it produces certain patterns of behaviour:

> Space commands bodies, prescribing or proscribing gestures, routes, and distances to be covered.
>
> (Lefebvre 1991: 143)

Lawson's example describes a pathway and a series of gates leading to a private house:

> [As an architectural system which] symbolizes and controls the transition from public through semi-public and semi-private areas to the private domain. It signals changes of possession, of control, and of behaviour.
>
> (Lawson 2001: 12)

Architectural 'control' can be experienced in a vast number of buildings in the constructed environment. For example, when entering a hospital building we may walk down a directed footpath, through an external covered entrance porch, through automated sliding doors, into a reception area with signs indicating a stated direction. This process again indicates and controls a transition and change in status from the autonomous to the institutional. Equally, site-specific dance performance by its very nature has the potential to challenge and disrupt the site's conventional norms of usage, a factor that can effectively operate as a choreographic 'device' in its own right as the choreographer explores alternative approaches to moving through, on and around the site.

Whilst recognizing the concept of the 'architect as author' it is also important to avoid the intentionalist assumption that a 'closed' or 'fixed' reading of any particular space is achievable or indeed desirable. Lefebvre argues that spaces themselves construct meanings (albeit influenced by the intentions of the architect/planner):

> a space is not a thing, but rather a set of relations between things (objects and products).
>
> (Lefebvre 1991: 83)

This suggests that constructed environments are not simply empty, passive spaces; instead, they actively engage with their contents, users, contexts and environments to construct meanings. Through this process of interaction, according to Michel de Certeau, place (stable, positional) becomes space (mobile, temporal):

> In short, *space is a practiced place*. Thus the street geometrically defined by urban planning is transformed into a space by walkers.
>
> (de Certeau 1984: 117)

The meanings and associations encountered in sites and places then are not absolute but are open to the further processes of individual interaction and interpretation resulting in multi-'readings'.

Internal and external space

As the concern of this chapter is with the concepts of experiencing and perceiving space, the notion of 'architect as author' is limiting, as observed by Mildred and Edward T. Hall,

> Far from being passive, environment actually enters into a transaction with humans.
>
> (Hall and Hall 1975: 9)

This 'transaction' is key, as acknowledged by Hall and Lefebvre: both place the individual at the core. Lefebvre refers to the concept of 'internal and external space' (1991: 82). In geographical terms, this could relate to indoor and outdoor spaces. In human terms, however, this can refer to 'internal' mental, cognitive space and 'external' physical and sensory space occupied by the individual. He adds:

> each living body *is* space and *has* its space; it produces itself in space and also it produces that space.
>
> (Lefebvre 1991: 170)

According to Lefebvre, therefore, the body *is* space – we consist of both internal (mental) and external (physical) space, we produce ourselves in the world whilst also physically constructing spaces and environments. This third stage, the production of space, can occur in several ways, the most literal of which is the architectural construction of towns, cities and buildings. We can also produce space through our external physical interactions with space. For example, the process of travelling from point A to point B is constructed conceptually as 'a journey'. 'Journeys' can vary in size and duration including movements from room to room or from country to country, consisting of both micro- and macro-forms connecting through both time and space. Accordingly, site-specific choreography presents a unique form of spatial production emerging from the dancer's movement interventions in the site, described by choreographer Carol Brown (2003) as a form of 'ephemeral architecture'.

The inside/outside interface perhaps becomes more complex when considering our 'internal' (mental/cognitive) construction of space. This internal construction of space is also influenced by external factors and combines with elements such as our sensory, kinaesthetic, and emotional responses to create a personal 'construction' of a particular space. In this sense we are referring to different ways of 'knowing' and experiencing a space, acknowledging the influence of sensory and 'other' forms of knowing upon the personal construction of space, in addition to the more formalized processes of experiencing such as the physical, visual and aural. Personal construction of space can be located as occurring at the point of interaction with environments and implies both an epistemological and physical approach to experiencing space.

Bloomer and Moore (1977) develop the discussion of 'inside' space by focusing on the more physical and anatomical elements of the experiencing process. They argue that our sense of internal space is created by a physical sense of space within the body. For example, in the common perception of the heart as the 'centre' of the body, referring to the heart and other major organs as 'landmarks':

> The heart, with its auditory and rhythmic presence, exemplifies the phenomenon of an internal landmark acquiring a universal spatial meaning in adult life.
>
> (Bloomer and Moore 1977: 30)

They discuss this type of knowing in conjunction with the type of knowing developed by the awareness of touch, the haptic sense,

> To sense haptically is to experience objects in the environment by actually touching them (by climbing a mountain rather than staring at it) … and thus it includes all those aspects of sensual detection which involve physical contact both inside and outside the body.
>
> (Bloomer and Moore 1977: 34–5)

This suggests that the inside/outside interface becomes permeable, with the boundaries between body and space becoming 'fluid' (Briginshaw 2001); sensations experienced on the outside of the body via the skin receptors are also experienced simultaneously on the inside of the body, often in a physical/sensorial manner such as shivering, excitement or revulsion. This further haptic information enables us then, as sensory beings, to locate and orient ourselves within general space. An internal 'grounding' provided by 'haptically perceived landmarks' (Bloomer and Moore 1977: 39) can serve to inform us of our own sense of internal space whilst processing 'external' spatial information. When combined with our 'internal' mental creation of space, these physical and haptic influences can begin to contribute towards our perception of space.

Further to the methods of experiencing space already identified, perhaps the most elusive concept to examine and identify is the sensory experiencing of space. Upon entering a space our senses are immediately challenged and engaged; amongst many elements we react to sight, sound, smell, taste, temperature and touch (our haptic sense referred to previously). This notion of bodily knowing and experiencing in relation to space is a concept, according to Lefebvre, which is often overlooked:

> When 'Ego' arrives in an unknown country or city, he first experiences it through every part of his body – through his senses of smell

> and taste, as (providing he does not limit this by remaining in his car) through his legs and feet.
>
> (Lefebvre 1991: 162)

Certainly, these sensory experiences can be seen to combine with those spatial, aesthetic and contextual images identified by Lawson when later attempting to re-create a mental image of a space. Similarly, certain smells and sounds can instantly evoke a recollection of place, highlighting the power of the senses. In addition, certain theorists have identified a link between space and the kinaesthetic sense, whereby an internal physical sense of motion and engagement is created whilst interacting with a space. Violet Paget, speaking of landscape in *The Beautiful* (1931), observes,

> You always, in contemplating objects, especially systems of lines and shapes, experience bodily tensions and impulses relative to the forms you apprehend, the rising and sinking, rushing, colliding, reciprocal checking … of shapes.
>
> (Paget 1931: 61)

This sense of motion can be linked to the physical aspects of scale and the participation of the body in the appreciation of size. For example, the kinaesthetic feeling induced when standing at the base of the Eiffel Tower in Paris, looking up through the steel structure to its summit. A sense of motion and bodily awareness is evoked, allowing comparison of the scale of the structure with our own human form. Yi Fu Tuan in *Topophilia* (1974) argues that the very words we use to describe certain spaces and environments imply a kinaesthetic relationship:

> The existence of a kinaesthetic relationship between certain physical forms and human feelings is implied in the verbs we use to describe them. For example, mountain peaks and man-made spires 'soar', ocean waves as well as architectural domes 'swell'.
>
> (Tuan 1974: 29)

Tuan's and Paget's acknowledgement of this type of kinaesthetic relationship is important as it serves to underline the existence of these types of knowing with their reliance upon sensation and bodily awareness that challenge the dominance of visual and formal factors. The kinaesthetic experience therefore can be added to the list of elements (sensory, cognitive, spatial, ideological and psychological) that combine and contribute towards our experiencing of space and explain why individuals perceive spaces differently through a 'process of experiencing'.

How all these contextual elements combine is the concern of the site-specific chorographer.

Site-specific dance performance

Site-specific dance performance is defined here as dance performance created in response to and performed within a particular site or location. Examples of this type of work include Tim Rubidge's *Footfalls Echo@Belsay* (2008) performed at Belsay Castle, Northumberland; Motionhouse's *Dreams and Ruins* (2005) performed at Witley Court, Worcestershire; *Genesis Canyon* (1996) choreographed by Stephan Koplowitz, performed at the Natural History Museum; and *Double Take* (2000) created by Suzanne Thomas for Seven Sisters dance group, performed in Selfridges department store, London. These works are inspired by and dependent upon their respective locations and differ from site-adaptive work whereby a preconceived work may tour to a variety of unconventional spaces, such as Siobhan Davies' *Plant and Ghosts* (2002). Whilst these spaces share similarities in their unorthodoxy as performance venues, such works cannot be deemed 'site-specific' in the true sense of the word as the essence of the work remains constant from location to location.

Site-specific choreography is influenced by the choreographer's response to a particular space and/or location, which presupposes an implied awareness from the choreographer when selecting spaces for site-specific performance. The choreographer 'tunes in' to this awareness on a conscious level, whilst simultaneously reacting to the 'processes of experiencing' operating at a subconscious level. Tangible elements will have an immediate impact on the conscious level. These include formal and structural elements of the site, architectural design, historical and contextual information and also the practicalities of staging including sight-lines and health and safety obstacles. At the same time, however, the other 'processes of experiencing', including personal aesthetic and artistic preferences will be informing the choreographer's choices and decisions. As Stephan Koplowitz (1997) observes:

> When creating a site-specific performance one is dealing with multiple levels at once: the architecture of the site, its history, its use, its accessibility. I'm interested in becoming a part of the design and rhythm of the site and amplifying that. This kind of work is not necessarily about big extensions and triple turns, but what is most appropriate for the site. The most virtuosic movements might simply be everyone raising their arms together.
>
> (Koplowitz 1997)

Koplowitz captures here the essence of successful site-specific work, the creation of a carefully constructed balance between the performance and the site. The final performance outcome is at once a reflection of the site and its architecture and the choreographer's personal and artistic response to the site.

For the choreographer, the processes of experiencing and perceiving space and the subsequent interpretation of these responses combine with aesthetic and artistic concerns to inform the creative process by providing stimuli both conscious and subconscious for movement content and creation. This process can operate on a number of levels and is dependent upon the choreographer's working methods and experience. On a simplistic level, the choreographer may be inspired by the function or the architectural design of a space, the shape, form and number of columns and arches, for example. These formal elements may directly relate to the number of sections of a dance work, or may provide a starting point for an improvisational task, improvising around the theme of 'planes' or on the theme of reaching and dropping. An example of such an exercise is described here following the choreographer's observation of a devising task in which dancers were required to respond to the architecture and form of a basement wine cellar:

> Twisting, touching the body, touching the walls. High-arch movements beginning to appear, arms raised to the ceiling whilst body curves over. Sinking, curved body, curved arms. Sliding of feet, turning and dropping, suspending and dropping, delicate.
>
> (Hunter 2004)[2]

In addition to formal and structural site-related components, the individual's kinaesthetic empathy with a space can also influence the dynamic content of the choreography. In *Architecture, Form, Space and Order*, Francis Ching (1996) describes how 'rows of columns can provide a rhythmic measure of space' (1996: 16); this 'rhythmic' information could be interpreted to produce rhythmic, repetitive movements. In addition, the sheer size and scale of a building may influence both the content and the form of a work, causing the choreographer to investigate and explore the concept of size and scale in a choreographic sense, moving from experimenting with large to small movements and gestures. Even the practical concerns of staging can act as a stimulus for creative solutions leading to further performance development. The intangible 'processes of experiencing' and the phenomenological resonances of 'place' also influence the creation of movement material. For example, the subterranean location of a basement or cellar may influence the choreographer's 'processes of experiencing' and trigger contextual associations, to produce a work with an air of mystery or foreboding. Therefore processes involved in the outside/inside interface combined with other sensory influences can combine and contribute to the underlying mood and 'feel' of a piece.

What then are the implications for the site? How does the site itself feature in such an interaction? Is its purpose merely to provide a stimulus and setting for a performance or does the interaction between the space and the performance develop further?

Whilst the site>performance relationship is perhaps relatively easy to visualize, the performance>site relationship could be viewed as more

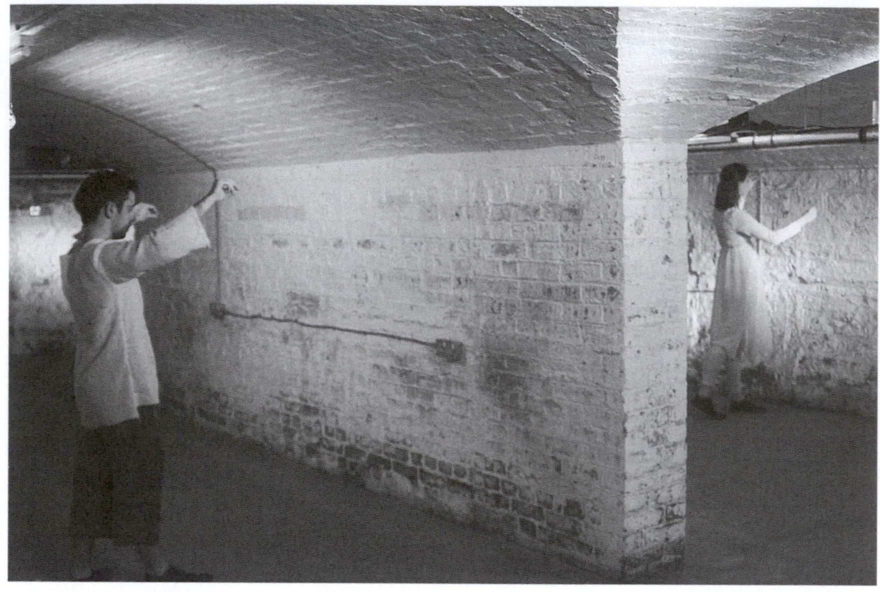

Figure 26.1 *Beneath* (2004). Dancers Sara Ginn and Stephen Musa. Photo: © A. Paul Davies.

complex. Essentially, the creative process can be viewed as a collaboration between site, choreographer and performer. Choreographer Carol Brown alludes to this process of interaction when discussing a dance-architecture workshop:

> In responding to the architecture of the site, the performers uncovered layers of embedded history and new trace-forms. The centre became an ear for the body, listening to the movements of the dancers. Architecture and anatomy traded places. We passed messages between them. The walls spoke.
>
> (Brown 2003: 2)

Drawing upon theories offered in this discussion and considering the relationship or interface between site and choreographer as one which combines a socially constructed space with a personally constructed one, we can begin to see how the dance performance can serve to 're-inscribe' the space (Briginshaw 2001: 57), thus challenging the context, dominant ideology and perception of a particular space or site. Site-specific dance performance situated within a church space, for example, can serve to challenge preconceptions concerning the form and function of the building as the audience use and view the building and its content from a different viewpoint, challenging the codes and conventions of usage. A pertinent example is Gerry Turvey's site-specific dance work *Fallen Angels* (2004) performed in Holy Trinity church, Leeds (www.turveyworld.co.uk.). In addition, the codes and conventions of performance spectatorship are also challenged. Gay McAuley discusses the conventions adopted in a traditional theatre setting:

> The behaviour of actors is marked; spectators know that it is to be interpreted differently from apparently identical behaviours occurring in other places. Spectators in the theatre both believe and disbelieve, they play a game in which they permit themselves to believe to a certain extent what is occurring.
>
> (McAuley 2001: 4)

This participation by the audience in a theatrical 'game' is challenged and heightened in site-specific performance as the rules are no longer defined according to the accepted conventions of theatre-going; they become fluid and ill-defined, opening up the interpretive possibilities.

Pioneered by the post-modernists in the 1960s and 1970s, site-specific art and performance provided the ideal genre for the challenging of artistic convention:

> The conceptual focuses of sixties artists on the avant-garde use of site specific performance spaces which stretched audience perception, on a particular urban sensibility and on blurring boundaries, such as inside/outside, private/public, and art/everyday life, paved the way for what was to follow.
>
> (Briginshaw 2001: 44)

Not only is the art form challenged and presented in a different format, but also the nature and definition of the performance site itself is questioned, presented and transformed. Site-specific performance, with its lack of proscenium arch and auditorium seating, actively encourages the audience's participation with both the site and the performance. The audience becomes actively engaged in the construction of meanings and interpretation; they have a greater sense of participation and ownership over the performance as they are often responsible for placing themselves physically in the space as observers. Similarly, they are required to be more proactive in the interpretation of the work, as the conventions of the traditional theatre venue are abandoned, leaving the observer to respond to the work independently. In this sense, site-specific performance, with its frequent inclusion of elements such as promenade, can be seen to challenge traditional Euclidean theory implying 'a single viewpoint in space from which all points converge' (Briginshaw 2001: 89). Instead, a multitude of viewpoints is created, effectively 'de-centering' the performance space and fundamentally challenging notions of performance and spectatorship.

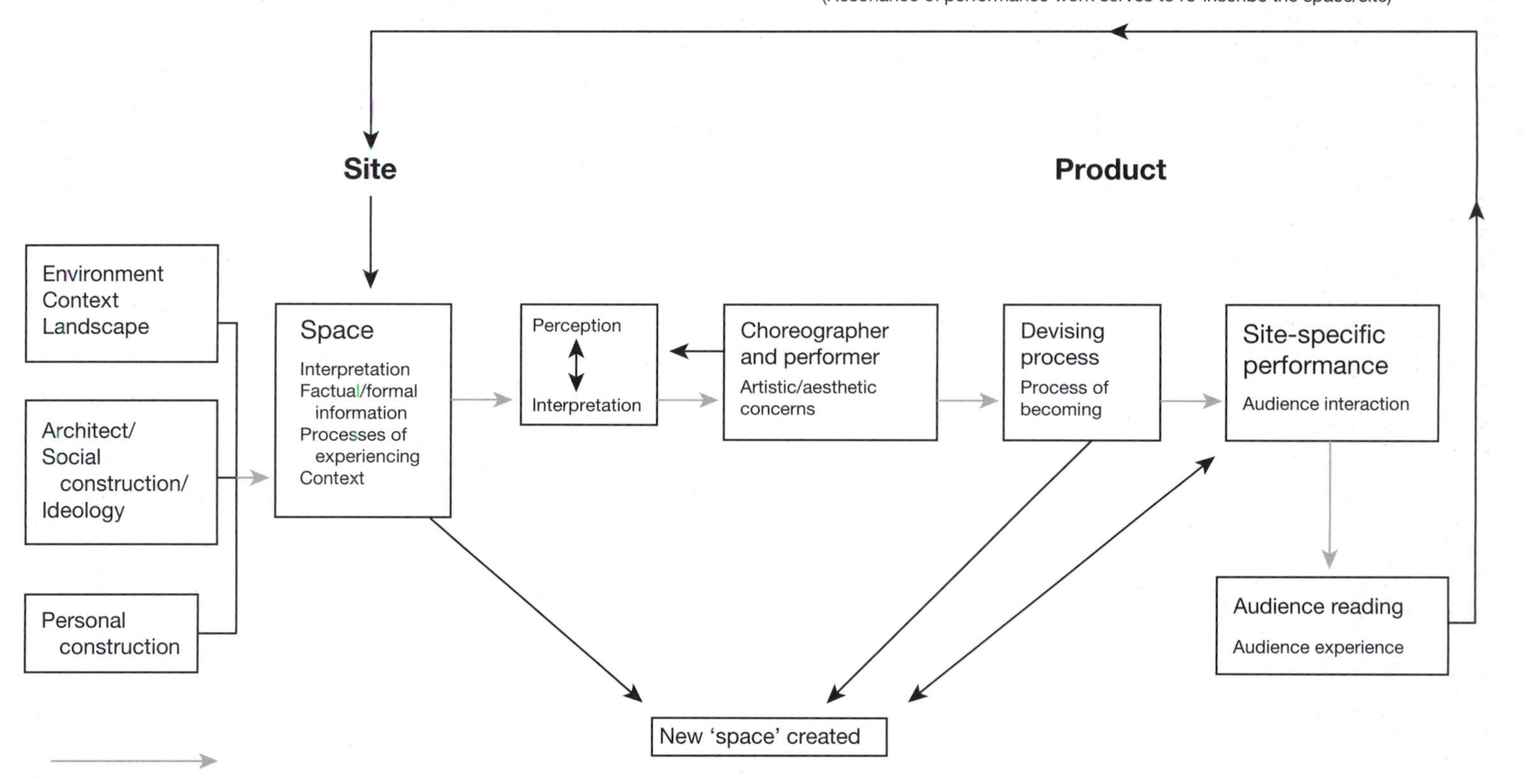

Figure 26.2 Hunter's model of influence. Detailing the relationship between the site and the creative process.

Therefore, we can begin to see how the site influences the dance, which in turn influences the site, each component informing and defining the other; the choreographer essentially enters into a 'dialogue' with the space whereby the performance works *with* the site as opposed to becoming imposed upon it. In this sense, both the concept and definition of the dance and the space is constantly shifting, becoming a fluid entity with no 'fixed' meaning. During the site-specific dance performance, both the site and the performance piece exist in a state of 'becoming-ness'; the readings are never fixed. Clifford McLucas, co-artistic director of Welsh performance company Brith Goff observes,

> The real site-specific works that we do, are the ones where we create a piece of work which is a hybrid of the place, the public, and the performance.
>
> (McLucas in Kaye 2000: 55)

In a sense, this interaction between site, performance and observer results in the creation of a new 'space', the conceptual space of performance, which exists only temporarily, yet brings a new dimension to the architectural location.

Conclusion – 'model of influence'

When considering the various elements involved in the creation of site-specific dance performance it is possible to identify a number of influencing factors involved in the production of a performance work. These factors are perhaps best illustrated via the presentation of a suggested 'model of influence', highlighting in linear form the relationship and interaction between the various components. This initial model focuses on the 'site to product' relationship, following the creative journey from the individual choreographer's interaction with the space/site to the creation of a final product/performance presented to an audience. When constructing this model, the various stages of spatial interaction were considered and the 'processes of experiencing' contained within these stages included. In this sense the 'through-line' of influence from space to choreographer becomes affected and embellished by the various sensory, formal, psychological and artistic elements collectively referred to here as 'processes of experiencing'. The interplay between these processes may vary from space to space and from site to site. In some spaces, for example, formal and thematic elements may serve to influence the choreographer predominantly; in other spaces, the sensory and personal construction of space may dominate. Whilst recognizing the existence and influence of these processes, the model does not suggest that all of these processes operate to influence the creative process at any one time. Whilst this *may* occur, it is more likely that the various processes of experience will serve to influence the choreographer in a process of ebb and flow. Some processes will be more dominant at certain stages of the experiencing and creative process and other factors will influence at other times. It is also necessary to acknowledge that the creative and devising process operates in a cyclical manner informed by the site-choreographer and site-performer relationship that develops and informs the creation of the final work. We recognize the existence of the choreographer and performers as living, breathing and creative individuals, susceptible to a variety of factors, which in turn will affect the processes of experiencing, perceiving and interacting with space and spaces.

In this model, a continuous through-line of influence can be witnessed, from the physical and social construction of space to the creation of a performance, and the audience's interaction with the performance. Prior to the presentation of the final performance product, however, a complex and creatively rich devising and creative exchange between the choreographer/performer and the space must occur; a process during which a temporary, new space of 'process' exists, inhabited by creative ideas and explorations which may or may not feature in the final performance outcome. Influencing factors, such as the various 'processes of experiencing' and the interpretive process together with aesthetic and artistic concerns, combine to contribute to the creation of performance material by the choreographer. This particular model reflects a devised approach to the creative process, thereby acknowledging the artistic and creative input of the performer. The active role played by the audience in the reading and interpretive process is also acknowledged in the model, a process which can carry resonances of the performance forward after the event, in turn serving to 're-inscribe' the original space with a variety of meanings. Finally, the creative potential presented by this type of interface between performance and space is alluded to via a reiteration of the suggestion that this type of interaction serves in itself to create a new type of 'space'. Preston-Dunlop captures the essence of this type of interaction:

> The body-in-space
> is the basic sculptural element of choreography.
> Bodies enter and move through, in and with a space
> turning the void into a place.
>
> (Preston-Dunlop 1998: 121)

In site-specific terms, the type of 'place' created is the 'place' of performance, transforming the accepted and conventional properties ascribed to a particular space, whilst simultaneously creating a temporary place of performance. This interaction between the spatial and the performative is ephemeral in nature, existing only in the moment of performance, and can be identified perhaps as the 'true' and desired outcome of site-specific performance, a perfect synthesis between space, performance and audience. In this sense, the role of choreographer can be viewed as that of an intermediary, providing a creative channel of communication between site and performance, informed and influenced by many varying factors that serve to enrich and enlighten the final performance outcome.

Notes

1 The idealized view of the countryside may be slowly eroding, however, following the wide-scale reporting of countryside flooding, erosion of farming traditions. etc. See: Appleton (1975), Bourassa (1991) and Brown (1982).

2 Choreographic journal notes, the *Beneath* project, a site-specific dance performance performed in the basement of the Bretton Hall mansion building, September 2004. The mansion building dates back to the eighteenth century and housed the University of Leeds School of Performance and Cultural Industries.

References

Appleton, J. (1975) *The Experience of Landscape*, London: John Wiley & Sons.

Bachelard, G. (1964) *The Poetics of Space*, New York: Orion Press.

Bloomer, K. C. and Moore, C. W. (1977) *Body, Memory, and Architecture*, New Haven: Yale University Press.

Bourassa, S. C. (1991) *The Aesthetics of Landscape*, London: Belhaven Press.

Briginshaw, V. (2001) *Dance, Space, and Subjectivity*, New York: Palgrave.

Brown, C. (2003) *Dance-Architecture Workshop, Isadora and Raymond Duncan Centre for Dance*. Available online at <http://www.Carolbrowndances.com> (accessed 9 December 2005).

Brown, J. (1982) *The Everywhere Landscape*, London: Wildwood House Ltd.

Ching, F. D. K. (1996) *Architecture, Form, Space, and Order*, New York and Chichester: John Wiley & Sons.

De Certeau, M. (1984) *The Practice of Everyday Life*, trans. S. Rendall, Berkeley, CA: University of California Press.

Goffman, E. (1969) *The Presentation of Self in Everyday Life*, London: Penguin.

Hall, M. and Hall, E. T. (1975) *The Fourth Dimension in Architecture: the Impact of Building on Behavior*, Santa Fe, Mexico: Sunstone Press.

Hunter, V. (2004) *Beneath*, choreographic diary entry, 9 September.

—— (2007) 'Public Space and Site-Specific Dance Performance: Negotiating the Relationship', *Research in Drama Education*, 12 (1): 112–15.

Kaye, N. (2000) *Site-Specific Art: Performance, Place, and Documentation*, London and New York: Routledge.

Koplowitz, S. (1997) *Project Interview*. Available online at <http://www.webbed-feats.org> (accessed 9 December 2005).

Lawson, B. (2001) *The Language of Space*, Oxford: Architectural Press.

Lefebvre, H. (1974) *La production de l'espace*, Paris: Anthropos.

—— (1991) *The Production of Space*, trans. D. Nicholson-Smith, Oxford: Blackwell.

McAuley, G. (2001) *Space in Performance: Making Meaning in the Theatre*, Ann Arbor: University of Michigan Press.

Norberg-Schultz, C. (1966) *Intentions in Architecture*, London: Allen & Unwin.

Paget, V. (1931) *The Beautiful: An Introduction to Psychological Aesthetics*, Cambridge: Cambridge University Press.

Preston-Dunlop, V. (1998) *Looking at Dances: A Choreological Perspective on Choreography*, London: Verve Publishing.

Tuan, Y.-F. (1974) *Topophilia: A Study of Environmental Perception, Attitudes, and Values*, Englewood Cliffs, NJ: Prentice-Hall.

27 Dancing with sprites and robots

New approaches to collaboration between dance and digital technologies[1]

Sita Popat and Scott Palmer

Creativity is not exclusive to any domain or discipline. We all regularly engage in activities that require us to be creative, seeking new ideas and ways of thinking, making new objects, events or artefacts. Historically the relationship between the arts and the sciences has been a stormy one, sometimes close and sometimes distinctly separated, but the last century has seen increasing levels of formal intersection between art and science (and also new technology) as discrete yet complementary disciplines. Ascott (1999: 2) argues that: 'art, technology and science are converging in important ways to produce new strategies, new theories and new forms of creativity, increasingly relying for their advance on a kind of trans-disciplinary consultation and collaboration'. Yet others have countered this argument, proposing that such collaboration relies on an underlying principle of commonality that can be difficult to achieve:

> The idea that science and art can somehow meet on common ground – that scientists can speak the same language as artists and vice versa – often entails compromise and more often than not it is the art that gets compromised.
>
> (Swain 2004: 63)

This chapter discusses the principles for establishing such 'common ground', and presents two case studies where cycles of iterative knowledge exchange were sought and places were found for performer/researchers and commercial sector technologists to play together as equals.

Playing (in) the field

A central element in the establishment of knowledge and understanding is the notion of play, a concept that is based on interactions rather than products. This is how children learn about the world, and it remains a fundamental basis of creativity throughout our lives. Play implies the freedom to experiment and the suspension of judgement that allows ideas to develop (Izzo 1997: 14; Abbs 1989). If judgement is suspended then the players can concentrate on a wider exploration of the medium. Swanwick (1982: 25), in his paper on music education, states the need for 'imaginative play' in the creative learning process, where the primary motivation is the discovery of the potential inherent in the medium rather than the production of a polished outcome. This is an essential part of exploring possibilities, and from the experience of playing the maturity of understanding arises. Playful interaction between the technological and the artistic should, in theory, lead to understanding and synthesis in the creative product, provided that the technical skills and qualities of both spheres are recognised and valued so that the widest points of intersection between the two can be explored.

Common ground has been established to varying degrees by collaborators with a willingness to play. One of the most prolific instigators of such collaborations over the past fifty years was scientist, Billy Klüver (1927–2004). Having a strong personal interest in the arts, he began collaborating with a series of artists in the 1960s. His collaborators over the years included a diverse range of individuals: Lucinda Childs, Yvonne Rainer, Robert Rauschenberg, John Cage, Andy Warhol. In 1966, he explained, 'All of the art projects that I have worked on have at least one thing in common; from an engineer's point of view they are ridiculous' (Klüver in Miller 1998). They were ridiculous because they appeared to serve no obvious purpose in the 'real' world. Why would a scientist be interested in making a tennis racket boom with sound when it hits a ball, or in making snowflakes fly upwards? Yet Klüver and his colleagues in 'Experiments in Art and Technology' (E.A.T.) maintained and developed science/art collaborations, because they recognised the value of this challenge to work in unfamiliar environments. Klüver originally had specific ideas about the relationship between artist and scientist:

> Once I gave a talk … and made the point that an engineer should just be another tool for the artist. But Bob [Rauschenberg] very specifically said, 'No! It has to be a collaboration.' I immediately understood what Bob was saying. The one-to-one collaboration between two people from different fields always holds the possibility of producing something new and different that neither of them could have done alone.
>
> (Klüver in Miller 1998)

Collaboration was most effective if it was not limited by the idea that one group 'serviced' the other. Together the collaborators could extend the possibilities beyond the boundaries apparently inherent in each discipline alone.

There are many examples of art/science/technology collaborations today, and it seems that some collaborators at least are able to transcend the practicalities and technicalities that Swain suggests can often lead to negative compromise (2004). Yet although collaborators often talk at length about the products that they have created, they seldom seem to focus on the route by which they achieved their successful collaboration, and even less so on the pitfalls or problems that arose. The following discussion addresses this paucity of information by presenting two collaborative case studies and exploring what made them effective in establishing common ground between artists and technologists.

Performance Robotics

The Performance Robotics Research Group's (PRRG) weeklong experimental laboratory at the University of Leeds in December 2003 provided a research context that supported a valuable playful interaction between participants. The PRRG consists of academics in performance, drama, puppetry and dance from the University of Leeds, Loughborough University and University of Kent, working with Shadow Robots Ltd, London.[2] On one level, we were seeking ways for humans and robots to function together socially, rather than trying to fuse one with the other in the cyborgian tradition practised by performance artist Stelarc in, for example, his work *Exoskeleton*.[3] On another level, we were exploring methodologies for mutual knowledge exchange between disciplines, building on an iterative cycle of research, that involved performance academics, robotics designers and engineers at all points (Popat *et al.* 2004). On both levels, we worked with principles of phenomenology and the experience of 'being there together'. This resulted in some unique experiences for the participants.

This was an open laboratory, with no specific aims other than trying to find a common language in order to develop ideas further. The participants were seeking to explore the spaces that their collaboration opened up between performance and robotics, which was a vague and uncertain place to start. At the beginning of the week we felt worryingly unprepared because the brief was so open. However, we also felt that this was an important aspect of the collaboration. We did not want to be tied by plans and expectations, but there was always the risk that nothing would be achieved because of this lack of focus, and so a wide range of materials was assembled to provide maximum flexibility. The Shadow Robots team brought three 'ready-made' robots and copious amounts of equipment, and set up a temporary workroom in a studio, with two larger studios available for practical workshops. Two dance students and two performance design students joined the team for the week, and all groups purposely tried to preserve open minds in order to see where our experiments would take us. Performers constructed bits of robots, and engineers took part in movement and drama workshops, in an effort to come to understand each other's disciplines and research imperatives.

A number of activities took place over that week, but one of the most interesting was the emergence of a relationship between Liz (a student

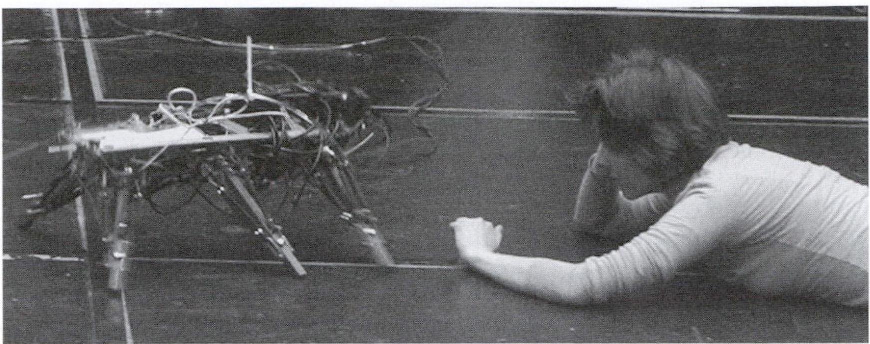

Figure 27.1 Zephyrus (robot) and Elizabeth Collier (dancer). Photo: © Scott Palmer.

dancer) and Zephyrus (a prototype robot) (see Fig. 27.1). Zephyrus had a rectangular body and six legs, with limited movement on the forwards/backwards plane and no knee-joints. This meant that in order to gain any forward motion it had to move its legs repeatedly over short distances, giving all its movement an impression of great effort and struggle. It was powered by air-muscle technology with compressed air, so it made regular and insistent hissing noises and clicks. This gave it a strong 'character', leading to much anthropomorphism during the course of the week. The relationship between Liz and Zephyrus developed throughout the laboratory, and demonstrated clearly the ways in which performance and robotics could achieve a synthesis that allowed knowledge to pass between the disciplines and a common ground to develop that could benefit both.

On the first day of the laboratory, an embodiment exercise was set up, and Liz chose to embody Zephyrus. Embodiment is beyond the act of 'copying' the movement, and requires the performer to gain a feel for the essence of the entity that they are embodying so that they can come to 'experience' what it is to 'be' that entity. Liz watched Zephyrus closely, trying to gain a feel for it, and to translate that experience into her own body. She took on the movement qualities and restrictions of the robot and experimented with the extremely limited possibilities. Her emerging embodiment was a demanding and intrusive character, with much action for little forward motion. At that stage, the performance researchers were more engaged in watching Liz's work than the engineers, as the full import of her actions had yet to dawn upon us.

As the week continued, the embodiment exercise became just one of a number of interactions that Liz had with Zephyrus. She also acted with it on two occasions and improvised a danced duet with it on a third. Liz became more comfortable moving in the embodiment of the robot, and began to find new options through experimentation. Her movement became richer and more complex, but still fairly closely within the robot's own constraints. Zephyrus itself was used in different workshop contexts, and in one of these it was discovered that the robot could balance on its back legs in a 'sitting' position and wave its 'arms', which then provided Liz with more alternatives for her movement vocabulary. Gradually it became apparent that her growing familiarity with the restrictions, but also with the possibilities, was leading her to develop movements that were currently beyond Zephyrus, but these movements could potentially become realised through changes in the robot's design. One of the engineers was astonished to recognise that Zephyrus might be made capable of jumping. The prospect had not occurred to him previously because there were no knee joints to bend. However, Liz discovered that, although her limbs were straight, if she pulled them together sharply when she was standing on her hands and feet then she was able to make small jumping movements. The engineer began to recognise the new design potentials in what was happening, and he started watching Liz and Zephyrus closely and making notes on what Liz was doing and how that could relate to robotic design principles.

On the final day of the laboratory, the same engineer asked tentatively if Liz could find a way to embody Zephyrus standing on its hind legs. He acknowledged that this was well beyond the design possibilities currently, but he wanted to see it anyway. Liz improvised for fifteen minutes, and she eventually used Zephyrus' insistent rhythmical sound to find a way to stand by working the rhythm through her hands and feet first on the floor and then up her body. The struggle that was evident in Zephyrus' movement at all times was particularly pronounced as she tried to achieve the task whilst staying within the movement parameters as far as possible. As she worked at this challenge, the engineers were sitting around the studio sketching and quietly discussing possibilities, looking at her movement from the point of view of mechanical joints, air-muscles and programming. Then gradually silence fell in the room as the suspense and concentration became palpable, until Liz finally managed to achieve a standing position. As she ended the improvisation there was a spontaneous round of applause from performers and engineers alike. This was an unplanned moment of performance, which had also generated pages of robotic design notes.

The engineers explained that normally changes in a robot's design require the building of new robots, which takes time and focuses on the components. The process is product-orientated because the design exists only in theory and there is little opportunity to see what will actually happen until the product is built. Three-dimensional (3D) modelling programmes now enable the designer to see the design on screen and alter it comparatively quickly, but Liz provided more than an approximation of the movement. As a dancer, she also brought to it her understandings of movement and the complex human body, which opened up the field of experimentation considerably. The engineers described how watching Liz embodying Zephyrus enabled them to have an overview of the potential within the whole of the robot. It enabled them to see new possibilities for design solutions, which they might not otherwise have predicted in their normal design process.

Equally, the embodiment of the independently moving, idiosyncratic robot extended both Liz's dance technique and choreographic skills. The robot's limited scope for movement placed her in a position where she had few options, and she had to investigate in great depth those movements that were available to her. She moved well beyond her standard personal movement style and found a range of movement that she would not normally have explored. Zephyrus had strong 'character' qualities that were completely attributable to its motion since it had no definable expression in its simple, mechanical appearance. Its independence, moving as it did through internal programming, gave it a sense of being a conscious entity that made its actions seem purposeful. Yet, its quirky style was an interesting embodiment task for a human dancer. The movement that was thereby produced by Liz was highly expressive but articulated the body in unusual ways, providing a vocabulary that stretched all those dancers present both choreographically and performatively. The purpose and expression inherent in the movement kept it from replicating choreographer Merce Cunningham's machinistic treatment of the human body, and yet it was disjointed and challenging to perform. The performers suggested that robots could be used to aid dance students and even professional dancers and choreographers in seeking diverse movement vocabularies either for specific works or for training purposes.

The experience of Liz working with Zephyrus opened up new options for our research and enabled us to see clearly how our research imperatives might intersect through the investigation of the human/robot relationship interface. At the same time, we found that the robotics specialist/performance academic interface could be the basis for exchanges that were profitable for all concerned. Although there was a performative outcome on the final day, this project was not particularly aimed at performance exploration. Instead, we were concerned with how knowledge could be transferred between the disciplines, and how this transference could become an iterative cycle of knowledge exchange that built up common ground between us. We were trying to find some focus that would not feel 'ridiculous' to the technologists in the way that Klüver described, but would still remain relevant to the performers. Above all, we wished to avoid one discipline 'servicing' the other.

The relationship between Shadow Robots and the performance academics was greatly enhanced by the fact that Shadow Robots were willing to embrace the 'ridiculous' as a part of their working processes. Because they customarily work with cheap materials (wood, plastic, string) in the early stages of designing and realising their robots, they were not averse to the idea of discarding or adapting items under construction. This gave their work a sense of improvisation and play at some levels that complemented the work of the performers. We did not know when Liz undertook the embodiment exercise that this would be the point from which the iterative knowledge exchange would become established, but the free-play situation allowed us to experiment and see where the moment of intersection arose. The engineers were patient and flexible enough to watch and see when it became relevant to them. It must also be explained that there were many other activities in the week's laboratory that were less successful in identifying common interests for all concerned, and this was equally important to us. At the end of the week's laboratory, we had a far stronger basis for communication, and we spent the final afternoon discussing what we had done and establishing the research questions that we have since used for further collaborative projects. These questions were firmly founded upon the common ground that had matured out of our period of 'play'.

Projecting Performance

Following the success of the Performance Robotics laboratory, the authors used a similar approach in their collaboration with KMA Creative Technology Ltd[4] in June 2004. Projecting Performance brought together software and graphics programmers from KMA with staff and students in dance and performance design at the University of Leeds. KMA are involved in a diverse range of creative work within the digital domain. Their more high-profile activities have included the design and manipulation of vibrant scenic projections for large-scale popular music events and the design of interactive abstract digital forms for use on websites. Through initial discussions, it emerged that there might be some interesting possibilities in combining these two products within a live performance setting. Ultimately, the project was realised because of this desire to explore synergies in the work that both parties were already undertaking, and this clear performative focus set it apart from the Performance Robotics project. The objective of Projecting Performance was to investigate the performance potential inherent in the combination of digital media and human dancers, and the stage picture maintained a primacy in this collaboration. KMA were specifically interested in working with dance researchers as they had recently begun a commercial project with Phoenix Dance Theatre that eventually resulted in the creation of Darshan Singh Bhuller's *Eng-er-land* (2005), performed as part of the *Inter Vivos* tour. The production required a sufficiently robust technical set-up to tour with the dance company without direct support from KMA staff. This pressure limited the possibilities for experimental work, as reliability and replication were primary requirements. Projecting Performance was therefore viewed as a research and development opportunity, allowing space and time to play with the technology without a fixed outcome in mind. We began by expecting to deal with 'mock-up' situations, where the human operator mimicked what would later be programmed for computerised control. However, as the project continued we realised that in our automatic assumption that a fully computerised system was preferable, we were overlooking an issue that engaged us far more in terms of the technical operator's relationship to the performance.

Similarly to the Performance Robotics project, a team of individuals was assembled with skills that seemed to be appropriate to the artistic and technological aspects of the project. Potential ways of investigating the interactivity between the digital space and the performance space were suggested but these ideas were registered only as possible starting points, not fixed outcomes. It was important that the project provided space for open-ended creative interaction and it was refreshing to observe that all members of the team were able to commit to working in such a divergent way. The main processes that we discussed were based on improvisation and devised dance performance. Kit Monkman, company director of KMA, admitted afterwards that he had had a few reservations, and he was initially concerned 'that it might be embarrassing (very English). That we might waste each other's time, that our working practices might prove to be fundamentally incompatible.'[5] The performance academics too were apprehensive that the collaboration might prove to become technology driven with little room for aesthetic exploration, despite the initial clarity about the need to achieve synthesis between the two. The technology would be clearly visible in the performance space, and the technicalities and practicalities of setting up and getting it to function could potentially take primacy. However, such fears proved unfounded, and the performance academics were surprised to find that we experienced much commonality with the way that KMA worked. Monkman describes their usual working techniques as 'experimentation and serendipitous discovery' – a process remarkably akin to devising and creating performance work.

The first day of the residency in the University of Leeds' lighting studio was reserved for KMA to set up their digital equipment and for the performance designers to prepare the space theatrically. A gauze (scrim) was rigged across the space to provide a semi-transparent wall as a surface for projection. Whilst this plane bisected the stage space, the dancers were still visible behind it. Theatrical lighting was prepared to allow for a variety of options in lighting both the space and the performers. The computers, which were to generate the projections, were set up and linked to a data projector that was then focused on the gauze. Initial software programming was undertaken in preparation for the arrival of the dancers. This preparation was important to ensure that the technical aspects of theatrical production work did not interfere with the momentum of creative discoveries. An important feature of the space was its flexibility; ideas could be tried out quickly and then be either discarded, recorded for future exploration or developed further. Ultimately, this potential for rapid experimentation contributed significantly to the range of discoveries that were made during the two further days of intensive work.

The KMA programmer, Tom Wexler, created a series of simple animated images as starting points for the exploration. Most of these

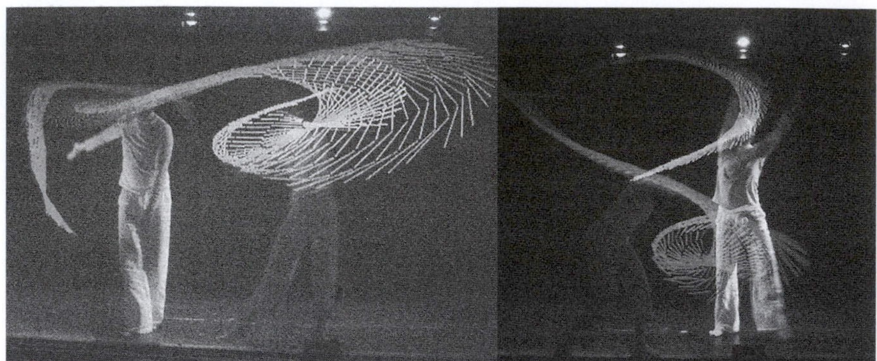

Figure 27.2 Elizabeth Collier and Paul Clark (dance students) interacting with yellow and blue sprites projected on the gauze in front of them. Note: some of the vibrancy in the images is lost in the transition to greyscale. Photo: © Scott Palmer.

digital creations or 'sprites' were based on basic geometric shapes, such as lines. They were then given a variety of parameters that created flowing abstract images when moved across the screen. The fluidity of this movement was produced by allowing each position of the sprite to be registered for a short time before allowing it to decay. Echoes of the sprite's movement were left as a trail that was visible temporarily across the monitor screen and duplicated in the performance space through its projection onto the gauze on stage (see Fig. 27.2). A second sprite was added, subsequently allowing more complex interactions to take place. Each sprite was controlled by an operator, working initially with a computer mouse. The operator used the mouse to draw the path of the sprite, leading it around the screen/gauze. The dancers could see the images on the gauze in front of them, and they were able to respond to the sprites, improvising movement with them in the performance space.

Key discoveries were made through allowing the dancers and operators to improvise freely within both the digital domain and the physical stage space, exploring how they could relate to each other through the performance medium. The experiments began with simple improvised movement from the dancer, which the operator of the sprite attempted to follow on-stage. This tracking process provided an almost instant mediatised echo of the movement content that was manifested in the space with the dancer via the gauze. At first, the dancers found the inter-relationship with the sprite a strange but exciting one, with one dancer commenting; 'I'm not used to dancing with a light'. This tendency at first to think of the sprite as being merely a scenographic element was gradually overcome to reveal a richer relationship between dancer and sprite as Tom, the programmer and operator from KMA, became more familiar with the

Figure 27:3 Tom Wexler (KMA) and Lisette Wright (design student) using WACOM tablets to operate the sprites. Photo: © Scott Palmer.

dancers' movements. His confidence increased as he came to 'trust' the dancers to move with him, and they to trust him to respond to them.

Gradually the relationship changed, and the operator discovered that he could lead the movement of the dancer, with the dancer responding to the speed, direction and qualities of the projected image's movement. The dancers reported that they felt increasingly as if they were dancing with another person, rather than a computerised image. The way that the sprite reacted to them and improvised with them was more akin to a human partner than a computerised interaction, as it had potential for the unexpected, the humorous, and the quirky. This realisation coincided with the operators removing their computer monitors altogether and working entirely by watching the sprites on the stage gauze in the performance space. This was a major breakthrough for the research, as it marked the point at which the operator moved from being the 'technologist' to being a performer, albeit by a proxy arrangement. It is in marked contrast to industry practice, where it is common for technical operation to occur away from the place of performance, removed physically from the stage space itself and distanced by glass screens and layers of technology. This practice has been criticised (Hunt 2001; White 1999: 10), since the operator often experiences little engagement with the creative act of performance and may simply be pushing buttons. In this project, however, the operators were engaging in dynamic creative expression, with a direct relationship between their embodied movements of mouse control and the sprites' movements. The dancers also explained that their awareness of the dancing partner slipped between the image and the operator, so that sometimes they felt that they were dancing with the sprite and sometimes with Tom. At this point, we ceased to think so much about how the movement would be simulated by a computer program, and focused our attention onto the relationship between performer-dancer and performer-operator.

This shift in focus led to the suggestion to replace the mouse-driven input device with a WACOM graphics tablet and pen (see Fig. 27.3). This allowed for more expressive movement as the pen was more intuitive and precise to use than the mouse, engaging the operator in a free-flowing action based on drawing or sketching. The sprite became gradually more infused with the operator's own movement style, which was not entirely clear until Lisette, a performance design student, joined Tom and started operating a second sprite. It was apparent which person was operating which sprite, as their styles were subtly different in quality and use of space. Other members of the team took turns to operate, resulting in some interesting observations about the performance skills of individuals from different disciplines. One of the dancers tried working with the pen, but his use of the space was clearly coloured by the experience of dancing. He found it difficult to use the whole of the screen, and his sprite seemed to be bound by a non-existent gravity that led him to use the lower section of the screen for most of the movement. His general awareness of the stage space was primarily as performer, and while performers are used to feeling the sensation of embodying movement in space, they are not necessarily used to visually engaging with the whole stage 'picture'. By contrast, the scenographers on the team were more able to construct a visual image that comprised the two sprites and the dancers in the performance space, using the full range of spatial availability. However, the most aesthetically interesting and sensitive performance was created by the KMA operator, Tom, who was also the designer and programmer of the sprites and therefore the most familiar with the technology and its possibilities. His use of space, quality of movement and sensitivity to the dancers was highly developed, despite his lack of dance or performance experience. Both Tom and scenographer Scott (co-author) reacted strongly to the experience of 'dancing' via their sprites with the performers on stage. Afterwards, they described the fluid interface that the pen provided allowing them to feel their movement embodied in the sprite. They were still sitting amongst the technical paraphernalia, but their experiences transcended that situation and they felt 'drawn in' to the image of the sprite on the stage. They were aware of the technicalities of what they were doing in one sense, but the differentiation between the performance and the technology had been erased in the moment, so that they considered themselves to be performers and experienced an intensity that they felt was akin to stage performance. The choreography that we created through the second day included both dancers and operators as choreographed performers.

The excitement at these discoveries was articulated at regular meetings to evaluate progress throughout the two days of experimentation. The team attempted to quantify what had been achieved and to identify likely avenues for further exploration. Alterations to the parameters of the sprite were suggested by all participants, in a spirit of open collaboration. Changes were undertaken through speedy programming and ideas were tested and modified further. Audience members from outside the research team were invited into the space to share examples of the work and to comment. This fed far more ideas into the process than we could use in the short period of the laboratory, but it aided us in establishing common ground on which to build. Our shift in focus to address the performer/operator relationship became the fundamental basis of our research, and proved to be more directly relevant to all disciplines (dance, scenography and technology) than had been apparent in the early stages of planning.

Despite the difficulties and necessary uncertainties in working in this way, the range and quality of the discoveries suggests that it has greater validity than a more prescriptive approach. Monkman described the process as 'an extraordinary valuable way of collaborating on projects'. He explained how much KMA valued the experience: 'Sadly the creative freedom that we all had … to play (with so much resource and support) without expectation is rarely possible in the commercial world'. However, the collaborative approach is not necessarily straightforward, nor easy to achieve within the rehearsal room, and much depends on the nature of the individuals involved. A level of honesty and trust is required between team members to enable truly exploratory work to develop and this openness of approach is difficult to attain, especially amongst individuals who are not familiar with the art form and language of dance or of this method of working. A longer timescale is also usually required for members of the team to build up a relationship and to appreciate individual skills and ways of working. Importantly for the outcome of this project, the technologists from KMA were both happy and, more fundamentally, able to work in this collaborative way.

The initial results of Projecting Performance were the product of careful preparation that established methods of working at the outset. This influenced the nature of the creative collaboration in which, despite the variety of experience and backgrounds, each individual's contribution was acknowledged on an equal basis within a supportive environment. There was a major reduction in the sometimes-intrusive distinction between the art and the technology, between the performers and the programmers. The focus remained on using the technology as an expressive tool to explore a performative outcome. At the end of the three days of intensive work, we had created a quartet performance in which two performer-dancers danced with two sprites controlled by two performer-operators, one of which was a member of KMA and the other a performance design student. It was unclear whether the quartet was between the dancers and the sprites, or the dancers and the performer-operators, and it seems likely that these relationships were in flux for much of the performance. Monkman described the outcome as being twofold: 'we ended the project with a very real and strong performance idea AND a strong working relationship, both of which we'd like to pursue'. As this book goes to print, the authors and KMA are continuing their collaborative research with the support of a grant from the Arts and Humanities Research Council.[6]

Conclusions

The Performance Robotics project and Projecting Performance both demonstrate models of effective working practice for collaboration between performers and scientists/technologists. Each discipline has so much to offer to the development of the other. However, it takes time and willingness to participate in dialogue and play. Too often individual agendas can intervene in the creative process, which can prevent collaboration and recognition of the value of all participating disciplines. This can particularly be the case where limited time and expensive resources are involved.

In Projecting Performance, it was the development of aesthetic empathy that enabled the KMA operator to engage in an improvised, embodied experience of performing through the technology with the dancers. This experience underscored the central aim to search for ways in which the performance and the technology could be integrated, focusing all participants on the aesthetic rather than the functional in the performance situation. In the Performance Robotics project, we looked instead at knowledge exchange, so that when we watched Liz's embodiment of Zephyrus the performance academics were primarily considering the dance performance and the roboticists were looking at the technical design implications. We were watching the same phenomenon, but drawing different information from the intersection of our disciplines. In both projects we have developed understandings not necessarily of each other's disciplines (which might be too much to expect in a week's laboratory) but of the points at which they intersect and the questions that arise for us at those points. We suggest that recognition of our inability to know everything but our willingness to bring our knowledge to the table and think flexibly and creatively is the key element of these collaborations.

Klüver's suggestion that the scientist or technologist sees the arts project as 'ridiculous' is founded on the basis that arts projects have no recognised 'real world' function, but successful collaboration surely arises when all participants can see a purpose behind their activities. Creativity in an arts project is centred on finding solutions to non-functional problems, problems associated with aesthetic outcomes. It promotes play and improvisation, since there are no definitive 'right' answers but there may be an interesting range of solutions that support the broader work of the scientist or technologist. We suggest that looking for some kind of relevance for all parties promotes enthusiasm for collaboration, and encourages creative engagement from all participants. This is the common ground that underpins the collaborative project, rather than direct knowledge of each other's disciplines. The projects described in this paper worked most effectively when the participants were able to avoid preconceptions and simply experience being there together and finding out what was important to each other; a process that felt unplanned, risky, and difficult to describe to funders. In both cases, the point of real interest grew out of an unexpected situation (the dancer's developed embodiment of the robot, the projection operator's sensitive improvisation with the dancers). We are not advocating that all research between artists and scientists/technologists should be 'woolly' and open-ended throughout the process, and both of these projects are now well advanced in establishing specific research questions and appropriate methodologies for further investigation. However, we would argue that without these periods of creative play, our understandings would be less rich and our research questions and methodologies less developed and informed. Swain (2004) suggests that compromise often arises out of the problematic assumption 'that scientists can speak the same language as artists and vice versa' (2004: 63). We do not yet speak the same language as our robotic or technology counterparts in these projects, but we do have sufficient words in common to communicate and learn more.

As students, researchers and practitioners of dance in all its various guises, we need to develop a deeper awareness of the flexibility of what we know and the transferability of that knowledge. Dance does not exist in isolation as an art form, and neither do art forms exist outside of the wider cultural context. In a world where so many scientists and technologists are programming objects and animations to move, who better to aid them in their understandings of the aesthetics and practicalities of motion than someone who has studied and explored the art of movement and choreography? The case studies in this chapter have demonstrated that collaborations can be both exciting and fruitful when dancers and technologists are able to play together, resulting in significant developments and quantifiable advances for all collaborators. The technologists are already trying to play in our field. We just need to have confidence in the value of our dance knowledge to join them.

Notes

1 An earlier version of this chapter was published under the title of 'Creating Common Ground: Dialogues between performance and digital technologies' in the *International Journal of Performance Arts and Digital Media* 1 (1), January 2005: 47–65.

2 Dr Gordon Ramsay, Dr Melissa Trimingham, Professor Mick Wallis and Dr Sita Popat are the academic members of the PRRG. Shadow Robots Ltd, <http://www.shadow.org.uk/index.shtml>.

3 See the Exoskeleton website for more information at <http://www.stelarc.va.com.au/exoskeleton/>.
4 More information about KMA can be found at their website at <http://www.kma.co.uk>.
5 Quotations from Kit Monkman, Director of KMA, are taken from his email to the authors on 15 September 2004.
6 Further details on Projecting Performance and ongoing work with KMA can be found at <http://www.leeds.ac.uk/paci/projectingperformance/home.html>.

References

Abbs, P. (1989) 'The Pattern of Art-Making', in P. Abbs (ed.) *The Symbolic Order: A Contemporary Reader on the Arts Debate*, London: Falmer Press.

Ascott, R. (ed.) (1999) *Reframing Consciousness*, Bristol: Intellect.

Hunt, N. (2001) 'A Play of Light', *Showlight 2001: International Colloquium on Entertainment Lighting*, Edinburgh Festival Theatre, Edinburgh, Scotland, 21–23 May.

Izzo, G. (1997) *The Art of Play: The New Genre of Interactive Theatre*, Portsmouth, NH: Heinemann.

Miller, P. (1998) 'The Engineer as Catalyst: Billy Klüver on working with artists', *IEEE Spectrum*, 35 (7): 20–9.

Popat, S., Ramsay, G., Trimingham, M. and Wallis, M. (2004) 'Robotics and Performance: a phenomenological dialogue', in the proceedings for *Pixelraiders 2 Conference*, Sheffield: Sheffield Hallam University.

Swain, M. (2004) 'Just Sugaring the Pill?' *Mute*, 27 (Winter/Spring): 56–63.

Swanwick, K. (1982) *The Arts in Education: Dreaming or Wide Awake?* University of London: Institute of Education, Special Professorial Lecture, 4 November 1982.

White, Christine (1999) 'The Changing Scenographic Aesthetic', *Scenography International, Issue 1, New Departures*. Available online at <http://www.lboro.ac.uk/research/scenography/> (accessed 7 October 1999).

28 Augmenting choreography

Insights and inspiration from science

Scott deLahunta, Phil Barnard and Wayne McGregor

This chapter concentrates on issues of collaboration between the arts and sciences, with special reference to Choreography and Cognition, a joint research project (see http://www.choreocog.net) initiated by arts researcher Scott deLahunta and choreographer Wayne McGregor that engaged practitioners from the field of cognitive science in seeking connections between creativity, choreography and the scientific study of movement and the mind. First, deLahunta describes briefly how initial ideas evolved into a six-month research project involving several cognitive scientists and the support of an Arts and Science Research fund.[1] There follows discussion about why a choreographer and a cognitive scientist might be interested in each other and in structured collaboration. Cognitive scientist Phil Barnard explains the background and one of the resulting experiments that took place and proposes further mutually beneficial research. In the final section, Wayne McGregor details his experience of working with cognitive scientists on Choreography and Cognition, which inspired the creation of *AtaXia* (2004) and motivated future plans.

Introduction to Choreography and Cognition

Choreography and Cognition began as a discussion about developing new understandings of the choreographic process that might lead to alternative creative approaches and enhance collaboration processes, initiated by Wayne McGregor's keen interest in Artificial Intelligence, the branch of computer science and engineering involved in creating intelligent machines, and the possibility of creating an *autonomous choreographic agent*. We knew that such an ostensibly impossible project would require not only a better grasp of the workings of the mind, the 'intelligences' involved in dance making, but would also rely on productive cooperation with scientists.

We organized a series of meetings with cognitive and neuroscientists in the United Kingdom and France. We visited their labs and gave each other short presentations, asked questions, described, explained; taking the initial steps towards mutual understanding. Since we knew relatively little about their field of expertise, and the scientists, in general, knew almost nothing about the field of contemporary dance, both sides had to construct new frames of reference.

As a point of entry into choreographic practice, we provided the scientists with verbal description of improvisation tasks/problems that McGregor normally gives his dancers to solve as a mode of generating movement sequences at the beginning of a creative process.[2] We tailored these by selecting examples of tasks involving a degree of complex mental work with specific cognitive requirements, for example visualizing shapes in space, to stimulate a focused conversation about how mind, brain and body interact.

We were fortunate to secure funding from a pilot Arts and Science Research Fellowship scheme in the UK to continue working over a period of six months with selected scientists: Alan Wing and Kris Hollands, SyMoN (Sensory Motor Neuroscience research group), University of Birmingham; Anthony Marcel and Phil Barnard, MRC Cognition and Brain Sciences Unit, Cambridge; Alan Blackwell of Crucible/Computer Lab, University of Cambridge; and Rosaleen McCarthy, Department of Experimental Psychology, University of Cambridge, where Wayne was hosted as a Research Fellow. In addition, James Leach, a social anthropologist doing fieldwork on arts and science collaborations, took part and made a significant contribution to our understanding of the nature of these exchanges (Leach 2006: 447–51).

The following three objectives guided the six-month project:

1 *Shared objective*: to seek connections between choreographic processes and the study of movement and the brain/mind that are scientifically and artistically interesting.
2 *Artistic objective*: to integrate the participation and contribution from the scientists into the fabric of the choreographic process while maintaining the integrity of the modes of looking and questioning pertaining to their respective research areas.
3 *Scientific objective*: to start to formulate specific questions and research methodologies that arise from the individual interests in this project in the context of the creative choreographic process.

In November 2003, the project began with a two-day shared session in London to watch McGregor and Random Dance working with some new scores and tasks for generating movement material. The goal was to elicit observations from the scientists as the basis for further investigation and experimentation. McGregor intended to use these interactions to conduct his own research into creative starting points and processes for his next piece, *AtaXia*. The project had several successful outcomes, which are documented on the Choreography and Cognition website (www.choreocog.net). The following sections of this chapter focus on some basic questions about shared interests and the collaborative organization of the project.

Why might a choreographer be interested in cognitive science?

There have been big advances in our understanding of the brain in the past fifty years, bringing with it new descriptions of what it is to think and how things like sensory perception, movement control and memory, as working parts of the mind as a whole, might interact. Research ranges from building intelligent computer models and developing clinical diagnostics to brain imaging and consciousness studies. For any artist interested in learning new things about creativity, cognitive science presents a possible pool of insights for both self-knowledge as well as understanding artistic collaborators, viewers and audiences better.

On teaching cognitive science and arts, Cynthia Freeland, University of Houston philosopher, writes that cognitive science:

> is revolutionizing our understanding of ourselves by providing new accounts of human rationality and consciousness, perceptions, emotions, and desires, with great consequences for our understanding of the creation, interpretation, and appreciation of artworks in all mediums.
>
> (Freeland 2001)

Freeland's three-part paper explores the idea of a course bringing cognitive science into relation with visual arts, film and music theory. The article's emphasis is on seeking connections between mind/brain research and art theory and less creative practice, and tackling some of the difficult problems of inter-disciplinary knowledge exchange.

In neuroscience, a discipline often seen to be part of the cognitive science field, a controversial new line of research has emerged in the last decade known as neuro-aesthetics, which attempts to explain some aspects of the perception of art based on scientific study of the brain. Early proponents include Zeki (1999) and Ramachandran (1999), focusing on visual arts with more emphasis on historical than on contemporary references, and there is some related research in music.[3] In the field of contemporary dance, independent researcher Ivar Hagendoorn has written articles about choreography drawing on the same fascination with the explanatory strength of cognitive neuroscience; some of his writings explore the possibility that such scientific study can inspire dance.[4] Indeed, William Forsythe's own curiosity about neuroscience stems from an interest in refining his intuition about what people watch in his dances through understanding some of the cognitive mechanisms of attention (Forsythe, personal communication, April 2006).

Why might a cognitive scientist be interested in choreography?

Phil Barnard's aim is to develop useful ways of thinking about the workings of the mind. His research programme is focused on meaning – not only the kind of meaning that is expressed in language and symbols, but also deeper meanings about the self – living, moving, thinking and feeling in a complicated social world. In his own work at the Cognition and Brain Studies Unit in Cambridge, Barnard first develops models of the healthy mind, and then considers how things might go wrong in clinical conditions such as major depression, mania, anxiety, anorexia or schizophrenia. One characteristic of the cognitive psychology community is that different groups of researchers focus on particular mental faculties – such as language, perception, memory, attention, motor skills or emotion. As a modeller interested in clinical conditions, Barnard seeks to understand how these individual mental faculties all work together in a unified mental system.

In these clinical cases, it is natural to emphasize dysfunctional thinking about the self, the world and other people and its emotional consequences. However, psychologists know that bodies clearly play an important role and that embodiment and multimodal sensation are an integral part of self-meaning. The difficulty is that any efforts to understand how bodies relate to meaning typically involve massive over-simplification. Against this background, choreography provides interesting research opportunities for Barnard:

> First, dance is inherently multimodal. In dance performance, thematic elements are packaged as movement, music and staging, all contributing to the viewer's emotional and intellectual experience. Secondly, this package challenges the psychologist's ability to think at the same time about many research topics embedded in a single rich context. Third, the experience of performing or viewing dance appears to provide conditions where, at least to some degree, it is possible to separate out the contribution of abstract senses of self and others from specific thoughts about those senses. Dance … can be performed or experienced without a continual flow of explicit verbal thoughts. Yet in domains of making dance, notating it, or discussing it those abstract senses of meanings are translated into verbal thoughts or graphic notations. Thus, dance and choreography provide a unique platform for studying, using both quantitative and qualitative methods on how thought and abstract senses of the embodied self work.
>
> (Barnard and deLahunta 2006)

Barnard's understanding of what dance had to offer to scientists developed quickly during the project. Other scientists similarly expressed their realization that dance and choreography involves an exceptional multimodal blend of physical and mental processes. Initially we had hoped that choreography would be an exciting research challenge for cognitive scientists already accustomed to working in an interdisciplinary mode. However, it was not yet known how this predisposition towards broad interdisciplinary research would work in collaboration with artists.

What might happen in the structure of a collaboration?

Having established points of mutual interest, we can say more about the set-up of the Choreography and Cognition project. We understand that arts and science collaborations will always encounter some generic points of difference. Both domains are involved in processes of investigation and creation, but these processes are markedly different in each field. For example, in order for science to make progress it needs to make a *simple* model of the problems it wishes to investigate; and it is a requirement in science that the same investigation gets the same result. For the artist, an investigation or research period may also involve breaking down a larger problem, but here the process tends to be dominated by internal self-referencing. As long as artwork is the outcome, this process can be unique; and no one else need assume the position of the artist in order to verify the working procedures. For the shared research we assumed and accepted these generic differences. Moreover, we extended this embrace of difference to the concept that any professional specialization, such as cognitive psychology, might effect a way of observing and describing phenomena in terms consistent with this specialization.

As Barnard noted, in the domain of making dance, verbal and graphic description is clearly part of the creation process even though the resulting performance can be experienced (on the part of both performer and audience) without the need for these explicit representations. For the cognitive scientist, these verbal and graphic elements provide clues to the processes of mind involved in dance making. This explains why we began our collaborative encounter by focusing on an early stage of the creative process, researching and making movement material that may be used in the final piece. When the cognitive scientists attended the two-day session to observe McGregor and his dancers generate new movement material, afternoon discussion sessions (which included McGregor and two of the dancers) allowed them to present responses based on their individual areas of specialization.

The scientists described what they had observed, using their own frames of reference, individually articulating the themes they thought of interest. Not surprisingly, this triggered a lively debate amongst the scientists, since they shared these references more immediately amongst each other than with the artists present. However, the shared respect and curiosity that drew us together during the initial meetings now provided a critical foundation for the project's success. Bridges of understanding were forged between artists and scientists through the mutual generation of what McGregor has described as 'conceptual frameworks, discussions, debate, explanation and dialogue that surround the practical events themselves'.

The aim was to elicit observations from the scientists that could become the basis for further investigation and experimentation; on the second day, they were invited to present a hypothesis or tentative theory to investigate through subsequent experimental or empirical methods. The ultimate goal was to arrive at different scientific starting points that might have implications for McGregor's creative research for *AtaXia*. Time was set aside over the next two months when each scientist could return to Sadler's Wells to work with McGregor and the dancers to pursue these lines of enquiry. Eventually, each scientist evolved a separate set of questions and a proposal for an experiment to investigate these further. The experiment devised by Barnard and his colleague Tony Marcel was the viewing and parsing exercise described in the following dialogue.

The viewing and parsing exercise: a dialogue between Phil Barnard (PB) and Scott deLahunta (SD)

SD: Can you briefly describe your experience of first encountering Wayne and the dancers creating dance material in the rehearsal studio?

PB: The invitation to observe Wayne generating movement material for a future dance piece came with the offer that we could each do some empirical research in collaboration with his dance company. I entered this enterprise with a vaguely formed and naive ambition to study how properties of movement influenced the emotional experience of the viewer. Unsurprisingly, the first thing to fall by the wayside is the predetermined plan. As I watched Wayne work developing his movement material with the dancers, I was quickly perplexed. Wayne briefed, observed and re-instructed the dancers and periodically interacted with his own notebook. But I realized I didn't have a clue what was going on in his mind. My questions suddenly changed. What was he 'seeing' in what the dancers were doing and how was he seeing it? When he saw something, what was he using to support his thought process and creativity? To what extent was there a shared understanding between the choreographer and dancers? How did the exploration of small phrases of movement like these relate to the wider context of creating and staging a piece intended to explore the theme of dysfunction (Wayne's starting point for the research for his next work)? Choreographers would no doubt have their own clearly framed ideas about this. As a cognitive scientist, I was entirely in the dark.

SD: Can you briefly describe the experiment you devised to investigate these questions further?

PB: We set out to develop a simple exploratory method for addressing some of these questions. Wayne and the dancers developed eight short

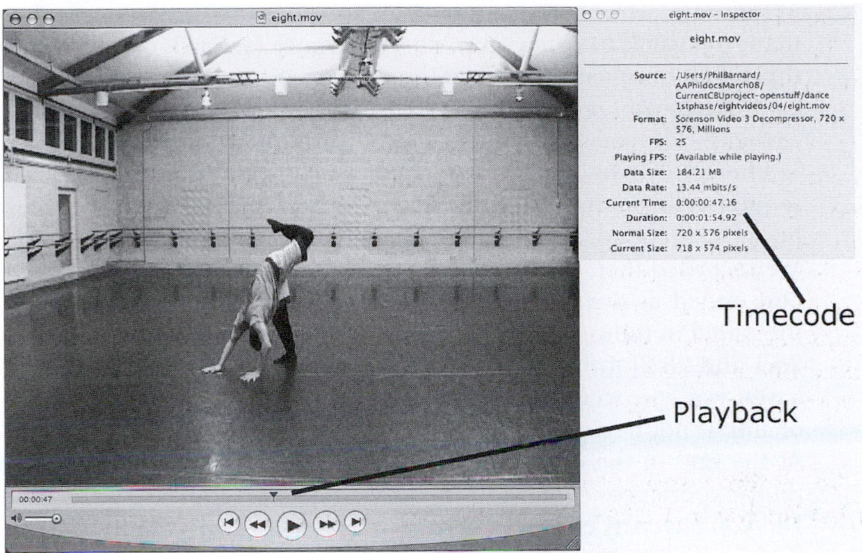

Figure 28.1 The Quicktime software used for the viewing and parsing exercise in the Choreography and Cognition project.

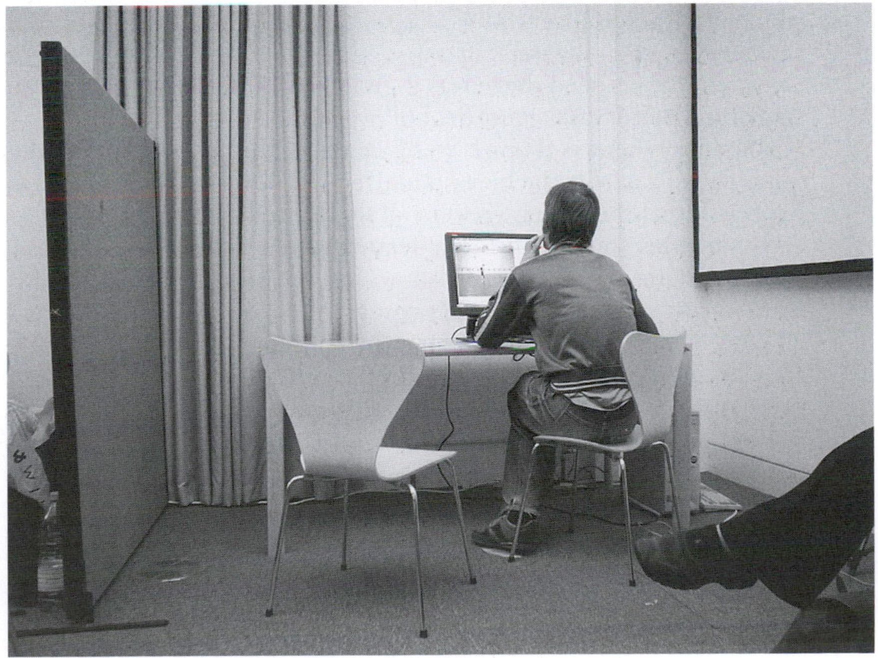

Figure 28.2 Image of Matthias Sperling watching the sequence.

dance sequences of between one and a half minutes and two minutes in duration, which we videotaped and digitized. Using software that made it possible to watch, stop, start and move forwards or backwards through the sequence we asked the ten dancers and Wayne to analyse each of the eight sequences and identify temporal units of movement in them – like parsing a sentence into words and phrases.

The study was as follows: first, each dancer watched each sequence through, indicating where the particular units they saw began and ended, stopping and starting the video when necessary. We recorded their judgements of where units of movement started and ended as our primary quantitative data; these were read off the panel in the right side of the interface shown here [see Figures 28.1 and 28.2]. Importantly, each individual could determine what a unit was – we were very careful not to bias them about what might or might not be a phrase or what properties they should focus on. At the end of the data collection, we asked the dancers to discuss their experiences of viewing the movement material.

SD: Did you have any expectations about what the results might be from this viewing and parsing experiment?

PB: One simple principle of cognitive psychology is that we can only 'think' about a limited range of things at a time. Movements of the kind the dancers were watching have many attributes, including bodily configurations, energy, use of space, or underlying intention and no one can attend to all at the same time. It would be astonishing if all ten dancers plus Wayne were to focus on exactly the same things: so in the parsing experiment we expected considerable variation. And indeed there was a great deal of variation; but at the same time there was a great deal of overlap.

Here are two ways [Figure 28.3] we developed for presenting the quantitative data. On the lower panel, eleven horizontal lines show, as expected, that the eleven viewers all segmented the sequence differently and this was a consistent feature across all eight sequences. Notice that the middle line only shows just seven black segments. This is the representation of Wayne's results. Whereas the other dancers all parsed the whole sequence, he, the choreographer, focused only on selecting the elements he found interesting. The upper panel is a new visualization invented by our statistician, Ian Nimmo-Smith, by placing time on both the vertical and horizontal axes. The pyramid-like structure that results uses greyscale to show the extent to which the dancers agreed. Regions where it is completely black index total agreement that adjacent frames were part of a coherent unit. The lightest shade of grey indicates where only one observer saw a coherent unit. Here in a single visualization is a statistical summary of the variation in phrase structure that we observed. Simultaneously, you can see multiple structures assigned to exactly the same movement sequence.

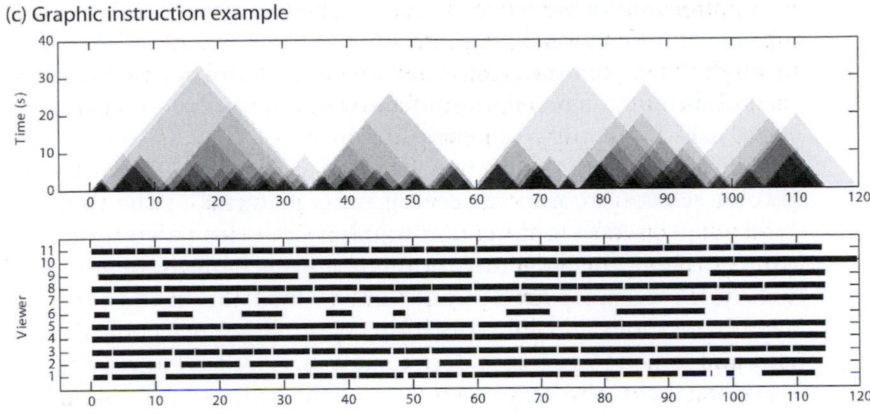

Figure 28.3 Graphic instruction example.

SD: It is fascinating how this single visualization captures all eleven viewers simultaneously; the exercise registers what each individual dancer sees in the movement sequence without resorting to verbal description making it possible to compare and contrast these different registrations. The set-up of the viewing experiment itself forces a unique mode of analysis using video, a common tool for dancers. I am tempted to see this representation of movement analysis as a sort of dance notation.

PB: What we have here is not a dance notation. These visualizations simply make explicit abstract properties of the perception of dance as seen by eleven different viewers. It makes it possible to directly see relationships that cannot be captured in simple numbers. For example, we see immediately from the branching structure that there are regions where there is agreement on where something starts but greater indeterminacy about its perceived end and vice versa. The visualization makes explicit attributes that might otherwise have remained implicit or difficult to articulate verbally in a discussion about the phrase. The pyramids expose contrasts within and between pieces and render them intellectually tangible. From this platform we can think back to the questions we posed initially.[5]

SD: This might have interesting consequences for students of choreography who might be encouraged through seeing this visualization of the parsing exercise not to get lost in the detail, to maintain an overview of the range of possible meanings of any one particular moment in a dance phrase. Our representations imply that while viewers are unlikely to agree on particular moments, they do agree in more general ways and that these densities of agreement can be featured hierarchically, making it possible to discuss more than one level of 'seeing' or noticing and noting how different levels might happen simultaneously.

PB: As a cognitive scientist, I have my own questions about attention and meaning. Of more significance to choreographic processes, we might ask: What properties applied in those regions that Wayne considered interesting and how did they differ from those that he did not select? Are dancers seeing units in terms of the same or different properties to the choreographer or even a naive audience? While it is tempting to speculate about the mechanisms of attention to movement, one area we would like to focus on in the future is how the methods and concepts from cognitive science could potentially be applied to augment dance analysis as well as choreographic construction.

SD: It would be fascinating if an experiment to try and generate valuable scientific results could also be used to augment the choreographic creation process. Can you explain what you mean?

PB: From this initial exercise, it became clear that through the parsing exercise the dancers had arrived at interesting insights about the movement they were looking at. Although they had obviously viewed dance material many times on video before, here they were asked to attend to many different features at any one of several 'levels' of decomposition *and* make decisions about what a unit of movement was for them individually. Additionally, using the software tool for viewing and marking times in the movement sequence rendered their observations explicit through non-verbal means. Here is one observation made during the post-data collection discussions:

> as the exercise went on, also *I felt my perspective of how I was looking at the exercise started to change a bit*. I think I started off feeling like a unit to me in the beginning was more of a chain of movement. Then *eventually it became not only just a chain of movement but perhaps looking at the intention of where the movement was coming from*. I guess that came out through the quality of what was happening. So it wasn't just about starting and stopping. ... There is another level that comes into it after a while, after you really watch it again and again.
>
> (Kham Halsackda in deLahunta and Barnard 2005)

Other similar observations were made by the dancers such as enhanced perception of movement features where initially they had only an 'implicit' feeling or empathizing in a new way with the point of view of the choreographer (deLahunta and Barnard 2005). We cannot be certain what it was about the parsing exercise that led to such changes in understandings. Perhaps it was the combination of specificity and ambiguity in the instructions combined with the ability to review detail many times over using the software tool that was significant. But the dancers' experience and our speculation about the various choreographic meanings that may be latent in the resulting visualizations suggest that students and mentors of choreography could benefit from sharing intellectual territory with cognitive science.

Developing augmentation techniques: a proposal by Phil Barnard

While interdisciplinary collaborations can focus on reciprocal exchange of concepts and ideas about the significance of movement and dance, there is an inherent danger that the different disciplines will tend to talk *at each other rather than with each other*. During our collaboration, it occurred to us that a useful approach to counter this would be to target future research on developing a range of techniques for augmenting choreographic processes. In this way we might develop the scientific study of choreographic cognition while offering back into the dance community something of immediate value – a possibility suggested by the apparent mutual benefits of the exercise just described.

The parsing exercise, while productive for us, dealt only with a tiny fraction of the full making process. To develop this as an area of research, we need also to explore how to visualize and summarize longer sequences in a much richer way. In order to work effectively, choreographers and dancers need to develop a frame of mind that supports analysis, creativity, criticism or just the replication of a performance. Already we have many clues about potentially productive avenues for future research. Reviewing and analysing dance on video is common practice in the dance community and technological support of various kinds is currently being explored (Forsythe 2000).

We all know that photographs provide powerful reminders of past experiences, and that trailers for TV shows will sample brief components of the previous episode to remind us where we are in the overall story. There is evidence that video snaps (very short time slices) of the recent past can help patients with severe memory problems to prompt recollections that otherwise would have been inaccessible. Annotated replays of short segments of action are now an integral part of commentaries on sport. Such observations raise the prospect of using dynamic images to reinstate past choreographic experiences and frames of mind in the context of making or discussing dance (Berry *et al.* 2007).

Imagine viewing a short part of a recent live performance you have seen. Then imagine how much you might be able to recall. To what extent can you reconstruct movements only in your mind's eye or through empathic bodily feelings? One approach we have been exploring to aid movement recollection is through making a temporal montage of video snaps from longer sequences with each snap lasting around one second.

In Figure 28.4, we reproduce a sequence of stills from one of the videos we used in our parsing exercise. Try to imagine how viewing these in sequence, like a series of almost arbitrary jump cuts, might bring certain parts of the movement sequence back to your mind. Unlike a succession of static stills (as seen in Figure 28.4), a short time slice of the video captures something of the dancer's dynamic, and his use of space. In our initial explorations, we sampled mechanically a small segment from every ten seconds of the kind of short sequences used in our parsing study, the average duration of a perceived unit in that study. We made no attempt to align the cuts with the perceived units that are represented in the graphic visualization. A sequence of dynamic snapshots effectively summarizes the whole movement sequence and its mechanical nature could be important partly because it can be easily automated at low expense in terms of time. Something that can be done quickly and rapidly reviewed may be more supportive to the creative process of making dances than techniques requiring an army of editors.

This rapid and disjointed juxtaposition of fragments brings together different yet related elements. It could be significant precisely because it does not allow time for thought about each one as it happens but rapidly reinjects or reinstates large amounts of movement material back from the past into the present moment. It is potentially a tool with properties that might be of interest to choreographers to stimulate recollection and creativity. If we can stimulate by reinstatement certain prior thinking states in the mind of the choreographer, we may be able to provide a range of technical resources for augmenting choreographic processes that are especially tuned to current understanding of how cognition works.

Notebooks full of words, sentences and graphical notations have one set of properties – they require time to inspect and mentally analyse and they omit the physical context from which they were derived. Perhaps they promote one particular slow mode of propositional thinking. It can even be argued that this mode could inhibit rather than promote creativity. Creativity seems to be linked to an alternative mode of thought in which generic and experiential senses in the mind are more prominent than specific propositions – intuition if you like. We are already researching how these modes of mind might work in psychopathologies such as the rapid and fragmentary thinking involved in mania or the slow propositional ruminations that accompany depression; and using that understanding to guide the development of new therapeutic interventions. It is potentially very exciting to uncover intellectual common ground between the domain of normal laboratory work and the world of dance.

Science/dance collaborations: a dialogue between Wayne McGregor (WM) and Scott deLahunta (SD)

SD: The process of making both *AtaXia* and *Amu* brought you into close working relationship with scientists.[6] Can you say something about

Figure 28.4 Twelve stills from the video of Kham Halsackda, a dancer with Random Dance, during the Choreography and Cognition project.

this working relationship, this collaboration, in general, e.g. how it started, what sustained it? What were some of your discoveries?

WM: All collaborations, whether they function between artists and other artists or artists and scientists, are demanding. Their success is based not so much on the nature of each individual's specialism or level of expertise but on an ability to communicate well, to share ideas and to listen. This openness of approach and willingness to think outside of the box is vital to true collaborative endeavour where all parties are taken on a journey of mutual exploration. The science/dance collaborations that have been the most productive for me have been those that tread this path of investigation in a dynamic, fluid and ever-evolving form. It is very difficult to establish exactly why a particular relationship works and why certain ones do not. The alchemy of collaboration, especially when you are blurring the boundaries of thinking, throws out new challenges for everyone and sets the tone for fruitful exchange. I understand from my investigation with Phil Barnard, for example, that what I *articulate* to be important in my creative process is, in retrospect, a memory of the process and often, if not always, *not* reflective of the actual creative decision-making process. It is a form of theatre in its own right, a construct. We have all acquired formulas to articulate our processes that are not accurate records, but traces of the events that take place. This is a fascinating revelation and pushes one to genuinely reflect on one's process utilizing a completely different intellectual framework. These encounters have the potential to change thinking and bring us to an altered state; this is what provides the biggest catalyst for creation.

SD: Could you say something about how both scientific processes (experiment/data collection) and outcomes (descriptions/explanations) informed your creative process? For example, I have heard you describe the idea of the prisms/vision disorientation for *AtaXia*. What information did you take back into the studio, and how did you use it?

WM: The scientific 'experiments' Random undertook during the *AtaXia* process directly fed back into the dance making to generate a new physical language. It's easy to see how and why this was possible. There was a very clear relationship between the aspiration of the research project and my interest in undermining the relationship between the body and the brain, quite literally making the behaviour of the body dysfunctional. Experiments were facilitated to disrupt the body's ability to coordinate its movements and these scientific choreographic interventions or perturbations actually made extremely able-bodied, virtuosic dancers unable to stand up, let alone balance. Through a series of dual tasks, vision disorientation techniques, motion capture/motor control experiments, etc. there was a very practical puzzle for the body and the brain to solve. The *process* of solving the puzzles, the time it took to see the body and brain attempt to come to terms with the difficulty and the ensuing solutions provided the most useful information to capitalize on in the studio. The journey of thinking through the unfamiliar was a greater resource than the actual end results. Because ultimately the brain finds a solution, it maps a framework that now easily facilitates the task – the brain learns fast.

This very practical experimentation is only one of the valuable aspects of a collaborative process with science. As important are the conceptual frameworks, discussions, debate, explanation and dialogue that surround the practical events themselves. This transfer of knowledge(s) permeates the process in many fundamental ways. Choreography is about making decisions, and decisions are shaped by immersing oneself in the actual content of the work. This total immersion allows strategies for making to emerge. It inspires new choreographic form with possibilities drawn from science but applied in dance; and opens up totally new territories of language because the currencies of language we expose ourselves to are non-arts-based. This was keenly seen in the *Amu* process where Random Dance were exposed to biological, medical, mechanical, spiritual 'learning' sessions focused around building a knowledge system for the heart. This included having our hearts scanned, watching open-heart surgery, understanding flow and dynamics of the heart, meditation techniques, etc. Each new session built a more dynamic, richer imagination for the heart and resonated very individually with each artist. This approach of immersion fuelled improvisations and physical investigations that drew directly upon our collective experience of learning about the functions of the heart and our individual experiences of building an empathy with our own heart. That is, science makes visible the unknown, art uses that discovery and translates it into something equally meaningful, but in a very different language. Sensibilities converge ...

SD: Where would you say the evidence of these projects (these working relationships) is demonstrated in both the choreography (the art) and the science?

WM: What is vital in genuine collaboration is the notion that science cannot be used merely to serve the artist in the same way that artists cannot merely provide data for the scientist. These may be outcomes or aspects of the collaboration, but not the points of departure. Therefore, in all of the collaborative processes undertaken with the scientists, I have not prioritized the making of a new work. New work has *resulted* from these dynamic exchanges but the focus has been a series of questions, propositions, ideas to be thrown between us, tested, examined and explored. Some questions lead to actual experiments, some remain in the abstract and are no less important. Equally, some of the scientists have published journal articles and given papers on work we have undertaken because during the evolution of our interchange particular points of interest converge with their science. Again, these have emerged and have not been a condition of collaboration. The outcomes of the science/dance collaborations have been varied and remain alive. The questions for all of us live on.

SD: You are about to embark on another period of research with scientists that will inform the creation of the new work ENTITY. Would you describe this is an evolutionary step?

WM: The intention to develop ENTITY, an autonomous choreographic agent, has been with me for some time. Both *AtaXia* and *Amu* helped provide a framework for this research. *AtaXia* looked at the direct connection between the body and the brain and discovered what happened when this connection was interfered with. The whole project was driven from the perspective of the brain being the central organism that controls everything the body experiences. *Amu* looked at the biological functions of the body through the filter of the heart and attempted to explore a connection between the heart and brain, ultimately exposing the generation of emotion. Both of these projects used kinaesthetic intelligence as a starting point for exploration. The human body, connected to itself and its environment, a complex, complicated, virtuosic, thinking, memory-laden entity, provides an unrivalled window into human experience. And dance – the most complete amalgam of all of the technologies of the body and brain – is a rich subject for never-ending research.

With this physical thinking in mind, the aspiration of building a new form of body, this ENTITY that has embedded inside it kinaesthetic intelligence, has come to fruition. We do not want to build a body that replicates human physical behaviour, but one that can do the unexpected, without the restrictions of a 'real' body. Its decision-making processes and learning, although based on human kinaesthetic intelligence, should surpass human capabilities with an embodied imagination of its own. ENTITY should be able to interact with us in the studio but provide us with challenging encounters with the alien, the unfamiliar, an uncertain artistic future that destabilizes our formulas of making and disrupts our aesthetic sensibilities.

Unfamiliar thinking territories: a brief glance back by Scott deLahunta

The Choreography and Cognition project was initiated in 2001 when we collaborated on the Software for Dancers project: a research into new concepts for digital creative tools for choreographers.[7] Now, we plan a ten-week research period at the University of California San Diego (UCSD) where Wayne will be Innovator-in-Residence, with the intention to conduct initial research on the ENTITY project. Again, the idea of the 'autonomous choreographic agent' is intended to be both a stimulus for shared dance and science research and creative impetus for a new artwork.

The urge to create this agent (or collection of agents) that can generate unique solutions to choreographic problems alongside his own decision-making processes, has been with Wayne for some time. It has taken several years, however, to gain enough collective experience and understanding to be able to approach the idea productively. Working together in the late summer of 2006 on a site visit to UCSD, Wayne, Phil and I drew on our past experiences to make concrete suggestions for the forthcoming residency. The proposal is to continue probing the interconnection of mental, emotional and physical processes involved in dance creation; Wayne outlined a three-stage development that emphasizes building conceptual frameworks through dialogue and practical investigation through various experimental formats. With the coordinators at UCSD, we identified key research areas and laboratories, which can bring interesting perspectives to bear on the ENTITY project, for example, memory, attention, distributed cognition, creativity, reasoning, decision making, protocol analysis in rich task environments, design rationale and cognitive design tools.

In the past, support for arts and science collaboration has often required increased public understanding of science as one of its key objectives; but as more collaborations are undertaken and more open-ended funding opportunities appear, it has become possible to pursue joint research under other terms.[8] This creates the possibility of doing collaborative research that, as Barnard states, uncovers intellectual common ground and leads to valuable outcomes in both domains. Interdisciplinary collaborations between artists and cognitive sciences in particular, in which differences are understood and exploited in shared description, research and creation processes, stand a chance of making unforeseen discoveries and of giving rise to new insights. Ultimately, this requires all involved to go beyond the clearly defined and relatively safe objectives outlined at the start of the Choreography and Cognition project, to follow the creative need to journey into unfamiliar thinking territory. This compels us, at least momentarily, to step away from the shelter of institutionalized categories. As Anthony Marcel wrote to Wayne, 'what you and the dancers are doing IS science. It's just another way of doing it' (Marcel, letter to Wayne McGregor, November 2003).

This chapter is adapted from presentations at the *Underskin Symposium*, La Biennale di Venezia Dance sector, Venice on 9 June 2006.

Notes

1 The pilot Arts and Science Research Fellowships scheme was jointly funded by the Arts Council England and the Arts and Humanities Research Board (now Council) of the UK.

2 The decision not to show video at this stage reduced the amount of information to process together; the descriptions coupled with some physical demonstration were thought sufficient.

3 For a bibliography related to neuro-aesthetics see <http://brainethics.wordpress.com/2006/09/27/a-short-bibliographic-guide-to-the-emerging-field-of-bioaesthetics/> (accessed 28 November 2006).

4 Ivar Hagendoorn organized an international symposium (January 2004), hosted by the Ballett Frankfurt with financial support by the Dana Foundation. Speakers: Marc Jeannerod, Julie Grèzes, Andrea Heberlein, Tania Singer, Petr Janata. Introduction and closing remarks Ivar Hagendoorn. For more information and related papers see: <http://www.ivarhagendoorn.com/> (accessed 28 November 2006).

5 See for more detailed discussion: deLahunta and Philip Barnard (2005) and deLahunta *et al.* (2006).

6 For information about AMU and the collaborative research with heart specialists see <http://www.oftheheart.org> (accessed 28 November 2006).

7 See the Software for Dancers project <http://www.sdela.dds.nl/sfd/> (accessed 28 November 2006).

8 In Australia, another extensive research project involving cognitive scientists and dancers took place. More information can be found online. Available at <http://www.ausdance.org.au/unspoken/> (accessed 28 November 2006). See also Grove, Stevens and McKechnie (2005).

References

Barnard, P. and deLahunta, S. (2006) Paper Presentation, *Underskin Symposium*, La Biennale di Venezia Dance sector, Venice (9 June 2006).

Berry, E. L., Kapur, N., Williams, N., Hodges, S., Watson, P., Smyth, G., Srinivasan, J., Smith, R., Wilson, B. and Wood, R. (2007) 'The use of a wearable camera, SenseCam, to aid autobiographical memory in a patient with limbic encephalitis', *Encephalitis*.

Choreography and Cognition website. Available online at <http://www.choreocog.net> (accessed 28 November 2006).

DeLahunta, S. and Barnard, P. (2005) 'What's in a Phrase?', in J. Birringer and J. Fenger (eds) *Tanz im Kopf/Dance and Cognition*, Jahrbuch der Gesellschaft für Tanzforschung 15, Münster: LIT Verlag.

DeLahunta, S., Barnard, P., Nimmo-Smith, I., Potts, J. and Ramponi, C. (2006) 'Densities of Agreement', *Dance Theatre Journal*, 21 (3).

Forsythe, W. (2000) Improvisation Technologies: A Tool for the Analytical Dance Eye (CD-ROM). Ostfildern, DE: Hatje Cantz Verlag.

Freeland, C. (2001) 'Teaching Cognitive Science and the Arts' I, II, III. Available online at <www.aesthetics-online.org/articles> (accessed 16 November 2006).

Grove, R., Stevens, C. and McKechnie. S. (eds) (2005) *Thinking in Four Dimensions: Creativity and Cognition in Contemporary Dance*. Carlton: Melbourne University Press. See the e-book online. Available online at <http://www.mup.unimelb.edu.au/ebooks/0-522-85144-4/index.html> (accessed 28 November 2006).

Leach, J. (2006) 'Extending Contexts, Making Possibilities: An Introduction to Evaluating the Projects', in the Special Section, Arts and Science Research Fellowships – Arts Council England and Arts and Humanities Research Board, in *Leonardo* 39 (5): 447– 51.

Ramachandran, V. S. (1999) 'Art and the Brain: Controversies in Science and the Humanities', *Journal of Consciousness Studies*, Imprint Academic, October.

Zeki, S. (1999) *Inner Vision: an Exploration of Art and the Brain*, Oxford University Press.

Index